Cases on Innovations in Educational Marketing:

Transnational and Technological Strategies

Purnendu Tripathi
IGNOU, India

Siran Mukerji
IGNOU, India

BUSINESS SCIENCE Reference

Senior Editorial Director:	Kristin Klinger
Director of Book Publications:	Julia Mosemann
Editorial Director:	Lindsay Johnston
Acquisitions Editor:	Erika Carter
Development Editor:	Myla Harty
Production Editor:	Sean Woznicki
Typesetters:	Keith Glazewski, Natalie Pronio, Deanna Jo Zombro
Print Coordinator:	Jamie Snavely
Cover Design:	Nick Newcomer

Published in the United States of America by
Business Science Reference (an imprint of IGI Global)
701 E. Chocolate Avenue
Hershey PA 17033
Tel: 717-533-8845
Fax: 717-533-8661
E-mail: cust@igi-global.com
Web site: http://www.igi-global.com/reference

Library of Congress Cataloging-in-Publication Data
Cases on innovations in educational marketing: transnational and technological strategies / Purnendu Tripathi and Siran Mukerji, editors.
p. cm.
Includes bibliographical references and index.
Summary: "This book provides comparative and comprehensive analysis of technological and transnational strategies in educational marketing on various issues across the world and also the best practices and experiences from a diverse range of countries"-- Provided by publisher.
ISBN 978-1-60960-599-5 (hardcover) -- ISBN 978-1-60960-600-8 (ebook) 1. Education, Higher--Marketing--Cross-cultural studies. 2. Education, Higher--Marketing--Technological innovations--Cross-cultural studies. 3. Transnational education--Cross-cultural studies. I. Tripathi, Purnendu, 1975- II. Mukerji, Siran. III. Title.
LB2342.82.C37 2011
338.4'3378--dc22

2011001300

British Cataloguing in Publication Data
A Cataloguing in Publication record for this book is available from the British Library.

Table of Contents

Detailed Table of Contents

The authors of the first chapter of this case book, Alan C. K. Cheung, Y. C. Cheng, Timothy W. W. Yuen and Celeste Y. M. Yuen, explore market strategies and supportive government policies for promoting Hong Kong's higher education in the three emerging Asian markets. Their analysis suggests extremely low visibility of Hong Kong's higher education due to a lack of concerted and coordinated effort between the Hong Kong government and higher education institutions. The study suggests coherent marketing strategies and government policies for attracting international students.

The second chapter, by Maria Fuentes Blasco, Irene Gil Saura and Beatriz Moliner Velásquez, attempts to make an in-depth examination of the viability of student perceptions of service quality as segmentation criterion while also analyzing how such dimensions can be used to segment effectively the collective of students' degrees using latent methodology.

The third chapter of this book, by Sven Tuzovic, Lyle Wetsch and Jamie Murphy, is a case about Google Challenge that gives undergraduate and graduate students hands-on experience on the world's fastest growing advertising mechanism, search engine advertising. The authors herein explore the challenge as an innovative pedagogical tool for marketing educators. This case study discusses the opportunities and challenges of integrating this dynamic problem-based learning approach based on the experiences of three instructors in Australia, Canada, and the United States.

Laurie Bedford, in the fourth chapter of this book, analyses efforts to promote the distinctiveness of online programs in an increasingly competitive market, focussing on instructor expertise and instructional quality. This case challenges the notion of part-time instructor as liability to the integrity of the instructional process by focusing on a single instructor categorized as a full-time, professional adjunct and is characterized by her colleagues as highly skilled. The case participant describes the challenges and the best practices that support her in providing quality instruction.

The authors of fifth chapter, Frank Wai-ming Tam and Paula Yu-Kwong Kwan, assert that in a highly competitive environment, schools need to find their institutional identities and strive for presenting a positive image to the community. This case focuses on how a school organization adapts itself to the environment and survives external competition. The authors also discuss the dilemma faced by schools in choosing between academic and pastoral ethos.

The authors, John Munro and Elena Verezub, in this case examine the influence of teaching individuals to read and comprehend hypertext. Its findings contribute to the advancement of knowledge in this area and indicate ways in which individuals can improve their capacity to convert e-text to knowledge.

The seventh chapter, by Kathleen A. Krentler and Albert Caruana, is a case study about transnational partnership between universities of Malta and USA for offering Master level degree. This paper charts the challenges faced and the hurdles encountered to develop the curriculum, launch the degree, recruit the students, undertake teaching, and ultimately, graduate the first cohort.

Manuel Cuadrado-García, María-Eugenia Ruiz-Molina, and Lourdes Hernández-Martín in this case aim to focus at students from two universities one each from UK and Spain taking part in an interdisciplinary project based on a real decision making process in the context of cultural management.

In the ninth chapter, Ken Stevens addresses the international problem of providing access to educational and vocational opportunities to small high schools in rural communities by repositioning these institutions as sites within teaching and learning networks. The small rural schools are repositioned as sites in teaching and learning networks on four inter-connected dimensions of change, i.e. technological, pedagogical, organizational and conceptual, and thereby, they enhance educational and vocational opportunities for senior students. The case further discusses the implications in these changes for the professional education of high school teachers teaching in networked classes as well as in traditional classrooms.

This case, by Francine Rochford, attempts to look at the academic freedom and ethical issues concerning marketing of university programs and services. The author suggests that mismatch between university objectives and choices made by them erode the effective protection of academic freedom. The paper highlights as to how casual approach of the university staff presents a problem for the real exercise of academic freedom, and is an abandonment of the ethical role of the university.

The fifteenth chapter of the book, by Shuyi Zhang and Li Zhao, focuses on a Chinese higher education scenario. The authors attempt to analyze the challenges towards internationalisation of Chinese higher education followed by suggesting the future trends.

In the sixteenth chapter, the authors Tom Bisschoff and Christopher Rhodes present and account of a school in South Africa that is faced with the demand to transform and become an agent of change in making its pupil profile multi-ethnic. According to the authors, this demand is driven by market oriented approach in which school must compete for pupil recruitment for their survival and also simultaneously demonstrate a willingness to change to multi-ethnic profiles and establish non-sexism and non-racialism as the dominating culture.

Paul Breen, Magdalena De Stefani, and Achilleas Kostoulas illustrate in this case how institutions can adapt, and indeed need to adapt, to the nature of society and education in the twenty first century by discussing a course of doctoral study through distance education by an institution of higher education in UK. These issues are discussed and analysed by three students who have participated in a programme of doctoral studies mainly conducted part time, by distance.

The eighteenth chapter, by Gonca Telli Yamamoto, Michael D. Featherstone, Faruk Karaman, and Patricia C. Borstorff, exemplifies an experiential case study of a multicultural virtual team project at two universities having students from very different cultural backgrounds. The authors suggest that virtual teams are needed by enterprises to compete in the global business environment.

Foreword

We live in times where knowledge is an ultimate power. It is now widely recognized that education in general and higher education in particular plays a crucial role in building knowledge societies. In a major restructuring of UNESCO's medium term strategy, the organization adopted "building inclusive knowledge societies" as one of its strategic objectives. This was clearly in recognition of the fact that in today's world, knowledge plays a key role in economic growth, social development, cultural enrichment, and political empowerment.

The world conference on Higher Education held at UNESCO in 2009 identified eight major trends in Higher Education. These are: rising demand and massification; diversification of providers and methods; private provision; open and distance education; cross-border higher education; quality assurance; teacher education; and changes in academic profession. These trends pose significant challenges and provide unprecedented opportunities to the institutions of higher education.

Knowledge acquisition and sharing, or in short, learning, is going through dramatic changes because of rapidly emerging new information and communication technologies and the social transformation that they generate. But what are the long term strategies to efficiently harness the enormous potential of ICT for developing new approaches to knowledge acquisition and sharing? What needs to be done to effectively integrate these strategies into forward and sustainable policy making? How can we harness the potential of ICTs to develop knowledge societies that are people centered, inclusive, and development oriented?

The traditional methods of teaching and learning can no longer cope with ever increasing demand for access to education. Many observers believe that knowledge acquisition and sharing, at all levels, will increasingly be technology mediated. This will have a transformational impact on traditional educational processes. It is likely to have profound impact on what we learn and how we learn. The traditional role of teachers and learners will undergo radial changes. The traditional classroom teaching will give way to education anytime, anywhere.

While these changes are inevitable, marketing the new brand of knowledge acquisition and sharing will be quite challenging. Change is unsettling by nature and brings uncertainty in its wake. Convincing parents and learners that technology-enhanced learning can be as effective, if not more effective, will require a group of marketing professionals who specialize in educational marketing. It will also require evidence-based innovative approaches and use of new ICTs to market new methods of knowledge acquisition and sharing.

This book presents examples of innovation in educational marketing based on studies by eminent scholars drawn from different parts of the world. The book is rich in its content and presents empirical evidence on a range of issues, including marketing strategies, learner perception, use of online marketing tools, distinctive features of online education, collaborative learning, cross cultural dimension of transborder education, and student experience management.

This book will be useful for a variety of audiences, including educational planners and policy makers, marketing professionals, researchers, learners, and parents. I congratulate the editors and the authors for presenting this book on an important and timely theme: educational marketing.

A. W. Khan
TAG University of Business, Kingdom of Bahrain

***Abdul Waheed Khan** is currently the President of Talal Abu-Ghazaleh University of Business, Bahrain and Senior Adviser to Arab Open University, and was the Assistant Director–General for Communication and Information of the United Nations Educational, Scientific and Cultural Organization (UNESCO) from July 2001 – 2010. In this capacity, Dr. Khan was responsible for leading UNESCO's program on "Building Inclusive Knowledge Societies," the primary focus of which was to harness the potential of Communication and Information Technologies (ICTs) to enhance access to quality education, facilitate acquisition of scientific knowledge, and promote cultural and linguistic diversity. Fostering digital opportunities for social and economic inclusion through public-private partnerships was also a key component of this programme.*

Preface

Today, in the era of global education and access to quality learning environment, education is truly transnational and has no geographical boundaries. Institutions of higher learning have off-shore campuses and international, students are one of the major sources of funding. Efforts have been taken to design, develop and market international educational programmes for the universities. Clearly, this envisages the fact that global institutions of learning are now devising new strategies to reach the unreached while marketing their educational products and promising to offer quality student services. With the passage of time, we can visualize these institutions as Multinational Institutions of Learning (MNIL) having subsidiaries in host countries and joint ventures with local institutions of learning. But, these developments should not only be limited to higher education, they should also cover the entire gamut of education, covering elementary education, K12, and even literacy enhancement and adult learning.

In the top 200 universities in Times Higher Education World University Rankings 2010-2011, the institutions of US, UK, Australia, Canada, and China have shown significant presence, and hence, they are the major attractions for international students. In Asia, besides China, Singapore, Taiwan, Hong Kong, Japan, and Korea have enormous potential to be the global centers for international education. India, having a network of over 400 universities and institutions of national importance, is one of the major sources of outbound mobile international students to US, UK, and Australia, and China has also responded to the need for having a future global center for international education. With the introduction of the Foreign Educational Institutions (Regulation of Entry and Operations) Bill, 2010, in the lower house of the Parliament of India (referred to the Department related Parliamentary Standing Committee on Human Resource Development for examination and report), the bill is intended:

"to regulate entry and operation of foreign educational institutions imparting or intending to impart higher education (including technical education and medical education and award of degree, diploma and equivalent qualifications by such institutions) and for matters connected therewith or incidental thereto" (p.1).

The present book, ***Cases on Innovations in Educational Marketing: Transnational and Technological Strategies***, addresses the prominent issues involved in marketing new educational approaches revolutionizing the entire education sector. The institutions highlighted in these cases are emerging as educational corporate entities with a bouquet of academic programs as products endeavouring to augment their presence worldwide with innovative technological and transnational strategies. This book provides comparative and comprehensive analysis of technological and transnational strategies in educational marketing on various issues across the world and also the best practices and experiences from a diverse range of countries. The participating authors have contributed interesting cases on varied nature of topics like advertising campaigns, benefits of e-learning, ethics of marketing education, global partnerships, government policies, marketing strategies, quality online instruction, school identity, service quality perceptions, teaching and learning networks, et cetera. The idea behind development of this book was that we should create an international platform for sharing of innovative cases on educational marketing with technological and transnational perspective so that readers from developing and developed world could equally benefit.

This case book has a total of 19 chapters, and functions as an excellent platform for exchange of innovative thoughts and brilliant ideas on educational marketing in the form of case studies from contributors of a number of countries, namely, the USA, Spain, China, Canada, Australia, Malta, UK, France, Rwanda, Uruguay, Greece, and Turkey. The cases focus on varied aspects of marketing of education, such as a comparative study of higher education services marketing in three Asian markets, quality of university services and market segmentation, search engine advertising in education, the role of a full time adjunct professional in providing quality educational services and its implication on institutional marketing, organizational survival techniques for competition in school education, e-text, and educational marketing, a transnational collaborative approach to providing higher education and creating new markets, collaborative marketing research, institutional repositioning and networked learning, academic freedom and ethics versus marketing techniques, social networking technologies as a medium for international marketing communications, student experience management for improved student relations, marketing techniques for online programs, marketing of doctoral programs, and e-learning in diverse international markets.

The first chapter, by Alan C. K. Cheung, Y. C. Cheng, Timothy W. W. Yuen, and Celeste Y. M. Yuen, provides a comparative study of current conditions of higher education services in three Asian markets while exploring effective market strategies and supportive government policies to further promote higher education in Hong Kong. The authors of this study highlight the need for wider range of coherent marketing strategies and adequate government policies for making the educational setup attractive thus promoting recruitment of international students.

The authors of second chapter, Maria Fuentes Blasco, Irene Gil Saura, and Beatriz Moliner Velásquez, present research on the transformations experienced by Spanish universities challenged by the changing environment and segmented demands, which together highlight the importance of becoming aware of the needs and wishes of students who are the main customers for the universities. They make an attempt to examine the viability of student perceptions of service quality as a segmentation criterion. While doing this, the present study deals with the dimensionality of university service quality, and analyzes how such dimensions can be used to segment effectively the collective of students' degrees using latent methodology.

In the third chapter of this collection, Sven Tuzovic, Lyle Wetsch, and Jamie Murphy have very succinctly presented the case of the Google Online Marketing Challenge, a collaborative partnership between Google and academia, which was one of the world's largest in-class competitions for higher education students. The study focused on undergraduate and graduate students' experiences of the world's fastest growing advertising mechanism, search engine advertising. This paper explores the challenge as an innovative pedagogical tool for marketing educators, and discusses the opportunities and challenges of integrating this dynamic problem-based learning approach into the classroom.

The fourth case chapter, by Laurie Bedford, is an effort towards understanding the nature of the motivations or competencies of the group of part-time instructors who are most often viewed as a liability to the integrity of the instructional process. Laurie Bedford states that these instructors of online programs are perceived as a homogeneous group with similar motivations and levels of expertise. However the author of this case challenges this notion by focusing on a single instructor categorized as a full-time, professional adjunct who describes the challenges and best practices that support her in providing quality instruction. These best practices are subsequently discussed as strategies to inform decisions upon which marketing efforts are dependent.

The authors of the fifth case, Frank Wai-ming Tam and Paula Yu-Kwong Kwan, suggest through their study that a school organization adapts itself to the environment and survives external competition through a series of self-organizing processes of differentiation and integration. They assert that in a fast changing and highly competitive environment like that in Hong Kong, schools need to find their institutional identities and thus present a positive image to the community, indeed a challenging and painful task. The authors make a study of a secondary school to illustrate how this can be done through a survey approach to ascertain needs and expectations of parents. They describe the dilemma schools face in choosing between academic and pastoral ethos and focus on the relations between important factors that impact perceptions of parents.

John Munro and Elena Verezub state that ability to convert information to knowledge is a key capacity in twenty-first century markets, and individuals who are able to read, comprehend, and execute the information more effectively can more efficiently use the resources available in the marketplace. The authors, through their study in the sixth chapter of this case book, examine the influence of teaching individuals to read and comprehend hypertext. The findings of the research contribute to the advancement of knowledge in this area and indicate ways in which individuals can improve their capacity to convert e-text to knowledge.

The seventh case study, by Kathleen A. Krentler and Albert Caruana, portrays the transnational partnership between the University of Malta in Malta and San Diego State University in the United States for commencing a Masters degree in Integrated Marketing Communications, offered in Malta. As a part of the agreement, the classes are delivered by faculty from both the universities, and students earn a degree from each of the two participating schools, thus providing recognition in both the US and the EU. This chapter highlights the challenges faced in this collaborative exercise.

In the eighth chapter, Manuel Cuadrado-García, María-Eugenia Ruiz-Molina, and Lourdes Hernández-Martín describe an interdisciplinary project focusing on the contribution in the teaching-learning process of students at the University of Valencia, in the context of the subject of marketing research. This was based on the collaborative agreement between the University of Valencia (UV) and the London School of Economics (LSE) in which students from both universities had an opportunity to take part in such projects based on a real decision making process, in the context of cultural management. The activities in this study proved to be a facilitator of learning in the field for the students.

Ken Stevens, in the ninth chapter, highlights the international problem facing small high schools in rural communities of providing access to educational and vocational opportunities that approximate those available to urban students. This issue has been addressed by repositioning these institutions as sites within teaching and learning networks in the Canadian province of Newfoundland and Labrador. This resulted in enhanced educational and vocational opportunities for senior students. Besides, the research study also demonstrated the important implications in these changes for the professional education of high school teachers who are increasingly likely to be required to teach in networked classes as well as in traditional classrooms.

Francine Rochford focuses on the important dimension of academic freedom in the university in the tenth case study of this volume. According to her, academic freedom is acknowledged to both define the university and to protect its status, and a commitment to academic freedom must be reflected in organisational structures and attitudes. However, often protection of this freedom is eroded by many factors. The author makes an exhaustive study of the implications of the use of marketing techniques, including that of technological advances, in university system as in private corporations, on academic freedom.

Iryna Pentina and Veronique Guilloux, the authors of the eleventh case study, discuss a class project on developing integrated marketing communications conducted by American and French cross-cultural student groups to promote environmentally-sustainable products in international markets. The authors feel that such research studies are of growing importance due to increased globalization of the world economy, making international aspects of marketing an important priority. As a part of the study, they used modern social networking technologies as tools for accomplishing the project, as means for presenting and displaying the results, and as a medium for international marketing communications.

The objective of the twelfth case study, by Chong Ho Yu, Samuel DiGangi, and Angel Jannasch-Pennell, is to illustrate how text mining of open-ended responses from student survey could yield valuable information for improving student experience management (SEM). To illustrate how text mining can be applied to SEM, the authors discuss an example from a campus-wide survey conducted at Arizona State University with the purpose of better understanding student experiences with instructional technology in order for administrators to make data-driven decisions on its implementation.

The thirteenth chapter by John Rutaisire highlights the importance of educational marketing through modern innovative technologies. The paper explores how teachers who mark Rwandan primary and secondary examinations perceive the Rwanda National Examinations Council and what the implications are for the effective management of the examinations system. The chapter acknowledges the challenges associated with post-conflict educational reconstruction focusing mainly on human resource capacity development and management, and highlights some lessons learned as Rwanda looks forward to the future.

Elizabeth Osika, Rochelle Johnson, and Rosemary Buteau, in the fourteenth chapter of this collection of case studies, have attempted to explore and identify the reasons behind the decline in enrolment in Southern State University, and in this process, have focused on the challenges faced in convincing the faculty and other stakeholders to move towards offering online programs, a vital aspect for the success of the university and for its future. They are of the opinion that online degree programs have the potential for enhancing student enrolment.

The fifteenth case study, by Shuyi Zhang and Li Zhao, focuses on the challenges and trends of Chinese higher education. It analyzes the challenges that the Chinese higher education faces and discusses a couple of issues of internationalization of higher education, and finally, discusses the future of Chinese higher education.

In the next chapter, Tom Bisschoff and Christopher Rhodes discuss the challenges and demands that a historically white school in a city setting in South Africa faces from a newly democratically elected government to transform and become an agent of change in making its pupil profile more representative of the demographics of the country as a whole.

The seventeenth chapter, authored by Paul Breen, Magdalena De Stefani, and Achilleas Kostoulas, describes and analyzes how an institution in the British higher educational sector has designed and provided a course of doctoral study, primarily by means of distance education. The chapter acts as an illustration of how institutions can and need to adapt to the nature of society and education in the twenty first century.

The eighteenth chapter, by Gonca Telli Yamamoto, Michael D. Featherstone, Faruk Karaman, and Patricia C. Borstorff, presents an experiential case study of a multicultural virtual team project conducted by educators at two countries of three universities whose students came from very different cultural backgrounds. The authors suggest that new technologies present businesses and the institutions charged with training business professionals with a significant paradigm shift. The case study details the experiences of students and instructors in creating and participating in a cross-cultural virtual team, conducted predominantly in a virtual environment.

The authors Felicia Blacher-Wilson, Evan G. Mense, and Michael D. Richardson, in the final chapter of the book discuss the growth of e-learning and distance learning technologies during the last decade. While doing so, they focus on the significant transformations in development and delivery of e-learning programs.

From the cases that have been presented in this book, it is evident that the field of educational marketing is quite dynamic and cases, research, and innovations can not be limited to only the present book. How can we continue to enrich our readers with latest developments? So, an idea of international journal on related areas of educational marketing emerged and finally it was conceived and developed as *International Journal of Technology and Educational Marketing (IJTEM)*(An Official Publication of the Information Resources Management Association). The journal is published semi annually by IGI-Global USA: the inaugural issue has been released in January 2011, and readers can access the journal at the following link: http://www.igi-global.com/IJTEM

Purnendu Tripathi
IGNOU, India

Siran Mukerji
IGNOU, India

REFERENCES

The Foreign Educational Institutions (Regulation of Entries and Operations) Bill. (2010). Retrieved January 11, 2011, from http://164.100.47.5/newsite/press_release/bill_committee.aspx

World University Rankings. (2010). Retrieved January 10, 2011, from http://www.timeshighereducation.co.uk/world-university-rankings/

Acknowledgment

We are indebted to the members of Editorial Advisory Board and members of review board of this book for their immense support and encouragement. We are indeed grateful to Dr. A. W. Khan, President, TAG University of Business, Kingdom of Bahrain for his kind consent to author the foreword. Our sincere thanks to Jan Travers, Director of Intellectual Property and Contracts, Kristin Klinger, Senior Editorial Director, Heather A. Probst, Director of Journal Publications, and Elizabeth Ardner, Director of Print Sales and Marketing for their invaluable support and cooperation. Our special gratitude to Myla Harty, Editorial Assistant to this book project for the much needed help at every stage of development of this book. Finally, we, the editors, are grateful to all the contributors for providing interesting and divergent case studies. We hope that readers will be benefited from our efforts and continue to offer their valuable suggestions.

Purnendu Tripathi
IGNOU, India

Siran Mukerji
IGNOU, India

Chapter 1
Exporting Hong Kong's Higher Education to Emerging Asian Markets:
Marketing Strategies and Government Policies

Alan C. K. Cheung
Johns Hopkins University, USA

Y. C. Cheng
Hong Kong Institute of Education, Hong Kong, PRC

Timothy W. W. Yuen
Hong Kong Institute of Education, Hong Kong, PRC

Celeste Y. M. Yuen
Hong Kong Institute of Education, Hong Kong, PRC

EXECTIVE SUMMARY

The purpose of this study is to examine the current conditions of higher education services in three Asian markets and to explore effective market strategies and supportive government policies to further promote Hong Kong's higher education in the region. It is evident from the findings that the visibility of Hong Kong's higher education in these Asian markets was extremely low. The low visibility of Hong Kong's higher education in the Asian region was due to a lack of concerted and coordinated effort between the Hong Kong government and higher education institutions in promoting their higher education. The study points to the need for more wide-ranging and coherent marketing strategies and government policies in order to attract the growing number of international students.

DOI: 10.4018/978-1-60960-599-5.ch001

ORGANIZATION BACKGROUND

Based on the latest statistics published by the Institute of International Education (2007, 2008a, 2008b, 2008c, 2009), the number of international students has been on the rise in many countries in the past two decades. For example, in 2005 the number of international students was 2.7 million, a significant 50% increase from 2000. It is estimated that the global demand for international education will grow to 3.7 million by 2025 (Banks, Oslen, & Pearce, 2009; Chow & Marcus, Winter 2008). According to the Organization of Economic Co-operation and Development (2007), there has been an increasingly high demand for international education from Asian markets such as India, Malaysia, and Indonesia in recent years. For instance, out of the top 14 sending countries, seven of them are from Asia. There is no doubt that the demand from the Asian regions will continue to dominate the markets in years to come (Bohm, Davis, Meares, & Pearce, 2002). To capture this growing market, many major hosting countries, such as the United Kingdom, Australia and the United States, have been stepping up their efforts to support the expansion of educational services to international students by developing favorable marketing strategies and government policies (Beaver, 2009; Carrington, Meek, & Wood, 2007; Obst, 2008).

Hong Kong is no exception. Since 2000, the Hong Kong government has initiated several measures to win market shares in Asia from its major competitors in the Asian regions. First, the Hong Kong government has recently raised the admission ceiling for non-local students from 10% to 20% starting with the 2008-2009 academic year. The second initiative that has been recently adopted was the establishment of funds to provide additional scholarships to both local and non-local students. Furthermore, the Hong Kong government has established a HK$18 billion Research Endowment Fund to further support the research work undertaken by higher education institutions (HEIs) in Hong Kong (Cheung, Yuen, & Yuen, 2008). In 2007, the Hong Kong government released its Action Agenda on China's 11th Five-Year Plan and the Development of Hong Kong, recommending the exploration of ways to attract more non-local students to study in Hong Kong and to develop Hong Kong into a regional education hub (The Hong Kong Government, 2007). In addition to the Mainland China market, the Hong Kong government is also increasingly interested in promoting their higher education services to other Asian regions. In 2009, education services had been identified by members of the Task Force on Economic Challenges (n.d.) as one of six major areas of economic development to be further developed. The objective of the present study is threefold: 1) to examine the condition of the three identified Asian markets, namely India, Indonesia, and Malaysia; 2) to examine the current strategies and government policies that were employed by key competitors such as the United Kingdom, Australia, and Singapore; and 3) to recommend appropriate marketing strategies and government policies to higher education institutions and the government in Hong Kong and elsewhere that are interested in expanding their efforts in recruiting the growing number of students from other countries, especially in Asian regions.

SETTING THE STAGE

Exporting educational services overseas can be of tremendous value to the countries involved. First, the industry can be economically important. For example, in Singapore, education has been taken as an important "knowledge industry" and accounts for more than 3% of the GDP (Yonezawa, 2007). Exporting education services, for instance, has already become Australia's third largest export (Luke, 2005). Its share in the cross-border degree study market rose quickly from 1% to 9% from 1990 to 2003 (Marginson, 2007). However, it should not be misunderstood that exporting educational services are targeted by exporting countries simply because of pecuniary benefits. Internationalization of higher education in fact can be seen as a response by academic institutions to a globalized world (Altbach and Knight, 2007). It is a response to a new age marked by globalization, competition, and marketization. Attracting foreign students to study in local universities and other forms of exporting educational services can foster the growth of the tertiary institutes on the one hand, and enhance the cultural sharing with other countries on the other. British Council Hong Kong, which is responsible for promoting British culture and education to Hong Kong, explained on its webpage: "We build engagement and trust for the UK through the exchange of knowledge and ideas between people worldwide" (British Council Hong Kong, n.d.).

Moreover, the international market for educational services is also expected to grow and the Asia Pacific Region is expected to be an area with huge increases in student numbers (Banks, et al., 2009; Bohm, et al., 2002). This is particularly the case with countries like India, Malaysia and Indonesia. But, the international market for educational services is in fact complicated. Marginson (2006) explained that the international market for educational services comprises at least a positional market of elite US/UK universities, which is now joined by an emerging commercial massive market. Against such a complicated market, success in exporting educational services often only comes with careful planning and investment in research. Kehm and Teichler (2007) noted that there has been an increasing body of research on internationalization of higher education. Marginson (2007) in fact explained Australia's achievement in exporting higher educational services against successful building up of a marketing niche: positioning herself as an Anglo-American system on the edge of Asia whilst differentiating herself from America and the UK in matters of price, location, safety, and climate.

The drive to export education services, particularly tertiary education service, has often involved an active supportive role of the government. The role of the government can be manifold.

The government can set up central agencies to facilitate the exporting of education services through providing collective research, promotion, and student services. In the case of Singapore, the Education Services Division under the Singapore Tourism Board works on competitive analysis and research (Singapore Education, n.d.). In a similar vein, the British Council of the United Kingdom and the Australian Education International of Australia (Australia Education International, n.d.) also study market trends on behalf of their countries. These efforts, in return, support the development of appropriate marketing strategies to penetrate the markets in the Asian regions.

On the other hand, the active support of the government can be the making of favorable education, population and employment policies that favor foreign students. Mok (2008) for example explained how the Singaporean and Malaysian governments in the past decade have worked towards the ideal of becoming a regional hub of education by reforming the national universities through the strategies of corporation and incorporation. Policy change can also be the reforming of university governance. The change in university governance is sometimes facilitated to encourage the universities to become more autonomous and entrepreneurial. Lee (2008) argued that universities in Singapore now enjoy a higher degree of institutional autonomy within a framework of public accountability.

There are many factors to explain why we can be optimistic about Hong Kong's potential to export her educational services. To begin with, the industry is now still in an infant stage and there is much room for development and growth. In 2007-2008, there were approximately 9,000 international students studying in Hong Kong. The number of students enrolled in publicly funded programs and self-financed programs were 6,000 and 3,000 respectively. On the other hand, Hong Kong possesses many favorable factors to attract overseas students. Among such factors are Hong Kong's reputation as a safe international city, its proximity and close relationship with Mainland China, and the rigorous quality assurance mechanism governing her tertiary institutes… etc. (Cheung, Yuen, and Yuen, 2008). In addition, Hong Kong has some of the world-renowned higher education institutions (HEIs) in the world. According to *Times Higher Education – QS World University Ranking 2009,* three out of the eight universities in Hong Kong were ranked as the world's top 50 in the world university league table (Times Higher Education, n.d.).

As mentioned earlier, the Hong Kong government has realized the importance of education service export and has already identified it as one of the major areas of growth for its economy (Task Force on Economic Challenges, n.d.). However, for a new-comer like Hong Kong to set foot in this international market of educational services, marketing research in fact is desperately needed, particularly because some players, like Australia, the U.K. and Singapore, are already becoming established and well known in the potential markets. McDonald and Dunbar (2004) explained that successful marketing hinges on understanding the market against such factors as market potentials, segments, and needs, etc. If Hong Kong is to develop into a regional hub of educational services, her efforts could be spearheaded by appropriate research and informed recommendation. It is against this the present study was undertaken.

CASE DESCRIPTION

Methods

This current chapter, which is a part of a larger study on the development of Hong Kong as a regional education hub, (Cheng, et al., 2009) focused on examining the current condition of the three target markets and generating effective marketing strategies and government policies recommendations to further promote Hong Kong's higher education to other Asian countries.

The data for this project was obtained from three major sources: surveys, in-depth interviews, and document analyses. The research team surveyed prospective students and parents in these three target markets. The in-depth interviews were conducted in Hong Kong as well as in the four studied cities—Mumbai, New Delhi, Jakarta, and Kuala Lumpur--between April 2007 to January 2008. Interviewees included government officials, academics, HEI's representatives, consulate generals, officials from policy bodies, and international students who were studying in Hong Kong. A total of 1,370 surveys and 121 in-depth interviews were conducted. For document analyses, the research team searched, collected, reviewed and analyzed all relevant documents related to policies and strategies used by these three countries via the Internet or provided by respective government officials or academics (see Cheng et al, 2009 for details).

The questionnaire survey had 28 questions covering the five major aspects: 1) demand for pursuing higher education overseas; 2) preferences when studying overseas; 3) general understanding and impressions of Hong Kong's higher education; 4) visibility of promotional activities of Hong Kong's higher education; and 5) personal demographic information. In addition, the interview guide consisted of 12 open-ended follow-up questions covering all major areas stated in the questionnaire survey.

Summary of Key Findings

The following section highlights the key findings from the surveys and interviews conducted in the three target markets and Hong Kong. These findings will generate insights into the discussion of marketing strategies and government policies which Hong Kong should adopt in the recommendation section.

Demand for International Education

It is clear from the findings that there was a high demand for international education in these target markets. A majority of students (over 80%) surveyed said that they were planning to study overseas. The findings of the focus group interviews with students and parents confirm the survey findings. When asked what were the main reasons to choose studying abroad instead of studying locally, most students and parents interviewed identified three reasons: 1) failing to secure a place at a local university due to a lack of university places in their hometown areas or keen competition, 2) obtaining a degree from overseas would make them more competitive when entering the labor force; and 3) not satisfied with the local higher education. Our findings are consistent with the broad literature that suggests there is an increasingly high demand for international education in these Asian markets.

Preferences When Studying Overseas

Preferred Degrees

When asked what kind of degree they were planning to pursue when studying overseas, more students preferred graduate degree to undergraduate degree. For example, over half of all respondents indicated that they preferred getting a graduate degree from an overseas institution to a local one. Approximately 35% said an undergraduate degree, and 12% and 4% said sub-degree and others, respectively. From the focus-group interviews with prospective students, the two main reasons for choosing a graduate program over an undergraduate program overseas were length of the study and its associated costs. It generally takes four years to finish an undergraduate degree as compared to two years for a graduate degree such as Masters' degrees. Though a doctoral degree takes 3-5 years, scholarships and assistantships are usually available.

The findings again are consistent with those of other studies. For example, since 2001/02, international graduate students outnumbered international undergraduate students in major hosting countries. Research shows that among all international students, close to half were pursuing graduate degrees, about 40% undergraduate degrees and only 14% non-degree/certificate studies or student on optional practical training (Chow & Marcus, Winter 2008). But it is noteworthy that, as revealed in our findings, around one-fourth of all respondents in Kuala Lumpur expressed an interest in pursuing a sub-degree overseas. It is not surprising given the fact that sub-degree programs and vocational studies are prevalent and popular in Malaysia.

Preferred Areas of Study

With regards to preferred areas of study, the top four majors among all respondents, in order of ranking, were Business Studies and Economics (24%), Medicine, Dentistry and Health Science (22%), Engineering (18%), and Computer Sciences (17%). (Figure 2) It is interesting to note that unlike other studied cities, there seems to be a high demand (21%) in Social Sciences such as Psychology, Political Sciences, and Sociology in Jakarta. Again, our current findings were in sync with a study by the Institute of International Education (2008b) that shows that Business, Engineering, Physical Sciences, and Computer Sciences were the top four majors among international students in the U.S.

Preferred Modes of Study

According to the General Agreement of Trade in Services (GATS), there are a few modes of supplying education services from one country

Figure 1. Degrees preferred

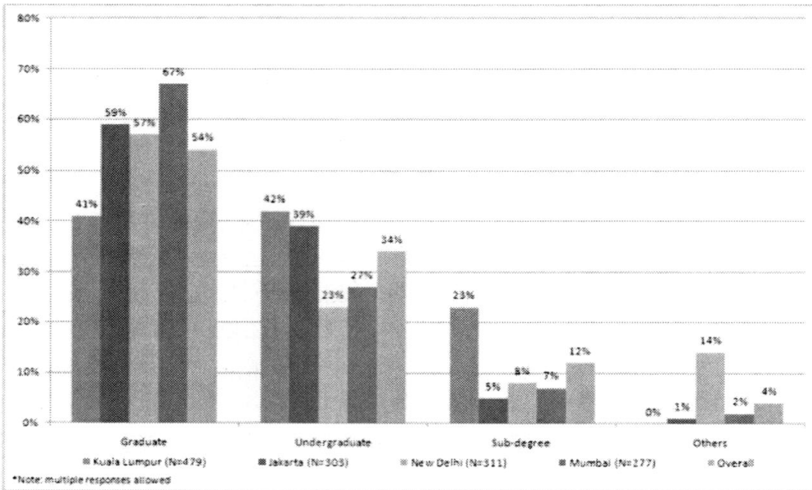

Figure 2. Majors preferred

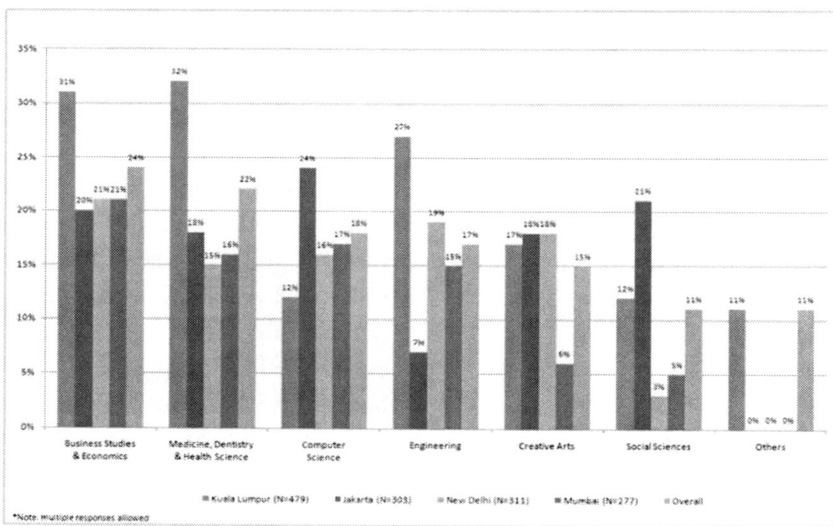

to another: 1) inbound mode, 2) outbound mode, and 3) mixed mode. In the context of the present study, inbound mode refers to the consumption of Hong Kong's higher education by overseas students in Hong Kong. In contrast, outbound mode refers to the consumption of Hong Kong's higher education by overseas students in their own countries. Students in mixed mode study partly in Hong Kong and partly in their home country.

When interviewing prospective students and their parents at education expos in the four studied cities, the majority indicated that they preferred inbound mode to outbound mode. Some interviewees believed that the outbound programs were not as good as the inbound programs due to a lack of both international exposure and overseas faculty members. In addition to inbound mode, a good number of respondents were in favor of a mixed mode approach. Some of the advantages of the mixed mode include familiar educational setting, more affordable tuition fees and staying close with family members during the major trunk of studies and gaining overseas exposure/internship. Outbound mode seems to be the least favorable choice among all interviewees.

Preferred Countries/Cities

In terms of countries/cities preferred, overall more students preferred Western countries like Australia (30%), the United Kingdom (26%), and USA (25%) to Singapore (18%) and Hong Kong (13%). (Figure 3) When asked why many students preferred Western countries to Asian countries, most interviewees believed that it was due to the fact that the U.K., Australia, and the U.S. are the world leaders in higher education. One student group in India best summed up this general perception by saying:

Both the U.S. and the U.K. are the two best countries when it comes to higher education. These countries are also the leaders in several disciplines such as medicine, engineering, and business. In addition, there are also abundant job opportunities.

A study conducted by the Australia Education International in 2007 also reached a similar conclusion with our current findings. In 2005-06, the number of annual enrollments of Indian students in the United States was 76,503; the U.K., 19,250 and Australia, 25,431 respectively (Australia Education International, 2007). Students interviewed in these three markets indicated that Singapore and Hong Kong were also attractive alternatives due to their close geographical proximity to their home countries and relatively low tuition fees and living costs compared to the U.K., U.S., and Australia.

Preferred Financial Assistance

Another consistent pattern found among all three studied markets is the importance of offering scholarships to these students. Seventy percent of all respondents said scholarship was their preferred financial assistance and 20% said assistantship/part-time job was important while studying overseas (Figure 4). There was also some demand for low-interest loans, especially in Mumbai and Kuala Lumpur. Approximately 15% of all respondents said low-interest loans were important to finance their further education overseas. When conducting fieldwork in these studied cities, the research team noticed there was

Figure 3. Countries preferred

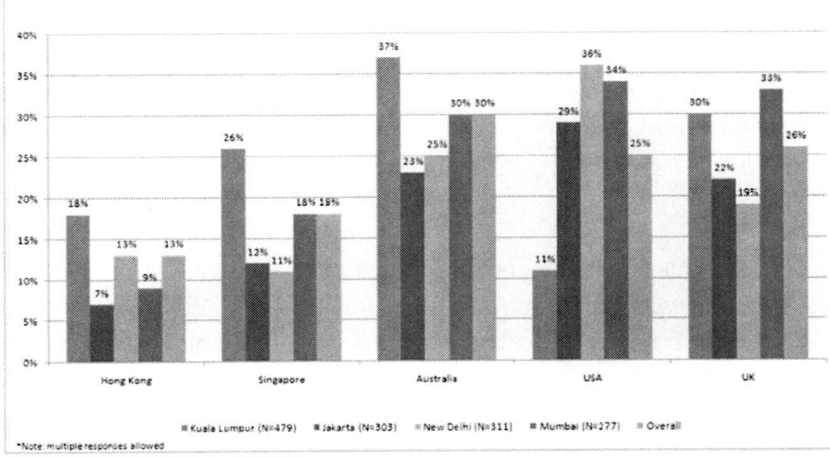

Figure 4. Financial assistantship preferred

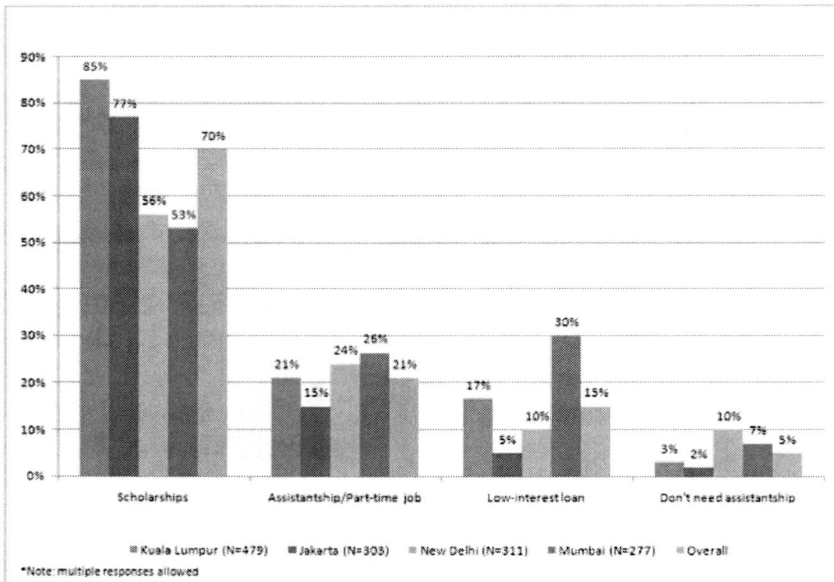

a strong presence of lending institutions and banks offering low-interest loans to target students at the expos in India. When interviewing with students in Kuala Lumpur, they said that the Singaporean government offered very low-interest loans to international students. This finding highlights the importance of offering low-interest loans, possibly at the government level, in exporting higher education to these target markets, especially in India.

Furthermore, similar findings were found during interviews with students and government officials in all three markets. As one student group interviewed in Mumbai commented:

Without scholarship aid, many parents would not be able to afford to send them to study overseas because of the high tuition cost and other associated expenses.

In addition to scholarships, the other most often-mentioned suggestion was part-time on-campus jobs. As one student group commented:

If HEIs in Hong Kong could offer part-time jobs to international students, that would be great because it would not only help us financially, but more importantly, it would also help broaden our learning and cultural horizons.

General Understanding and Impression of Hong Kong's Higher Education

General Understanding

When it comes to general understanding of Hong Kong's higher education among all respondents, our findings suggested that students from these three Asian markets knew very little about Hong Kong's higher education. According to the survey findings (Figure 5), close to 80% of all respondents said that they knew little or very little about the Hong Kong higher education system. Only 12% said adequate and 9% very well and fairly well.

The data from the focus group interviews also generated similar results. Most students inter-

Figure 5. General understanding of Hong Kong's higher education

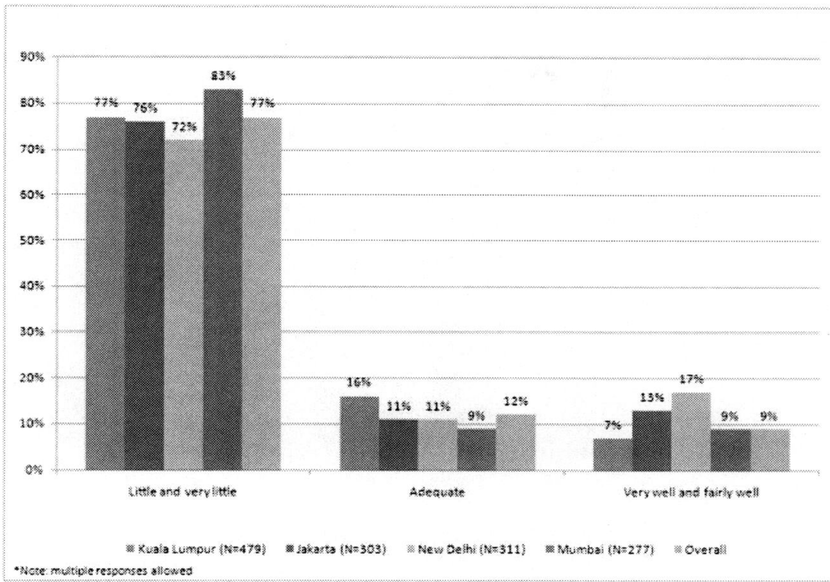

viewed said that they knew Hong Kong was a well known city in Asia but they knew very little about Hong Kong's higher education. One student in Malaysia put it well:

I think very few of my friends including myself would say they know much about Hong Kong's higher education. All they know is that Hong Kong is a shopping paradise and a well-known financial center.

Overall Impression

Though few respondents were familiar with higher education in Hong Kong, a good number of them had a good overall impression of Hong Kong's higher education. Based on the returned survey, an average of 30% of all respondents said their impression of Hong Kong's higher education had been good or very good (Figure 6). Close to half of the respondents said no idea, and about one fourth said average and not so good. When asked why they had a good impression of Hong Kong's higher education during our focus group interviews, the majority of interviewees said that Hong Kong was one of the most well-known and successful cities in the world, it must have a great higher education system to support its prosperity.

Promotional Activities of Hong Kong's Higher Education

Visibility of Hong Kong's Higher Education

In terms of visibility and the overall impression of promotional activities of Hong Kong's higher education in these markets, the findings clearly indicated that both of these items scored extremely low. Over 75% of all respondents stated that they were either not being informed or promotional activities were not visible to them (Figure 7). The qualitative data from our in-depth focus group interviews with various stakeholders generated similar results as the survey data. As one parent in Jakarta noted:

Figure 6. Overall impression of Hong Kong's higher education

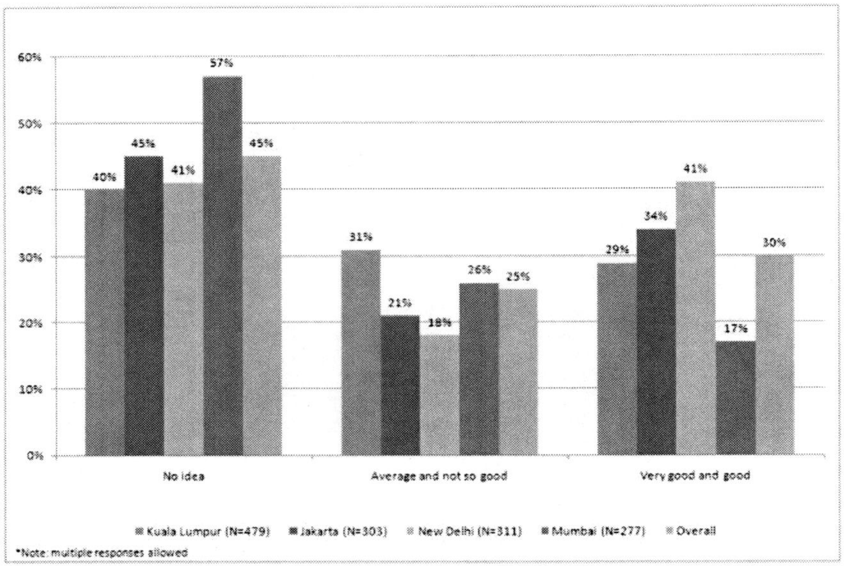

Figure 7. Visibility of Hong Kong higher education

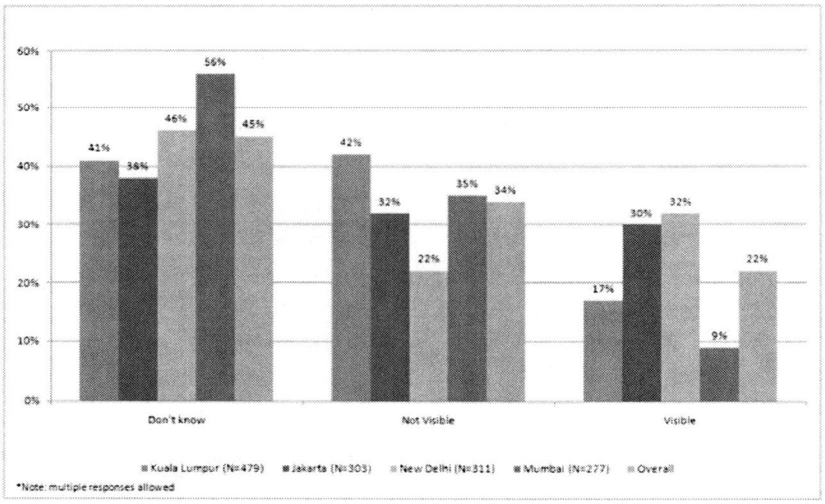

I have been attending education expos in the last few years and I didn't see a lot of promotional activities going on at the expos here in Indonesia by higher education institutions from Hong Kong.

Another education consultant in India echoed this comment by saying:

Compared to other countries such as Singapore and Australia, the visibility of Hong Kong's higher education in Asian markets is relatively weak. For example, Singapore has been campaigning aggressively in Asia over the past ten years to attract international students to their country. They also have a strong presence in major promotional outlets and channels in India such as

Internet, educational expos, TV ads, etc. If Hong Kong wants to enter these markets and compete with other competitors, they need to do a lot of catch-up work to raise their visibility.

Preferred Channels

When asked their preferred channels to obtain information for their overseas education, over 75% of all prospective students in these studied markets first considered Internet. About 30% said exhibitions, 20% newspaper, 18% TV, and 18% friends and relatives (Figure 8). Again, our interview data suggested similar results. In addition to the aforementioned channels, an increasing number of universities have become more proactive by paying regular visits to potential high schools in these markets and giving presentations to students and parents at the school. Some parents and principals interviewed also suggested that overseas offices could be another effective channel to reach out to disseminate useful information to prospective students and their parents.

The Decision of Studying Higher Education

When it came to making the decision to study overseas, 65% of all respondents said that the decision was more likely to be made jointly by parents and students (Figure 9). Approximately 20% of prospective students said the decision was made solely by them and only 11% solely by parents. Students, parents, and principals interviewed, confirmed the survey findings. During a focus group interview with prospective students in Kuala Lumpur, almost all the students indicated that parents played a very key role in the decision making process. As one student said:

My parents, of course, play a significant role in the decision making process when it comes to overseas study because they are the ones who will be footing the bills. Having said that, they will definitely consult with and involve me in the process.

Figure 8. Preferred channels to obtain information

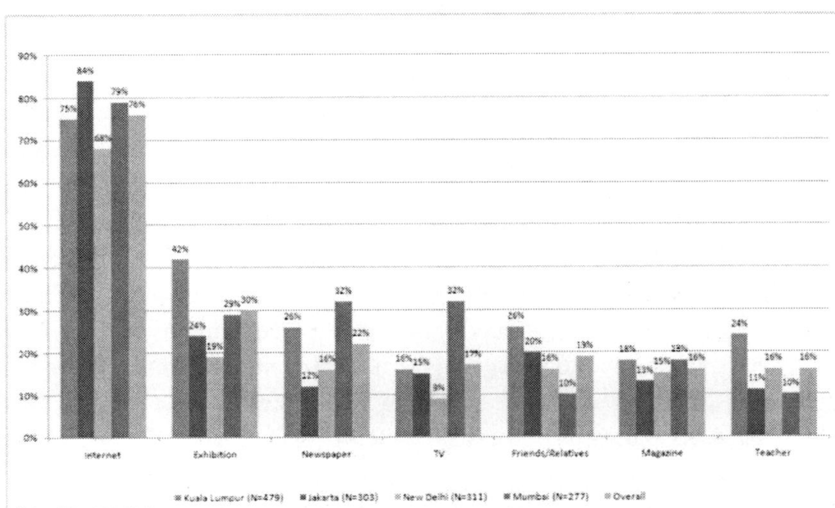

Figure 9. Decision makers when choosing higher education overseas

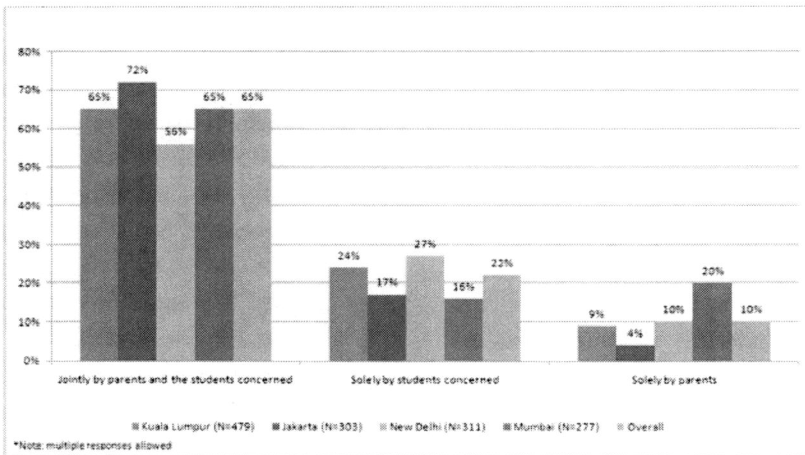

Other Observations

In addition to the above findings, the research team had made a few additional observations that stood out in these three markets during our fieldwork. First, bank loans were very common in India, but not so much in Indonesia and Malaysia. When attending the education expos in both cities in India, there was a strong presence of lending institutions at the sites.

Second, when interviewing government officials in Malaysia, we learned that there were over 50 degree programs offered by universities in Hong Kong that were recognized by the Malaysian government. However, no such information was obtained in the other two target markets.

Finally, there is a sizable population in Jakarta and Kuala Lumpur that is of Chinese descent. For example, over 60% of all respondents in Kuala Lumpur claimed themselves to be ethnic Chinese. During our interviews with other stakeholders in Malaysia, we were told that these Chinese ethnic students were generally well off and more inclined to study abroad due to political and economic reasons. Approximately 6 million Chinese reside in various parts of Malaysia. A good portion of these Chinese were studying in Chinese Independent Schools run by a private organization. According to a Chinese high school principal in Jakarta, a high percentage of these Chinese students were in fact planning to study overseas. For example, in 2005, out of the 6,000 Chinese high school graduates, approximately 30% chose to study abroad. Like Malaysia, Indonesia also has a decent number of ethnic Chinese, approximately 5 million. Out of the 20,000 Indonesian students studying abroad, half of them are ethnic Chinese. In contrast, there were very few ethnic Chinese living in these two studied cities in India.

DISCUSSION

Based on our key findings, the following section will be focusing on exploring effective marketing strategies and supportive government policies to penetrate these emerging markets. To this end, the widely accepted 4Ps model will be used as a framework to organize the marketing strategies and policies (McCarthy, 2001). The 4Ps are product, price, place, and promotion. The term "product" refers to tangible, physical products and services. Place refers to the channels of distribution that serve as the means for getting the product to the target customers. Price is the amount that target consumers are willing to pay for the product or services provided. In the context of marketing mix, promotion represents the various aspects of marketing strategies.

Products

Degrees Offered

In terms of degrees offered, it is clear from the findings that both undergraduate and graduate degrees are of high demand. Therefore, both undergraduate and graduate programs should be given a high priority in these three target markets. Sub-degree or diploma programs would be the second priority. Among the three target markets, the findings suggested that a good portion of prospective students, especially in Malaysia, were interested in overseas studies at the sub-degree level, both with academic and vocational orientations. This seemed to be a potential market especially if these programs could be linked to top-up undergraduate programs that, with an additional one to two years, can award students with first degree of Hong Kong or overseas universities. In order to cater to the diverse and unmet international education demands, HEIs should consider strengthening and diversifying their existing program pathways to accommodate a wide range of sub-degree/diploma graduates. This is also a common practice of the competitors to provide flexible pathways to international students to finish their degree study (Cheung, Yuen, Yuen, & Cheng, in press-b). In addition, HEIs may consider developing degrees of professional and vocational education (PVE).

Programs Offered

As mentioned earlier, the top four popular programs among all respondents were business, medicine, engineering, and computer science. Hong Kong has received high recognition and ranking in these majors both internationally and regionally. For example, the Economist Intelligent Unit ranked the MBA program offered by one HEI in Hong Kong among the 100 best in the world and first in Asia (Cheung, et al., 2008). The strong reputation of these programs, if promoted effectively, could be one of the strongest selling points.

In addition to academic excellence, HEIs in Hong Kong should also be focusing on their unique advantages and strengths when promoting their products in these markets. For example, Hong Kong is an international world class city, which has excellent infrastructure and excellent law and order. In addition, it also has a long history of engaging in international trade and is well-connected with the globe. Furthermore, Hong Kong serves as a gateway and springboard to Mainland China. These unique strengths are Hong Kong's competitive advantages over its competitors.

Place

Inbound Mode

When it comes to modes of study, it is evident from the findings that inbound mode should be given the first priority. According to school principals, government officials, and some HEIs representatives in these studied markets, in order to make Hong Kong more competitive, HEIs in Hong Kong need to consider establishing a credit transfer system between Hong Kong and the target markets. In addition, HEIs in Hong Kong should consider flexible admission (e.g. Fall and Spring admission) to accommodate students with different graduation dates. Furthermore, to provide a safe and multi-culturally sensitive campus to international students, Hong Kong HEIs should set up an international student office to provide one-stop on-campus support services to these students, ranging from orientation of university life, accommodation (home stay), library facilities, language support, academic and personal counseling services.

Mixed Mode

In addition to inbound mode, HEIs in Hong Kong may also consider offering mixed mode as a secondary priority to prospective students in these three target markets. A mixed mode should be offered in different structures to accommodate diverse needs of international students. For example, some competitors, such as Australia and the UK, offer a so-called 2+1 program to their international students, i.e. doing the first two years of studies in their home country and the last year overseas. Although some respondents opted for doing the whole overseas degree locally (3+ 0), this seems to be less attractive in the long run due to a lack of international exposure. Curriculum monitoring and the physical presence of professors to deliver the services within the territory of the member would be important. Preferably, the joint programs should be taught by local faculty members of high caliber and with international exposure. Besides, the frequent communications between the degree offering institutions and the market academics on program quality issues will be critical to address the quality assurance issues.

Outbound Mode

Based on our findings, outbound mode, i.e. foreign institutions offering programs locally in local markets, is the least favorable among all participants. However, if individual HEIs in Hong Kong decide to pursue this mode, the practice of other competitors has suggested that it should begin as a partnership with renowned overseas institutions to offer joint programs in the target markets to uphold its academic rigorousness.

Price

Among the 4Ps, price is a critical factor for prospective international students to consider when pursuing education overseas. Since Singapore is one of the favorite study destinations to many students in these Asian markets and Hong Kong's key competitor, it is important to make our tuition costs as comparable as to that of Singapore to remain competitive. In addition, the Singaporean government often provides international students scholarships, grants and financial aids to reduce their financial burden. Furthermore, the Singaporean government also offers low-interest loans to international students. The Hong Kong government may also consider working with banks and credible lending institutions to provide loans for international students. In the case of India where banking institutions often make loans to help Indian students seek overseas study, attempts should be made to work with these lending institutions to make sure students who are planning to pursue overseas education in Hong Kong are qualified for such loan.

Price differentiation (including providing more favorable rates to students from less-developed countries) is also recommended. This may help to attract international students in the target markets to choose Hong Kong as their potential destination. Moreover, bursaries for non-local eligible applicants are also important to encourage them to consider Hong Kong as their potential destination for higher education. Besides, to help non-local students to finance their studies and gain more exposure to Hong Kong society, restrictions on studentship and part-time work should be relaxed.

Promotion

Promotion represents the various aspects of marketing communications and perhaps has become the most important component among the 4Ps. One of the major drawbacks of exporting Hong Kong higher education is a lack of visibility of Hong Kong's higher education in these markets. Our findings revealed that around 70% of all student respondents from the four target cities indicated that they had no knowledge of higher education in Hong Kong. To facilitate the export of Hong Kong's higher education services, the

Hong Kong government and HEIs should increase the visibility of Hong Kong's higher education in these target markets. Based on the findings of the study and with reference to the best practices from other countries, below are some of the workable promotional initiatives.

Maximizing the Advantages of the Special Administrative Region: Hong Kong

First of all, Hong Kong should maximize the competitive advantages over its competitors when promoting their higher education overseas. For example, Hong Kong is one of the leading financial centers in the world. Being an international city with its excellent location and infrastructures, Hong Kong enjoys the benefits of its well-connected transport systems. The Hong Kong International airport is a leading air passenger gateway and logistic hub in Asia. It is trouble free and affordable for international travelers or frequent flyers to arrange their flight journeys both coming from the Asian Pacific rim and the West. Moreover, Hong Kong is known as a safe and East-West mixed place with a wide variety of international foods and entertainments. In terms of education, Hong Kong might be a new player in the international education exportation market, but it has nine well-established universities and a number of private higher institutions. As mentioned earlier, three of these HEIs were ranked in the world's top 100. Together they offer a wide range of degrees at undergraduate, postgraduate, associate degrees and diplomas levels. Each of the nine universities has established a sound self-accredited mechanism and their qualifications are in alignment with international standards. As its education system is modeled after the British one, it is easy for international students to adjust and engage in various academic activities. Moreover, being a special administrative region of and due to its geographical proximity to the Chinese Mainland, many academics take these advantages to develop their mainland connections, academically and socially. It is very common for HEIs to provide internships based in the Chinese Mainland. This China factor has been well acknowledged and will increasingly be seen as the key benefit to study in Hong Kong.

Strengthening the Partnership with Local Agencies in Target Markets

During our fieldwork in these four studied cities, we learned that many foreign institutions worked closely with local agencies in their target markets to promote their education services. Thus, it would be strategic to strengthen the connections with local popular agencies in these target markets. Agencies which have established a brand name in their country would offer wisdom as to how to target prospective students in the regions. For example, their connections with local schools, education authorities and banks would be invaluable for strategic positioning and development planning. Moreover, there are cultural issues in serving students from the target markets in terms of life-style, diet and religions. These could also be informed by the local agencies for all necessary preparatory works.

Widening the Clientele and Providing an Integrated Outreach Approach

As indicated in our survey data, the majority of participants said that the decision of studying abroad was often made jointly by parents and students. In this new era, the clientele of the market has been widened to include not only their prospective students, but also their families, friends, and relatives. In the Asian contexts, parents are often the sole financial providers for paying the tuition fees and therefore they play an important role in deciding where and what their children study in further education. Hence, it is important to be sensitive to the needs and concerns of prospective students and their families so as to provide a holistic service for them.

Continuing to Pursue Publicity through Various Channels Locally and Internationally

As indicated previously, publicity is the key to accelerate the development of the education industry locally and internationally. According to our findings, word of mouth, Internet, media advertisement and education expos are perceived as effective means to reach out to the target students and their parents. In addition, people networking can also contribute to publicity by inviting current international students to share their experience in Hong Kong with their own people in their hometowns. The wider the circulation of information, the better will be the results in reaching out to the prospective students and families for them to make an informed choice.

Collaborating with International Schools and School-Sponsoring Bodies in Target Markets

Establishing partnerships with international schools, school-sponsoring bodies and higher education institutions in the target markets is felt increasingly important. This could be a mutually beneficial joint venture. For example, Malaysia has a large portion of Chinese population and most of the school-age children are educated in schools run by the Chinese association, Dong Jia Zong. It has connection with Independent High Schools and universities for the Chinese communities. Fostering the partnership with the Association could be a good entry point to promote Hong Kong's higher education industry to this high potential group.

Providing Support Services for Cultural and Social Adjustment

Whilst much attention has been paid to overseas promotion and publicity, it is too imperative not to ignore the needs of the international students who are currently studying in Hong Kong. In order to help international students mix and share with one another and with local students, educational institutions should provide more exchange and leisure activities on campus. People networking will certainly help them settle into the new society, academically and socially. Other practical supporting services may include study skills, help in finding accommodation, academic placement, career-path information and assistance in student visa applications.

Government Policies

In addition to marketing strategies, the Hong Kong government should also consider working with HEIs and other bureaus to formulate favorable policies and measures to make Hong Kong a more attractive place to international students.

Expanding Subsidizing University Admission Quotas

In recent years, there has been a trend in Singapore to attract more non-local students to their undergraduate programs. For example, there is an expansion of the subsidized university admission quotas in Singapore. Likewise, enrollment quotas have been relaxed. These include an increase in the admission quota of non-local students from 10% - 20% of the approved student numbers for publicly funded programs from the 2008-2009 academic year at the undergraduate level. There was also an expansion of places in private universities. These are significant steps to respond to the perceived needs, but Hong Kong still lags far behind in this regard. In the 2009 policy address, for example, the Hong Kong government aspired to expand the education exportation market to include senior secondary students onwards. In response to this wake up call, the existing policy that 18% of the local students at the relevant age-group could only get access to 14,500 publicly-funded first-year undergraduate admission quotas should no longer be seen as sufficient. The Hong Kong government should consider a further increase in the admission of non-local students by increasing the total number of government funded places while keeping the admission quota of non-local students at the 20% level.

Investing in Higher Education and Research and Development

Second, research into higher education is one of the key areas for future research development. Although the Hong Kong government has granted HK$18 billion dollars to the higher education sector for research and development, compared with the investment of higher education in Australia, Britain and Singapore in terms of GDP, this is still far behind. In fact, local higher education institutions have suffered from inadequate research funding in academic activities such as exchanges, new projects and scholarships to attract internationally renowned scholars. It is well acknowledged that university reputation is a strong impact factor as far as recruiting international students is concerned (Mazzarol, Soutar, Smart, & Choo, 2001; Mullins, Quintrell, & Hancock, 1995). One of the key factors for making a good reputation is the amount of grants that the government invests in the higher education sector.

Providing Scholarship and Assistantships

It is evident from the findings that scholarships and assistantship were also great importance to many prospective international students. The Australian government hands out scholarships and grants on a competitive and selective basis and the Singaporean government offers a comprehensive package of financial aid to non-local students. Again, Hong Kong offers relatively stringent funds compared to Australia and Singapore. However, there was a change in the recent policy when the government established additional funds to provide more attractive scholarships to all students (Cheung, et al., 2008). With reference to the data collected from the on-site markets such as Singapore and Malaysia, the availability of low-interest loans is another determinant factor to help non-local students decide where and what to study. The local government should start working collaboratively with local banks and offering something comparable to any interested and selected non-local students planning to study any recognizable and qualified degrees.

Easing Population and Immigration Policies

The shortage of student accommodations has also been one of the main concerns of non-local students and the higher institutions as indicated in many of our personal interviews with non-local students in Hong Kong. Failure to address this issue properly could impede the development of education industry. Currently, some measures are being taken to address this need, such as building more hostels/joint hostels across institutions, provision of accommodation subsidies etc. (Cheng et al., 2009). However, these measures should not be done piece-meal and need to be on a larger scale. The government should consider including this element in its long term city planning and education industry development.

The findings also revealed that population and immigration policies are closely linked to the decision of the non-local students of where and what to study. Because of improvements in transportation, cross-border higher education has been promoted and intensified in recent decades. Apart from Australia and the United States, many countries in the West such as Ireland and the United

Kingdom are beginning to relax their immigration policies to allow international students to take up part-time jobs and/or allow them to work after their first year of graduation. The British Council has noted that easing immigration and job hunting procedures both during and after the period of study would facilitate and attract international students (Cited inBinsardi & Ekwulugo, 2003). In this regard, non-local students will regard Hong Kong's current immigration policies as unwelcoming as there are restrictions on part-time jobs during their study. Moreover, many of them have to wait a long time in order to obtain necessary work visas; it would be problematic to stay behind for job hunting even though they are allowed to do so after their graduation (Cheung et al., 2008). To make the immigration policy more welcoming and responsive to the international students, the government should consider reviewing the current practices and make necessary amendments so as to be more competitive. The talent migrant scheme should also be reviewed and lower its requirements so as to attract more qualified international talents to make Hong Kong their destination.

Entering into Policy Dialogues and International Agreements with Other Countries

Fifth, our findings clearly suggest that the governments of these three studied markets have been actively collaborating with other governments to promote their higher education. While interviewing representatives from various HEIs in Hong Kong, one of the recommendations was that the Hong Kong government should take a more active role in initiating communications and conversations with other governments to discuss issues such as credit transfers, recognition of degrees, and joint programs to further promote their higher education in these Asian markets. It is recommended that the government enter into policy dialogues and international agreements regarding these aforesaid issues in the form of a Memorandum of Understanding with the Ministry of Education of selected Asian countries at the Government-to-Government level. The Hong Kong government should continue to expand its network to other potential countries by tapping into existing economic and political relationships with countries throughout the world.

Establishing a Central Agency to Coordinate Exporting Higher Education

Mazzarol (1994) envisages that there is also a need to obtain sufficient, reliable and timely information on the education activities and national education systems of the potential competitors. In this regard, to develop Hong Kong as an education hub, the experience of Singapore and Australia in exporting higher education services should be taken into account. The past decades have seen strident advances made in this area by the leading central coordinating agencies of Australia, Britain and Singapore. For example, the Australian Education International, the British Council and Singapore Tourism Board all play a very critical role in promoting and developing strategies for exporting their higher education to non-local students and the education industry has become one of the major sources of income for their respective nations. With reference to these competitors, it is clear that without concerted efforts made by various key players it would be difficult to provide a comprehensive one-stop service to prospective students and their families. It is highly recommended, therefore, to set up a designated agency to coordinate efforts for researching, developing and promoting the market policy and implementation strategies. This agency should be of a multi-dimensional nature serving at the levels of policy making, research and development, promoting, crisis management as well as implementation (Cheng et al, 2009). Its mission can only be achieved by obtaining the endorsement and support from all the key players, for example and with regard to Hong

Kong, the higher education institutions, Hong Kong Trade Development Council, Hong Kong Tourism Board, the Hong Kong Education Bureau and the industry. The key responsibilities of the agency would include research into global trends and competitive analysis for promotion strategies, advertising for the Hong Kong education brand, free educational consultations, information sharing and dissemination, creating and updating databases and organizing educational expos and talks, both locally and internationally.

Establishing Overseas Offices

Furthermore, consideration should be given to establishing overseas offices to provide and disseminate important educational information to prospective students and their parents in selected Asian markets. Parents and students interviewed in these four target cities indicated that a local information center is extremely helpful to prospective students and their parents when choosing their study destination. In addition to providing general educational information, other basic related information such as employment and immigration should also be offered. The Hong Kong government could further explore and examine the feasibility of providing one-stop service to prospective students in these overseas offices. Using existing overseas offices run by other agencies (e.g. Hong Kong Trade Development Council) to serve as an information center for international students could be cost-effective because it does not require extensive investments.

Investing in Systematic Marketing Research

Finally, it is also imperative that the Hong Kong government and HEIs should equip themselves with the necessary marketing information and intelligence to position them in this increasingly intensified market. This may mean a substantial investment in conducting systematic marketing research in the selected markets. Few empirical studies have been conducted in these Asian markets. Further research is needed to fully understand the needs of prospective students. Of benefit would be an examination of the critical factors that may influence the decisions of prospective students in the selected markets.

CONCLUSION

The purpose of the current study is to examine the current condition of three Asian markets and explore effective marketing strategies and supportive government policies to further promote Hong Kong's higher education in the Asian regions. Overall findings of the study clearly indicate that there is a high demand for higher education services in these target markets. However, there was a widely shared view of a lack of general understanding and visibility of Hong Kong's higher education in the regions. In contrast, key competitors like the UK, Australia and Singapore have been stepping up their efforts in promoting their higher education by implementing effective marketing strategies and formulating favorable education, immigration, and population policies to support the export of their higher education for over a decade or more (Cheung, Yuen, Yuen, & Cheng, in press-a; Cheung, et al., in press-b)

Though Hong Kong is lagging behind other key competitors in terms of visibility and promotional efforts, it has several key competitive advantages: international world-class city, excellent marketing infrastructure, high-quality education with affordable costs, and well-established quality assurance mechanisms (Cheung, et al., 2008). In addition to these competitive advantages, the recent measures such as increased research funding and scholarship and ease of immigration policies initiated by the Hong Kong government have added much needed strengths to their overall competitiveness. The competition of international education will continue to be intensified as more countries enter into the race. This study points to the need for more wide-ranging and coherent policies in order to compete with other key competitors. Not only does the implementation of these strategies and policies require additional investment, but perhaps more importantly, it also requires more careful planning and coordinated efforts by the Hong Kong government, HEIs, other associated bureaus, and the support of the general public as a whole.

REFERENCES

Altbach, P., & Knight, J. (2007). The internationalization of higher education: Motivation and realities. *Journal of Studies in International Education*, *11*(3/4), 290–305. doi:10.1177/1028315307303542

Australia Education International. (2007). *International students in higher education-comparison of main English speaking destination countries*.

Australia Education International. (n.d.). *Market information package*. Retrieved on February 3, 2009, from http://www.aei.gov.au/AEI/MIP/Default.htm

Banks, M., Oslen, A., & Pearce, D. (2009). *Global student mobility: An Australia perspective five years on.* Retrieved December 14, 2009, from http://www.idp.com/pdf/GSM_Brochure_Oct07.pdf

Beaver, C. (2009). *The UK's international education s*trategy. Retrieved June 5, 2009, from http://www.iienetowrk.org/page/116258

Binsardi, A., & Ekwulugo, F. (2003). International marketing of British education: Research on the students' perception and the UK market penetration. *Marketing Intelligence & Planning*, *21*(5), 318–327. doi:10.1108/02634500310490265

Bohm, A., Davis, T., Meares, D., & Pearce, D. (2002). *Global student mobility 2025: Forecasts of global demand for international higher education*. IDP Education Australia.

British Council Hong Kong. (n.d.). About us. Retrieved January 14, 2010, from http://www.britishcouncil.org/hongkong

Carrington, R., Meek, V. L., & Wood, F. Q. (2007). The role of further government intervention in Australian international education. *Higher Education*, *53*, 561–577. doi:10.1007/s10734-005-8755-0

Cheng, Y. C., Ng, S. W., Cheung, A., Choi, P. L., Tang, Y. F., & Yuen, W. Y. (2009). *A technical research report on the development of Hong Kong as a regional education hub*. Hong Kong: Hong Kong Institute of Education.

Cheung, A., Yuen, W. W., & Yuen, Y. M. (2008). Exporting Hong Kong's higher education in Asian markets: Strengths, weaknesses, opportunities, and threats. *International Journal of Educational Reform*, *17*(3), 308–326.

Cheung, A., Yuen, W. W., Yuen, Y. M., & Cheng, Y. C. (in press). -a). Promoting Hong Kong's higher education to Asian markets: Market segmentations and strategies. *International Journal of Educational Management*.

Cheung, A., Yuen, W. W., Yuen, Y. M., & Cheng, Y. C. (in press). -b). Strategies and policies for Hong Kong's higher education in Asian markets: Lessons from the United Kingdom, Australia, and Singapore. *International Journal of Educational Management*.

Chow, P., & Marcus, R. (2008). International student mobility and the United States: The 2007 open doors survey. Retrieved from www.bc.edu/bc_org/avp/soe/cihe/newsletter/Number50/p13_Chow_Marcus.htm

Institute of International Education. (2007). *Open doors 2007: Report on international educational exchange*. New York, NY: Institute of International Education.

Institute of International Education. (2008a). *Global destinations for international students at the post-secondary (tertiary) level*, 2007. Retrieved Nov 11, 2008, from http://www.atlas.iienetwork.org/?p=48027

Institute of International Education. (2008b). *IIE study abroad white paper series*. New York: NY Institute of International Education.

Institute of International Education. (2008c). *Open doors: Statistics on international study mobility*. New York, NY: Institute of International Education.

Institute of International Education. (2009). *Global destinations for international students at the post-secondary (tertiary) level,* 2008. Retrieved April 17, 2009, from http://www.atlas.iienetwork.org/?p=48027

Kehm, B. M., & Teichler, U. (2007). Research on internationalisation in higher education. *Journal of Studies in International Education, 11*(3-4), 260–273. doi:10.1177/1028315307303534

Luke, C. (2005). Capital and knowledge flows. *Global Higher Education Markets, 25*(2), 159–174.

Marginson, S. (2006). Dynamics of national and global competition in higher education. *Higher Education, 52*, 1–39. doi:10.1007/s10734-004-7649-x

Marginson, S. (2007). Global position and position taking: The case of Australia. *Journal of Studies in International Education, 11*(1), 5–32. doi:10.1177/1028315306287530

Mazzarol, T. W. (1994). *A model of sustainable competitive advantage for service exporters*. Perth, Australia: Curtin University of Technology.

Mazzarol, T. W., Soutar, G., Smart, N., & Choo, D. (2001). *Perceptions, information and choice: Understanding how Chinese students select a country for overseas study. Commonwealth of Australia: Australian Education International.* Department of Education, Training and Youth Affairs.

McCarthy, J. (2001). *Basic marketing: A managerial approach*. Homewood, IL: Irwin.

McDonald, M., & Dunbar, I. (2004). *Market segmentation: How to do it, how to profit from it?* Amsterdam, The Netherlands: Elsevier.

Mok, K. H. (2008). Positioning as regional hub of higher education: Changing governance and regulatory reforms in Singapore and Malaysia. *International Journal of Educational Reform, 17*(3), 230–250.

Mullins, G., Quintrell, N., & Hancock, L. (1995). The experiences of international and local students at three Australian universities. *Higher Education Research & Development, 14*(2), 201–231. doi:10.1080/0729436950140205

Obst, D. (2008). *National policies for international education.* Retrieved Nov 8, 2008, from http://www.iienetwork.org/page/116248

OECD. (2007). *Share of tertiary foreign students in OECD countries*. Retrieved October 11, 2007, from http://www.oecd.org/document/54/0,3343,en_2649_37455_38082166_1_1_1_37455,00.html

Singapore Education. (n.d.). *Roles and responsibilities of Education Services Division.* Retrieved February 3, 2009, from http://www.singaporeedu.gov.sg/htm/abo/abo01.htm

Task Force on Economic Challenges. (n.d.). *Six economic areas identified by task force on economic challenges for further development.* Retrieved April 29, 2009, from http://www.fso.gov.hk/tfec/eng/press.html

The Hong Kong Government. (2007). *Report on economic summit on China's 11th five-year plan and the development of Hong Kong*. Retrieved September 22, 2009, from http://www.info.gov.hk/info/econ_summit/eng/pdf/tb_aa.pdf

Times Higher Education. (n.d.). *Times higher education - QS world university ranking* 2009. Retrieved January 14, 2010, from http://www.timeshighereducation.co.uk/Rankings2009-Top200.html

Yonezawa, A. (2007). Strategies for the emerging global higher education market in East Asia: A comparative study of Singapore, Malaysia and Japan. *Globalisation, Societies and Education*, *5*(1), 125–136. doi:10.1080/14767720601133561

ADDITIONAL READING

Altbach, P. G. (1998). *Comparative higher education: Knowledge, the university, and development*. Hong Kong: Comparative Education Research Centre, The University of Hong Kong.

Altbach, P. G. (2004). Higher education crosses borders. *Change*, *36*(2), 18–24. doi:10.1080/00091380409604964

Bennell, P., & Pearce, T. (2003). The internationalisation of higher education: Exporting education to developing and transitional economies. *International Journal of Educational Development*, *23*(2), 215–232. doi:10.1016/S0738-0593(02)00024-X

Bolsmann, C. (2008). International student recruitment to universities in England: Discourse, rationales and globalisation. *Globalisation, Societies and Education*, *6*(1), 75–88. doi:10.1080/14767720701855634

Brooks, J. H., & DuBois, D. L. (1995). Individual and environmental predictors of adjustment during the first year of college. *Journal of College Student Development*, *36*, 357–360.

Edwards, J. (2007). Challenges and opportunities for the internationalization of higher education in the coming decade: Planned and opportunistic initiatives in American institutions. *Journal of Studies in International Education*, *11*(3-4), 373–381. doi:10.1177/1028315307303920

Eggins, H. (2003). Globalization and reform: Necessary conjunctions in higher education. In Eggins, H. (Ed.), *Globalization and reform in higher education* (pp. 1–8). Glasgow, UK: Bell & Bain Ltd.

Gibbs, P., & Knapp, M. (2002). *Marketing higher and further education*. London, UK: Kogan Page.

Harman, G. (2004). New directions in internationalizing higher education: Australia's development as an exporter of higher education services. *Higher Education Policy*, *17*(1), 101–120. doi:10.1057/palgrave.hep.8300044

Hung, F. S., Shive, G., Wang, X., & Diu, J. (2005). *Export potential of Hong Kong's education services*. Hong Kong: Hong Kong Institute of Educational Research, The Chinese University of Hong Kong, and Hong Kong America Center.

Kau, A. K. (2005). Developing Singapore as an education hub in Asia: Opportunities and challenges. Department of Marketing and IB, Lingnan University. Retrieved from http://www.In.edu.hk/mkt/Seminar7Dec05.pdfKehm, B. M., & Teichler, U. (2007). Research on internationalisation in higher education. *Journal of Studies in International Education*, *11*(3-4), 260–273.

Knight, J. (2006). *Internationalization of higher education: New directions, new challenges. The 2005 IAU global survey report*. Paris, France: International Association of Universities.

Knight, J., & De Wit, H. (Eds.). (1997). *Internationalization of higher education in Asia Pacific countries*. Amsterdam, The Netherlands: European Association for International Education.

Li, M., & Bray, M. (2007). Cross-border flows of students for higher education: Push-pull factors and motivations of mainland Chinese students in Hong Kong and Macao. *Higher Education*, *53*, 791–818. doi:10.1007/s10734-005-5423-3

Linacre, S. (2007). *International students in Australia*. Australian Bureau of Statistics.

Luke, C. (2005). Capital and knowledge flows. *Global Higher Education Markets*, *25*(2), 159–174.

Mazzarol, T. W. (1998). Critical success factors for international education marketing. *International Journal of Educational Management*, *12*(4), 163–175. doi:10.1108/09513549810220623

Mazzarol, T. W., & Soutar, G. (2001). *The global market for higher education: Sustainable competitive strategies for the new millennium*. Northampton, UK: Edward Elgar.

Mazzarol, T. W., & Soutar, G. N. (2002). Push-pull factors influencing international student destination choice. *International Journal of Educational Management*, *16*(2), 82–90. doi:10.1108/09513540210418403

Mazzarol, T. W., & Soutar, G. N. (2008). Strategy matters: Strategic positioning and performance in the education services sector. *International Journal of Nonprofit and Voluntary Sector Marketing*, *13*(2), 141–151. doi:10.1002/nvsm.313

Mok, K. H. (2007). Questing for internationalization of universities in Asia: Critical reflections. *Journal of Studies in International Education*, *11*(3-4), 433–454. doi:10.1177/1028315306291945

Mok, K. H. (2008). Positioning as regional hub of higher education: Changing governance and regulatory reforms in Singapore and Malaysia. *International Journal of Educational Reform*, *17*(3), 230–250.

Mullins, G., Quintrell, N., & Hancock, L. (1995). The experiences of international and local students at three Australian universities. *Higher Education Research & Development*, *14*(2), 201–231. doi:10.1080/0729436950140205

Scott, P. (1998). Massification, internationalisation and globalisation. In Scott, P. (Ed.), *The meanings of mass higher education* (pp. 108–129). Buckingham, UK: OUP and SRHE.

Shieh, C. J., & Wang, I. M. (2007). *Development of export of China's higher education*. The National Council of the Professors of Educational Administration.

Teichler, U. (2004). The changing debate on internationalisation of higher education. *Higher Education*, *48*, 5–26. doi:10.1023/B:HIGH.0000033771.69078.41

Van Damme, D. (2001). Quality issues in the internationalisation of higher education. *Higher Education*, *41*, 415–441. doi:10.1023/A:1017598422297

van der Wende, M. (2007). Internationalization of higher education in the OECD countries: Challenges and opportunities for the coming decade. *Journal of Studies in International Education*, *11*(3-4), 274–289. doi:10.1177/1028315307303543

van der Wende, M. C. (2003). Globalization and access to higher education. *Journal of Studies in International Education*, *2*, 193–206. doi:10.1177/1028315303007002006

KEY TERMS AND DEFINITIONS

Export of Education Services: Refers to all services rendered to non-local students. According to the General Agreement on Trade in Services (GATS) for a country that exports education services, there are four modes of supplying education services: cross border supply, consumption abroad, commercial presence, and presence of natural persons.

Globalization: Refers to the integration of economies and societies among countries.

Inbound Mode: Refers to consumption of education services by non-local students in host country can be considered as the inbound mode.

Internationalization of Higher Education: Refers to bringing international and intercultural dimension into teaching and research to enrich the learning environment of an institution.

Mixed Mode: Refers to consumption of education services by non-local students in a foreign institution partly in the host country and partly in their own country.

Outbound Mode: Refers to consumption of education services by non local students in a foreign institution in their own country.

The 4Ps Model: It is a model or framework to organize marketing strategies and government policies. The 4 Ps are product, price, place, and promotion.

Chapter 2
Heterogeneity Analysis in the University Context: A Proposal Based on Service Quality Perceptions

Maria Fuentes Blasco
Universidad Pablo de Olavide, Spain

Irene Gil Saura
Valencia University, Spain

Beatriz Moliner Velásquez
Valencia University, Spain

EXECUTIVE SUMMARY

The transformations being experienced by Spanish universities faced with the challenge of adapting to a changing environment and increasingly discerning and segmented demand highlights the importance of knowing the needs and wishes of students as main customers. The present study attempts an in-depth examination of the viability of student perceptions of service quality as a segmentation criterion. We go deeply into the dimensionality of university service quality and we analyze how such dimensions can be used to segment effectively the collective of students' degrees using latent methodology. The results based on information gathered from 287 questionnaires permit analysis of existing heterogeneity and a set of recommendations to be made for strategic management in the area of university services.

DOI: 10.4018/978-1-60960-599-5.ch002

ORGANIZATIONAL BACKGROUND

Spanish University

Global social, economic and technological change since the late 20th Century such as globalisation of the economy, social and business fabric trends towards increased competition and the search for organisational excellence (Cheng, 2000), are affecting education and more specifically, university education. The internationalisation of university education and the growth in educational supply in recent years are some of the limitations encountered by institutions as they attempt to maintain their market share in the face of competition. Spanish universities are also facing the same challenges and have undergone substantial change recently since the construction of the European Higher Education Area which was promoted with the Bologna Declaration signed on 19 June 1999 by 29 European Ministers with competences in Higher Education. The Bologna process aims to increase compatibility and comparability of Higher Education systems while respecting their diversity and its introduction is planned for 2010. Current changes are mainly based on the following pillars: the elimination of obstacles to the movement of students, university teachers and administrative staff, recognition of higher education qualifications, the start up of a system of qualifications organised in three cycles, and European cooperation.

According to the Spanish Ministry of Science and Innovation, there are 77 universities in Spain - 47 of them are state universities, 23 are private universities, 5 are distance learning universities and 2 are specialized colleges. Out of the 23 private universities, 74% of them were created in the last fifteen years. Over a million and half students enrolled in universities in the academic year 2008-09 (1,500,069 students in first and second cycles: 89.2% enrolled in state universities and 10.8% in private universities).

In Spain there are 32.81 university students per 1,000 inhabitants. This ranking is higher than that in Germany (23.75), France (26.01) or UK (28.55). Despite these data, investment from GDP of the Spanish State in higher education was 0.9% in 2006, lower than the EU average (1.30%), Sweden (1.9%), and Norway (2.3). Spain also devotes only 0.08% to scholarships and grants to university students, while the OECD average is 0.25.

According to the Spanish Secretariat of State for Universities, the most significant weaknesses of Spanish universities system are lack of identity, academic failure, low academic standards, poor job placement, inadequate mobility, and above all, the resistance to change for adapting to the European Higher Education Area. These weaknesses would mean a less competitive and lower quality university education levels. Thus, the necessary investment in higher education and its efficient management are the keys for the success of Spanish universities integration into the European Credit Transfer System (ECTS) Programme.

The basic elements of quality in university education can be grouped into human factors (attitudes, teaching design, operation and competence of faculty), technical factors (infrastructure and equipment), and management factors (teaching programmes, organizing teaching quality assessment, information transparency and participation of everybody involved). Traditionally, the indicators used to measure quality in universities have been internal ratios to assess the demand-oriented students, human resources, physical resources, curriculum and academic achievements. However, with the growth of new information technologies and communication and the development of Educational Psychology, there is a need to better organize the higher education system that would include the specificities of each institution, faculty and students from a more qualitative perspective.

In view of all this, Spanish universities are increasingly aware of the need to maintain and/or improve the quality of their services. However, the most recent literature on service quality in the educational context criticises the lack of customer-friendliness, indicating that universities should focus not only on the skills and knowledge demanded by society, and which students must have, but also on students' attitudes and perceptions of the educational experience (Abdullah, 2006). Thus, management of the institutions from a student-friendly perspective provides a more integral dimension for planning actions in universities.

One of the areas of interest for academic research in education is to identify the aspects which condition students' choice of education provider. For example, in the study by Binsardi and Ekwulugo (2003) on students in the United Kingdom, the main determinant in the choice of university was found to be perception of the level of qualifications. Mazzarol and Soutar (2002) researched education in Australia and found that the quality and reputation of the institution also contributed to the choice. Previous studies have pointed out that the image of the educational service provider enables a competitive advantage to be developed in this type of market. However, the perception of service quality is a construct which has received special attention in the service marketing literature and specifically in research into university education. From both an academic and business management perspective, service quality permits increased profitability because it generates repeat purchase, positive recommendations, loyalty and contributes toward differentiating the service (Zeithaml & Bitner, 1996). In the last decade, many works have been published which have evaluated service quality in higher education, not only globally but also in different areas such as computer technologies, distance learning and student accommodation services, among others (Fuentes, Gil, Berenguer, & Moliner, 2007).

Furthermore, effective segmentation of the market enables organisations to adapt their supply to demand from profitable consumer groups, creating and maintaining competitive advantages in order to develop in the current business environment. Despite the importance attributed to segmentation as a strategy, there has been little in-depth exploration in the area of university education (Fuentes & Gil, 2006).

SETTING THE STAGE

Service Quality in Higher Education

In the service literature, service quality is generally understood to be "*a global judgement or attitude, concerning the superior nature of the service*" (Parasuraman, Zeithaml, & Berry, 1988, p.16). It has a technical and a functional dimension which are associated respectively with the result ("what" the consumer is receiving) and the process ("how" the service is being received) (Grönroos, 1984). It is therefore commonly accepted that assessment of service quality must include not only service design, that is, the most tangible aspects of the service, but also how it is performed and in particular, the interaction between the customer and service provider staff.

Higher education is considered to be a pure service as this personal interaction component is particularly relevant (Oldfield & Baron, 2000). The different figures participating in university education service (students, government, teachers, staff, etc.) are one of the reasons why service quality in this field of research is considered to be a complex, multidimensional concept which is still awaiting definition and measurement in the literature. The different proposals, in the context of conceptualising quality in the university sphere include the one by O'Neill and Palmer (2004) who define service quality in higher education as "*the difference between what students expect to receive and their perception of the service delivery*" (p.42). This approach which links expectations and perceptions by attributing judgements of high or low quality depending on "*how consumers perceive the actual result of the service in the context of what they were expecting*" (Parasuraman, Zeithmal, &

Berry, 1985, p.46), has its origins in the research tradition developed by Parasuraman et al. (1988) and in the assessment proposals based on the SERVQUAL scale.

In recent decades, different measurement instruments have been produced to evaluate service quality, such as SERVQUAL (Parasuaraman et al., 1988), SERVPERF (Cronin & Taylor, 1992) and evaluation of performance (EP) (Teas, 1993). Whereas the SERVPERF scale measures service quality using only assessment of perception, the EP scale analyses the gap between perception of performance and the ideal level of each service attribute, while the SERVQUAL scale quantifies quality by comparing normative perceptions and expectations.

Measurement of service quality has been mainly dominated by the use of this last scale and by the subsequently renewed Three-Column format SERVQUAL, which includes desired expectation and minimum expectation (Parasuraman, Zeithmal, & Berry, 1994); since the 1990s many applications have been developed on the basis of this proposal in the sphere of university education (see Table 1).

However, many works point out certain conceptual and operational limitations in these service quality measurement instruments (Gil, 1996). For example, one of the main criticisms of the SERVQUAL scale refers to the role of expectations (Carman, 1990; Teas, 1993). The main criticism is based on the interpretation of the expectation concept as the ideal standard and its operationalisation in the SERVQUAL instrument. It is argued that the conception of ideal comparison standard, interpreted as the classical ideal point or weak ideal point in the classical models for ideal attitude point is not compatible with the measurement of perceived service quality obtained from the discrepancy (P – E) which is specified in SERVQUAL. In this sense, the concept of service expectation has been extensively debated, however, there is no clear consensus on the specific nature of the expectation variable as a standard of comparison. Furthermore, more recent works question the importance attributed to the role of expectations especially in the area of quality assessment. Thus, several authors conclude that although a wide variety of expectations have been defined, there is no structure which permits different standards to be joined or which indicates their interactions with service performance (Kalamas, Laroche, & Cézard, 2002). After analysing the above conceptual and operational problems of SERVQUAL, Teas (1993) develops a probabilistic model of perceived quality based on the perception of the service received (P) and expectation as ideal point (I), the scale of Evaluated Performance (EP). The author points out that although the final model is similar to the operationalisation proposed in SERVQUAL, it must not be forgotten that it is assumed that the attributes have infinite classical ideal points and that SERQUAL'S concept of normative expectation is redefined as "excellence norm". Teas (1993) examines the validation of the conceptual model for perceived service quality (P – E) as specified in the service quality literature and that of two proposed alternative models. The author evaluates the validity of the construct by correlation between the scales and a global satisfaction measurement, pointing out that the SERVQUAL scale construct, while when valid, is inferior to the Evaluated Performance Scale (EP).

The same occurs in the analysis of concurrent validity though there is a correlation index between global quality and the two scales. These results are also compared by other authors such as Fuentes and Gil (2006) who award construction superiority to the EP scale over the SERVQUAL scale in Spanish higher education context.

Also, some research suggest that service quality measures based only on assessment of performance such as the SERVPERF scale are more valid and offer greater explained variance than SERVQUAL and EP. As an alternative model, Joseph and Joseph (1997) propose the importance/performance paradigm to measure service quality

Table 1. Empirical research on service quality in higher education

Study	Concept investigated	Conceptualisation	Operationalisation	Sample	Sampling technique	No. items	Response scale	Information analysis
Shank, Walker, and Hayes (1995)	Perceived Quality Service (student-faculty)	Perceptions - Expectations	Adapted Servqual	686 students from 4 different universities, 13 faculty	Not specified	23	7 points	Parametric and non-parametric statistic tests
Casanueva, Periáñez, and Rufino (1997)	Teaching service quality provided by the professor	Perceptions	Own scale	954 statements from 120 students	Not specified	28	Not described	Exploratory Factorial Analysis (PCA) ANOVA Regression Analysis
Owlia and Aspinwall (1998)	Engineering teaching quality	Perceptions Importance	Own scale	94 students in the final year of Engineering	Random sampling	19	5 points	Exploratory Factorial Analysis (PCA) Regression Analysis
Camisón, Gil, and Roca (1999)	State university service quality	Perceptions – Expectations, Perceptions	Adapted Servqual plus own items	400 students from two different degree courses	Stratified random sampling	37	7 point Likert	Factor Analysis and Linear Regression
Engelland, Workamn, and Singh (2000)	Qualification services centre quality	Perceptions - Expectations	Adapted Servqual	237 students who had used the services	Not specified	50-22	Not specified	Exploratory Factorial Analysis (PCA) and Confirmatory Analysis
Comm and Mathaisel (2000)	Service quality in higher education employees	Perceptions - Expectations	Adapted Servqual plus own items	473 employees in a private higher education institution	Not specified	70	5 point Likert	Not specified
Long, Tricker, Rangecroft, and Gilroy (2000)	Distance Learning Service Quality	Perceptions - Expectations	Own scale	Students and professors	Not specified	36	No especifica	Descriptive analysis
Bekkering and Engelland (2002)	Technology service quality in university computer classrooms	Perceptions - Expectations	Adapted Servqual plus own items	278 students from state university	Not specified	42	7 point Likert	Exploratory Factorial Analysis (PCA) and Confirmatory Analysis

continued on following page

Table 1. continued

Study	Concept investigated	Conceptualisation	Operationalisation	Sample	Sampling technique	No. items	Response scale	Information analysis
Capelleras and Veciana (2004)	University teaching service quality	Perceptions	Own scale	8026 students from 3 scientific disciplines	Stratified random sampling	22	5 point Likert	Exploratory Factorial Analysis (PCA) and Confirmatory Analysis
Russell (2005)	Service quality for international university students	Perceptions - Expectations	Own scale	27 postgraduate international students and 25 undergraduate international students	Non random sampling	Not specified	Not specified	Crosstabs and Pearson chi-square test
Abdullah (2006)	State and private university teaching service quality	Perceptions	Adapted Servperf (HEdPERF scale)	381 students	Random sampling	22	7 point Likert	Exploratory Factorial Analysis (PCA), Confirmatory Analysis and Regression Analysis
Fuentes and Gil (2006)	University students' service quality expectations	Minimum, Desired and Ideal Point Expectations	Adapted Servqual Evaluated Performance Model	287 students at a university centre	Stratified random sampling	18	5 point Likert	Confirmatory Analysis
Prugsamatz, Pentecost, and Ofstad (2006)	University students' service quality expectations	Expectations	Adapted Servqual	133 students from two universities	Random sampling	16	7 point Likert	Exploratory Factorial Analysis (PCA), MANOVA
Smith, Smith, and Clarke (2007)	Information Technology service department in a Higher Education Institute	Perceptions – Expectations	Servqual	314 students and 152 staff	Not specified	22	7 point Likert	Exploratory Factor Analysis
Brochado (2009)	University students' service quality	Perceptions – Expectations	Adapted Servqual, Servperf and HEdPERF	360 university students	Not specified	41 (HEdPERF) 22 (Servqual)	7 point Likert	Confirmatory Analysis and Regression Analysis

continued on following page

Table 1. continued

Study	Concept investigated	Conceptualisation	Operational-isation	Sample	Samplingtechnique	No. items	Response scale	Information analysis
Nadiri, Kan-dampully, and Hussain (2009)	perceived service quality of staff, faculty and dormitories, sports and health centre.	Perceptions	Servperf	492 stu-dents	Non random sam-pling	22	5 point Likert	Exploratory Factor Analy-sis and Linear regression
Radder and Han (2009)	Service Quality of On-Campus Student Hous-ing	Perceptions – Expectations	Adapted Servqual	430 residential students	Stratified random sampling	24	5 point Likert	Exploratory Facto-rial Analysis (PCA) and Confirmatory Analysis ANOVA
Trivellas and Dargenidou (2009)	Organisational culture and job Satisfaction on the quality of services pro-vided in higher education	Perceptions	Own scale	134 faculty and staff	Not specified	24	7 point Likert	Exploratory Facto-rial Analysis (PCA) and Regression Analysis
Bayraktaro-glu and Atrek (2010)	State univer-sity teaching service quality in faculty of business	Expectations, Perceptions and Importance	Adapted Serqual and Servperf	421 stu-dents	Not specified	21	5 point Likert	Confirmatory Analysis,

Source: adapted from Fuentes et al. (2007).

in education. This instrument, applied in some studies, permits detection of students' tolerance zone in order to identify areas of satisfaction and dissatisfaction. Thus, despite the extensive literature on service quality assessment, some theoretical and empirical aspects are still unresolved and measurement is the most debated controversial aspect in the theory (Abdullah, 2006). Apart from the debate among the above researchers for the merits of SERVQUAL over SERVPERF and vice versa, it seems, however, that on balance the emerging literature supports the performance-based paradigm over the disconfirmation-based paradigm (Nadiri et al., 2009).

Furthermore, from a conceptual perspective and addressing the idea of variable multidimensionality, quality components need to be adapted to each service area and specifically in the context of education (Capelleras & Veciana, 2004). The literature offers a wide variety of service quality dimensions in higher education. One of the most recent contributions is by Russell (2005) who points out that the following are particularly relevant in educational services experiments: the service delivery process, physical and technological facilities, and the human factors given that interaction with the teacher is the main component in the service provision. One of the recent adaptations in the context of university education is the scale HEdPERF (Higher Education PERFormance) which measures service quality based only on assessment of performance which represent factors on academic, non academic, reliability and empathy aspects (Abdullah, 2006).

Service Quality and Latent Segmentation

The need to study consumer differences has been widely recognised in the face of growing heterogeneity in consumer behaviour patterns and strong competition in consumer markets (Wedel & Kamakura, 2000). For organisations, this heterogeneity suggests the need to develop segmentation strategies for services in order to adapt their offer as far as possible to the needs and desires of target groups in relation to their limited resources. This fact has been particularly relevant in the sphere of university education, where it has been suggested there is a need to provide offers which adapt closely to the target groups (Fuentes et al., 2007).

Wedel and Kamakura (2000) argue that identifying internally homogenous and heterogeneous segments with each other depends on the basis and procedures used to define them, in accordance with the strategic aim of the study and the market in question.

In relation to the criteria, Webster (1989) recognises that any hypothetical construction could be used as a segmentation variable, provided it is operational and can be measured. Despite that, the literature on market segmentation underlines the importance of criteria regarding consumer behaviour and consumer response to the service provision. Specifically, recent works on these lines highlight the utility of the resulting segments when considering uneven influence of consumer behaviour based on the perception of the received service quality (see Fuentes & Gil, 2006; Fuentes et al., 2007; Sánchez, Sánchez, Marín, & Gázquez, 2007).

Segment identification has evolved towards modelising non observed heterogeneity characteristic of behavioural bases using latent methodology. This type of procedure means that consumers can be assigned to segments on the basis of likelihood of belonging, thereby eliminating the restriction of deterministic assignation characteristic of non hierarchical cluster analysis (Dillon & Kumar, 1994). This methodology assigns individuals to different segments, under the supposition that the data comes from a mixture of probability distributions, that is from different homogenous groups or segments which are mixed in unknown proportions (McLachlan & Basford, 1988). As neither the segment to which each individual belongs nor the number of segments is known beforehand, the aim is to "undo the mixture" or recognise sample heterogeneity, identifying the different groups by estimating the parameters for the density function underlying each segment (Wedel & Kamakura, 2000). The segments thus identified are "*intuitively more attractive, more realistic and theoretically more precise*" (Lilien & Rangaswamy, 1998, p.60). Furthermore, the latent focus provides other advantages over traditional segmentation techniques. The main of these being that they are based on a probabilistic distribution model, *parametric* or *semi-parametric,* on the population from which the sample is extracted which makes it possible to describe the segments and estimate the unknown parameters using the likelihood principle (Dillon & Kumar, 1994), and therefore make predictions with a common model structure (Magidson & Vermunt, 2002). From this utility derive other advantages of latent segmentation over traditional segmentation techniques such as: (1) a posterior classification of individuals based on the likelihood of belonging, an individual can be assigned to one or more groups, where the likelihood of each individual belonging to the total of groups is one; (2) unlike traditional cluster analysis, latent modelisation *offers different diagnosis and validation criteria* to determine the resulting solution, for example the Bayesian information criterion (BIC) is highly useful for validating the number of segments, since latent model involves parametric or semi parametric distributions; (3) they are *more flexible techniques* than traditional cluster techniques on the nature of the study variables as they are not limited to quantitative variables. In addition, it is not necessary to standardise the variables in the analysis as the solution of groups from the mixture models is invariant to linear transformations (Magidson & Vermunt, 2002); (4) furthermore exogenous variables (known as covariables) can be included to classify and describe the segments using a single estimation algorithm. This makes it possible to define the profiles for the resulting segments more clearly which is crucial for the correct introduction of the segmentation strategy in a company (Wedel & DeSarbo, 2002); (5) latent models *can be estimated when the number of latent variables is even higher than the number of segments* (Magidson & Vermunt, 2002); (6) conditioned mixture models and finite mixture models with structural equations permit *determination of the belonging* of individuals to the segments in terms of likelihood and *estimation of the influence* of the independent variables on the dependent variables *in a single step*, unlike the tandem approach, thereby limiting problems of measurement error.

The advantages of latent segmentation methodology have promoted research into statistical techniques for identifying heterogeneity at segment level by estimating finite mixture models. These models are based on the premise that sample observations come from two or more groups and are mixed in unknown proportions. It is therefore a question of dividing the sample, identifying and estimating the parameters in relation to the underlying density of the data observed in each group or segment. Therefore the unconditional likelihood of the values observed is defined as a mixture of the densities in each segment and the mixture weightings, thus defining the relative size of each group (Wedel & Kamakura, 2000).

CASE DESCRIPTION

Objective and Methodology

According to the theoretical background, this case attempts to make contributions to service quality for higher education. It is aimed to evaluate the utility of university student perceptions on service quality to establish the basis for developing strategies based on the delivery of quality and to analyse the functionality of perceptions in service evaluation as a behavioural segmentation criterion.

In this epigraph, an attempt is made to show the research design and methodology and the validity of the proposed scale to achieve our objective.

Measurement Scale and Information Collection

In order to obtain a battery of questions which would capture all the essential aspects of university teaching service quality, the domain and the identification of main dimensions which composed this domain were defined. Service quality perceived by students (specified consumers in the present study) was defined as the students' judgment about overall excellence or superiority of educational service.

From this definition, the literature allowed to identify a battery of items on the five dimensions of service quality (Parasuraman et al., 1988) which included specific attributes for the higher education context (Carman, 1990). In this sphere, several authors have highlighted the importance of dimensions such as the university teacher's teaching work (Camisón et al., 1999) and the study support services – libraries, computer and language laboratories – (Bekkering & Engelland, 2002).

On the basis of this information, a 25 item scale was considered that was generated from the review of the literature and the accumulated experience of the teaching quality evaluation processes undertaken by the university centre where this study took place. The initial scale was pre-tested to enhance the content validity of the attributes investigated and the clarity of wording. As a result, the scale was made up of 18 items (see Table 2).

We used the 5-point Likert format to reflect the perception of each measured variable, where 1 is "strongly disagree" and 5 "strongly agree".

Table 2. Attributes used in the study

Items	Meaning	Source
P1	Have modern looking equipment	Adapted from Engelland *et al.* (2000) and Bekkering and Engelland (2002)
P2	Have suitable classrooms to teaching or study	
P3	Have updated bibliographical batches of documents	
P4	Present a full range of career-planning resources	
P5	Have information readily for job searches	
P6	Have faculty who have an adequate level of theoretical-practical knowledge	Adapted from Capelleras and Veciana (2004)
P7	Have faculty who have an adequate ability to transmit concepts	
P8	Have faculty who explain the concepts with sufficient clarity	
P9	Have faculty who prepare their sessions suitable	
P10	Have employees who give personal attention	Adapted from Parasuraman *et al.* (1988) and Camisón *et al.* (1999)
P11	Have employees who know the needs of their students	
P12	Promise to do something by a certain time, then do it	
P13	Have complete information on employers	
P14	Show a sincere interest in solving the students problems	
P15	Be consistently courteous with students	
P16	Tell students when they will be served	
P17	Serve students promptly	
P18	Have the student's best interest at heart	Adapted from Engelland *et al.* (2000)

The response rate to the questionnaires was high at 94% (287 questionnaires were returned and analyzed, so there was a sample error of approximately ± 3.67%, for a significance of 0.05).

Measurement Scale Reliability, Dimensionality and Validity

The preliminary study on dimensionality and possible refinement of the scale was conducted by an exploratory factor analysis (Maximum Likelihood Method with Varimax Rotation), using the criteria of eigenvalues greater than 1 (Hair, Anderson, Tatham & Black, 1999). In terms of the dimensionality, the items were grouped in four dimensions (see Table 3). With regard to the scale refinement, the items eliminated were those which, when eliminated, considerably increased the alpha reliability indicator[1].

The global results in Table 3 reflect the satisfactory values for scale dimensionality, as the total explained variance for the four dimensions is over 50% (Hair et al., 1999) and reliability values show good internal consistency over 0.7 (Nunnally, 1987).

The results extract four dimensions to define service quality in the higher education context.

The first factor is made up of the variables relating to *fulfilment and attitude of contact staff and faculty* such as ability to provide the promised

Table 3. Initial analysis of scale dimensionality

Items	F1	F2	F3	F4
P1	0.206	0.150	0.218	0.108
P2	0.236	0.293	0.191	0.074
P3	0.187	0.241	0.511	0.080
P4	0.209	0.247	**0.750**	0.202
P5	0.205	0.180	**0.759**	0.132
P6	0.222	**0.636**	0.277	0.155
P7	0.108	**0.813**	0.162	0.163
P8	0.280	**0.721**	0.252	0.127
P9	0.251	**0.629**	0.167	0.192
P10	**0.658**	0.223	0.188	0.329
P11	**0.643**	0.276	0.302	0.155
P12	**0.675**	0.268	0.105	0.127
P13	**0.608**	0.279	0.173	0.182
P14	**0.656**	0.113	0.225	0.206
P15	**0.712**	0.091	0.251	0.340
P16	0.348	0.279	0.170	**0.800**
P17	0.266	0.188	0.157	**0.932**
P18	0.379	0.306	0.277	0.442
Factor	Fulfilment and attitude of contact staff and faculty	Technical dimension of faculty	Tangible aspects	faculty attitude and behaviour
Conbrach's Alpha	0.841	0.819	0.783	0.778
Explained Variance	15.43%	14.00%	11.60%	10.21%
Alpha: 0.902; Test Barlett Chi² (g.l. 153)=2343.31 (p-valor=0.000) Índice KMO: 0.891				

service reliably, correct manner to inform and the interest in solving students' problems. The second dimension refers to *technical dimension of faculty*, including aspects such as adequate level of knowledge, ability to transmit concepts and to explain with clarity. In the third place, the factor relating to the *tangible aspects of service* includes attributes with regard to career-planning and information for job searches. Finally, the dimension of *faculty attitude and behaviour* includes variables such as availability of faculty to meet the students.

This initial dimensionality proposal was confirmed after confirmatory factorial analysis with software EQS 6.1. The measurement model was estimated with the robust maximum likelihood method, using the covariance matrix from the outset. First we calculated internal consistency of the dimensions considering two indicators: composed reliability coefficient with a minimum threshold of 0.7 (Anderson & Gerbing, 1988) and the variance extracted for each factor, whose value must be over 0.5 (Fornell & Larcker, 1981). These indexes, shown in Table 4, are acceptable for all dimensions.

Table 4. Measurement model (scale dimensionality, reliability and validity)

	Items	Standardized factor loadings	Correlation² (CI at 95%)
Fulfilment and Attitude Staff (F1)	P10	0.637	F1-F2=0.465 (0.407; 0.523) F1-F3=0.378 (0.302; 0.454) F1-F4=0.567 (0.485; 0.649) F2-F3=0.360 (0.284; 0.436) F2-F4=0.367 (0.295; 0.439) F3-F4=0.315 (0.223; 0.407)
	P11	0.679 (11.94**)	
	P12	0.686 (8.77**)	
	P13	0.725 (9.75**)	
	P14	0.677 (9.20**)	
	P15	0.608 (8.66**)	
	Composed reliability	0.856	
	Extracted Variance	0.501	
Technical dimension of faculty (F2)	P6	0.655	
	P7	0.789 (10.69**)	
	P8	0.838 (10.83**)	
	P9	0.657 (8.88**)	
	Composed reliability	0.826	
	Extracted Variance	0.546	
Tangible aspects of Service (F3)	P4	0.892	
	P5	0.766 (12.12**)	
	Composed reliability	0.817	
	Extracted Variance	0.691	
Faculty Attitude and Behaviour (F4)	P16	0.787	
	P17	0.810 (10.89**)	
	Composed reliability	0.779	
	Extracted Variance	0.638	
Global measurement model fit measurements: Chi² Sat.(g.l.=71)=144.98 (p-valor=0.008); RMSEA=0.062; CFI=0.948; BB-NFI=0.906; BB-NNFI=0.931; GFI LISREL = 0.920; AGFI LISREL = 0.879			
**: t-statistic values between brackets (p-value<0.01)			

Moreover, the estimated model was evaluated by the internal consistency criteria set proposed by Jöreskog and Sörbom (1993): (1) *weak convergence criterion* (Steenkamp & Van Trijp, 1991) involves eliminating indicators that do not show significant estimation parameters (associated statistic t-student lower than 1.96); (2) *strong convergence criterion* (Steenkamp & Van Trijp, 1991) means eliminating non-substantial indicators (those standardized coefficients are lower than 0.5); (3) Jöreskog and Sörbom (1993) suggest eliminating the indicators that contribute least to the explanation of the model, taking as a cut-off point $R^2 \leq 0.3$.

Finally, we analysed scale construct validity (convergent and discriminant) for factors which make up the latent variables. Convergent validity is confirmed as all the variables had significant and high loadings (t>2.58) (Anderson & Gerbing, 1988). With regard to discriminant validity -that is to say, verification that each factor represents a separate dimension- was analysed through the standardised linear correlations or covariances between first order latent variables. These values show signs of discriminant validity as they took values away from 1, which in all cases is indicative of discrimination between the different dimensions analysed. After being squared, they are lower than the variance extracted and therefore we can guarantee discriminant validity in the latent variables. To analyse this type of validity in depth, it was verified that the confidence interval for the correlation between each pair of latent factors did not contain the value 1 (see Table 4), showing that said factors represent significantly different concepts (Anderson & Gerbing, 1988).

The fit indexes obtained in the measurement model estimation show that the variables measured converge perfectly towards the factors established in the exploratory factor analysis (see Table 4). The robust Chi-Square test allows us to state that global fit is correct with a confidence level of 95%. This was further corroborated by the other global fit indicators (RMSEA<0.08; GFI and AGFI greater than 0.9; CFI>0.9; and incremental fit indices -BBNFI and BBNNFI- greater than 0.9).

SEGMENTATION PROCESS

After checking the reliability and validity of the proposed scales, we proceeded to verify the hypotheses by analysing the non observed heterogeneity by means of identifying latent segments. In other words, we tried to determine if students had a heterogeneous perception of service quality. The analysis of the latent heterogeneity allows us to establish the effectiveness of quality service perceptions as behavioural criteria of segmentation.

With this objective in mind, we examined the heterogeneity in perceptions by means of a finite mixture model (predictive post-hoc technique). This model allows us to classify the students according to their membership probabilities – opposite deterministic classification of traditional cluster analysis. Moreover, the finite mixture model shows several measures of performance to evaluate the discriminant capability of segmentation criteria.

Variables introduced in the analysis were the dimensions that define service quality in higher education context: *fulfilment and attitude of contact staff and faculty*, *technical dimension of faculty*, *tangible aspects of service,* and *faculty attitude and behaviour*. Factorial loadings of the dimensions resulting from measure model were used to estimate the finite mixture model (see epigraph *Measurement scale reliability, dimensionality and validity*), so these variables are continuous and they are defined as real numbers.

In addition, due to the wide acceptance of the effectiveness of descriptive segmentation criteria (Wedel & Kamakura, 2000), three variables were included as covariates to attempt to describe the resulting segments: *gender* as general variable, and *degree* and *year* as specific variables.

We assumed that the students' perceptions about service quality dimensions come from *s*

Table 5. Measures of performance to determinate the optimal number of latent classes

	-LL	BIC	AIC	AIC3	CAIC	E_s	R^2	NP
1 clase	-1171.45	2388.19	2358.92	2366.92	2366.92	1.00	1.00	8
2 clases	-1025.42	2185.85	2098.12	2122.02	2209.85	0.73	0.77	24
3 clases	-970.63	2167.64	2021.26	2061.26	2207.64	0.76	0.77	30
4 clases	-933.69	2184.30	1979.37	2035.37	2240.30	0.77	0.76	56
5 clases	-920.38	2248.25	1984.76	2056.76	2320.25	0.79	0.76	72
NP: number of free parameters.								

latent segments that are merged in unknown proportions π_s. The estimation of the different latent classes was carried out with software LATENT GOLD 3.0. The first step of the analysis was to choose the optimal number of segments, so the model was estimated from $s=1$ (no heterogeneity) to $s=5$ (there were five latent segments or classes). Table 5 shows the estimation summary and the performance measures for each model.

Overall, goodness of fit measures which take into account model parsimony (BIC, AIC, AIC and CAIC), standardised measure of how accurately participants are classified (Entropy E_s), and coefficient of determination show that 3-classes-model is the best estimation. Considering this solution, the resulting three segments have a size of π_1=47.24% (136 students), π_2=34.30% (98 students) and π_3=18.46% (53 students) respectively.

Table 6 presents the profiles and the estimated parameters in each latent class. The profile corresponds to the average value of latent factor in each segment (i.e. the position of factor with respect to the centroid of segment).

The estimated parameter represents the effect of this factor on the segment. With regard to the discriminant ability of the four dimensions that define service quality, Wald-statistics show that there are significant differences on the position of each dimension among the three latent segments (see Table 6). That is to say, the p-value associated with Wald-statistic indicates that *fulfilment and attitude of contact staff and faculty*, *technical dimension of faculty*, *tangible aspects of service* and *faculty attitude and behaviour* discriminate significantly throughout the three segments.

In order to complete the composition of the segments, the profile of latent classes was analyzed according to the information of the covariables included in the estimation model. Table 7 shows the composition of each segment in terms of descriptive criteria.

Table 6. Latent Class Scores

	Mean (Estimated Parameter)			Wald	p-value	R^2
	Class 1	Class 2	Class 3			
F1	3.167 (0.0428)	2.576 (-0.5521)	3.633 (0.5092)	143.44	7.1e-32	0.472
F2	3.170 (-0.0093)	2.589 (-0.5897)	3.778 (0.5990)	222.95	3.9e-49	0.630
F3	3.757 (0.0633)	2.898 (-0.7958)	4.426 (0.7325)	95.95	1.5e-21	0.379
F4	3.875 (-0.0132)	3.213 (-0.6751)	4.577 (0.6883)	135.40	4.0e-30	0.394

Table 7. Latent segments profiles

Descriptive Variable	Categories	Class 1	Class 2	Class 3
Gender	Man	44.37%	**48.39%**	34.62%
	Woman	55.63%	51.61%	**65.38%**
				χ^2 (g.l.=2)= 2.59
Degree	Business Administration	**14.08%**	10.75%	19.23%
	Business studies	34.51%	33.33%	**42.31%**
	Tourism	20.42%	8.60%	21.15%
	Translation & Interpreting	19.72%	**31.18%**	17.31%
	Business Administration + Law	7.75%	11.83%	0.00%
	Law	3.52%	4.00%	0.00%
				χ^2 (g.l.=10)= **20.03***
Year	1º	26.76%	30.11%	**40.38%**
	2º	39.44%	**41.91%**	28.85%
	3º	**28.17%**	24.73%	26.92%
	4º	**4.23%**	3.23%	3.85%
	5º	**1.41%**	0.00%	0.00%
				χ^2 (g.l.=8)= 6.35

From the information gathered in Tables 6 and 7, the final configuration of the three latent classes has been interpreted. The first segment is the largest of the three since it contained 136 students (47.24% of sample). The average values of the four factors that define service quality were higher than 3 out of 5-point Likert scale. The highest value is reached in the dimension relating to *faculty attitude and behaviour* (3.88). This factor corresponds to the dimensions of security and empathy proposed by Parasuraman et al. (1988). This latent class contains higher percentage of women than men (55.6% versus 44.4%). It is the only group that contains all the degrees of students tested, and it has the highest percentage of students enrolled in Business Administration. It also includes students from the five years and it shows the highest percentage of students in last years of degree.

The second segment is composed by 98 students (34.3% of the sample). This group of students shows the worst perceptions of dimensions that define service quality. Except for the fourth factor, average values do not reach 3 out of 5-point scale and they are significantly lower than the scores reached in the other two groups. As Table 6 shows, the worst assessments correspond to *fulfilment and attitude of contact staff and faculty* and *technical dimension of faculty* since their average values are 2.58 and 2.59 respectively. This latent class contains a large percentage of students who are enrolled in Traduction & Interpretating in the first three years. Another feature of this segment is the highest proportion of men compared to the rest of groups.

Finally, 53 students form the third segment (18.46% of the sample). This latent class presents the significantly best assessments of service quality perceptions, with average scores higher than 3.5 points out of 5. Specifically, the best evaluated dimensions are *faculty attitude and behaviour* (4.58) and *tangible aspects of service* (4.43). This segment presents a significant percentage of women (65.4%) and it does not contain any student enrolled in Law and Business Studies & Law degrees. Overall, students in this group are enrolled in Business Studies degree (over 40%), Tourism degree (over 20%) and Business Administration degree. Over 40% of students are enrolled in the first year of the degrees.

The results indicate that there are three latent segments clearly differentiated according to the students' perceptions of the service quality dimensions. Therefore, we can conclude that these identified four dimensions *fulfilment and attitude of contact staff and faculty*, *technical dimension of faculty*, *tangible aspects of service,* and *faculty attitude and behaviour* are perceived by students differently, and these four factors are able to discriminate the students in three segments. This result allows us to test our research hypothesis in an affirmative way.

SOLUTIONS AND RECOMMENDATIONS

This case aimed to contribute to the analysis of market segmentation and perceived service quality in the higher education context. We pretended to analyse the utility of heterogeneous university student perceptions on service quality to establish the segmentation criteria for developing strategies based on delivery of quality. To do so, a multidimensional measure scale of perceived service quality was developed on the five dimensions of service quality (Parasuraman et al., 1988) including specific attributes for this kind of service (Capelleras & Veciana, 2004; Russell, 2005; Abdullah, 2006). The dimensionality study enabled us to identify four dimensions which comprise the service quality perceived by students. The factors identified are: *fulfilment and attitude of contact staff and faculty*, *technical dimension of faculty*, *tangible aspects of service,* and *faculty attitude and behaviour*. This result is in line with the results reported by Camisón et al. (1999) and Capelleras and Veciana (2004), who identify two dimensions in the evaluation of purely teaching service: *technical dimension of the teaching staff* and what is known as *teaching staff attitudes* related to how the service is perceived.

With regards to the utility of quality perceptions as behavioural criteria for segmenting, the results show that students are able to be put into groups based on quality dimensions scores. Specifically, mixture model estimation which includes the four quality dimensions as discriminant variables allowed us to identify three latent segments –with sizes 47.24%, 34.30% and 18.46% respectively. These latent classes show significant differences among service quality perceptions and among descriptive criteria used as covariables. The most important differences are found between the second and third class. Thus, third group presents average scores exceeding 3.5 out of 5-point scale for all the dimensions tested, while second group does not reach 3 out of 5 for the first three dimensions. With regard to descriptive characteristics, the result shows that the segment with highest average values of quality dimensions is made up by students which are enrolled in Business Studies and Tourism - 40% of this group is enrolled in the first year. On the other hand, the feature that defines the segment with the worst average values of quality dimensions is the significant proportion of students enrolled in Translation & Interpreting in the first three years of this degree. This is vital for university managers, since the identification of the heterogeneity of consumers allows them to develop differentiated marketing strategies. That is why managing service quality perceptions may help to design ongoing improvement processes in the organisation's services, especially the teaching service. To do so, after classifying the students into the different segments according to their levels of service quality perceptions, it would be advisable to make an in-depth study of each group's typology, analysing the effect of other influential factors on their levels of perceived service quality.

In addition, according to Joseph, Yakhou and Stone (2005), developing service quality improvement programmes focused on a single student typology is risky. This therefore, creates the need for periodic study of their needs and expectations and their evaluations of quality service performance.

The higher education policy-makers need to adopt more formal approaches to provide a guarantee of quality services. Besides, there has also been increased internationalization of the labour-market, international mobility of teachers or lecturers, researchers, students and competitive education programmes. Service quality is important to institutions of higher learning for a number of reasons, including competitive advantages, satisfying government requirements, and meeting the ever-increasing public expectations. As far as higher education is concerned, students are the key stakeholders, and yet there is very little research literature on the voices of students. The core business of institutions of higher learning should indeed be serving the students. Therefore, the units of analysis or the major customers of the institutions of higher learning are the students. They are the "daily customers" and informed respondents who can most probably able to tell the service beliefs, practices and processes (Voon, 2006).

Institutions of higher education need to emphasize and ensure a high level of service quality because the improved service quality may have a positive and significant effect on student satisfaction and loyalty. The long-term orientation component is specifically critical for higher education responsible for shaping future leaders and managers. An institution of higher learning which is customer oriented will seriously try to understand students' current and future needs and wants, discuss or share among the various functional units about their needs, and respond rapidly to meet those needs relatively better than the competitors.

ACKNOWLEDGMENT

The authors are grateful to the Spanish Ministry of Science and Innovation for financial support for this work (SEJ2007-66054/ECON).

REFERENCES

Abdullah, F. (2006). Measuring service quality in higher education: HEdPERF versus SERVPERF. *Marketing Intelligence & Planning*, *24*(1), 31–47. doi:10.1108/02634500610641543

Anderson, J. C., & Gerbing, D. W. (1988). Structural equation modeling in practice: A review and recommended two-step approach. *Psychological Bulletin*, *103*(3), 411–423. doi:10.1037/0033-2909.103.3.411

Bayraktaroglu, G., & Atrek, B. (2010). Testing the superiority and dimensionality of SERVQUAL vs. SERVPERF in higher education. *The Quality Management Journal*, *17*(1), 47–59.

Bekkering, E., & Engelland, B. (2002). Extending quality assessment beyond the classroom: The campus computer lab scale. *Journal of Advancement of Marketing Education*, *2*(1), 18–24.

Binsardi, A., & Ekwulugo, F. (2003). International marketing of British education: Research on the students' perception and the UK market penetration. *Marketing Intelligence & Planning*, *21*(5), 318–327. doi:10.1108/02634500310490265

Brochado, A. (2009). Comparing alternative instruments to measure service quality in higher education. *Quality Assurance in Education*, *17*(2), 174–190. doi:10.1108/09684880910951381

Camisón, C., Gil, M. T., & Roca, V. (1999). Hacia modelos de calidad de servicio orientados al cliente en las universidades públicas: El caso de la Universitat Jaume I. *Investigaciones Europeas de Dirección y Economía de la Empresa*, *5*(2), 69–92.

Capelleras, J. L. L., & Veciana, J. M. (2004). Calidad de servicio en la enseñanza universitaria: desarrollo y validación de una escala de medida. *Revista Europea de Dirección y Economía de la Empresa*, *13*(4), 55–72.

Carman, J. M. (1990). Consumer perceptions of service quality: An assessment of the SERVQUAL dimensions. *Journal of Retailing*, *66*(1), 33–55.

Casanueva, C., Periáñez, R., & Rufino, J. E. (1997). Calidad percibida por el alumno en el servicio docente universitario: Desarrollo de una escala de medida. In *XI Congreso Nacional AEDEM* (pp. 27-34). Spain: Lleida University.

Cheng, Y. C. (2000). CMI-triplization paradigm for reforming education in the new millennium. *International Journal of Educational Management*, *14*(4), 156–174. doi:10.1108/09513540010371975

Comm, C. L., & Mathaisel, D. F. (2000). Assessing employee satisfaction in service firms: An example in higher education. *Journal of Business and Economic Studies*, *6*(1), 43–53.

Cronin, J. J., & Taylor, S. A. (1992). Measuring service quality: A reexamination and extension. *Journal of Marketing*, *56*, 55–68. doi:10.2307/1252296

Dillon, W. R., & Kumar, A. (1994). Latent structure and other mixture models in marketing: An integrative survey and overview. In Bagozzi, R. P. (Ed.), *Advanced methods of marketing research* (pp. 295–351). Cambridge, MA: Blackwell Business.

Engelland, B. T., Workman, L., & Sing, M. (2000). Ensuring service quality for campus career services centers: A modified SERVQUAL scale. *Journal of Marketing Education*, *22*(3), 236–245. doi:10.1177/0273475300223007

Fornell, C., & Larcker, D. F. (1981). Evaluating structural equation models with unobservable variables and measurement error. *JMR, Journal of Marketing Research*, *28*, 39–50. doi:10.2307/3151312

Fuentes, M., & Gil, I. (2006). Segmenting university students on the basis of their expectations. *Journal of Marketing for Higher Education*, *16*(1), 25–45. doi:10.1300/J050v16n01_02

Fuentes, M., Gil, I., Berenguer, G., & Moliner, B. (2007). Expectations as the basis for predictive segmentation of university service quality. *International Review of Public and Non Profit Marketing*, *4*(1/2), 47–64.

Gil, I. (1996). La evaluación de la calidad de servicio percibida y limitaciones de la herramienta SERVQUAL. *Revista Europea de Dirección y Economía de la Empresa*, *2*, 19–32.

Grönroos, C. (1984). A service quality model and its marketing implications. *European Journal of Marketing*, *18*, 36–44. doi:10.1108/EUM0000000004784

Hair, J. F., Anderson, R. E., Tatham, R. L., & Black, W. C. (1999). *Análisis multivariante*. London, UK: Prentice Hall.

Jöreskog, K. G., & Sörbom, D. (1993). *Lisrel 8 structural equation modeling with the Simplis command language*. Chicago, IL: Scientific Software International.

Joseph, M., & Joseph, B. (1997). Service quality in education: A student perspective. *Quality Assurance in Education*, *5*(1), 26–37. doi:10.1108/09684889710156549

Joseph, M., Yakhou, M., & Stone, G. (2005). An educational institution's quest for service quality: Customers' perspective. *Quality Assurance in Education*, *13*(1), 66–82. doi:10.1108/09684880510578669

Kalamas, M., Laroche, M., & Cézard, A. (2002). A model of the antecedents of should and will service expectations. *Journal of Retailing and Consumer Services*, *9*, 291–308. doi:10.1016/S0969-6989(02)00016-4

Lilien, G. L., & Rangaswamy, A. (1998). *Marketing engineering: Computer-assisted marketing analysis and planning*. Reading, MA: Addison Wesley Educational Publishers.

Long, P. D., Tricker, T., Rangecroft, M., & Gilroy, P. (2000). Satisfaction with distance education: Evaluation of a service template. *Total Quality Management, 11*(4/6), 530–536.

Magidson, J., & Vermunt, J. K. (2002). Latent class models for clustering: A comparison with K-means. *Canadian Journal of Marketing Research, 20*, 37–44.

Mazzarol, T., & Soutar, G. N. (2002). Push-pull' factors influencing international student destination choice. *The International Journal of Education, 16*(2), 82–90.

Nadiri, H., Kandampully, J., & Hussain, K. (2009). Students' perceptions of service quality in higher education. *Total Quality Management & Business Excellence, 20*(5), 523–535. doi:10.1080/14783360902863713

Nunnally, J. C. (1987). *Teoría psicométrica*. Mexico: Trillas.

O'Neill, M. A., & Palmer, A. (2004). Importance-performance analysis: A useful tool for directing continuous quality improvement in higher education. *Quality Assurance in Education, 12*(1), 39–52. doi:10.1108/09684880410517423

Oldfield, B. M., & Baron, S. (2000). Student perceptions of service quality in a UK university business and management faculty. *Quality Assurance in Education, 8*(29), 85–95. doi:10.1108/09684880010325600

Owlia, M. S., & Aspinwall, E. M. (1998). Quality in higher education: A survey. *Total Quality Management, 7*(4), 161–171.

Parasuraman, A., Zeithaml, V. A., & Berry, L. L. (1985). A conceptual model of service quality and its implications for future research. *Journal of Marketing, 43*, 41–50. doi:10.2307/1251430

Parasuraman, A., Zeithaml, V. A., & Berry, L. L. (1988). SERVQUAL: A multiple-item scale for measuring consumer perceptions of service quality. *Journal of Retailing, 64*, 39–48.

Parasuraman, A., Zeithaml, V. A., & Berry, L. L. (1994). Alternative scales for measuring service quality: A comparative assessment based on psychometric and diagnostic criteria. *Journal of Retailing, 70*(3), 201–230. doi:10.1016/0022-4359(94)90033-7

Prugsamatz, S., Pentecost, R., & Ofstad, L. (2006). The influence of explicit and implicit service promises on Chinese students' expectations of overseas universities. *Asia Pacific Journal of Marketing and Logistics, 18*(2), 129–145. doi:10.1108/13555850610658273

Radder, L., & Han, X. (2009). Service quality of on-campus student housing: A South African experience. *The International Business & Economics Research Journal, 8*(11), 107–119.

Russell, M. (2005). Marketing education: A review of service quality perceptions among international students. *International Journal of Contemporary Hospitality Management, 17*(1), 65–77. doi:10.1108/09596110510577680

Sánchez, M., Sánchez, R., Marín, G., & Gázquez, J. C. (2007). Service quality in public services as a segmentation variable. *The Service Industries Journal, 27*(4), 355–369. doi:10.1080/02642060701346771

Shank, M. D., Walker, M., & Hayes, T. (1995). Understanding professional service expectations: Do we know what our students expect in a quality education? *Journal of Professional Services Marketing, 13*(1), 71–89. doi:10.1300/J090v13n01_08

Smith, G. S., Smith, A., & Clarke, A. (2007). Evaluating service quality in universities: A service department perspective. *Quality Assurance in Education, 15*(3), 334–351. doi:10.1108/09684880710773200

Steenkamp, J. B., & Van Trijp, H. C. M. (1991). The use of Lisrel in validating marketing constructs. *International Journal of Research in Marketing*, *8*(4), 283–299. doi:10.1016/0167-8116(91)90027-5

Teas, R. K. (1993). Expectations, performance evaluation and consumers' perceptions of quality. *Journal of Marketing*, *57*(4), 18–34. doi:10.2307/1252216

Trivellas, P., & Dargenidou, D. (2009). Organisational culture, job satisfaction and higher education service quality. The case of Technological Educational Institute of Larissa. *The TQM Journal*, *21*(4), 382–399. doi:10.1108/17542730910965083

Voon, B. H. (2006). Linking a service-driven market orientation to service quality. *Managing Service Quality*, *16*(6), 595–619. doi:10.1108/09604520610711927

Webster, C. (1989). Can consumers be segmented on the basis of their service quality expectations? *Journal of Services Marketing*, *3*(2), 35–53. doi:10.1108/EUM0000000002485

Wedel, M., & DeSarbo, W. S. (2002). Market segment derivation and profiling via a finite mixture model framework. *Marketing Letters*, *13*(1), 17–25. doi:10.1023/A:1015059024154

Wedel, M., & Kamakura, W. A. (2000). *Market segmentation. Conceptual and methodological foundations*. London, UK: Kluwer Academic Publishers.

Zeithaml, V. A., & Bitner, M. J. (1996). *Services marketing*. New York, NY: McGraw-Hill.

ADDITIONAL READING

Clewes, D. (2003). A student-centred conceptual model of service quality in higher education. *Quality Assurance in Education*, *9*(1), 69–85.

DeShields, O. W., Kara, W. J. A., & Kaynak, E. (2005). Determinants of business student satisfaction and retention in higher education: Applying Herzberg's two factor theory. *International Journal of Educational Management*, *19*(2), 128–139. doi:10.1108/09513540510582426

European Higher Education Area. Spanish Ministry of Education. From http://www.educacion.es/en/boloniaeees/inicio.html

European Research Area. (2000).Spanish Ministry of Science and Innovation. From http://www.micinn.es/

LeBlanc, G., & Nguyen, N. (1999). Listening to the customer's voice: examining perceived service value among business college students. *International Journal of Educational Management*, *13*(4), 187–198. doi:10.1108/09513549910278106

Quester, P., Wilkinson, J. W., & Romaniuk, S. (1995). A test of four service quality measurement scales: the case of the Australian advertising industry. Working Paper 39, Centre de Recherche et d'Etudes Appliquees, Group esc Nantes Atlantique, Graduate School of Management, Nantes.

Rodríguez, J., Mira, J., Gómez, J. M., García, A., & Pérez-Jover, V. (2003). Implantación de un sistema de calidad en la enseñanza superior basado en el Modelo Europeo de Excelencia. *ESIC Market*, *114*, 243–252.

Teas, R. K. (1994). Expectations as a comparison standard in measuring service quality: an assessment and re-evaluation. *Journal of Marketing*, *58*(1), 132–138. doi:10.2307/1252257

Zeithaml, V. A. (2000). Service quality, profitability, and the economic worth of customers: What we know and what we need to learn. *Journal of the Academy of Marketing Science*, *28*(1), 67–85. doi:10.1177/0092070300281007

KEY TERMS AND DEFINITIONS

Behavioural Segmentation Basis: Knowledge, attitudes, uses or perceptions about a product/service used to divide potential consumers into groups.

Bologna Process: European Higher Education Area, in which students can choose from a wide and transparent range of high quality courses and benefit from smooth recognition procedures. The Bologna Declaration of June 1999 has put in motion a series of reforms needed to make European Higher Education more compatible and comparable, more competitive and more attractive for Europeans and for students and scholars from other continents. Reform was needed then and reform is still needed today if Europe is to match the performance of the best performing systems in the world, notably the United States and Asia.

Latent Class Analysis (LCA): Multivariate technique which can be applied for cluster, factor, or regression analytic purposes. It is commonly used to classify cases into a set of latent classes, based on categorial indicator variables such as survey items. After cases are so classified, then in regression models, LCA with covariates uses additional variables to predict class membership.

Market Segmentation: Consists of viewing a heterogeneous market (one characterized by divergent demand) as a number of smaller homogeneous markets in response to differing product preferences among important market segments. It is attributable to the desires of consumers or users for more precise satisfaction of their varying wants.

Perceived Service Quality in Higher Education: The difference between what students expect to receive and their perception of the service delivery.

Perceived Service Quality: The consumer's judgment about an overall excellence or superiority of service. It's a form of attitude, related but not equivalent to satisfaction, and results from a comparison of expectations with perceptions of performance.

Service: Are behavioural rather than physical entities, and have been described as deeds, acts, performances, processes, activities or effort.

SERVQUAL: 22-item instrument for assessing customer perceptions of service quality in service and retailing organizations along the five service dimensions (tangibles, reliability, responsiveness, assurance, and empathy).

ENDNOTE

1. Specifically, items p1, p2, and p18 were eliminated since they showed an insufficient loading (lower than 0.05). Item p3 was eliminated since the alpha reliability indicator considerably increased.

Chapter 3
The Google Online Marketing Challenge:
A Transnational Comparison of Classroom Learning with Real Clients, Real Money, and Real Advertising Campaigns

Sven Tuzovic
Pacific Lutheran University, USA

Lyle Wetsch
Memorial University of Newfoundland, Canada

Jamie Murphy
Murdoch Business School, Australia

EXECUTIVE SUMMARY

In 2008, a collaborative partnership between Google and academia launched the Google Online Marketing Challenge (hereinafter Google Challenge), perhaps the world's largest in-class competition for higher education students. In just two years, almost 20,000 students from 58 countries participated in the Google Challenge. The Challenge gives undergraduate and graduate students hands-on experience with the world's fastest growing advertising mechanism, search engine advertising. Funded by Google, students develop an advertising campaign for a small to medium sized enterprise and manage the campaign over three consecutive weeks using the Google AdWords platform. This article explores the Challenge as an innovative pedagogical tool for marketing educators. Based on the experiences of three instructors in Australia, Canada and the United States, this case study discusses the opportunities and challenges of integrating this dynamic problem-based learning approach into the classroom.

DOI: 10.4018/978-1-60960-599-5.ch003

BACKGROUND

Google Online Marketing Challenge

The *Google Online Marketing Challenge* is a global business student competition developed by professors in collaboration with Google. Unlike most student competitions with hypothetical scenarios or simulations, the Google Challenge gives students US$200 to work with real businesses, in real-time, to create an online marketing campaign using Google's advertising platform, AdWords (Flaherty et al., 2009).

Review of Experiential Learning

To maintain student interest and create a memorable encounter, instructors increasingly face the challenge of providing innovative and stimulating educational experiences for students (Elam & Spotts, 2004; Matulich, Papp & Haytko, 2008; Ueltschy, 2001). Scholars argue that "(...) the lecture format is not the most effective educational delivery mechanism, particularly in marketing" (Helms, Mayo & Baxter, 2003, p. 18). Instead, active learning methods that empower students to think and learn for themselves are increasingly recommended as an alternative (Johnson, Johnson & Smith, 1991).

Critics often lament that universities provide insufficient real-world experiential learning (Kelley & Gaedeke, 1990; Thomas, 1995). Traditional learning methods such as lectures still seem appropriate in some environments such as large or introductory-level classes, yet students have different learning styles (Karns, 2006; Kolb & Kolb, 2005). Students often prefer experiential learning, through activities such as field trips, case studies, business audits, internships, simulations, competitions, live projects, community-based service learning and student-operated businesses (Andrews, 2007; Doren & Corrigan, 2008; Drea et al., 1997; Govekar and Rishi, 2007; Hamer, 2000; Karns, 2005; Kennedy, Lawton & Walker, 2001; McIntyre, Webb and Hite, 2005).

Experiential learning is a pedagogical approach whereby students experience "a task or set of tasks, and ultimately learn from their actions" (Neale et al., 2009, p. 7). Simpson and Pham (2007) note that such "learning strategies are based on application (using knowledge to solve problems) and analysis" (p. 1). Experiential learning helps grasp the relevance of information from situations encountered (McKeachie, 2002) and transform knowledge into know-how (Katula & Threnhauser, 1999). Many university educators advocate and incorporate real-world experiential learning in various disciplines including marketing related courses such as: marketing (Bobbitt et al., 2000; Drea et al., 1997; Munoz & Huser, 2008), marketing research (Bove & Davies 2009; Bridges, 1999), marketing communications (Luck & Chalmers, 2007), personal selling and purchasing (O'Hara & Shaffer, 1995), services marketing (Gremler et al., 2000), economics (Hawtrey, 2007), and entrepreneurship and retail management (Daly, 2001).

Students perceive experiential methods, particularly real-world projects, as more effective for their learning (Karns, 2005; Navarro, 2008). Relative to traditional lectures, students become more engaged with problem-based/problem-centered teaching (Gilbert & Andrew, 2004). For example, Rosso et al. (2009) report that MBA students demonstrated a high level of comprehension thanks to a search-advertising project in their course.

One way to link marketing theory with 'real-world' application is to involve students in service learning projects or "living cases" (LeClair & Stöttinger, 1999, p. 31), also referred to as *client-sponsored projects* (Humphreys, 1981). *Community-based service learning* programs focus on student involvement in community service within a credit-earning educational experience (Berry & Workman, 2007; Govekar & Rishi, 2007; Petkus, 2000). *Living cases* combine traditional case study elements with a unique real-world business environment in which students learn to solve complex and unstructured problems (LeClair & Stöttinger, 1999).

Many students are fearful and uncertain when they realize they will work with a real business (Rosso et al., 2009). "Students are not working in a clean, tidy environment when dealing with a live case; rather, they are dealing with variable situations, uncertainty, and incomplete information" (Elam & Spotts, 2004, p. 52). Yet, this fear and anxiety turns into excitement and engagement once students apply their knowledge and make a meaningful contribution for their business (Rosso et al., 2009). Similarly, Bourner, Hughes & Bourner (2001) illustrate that students highly value coursework that incorporates a real organization. Students particularly appreciate the lifetime benefits of real-world projects such as self-confidence, entrepreneurial skills, access to mentors and networking opportunities (Russell, Atchison & Brooks, 2008). Compared to classroom education, client projects "challenge students in ways that not even the best-written case study or end-of-the textbook chapter exercise can duplicate" (McEachern, 2001, p. 211).

Academic literature also suggests that students learn more through competitive projects (Rundle-Thiele & Kuhn, 2008; Stutts & West, 2003; Zabkar, 2008). Flaherty et al. (2009) in their review of student competitions concluded that "extending the classroom experience from simulations to national or global competitions adds the benefits of real world applications, industry standards for grading students, and a compelling learning experience in an industry context" (p. 447). The authors further suggest that competitions enhance education and benefit three different constituents: students, industry and the educational institution (Flaherty et al., 2009).

Experiential learning, however, has critics. Relative to traditional instruction, at its extreme, experiential learning may lead to less effective outcomes due to its self-discovery methods with little or no guided instruction (Kirschner, Sweller & Clark, 2006; Mayer, 2004). Other critics note undesirable student behaviors such as free-riding in groups, recycling student papers from previous terms and repeatedly overplaying simulations (Schibrowsky & Peltier, 1995). The Google Challenge, developed by academics in collaboration with Google, helps overcome these experiential learning weaknesses through guided instruction enhanced by self-discovery (Flaherty et al., 2009; Neale et al., 2009). The Challenge merges marketing education with problem-based and technology-enhanced learning in a real-world environment with real money and real clients (Flaherty et al., 2009; Murphy et al., 2008; 2009a; 2009b).

The developers of the Google Challenge addressed these issues in several articles (e.g. Neale et al., 2009). For example, unlike simulated or fabricated competitions, student teams cannot overplay because the Challenge is a live competition with a finite budget and finite timeline. Students cannot reuse old papers since each team works with a unique organization. A written reflective paper in which students evaluate group dynamics helps address the common free-riding problem. Overall, the Google Challenge leverages the best of experiential learning by blending client-sponsored living cases, community-based service learning and a global student competition (see Figure 1).

Learning Objectives

The Challenge has three main *objectives* (Neale et al., 2008):

1. To provide students with an engaging and effective real-world exercise preparing them as cutting-edge online marketers;
2. To connect Higher Education institutions with local businesses in the community; and
3. To provide instructors with a theory-based yet commercially practical assessment item for their students.

Figure 1. Google challenge as a pedagogical tool

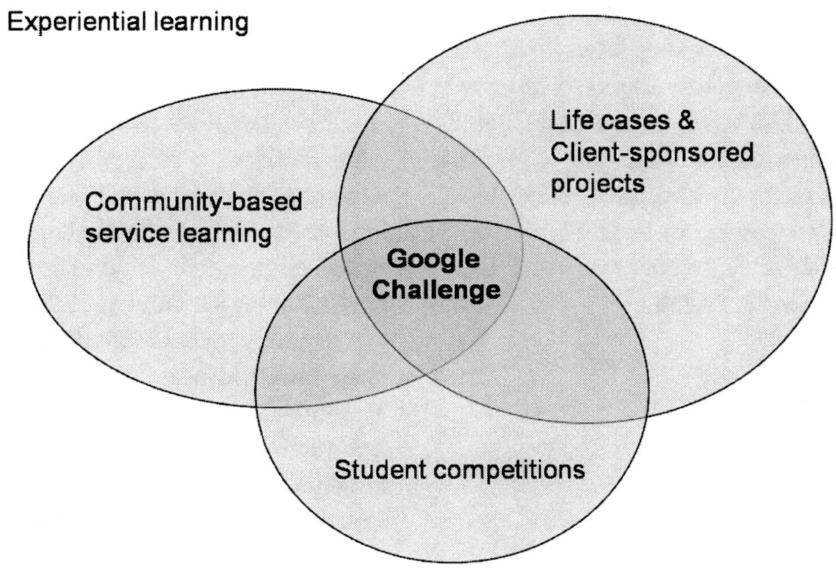

As discussed in the next section, the Google Challenge introduces students to the most important and fastest growing sector in online marketing, keyword/search advertising (Flaherty et al. 2009). Due to the Internet's rapid growth and evolution, instructors should stay up-to-date with the content and also the delivery of classroom material. Keyword advertising, now essential for many businesses, provides a major revenue source for all search engine companies. For instance, Google derives over 95 percent of its $20+ billion in revenue from search advertising (Jansen et al., 2008; Lavin et al., 2009).

This paid search has become an important topic for all business students – regardless of their major (Rosso et al., 2009) – and offers attractive job opportunities in a growing industry (Levisohn 2009). Students participating in the Google Challenge consult with businesses and provide them with online marketing advice. For example, they collect real-world data and use Google's AdWords platform to develop a real online advertising campaign for their client. Thus, students both gain practical experience and build a beneficial network when applying for internships and jobs. Instructors using the Challenge teach traditional advertising concepts such as copywriting, cost per thousand (CPM), return on investment as well as specific online marketing concepts such as click-through-rate (CTR), cost-per-click (CPC) and optimization techniques (Flaherty et al., 2009).

After participating in the Google Challenge, students should accomplish the following *learning objectives* (see Flaherty et al., 2009):

- Understand the complexity of developing and implementing an online marketing campaign;
- Confidently discuss online marketing and media planning issues with their client;
- Create a practical and successful campaign that fits with the objectives of their client;
- Illustrate the technical and cultural factors that affect the success of online marketing campaigns
- Maximize targeted and relevant traffic to their client's website; and
- Use optimization techniques to refine and improve campaign effectiveness over the three-week competition period.

Instructors assess student understanding of these concepts by grading two mandatory Google Challenge reports: a *Pre-campaign Strategy Report* and a *Post-campaign Summary Report* (discussed in section 3). Scholars argue that these written reports enhance the academic value of experiential learning as students must reflect and communicate their experiences (e.g., Flaherty et al., 2009; Hawes & Foley, 2006; Matulich, Papp & Haytko, 2008; Young, 2002).

ONLINE AND SEARCH ADVERTISING

Review of Sponsored Search Advertising

Over the last six years *online advertising* has had annual double-digit growth (Lavin et al., 2009). The Interactive Advertising Bureau (IAB) reports that 2008 Internet advertising in the U.S. grew 10.6 percent to US$ 23.4 Billion (IAB, 2009). According to projections, spending will reach US$ 51.0 Billion in 2012 (eMarketer, 2008). Online advertising includes various forms including display, rich media, video, sponsorships, classified, email and search advertising. These ad forms vary in success (Lavin et al., 2009). *Search advertising* is the leading format, with 45 percent of the total Internet advertising market share (IAB, 2009).

The concept of *sponsored search* advertising (also referred to as paid search, pay-per-click, keyword advertising, and search engine advertising) aligns online advertisements with a user's search engine query (Lavin et al., 2009; Murphy et al., 2009a; Rosso et al., 2009). A *query* refers to (typically one to three) words or a phrase describing the users' information need (Jansen & Spink, 2006). The user initiates the quest for information by entering a keyword or phrase in the search engine, then the search engine returns a results list (see Figure 1). Each result typically consists of three elements: the title of the webpage, a two-to-three line text description and the web address of the page (Rosso et al., 2009). Besides the normal (or "organic") search results, specially labeled results ("sponsored ads") appear on the same page, usually at the top or the right hand side (Note the outlined areas in Figure 2).

Figure 2. Sponsored search results for the keyword 'Chocolate' with Google AdWords

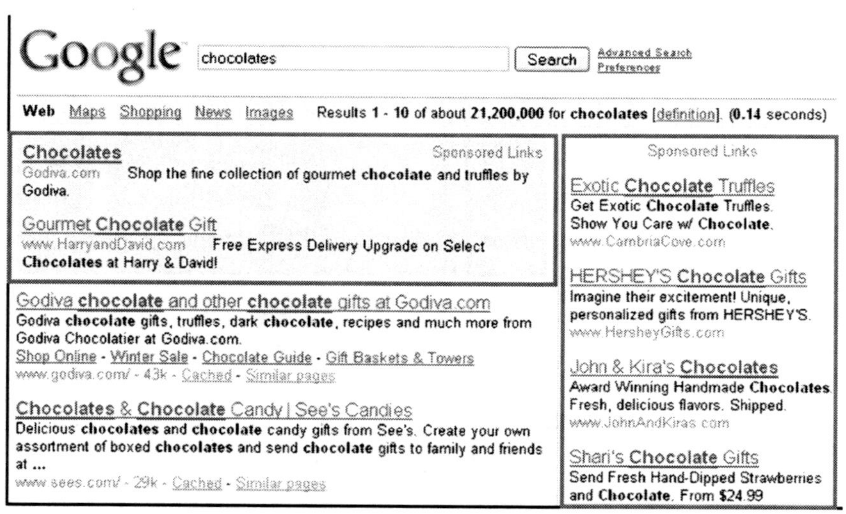

Basics of Google AdWords

As the leading search engine with a 72 percent U.S. market share (McGee, 2010) and 83 percent globally (Marketshare.hitslink.com, 2009), Google drives keyword advertising development with its flagship products AdWords (adwords.google.com/) and AdSense (www.google.com/adsense/). AdWords is Google's text-based system for advertising on search engine result pages such as Google.com and partner sites (e.g. AOL.com). Advertisers create ads for display alongside the keywords related to user queries. AdSense is similar, except that the ads appear on Google's content network of millions of Websites in over 100 countries and 20 languages (Jansen et al., 2008). For example, the newspaper The New York Times earns revenue by placing 'Ads by Google' on Times' web pages.

The process of a traditional AdWords advertising campaign follows (Murphy, Hudson & Hunter, 2008; Rosso et al., 2009): Advertisers develop simple text-based ads with four lines of copy. Each ad consists of a (25 character or less) headline, a two-line description (each a maximum of 35 characters) and a URL (uniform resource locator) that indicates the landing page. Table 1 illustrates two sample AdWords ads for the fictitious business, Melbourne Flowers. The copy is identical except for the second half of the second line: *reasonable prices* vs. *wedding specials*. The first ad should interest value conscious market segments, whereas the second ad targets consumers interested in weddings (Murphy, Hudson & Hunter, 2008; for a similar example see Murphy et al., 2009a).

Table 1. Sample AdWords for a fictitious business, Melbourne Flowers (Murphy, Hudson & Hunter, 2008)

Campaign 1	*Campaign 2*
Melbourne Flowers Great flowers; reasonable prices Central location near MCG MelbourneFlowers.com.au	**Melbourne Flowers** Great flowers; wedding specials Central location near MCG MelbourneFlowers.com.au

Google AdWords offers the option to create ad campaigns of one or more ad groups (Jansen et al., 2008; Rosso et al., 2009). Each ad group can contain one or more ads with one or more related keywords. Figure 3 illustrates the basic structure of an AdWords account.

To place sponsored ads on Google, advertisers participate in a live auction with all advertisers who chose a given keyword that determines "which ads run in which positions on which pages and at what prices" (Rosso et al., 2009). First, Google considers the maximum cost-per-click (Max CPC) bid for the keyword entered of each advertiser. Then, Google evaluates the relevance of the keyword, its "Quality Score" or rating of how well each keyword and its related ad match (Google, 2009b). The CPC model is efficient as marketers pay only if the ad is clicked. While AdWords

Figure 3. Basic structure of a Google AdWords account

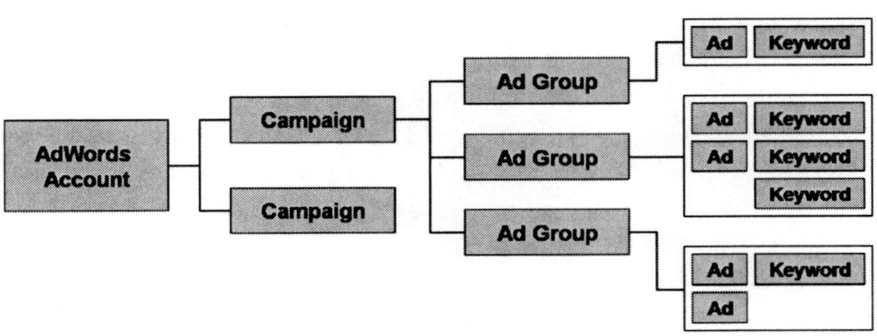

usually operates on a CPC basis, the CPM (cost per thousand impressions) model is also available for placement targeting on Google's content network (Murphy, Hudson & Hunter, 2008). Scholars argue that performance-based costing, usually CPC, continues to grow while display-based costing, usually CPM, continues to decline (Murphy, Hudson & Hunter, 2008).

AdWords offers several major advantages over traditional advertising media such as print or television. First, the ads are simple and nonintrusive. Second, AdWords offers enhanced segmentation and targeting opportunities (Murphy, Hudson & Hunter, 2008; Murphy et al., 2009a). For instance, advertisers can select keywords and the geographical location in which its ads appear. In the Melbourne Flowers example (see Table 1), results may be limited to people living within 30 kilometers of Melbourne's central business district. With regard to targeting, the florist could choose keywords such as *florist*, *flowers* and *weddings*.

OVERVIEW OF THE GOOGLE CHALLENGE

Evolution of the Challenge

Neale et al. (2009) overview the evolution of the Google Challenge. The idea originated in March 2007 when a Google employee and his former professor discussed giving students a real-world online marketing exercise. Influenced by the Association to Advance Collegiate Schools of Business (AACSB) standards, the "practitioner and academic envisioned the Challenge as a fun and exciting competition that helped students learn experientially, working in groups with real clients and spending real money" (Neale et al., 2009, p. 76). More importantly, the two originators as well as a small team of Google employees and other academics designed the Challenge as an academic exercise, and to target academics more than students or businesses (Neale et al., 2009). Next, 14 academics from eight countries formed a *Global Academic Panel* (www.google.com/onlinechallenge/panel.html) that helped develop pedagogical materials for students, instructors and businesses. The panel also selects regional and global winners (Neale et al., 2009). The theoretical underpinnings of the Challenge stem from Kolb's experiential learning theory of experiencing-reflecting-thinking-acting (Kolb, 1984; Kolb & Kolb, 2005, 2008; see also Neale et al., 2009, who discuss the experiential learning cycle and the Challenge).

How the Challenge Works

The Challenge combines an experiential, "problem-based learning approach" (Hmelo-Silver, 2004) with a global competition. Teams of three to six students engage in a facilitated, self learning experience to solve a complex problem with no single answer (Flaherty et al., 2009). Participating students have a real-world project covering all phases of marketing planning: from market analysis and marketing strategy to implementation and evaluation. Google gives each team US$ 200 in AdWords, to run an online advertising campaign for a small- to medium-sized enterprise. The campaign can run any three consecutive weeks from late January to early June (Murphy et al., 2009a; Neale et al., 2009). As students spend real money for real clients, they employ marketing skills to develop, implement, refine and improve their AdWords campaigns. As a result, students become active learners trying to maximize the targeted and relevant traffic to a client's website.

The Google Challenge is designed as a undergraduate or graduate in-class exercise for myriad classes, such as online marketing, consumer behavior, advertising, integrated marketing communications, e-commerce, and marketing strategy (Murphy et al., 2009a). Instructors who wish to participate in the Challenge can register their class online starting around October on the Google

Website (www.google.com/onlinechallenge). Challenge registration ends in late January. Once registered, the Challenge follows six major steps (see Table 2; Google, 2010; Jansen et al., 2008; Neale et al., 2009; Rosso et al., 2009). On request, Google provides a US $50 voucher for professors to gain hands-on experience before their students participate in the Google Challenge.

Selecting the Google Challenge winners is a three-step process. First, Google evaluates campaign performance based on an algorithm of around 30 factors across five criteria: account structure, optimization techniques, account activity and reporting, performance and budget, and relevance (Neale et al., 2009). The algorithm results narrow the field to 150 teams – the top 50 teams in each of three regions (Americas, Europe/Middle East/Africa, and Asia-Pacific). Google AdWords specialists then judge these top 150 teams qualitatively, reducing the field to five teams in each region. Finally, the academic panel evaluates solely the quality of the two written reports from the top 15 teams.

The Google Challenge after Two Years

After two years, the Google Challenge has established itself as an ongoing and innovative educational exercise. In the inaugural 2008 Challenge, over 8,000 students participated along with around 340 instructors and 1,620 businesses from 47 countries (Jansen et al., 2008; Murphy et al., 2009a; Neale et al., 2009). In 2009, participating students increased to over 10,000 from 57 countries. In addition, *student-led learning communities* – open access learning communities initiated and driven by students (Neale et al., 2009) – have evolved around the Challenge (e.g. GOMCHA.com).

Rosso et al. (2009) note that Microsoft and Yahoo also offer search advertising that could be used in the classroom. Thus, keyword advertising as a pedagogical tool extends beyond Google. However, the authors argue that based on (1) Google's overwhelming search market share and (2) the pedagogical support offered by Google, educators have little reason at this time to prefer another program. However, Microsoft with the release of its new search engine Bing, started in fall 2009 to sponsor the *DMEF Collegiate ECHO*

Table 2. Major steps of the Google challenge

Step	*Description*
1. Student teams	At beginning of the class, instructors divide students into groups of three to six students.
2. SME recruitment	The teams or professors recruit a SME (profit or non-profit) as a client. The criteria for eligibility as a client for the Challenge are that the SME employs less than 100 people, has a Website, and has not used Google AdWords in the last six months.
3. AdWords account and voucher	Teams work with their client to set up an AdWords account for an online marketing campaign. Google then credits each team with US$ 200 for the campaign.
4. Pre-campaign strategy	Each team develops a campaign strategy. Based on meetings with the client and an analysis of the client's business and website, each team has to submit a 4-page pre-campaign report outlining the proposed strategy.
5. Campaign	For three consecutive weeks teams run a real AdWords campaign using the US$ 200 budget that is provided by Google. Groups spend their AdWords budget bidding for keywords. They refine and optimize their campaigns on the basis of real-time campaign results.
6. Post-campaign evaluation	After the end of the campaign teams have to submit an 8-page post-campaign report both to the instructor and to Google. This report contains both campaign results and recommendations for the client as well as a reflection on what students learned by covering three main topics: learning objectives and outcomes, group dynamics and client dynamic.

Direct & Interactive Marketing Challenge, also for undergraduate and graduate students worldwide (DMEF, 2010). This competition, however, does not provide the execution of an actual campaign.

TRANSNATIONAL COMPARISON OF CLASSROOM LEARNING

Integrating the Google Challenge into marketing courses offers great pedagogical opportunities but also challenges. In the following sections, three marketing educators from Australia, Canada and the U.S. reflect on the classroom preparation and implementation of the Google Challenge as well as lessons learned. In all three cases, the Google Challenge in the course curriculum was overwhelmingly positive. Table 3 briefly compares the three course settings.

Learning Experiences from the United States

The Google Challenge ran in a class of 15 students in the course *e-Marketing*, an elective for the Marketing concentration at Pacific Lutheran University (Tuzovic, 2009). The course introduces students to the use of the Internet and other online and mobile technologies for marketing, in particular the planning, design and execution of

Table 3. Comparison of PLU, MUN and UWA courses and instructors' Google challenge implementation in the classroom

	Pacific Lutheran University (PLU)	*Memorial University of Newfoundland (MUN)*	*University of Western Australia (UWA)*
Course title	e-Marketing	Two courses: 1. Channels and Internet Marketing 2. Internet Marketing Management	Electronic Marketing
Level	Undergraduate	Undergraduate and MBA	Graduate
Number of students	15	90 over two years	15
Mandatory or optional class project?	Mandatory	Mandatory	Mandatory
Grade	1/3 of overall grade	20-30% (depending on course)	1/4 of overall grade
Number of teams	5	24 over 2 years	3
Picking teams	Students self-selected their teams	Student selected teams	Students assigned based on nationality, work experience, gender and IT skills
Recruiting clients	Each student team recruits a SME or nonprofit	Clients recruited through alumni affairs to provide list for students to choose from	Two suggestions prior to class and one client aligned with a student
Integration of Challenge in course	Partially in class, with several class sessions devoted to work on the project	Learning provided though self study, online resources, and class presentations. Execution of Challenge on student time	Partially in class, mostly with presentations of pre- and post-campaign reports
Overview of clients	Cupcake bakery, comic book store, nut-roasting company, electronic medical records and practice management service, nonprofit child placement agency	Wide range of clients from professional services, tourism, clothing manufacturing, engineering firms, educational institutions, etc.	Local private high school (AU), swim wear franchisee (AU) and a forestry company (TH)

marketing strategies and programs. After discussing topics such as Internet macro-environment, Internet marketing strategy and the marketing mix, the course emphasized different online marketing communication forms, in particular, search engine optimization and keyword advertising. However, Jansen et al. (2008) point out that "the dynamic nature of online advertising and the inherent lag in updating textbooks (…) makes discussing keyword advertising in the classroom a challenging task" (p. 5). Due to the rapid growth and evolution of search advertising, the Challenge seemed a fitting class project.

Based on results of the 2008 Google Challenge *Post-Participation Survey Datasets* (see http://www.google.com/onlinechallenge/research.html), which show that 51 percent of the instructors incorporated the Challenge as a mandatory class project in their curricula, the Challenge was a mandatory class project worth one-third of the students' overall grade. In the first week of class, teams were set up. Based on the regulation of teams of three to six, there were five teams. Given that the students knew each other from other courses, students self-selected into teams (see Rosso et al., 2009, for a similar approach). Four of the five teams seemed to work well throughout the semester.

Each team recruited a client from the community: (1) a cupcake bakery, (2) a comic book store, (3) a nut-roasting company, (4) an electronic medical records and practice management service and (5) a non-profit child placement agency and international adoption programs. Overall, client recruitment posed no difficulties for the students.

Google provides free materials, for example, the Student Guide 2009 (Google 2009a) and Challenge Handbook (Google 2009b), which were distributed to the students at the beginning of the semester. Due to a large amount of information to absorb in addition to textbook material, as well as learning the AdWords platform, students worked on their pre-campaign strategy in class during February and March. All teams ran their 3-week campaigns from March 31 through April 21, when students had additional class time to optimize their online advertising strategy. Table 4 shows two sample AdWords ads for the nonprofit organization. The ads differ slightly as two different programs were promoted.

Figure 4 illustrates the results of one student campaign as an example. For the nonprofit organization, students started their campaign with two ad campaigns, one for China adoptions and one for a Nepal sponsorship program. In the first week, the team "tested the waters", investing above their average budget to find which keywords worked and what they cost. After a few days, the students recognized that most traffic stemmed from ten keywords. As a result, the team monitored those keywords closely each day and adjusted their pricing strategy accordingly. Table 5 summarizes the team's main keywords and phrases, along with the bid prices after the first week of the campaign.

At the end of the 3-week campaign, the student team generated the following statistics for their client:

- Total Cost: $200
- Impressions: 654,433
- Clicks: 862
- CTR: 0.13%
- Avg. CPC: $0.23

Table 4. Exemplary AdWords ads of one student team

Client	*Ad campaigns*	
Nonprofit child adoption programs	**Adopt a Child from China** Faith International can help you With adopting a child from China www.FaithAdopt.org/China	**Nepal Child Sponsorship** Every child deserves a chance See how you can help right now www.FaithAdopt.org/Sponsor-a-Child

Figure 4. Campaign results for the nonprofit organization (based on students' in-class presentation)

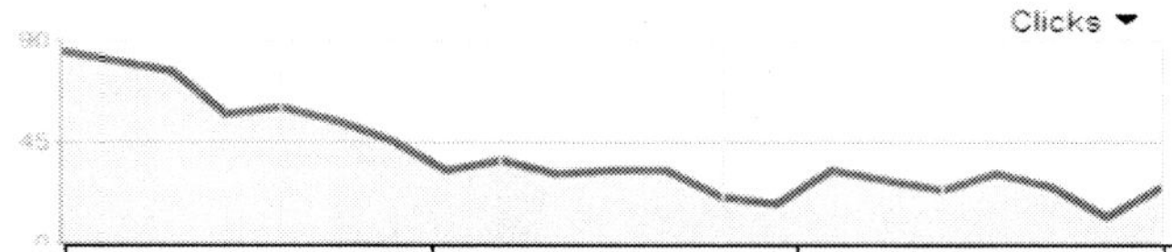

Week 1	Week 2	Week 3	All weeks
Total cost: $71.49	Total cost: $57.40	Total cost: $71.11	Total cost: $200
Total clicks: 469	Total clicks: 210	Total clicks: 183	Total clicks: 862
CTR: 0.11%	CTR: 0.15%	CTR: 0.21%	CTR: 0.13%
Avg. CPC: $0.15	Avg. CPC: $0.27	Avg. CPC: $0.38	Avg. CPC: $0.23
Bounce Rate: 58%	Bounce Rate: 52%	Bounce Rate: 51%	Bounce Rate: 55%
Imps: 430,712	Imps: 136,641	Imps: 87,080	Imps: 654,433
Avg. Time: 02:09	Avg. Time: 02:06	Avg. Time: 02:48	Avg. Time: 02:17

The bounce rate was 55 percent with an average time on site of 2 minutes 7 seconds. The *bounce rate* measures the percentage of people who come to a website and leave instantly, rather than navigate on to other pages within the same site. In other words, they "bounce" away immediately to a different website. A high bounce rate signals that the entry-page of the website is not effective as users seem not to find the information they seek. Compared to another team that achieved a percent bounce rate, this team performed well with a bounce rate of 55 percent. Figure 4 illustrates the campaign results summarizing the analytical data for each week.

STUDENT PERCEPTIONS OF THE COURSE

Students widely agreed that they gained *valuable knowledge* in online marketing, such as the following comments:

Before taking this class and doing this project I didn't really know anything about online marketing. This class and project has helped give me a general understanding about how online marketing works and what companies can do to improve their online marketing.

Table 5. Summary of keywords and bid prices of the campaign for the nonprofit organization (based on students' post-campaign summary)

China Campaign (End of 3 weeks)	*Top bid price/ Average CPC*	*Nepal Campaign (End of 2 weeks)*	*Top bid price/ Average CPC*
Adoption	$0.70/$0.40	Adoption	$0.60/$0.20
Adopt a child	$0.90/$0.39	Orphanages	$0.65/$0.29
International adoption	$0.95/$0.54	Adopting a child	$0.25/$0.12
Chinese adoption	$0.85/$0.37	Adopt a child	$0.15/$0.08
Adopting from china	$0.60/$0.38	Nepal adoption	$0.40/$0.38
Adoption from	$0.75/$0.36	Nepal sponsorship	$0.40/$0.36
Children for adoption	$0.80/$0.46	Child sponsorship	$0.15/$0.15
Adoption china	$0.75/$0.21	Overseas adoption	$0.35/$0.12
Orphanages	$0.70/$0.32	How to adopt	$0.15/$0.13
Adoption from china	$0.70/$0.32	Adoption information	$0.35/$0.15

It improved my knowledge by using real tools to increase traffic and clicks to a website. Before this project I did not know anything about how Google worked. Now I feel more knowledgeable about Google and how internet advertising works.

Students widely acknowledged the *real-world aspects* of the Google Challenge:

I liked the fact that we actually got to deal with a REAL company and were given a budget rather than just having a mock project like most other classes have. It helped give you a real sense of how online marketing works and that you were competing with people across the globe.

One thing I found very interesting about this project is the fact that you can see progress. I have worked on many other projects (...) but with this project I was very happy to see progress. It was fun tweaking and estimating costs for this project as well.

It felt like we were a professional team who was hired to do this advertising for a company. We had to make many decisions throughout the campaign that had to be made on the fly so that we could keep things on track as best as possible, and this was a great experience.

Another positive learning experience was the "freedom" students had on this project. Even though teams had to follow certain guidelines, the Challenge provides students with wide *flexibility*.

I like the freedom that Google gave us to run our own campaign. Yes, there were guidelines, but for the most part we were on our own to try and help the company's website receive more traffic.

Since this is an online campaign, each member can manage, run, and check the campaign at anywhere and anytime. We all love the dynamic and flexibility of the online service.

CONCLUSION OF THE INSTRUCTOR

A Challenge learning objective was to engage students in creating a practical, hands-on online advertising campaign in a real-world environment, thus extending the traditional classroom experience. In summary, the implementation of the Google Challenge in the course curriculum was overwhelmingly positive. As a result of this experience, the instructor will participate with his e-Marketing course again in the 2010 Google Challenge.

Learning Experiences from Canada

The Google Challenge came to the course professor's attention in early December of 2007. Although course outlines for both a senior undergraduate course "Channels and Internet Marketing" and MBA elective course "Internet Marketing Management" offered in January 2008 were in place and circulated, the Google Challenge's potential for students initiated an immediate redesign of both scheduled courses.

As the sole university in the province of Newfoundland and Labrador in Canada, strong connections with the local community exist; the majority of local business leaders with university education earned their degree locally. Opportunities to enhance local connections are always encouraged by the university and received well by the business community. Consultation with Alumni Affairs led to a targeted email for university alumni involved in local businesses, which potentially met the criteria for participation in the Google Challenge.

Although the email was sent at 10:00 am a few days before Christmas, within 20 minutes eight businesses responded that they wanted to be involved! The speed and receptiveness of the response was very positive. Before the classes began in the New Year, over 40 alumni businesses requested to be involved. The diversity and quantity of businesses gave student teams the opportunity to select a business that fit their interests to facilitate potential business connections.

Between the two courses that participated in the Google Challenge the first year there were 48 students involved (40 undergraduate and 8 MBA). Students formed their own teams, four per team undergraduate, and two per team MBA. The order of selecting a business was based on the order of team names submitted by email, first come – first served.

The content of the course was delivered through a variety of self-study of the Google Challenge materials and online videos, as well as in class introductions of some search advertising elements. Class time was available during the three weeks that the campaigns were live, for students to discuss and share insights on their trials and tribulations.

At the beginning of the Google Challenge, students met with their client and the course instructor who provided initial guidance and assistance. For many students, this was their first experience with any form of 'consulting' and working with real clients.

At the completion of the course, all teams presented to their clients during class. This formal presentation allowed the students to see the different techniques utilized for different types of clients and the impact that the techniques had on the results. Without exception, all clients made the time and effort to come to the class, further enhancing the alumni and student connections.

STUDENT PERCEPTIONS OF THE COURSE

The students in both courses had unanimously *positive feedback* on the incorporation of the Google Challenge into the course.

Google AdWords was a very valuable learning experience, it was a great opportunity to get real world experience.

Google AdWords was the best part of this course, really puts theory into practice and makes it more interactive.

I can't believe how much time and effort I am putting into the Google AdWords. I feel that I have to because if I do not do my best, it is not just marks on the line; it is someone's business. I have never taken an assignment this seriously during my entire degree.

The Google AdWords Challenge was a lot of work but a great way to incorporate a lot of different experiences and tasks into one major project. I think that it could have even been manageable as an individual project.

The hands on aspect with Google AdWords was awesome, it was a good way to learn, in complete control of the campaign was good, nice having a real responsibility for a real business.

Some students recognized the opportunity that participating in the Google Challenge would provide in their quest for employment post graduation.

The Google AdWords campaign was very interesting and I feel it will be beneficial knowledge for my future career path.

The potential *benefit for future employment* was validated in the months following the initial application of the Google Challenge into the undergraduate course. Of the 40 undergraduate students who participated in the Google Challenge, eight of them either secured a work term appointment or a job offer post graduation specifically because of their Google Challenge experience. The employment impact on the students is summed up in the following student comment.

After a four year degree, what is came down to is that I was able to find a job simply because I had participated in one assignment as part of a single course. I am so glad that I had the chance to participate in the Google AdWords Challenge as it was entirely responsible for my ability to secure full time employment after my graduation."

CONCLUSION OF THE INSTRUCTOR

The feedback from the businesses and students who participated was so positive that the Google Challenge has been included in both the undergraduate and MBA courses for the past two years and 2010. Students are very excited about participating in the Google Challenge once again. There is no doubt in the instructor's mind that for as long as Google offers the Challenge, that he will be involved, as the benefit of connecting students with alumni and the skills that it provides to students are too valuable to turn down.

Learning Experiences from Australia

Instructors at the University of Western Australia ran the Challenge in their classes in both 2008 and 2009. These classes included undergraduate and graduate classes, on the main campus in Perth and overseas in Singapore. The undergraduate classes ranged from 25 to 200 students and the graduate classes ranged from 15 to 25 students. The campaign results and overwhelmingly positive feedback resemble the United States and Canada examples above. This short section focuses on implementing the Challenge in the graduate classes.

Client recruitment was easy, with the instructor and students nominating possible clients. Furthermore, students that participated in the 2008 Challenge recommended clients for the 2009 Challenge. For example, ex-students suggested a swim wear and forestry company. For the latter, the ex-student worked with the current students. There was an oversupply of clients in both years, which enabled student teams to choose clients that they wanted to collaborate with.

In both years there was an overseas client, from France in 2008 and Thailand in 2009. Students used Skype and email for communication with their clients, who spoke English. These overseas clients reinforced key class themes. Students appreciated, and grasped, that thanks to the Internet they lived in a fast moving and ubiquitous global economy. In addition, these overseas clients underscored geo-targeting via online advertising.

The classes also had an overseas composition. Over half the students were international, particularly from Southeast Asian countries such as China, Malaysia, Indonesia and India. As these students often knew few other students, the instructor assigned student teams. In addition to nationality, gender, work experience and computer skills helped balance the teams. The first few team meetings were awkward but after a few weeks, students relished the opportunity to meet and collaborate with other nationalities.

The Challenge was the major project worth 25 percent of the overall grade. The classes met weekly for three hours and each week the students had five to ten minutes to ask questions and share insights on the Google Challenge. There was no single class devoted to the Challenge or keyword advertising. The Challenge did, however, serve as a great theme unifying online marketing throughout the term. For example, web page content is important in general and for keyword advertising.

Although there was no class dedicated to keyword advertising, there were ten minute formal presentations of the Pre-Campaign Strategy and the Post-Campaign Summary. The client was often present for both presentations, which was great. The local clients attended both report presentations. The overseas clients sort of attended via Skype. The students gave that extra effort to impress their client, and they felt professional. The clients enjoyed being back in the classroom and interacting with students. Perhaps the best part was the short discussion after students presented. The clients got a feel for improvements to their website and business; the students got a feel for the real world.

CONCLUSION

Reflecting on the authors' experiences, students widely enjoyed this *real-life project* and gained important learning outcomes such as *reflective and critical thinking, self-directed learning, teamwork dynamics*, and the *use of cutting-edge technology*. Providing the connection to the business community, the real world critique of their work and the reality of the 24-7 operation allows students with crucial experiences to assist with their transition to the real world. As some of the experiences showed, the connections have the potential to provide students with real world experience and significant business connections that can lead to *employment opportunities post graduation*.

REFERENCES

Andrews, C. P. (2007). Service learning: Applications and research in business. *Journal of Education for Business, 83*(1), 19–26. doi:10.3200/JOEB.83.1.19-26

Berry, G. R., & Workman, L. (2007). Broadening student societal awareness through service-learning and civic engagement. *Marketing Education Review, 17*(3), 21–32.

Bobbitt, L. M., Inks, S. A., Kemp, K. J., & Mayo, D. T. (2000). Integrating marketing courses to enhance team-based experiential learning. *Journal of Marketing Education, 22*(1), 15–24. doi:10.1177/0273475300221003

Bourner, J., Hughes, M., & Bourner, T. (2001). First-year undergraduate experiences of group project work. *Assessment & Evaluation in Higher Education, 26*(1), 19–39. doi:10.1080/02602930020022264

Bove, L. L., & Davies, W. M. (2009). Teaching marketing research using client-sponsored projects: Method, challenges and benefits. *Journal of Marketing Education, 31*(3), 230–239. doi:10.1177/0273475309344999

Bridges, E. (1999). Experiential learning and customer needs in the undergraduate marketing research course. *Journal of Marketing Education, 21*(1), 51–59. doi:10.1177/0273475399211007

Daly, S. P. (2001). Student-operated Internet businesses: True experiential learning in entrepreneurship and retail management. *Journal of Marketing Education, 23*(3), 204–215. doi:10.1177/0273475301233006

DMEF. (2010). DMEF collegiate ECHO direct & interactive marketing challenge. Retrieved January 18, 2010, from http://www.directworks.org/uploadedFiles/Students/COMEPTITIONS_and_AWARDS/Collegiate_ECHO/Bing%20ECHO%20Competition%20Case%20Study%2008-25-09.pdf

Doren, D. V., & Corrigan, H. B. (2008). Designing a marketing course with field site visits. *Journal of Marketing Education, 30*(3), 189–206. doi:10.1177/0273475308318071

Drea, J., Engelland, B. T., & Singh, M. (1997). Using experiential learning in a principles of marketing course: An empirical analysis of student marketing audits. *Marketing Education Review, 7*(2), 53–59.

Elam, E. L., & Spotts, H. E. (2004). Achieving marketing curriculum integration: A live case study approach. *Journal of Marketing Education, 26*(1), 50–66. doi:10.1177/0273475303262351

eMarketer. (2008). *US online advertising spending, 2006-2012*. Retrieved January 10, 2010, from http://www.marketingcharts.com/wp/wp-content/uploads/2008/03/emarketer-us-online-advertising-spending-2006-2012.jpg

Flaherty, T. B., Jansen, B. J., Hofacker, C., & Murphy, J. (2009). Insights on the Google Online Marketing Challenge and its successful classroom implementation. *MERLOT Journal of Online Learning and Teaching*, *5*(2), 446–457.

Gilbert, W. L., & Andrew, J. W. (2004). Real world problems bringing life to course content. *Proceedings of the 5th Conference on Information Technology Education*, Salt Lake City, UT.

Google. (2009a). *Student guide 200*. Retrieved January 15, 2010, from www.google.com/onlinechallenge/files/student_guide.pdf

Google. (2009b). *Marketing and advertising using Google*, 2nd ed. Retrieved January 15, 2010, from http://www.google.com/onlinechallenge/files/MarketingAndAdvertisingUsingGoogle2.pdf

Google. (2010). *About the challenge*. Retrieved January 15, 2010, from http://www.google.com/onlinechallenge/about.html

Govekar, M. A., & Rishi, M. (2007). Service learning: Bringing real-world education into the B-school classroom. *Journal of Education for Business*, *83*(1), 3–10. doi:10.3200/JOEB.83.1.3-10

Gremler, D. D., Hoffman, K. D., Keaveney, S. M., & Wright, L. W. (2000). Experiential learning exercises in services marketing courses. *Journal of Marketing Education*, *22*(1), 35–44. doi:10.1177/0273475300221005

Hamer, L. O. (2000). The additive effects of semistructured classroom activities on student learning: An application of classroom-based experiential learning techniques. *Journal of Marketing Education*, *22*(1), 25–34. doi:10.1177/0273475300221004

Hawes, J. M., & Foley, L. M. (2006). Building skills with professional activity reports. *Marketing Education Review*, *16*(1), 35–40.

Hawtrey, K. (2007). Using experiential learning techniques. *The Journal of Economic Education*, *38*(2), 143–152. doi:10.3200/JECE.38.2.143-152

Helms, M., M., Mayo, D. T., & Baxter, J. T. (2003). Experiential learning: The benefits of trade shows for marketing students and faculty. *Marketing Education Review*, *13*(3), 17–25.

Humphreys, M. A. (1981). Client-sponsored projects in a marketing research course. *Journal of Marketing Education*, *3*(10), 7–12. doi:10.1177/027347538100300203

IAB. (2009). *IAB Internet advertising revenue report*. PricewaterhouseCoopers, March 2009.

Jansen, B., & Spink, A. (2006). How we are searching the World Wide Web? A comparison of nine search engine transaction logs. *Information Processing & Management*, *42*(1), 248–263. doi:10.1016/j.ipm.2004.10.007

Jansen, B. J., Hudson, K., Hunter, L., Liu, F., & Murphy, J. (2008). The Google Online Marketing Challenge: Classroom learning with real clients, real money, and real advertising campaigns. *Journal of Interactive Advertising*, *9*(1). Retrieved November 22, 2009, from http://www.jiad.org/article109

Johnson, D. W., Johnson, R. T., & Smith, K. A. (1991). *Active learning: Cooperation in the college classroom*. Edina, MN: Interaction Book Company.

Karns, G. L. (2005). An update of marketing student perceptions of learning activities: Structure, preferences, and effectiveness. *Journal of Marketing Education*, *27*(2), 163–171. doi:10.1177/0273475305276641

Karns, G. L. (2006). Learning style differences in the perceived effectiveness of learning activities. *Journal of Marketing Education*, *28*(1), 56–63. doi:10.1177/0273475305284641

Katula, R. A., & Threnhauser, E. (1999). Experiential education in the undergraduate curriculum. *Communication Education, 48*(3), 238–255. doi:10.1080/03634529909379172

Kelley, C. A., & Gaedeke, R. M. (1990). Student and employer evaluation of hiring criteria for entry-level marketing positions. *Journal of Marketing Education, 12*, 64–71. doi:10.1177/027347539001200309

Kennedy, E. J., Lawton, L., & Walker, E. (2001). The case for using live cases: Shifting the paradigm in marketing education. *Journal of Marketing Education, 23*(2), 145–151. doi:10.1177/0273475301232008

Kirschner, P. A., Sweller, J., & Clark, R. E. (2006). Why minimal guidance during instruction does not work: An analysis of the failure of constructivist, discovery, problem-based, experiential, and inquiry-based teaching. *Educational Psychologist, 41*(2), 75–86. doi:10.1207/s15326985ep4102_1

Kolb, A. Y., & Kolb, D. A. (2005). Learning styles and learning spaces: Enhancing experiential learning in higher education. *Academy of Management Learning & Education, 4*(2), 193–212.

Kolb, A. Y., & Kolb, D. A. (2009). *Experiential learning theory: A dynamic, holistic approach to management learning, education and development.* Retrieved January 15, 2010, from http://www.learningfromexperience.com/images/uploads/ELT-Hbk-MLE&D-LFE-website-2-10-08.pdf

Kolb, D. (1984). *Experiential learning. Englewood.* Cliffs, NJ: Prentice Hall.

Lavin, M., Van Alstine, L., Scott, A., Oliver, J., & Murphy, J. (2009). The Google Online Marketing Challenge: Fostering student learning of search advertising. *Journal of Advertising Education, 13*(1), 38–43.

LeClair, D. T., & Stöttinger, B. (1999). Using an intensive living case in graduate marketing courses: Experiences from an international project. *Marketing Education Review, 9*(3), 31–40.

Levisohn, B. (2009, February 9). Web work: Searching for hitmakers. *Business Week.*

Ling, P. (2008). *The first global Google Online Marketing Challenge 2008: Perspectives of ECU student participants*. ECULTURE 2008, Joondalup, Australia, November 5. Retrieved January 15, 2010, from http://www.ea.ecu.edu.au/staffdir/data/tmp/lingecu_google_participants_2008.pdf

Luck, E., & Chalmers, W. (2007). Making education relevant. A SMART collaborative project: School marketing and real-world teaching. *Proceedings of the Australian and New Zealand Marketing Academy (ANZMAC) Conference* 2007, Dunedin, New Zealand. Retrieved January 20, 2010, from http://eprints.qut.edu.au/13097/1/13097.pdf

Marketshare.hitslink.com. (2009). *Top search engine share trend.* Retrieved January 30, 2010, from http://profitadz.com/pdf/MarketShare.pdf

Matulich, E., Papp, R., & Haytko, D. L. (2008). Continuous improvement through teaching innovations: A requirement for today's learners. *Marketing Education Review, 18*(1), 1–7.

Mayer, R. E. (2004). Should there be a three-strikes rule against pure discovery learning? The case for guided methods of instruction. *The American Psychologist, 59*(1), 14–19. doi:10.1037/0003-066X.59.1.14

McEachern, R. W. (2001). Problems in service learning and technical / professional writing: Incorporating the perspective on nonprofit management. *Technical Communication Quarterly, 10*(2), 211–225. doi:10.1207/s15427625tcq1002_6

McGee, M. (2010). *Experian gitwise: Google passes 72% U.S. market share*. Retrieved January 20, 2010, from http://searchengineland.com/google-passes-72-us-market-share-33545

McIntyre, F. S., Webb, D. J., & Hite, R. E. (2005). Service learning in the marketing curriculum: Faculty views and participation. *Marketing Education Review, 15*(1), 35–45.

McKeachie, W. J. (2002). *McKeachie's teaching tips: Strategies, research, and theory for college and university teachers* (11th ed.). Boston, MA: Houghton Mifflin.

Munoz, C., & Huser, A. (2008). Experiential and cooperative learning: Using a situation analysis project in principles of marketing. *Journal of Education for Business, 83*(4), 214–220. doi:10.3200/JOEB.83.4.214-220

Murphy, J., Hudson, K., & Hunter, L. (2008). Google AdWords: Case study. In Summers, J., Gardiner, M., Lamb, C. W., Hair, J. F., & McDaniel, C. (Eds.), *Essentials of marketing* (3rd ed.).

Murphy, J., Hudson, K., Hunter, L., & Neale, L. (2009a). The Google Online Marketing Challenge: Hands on teaching and learning. *Journal of Hospitality and Tourism Education, 21*(1), 44–47.

Murphy, J., Hunter, L., Hofacker, C., Lavin, M., Voorhees, C., & Canhoto, A. I. (2008). *The Google Online Marketing Challenge: A global teaching and learning initiative*. Special Session at the American Marketing Association Summer Educator's Conference, August 10, San Diego, CA.

Murphy, J., Tuzovic, S., Ling, P., & Mullen, L. (2009b). *Incorporating the Google Online Marketing Challenge into classes*. Special Panel at the Marketing Educators' Association Conference, April 23-25, Newport Beach, CA. Retrieved August 5, from 2009http://www.google.com/onlinechallenge/research_files/MEA_Google_Challenge_Incorporating.pdf

Navarro, P. (2008). The MBA core curricula of top-ranked U.S. business schools: A study in failure? *Academy of Management Learning & Education, 7*(1), 108–123.

Neale, L., Hofacker, C., Hunter, L., Hudson, K., Canhoto, A. I., & Murphy, J. (2008). The Google Online Marketing Challenge: A global real-world teaching and learning tool. In Kehoe, W. J., & Whitten, L. K. (Eds.), *Advances in marketing: Issues, strategies and theories* (p. 30). Tuscaloosa, AL: Society for Marketing Advances.

Neale, L., Treiblmaier, H., Henderson, V., Hunter, L., Hudson, K., & Murphy, J. (2009). The Google Online Marketing Challenge and research opportunities. *Journal of Marketing Education, 31*(1), 76–85. doi:10.1177/0273475308329534

O'Hara, B. S., & Shaffer, T. R. (1995). Details and student perceptions of an experiential program for personal selling and purchasing classes. *Journal of Marketing Education, 17*(Spring), 41–49. doi:10.1177/027347539501700106

Petkus, E. (2000). A theoretical and practical framework for service-learning in marketing: Kolb's experiential learning cycle. *Journal of Marketing Education, 22*(1), 64–70. doi:10.1177/0273475300221008

Rosso, M., McClelland, M. K., Jansen, B. J., & Fleming, S. W. (2009). Using Google AdWords in the MBA MIS course. *Journal of Information Systems Education, 20*(1), 41–50.

Rundle-Thiele, S. R., & Kuhn, K.-A. L. (2008). Challenging first year marketing students using a tournament style competition. *Proceedings of the 2008 Annual Conference of the Academy of Marketing Science: Creating Value in a Global Marketplace*, May 28-31, 2008, Vancouver, BC, Canada.

Russell, R., Atchison, M., & Brooks, R. (2008). Business plan competitions in tertiary institutions: Encouraging entrepreneurship education. *Journal of Higher Education Policy and Management, 30*(2), 123–138. doi:10.1080/13600800801938739

Schibrowsky, J. A., & Peltier, J. W. (1995). The dark side of experiential learning activities. *Journal of Marketing Education, 17*(1), 13–24. doi:10.1177/027347539501700103

Simpson, M. C., & Pham, K.-Q. (2007). *The creative campus: Experiential learning by short study-abroad courses*. Paper presented at 32nd Improving University Teaching Conference, Jaén, Spain.

Stutts, M. A., & West, V. (2003). *Competitive learning: Beyond project-based classes*. Retrieved January 15, 2010, from http://www.sbaer.uca.edu/research/acme/2003/papers/new/29.pdf

Tuzovic, S. (2009). Google mania in higher education: Sharing the excitement and the nuts and bolts of incorporating the Google Online Marketing Challenge in the classroom (pp. 73-82). In D. Gómez Chova, M. Belenguer, & I. Candel Torres (Eds.), *Proceedings of EDULEARN 09: International Conference on Education and New Learning Technologies*, July 6-8, 2009, Barcelona, Spain: International Association of Technology, Education and Development.

Ueltschy, L. C. (2001). An exploratory study of integrating interactive technology into the marketing curriculum. *Journal of Marketing Education, 23*(1), 63–72. doi:10.1177/0273475301231008

Young, M. A. (2002). Experiential learning = hands-on + minds-on. *Marketing Education Review, 12*(1), 43–51.

Zabkar, V. (2008). Advertising education in Central and Eastern Europe: A case study. Retrieved January 15, 2010, from http://www.eacaeducation.eu/download/pdf/Vesna_Zabkar.pdf

ADDITIONAL READING

Abraham, M. (2008). Why Google's surprising paid click data are less surprising. comScore Voices. Retrieved February 29, 2008, from http://blog.comscore.com/2008/02/why_googles_surprising_paid_cl.html

Berman, S. J., Battino, B., Shipnuck, L., & Neus, A. (2007). The End of Advertising as We Know It. *IBM Institute for Business Value*, 1-28, Retrieved from http://www-05.ibm.com/de/media/downloads/end-of-advertising.pdf.

Chaffey, D., Ellis-Chadwick, F., Johnston, K., & Mayer, R. (2009). *Internet Marketing. Strategy, Implementation and Practice* (4th ed.). Pearson/Prentice Hall.

EConsultancy. (2008). Paid Search Marketing. Best Practice Guide. Retrieved from www.e-consultancy.com

Google AdWords Beginner's Guide. Retrieved from https://adwords.google.com/support/aw/bin/static.py?page=guide.cs&guide=21899&hl=en_US.

Google AdWords Case Study of Roses Only. Retrieved from https://adwords.google.com/select/rosesonly.html IAB (2007). Internet Advertising Revenue Report. An Industry Survey Conducted by PricewaterhouseCoopers and Sponsored by the Interactive Advertising Bureau. 2007 Second-Quarter and First Six-Month Results. Retrieved from http://www.iab.net/media/file/IAB_PwC_2007Q2.pdf

Google AdWords Content Network. Retrieved from https://adwords.google.com/select/afc.html

Google AdWords Contextual Targeting. Retrieved from https://adwords.google.com/select/afc/contextual.html

Google AdWords Help Center. Retrieved from https://adwords.google.com/support/

Google AdWords Learning Center. Retrieved from http://www.google.com/intl/en/adwords/learningcenter/

Google AdWords Placement Targeting. Retrieved from https://adwords.google.com/select/afc/site.html

Google Financial Statements. Retrieved from http://investor.google.com/fin_data.html

Google Groups AdWords Help. Retrieved from http://groups.google.com/group/adwords-help/

Murphy, J., & Forrest, E. (1996). Hits, Views, Clicks and Visits: Web Advertisers Face Data Jungle. *The New York Times on the Web*, May 26, 1996. Retrieved from http://www.nytimes.com/library/cyber/week/0526measure.html

Murphy, J., & Forrest, E. (1996). Banners: Bullying, Boosting and Blocking. *The New York Times on the Web*, May 26, 1996. Retrieved from http://www.nytimes.com/library/cyber/week/0526measure-side2.html

Ramos, A., & Cota, S. (2009). *Search Engine Marketing*. New York, NY: McGraw-Hill.

Strauss, J., & Frost, R. (2009). *e-Marketing*. 5th ed., Pearson/Prentice Hall.

KEY TERMS AND DEFINITIONS

Bounce Rate: This term refers to the percentage of visitors who enter a website and exit instantaneously; that means, they "bounce" away within a few seconds without visiting any other pages on the site in between. The bounce rate is a metric used in website traffic analysis. A high bounce rate indicates that the site entrance page (or landing page) is not relevant to the visitors.

Click-Through-Rate (CTR): The percentage of visitors who click on an advertisement they see on search engine result pages and content pages. CTR is calculated as the number of clicks an ad receives divided by the number of times the ad is shown (referred to as impressions). CTR is a way to measure how relevant keywords are. Compared to traditional banner ads which have a very low CTR, ads on search engines have a higher CTR since they are highly relevant to the associated search.

Cost-Per-Click (CPC): This is the amount of money an advertiser pays each time when a user clicks on an advertisement on search engines and content pages.

Organic Search Results: The unpaid, algorithmic search engine results which appear because of their relevance to the search terms.

Pay-Per-Click (PPC): This refers to a pricing model for advertising on search engines (e.g. Google, Bing, Yahoo!) in which advertisers pay their host every time someone clicks on their advertisement.

Quality Score: A variable used by Google that can determine the rank and the cost-per-click of ads placed in Google AdWords.

Search Marketing: The marketing of a website on search engines. This includes search engine optimization (SEO) and pay-per-click advertising.

Chapter 4
The Adjunct's Role in Delivering Quality Online Instruction

Laurie Bedford
Professional Development Consultant and Adjunct Faculty, USA

EXECUTIVE SUMMARY

Efforts to promote the distinctiveness of online programs in an increasingly competitive market have led to a focus on instructor expertise and instructional quality. The part-time instructor, who is most often charged with facilitating online courses, is commonly viewed as a liability to the integrity of the instructional process. However, little is known about the true nature of the motivations or competencies of this group of instructors. Most often, they are perceived as a homogeneous group with similar motivations and levels of expertise. This case challenges this notion by focusing on a single instructor categorized as a full-time, professional adjunct and is characterized by her colleagues as highly skilled. The case participant describes challenges and best practices that support her in providing quality instruction. These best practices subsequently are discussed as strategies to inform decisions upon which marketing efforts are dependent.

BACKGROUND

Technology has impacted education in diverse ways. Since the first media devices were integrated into instructional activities, learning has evolved into a multi-faceted phenomenon with the potential to meet the unique needs of students, regardless of their learning style or preference. These technological advancements have created educational opportunities that would not have been possible otherwise. Technology is an important factor in higher education marketing because it is often juxtaposed with a progressive curriculum and used to highlight the distinctiveness of a program. While universities have capitalized on contemporary technological advancements for decades,

DOI: 10.4018/978-1-60960-599-5.ch004

perhaps no technology has changed the nature of how we design, deliver and market education as those associated with online learning have.

Since beginning its rise to mainstream acceptance in the mid-1990s, online education has mushroomed into one of the industry's most promising practices in terms of recruiting, retaining and graduating students from diverse backgrounds and with diverse needs. Consequently, as the demand for online education increases, the need to identify qualified faculty to assume the increasing workload becomes critically important (Allen & Seaman, 2008). To complicate the challenge, tenured or full-time faculty are often unable to fill this need due to workload or resistance. To fill the void, organizations are more frequently turning to adjuncts to meet the needs of their online learners (Milliken & Jurgens, 2008). In 2008, the National Center for Education Statistics estimated that 48 percent of instructional faculty across degree-granting universities held adjunct status. This, in turn, has resulted in an increasing concern regarding the nature of the adjunct-university relationship as well as the ability of part-time faculty to guide learners towards appropriate levels of competencies. The two primary considerations within this discourse are whether part-time faculty members are sufficiently prepared to provide quality instruction and whether organizations have built appropriate capacity to support their efforts (Shakeshaft, 2002; Bedford, 2009).

SETTING THE STAGE

In the early stages of the growth of online education, the programs themselves could be marketed as unique because of their convenience and flexibility (Garrett, 2008). However, as online education has proliferated, it has become clear that these arguments alone will not continue to be sufficient evidence of a distinctive program that will offer unique opportunities. Nor do they address issues of the quality of instruction executed by adjunct instructors. Organizational leaders need to recognize that their marketing efforts must be adjusted for a new and savvier audience. This audience is not bound by time or place but represents a growing number of individuals for whom choice is unlimited. In addition, this audience is characterized by a trend in which adult learners expect an education with broad and personal meaning attached (Forest & Peterson, 2006). For these adult learners, quality programs are a distinguishing factor in their decision about which online program will best meet their academic needs (Gibbons & Wentworth, 2002).

The proliferation of online education has led to a better understanding of best practices (Kupczynski & Hooper, 2006). Consequently, online programs have become more standardized as developers strive to align their practices with those identified as most promising. This means that courses across institutions have similar content and structure. As a result, organizations that enjoyed a market niche in the early days are finding it more difficult to differentiate themselves among their competitors (Allen & Seaman, 2008). As in traditional education, when program offerings and course content can no longer be the distinctive factor, organizations must look to broader aspects of their programs that make them stand out as high quality among many. Efforts to differentiate programs in an increasingly competitive market have led to a focus on a wide assortment of instructional features. According to Garrett (2008), these include institutional type, programs of study, levels of study and cost. However, as more programs become available, the range and scope become increasingly similar. Potential students are faced with larger numbers of schools and programs for which there seems to be no clear differentiating factor.

In higher education, marketing can be a way to create a unique identity and differentiate the focal organization from the distracters. According to Anctil (2008):

Marketing helps organizations identify needs, develop products and services to address those needs, and puts those goods and services into the hands of people in need. When seen in this context, marketing is a dynamic process that is responsive and innovative. (p. 26)

While there is little evidence to inform marketers of which specific practices might draw potential online students to certain programs or types of programs, we do know that the majority of online learners fit into the category of non-traditional (Gibbons & Wentworth, 2002). Non-traditional students seek education for a variety of reasons, including professional advancement and economic stability. Whatever the reason of entry, they bring the expectation that they will work to successful completion. Since, as Robinson and Doverspike (2006) found, online learners are more likely to enroll if they believe they can complete, it makes logical sense to engage in marketing practices that demonstrate the organization's ability to assist learners toward that goal.

However, as Nichole (2010) concludes, the issues regarding student retention in online learning are complex, and the number of students who do not complete outnumber those in traditional settings significantly. Many of the reasons for the considerable dropout among online learners are related to personal circumstances and are beyond the immediate control of the institution. These include time management, family responsibilities and financial difficulties (Ashby, 2004; Nash, 2005). Other key issues however, can be used to assess how an organization's instructors might impact persistence and ultimate retention among the learners.

In an effort to categorize the issues related to student completion so that they may be addressed by appropriate stakeholders, Garland (1993) identified four types of barriers to student success in online programs. These include situational barriers related to the context of the learner; institutional barriers associated with the rules that the institution offering the program wants to enforce; dispositional barriers related to learner attitude and work habits; epistemological barriers related to the content of the course. Institutional and epistemological barriers as defined by Garland (1993) are most closely associated with instructional issues and within control of the organization. Shin (2002, 2003) concurs that these internal factors, such as relationships with instructors, can have an important impact on retention. As such, quality instruction should be considered one of the key components in student-retention practices that are within the immediate control of the organization.

Quality instruction, like many facets of student recruitment and retention, is multi-faceted and complex. A central feature unique to quality online instruction draws on the knowledge that how technology is incorporated into the instruction is more important than the technology itself (Schroeder, 2008). Without the teacher, the technology is a mere repository for the content (Clark, 1983). Quality instruction therefore can be defined as the combined result of specific practices that lead to learner success, persistence and ultimate program completion. Angelino, Williams and Natvig (2007) describe some of these best practices as timely feedback and social presence in relation to desired outcomes. Akridge, DeMay, Braunlich, Collura and Sheaha (2002) add to the discourse by suggesting that instructors can impact instruction through relevant content, motivational strategies and engaging learning experiences—which, they conclude, are the foundation of a quality educational environment. Through this process, the teacher, along with her repertoire of pedagogical knowledge, will continue to have the most significant impact on the learning process. As an empirically sound philosophy, organizations have an opportunity to capitalize on instructor capabilities as a discriminating factor than can be traced to overarching learning outcomes. This cannot be done, however, unless these same organizations can demonstrate that their instructors do, in fact, have those coveted capabilities. Furthermore, organizations must be in a position to attract and retain these qualified candidates.

CASE DESCRIPTION

According to Lewis (2008), quality teachers choose organizations based on specific factors that appeal to them, including the extent to which they feel valued as professionals. Therefore, organizations that desire to define themselves based on the qualifications of their instructors must evaluate their practices to attract the best candidates for their online programs.

Simpson (2004) suggests that progressive online schools be intentional in their interventions for student-retention practices related to quality instructional practices. This process includes a focus not only on the student but on the individual instructor as well. Since the many schools employ a majority of instructors as adjunct (Wilson, 2009, Milliken & Jurgens, 2008, National Center for Education Statistics, 2008), it is important to understand and recognize the unique instructional expertise that these individuals bring to the learning environment. For example, Puzziferro and Shelton (2009) describe the adjunct as being able to better attend to the needs of non-traditional learners because of their multiple professional roles within diverse organizations. Furthermore, organizations can also capitalize on the significant role that these employees play in advancing the goals and visions of the university (Tipple, 2010; Puzziferro & Shelton, 2009).

Without consideration for the diverse motivations and levels of expertise of adjunct faculty, they are most often perceived as a homogeneous group with similar levels of expertise, instructional knowledge and enthusiasm for teaching/learning. Often, they are collectively characterized as unprepared to teach, less motivated to put forth extended effort and possessing a negligible appreciation for organizational culture (Bedford, 2009; Shakeshaft, 2002; Shelton & Saltsman, 2006). Other literature points to the adjunct status as a way to marginalize individuals based on characteristics such as gender (Wolfinger, Mason & Goulden, 2009). These notions are often juxtaposed with a perception that adjuncts are those who lack the capacity to secure full-time positions. This positions the adjunct in a tenuous position with vague and intangible professional identity and no clear career path or status.

As a result of these perceptions, stakeholders in educational excellence frequently view the increased use of adjuncts as an obstacle in the retention and successful outcomes of learners. Although full-time tenured instructors are often steeped in the traditions of the face-to-face research university, they are most often identified as possessing the most desirable qualifications for teaching in the online environment (Puzziferro & Shelton, 2009). However, when traditional, tenured faculty cannot be secured for such instructional purposes, organizations often take a defensive posture, situating the adjunct as a practitioner who brings knowledge from the field to the learning environment. This is often done without regard for parallel issues that relate to the delivery of quality instruction. At the same time, organizations sustain the notion that adjuncts lack instructional expertise by suggesting that their training efforts bring the adjuncts' expertise in line with their full-time counterparts. These arguments situate the use of adjuncts in a deficit model that suggests that the organization can make up for inadequacies in their faculty. The deficiency model paradigm yields to the notion that the use of adjuncts is less than ideal and perpetuates the uncertainty that adjuncts bring to the learning environment.

None of these arguments, however, acknowledges the adjunct as a unique individual with diverse motivations, varying levels of instructional expertise and distinct experiences. Rather, defending the concerns about the reliance on adjuncts with organizational attempts to compensate, the deficiency paradigm overlooks the individual contributions that faculty members bring to the instructional environment. This creates additional dilemmas for an organization trying to establish a reputation of quality when the instructional base primarily relies on the use of part-time instructors. The focus on what is absent neglects instructors who purposely build new skill sets to bring contemporary strategies to their instruction (Bedford, 2009). It also positions the adjunct as having to prove her worth through creativity and persistence, which, ironically, has allowed many adjuncts to become experts in online models for quality instruction (Puzziferro & Shelton, 2009).

It has been long understood that the most important factor in learning is the instructor and the instructional practices on which he or she draws (Clark, 1983). As online programs continue to mature and become more competitive, leaders in the field are recognizing this. For the organization, this means that leadership needs to understand and document the instructor role in the tradition of the mission of the organization (Puzziferro & Shelton, 2009; Tipple, 2010) and the ultimate success of their learners. In particular, with the increasing number of adjuncts assuming online teaching responsibilities, the ability to respond to the unique needs associated with this growing trend is at stake. Of particular importance is the understanding of the professional and personal situations from which adjuncts emerge. These have been summarized by Schnitzer and Crosby (2003) and include:

- Those who accept adjunct positions with the goal of becoming full-time instructors.
- Instructors who teach in a traditional venue but want to add online opportunities to their repertoire of experiences.
- Administrators who desire to have continued contact with students.
- Recent graduates seeking experience.
- The full-time, part-timer for whom a series of adjunct responsibilities constitutes full-time employment.

Some organizations have taken proactive steps to ensure that the stakeholders value and understand the importance of faculty by situating adjuncts as partners rather than outsiders. These progressive organizations seek to purposefully identify and categorize adjuncts similar to Schnitzer and Crosby (2003) in order to determine how they can best meet their instructional responsibilities. As the commonly used categories of adjunct instructors become mainstream in the discourse, one group that is rising to the forefront is commonly referred to as the "*full-time part-timers.*" This group is characterized by instructors who neither rely on part-time teaching appointments for supplemental income nor as a means to position themselves for subsequent full-time employment. These full-time, professional adjuncts, according to Bedford (2009), are content with their part-time status as they respond to the needs of organizations. Embracing an entrepreneurial spirit, full-time professional adjuncts maintain long-term relationships with organizations as consumers of their services. As more individuals are exploring the full-time professional adjunct option as a career choice with the potential for diverse work, flexible scheduling, fair compensation and professional growth, organizations are recognizing that they need to consider how to best negotiate their relationship with this group of professionals and to capitalize on their contributions to recruit and retain students. At stake is both the delivery of quality instruction as well as the reputation of the organization at which they are employed.

The growing body of evidence attempting to categorize adjuncts, such as the full-time professional, suggests that there is an increasing trend towards the recognition that adjuncts emerge from diverse situations. Since their needs can vary greatly, attending to them is a complex task. Further complicating the process, in order to determine needs, first motivations must to be more clearly understood. A few studies (for example, Shiffman, 2009, Bedford, 2009) have investigated the motivations of online faculty.

However, these studies attempt to identify needs based on arbitrary categories of adjuncts and fail to consider the adjunct as an individual (Wilson, 2009). Without a more specific focus on individual needs, organizations lack the evidence to facilitate the decision-making process in this area. To ensure that those who recruit, hire and work to retain online instructors are effective in their efforts, appropriate tools need to be developed to ensure that all aspects of adjunct support and development are addressed. This will, in turn, allow the organization to be able to make marketing claims based on data regarding the characteristics of their adjuncts rather than draw on assumptions that may be accurate for one individual but not another.

It is clear that little data exists to determine how adjuncts might be individually supported as necessary for them to manifest those motivations as best practices in the learning environment. Best practices are often determined by a variety of stakeholders. While the ultimate goal of the development and implementation of support structures for adjunct faculty is the success of the learners, from a marketing perspective, the adjunct herself should also be viewed as an important stakeholder. This is critical because adjuncts—who may deliver a significant level of instruction—are the individuals with whom students most closely work. Students will evaluate the effectiveness of the overall organization (as well as their ability to successfully complete) most often by the value they place on individual instructors with whom they interact (Shin, 2002, 2003; Angelino, Williams,& Natvig, 2007; Rovi, 2003). Therefore, identifying the needs of those providing the instruction should be of primary consideration in determining how best to support their efforts.

While adjuncts can be placed into many diverse categories, this case study examined best practices associated with the specific needs of one full-time, professional adjunct. This included inquiry into the level of instructional opportunities, support for scholarly activities and a reciprocal method of communication that respects the individual's contributions to the organization. It was developed through the perspective of an online instructor, Naomi, who characterizes herself a self-employed, scholar consultant. Naomi is 56 years old and resides in the Southwest United States with her husband—a full-time public school administrator--and her teenage daughter. She also has two grown children and an infant grandson.

Naomi was identified as the focal participant for this case based on a number of pre-determined criteria. First, potential participants were selected from a sample of candidates who met the characterization of full-time, professional adjunct status as outlined by Bedford (2009). These individuals consider the organizations with which they engage consumers of their services. They situate themselves as consultants with the potential to bring expertise and innovation to the organization. Specifically, according to Bedford (2009), these individuals:

- Provide instruction for two to four universities.
- Often also engage in other instructional development and consulting.
- Do not actively seek full-time, traditional employment.
- Consider themselves entrepreneurs.

Naomi works virtually for two, fully online universities. Her teaching load at each is one to three courses per term. In addition, she teaches for a local community college, where she designs and facilitates one or two hybrid courses per year. These courses combine both online and traditional, face-to-face instruction. Finally, Naomi consults for a handful of organizations, primarily engaging in faculty training with some course development when needed. These work assignments result in what Naomi considers to be full-time compensation but accounts for about 75 percent to 80 percent of her actual work time. The remaining workday is used for scholarly engagement, service activities and personal responsibilities.

It was also important that the focal participant be recognized as a highly qualified instructor who brings rigor to the instructional process. The level to which the participant met this criterion was established through a series of questionnaires with administrators and colleagues. The purpose of these questionnaires was to ensure that the recommendations based on the motivations and needs for support were aligned with efforts to attract and retain faculty with these characteristics.

Overwhelmingly, Naomi's supervisors and colleagues described her as "*dedicated,*" "*intelligent,*" "*an asset to the program*" and "*highly motivated to provide quality instruction.*" One particularly salient response was as follows:

Having instructors as qualified, engaged, and committed as Naomi, allows us to stand out in the field. Many institutions have online programs that offer similar degrees. What we can offer is the best instruction and highest level of support for our students. We can confidently say this because of instructors like Naomi in our online classrooms.

These comments demonstrate that not only does Naomi possess the demographics of an instructor who is committed to the instructional process and success of her students but that her efforts have positive results. This situates Naomi to be a voice for adjuncts within the context of improved organizational relationships as well as increased market value for the programs with which she affiliates.

CASE FINDINGS

Ensuring that students have the opportunity to interact with highly qualified instructors is critical to the success of online programs in the contemporary, competitive environment (Shin, 2002, 2003; Angelino, Williams & Natvig, 2007). Recruiting, selecting and retaining qualified instructors are at the forefront of the efforts of many institutions that offer online programs (Garrett, 2008). The extensive use of adjuncts complicates the issue but provides potential benefits to the organization as research continues to add to what we know about their motivations.

This case was intended to identify how organizations can build capacity to support adjuncts with regard to their diverse motivations. Its overarching purpose was to inform the development of comprehensive supports and partnerships with the instructors who work closely with the organization's consumers. Marshall and Rossman (2006) argued that a qualitative study should utilize techniques in which the complexity of human actions can be addressed. Furthermore, as Merriam (1995) explained, case study is one of the most ideal designs for understanding and interpreting these types of phenomena. With this in mind, the case-study approach was incorporated into the design of this study and was based on a unit of analysis of a single individual from whose perspective best practices for supporting full-time, professional adjunct faculty were examined.

To best give voice to the adjunct needs, several issues were considered. First, the design of the case recognized that adjuncts cannot be considered a homogeneous group. While adjuncts can be categorized in many ways (Schnitzer & Crosby, 2003), the full-time, professional adjunct was identified as the category of choice for this case. Since full-time professional adjuncts by definition have experiences with multiple organizations, this was considered an ideal perspective from which to analyze the issues with respect to multiple organizations.

The case study relied on a series of in-depth interviews with the focal participant. The interviews revolved around four primary considerations that, according to Bedford (2009), provide a framework from which to develop appropriate practices for supporting full-time professional adjuncts. This framework includes concerns about overcoming barriers; developing a professional identity; balancing personal and professional matters; and providing for opportunities to engage in scholarly activities. The Bedford (2009) framework establishes structure for supporting adjunct faculty for whom participating in several part-time contracts constitutes their full-time, articulated profession. Although each of the constructs within the framework is intertwined and dependent upon the others, they were considered separately for data collection, analysis and discussion. This structure provided for a comprehensive view of what motivates the full-time professional adjunct as well as gave insight into which issues are most important.

The interview protocol was divided into four segments that represented the foundation for four separate interviews based on Bedford's (2009) framework. Interview data was analyzed prior to subsequent interviews to provide opportunities for follow-up and clarification questions. The analysis of the transcribed interview data involved a symbiotic process in which the first step was axial coding. Next, content analysis was implemented in an effort to reveal patterns and themes among the codes. Content analysis, according to Patton (2002) refers to a process that resulted in the identification of core consistencies and meanings through the reduction of a large quantitative or qualitative material. These core consistencies and meanings—or themes—were reached from a deductive analysis perspective in which the data were analyzed within Bedford's (2009) framework. Both challenges and best practices identified by the participant were considered and are included in the detailed descriptions of the findings presented in the following sections.

Seeking a Professional Identity

Perhaps one of the most salient issues emerging from the case study was Naomi's desire to be viewed as a professional instructor-consultant with talents, expertise and abilities coveted by organizations of higher learning. She described professional identity in many ways but overall posited within the context of being a participant and expert in a discipline. This also included a sense of belonging. However, she did not explicitly assign this sense of belonging to a single organization or entity. Rather, she described belonging as a sentiment that could be realized through a network of colleagues, peers and others within a hierarchical structure for the purpose being collegial and supportive.

While she described her current professional network as dynamic and synergistic, she juxtaposed that with a discussion annotated by terms such as "*isolation*" and "*lack of connection.*" These were both cited as issues that she continually struggled with in efforts to build her professional identity. She described this as follows:

A professional identity is something that's not easily definable. I know that I am highly skilled and have considerable expertise in my discipline, but it's often hard to make that fit into a description of myself.... I think that this is often resolved through academic discourse that emerges from informal, spontaneous and reflective conversation. Since the majority of my work is virtual, most days ... [I often don't] have opportunities to engage with colleagues in this way. Furthermore, since I work with many organizations, most of my collegial relationships are fragmented. This makes it difficult to have a voice in the academic world. I think that's important in professional identity—to have someone recognize your expertise and contributions.

For Naomi, another issue was in the lack of an official, recognized title. While she was initially hesitant to bring the issue to the discussion, she reflected on the implications in a number of ways. She explained:

On the surface, this really doesn't seem like a big deal—and shouldn't be. However, our society and the world of academia thrive on professional identities recognized by labels. For example, if you're a Dean or a Provost, people know what that means and respect that. However, the term "adjunct" has many different connotations. An adjunct can be anyone that teaches one or two classes per year to someone like me who makes it their career. It seems like there should be some differentiation among us.... Often, when I tell people I'm an adjunct, they think that I do this part-time and wonder what my "real job" is.

The idea of an official title was closely connected to Naomi's concern that she be engaged in a legitimate, recognized career path. She stated:

I know that things are always changing. Jobs of the future haven't even been thought of today. I guess I'm in that category. Teaching online for many schools is not something that[I] would have ever thought I would be doing ten years ago. Even today, it's not something that people recognize as even being possible.... Together with the bad press that adjuncts get, it's hard to be convincing that I am building a reputable career.

More significant to Naomi's sense of personal identity, however, were organizational attempts at creating transparency between part-time and full-time responsibilities. She explained:

I want to work for organizations who respect and recognize me as a professional. In some schools, they give lip service to this, but administrative actions prove otherwise. These organizations will make statements about how much the adjuncts are appreciated and how they are important partners, but when it comes right down to it, our voices are not heard. Decisions are made without our input, and we're informed of policies after they are implemented. This doesn't make me feel like much of a partner. In my mind, this is what happens to a part-time employee who's not invested in the work. This isn't what I want to be. I try to avoid organizations like this, but it isn't always possible. You don't always know the culture until you get involved with them.

In contrast, Naomi shared her insight about more progressive organizations that make it a priority to involve part-time instructors at all levels. These organizations, as described by Naomi, allow for part-time instructors to be involved in policy and curriculum committees as equal partners without regard for their status. She stated:

For example, at one school, I was asked to be part of a committee to revise enrollment policies. I knew that my ideas were valued, and I saw many of them incorporated into the final draft. These schools also conduct frequent surveys to find out what issues all faculty think are important. Everyone completes all surveys—not just a distinct group--because we know that we will be taken seriously.

Fortunately, organizations with which Naomi is engaged are making purposeful efforts to support adjunct faculty in these areas. Naomi cited a number of strategies that promote camaraderie and feelings of partnership with the organizations with which she works. These strategies included simple practices such as creating a unique title for their part-time instructors. In organizations with which Naomi is affiliated, adjuncts are described as contingent faculty or partner faculty—titles that differentiate them from their full-time counterparts yet affirm their status in the organization. In addition, Naomi also discussed efforts to use Web 2.0 and other contemporary strategies to engage adjuncts. For example, Naomi described networking groups and informational links on sites such as LinkedIn, Facebook, Twitter and other sites commonly used by virtual professionals. She stated that these opportunities are often "*similar to watercooler conversations that happen in traditional environments.*"

Establishing a professional identity was something clearly important to Naomi. She clearly viewed this as a part of her overall effort to develop a repertoire of professional responsibilities that lead to a sense of fulfillment and accomplishment. Throughout her interviews, she was very clear that she wanted to be perceived as a professional by both the organizations with which she affiliates herself and the lay community. At the same time, she acknowledged that, as a part-time employee, there needs to continue to be a balance between being a partner and understanding that her part-time status has the potential to situate her as an outsider. She explained:

I realize that I've chosen this career path. This means that I am a part-time contractor without employee status anywhere. Many adjuncts complain about benefits and security. I thought about this carefully when making my career decisions, and I can live with that. So, it really bothers me when people categorize me as something I'm not. This is often made worse by the vocal adjuncts who want the benefits of full-time work but are not full-time employees. Perhaps as time goes on and my career choice becomes more mainstream, organizations will more frequently be in a position to support these concerns.

It was clear that while Naomi didn't consistently feel supported in these areas, she understood that progressive organizations recognized the problem. She felt convinced that the situation is a result of the novelty of online education issues and that as online education continues to become more mainstream, the situation will be resolved. Naomi also articulated how these issues impact her professional identity within the context of her challenges in overcoming barriers—which was the focus of the second interview.

Overcoming Barriers

Closely associated with the need to develop and maintain a professional identity was Naomi's concern with overcoming barriers associated with adjunct status. While adjuncts have varying levels of expertise, many have those equivalent of full-time or tenured faculty. However, they are rarely recognized as such. Naomi explains:

Throughout the academic discourse—both in the literature and in the dialogue—the use of adjuncts is seen as a crisis in education. Those who are uninformed make broad, sweeping claims that a part-time professional cannot have the motivation or capacity to provide high quality, rigorous instruction. At best, a few adjuncts might be recognized as "outliers" so to speak. These individuals are seen as exceptions rather than the norm.

Naomi stressed throughout the interviews that she sees this as important not only to her current sense of professional identity but to her ability to continue to develop in her discipline and perhaps, advance in her field. She cited concerns about being considered a serious candidate for a full-time, traditional faculty position or an administrative position in the future. Specifically, she stated:

I'd like to think that if at some point, I decide to go a different direction in my career, I'll be taken seriously. Since adjuncts are so often perceived as somebody who couldn't make it as a "real" instructor, I'm concerned that I'll be overlooked as somebody who's already been labeled as such....[I think that] it is important for the world of academia and in the lay community that part-time instructors can be thought of as competent. I certainly believe that I am and that I am capable of many things. At this point in my career, I am focusing my expertise on online students. This should not create barriers for me in the future, but I think it will.

Juxtaposed with personal concerns, Naomi also acknowledged the importance of instructor image to the organization and to online programs as a whole. She continued:

Despite what we've learned about the quality of online education, there continue to be skeptics. These are individuals who perceive the online degree as something less than the traditional degree. Being an instructor in online education—and an adjunct at that—I sometimes feel that I am consistently defending what I do. Online organizations have an equal, if not greater stake in resolving this.

Throughout the remainder of this interview, Naomi suggested ways in which she observed online schools addressing this issue. She felt that online schools are in a position to partner with all faculty to demonstrate the quality and rigor of online education. Rather than take a defensive posture, Naomi characterized progressive schools as those willing to work with adjuncts to ensure that courses, programs and instruction met or exceeded expectations of traditional education. At one point, Naomi indicated that while she held concerns about the fairness of this position, it also gave her greater motivation to succeed. She stated:

Online schools are in a position to have to prove that they have quality. While this might be perceived as a negative, I've observed the best schools accepting the challenge in positive ways. Rather than defend their services, they rise to the occasion to provide the best instruction for the students. This, in turn, makes me a better teacher. As expectations rise, I do whatever I can to meet them. I think that this also exemplifies how really good schools create partnerships with us. All this only serves to better educate our students.

Balancing Professional and Personal Commitments

Like many contemporary professionals, Naomi expressed concerns about her ability to balance her professional and personal commitments. With a newborn grandchild and a daughter in high school, she cited a need to be able to provide for their needs. She expressed a sense of relief that online teaching gives her the flexibility to ensure that she balance that with a professional presence connected to developing a sense of professional identity. She stated:

I feel very lucky that I can be engaged in meaningful work but can also take the afternoon off to babysit or go to my daughter's game. I don't have to ask for time off or explain to anyone what I need. That gives me a great sense of independence.... I also think that this... affects my performance. I'm not worried about what else I need to do because I can prioritize. My work and my professional lives intermingle, and I don't have to be cognizant about which eight hours in a day I'm obligated to be sitting at a desk.

However, Naomi also referred to obstacles to this flexibility inherent in the adjunct teaching role. Of significant concern is her ability to schedule time away from her work for any length of time. The following passage highlights the situation:

Certainly, teaching online gives me a certain amount of flexibility. Since I have no set working hours, I can work around my personal life. However, I still have deadlines and responsibilities. I am committed to my instruction and my students. I am obliged to check in with them frequently, and some of the schools that I work for require certain time frames... [in which to do that]. In addition, other contractual obligations need to be addressed. One of the skills necessary for this kind of work is to be able to multi-task and prioritize. With all of the various professional activities going on I also need to be in a position to identify those personal issues as priority.

She continued:

When I work for several organizations, the quarters or semesters overlap. So, even when I have a break at one University, my teaching responsibilities at others continue. When you're a part-time employee, you don't get benefits—and that's fine. But not having time off sometimes can present problems. Since I work virtually, I'm not bound to an office, but I am bound to be online almost every day.

Complicating the matter, Naomi cited differences and sometimes unreasonable expectations for interaction. She explains:

One school I worked for expected me to be online every day. That's just not reasonable. I believe that every effort should be made to support students, but I also think that there needs to be a balance between that and the instructor needs.

This situation creates a dilemma that Naomi described as one in which she continually needs to be cognizant of her interactions online. This prevents her from having an opportunity to completely separate from work and be able to focus on her family. As Naomi states, "*I cherish the time that I have with my new grandson. But I'm always thinking about what I need to do online.*"

Naomi also described innovative steps that schools are taking to ensure that faculty in her situation have opportunities for pursuits outside of academia. She provides examples such as options for taking a term off without fear of dismissal and opportunities to engage substitutes in her classrooms for short periods of time as best practices to support part-time faculty. In addition, she offered, "*some schools are providing more flexibility in how often we're required to interact online. For example, they may require that I participate every day for the first week or two, [and] then level off as the students get more comfortable.*" She concluded, "*This is a great compromise to ensure that all stakeholders are getting what they need. Especially when schools plan ahead of time, I can schedule this in and know when the work will be most intense.*"

Scholarly Engagement

Throughout the interviews, Naomi was continually clear about and often came back to the point that she sees herself as a scholar. She indicated:

Being a part-time teacher doesn't mean that I'm not interested in furthering the discipline. In fact, I think that my professional status puts me in a great position to engage in research in ways that might not be possible if I were bound by specific organizational policies. Being a part-time teacher means that I'm not involved with issues complicated by political or personal agendas. In my opinion, that gives me more time and energy to focus on my research.

It was also clear that Naomi's desire to engage in research and other scholarly activities was closely connected to her desire to provide effective and relevant instruction for her students. She expressed this in several ways, including her currency in her field, having practical experience to share with her learners, and being viewed as a contributor in the academic arena. She compared herself to other professionals who maintain their credentials in an effort to ensure that contemporary knowledge is embedded into their practice. She also articulated her belief in the importance of her role as an academic contributor as well as her potential to bring fresh dynamics to scholarly discourse. She stated:

I engage in all of the scholarly activities that I would if I was vying for a tenure role—research, publishing, service, etc. The only difference is that I engage in the activities that I enjoy and interest me with no pressure from an organization to find something that will benefit them .... What I do benefits everyone—I don't have to worry about what any single organization thinks.

She added, "*As an independent adjunct, I am not obligated to attend campus activities, meetings, social events, etc. as part of [my] professional obligations."* This, she continued, provided her with the "*flexibility to build into ... [my] schedule opportunities to regularly interact with colleagues across diverse organizations and networks that will best meet ... [my] professional needs."*

As with many other professional issues, Naomi also expressed barriers to her participation in meaningful scholarly activities. She articulated her belief that this type of independent scholarly activity would lead to broad-based skill and, ultimately, significant academic growth and development over time. At the same time she acknowledged disappointment with regard to the lack of support organizations provided for these activities. In some cases, these barriers could be mitigated because of efforts being made by organizations to ensure access to academic libraries, institutional review boards and even research funding opportunities. However, these opportunities were described as "*intermittent and unreliable."*

Connections to Quality Instruction

During her discussion with regard to each of the four areas of instructor support as identified by Bedford (2009), the participant discussed both her challenges and what she considers to be organizational successes. While many of these issues are not directly related to instructional quality, the implication is that they support the instructor who has already been identified as possessing coveted instructional characteristics and is concerned with the continued development of her skills and expertise. For example, in her discussion of her need for professional identity, Naomi identifies her desire to have her expertise acknowledged. This would assume that she already believes she has developed or is willing to develop that expertise to the performance level indicative of quality instruction that would enable persistence and lead to organizational respect by potential students. The acknowledgement of this by her supervisors and colleagues supports this assumption and validates how a professional identity might be important to instructors who are concerned about quality in their instructional processes.

Naomi also stated concern with overcoming stereotypes of adjuncts as providing poor quality. Since her perceptions and that of her supervisors and colleagues would suggest that these characteristics do not describe Naomi's performance, addressing this issue has potential positive impacts for both the individual faculty member and for the organization. Rather than acknowledging the deficient and attempting to compensate for it, it appears that there is an opportunity for organizations to work directly with adjuncts to identify and address the rhetoric. The focus of these conversations could involve instructional quality and can potentially be used to differentiate programs from the competitors based on the perception and performance of the learners.

Similarly, working with individuals on issues of flexibility can lead to increased instructional quality. According to Testa, (2010) flexibility in a work schedule results in higher levels of productivity and increased efficiency. Since two of Naomi's concerns are her desire to provide quality instruction and have availability to attend to family issues, organizations have an opportunity to partner with adjuncts to ensure a proper balance between a professional and personal life. Such a partnership would provide the support necessary for both the faculty and the organization to ensure that appropriate time and resources are dedicated to the instructional process and that personal commitments will not interfere.

The final category, scholarly engagement, likely has the most salient implications with regard to the relationship between the adjunct's needs and instructional quality. As instruction is an evolving and dynamic process, best practices continue to emerge through the scholarly process. While all instructors need to be responsible for being familiar with the most current practices, engagement in the research process has the most promise in terms of transferring that information into the classroom environment (Stringer, 2008). When instructors such as Naomi suggest that scholarly engagement is an important aspect of their professional identity, organizations can capitalize upon those aspirations with the knowledge that improved instruction may very well be a likely outcome of the undertaking. Furthermore, as instructors—adjunct or otherwise—become known within the professional community for their scholarly contributions, those accomplishments can be shared across the organization.

A focus on these articulated needs as related to instruction can provide the evidence to counter the argument that adjuncts negatively affect the quality and ultimate success of students. Rather, adjuncts can begin to be seen as valuable assets in demonstrating student competence and increasing the completion rate among them. Furthermore, as a valued partner with a better understanding of the organizational culture through participation and engagement, adjuncts are in the position to serve the organization in a variety of other ways (Puzziferro & Shelton, 2009; Tipple, 2010). This includes supporting the goal of demonstrating student success that perpetuates a positive impression of a program concerned with instructional quality (Gibbons & Wentworth, 2002) and promoting organizational recognition through scholarly engagement and a reputation of excellence.

CURRENT CHALLENGES FACING ORGANIZATIONS

Recent technological advancements in education—particularly those related to online learning—have created incalculable opportunities for all stakeholders. As with any innovation, however, the evolution and increased interest in technology-driven instruction has also created challenges. For online education programs, one of the most salient challenges involves the substantial increase in enrollment in recent years (Allen & Seaman, 2008). This concurrently creates marketing challenges for institutions of higher education as new programs are being developed to meet the demand. As online technologies become more mainstream and available, so does the opportunity for organizations to offer online courses and programs. At the same time, program and course content is becoming more standardized based on industry standards and credentialing agencies. Organizations that once enjoyed little to no competition in online programs are finding it more difficult to market their programs as unique (Garrett, 2008). As a result, organizations need to examine diverse program components to determine how best they can articulate the advantages of their programs to potential students as well as maintain the standards of excellence—including student recruitment, retention and program completions—that all stakeholders demand.

According to Allen and Seaman (2008), the organization's ability to recruit and retain students is among the primary marketing concerns related to the continued success and growth of online programs. As the volume of potential students comes into balance with opportunities for enrollment, the organization's ability to recruit and retain students becomes more difficult. In addition, geography no longer limits the potential students' choice, allowing them to receive education from unlimited sources. Consequently, online programs need to determine how best to structure their efforts to ensure that they articulate and, ultimately, address the needs of their contemporary constituents. This can most effectively be done at an organizational level by addressing institutional and epistemological barriers (Garland, 1993).

The quality and expertise of faculty and the effectiveness of the instruction they provide are two distinctive characteristics that program administrators are beginning to recognize as differentiating factors that lead to successful student completion. However, since much of the instruction in online education is facilitated by adjuncts, rhetoric concerning the reliance on these professionals becomes a barrier in promoting programs as high quality and rigorous. The literature overwhelmingly positions adjuncts as providers of mediocre instruction at best (; Shakeshaft, 2002; Shelton & Saltsman, 2006; Schnitzer & Crosby, 2003). This creates challenges as stereotypes and perceptions of adjunct faculty as a collective continue to be perpetuated.

Marketing strategists, who are challenged by these issues, currently draw on a number of techniques to ensure that they are addressing the concerns of educational quality provided by adjuncts. They understand that the structure of their marketing techniques cannot ignore the rhetoric surrounding the conditions and status of their faculty. Strategies to address these concerns, however, are often created from a deficiency perspective that strives to compensate for an articulated concern rather than address the problem at the source. Arguments based on this model situate the use of adjuncts as a defensible strategy for the organization. Furthermore, they portray adjuncts as a homogeneous group without regard for individual contribution, expertise or motivation. Finally, it serves to perpetuate stereotypes about the quality of instruction provided by adjuncts.

SOLUTIONS AND RECOMMENDATIONS

Organizations that once enjoyed little to no competition in online programming need to adjust their strategies to redefine their programs as unique. Perhaps the most salient consideration in accomplishing this might be to determine how to best capitalize on the strengths that instructors bring to the learning environment. The reliance on adjunct faculty, however, brings unique complexities to the issues because of their multi-faceted experiences and motivations. To recognize each adjunct for her contributions to the organization, the distinctive characteristics and associated motivations of adjuncts within its faculty ranks must first be identified. By examining the professional needs and best practices for supporting instructional efforts as articulated by one professional adjunct, organizations can begin to see how they need to differentiate adjuncts by more than situational characteristics. Within these categories, adjuncts are driven by diverse motivations, articulated needs and demonstrated expertise. A better understanding of what makes adjuncts unique can lead to an identification of the characteristics coveted by the organization. Then, the organization can begin to develop supports and structures that align with those needs in an effort to recruit and retain appropriate faculty.

Rather than consider all adjuncts as a homogeneous group, capitalizing on and supporting adjuncts specific and individual needs could strengthen the adjunct-organizational relationship considerably. This strength can create a niche in the marketplace for online programs by being recognized as employing highly qualified instructors who are concerned about issues of academia. As partners, they can also be in a position to perpetuate the culture of the organization (Puzziferro & Shelton, 2009; Tipple, 2010). Furthermore, these instructors can be viewed as professionals with diverse interests and an ability to bring best practices to organizations. By focusing on individuals rather than collectives, the organization stands to enhance its relationship with all stakeholders, including potential students and financial contributors.

The solution to differentiating and marketing online programs based on instructional quality and rigor is multi-faceted. A critical component is to integrate this paradigm into the overall structure and management of the organizational-adjunct relationship. To attract and retain the adjunct who is in a position to bring expertise and quality instruction, leadership must recognize how interactions with these individuals can lead to a synergistic partnership in which skills can best be maximized.

Initially, the organization must make efforts to assess those structures already in place to determine the level of commitment currently being afforded to adjuncts. Bedford's (2009) framework appears to provide a context in which to juxtapose and organize the issues. Questions that determine the level to which the organization fosters the adjuncts' professional identity, addresses barriers, considers the adjuncts' professional and personal needs, and provides for scholarly activity include:

1. How do we define adjunct instructors? How do we differentiate adjuncts from full-time instructors or other staff? To what extent are adjunct instructors' included in decision making processes? Do we categorize adjuncts as a single category of instructor? How might we better perceive adjuncts to enhance their relationship with the organization?
2. In what ways to we provide networking opportunities for adjuncts? Are those opportunities centered on the organizational agenda? Are opportunities for diverse discourse presented? How might we connect adjuncts both within and outside our organization?
3. How do we support adjuncts in their efforts in professional development? Do we consider adjuncts professional-development needs individually? Do we help adjuncts build professional-development plans?
4. What efforts do we make to recognize the benefits that adjuncts bring to the organization? How do we describe our use of adjuncts? Do we perceive the use of adjuncts as strength? How do we articulate those perspectives? What is the adjuncts' role in this process?
5. Do we view adjuncts as possessing expertise that can benefit the instructional process? How do we incorporate that expertise into our overall programming? What is the adjunct role in program, curriculum and instructional development?
6. Do our adjuncts have opportunities for breaks from instructional responsibilities? What systems do we have in place to provide flexibility for adjuncts? How do we recognize adjuncts' multiple commitments (both personally and professionally)?
7. In what ways to we support adjuncts in their scholarly pursuits? Do we offer flexibility? Do we facilitate opportunities for adjuncts to engage in discourse that leads to scholarly activity? In what ways do we promote opportunities for adjuncts to share their work within their academic discipline? Do we recognize adjuncts for their academic achievements?

Analyzing current practices in this way can lead to critical information needed to construct an overall strategy that ensures highly qualified instructors are in place and are maintained. It can provide valuable information with regard to how adjuncts currently view the organizational efforts at support and collaboration. In addition, organizations can then focus on those issues and needs viewed as important by faculty with efforts to build and maintain structures to support them. Finally, this process can also provide opportunities to identify gaps in supports created by diverse motivations and develop opportunities to fill them.

CONCLUSION

The key to successful marketing of online programs in the current climate may be to capitalize on those program features that cannot easily be replicated at other sites. Since faculty bring individuality and creativity to the learning situation, they should be considered an organization's most valuable asset (Puzziferro & Shelton, 2009). This will require that organizations take steps to attract and retain the most qualified instructors with attributes identified as desirable and aligned with organizational values. To facilitate this process, organizations must first assess current practices to determine the extent to which they already meet the articulated needs of adjunct faculty. Next, efforts must be made to identify additional structures that support the adjuncts' needs in each of the categories described within Bedford's (2009) framework. By building structures based on categories of need, the organization is then situated to add structures that align with individual aspiration in a more comprehensive and dynamic manner.

While this case represents a single instructor's perspective, lessons can be learned and transferred to the overall organization-adjunct relationship. The focal participant identified specific practices which she perceived that best support her as an individual, instructor and scholar. In many cases, these practices may require organizations to implement small changes in policy. In other situations, comprehensive reform might be necessary to provide solutions to barriers and concerns expressed by a single individual who brings the desired instructional quality to the learning environment.

The ultimate goal of the organization should be to assess current practices as they relate to the organization-adjunct relationship and to revise those practices accordingly. This will ensure that the organization has a comprehensive repertoire of policies and procedures that address individual needs based on those issues articulated as important. The organization will then be in a position to demonstrate the level of commitment to those instructors who bring best practices in instruction, quality engagement with learners and strong partnership with the organization as a whole. These characteristics are critical factors to the success of learners, which leads to positive perceptions about the organization on many levels. This will lead to practices that marketing strategists can capitalize upon to promote their programs in the contemporary, competitive online environment.

REFERENCES

Akridge, A., DeMay, J., Braunlich, L., Collura, M., & Sheaha, M. *(2002).* Retaining adult learners in a high-stress distance education learning environment: The Purdue University Executive MBA in Agribusiness. In V. Phillips, B. Elwert, L. Hitch, & C. Yager (Eds.), *Motivating and retaining adult learners online.* Essex Junction, VT: Geteducated.com. Retrieved from http://www.geteducated.com/images/pdfs/journalmotivateretain.pdf

Allen, E., & Seaman, J. (2008). *Staying the course: Online education in the United States*, 2008. Needham, MA: The Sloan Consortium. Retrieved from http://www.sloan-c.org/publications/survey/pdf/staying_the_course.pdf

Anctil, E. (2008). Marketing and advertising higher education. *ASHE Higher Education Report*, *34*(2), 19–30.

Angelino, L. M., Williams, F. K., & Natvig, D. (2007). Strategies to engage online students and reduce retention rates. *Journal of Educators Online*, *4*(2), 1–14.

Ashby, A. (2004). Monitoring student retention in the Open University: Definition, measurement, interpretation and action. *Open Learning*, *19*(1), 65–77. doi:10.1080/0268051042000177854

Bedford, L. (2009). The professional adjunct: An emerging trend in online instruction. *Online Journal of Distance Learning Administration, 12(*3). Retrieved from http://www.westga.edu/~distance/ojdla/fall123/bedford123.html

Carnevale, D. (2004). For online adjuncts, a seller's market. *The Chronicle of Higher Education*, *50*(34).

Clark, R. E. (1983). Reconsidering research on learning from media. *Review of Educational Research*, *53*(4), 445–459.

Forrest, S., & Peterson, T. (2006). It's called andragogy. *Academy of Management Learning & Education*, *5*(1), 113–122.

Garland, M. R. (1993). Student perceptions of the situational, institutional, dispositional, and epistemological barriers to persistence. *Distance Education*, *14*(2), 181–198. doi:10.1080/0158791930140203

Garrett, R. (2008). Marketing online programs: Differentiation versus technique. *Sloan-C View, 5*(7). Retrieved from http://www.sloan-c.org/publications/view/v7n5/viewv7n5.htm

Gibbons, H. S., & Wentworth, G. (2002). Processes for motivating online learners from recruitment through degree completion. In V. Phillips, B. Elwert, L. Hitch, & C. Yager (Eds.), *Motivating and retaining adult learners online.* Essex Junction, VT: Geteducated.com. Retrieved from http://www.geteducated.com/images/pdfs/journalmotivateretain.pdf

Jaschik, S. (2006). Adjuncts and graduation rates. *Inside Higher Ed.* Retrieved from http://insidehighered.com/layout/set/print/news/2006/10/16/parttime

Kupczynski, L., & Hooper, B. (2006). The internet as a path to adult learning. *New Horizons for Learning Online, 12*(3). Retrieved from http://www.newhorizons.org/journal/journal50.htm

Lewis, A. (2008). A new look for the teaching profession. *Phi Delta Kappan*, *89*(7), 467–468.

Marshall, C., & Rossman, G. B. (2006). *Designing qualitative research* (4th ed.). Thousand Oaks, CA: Sage Publications.

Merriam, S. B. (1995). What can you tell from an N of 1?: Issues of validity and reliability in qualitative research. *PAACE Journal of Lifelong Learning*, *4*, 51–60.

Milliken, T. F., & Jurgens, J. C. (2008). Assessing the needs of human services adjunct faculty: Uncovering strategies for retaining quality instructors. *Human Service Education*, *28*(1), 29–43.

Nash, R. D. (2005). Course completion rates among distance learners: Identifying possible methods to improve retention. *Online Journal of Distance Learning Administration*, *8*(4). Retrieved from http://www.westga.edu/distance/ojdla/.

National Center for Education Statistics. (2008). *Digest of educational statistics*. U.S. Department of Education Institute of Education Sciences. Retrieved from http://nces.ed.gov/programs/digest/d08/tables/dt08_248.asp

Nichols, M. (2010). Student perceptions of support services and the influence of targeted interventions on retention in distance education. *Distance Education*, *31*(1), 93–113. doi:10.1080/01587911003725048

Patton, M. (2002). *Qualitative research and evaluation methods* (3rd ed.). Thousand Oaks, CA: Sage Publications.

Puzziferro, M., & Shelton, K. (2009). Supporting online faculty: Revisiting the seven principles (A few years later). *Online Journal of Distance Learning Administration*, *12*(3). Retrieved from http://search.ebscohost.com/login.aspx?direct=true&db=eric&AN=EJ864301&site=ehost-live.

Robinson, R., & Doverspike, D. (2006). Factors predicting the choice of an online versus a traditional course. *Teaching of Psychology*, *33*(1), 64–68. doi:10.1207/s15328023top3301_10

Schnitzer, M., & Crosby, L. (2003). Recruitment and development of online adjunct instructors. *Online Journal of Distance Learning Administration*, *6*(2). Retrieved from http://www.westga.edu/~distance/ojdla/summer62/crosby_schnitzer62.html.

Schroeder, R. (2008). Teaching and learning: What does technology have to do with it? *Sloan-C View, 7*(1). Retrieved from http://www.sloan-c.org/publications/view/v7n1/viewv7n1.htm

Shakeshaft, C. (2002). The shadowy downside of adjuncts. *The School Administrator.* Retrieved from http://www.interactiveinc.org/Publications/downsideofadjuncts.pdf

Shelton, K., & Saltsman, G. (2006). An administrator's guide to online education. *University Business, 8*(9), 73–76.

Shiffman, C. (2009). The emerging academician: The rise of the online adjunct faculty. *Dissertation Abstract International, 70*(2). (UMI No. AAT 3344730).

Shin, N. (2002). Beyond interaction: The relational construct of transactional presence. *Open Learning, 17*(2), 121–137. doi:10.1080/02680510220146887

Shin, N. (2003). Transactional presence as a critical predictor of success in distance learning. *Distance Education, 24*(1), 69–86. doi:10.1080/01587910303048

Simpson, O. (2004). The impact on retention of interventions to support distance learning students. *Open Learning, 19*(1), 79–95. doi:10.1080/0268051042000177863

Strauss, A., & Corbin, J. (2007). *Basics of qualitative research: Techniques and procedures for developing grounded theory* (3rd ed.). Thousand Oaks, CA: Sage Publications.

Testa, B. (2010). No mere perk: Flex-work as a strategic tool. *Workforce Management, 89*(3), 4.

Tipple, R. (2010). Effective leadership of online adjunct faculty. *Online Journal of Distance Learning Administration, 13*(1). Retrieved from http://www.westga.edu/~distance/ojdla/spring131/tipple131.html.

Wilson, C. (2010). Fighting back: The human cost of layoffs. *Academe, 95*(4).

Wolfinger, N., Mason, M., & Goulden, M. (2009). Stay in the game: Gender, family formation and alternative trajectories in the academic life course. *Social Forces, 87*(3), 1591–1621. doi:10.1353/sof.0.0182

ADDITIONAL READING

Allen, E., & Seaman, J. (2008). *Staying the course: Online education in the United States*, 2008. Needham, MA: The Sloan Consortium. Retrieved from http://www.sloan-c.org/publications/survey/pdf/staying_the_course.pdf

Anonymous. (2010). Distance learning program success: A matter of perception? *University Business, 13*(1), 18.

Beck, E., & Greive, E. (2005). *Going the distance: A handbook for part-time and adjunct faculty who teach online*. Part-Time Press.

Bedford, L. (2009). The professional adjunct: An emerging trend in online instruction. *Online Journal of Distance Learning Administration, 12(*3). Retrieved from http://www.westga.edu/~distance/ojdla/fall123/bedford123.html

Beqiri, M., Chase, N., & Bishka, A. (2009). Online course delivery: An empirical investigation of factors affecting student satisfaction. *Journal of Education for Business, 85*(2), 95–100. doi:10.1080/08832320903258527

Carnevale, D. (2004). For online adjuncts, a seller's market. *The Chronicle of Higher Education, 50*(34).

Carr, S. (2000). A day in the life of a new type of professor. *The Chronicle of Higher Education, 47*(16), A47.

Conceição, S. (2006). Faculty lived experiences in the online environment. *Adult Education Quarterly, 57*(1), 26–45. doi:10.1177/1059601106292247

Curtis, J., & Jacobe, M. F. (2006). *AAUP contingent faculty index*. Washington, DC: American Association of University Professors. Retrieved from http://www.aaup.org/NR/rdonlyres/F05FF88E-B2A8-4052-8373-AF0FDAE060AC/0/ConsequencesAnIncreasinglyContingentFaculty.pdf

Dahl, J. (2005). Boosting faculty participation in support activities. *Distance Education Report, 9*(19), 4–7.

Garrett, R. (2008). Marketing online programs: Differentiation versus technique. *Sloan-C View, 5*(7). Retrieved from http://www.sloan-c.org/publications/view/v7n5/viewv7n5.htm

Howell, S. (2006). Reflections on research, faculty and leadership in distance education. *Quarterly Review of Distance Education, 7*(3), 331–334.

Keown, P. (2009). The tale of two virtual teacher professional development modules. *International Research in Geographical and Environmental Education, 18*(4), 295–303. doi:10.1080/10382040903251166

Lewis, A. (2008). A new look for the teaching profession. *Phi Delta Kappan, 89*(7), 467–468.

Lorenzetti, J. (2003). Getting the best out of online adjunct faculty: A guide. *Distance Education Report, 7*(14), 1–6.

Lyons, R. (2007). *Best practices for supporting adjunct faculty*. San Francisco, CA: Jossey-Bass.

Milliken, T. F., & Jurgens, J. C. (2008). Assessing the needs of human services adjunct faculty: Uncovering strategies for retaining quality instructors. *Human Service Education, 28*(1), 29–43.

Mitchell, R. (2009). Online education and organizational change. *Community College Review, 37*(1), 81–101.

Perreault, H., Waldman, L., & Alexander, M. (2002). Overcoming barriers to successful delivery of distance-learning courses. *Journal of Education for Business, 77*(6), 313. doi:10.1080/08832320209599681

Puzziferro, M. (2004). Online adjunct faculty: Issues and opportunities. *Academic Exchange Quarterly, 8*(3), 125–130.

Restauri, S. (2004). Creating an effective online distance education program using targeted support factors. *TechTrends: Linking Research & Practice to Improve Learning, 48*(6), 32–39.

Rovai, A. (2003). In search of higher persistence rates in distance education online programmes. *The Internet and Higher Education, 6*, 1–16. doi:10.1016/S1096-7516(02)00158-6

Scarafiotti, C. (2004). Five important lessons about the cost of e-learning. *New Directions for Community Colleges*, (128): 39–46. doi:10.1002/cc.173

Schnitzer, M., & Crosby, L. (2003). Recruitment and development of online adjunct instructors. *Online Journal of Distance Learning Administration, VI*(II). Available online at http://www.westga.edu/~distance/ojdla/summer62/crosby_schnitzer62.html

Schroeder, R. (2008). Teaching and learning: What does technology have to do with it? *Sloan-C View, 7*(1). Available online at http://www.sloan-c.org/publications/view/v7n1/viewv7n1.htm

Shakeshaft, C. (2002). The shadowy downside of adjuncts. *The School Administrator.* Available online at http://www.interactiveinc.org/Publications/downsideofadjuncts.pdf

Sharma, R. (2008). The tools for successful online teaching. *British Journal of Educational Technology, 39*(5), 951–952. doi:10.1111/j.1467-8535.2008.00890_4.x

Shelton, K., & Saltsman, G. (2006). An administrator's guide to online education. *University Business*, *8*(9), 73–76.

Stringer, E. (2008). *Action research in education* (2nd ed.). Upper Saddle River, NJ: Person, Merrill, Prentice Hall.

KEY TERMS AND DEFNITIONS

Adjunct: Part-time teacher.

Expertise: Level of discipline specific and pedagogical knowledge of the faculty member.

Full-Time Professional Adjunct: Teachers who maintain several part-time teaching relationships to create a full-time work load.

Marketing: Techniques used by organizations to recruit and enroll prospective students.

Online: Courses or programs delivered electronically via the Internet.

Quality Instruction: Pedagogical practices that result in student satisfaction and learning.

Recruit: Soliciting interest in faculty positions from qualified applicants.

Retain: Maintaining current faculty employees within the organization.

Chapter 5
School Images, School Identity, and How Parents Select Schools for Their Children:
The Case of Hong Kong

Frank Wai-ming Tam
The Chinese University of Hong Kong, Hong Kong

Paula Yu-Kwong Kwan
Hong Kong Institute of Education, Hong Kong

EXECUTIVE SUMMARY

The case suggests that a school organization adapts itself to the environment and survives external competition through a series of self-organizing processes of differentiation and integration. Differentiation is the process through which the school develops its own identity and core competencies through trial and error, whereas integration is the process through which the school develops stable and sustaining relationships with parents and other strategic partners within the community. The authors assert that in a fast changing and highly competitive environment like that in Hong Kong, schools need to find their institutional identities and to present a positive image to the community. This endeavor is often a challenging and painful task. The authors study the case of a secondary school to illustrate how this can be done, employing a survey approach to ascertain needs and expectations of parents. The dilemma schools face in choosing between academic and pastoral ethos is described and relations between important factors that impact perceptions of parents are discussed.

DOI: 10.4018/978-1-60960-599-5.ch005

INTRODUCTION

Image and identity are important considerations for parents when choosing a school for their children, and also for teachers when considering joining or leaving a school. These factors affect student satisfaction also. Although school image and school identity are two different constructs, they are interrelated. The way a school constructs its identity determines its image; a positive school image can facilitate the process of identity formation.

In research literature, currently there are three schools of thought regarding corporate image: relational, evaluative and impressional, the differences among them resting mainly on the nature of the target audience or stakeholder. The relational school is mainly concerned about different expectations of different stakeholders (Freeman, 1984). When applied to school settings, it focuses on views of both internal stakeholders (teachers and students) and external stakeholders (parents and the community). In the evaluative school, assessment of image of an organization is based on financial performance or value of the organization. Under school settings, it focuses on academic performance of students in public examinations, and/or other tangible performance measures. In a schooling system which emphasizes competition among students and between schools, tangible measures of student performance often become a school's 'competitive advantage' (Hall, 1992). In recent years, there has been an increasing interest in stakeholders' emotional association with an organization, which influences the organization's performance and long-term sustainability. In the impressional school, corporate image, corporate identity and personality become importance factors in determining an organization's long-term survival in a competitive environment (Dutton et al, 1994).

How do organizations adapt themselves to the environment? Bateson (1985) and Csikszentmihalyi (1993) have proposed that biological and social systems are rather similar in their self-organizing processes because they all follow two distinctive dimensions: integration and differentiation. Integration is the development of partners, coalitions, and collaborators within a social network. The resource dependency theory pointed out that survival and development of social institutions is dependent on acquisition of resources by interacting with the environment, and the nature of these interactions often determines the structure and behavior of these institutions (Pfeffer & Salancik, 1978). Therefore, in order to reduce dependency and uncertainty, institutions often need to develop stable and sustainable relationships, such as strategic partners, working collaborators, and social networks. It has been pointed out that such relationships can help an institution not only to acquire outside resources, but also to innovate (Tam, 2007).

Differentiation is the internal transformation that an institution needs to go through in order to improve its effectiveness. There may be several types of differentiation; the most common are horizontal, vertical, functional and programme (Holland, 1995). Programme differentiation is very important in a school's image formation because it is the means to gain the attention of outsiders. Because public schools in Hong Kong are following the same operational framework and curriculum guides, and are receiving the same amount of resources from the government, unless a school can develop some distinctive characteristics in its programmes, there is little chance it can assert itself in the community.

The processes of differentiation and integration can be seen as two distinctive but interactive dimensions of ways in which a school develops its identity in the community. This is similar to a person interacting with the environment during the process of his or her maturation (Kegan, 1982). Table 1 shows a conceptual framework that describes four potential states of fitness based on the different degrees of differentiation and integration of a school. The integration dimension is

Table 1. Four types of school images

		Integration dimension	
		Low	**High**
Differ-entiation dimension	Strong	Self-sufficient	Synergetic
	Weak	Bureaucratic	Opportunistic

the degree of interaction of the school with the community. At one extreme is total isolation, and at the other, total absorption. The differentiation dimension is the degree of organizational identity, from one extreme of a total lack of identity to the other extreme of a clear and strong school image. Consequently, four categories of school images may be derived from these two dimensions: bureaucratic, opportunistic, self-sufficient, and synergetic (see Table 1).

A bureaucratic image is characterized by fuzziness where a school is alienated from the community. Schools that possess this characteristic operate by bureaucratic routines, follow the standardized curriculum and teaching procedures, and have very limited sense of pride or uniqueness. The members do not see a need to develop a close relationship with the community, beyond the minimum required. As suggested by Jaques (1953) and Hirschhorn (1988), this mode of operation alienates the school from the community and helps reduce much of the anxiety of teachers and school administrators.

Opportunistic images are characterized by schools actively organizing programs for the community and participating in local events, but without a clear vision of what they are trying to accomplish, i.e. with incoherent goals and priorities. Schools that possess these characteristics basically operate in a bureaucratic mode but participate in the community in order to survive. They are very concerned about their projected image and their acceptance by parents in the community, but they rely mainly on instrumental means to achieve these ends. To seek conformity, they provide educational programs that satisfy parents' wants for their children, regardless of how distorted these desires may be, sometimes even at the expense of educational benefits to the students.

Self-sufficient school images are characterized by schools having developed their own distinctive character, vision, and identity. However, these are developed without consideration of what the community actually needs; these schools do not see a clear need to be involved in the community. Schools that possess these characteristics develop unique educational programs based on their school vision and philosophy, and they may actually have a good reputation in the community. Yet, without good relations with the community, these schools might give people the impression of being unapproachable and incomprehensible.

Synergetic school images are characterized by schools having a distinctive character and uniqueness in their educational programs, and at the same time developing a vibrant relationship with the community. Schools that possess this characteristic constantly communicate with the community and understand its needs. In this process, the schools have developed their identity and goals in harmony with their educational philosophy, and seek to satisfy educational needs of the community. These are the schools that are able to co-evolve with, and become part of, the community.

Notwithstanding the above described four conceptual types of school images, in reality, no school is totally isolated or totally integrated; most schools are continuously searching for their identities and constantly try to find their standing in the community. This can be employed as a conceptual framework to examine the evolving nature of school and community relations. The present chapter employs the impressional perspective to investigate how parents in Hong Kong construct images of secondary schools when they select schools for their children, and how these images are related to internal and external characteristics of the schools. A cross-sectional survey of parents whose children were studying in primary six (the last year of primary school) was conducted in 2009. Results of the study suggest that there may be two main dimensions of school image as perceived by parents in Hong Kong: academic dimension and pastoral dimension. The strength of the two dimensions of school image is related to social backgrounds of families, their parenting approaches, as well as academic abilities of their children. Findings of the present study are expected to have important implications for schools wanting to align their internal processes with perceptions and concerns of parents, and to educate parents to gain a more perceptive understanding of what school image represents and how school image is related to the educational processes in the school.

CASE DESCRIPTION

The Hong Kong Education System

In Hong Kong there are three major types of schools, the difference being modes of finance and the students they serve. The first type is government schools, established by the government and funded by public revenue, where the teachers are hired as civil servants. The second type is subsidized schools, which are similar to the grant-maintained schools in the U.K. Subsidized schools are established with provisions similar to government schools, but are different in that they are sponsored and governed by charitable organizations. However, they are not private schools because they obtain most of their funding from public revenue. This mode of operation is very popular in Hong Kong as most of the schools in the territory started as private schools when the government implemented the nine year compulsory education back in the mid-1970s. Now close to 70% of schools in operation are being funded in this mode. The advantage of this funding mode is that the school can draw rich resources of social capital from the school sponsoring body to support its operations and at the same time the government does not have to be responsible for teachers' employment in case the school needs to close down due to decline of its student population. Students are allotted to government and subsidized schools centrally by the government. The third type is private schools which have the freedom of recruiting students in their own way. There are two sub-types of private schools, namely, international schools and direct subsidy schools. International schools are private schools adopting non-local curriculum and mainly cater to expatriate families. However, an increasingly large number of local families now prefer to send their children to international schools despite tuition fees in international schools being unaffordable for most families in Hong Kong. Direct subsidy schools are private schools which can charge a school fee and receive a matching subsidy from the government. However, these schools operate with the risk of unstable enrollment because whenever there is an economic recession, parents tend to withdraw students from private schools to put them in public schools.

Government and subsidized schools enroll their students from the local community through the centrally administered secondary allocation system of the government. The system works in such a way that a school may enroll up to 20% of its students in secondary one through direct admission while the remaining 80% are allocated through the centralized allocation system. Students in Hong Kong are equally divided into three bands in accordance with their academic abilities. The band one comprising the top one-third students in terms of academic strength whereas band three comprises the bottom one-third who are academically the weakest. The scaling mechanism is a standardized aptitude test administered to all primary six students and the result is used to adjust the internal assessment results of students coming from different schools. Parents are required to fill out a choice form to indicate secondary schools they prefer for their children in the geographic district they belong to. Allocation is based on the academic ability of students; band one students will be allocated to schools of their choice first, then band two students will be allocated to schools they prefer, to the extent room is available, and so on and so forth. In fact, one may estimate the popularity of a school by knowing the percentages of band one and band two students it takes in.

Since its original conception in the mid-1970s, the secondary student allocation system has been well received by the education community. Parents and teachers saw this as a fair system because the screening and allocation mechanisms were based on meritocratic principles. However, the allocation system soon became an important source of motivation behind the efforts of teachers, students and parents. First, secondary school administrators and teachers often set their goals to attract as many band one students as they can. In other words, within the education community, the driving ethos among secondary schools is to move towards becoming a band one school, and in order to do this, they must maintain good public examination results and high university entrance record. Second, parents tended to put pressure on their children very early in their primary years to outperform their fellow schoolmates in examinations in order to be counted in band one. However there is always an element of risk in the school selection process that parents have to consider. Since allocation to schools is hinged on supply and demand functions, higher performing schools usually attract a higher number of applications which, in turn, lead to a lower rate of success. In addition, the allocation system also has an undesirable labeling effect on students who attend lower band schools, which is considered damaging to their self-esteem.

Given the recent shrinkage of population growth in Hong Kong, schools in general and band three schools in particular are increasingly concerned about successfully recruiting new students. Although marketing concepts are traditionally not practiced in the Hong Kong educational community, many school principals have started seeing it as a possible avenue to improve the popularity of their schools amongst parents and students in the wake of an increasingly intense competitive environment. However, school principals are generally trained in their own areas of academic expertise and are preoccupied with teaching and student matters in their early careers. They usually lack knowledge and skills to effectively apply marketing concepts. More often than not, strategies used by schools are more for selling rather than marketing. In other words, there is a lack of customer orientation in the strategies; schools only focus on providing information they believe is important to the public, without considering the value of this information to parents and students. The most commonly used selling strategies adopted by schools are hanging eye-catching banners in school campuses describing various school activities, organizing open days inviting prospective primary students to visit the schools, and placing special advertisements in the media. Due to the neglect of expectations of target recipients and/or participants, these activities can at best make them aware of a school; they cannot convince them the school is a better choice. More importantly, schools rarely position themselves amongst all competing schools in the school community on the basis of their strengths and weaknesses.

The School

Blue Bay School (BBS, a disguised name) is a subsidized secondary school with 26 years of history in the Bay area of Hong Kong. As a subsidized secondary school, BBS enrolls students from the local community through the secondary students allocation system. It has over 1000 students enrolled, ranging from secondary one (year 7) to pre-university (year 13). Most of the students come from families with low socio-economic backgrounds residing in the surrounding area. BBS used to be a popular choice for children's education among parents in the Bay area when it was a new school. However, its popularity dropped when newer schools were opened in the surrounding areas. In the current school year, the school is admitting students who are mainly in the lowest (band three) category. According to government planning, the school has no immediate danger of closing down because the demand for admissions in secondary schools in the Bay area still matches the supply. However, once there is any decrease in demand of secondary schools in this area, the school will face the risk of having to discontinue operations.

The school sponsoring body of BBS is a large charitable organization in Hong Kong. The organization appointed Mr. Hosea Yeung as chairman of the management of BBS. Mr. Yeung is the owner of a successful family business and because of his busy schedule, he can squeeze out only a little time to care for BBS. In fact it is generally observed that chairmen of most of the school management boards in Hong Kong are not career educators; they consider taking up the appointment as a service to the community. Because of their lack of training in educational administration, they often delegate most of the management responsibilities to the principal and the management team. Mr. Yeung also knows that apart from attending the board of management meetings and donating money to the school, he would not be able to do much for the school. This is why he knows that he will have to select the principal for the school very carefully.

Mr. Daniel Chan, now in his late 40's, was appointed principal of the school six months ago. When he assumed charge, the school supervisor gave him two targets to work on. The first was to enhance the school image in the community through improving student performance, and the second was to maintain a harmonious environment in the school. Mr. Chan guessed that perhaps the contradictory nature of these two targets is the reason why his immediate predecessor resigned even before completing her two-year probationary term. Schools in Hong Kong, as those in many other school systems in the world, have undergone enormous educational reforms recently. Teachers in general do not welcome these changes as they are either not motivated or are not competent to meet the requirements set by the government. The principal may have to develop special measures to have the prescribed initiatives successfully implemented in the school. Therefore, it would be a difficult task for school principals in Hong Kong to maintain harmonious working relationships with colleagues on the one hand, and to enhance the school image through improving student performance on the other. Mr. Chan assumes that if he is unable to achieve these two targets in two years time, he too will probably need to look for another job.

In the first year of his principalship at BBS, Mr. Chan decided not to introduce too much changes, with a view to preserving the harmony. Yet he also knows that he needs to move strategically. In order to gain a more realistic view of the current situation of the school, Mr. Chan did two things which his colleagues considered unconventional. First, he formed an ad hoc group to conduct an internal review of the school. The review consisted of two major components: (i) To critically review the performance of the school based on the available documents, external school review reports and public examination results; and (ii) To conduct individual interviews among representative samples of teachers, students and parents. Second, he sought help from a university researcher to conduct an opinion survey among parents whose children were studying in nearby primary schools. The following section describes the results of the internal review process.

Internal Review of School Performance

In the junior section, BBS streams students into different classes based on their abilities. There are two high ability classes and three low ability classes. In Hong Kong, all students are required to sit for the Secondary One Entry Examination

(Chinese, English and Mathematics). The results are used to ascertain the value-added by a school in terms of academic performance of its students. The performance of BBS students in the junior section ranged from 25 percentile to 35 percentile; performance in English was the highest, followed by Chinese and Mathematics. When these cohorts of students were assessed again three years later, it was discovered that average performance in Mathematics had improved by 20 percentile, in Chinese it remained about the same, and performance in English had dropped by an average of 10 percentile. In other words, in the junior secondary years, highest value addition was realized in Mathematics, while value addition in English was the lowest.

In Hong Kong, students' passing percentages in public examinations are often considered by parents to be acid tests of the effectiveness of a school. Although it is not realized by many, parents construct an informal image of the school their children attend through observing their performance and engaging in gossip. They often rank a school based on perceptions so formed. In the case of BBS, performance of students in the public examination has not been stable in the past few years. In many of the subjects, performance in different years fluctuates in a wide range, sometimes up to 40 percent. Subjects which have higher passing percentages are principles of accounting, commerce, information technology and graphic communication. Student performance in subjects which require a good foundation in language and science has been very poor.

Results of the stakeholder survey (conducted for the External School Review), however, indicate that the students like their school life, and their sense of satisfaction and behavioral conducts are significantly higher than the territory norm. Students have low global and academic self-concepts and they do not feel much pressure of school work as they are given very little homework and tests. Results of the survey also suggest that the students feel their teachers care about their development, have arranged various types of extra-curricular activities, and are willing to spend extra time to help them, but they seldom give positive feedbacks (such as rewards and praises) to the students. The students also claimed that they had learning motivation, lack self-initiation and seldom raise questions in class.

In sum, the available evidences appear to be indicating that BBS is not an effective school. Students come to BBS with weak academic foundations, low self-concept and probably poor learning habits as well, which are typical for families with low socio-economic backgrounds. This is perhaps the reason why their performances in languages and other academic subjects are difficult to improve. They are able to achieve higher passing rates in practical subjects, such as accounting, commerce and graphic communication since performance in these subjects is less inhibited by inadequate language proficiency. Language efficiency is generally affected by social backgrounds. Mathematics is the only academic subject which stood out among other subjects to maintain a high performance in both junior and senior secondary levels.

REPORT OF THE SURVEY OF PARENTS IN THE COMMUNITY

For assessing perceptions of parents regarding the choice of secondary schools for their children, the research team conducted a survey among parents whose children were studying in nearby primary schools. The survey questionnaire was compiled by the research team; the contents were adapted from previous researches conducted by the research team members. Appendix A presents the English version of the survey questionnaire. There are six parts in the questionnaire. Part I contains eight items pertaining to the respondent's degree of involvement in the child's schooling. Part II contains four items which cover the respondent's level of expectations in terms of the child's education. Part III contains ten items which seek to identify the approach the respondent uses when having conflict with the child. Part IV covers parents order of preference for the 13 secondary schools (these are all the choices they can pick under the prevailing secondary school allotment system) in the surrounding areas that they can send their children to. The respondents were asked to specify whether they considered the specified characteristics of the schools to be important and appealing. The characteristics include academic ethos, stable administration, caring and support, close distance, educational innovation, sports and extracurricular activities, campus environment, and public examination results. Part V contains eight items which address the extent to which the child had exhibited certain deviant behaviors. Part VI contains ten items which ask the respondents to provide demographic information of the family.

A total of 700 survey forms were sent out to parents of all primary six students in the five sampled primary schools. 595 parents responded to the survey, resulting in a response rate of 85%. 72.8% and 21.7% of the respondents were mothers and fathers, respectively, of the children who carried home the survey questionnaire; the remaining 2.2% were grandfathers, grandmothers or other relatives. The average age of the respondents was 42.5 years. Among the respondents, 51.7% were born in Hong Kong, 39.9% had lived in Hong Kong for more than 7 years, and 5.6% had lived in Hong Kong for 3 to 6 years. 85.4% of the respondents were married and were living with their spouses, 10.9% were single, separated or divorced, and the remaining were mainly widows. More than half of the respondents (50.3%) had a senior secondary education, 28.3% had junior secondary, 10.6% had only primary and the remaining 10.8% had university education or above.

Results of the survey suggest that BBS was ranked 10th among the 13 secondary schools in the Bay area. The schools were ranked on the basis of weighted average of their performances. Rank 10 in 13 schools means BBS was in the below 33 percentile. However, one needs to note that the school with the highest ranking may not necessarily be the best school or the most competitive school in the community. It only means that it is the most popular when academic abilities of students has been taken into consideration by their parents when ranking the schools. When some parents know that their children may not do well in an academically competitive school, they will tend to choose a school which is less competitive.

Furthermore, parents were divided into three groups, namely, high, medium and low, based on their assessment of the academic performance of their children, and then first 5 rankings of schools were calculated again. The result of the recalculation was that among parents who assessed their children as high ability students, BBS was not ranked within the top five schools of their choices. Among parents who assessed their children as medium ability students, BBS was still not ranked within the top five schools.

Table 2. Summary of respondents demographic profiles

Relationship with student	Mother 433 (72.8%)	Father 129 (21.7%)	Other relatives 33(5.5%)	
Years of residency in Hong Kong	Since born 308 (51.8%)	Immigrated and stayed for more than 7 years 237 (39.8%)	Immigrated and stayed for less than 7 years 50 (8.4%)	
Marital status	Married 508 (85.4%)	Single 65 (10.9%)	Widow 22 (3.7%)	
Education	University 64 (10.8%)	Senior Secondary 299 (50.3%)	Junior Secondary 169 (28.3%)	Primary 63 (10.6%)

However, it was ranked second among the top five schools by parents who assessed their children as low ability students. Hence, it appears that BBS is not a popular school among parents who expect their children to have high academic performance. Yet, it is popular among parents whose children belong to the low academic abilities group. Table 3 reports the results of this comparison.

Factor analysis was then conducted on the eight school characteristics rated by parents. Two distinctive factors emerged from the analysis. Factor one: academic ethos, public examination result and stable administration; and Factor two: caring and support, close distance, education innovation, sports and extracurricular activities, and campus environment. Factor one can be taken as academic ethos of a school and factor two as its pastoral ethos. What this result appears to be saying is that academic ethos and pastoral ethos are two main school characteristics that parents are concerned about when deciding the school they send their children to. A school which is strong in academic ethos will tend to put strong emphasis on competition within the school, require students to spend much of their time on homework and tests, and to develop students' identity in academic performance, which is typical of a traditional Chinese school. On the other hand, a school which is strong in pastoral ethos will tend to put more emphasis on other aspects of adolescent development, such as organizing more sports and extracurricular activities for the students, deploying more manpower for discipline and counseling, and paying more attention to making the school more inviting to the students. Perceivably, academic ethos and pastoral ethos are not necessarily exclusive of each other in the operation of a school. Every school will need to have some academic thrust and some caring elements. Nevertheless, when a school has limited resources and wants to be effective in whatever it does, then one of the two aspects will tend to stand out clearly. Table 4 shows the relative ranking of the thirteen schools in the community and their relative strengths in academic and pastoral ethos.

Table 3. Choices of secondary schools made by parents whose children were classified by them as high ability, medium ability and low ability

	Name of school	First choice	Second choice	Third choice	First 3 choices
High ability	School K	127	27	33	187
	School B	48	61	70	179
	School L	25	65	71	161
	School G	26	41	27	94
	School C	6	16	9	31
Medium ability	School C	39	41	19	99
	School B	27	29	28	84
	School K	40	17	23	80
	School E	28	23	21	72
	School G	24	24	21	69
Low ability	School C	9	5	11	25
	SchoolM (BBS)	11	4	2	17
	School B	7	5	4	16
	School G	2	5	7	14
	School K	4	7	2	13

Table 4. Ranking of schools in Bay area and their average academic ethos and pastoral ethos scores

School	Rank order	Academic ethos	Pastoral ethos
School A	6	1.04	1.30
School B	2	2.48	1.65
School C	4	1.23	1.90
School D	11	0.49	0.90
School E	7	1.36	1.59
School F	8	0.70	1.15
School G	3	1.85	1.88
School H	12	0.39	0.87
School I	9	0.97	1.08
School J	13	0.45	0.88
School K	1	2.77	1.84
School L	5	2.33	1.43
School M (BBS)	10	0.59	1.19

Analysis of the relationship between family socio-economic background (sum of household income and educational attainment of parents) and of the characteristics of secondary schools parents consider while choosing schools for their children found that families with higher socio-economic backgrounds tend to choose schools with stronger academic ethos, and families with lower socio-economic backgrounds tend to choose schools with stronger pastoral ethos. Hence there is reason to believe that schools with stronger academic ethos, as perceived by parents, will have higher concentration of students from middle class families and are more sought after in the community, whereas schools which emphasize pastoral ethos (as perceived by parents) will have a high concentration of students from lower class families.

For the case of BBS, its average academic ethos score is low while the average pastoral ethos score is moderately high. In other words, parents in the community look at BBS mainly as a school which does not emphasize academic performance, but provides care and support to its students. There are many reasons why a school such as BBS ends up emphasizing pastoral ethos instead of academic ethos. Firstly, it has been well documented that schools which enroll lower ability students have much difficulties building a strong academic ethos because teachers' efforts in schools with low ability students are constrained by the students' socio-economic backgrounds; teachers may need to put in much more effort in their work but still may be unable to achieve results comparable to schools with high ability students (Anyon, 1980; Gamoran, 1995). Secondly, students of low academic ability often have problems of learning motivation and misbehaviors in the classroom, causing considerable disruption in the teaching and learning process. Thirdly, teachers working in schools with low ability students are often emotionally more involved in their work and spend longer time counseling students, organizing extra-curricular activities, and dealing with discipline issues (Macbeath et al., 2006). Hence they tend to consume more energy in school and they also experience burn outs more easily. A comparison was made between perceptions of parents who have selected BBS as one of the top three choices with choices of all parents in the community. It was found that parents who had selected BBS as one of the top three choices were weaker in their involvement

Table 5. Perceptions of parents who had chosen BBS as one of top three choices as compared to choices of all parents in the community

Factors	All parents	Parents who have chosen BBS as one of top three choices
Parental involvement (at home)	3.87	3.33
Parental involvement (in school)	3.26	2.88
Dependency on teachers and school	3.78	4.45
Expectation of the child	4.01	3.83
Self-report deviant behaviors exhibited by the child	1.91	2.35

with children both at home and in school, and had lower expectations of their children in academic terms (see Table 5.) Also these parents appeared to be more dependent on the schools and their children's teachers to provide information about future schooling, and reported that their children had more deviant behaviors.

QUESTIONS TO PONDER

Available evidences suggest that BBS is not a popular school in the community. The school is being perceived as academically weak, but at the same time, caring for non-academic development of the students. However, BBS did not choose to be like this. The fact that it is unable to break the spell of (social) class influence on students' academic performance causes its operations to be ineffective. On the one hand, maintaining the status quo appears to be the natural thing to do, but it is running the risk of closing down if there is decline of student population in the community. On the other hand, trying to reshape the culture of the school to build an academically strong image in the community appears to be unrealistic. Is there a third way out for BBS? This third way is particularly important to schools which are serving lower ability students. When academic excellence (or being band one) becomes the only driving force in education, the schooling system runs into a dead knot. When a school sets its educational goal to become a band one school, it has no alternative but to put pressure on its students to achieve better examination results, as a result of which, the schooling process becomes rather monotonous as all activities other than those that can improve students' examination results are suppressed. A monotonous schooling process will tend to marginalize many at-risk students or students who have less family support. More specifically, the 'third way' has several implications for BBS:

1. Is it really impossible for BBS to operate more effectively for socially disadvantaged students?
2. Why are parents set in the two images of schooling (academic and pastoral)? Is it possible for them to develop a third image? If yes, how?
3. How does professionalism come into the picture when a school tries to build its image in the community?

RECOMMENDATIONS AND CONCLUSION

The classical view of school management suggests that schools should consolidate human and physical resources internally and focus on the key tasks of learning and teaching in the classroom. Yet, recent developments in education policy have compelled schools to develop their unique characteristics and try various means to promote their images in order to survive. Therefore there appears to be some contradiction in what school administrators should focus their energy on.

Nevertheless, this contradiction is not altogether unproductive. Although pressure to survive has put much stress on teachers and school administrators, it has also forced schools to emerge from their bureaucratic shells, to change their detached and indifferent attitudes towards parents' expectations, and be concerned about how to develop productive relations with the community. Yet, in order to develop and operate sustainably, a school should develop its uniqueness by examining its strengths and weaknesses, sharing a set of core values and beliefs with its core members, and developing special characteristics of its program. Without this process of self-exploration, a school could spend endless amount of energy creating programs to attract the attention of the public, without actually bringing long-term benefits to the school itself, or the students, for that matter.

REFERENCES

Anyon, J. (1980). Social class and the hidden curriculum of work. *Journal of Education*, *162*(1), 67–92.

Bateson, G. (1985). *Mind and nature: A necessary unity*. London, UK: Fontana Paperbacks.

Csikszentmihalyi, M. (1993). *The evolving self: A psychology for the third millennium*. New York, NY: HarperCollins Publishers, Inc.

Dutton, J. E., Dukerich, J. M., & Harquail, C. V. (1994). Organizational images and member identification. *Administrative Science Quarterly*, *39*(34), 239–263. doi:10.2307/2393235

Freeman, R. E. (1984). *Strategic management: A stakeholder approach*. Boston, MA: Pitman.

Gamoran, A. (1995). *Effects of schooling on children and families. Family-school links: How do they affect educational outcomes?* Hall, R. (1992). The strategic analysis of intangible resources. *Strategic Management Journal*, *13*, 135–144.

Hirschhorn, L. (1988). *The workplace within*. Cambridge, MA: MIT Press.

Holland, J. H. (1995). *Hidden order*. Reading, MA: Addison-Wesley.

Jaques, E. (1952). *The changing culture of the factory*. London, UK: Tavistock.

Kegan, R. (1982). *The evolving self: Problems and process in human development*. Boston, MA: Harvard University Press.

MacBeath, J., Gray, J. M., Cullen, J., Frost, D., Steward, S., & Swaffield, S. (2007). *Schools on the edge: Responding to challenging circumstances*. London, UK: Paul Chapman Publishing.

Tam, W. M. (2007). Rethinking school and community relations in Hong Kong. *International Journal of Educational Management*, *21*(4), 350–366. doi:10.1108/09513540710749555

ADDITIONAL READING

Bagin, D., & Gallagher, D. R. (2001). *The school and community relations* (7th ed.). Boston, MA: Allyn & Bacon.

Balmer, J. M. T. (2001). From the Pentagon: A new identity framework. *Corporate Reputation Review*, *4*(1), 11–22. doi:10.1057/palgrave.crr.1540129

Chester, E. F. (2000). *Reinventing public education via the marketplace*. Canada: Fraser Institute.

Chubb, J., & Moe, T. M. (1988). Politics, markets and the organization of schools. *The American Political Science Review*, *82*(4), 1065–1087. doi:10.2307/1961750

Chun, R. (2005). Corporate reputation: Meaning and measurement. *International Journal of Management Reviews*, *7*(2), 91–109. doi:10.1111/j.1468-2370.2005.00109.x

Crowther, F., & Caldwell, B. J. (1998). *The entrepreneurial school: A handbook for dynamic school management*. Sydney, Australia: Ashton Scholastic.

Dewhirst, T., & Davis, B. (2005). Brand strategy and integrated marketing communication. *Journal of Advertising*, *34*(4), 81–92.

Firestein, P. (2009). *Crisis of character: Building corporate reputation in the age of skepticism*. NY: Union Square Press.

Gray, L. (1991). *Marketing education*. Philadelphia, PA: Open University Press.

Kay, M. J. (2006). Strong brands and corporate brands. *European Journal of Marketing*, *40*(7/8), 742–760. doi:10.1108/03090560610669973

Levinson, H. (2002). Assessing organizations. In Lowman, R. L. (Ed.), *Handbook of organizational consulting psychology* (pp. 315–343). San Francisco, CA: John Wiley & Sons, Inc.

Meewar, T. C., & Karaosmanglu, E. (2006). Seven dimensions of corporate identity. *European Journal of Marketing*, *40*(7-8), 846–869. doi:10.1108/03090560610670025

Merz, C., & Furman, G. (1997). *Community: Promise and paradox*. New York: Teachers College Press.

Mitchell, R. K., Agle, B. R., & Wood, D. J. (1997). Toward a theory of stakeholder identification and salience: Defining the principle of who and what really counts. *Academy of Management Review*, *22*(4), 853–885. doi:10.2307/259247

Murphy, J. (1999). New consumerism: Evolving market dynamics in the institutional dimension of schooling. In Murphy, J., & Louis, K. S. (Eds.), *Handbook of research on educational administration* (2nd ed., pp. 405–419). San Francisco, CA: Jossey-Bass.

Nkomo, S. M., & Cox, T. Jr. (1996). Diverse identities in organizations. In Clegg, S. R., Hardy, C., & Nord, W. R. (Eds.), *Handbook of organization studies*. London: Sage Publications.

Stapley, L. F. (1996). *The personality of the organization: A psychodynamic explanation of culture and change*. London: Free Association Books.

Trist, E. (1990). Culture as a psychosocial process. In Trist, E., & Murray, H. (Eds.), *The social engagement of social science*. London: Free Association Books.

KEY TERMS AND DEFINITIONS

Academic Ethos: The academic ethos of a school is measured against its student achievement in public examinations, instructional innovation, and medium of instruction (either Chinese or English) by Hong Kong parents.

Differentiation Process: It is the process through which a school develops identify its unique characteristics which differentiates from others schools.

Integration Process: It is the process through which a school develops partners, coalitions, and collaborators within a social network.

Labeling Effect: Students studying in less performing schools are considered inferior to their counterparts in better performing schools.

Pastoral Ethos: The pastoral ethos of a school is measured against its special care to students and amount of extra-class activities provided by Hong Kong parents.

School Identity: It is the way members of a school feel being associated with the school and make sense of their school in interacting with others.

School Image: It is the representation which a school creates about itself to parents, students, teachers and the community.

School Sponsoring Body: A school sponsoring body is the governing body of a school in Hong Kong. It is responsible for the appointment of the principal and through monitoring the performance of the principal it oversees school operations and management.

APPENDIX

Secondary School Choice Questionnaire for Parents of Primary Six Students

Please indicate whether the following statements can accurate describe your relationship with your child (the one who brought home this survey form) or your interaction with your child's school.

1 Very inaccurate
2 Inaccurate
3 Partly accurate
4 Accurate
5 Very accurate

1a. I frequently ask about his/her conditions in school.
1b. I understand my children's conditions in school through school reports and announcements.
1c. I spend time to talk with him/her everyday to understand his school life.
1d. I cooperate with my child's school to solve his/her difficulties in learning.
1e. I initiate contact with teachers in school to understand the learning conditions of my child.
1f. I will participate in the parent activities organized by my child's school.
1g. I will take time to involve as a volunteer in my child's school.
1h. I will express my opinions to my child's school regarding his/her learning.

In questions 2a - 2c, please indicate whether the statements accurately describe your feelings?

1 Very inaccurate
2 Inaccurate
3 Partly accurate
4 Accurate
5 Very accurate

2a. I have high expectations about my child.
2b. I expect my child to have good performance among his/her peers.
2c. I expect my child to live a meaningful life.
2d. Please indicate the level of education that you expect your child to complete:
__ primary __ secondary __ community college
__ university __ graduate school __ never thought about this

When you are in conflict with your child, will you use the following methods?

3a. Analyze the problem with your child, and come up with a mutually acceptable solution.
3b. Scold the child and forbid him/her to engage in similar behaviors again.
3c. Ignore the child, let him/her throw tantrum or cry by himself/herself.
3d. Let the issue suspend temporarily, allow everybody to cool down and think of a solution.
3e. Discus with the child patiently and peacefully.
3f. Engage in mutual accusation with your child.
3g. Ask your spouse to help to discuss with your child.
3h. Keep your anger inside, such as being silent, upset, cry alone.
3i. Use language or body language to scold your child, such as threaten him/her, act as if you are throwing something at him/her, etc.
3j. Find the teacher or the social worker to discuss how to deal with it

Choice of School

There are a total of 13 secondary schools in the Bay Area (the list of school is attached.) Suppose you are choosing a secondary school for your child among these school, please place these schools in order of your choice (1 is the highest, 13 is the lowest) according to your understanding and perception of these school and according to your child's ability. Also, based on your knowledge, please check the characteristics of the schools that cause you to make the choice. If you would like to obtain more information about these schools, please refer to the Secondary School Profiles of Bay Area, or go to the school website

Priority	School name or school code	School characteristics (Please check whether the following schools contain the characteristics below)									
		A	B	C	D	E	F	G	H	I	J
1											
2											
3											
4											
5											
6											
7											
8											
9											
10											
11											
12											
13											

A. Academic ethos; B. Stable administration; C. Caring ethos
D. Distance from home; E. Instructional innovation; F. Extra-class activities
G. Campus environment; H. Public examination results; I. English medium of instruction

In your parenting experience, did the following behavior(s) occur in your child (the one who brought the survey home)?

5a. He (or she) was in the company of deviant friends.
5b. His (or her) academic performance was getting worse.
5c. He (or she) did not want to do homework or did not want t go to school
5d. He (or she) developed bad habits, such as foul language, smoking, drinking, gambling, etc.
5e. He (or she) was disrespectful to the parents, frequently talked back or throw tantrum.
5f. He (or she) did not want to talk with the parents.
5g. He (or she) constantly watched TV, talked on the phone, played video games or went online.
5h. He (or she) dressed up strangely.
5i. He (or she) was obsessed with idol worshiping.
5j. He (or she) was being complained for problem behaviors at school.

Please check or fill in the information according to your family condition.

6. You are □ Father □ Mother □ Other (Please indicate)________________
7. Your age is __________years Spouse's age is __________years
8. Years of resident in Hong Kong
   Myself □ Since birth □ 7 years or above □ 3 to 6 years □ Less than 3 years
   Spouse □ Since birth □ 7 years or above □ 3 to 6 years □ Less than 3 years
9. Education
   Myself □ Primary or below □ Junior secondary □ Senior secondary □ University or above
   Spouse □ Primary or below □ Junior secondary □ Senior secondary □ University or above
10. Marital status
    Married □ Single or separated □ Divorced □ Widow □ Married (spouse live in a different place □ Other (Please explain: ______________________)
11. Major source of family income
    Personal income □ Spouse's income □ Our total income □ Saving
    Public assistance □ Other source (Please explain: __________________)
12. Average monthly household income (HK$)
    Less than 5,000 □ 5,000 - 9,999 □ 10,000 - 3,999 □ 5,000 - 19,999
    20,000 - 29,999 □ 30,000 - 39,999 □ 40,000 - 49,999 □ 50,000 or above
13. Number of children in the family _____________
14. My child's (The one who brought this survey home) position in the family
    The eldest □ The second □ The third □ Other (_________)
15. My estimate is that he/she should belong to which allocation band:
    Band 1 (upper) □ Band 1 (middle) □ Band 1 (lower)
    Band 2 (upper) □ Band 2 (middle) □ Band 2 (lower)
    Band 3 (upper) □ Band 3 (middle) □ Band 3 (lower)
    Unclear □ Others (Please explain: __________________)

Chapter 6
Technology in the Development and Teaching of a Literacy Program for XXI Century Education

John Munro
The University of Melbourne, Australia

Elena Verezub
Swinburne University of Technology, Australia

EXECUTIVE SUMMARY

A key capacity in twenty-first century markets is being able to convert information to knowledge. This information is frequently a written form in e-text contexts. Individuals able to read, comprehend, and execute the information more effectively can use more efficiently the resources available in the marketplace. The study examined the influence of teaching individuals to read and comprehend hypertext. Its findings contribute to advancement of knowledge in this area and indicate ways in which individuals can improve their capacity to convert e-text to knowledge.

ORGANISATIONAL BACKGROUND

This study was conducted as a part of the research program of the Melbourne Graduate School of Education (MGSE) in the University of Melbourne. The University of Melbourne is a leading international university, with links to the Universitas 21 and Association of Pacific-Rim Universities networks of research-led universities. It is consistently ranked among the leading universities in the world. It is rated in the top 20 worldwide by international peer assessment and employer rating locates it in the top 10 (At a Glance, 2008). It has achieved this evaluation through its tradition of excellence in teaching, research and research training and knowledge transfer.

DOI: 10.4018/978-1-60960-599-5.ch006

The MGSE has the organisational culture, economic climate, business and management structure, financial status that one would expect of an international graduate school in a Twenty first century school of education. Its work is founded on explicit regular strategic planning, with a focus on excellence in the three aspects, teaching, research and knowledge transfer as its key institutional goal.

This study was implemented in this context and brings together the focus on these three main activities. It investigates factors that influence the comprehension of text presented in hypertext formats and conventional written. Its findings contribute to advancement of knowledge in this area and provide the basis for future research. Given their ready mapping into instruction, they provide a basis for improved performance through the use of hypertext throughout the community.

SETTING THE STAGE

The advent of new technologies has brought changes to the market environment. In the Australian system of education, a strong focus is placed on the development, marketing and teaching new literacy programs which enhance the quality of education. Although the overall results in literacy are good, quite a number of students cannot reach the standards. International data shows that in Australia the overall students' performance in literacy is falling behind other countries. Between 2003 and 2006 "...Australia declined in both its absolute and relative performance in reading literacy, with the proportion of students at the high end of achievement also declining." (Importance of Literacy and Numeracy, 2009).

The ability to comprehend written text is important for effective learning and performance. It includes three dimensions: the reader who comprehends, the text that is to be comprehended and the activity in which comprehension is embedded (Block, Gambrell and Pressley, 2002).

It is influenced by several factors that are both internal and external to the reader. Relevant internal variables include one's purpose for reading and their existing knowledge of the context, text structures and motivation (Block, Gambrell and Pressley, 2002; Greasser, 2007; Kintsch, 1995; Tapicro, 2007). External factors include the texts available for reading, text readability and the reading programs used to foster reading ability.

Reader activity during comprehension can be described in terms of the actions readers employ to link concepts both within the text they read and with what they know. They learn more comprehension strategies over time, that they use with texts of increasing complexity. They develop a wide repertoire of reading strategies that they use selectively, based on judgments they make of the reading demands of a particular situation. Both "meaning making strategies" (cognitive) and the management of these strategies (metacognitive) can be used in the process of instructing learners to improve the learning process (McNamara, Ozuru, Best, & O'Reilly, 2007; Vaidya, 1999; Williams & Atkins, 2009).

The advent of new technologies has introduced new contexts in which individuals need to read and comprehend. One of these has been the use of hypertext, the format used to organise written information in the computer context. Hypertext is defined in two ways: in terms of its functional components and construction (Jonassen, 1991; Sweeters, 1994) and in terms of how its links are used for comprehension, (Tolhurst, 1995), that is, the semantic use of its links. ICT has gradually included multimedia contents, such as video and audio clips, animations, and pictures in hypertext. Therefore, the term hypermedia has been used to describe this phenomenon (Landow, 2006). Researchers use hypertext and hypermedia interchangeably since they share the same technological foundation.

The present study is based on a conceptualization derived from the semantic definitions. Hypertext refers to an information data source in which the ideas are linked principally in linear sequential, hierarchical or in referential relationships (Oliver and Herrington, 1995). Market practice frequently assumes that readers can comprehend the types of links between the ideas in hypertext. Their prior knowledge influences how they do this. Those with higher prior knowledge of a topic select hyperlinks according to their individual interests, while those with low prior knowledge with the topic choose hyperlinks based on coherence they have established during reading (Salmeron, Canas, Kintsch, & Fajardo, 2005).

The rapid evolution of ICT has impacted on the information sources that need to be handled in the market place and in everyday life. The demands of a technologically capable workforce has been expanding globally (Baskin & Williams, 2006). Students need to become sophisticated in using ICT as their primary learning instruments (McNabb, 2005 - 2006). Students as young as pre-schoolers now need to process information via computers and the Internet. The use of ICT to communicate everyday information and instructions and equipping individuals to read and comprehend this information has put extra pressure on educational provision (Cartwright & Hammond, 2007; Watson & Hempenstall, 2008; Way & Webb, 2007).

Comprehension of hypertext requires the use of different skills from those used to understand conventional written text. Readers who use hypertext produced better structured and more thorough conceptual representations of the topics they studied than readers reading traditional text (Intrator, 2000; Spoehr, 1994). Without using adequate data processing strategies, readers are less likely to focus and direct their learning activity or to analyse and evaluate the information in deeper, conceptual ways (Edwards and Hardman, 1989; Foss, 1989).

A range of factors influence readers' hypertext comprehension. Interface design, for example, the mismatch of background and character colours and the use of irregular fonts, can affect hypertext reading efficiency (Thurstun, 2004; Tindale, 2006). The number of links used in hypertext can impact on hypertext reading performance, depending on how the links are organised. Increase in the number of links, when embedded in hypertexts, increase readers' cognitive load and opportunities of disorientation (McDonald and Stevenson, 1996) but not when the links are presented in a menu bar (Madrid, Van Oostendorp & Melguizo, 2009). Readers' hypertext reading performance is higher for linearly structured hypertext than for hierarchically or referentially structured hypertext (McDonald & Stevenson, 1996).

Various cognitive and metacognitive reading strategies have been shown to influence text comprehension (Mastropieri and Scruggs, 1997; Presley, 2000; Pressley, Brown, El-Dinary, and Afflerbach, 1995; Swanson, de La Paz, 1998, Vaidya, 1999). The present study selected three that facilitate reading comprehension for conventional written text; summarizing, paraphrasing, and predicting. The rationale for the selection of the strategies is as follows.

To understand how teaching these strategies may improve readers' understanding of hypertext, it is useful to examine how they change the text on which they are used. Paraphrasing is a strategy for processing sentences in the text (Katims & Harris, 1997). It allows readers to 'translate' a sentence into their own words and re-describe it. Predicting allows readers to take each sentence further (Kintsch 1995). They link the sentence with their existing knowledge. This allows them to expect or anticipate concepts not mentioned explicitly in the text and facilitates comprehension (Schmitt & Baumann, 1986).

The summarizing strategy involves synthesising individual sentence meanings into a theme or summary (Kintsch's (1995). Readers need to re-organise what they have been reading into a concise form. They may need to select topic sentences and delete unimportant information, etc. (Kletzien, 2009). It is an important ability for primary school students reading to learn (Malone and Mastropieri, 1992; Simmons, Kuchs, Fuchs, Hodge and Mathes, 1994).

The three strategies lead to different reading comprehension outcomes. Paraphrasing can be linked with literal comprehension outcomes. Predicting and summarizing permit the reader to 'go beyond the information stated in the text' and to infer or predict.

To investigate the comparative ease with which these three strategies are learnt, a study was planned to examine developmental trends in how the three strategies are learnt. Earlier research had shown that readers as young as second-graders benefit from strategy instruction (Brown, Pressley, van Meter & Schuder 1996) and this improvement continues across the primary years (Pressley, 1998). The present study examined the comparative facilitation of the three strategies from the period when students characteristically begin to develop as self-managing reading comprehenders (Munro, 2002).

The text to be read was expository or factual text, the general type usually used to enhance one's knowledge of particular topics (Stanovich and Siegel, 1994). This type of text has become increasingly important as our society advances technologically (Lapp, Flood & Ranck-Buhr, 1995).

CASE DESCRIPTION

Method

This section presents a study conducted in The University of Melbourne, Australia. The aim of the study was to develop and teach a training literacy program. It compared the effectiveness of training either to summarize, paraphrase and predict on both expressive and recognition comprehension for the expository and factual conventional written texts and hypertexts. The data were used to formulate recommendations for teaching students to comprehend e-text. The teaching could be packaged into an instructional program that could potentially be marketed and used to improve reading more broadly.

Participants

The participants were 60 third graders (age range 8-9 years old, mean age 8.6 years) and 60 sixth graders (age range 11-12 years old, mean age 11.3 years) who attended state schools in Melbourne. They were taught to use one of three alternative strategies; summarizing, paraphrasing or predicting. They displayed reading comprehension for both conventional written text (CWT) and hypertext (HT). Their reading comprehension performance was tested before and after the training.

Children in the younger age range are frequently characterized as beginning to develop as self-managing reading comprehenders while those in the older age range are characterized as possessing a repertoire of reading strategies (Munro, 2002). Comparison of strategy use for the two age ranges was expected to permit an investigation of developmental trends. The ratio of male to female students was 26:34 and 31:29 for the third and sixth grades respectively.

The schools' demographics reflected an average socio-economic background. The students did not have emotional difficulties or learning disabilities and attended school regularly. The reading knowledge and skills of the students lay within the average span, as indicated by performance on appropriately normed reading tests; all students had a reading comprehension score in the 23rd to 95th percentile rank range, according to the TORCH Reading Comprehension Test (Mossenson, Hill and Masters, 1987).

The Tasks Used to Assess Reading Comprehension

A variety of reading comprehension task formats are available. One means of categorizing the tasks is in terms of whether readers need to recognize ideas that are consistent with the text read or by answering questions that express their comprehension. Both were used here. The cloze procedure, in which students select words and phrases to complete written prose so that it matches the meaning of prose they have read earlier was used as a recognition comprehension task. Answering questions about the text by framing a verbal response is a task that assesses expressive comprehension.

As noted, the type of links used may influence text comprehension and the use of the reading comprehension strategies. The majority of hypertexts developed for classroom have the linear format (Oliver and Herrington, 1995), with links between nodes in planned sequences. The present study examines hypertext that uses the linear linking format.

Use of the summarizing strategy is facilitated when students can identify easily the key words in a text and synthesise them into a sequence of ideas. Given that some of the key words in hypertext are highlighted perceptually, it is expected that some of the sentence elements can be transferred into a summary.

Use of the paraphrasing strategy requires students to generate synonyms in order to say the ideas in other words. This in terms may require more extensive vocabulary knowledge. The hypertext structure does not, it would seem, facilitate the use of the paraphrasing strategy.

The predicting strategy requires the use of a 'thinking ahead' or an 'anticipatory' mindset. This is cued in the hypertext by offering the reader options for making physical links. It could be argued that the hypertext linkage system symbolizes a set of possible predictions that readers might make while reading conventional written text.

A key aspect of self managed reading is the capacity of readers to decide when to use particular strategies selectively. Of the three strategies in the hypertext context, it would seem that predicting makes the least cognitive demand. The hypertext design cues readers to predict more than it cues them to summarize or to paraphrase. In other words, the need for readers to select spontaneously the most appropriate strategy is reduced for the predicting strategy.

This leads to the expectation that when the three strategies are taught in conventional written text, the predicting strategy would transfer first, followed developmentally by summarizing and then by paraphrasing. The present study investigates this expectation.

Materials

Assessment of Comprehension

Two task contexts were chosen to measure reading comprehension of a conventional written text and a hypertext: (1) the cloze procedure was used to measure recognition comprehension; and (2) the comprehension question procedure was used to measure expressive comprehension. Each context included items that assessed both literal and inferential comprehension. The literal items targeted information stated explicitly in the text. The inferential items required students to 'go beyond' the literal content of a text and infer ideas not stated explicitly, for example, to infer intention.

Instructional Materials

Factual texts were used to investigate students' use of the targeted strategies in a conventional written text and a hypertext. The texts were selected in consultation with the students' teachers and were edited and adapted to each grade level using the Fry readability formula (Fry, 1977).

In the present study, the structure of hypertext was represented by linear links. The choice of linear linking for hypertexts was made for the following reasons. First, simplicity in navigation is essential for learners. Linear linking involves the lowest levels of learner decision-making and control. When the text is prepared in this form, the instructor can exert the greatest influence on the information that will be assessed by the learners. The less users have to think about navigation related issues, the more they can concentrate on the subject matter and hence the greater their learning (Apple Computer Inc., 1990). Second, many hypertexts, especially those developed for reading and comprehending in the classroom, are of the linear form (Oliver and Herrington, 1995). Third, hypertext reading material with linear links typically follows a planned sequence with links to other sites and nodes. Hypertext with linear links most resembles conventional written text.

Based on the earlier review that identified the optimal forms and conditions for presenting hypertext (Johnson-Sheehan and Baehr, 2001), the characteristics for hypertext displays used in the present study are as follows: left justified text; a character density of 80 characters per line, double spacing and proportionally spaced characters.

Instructional Phases

At each grade level the students were divided into three instructional groups of 20, one each of which was taught to summarize, to paraphrase and to predict. To allocate students to an instructional regime, the students were matched on reading comprehension score, grouped into triads of similar reading ability and allocated randomly. The three groups at each year level did not differ in comprehension and the sets of scores were approximately normally distributed.

The three phases of the study, at each year level, involved the following student activities:

1. At the pre-instructional phase students' reading comprehension was assessed using (1) the TORCH Reading Comprehension Test and (2) a typical comprehension task that assessed their performance on the comprehension strategy to be taught (either paraphrasing, summarizing or predicting) in both the CWT and HT contexts. As well, information about students' history of the use of computers was collected by questionnaire.
2. At the instructional phase students were taught the relevant strategy in small groups using a teaching regime that extended over five sessions.
3. At the post-instructional phase students' reading comprehension was assessed using a second typical comprehension task in both the CWT and HT contexts.

Thirty-five to 45 minute training sessions were conducted with each group in their classrooms during regular school hours. Training was based on the principles of explicit or direct instruction (Pearson, 1984; Rosenshine, 1986; Rosenshine and Stevens, 1984) which were as follows:

1. Explicit explanation of the rules. Each to-be-mastered skill was defined explicitly. The students were told why each skill would be useful, what types of materials it might be used with, and when to apply it.
2. Modeling the strategy. Each skill was modeled using a talk-through procedure in which the researcher attempted to make explicit the processes used in applying the skill to text. Individual students were also called upon to do talk-throughs in some of the sessions.
3. Guided practice with corrective feedback. The students were given the opportunity to practise each skill and were given appropriate and immediate feedback.
4. Independent practice. By the end of the training, the students had learned to use the skill independently.

Results

The Validity of Comprehension Tasks

Prior to reporting student performance on the comprehension tasks, estimates of their validity are examined. The level of the associations between the various measures of reading comprehension, using Pearson product-moment correlation coefficients, is as follows:

1. TORCH reading comprehension score and comprehension of a conventional written text or a hypertext before and after training sessions were correlated for both grade levels.
2. Comprehension of a written text before training was correlated with comprehension of text after training.
3. Comprehension of a hypertext was correlated with comprehension of the conventional written text both before and after training.

These data are consistent with the assumption that comparative performance on the traditional reading comprehension task (that is TORCH comprehension) draws on essentially similar processes to those underpinning comprehending the conventional written texts and the hypertexts used in the study. Similarly, the associations between comprehension of the conventional written text and the hypertexts before and after training sessions draw on the same reading comprehension process for the students at each grade level are consistent with this expectation.

The Effect of the Strategy Taught and Type of Text on Comprehension

Changes in comprehension performance for each strategy training condition for third and sixth graders were computed. Mean comprehension performance prior to and after each training regime and the corresponding effect size of the training (*eta*^{2}) for each grade level are shown in Table 1. In all the cases, the skewness and kurtosis were consistent with the distribution having an approximately normal distribution (Tabachnik & Fidell, 1996).

The difference between pre- and post-test scores indicates the comparative effectiveness of the various types of strategy training for each type of text at each year level. The effect size measures indicate that teaching third graders to both summarise and paraphrase improved their comprehension of conventional written text while teaching

Table 1. Means, standard deviation and size effect for a conventional written text and a hypertext comprehension by Grades 3 and 6 students before and after training

Grade level	Type of text	Instructional condition	Comprehension score				
			before		after		effect size
			mean	SD	mean	SD	
3	Cwt	summarizing	4.65	1.23	5.80	1.32	0.48
		paraphrasing	4.05	0.95	5.35	1.35	0.39
		predicting	3.75	1.29	5.20	1.67	0.47
	Ht	summarizing	4.25	1.21	4.60	1.35	0.05
		paraphrasing	4.40	1.23	4.75	1.25	0.11
		predicting	3.70	1.17	4.65	1.39	0.42
6	Cwt	summarizing	12.70	1.87	13.40	1.50	0.18
		paraphrasing	12.20	1.51	12.60	1.64	0.11
		predicting	11.65	1.50	12.40	1.82	0.14
	Ht	summarizing	12.10	2.10	14.15	1.69	0.52
		paraphrasing	11.10	1.41	11.55	1.54	0.1
		predicting	11.35	1.79	11.90	1.86	0.1

them to predict also improved hypertext comprehension. At the sixth grade level, on the other hand, instruction in summarizing only influenced reading comprehension and for the hypertext context.

The influence of strategy training on text comprehension was analyzed in terms of two factors; the type of strategy taught (summarizing, paraphrasing or predicting) and the type of text (conventional written text and hypertext). For the third graders, the type of text influenced reading comprehension. Training to predict was associated with improved comprehension for both conventional written text and hypertext contexts while training to summarise and to paraphrase improved comprehension in the conventional written text context but not in the hypertext context.

For the sixth graders, training to summarize improved comprehension for hypertext. Training to paraphrase and predict did not improve comprehension of either a conventional written text or a hypertext.

The study also examined whether computer use for various purposes both at home or at school influenced the effectiveness of the training. The improvement in hypertext comprehension score, for any of the strategies, was generally not influenced by the readers' computer-using habits. The frequency of using computers for a range of purposes, such as playing games, e-mailing, finding new information, writing what has been learnt, either at home or at school, did not influence improvement in hypertext comprehension. The only activity that influenced comprehension gains was using computers at school for looking for answers to questions by Grade 6 students.

Discussion

The results show that teaching students to summarize, paraphrase or predict in the conventional written text context transfers to the hypertext context. The transfer shows a developmental trend. Training to predict transferred first, followed later by training to summarise.

These findings extend the findings of similar investigations of comprehension of a conventional written text at different grade levels (Fountas and Pinnell, 2001; Katims and Harris, 1997). The finding that Grade 3 students improved comprehension of a conventional written text after being trained to summarise, paraphrase and predict is consistent with findings that teach reading comprehension strategies for younger students (Brown, Pressley, van Meter and Schuder, 1996). Conventional written texts are understood more effectively because of the readers' familiarity with their structure. As reported earlier, no studies have investigated the application of these strategies to hypertext.

This trend indicates an appropriate direction for the teaching. To comprehend using the paraphrasing strategy, readers need to be guided to link text items with synonyms they know and sequence these into an 'alternative' sentence. To comprehend using the predicting strategy, they need to link the text with meanings in their existing knowledge that are not mentioned in the text. To comprehend using the summarizing strategy, they need to be guided to synthesize the sentences into a 'big idea' as they progress through the text, by selecting, reorganising and deleting.

The results of the present study showed that training to predict transferred to the hypertext context for the third-graders. The predicting strategy is one of the first reading comprehension strategies young readers learn in the conventional written text (Munro, 2002). The transfer of the predicting strategy to the hypertext context is related to how students make connections between their existing knowledge and knowledge gained from the text read. The hypertext linkage system allows students to predict the meaning of a link. At the same time, no transfer of the summarizing and paraphrasing strategies to the hypertext context was found. This is consistent with more complex cognitive processes while using these strategies. Paraphrasing requires the ability to say in other words the ideas in the text and summarizing requires readers to identify the main ideas and then summarise them.

Researchers argue that the Internet forces us to expand our understanding of a text, and to synthesize a microstructure (parts of a text) into a macrostructure (summary of a text) by means of links (Coiro, 2003; Sutherland-Smith, 2002). The transfer of the summarizing strategy to the hypertext context for Grade 6 students suggests the student' ability to identify the main ideas from the hypertext and summarise them. Also, it may be suggested that the sixth-graders would require more training to paraphrase and predict in the hypertext context.

It was found that training Grade 6 students either to summarise, paraphrase or predict did not enhance comprehension in the conventional written text context. It is possible that the older students had mastered and used these strategies in the conventional written text context.

CURRENT CHALLENGES FACING THE ORGANISATION

International schools of education continually set themselves the challenge of knowledge enhancement. A key goal they share is how to contribute to the improvement of educational practice, both locally and internationally, through validated research. They achieve this in part through the provision of a robust graduate research training program.

This study identifies key processes in the comprehension of hypertext. An awareness of them can potentially improve the efficiency of reading comprehension outcomes. The challenge facing the MGSE is multifaceted: (1) how to communicate the outcomes so that they could have maximal application through knowledge transfer; (2) how to map them into teaching programs so that students could improve their ability to learn by reading hypertext; and (3) how to extend the research further.

SOLUTIONS AND RECOMMENDATIONS

The findings of the study have substantial implications for practice. They indicate that readers can improve the efficiency with which they comprehend and use factual e-text by being taught particular reading comprehension strategies.

The teaching of reading comprehension strategies in the hypertext context is a new and exciting concept in the field of computer use in education. In terms of teaching reading comprehension in the 21st century, 'The question of what to teach is accompanied by one just urgent: how to teach' (Wood, 2000, p. 119). The following strategy teaching plan is proposed based on recommendations suggested by Munro (1996):

a. show the order in which you will teach strategies and how you will teach each one, first for familiar hypertext. In individual teaching, the order will be determined by what the reader knows about each of these strategies. In group teaching contexts, an order more appropriate to group knowledge will be necessary.
b. introduce one new strategy and allow it to be consolidated before introducing the next.
c. ask students to evaluate the effectiveness of the strategy, to monitor its effectiveness.
d. encourage students to discuss with peers how they use the strategies, share their strategies with each other, teach each other strategies, model them.
e. revise regularly earlier strategies.
f. integrate the new strategy with existing strategies, to decide when and how to use each.
g. allow students to practise remembering them.

There are number of possible avenues of future research. One is to explore experimentally the value of using other reading comprehension strategies in the hypertext context. These investigations could include the application of a single strategy as well as multiple strategies for reading and comprehending a hypertext.

A second is to elaborate Internet-based training sessions for teaching reading comprehension strategies. This could prove useful for several reasons. Interacting with a hypertext differs from a conventional written text in particular ways. If, for example, students are unable to match their task goals to the structure of information and activities offered by the system, navigational difficulties may arise. Unfamiliar or large hypertext structures can lead to these difficulties. Internet training that is successful for all learners needs to cater for learners' individual characteristics and their differing ability to interact with hypertext. The amount of time spent teaching comprehension strategies on the Internet differ from the time required for conventional written text context. Students may benefit if they were trained and then tested in the hypertext environment.

A third avenue, for research, is the applicability of the reading comprehension strategies hypertexts of any structure: either linear, or hierarchical, or referential. These could include narrative and expository hypertexts. A combination of narrative and expository text can promote an wider range of thinking and comprehension skills.

REFERENCES

Apple Computer Inc. (1989). *HyperCard stack design guidelines*. Cupertino, CA: Apple Computer Inc.

At a Glance. (2008). *The University of Melbourne*. Retrieved from http://www.unimelb.edu.au/publications/docs/AtAGlance.pdf

Baskin, C., & Williams, M. (2006). ICT integration in schools: Where are we now and what comes next? *Australiasian Journal of Educational Technology, 22*, 455 - 473. Retrieved 12 October, 2009, from http://www.ascilite.org.au/ajet/ajet22/baskin.html

Block, C. C., Gambrell, B. L., & Pressley, M. (2002). *Improving comprehension instruction: Rethinking research, theory, and classroom practice*. Jossey-Bass.

Brown, R., Pressley, M., van Meter, P., & Schuder, T. (1996). A quasi-experimental validation of transactional strategies instruction with low-achieving second-grade readers. *Journal of Educational Psychology, 88*, 18–37. doi:10.1037/0022-0663.88.1.18

Cartwright, V., & Hammond, M. (2007). Fitting it in: A study exploring ICT use in a UK primary school. *Australiasian Journal of Educational Technology, 23*, 390-407. Retrieved 12 October, 2009, from http://ascilite.org.au/ajet/ajet23/cartwright.html

Coiro, J. (2003). Exploring literacy on the Internet. *The Reading Teacher, 56*(5), 458–464.

Department of Education. Employment and Workplace Relations. (2009). *Importance of literacy and numeracy*. Retrieved from http://www.deewr.gov.au/Schooling/LiteracyandNumeracyPilotProject/Pages/ImportanceLandN.aspx

Edwards, D., & Hardman, L. (1989). Lost in hyperspace: Cognitive mapping and navigation in a hypertext environment. In McAleese, R. (Ed.), *Hypertext: Theory into practice* (pp. 105–125). London, UK: BSP.

Foss, C. L. (1989). Tools for reading and browsing hypertext. *Information Processing & Management, 25*(4), 407–418. doi:10.1016/0306-4573(89)90068-X

Fountas, I., & Pinnell, S. G. (2001). *Guiding readers and writers grades 3-6: Teaching comprehension, genre, and content literacy*. Portsmouth, NH: Heinemann.

Fry, E. (1977). Fry's readability graph: Clarifications, validity, and extension to level 17. *Journal of Reading*, *21*, 242–252.

Greasser, A. C. (2007). An introduction to strategic reading comprehension. In McNamara, D. S. (Ed.), *Reading comprehension strategies: Theories, interventions, and technologies* (pp. 3–26). Abingdon, UK: Lawrence Erlbaurn Associates.

Intrator, S. M. (2000). Click, click, click... what do we know about reading hypertext? *Knowledge Quest*, *28*(4), 31–34.

Johnson-Sheehan, R., & Baehr, C. (2001). Visual-spatial thinking in hypertexts. *Technical Communication*, *48*(1), 22–30.

Jonassen, D. H. (1991). Evaluating constructivist learning. *Educational Technology*, *31*, 28–33.

Katims, S. D., & Harris, S. (1997). Improving the reading comprehension of middle school students in inclusive classrooms. *Journal of Adolescent & Adult Literacy*, *41*(2), 116–123.

Kintsch, W. (1995). *Discourse comprehension: Essays in honor of Walter Kintsch* (Weaver, C. A. III, Mannes, S., & Fletcher, C. R., Eds.). Hillsdale, NJ: L. Erlbaum.

Kletzien, S. B. (2009). Paraphrasing: An effective comprehension strategy. *The Reading Teacher*, *63*(1), 73–77. doi:10.1598/RT.63.1.7

Landow, G. (2006). *Hypertext 3.0: Critical theory and new media in an era of globalisation* (3rd ed.). Baltimore, MD: The Johns Hopkins University Press.

Lapp, D., Flood, J., & Ranck-Buhr, W. (1995). Using multiple text formats to explore scientific phenomena in middle school classrooms. *Reading and Writing Quarterly: Overcoming Learning Difficulties*, *11*, 173–186.

Madrid, R. I., Van Oostendorp, H., & Melguizo, M. C. P. (2009). The effects of the number of links and navigation support on cognitive load and learning with hypertext: The mediating role of reader order. *Computers in Human Behavior*, *29*, 66–75.

Malone, L. D., & Mastropieri, M. A. (1992). Reading comprehension instruction: Summarisation and self-monitoring training for students with learning disabilities. *Exceptional Children*, *58*, 279–279.

Mastropieri, M. A., & Scruggs, T. E. (1997). Best practice in promoting reading comprehension in students with learning disabilities. *Remedial and Special Education*, *18*, 197–213. doi:10.1177/074193259701800402

McDonald, S., & Stevenson, R. (1996). Disorientation in hypertext: Effects of three structures on navigation performance. *Applied Ergonomics*, *27*(1), 61–68. doi:10.1016/0003-6870(95)00073-9

McNabb, M. (2005. (2006). Navigating the maze of hypertext. *Educational Leadership*, (December - January): 76–79.

McNamara, D. S., Ozuru, Y., Best, R., & O'Reilly, T. (2007). The 4-pronged comprehension strategy framework. In McNamara, D. S. (Ed.), *Reading comprehension strategies: Theories, interventions, and technologies* (pp. 465–496). Abingdon, UK: Lawrence Erbaurn Associates.

Mossenson, L., Hill, P., & Masters, G. (1987). *Tests of reading comprehension: Manual*. Australian Council of Educational Research.

Munro, J. (1996). *Teaching reading strategies*. Australia: Hawthorn.

Munro, J. (2002). *Leading learning communities*. Jolimont, Australia: Incorporated Association of Registerd Teachers of Victoria.

Oliver, R., & Herrington, J. (1995). Developing effective hypermedia instructional materials. *Australian Journal of Educational Technology*, *11*(2), 8–22.

Pearson, P. D. (1984). Direct explicit teaching of reading comprehension. In Duffy, G. G., Roehler, L. R., & Mason, J. (Eds.), *Comprehension instruction: Perspectives and suggestions* (pp. 222–233). New York, NY: Longman.

Pressley, M. (1998). *Reading instruction that works: The case for balanced teaching*. New York, NY: Guilford Press.

Pressley, M. (2000). What should comprehension instruction be the instruction of? In Kamil, M., Mosenthal, P., Pearson, P. D., & Barr, R. (Eds.), *Handbook of reading research* (*Vol. 3*, pp. 545–562). Hillsdale, NJ: Erlbaum.

Pressley, M., Brown, R., El-Dinary, P. B., & Afflerbach, P. (1995). The comprehension instruction that students need: Instruction fostering constructively responsive reading. *Learning Disabilities Research & Practice*, *10*, 215–224.

Rosenshine, B. (1986). Synthesis of research on explicit teaching. *Educational Leadership*, *43*, 60–69.

Rosenshine, B., & Stevens, R. (1984). Classroom instruction in reading. In Pearson, P. D. (Ed.), *Handbook of reading research* (pp. 745–798). New York, NY: Longman.

Salmeron, L., Canas, J. J., Kintsch, W., & Fajardo, I. (2005). Reading strategies and hypertext comprehension. *Discourse Processes*, *40*(3), 171–191. doi:10.1207/s15326950dp4003_1

Schmitt, C. M., & Baumann, F. J. (1986). How to incorporate comprehension monitoring strategies into basal reader instruction. *The Reading Teacher*, *40*, 28–31.

Simmons, D. C., Kuchs, D., Fuchs, L. S., Hodge, J. P., & Mathes, P. G. (1994). Importance of instructional complexity and role reciprocity to classwide peer tutoring. *Learning Disabilities Research & Practice*, *9*, 203–212.

Spoehr, K. T. (1994). *Enhancing the acquisition of conceptual structures through hypermedia, in classroom lessons: Integrating cognitive theory and classroom practice*. Cambridge, MA: Mcgilly.

Stanovich, K. E., & Siegel, L. S. (1994). Phenotypic performance profile of children with learning disabilities: A regression-based test of phonological-core variable-difference model. *Journal of Educational Psychology*, *86*, 24–53. doi:10.1037/0022-0663.86.1.24

Sutherland-Smith, W. (2002). Weaving the literacy web: Changes in reading from page to screen. *The Reading Teacher*, *55*, 662–669.

Swanson, P. N., & De La Paz, S. (1998). Teaching effective comprehension strategies to students with learning and reading disabilities. *Intervention in School and Clinic*, *33*, 209–219. doi:10.1177/105345129803300403

Sweeters, W. (1994). Multimedia electronic tools for learning. *Educational Technology*, *34*(5), 47–52.

Tabachnik, G. B., & Fidell, S. L. (1996). *Using multivariate statistics*. New York, NY: Harper Collins College Publishers.

Tapicro, I. (2007). *Situational models and levels of coherence: Towards a definition of comprehension*. Abingdon, UK: Lawrence Erlbaurn Associates.

Thurstun, J. (2004). Teaching and learning the reading of homepages. *Prospect*, *19*(2), 56–71.

Tindale, J. (2006). Reading print and electronic texts. In Murray, D. (Ed.), *Navigating to read - reading to navigate* (pp. 2–15). Sydney, Australia: Sydney AMEP Research Centre.

Tolhurst, D. (1995). Hypertext, hypermedia, multimedia defined? *Educational Technology, 15*(2), 21–26.

Vaidya, S. R. (1999). Metacognitive learning strategies for student with learning disabilities. *Education, 120*, 186–189.

Watson, T., & Hempenstall, K. (2008). Effects of a computer based beginning reading program on young children. *Australiasian Journal of Educational Technology, 24*(3), 258–574.

Way, J., & Webb, C. (2007). A framework for analysing ICT adoption in Australian primary schools. *Australiasian Journal of Educational Technology, 23*, 559-582. Retrieved 12 October, 2009, from http://www.ascilite.org.au/ajet/ajet23/way.html

Williams, J. P., & Atkins, J. G. (2009). The role of metacognition in teaching reading comprehension to primary schools. In Hacker, D. J., Dunlosky, J., & Graesser, A. C. (Eds.), *Handbook of metacognition in education* (pp. 26–43). Hoboken, NJ: Routledge.

Wood, J. (2000). Literacy: Charlotte's Web meets the World Wide Web. In Gordon, D. T. (Ed.), *The digital classroom* (pp. 117–126). Boston, MA: Harvard Education Letter.

ADDITIONAL READING

Akbulut, Y. (2008). Predictors of Foreign Language Reading Comprehension in a Hypermedia Reading Environment. *Journal of Educational Computing Research, 39*(1), 37–50. doi:10.2190/EC.39.1.c

Antonenko, P. D., & Niederhauser, D. S. (2010). The influence of leads on cognitive load and learning in a hypertext environment. *Computers in Human Behavior, 26*(2), 140–150. doi:10.1016/j.chb.2009.10.014

Calisir, F., Eryazici, M., & Lehto, M. R. (2008). The effects of text structure and prior knowledge of the learner on computer-based learning. *Computers in Human Behavior, 24*(2), 439–450. doi:10.1016/j.chb.2007.01.032

Defays, J.-M. (2009). Text and Hypertext: Function, Reading, Learning. *Belgian Journal of Linguistics, 23*(1), 103–114. doi:10.1075/bjl.23.09def

Fontanini, I., & Tomitch, L. M. B. (2009). Working Memory Capacity and L2 University Students' Comprehension of Linear Texts and Hypertexts. *International Journal of English Studies, 9*(2), 1–18.

Ignacio Madrid, R., Van Oostendorp, H., & Puerta Melguizo, M. C. (2009). The effects of the number of links and navigation support on cognitive load and learning with hypertext: The mediating role of reading order. *Computers in Human Behavior, 25*(1), 66–75. doi:10.1016/j.chb.2008.06.005

Kester, L., & Kirschner, P. A. (2009). Effects of Fading Support on Hypertext Navigation and Performance in Student-Centered E-Learning Environments. *Interactive Learning Environments, 17*(2), 165–179. doi:10.1080/10494820802054992

Liu, P.-L., Chen, C.-J., & Chang, Y.-J. (2010). Effects of a computer-assisted concept mapping learning strategy on EFL college students' English reading comprehension. *Computers & Education, 54*(2), 436–445. doi:10.1016/j.compedu.2009.08.027

Mariotti, A. P. (2010). Sustaining Students' Reading Comprehension. *Kappa Delta Pi Record, 46*(2), 87–89.

McCollin, M., O'Shea, D. J., & McQuiston, K. (2010). Improving Vocabulary and Comprehension Skills of Secondary-Level Students from Diverse Backgrounds. *Preventing School Failure*, *54*(2), 133–136. doi:10.1080/10459880903217846

Naumann, J., Richter, T., Christmann, U., & Groeben, N. (2008). Working memory capacity and reading skill moderate the effectiveness of strategy training in learning from hypertext. *Learning and Individual Differences*, *18*(2), 197–213. doi:10.1016/j.lindif.2007.08.007

Protopsaltis, A. (2008). Reading Strategies in Hypertexts and Factors Influencing Hyperlink Selection. *Journal of Educational Multimedia and Hypermedia*, *17*(2), 191–213.

Salmerón, L., Baccino, T., Cañas, J. J., Madrid, R. I., & Fajardo, I. (2009). Do graphical overviews facilitate or hinder comprehension in hypertext? *Computers & Education*, *53*(4), 1308–1319. doi:10.1016/j.compedu.2009.06.013

KEY TERMS AND DEFINITIONS

Conventional Written Text: A hard-copy text.

Expository or Factual Text: a text that explains something.

Hypertext: An e-text in which the ideas are linked principally in linear sequential relationships, in hierarchical relationships or in referential relationships.

Paraphrasing: Re-stating information using synonymous words and expression; does not require readers to organise info in a short format.

Predicting: Thinking ahead; trying to foresee what comes next in the text based on prior knowledge.

Summarizing: Re-organizing information using your own words into a concise form, omitting detail.

Chapter 7
An International Collaborative Masters Degree in Integrated Marketing Communications:
A US-EU Program in the Mediterranean

Kathleen A. Krentler
San Diego State University, USA

Albert Caruana
University of Malta, Malta

EXECUTIVE SUMMARY

A transnational partnership between the University of Malta in Malta and San Diego State University in the United States resulted in an agreement to commence a Masters degree in Integrated Marketing Communications. The degree is fully delivered in Malta, a Mediterranean island state and a full member of the European Union. In Malta, the program is held not at the main campus of the University but at the historical campus of the University of Malta in Valetta that dates back to 1592. Classes are in English and are taught by faculty from both universities. Students earn a degree from each of the two participating schools thus providing recognition in both the US and the EU. This chapter charts the challenges faced and the hurdles encountered to develop the curriculum, launch the degree, recruit the students, undertake teaching, and ultimately, graduate the first cohort.

ORGANIZATION BACKGROUND

This case presents a program which is the result of a transnational partnership between the University of Malta (UM) and San Diego State University (SDSU) in the United States. It is a comprehensive post-graduate program in Integrated Marketing Communications (IMC). The effort is part of a series of post-graduate degree programs offered by

DOI: 10.4018/978-1-60960-599-5.ch007

the University of Malta in partnership with various US partner universities under its International Masters Programmes (IMP) portfolio. In the case of the IMP IMC program, students earn a Master of Science in Business Administration (MSBA), Marketing from San Diego State University and a Master of Arts (MA) in Integrated Marketing Communications from the University of Malta as they study in Malta for one year, taking courses from both UM and SDSU faculty. This case describes how the partnership was established, the development process, program details, the program's launch and its first year of operations. The benefits and challenges of developing and implementing such a program are highlighted throughout the case and insight into how such a transnational partnership can occur is provided.

SETTING THE STAGE

Partnership Establishment

Integrated Marketing Communications seeks to send a single, consistent message to a company's or organization's various publics. This approach has grown in importance in the realm of corporate communications and marketing in recent years as its value over piecemeal approaches to corporate communications has been recognized. Because the concept is relatively new, established corporate practitioners rarely have been educated in either the theory or practice of integrated marketing communications. Hence as demand for expertise in IMC has grown in companies and organizations there has been a concurrent need for educational offerings in the field. The discipline of integrated marketing communications in universities worldwide is a relatively new phenomenon but it is growing. IMC studies are sometimes housed in business schools, as an offshoot of marketing and advertising. Alternatively they are sometimes found in departments or schools of communications.

These two different approaches to the housing of IMC studies were found in the early 2000s on the campuses of San Diego State University, a public university located in San Diego, California, USA and at the University of Malta. At San Diego State University (SDSU) faculty interest and expertise within the Marketing Department of the College of Business Administration had resulted in the development of a Centre for Integrated Marketing Communications. At the time it was established in 2003 the Centre for IMC was the only such center in the US located in a business school. The Centre was developed to support research amongst faculty in IMC and education in IMC at the undergraduate, graduate, and executive levels. An undergraduate emphasis in integrated marketing communications within the marketing major had been offered for the first time two years prior to the establishment of the IMC Centre and was growing rapidly. In 2009 almost 50% of all marketing majors at SDSU chose the IMC emphasis. Under the centre's watchful eye, growth in IMC at SDSU continued. This growth included the development and offering of executive short courses. A strong community advisory board was established as part of the centre's development. The board was and remains instrumental in providing a connection between the academic programs that are under the auspices of the centre and the practice of IMC in the community.

At the University of Malta, the Centre for Communication Technology was established in 1991 and initially focused primarily on building its undergraduate program in communications. In the late 1990s when the Centre began contemplation of which post-graduate degrees to offer, considerations relating to expertise possessed and market opportunities identified IMC as an area worth pursuing. A masters program in Integrated Marketing Communications was first offered in 2002. Students in the program came from a variety of undergraduate academic backgrounds although communication studies and business were the two most frequently represented fields.

The program was offered as a part-time, evening program targeted at working professionals. By 2007 three cohorts of students had completed this program which was, at the time, the only masters program in IMC in Europe.

The faculties of the IMC programs at the two universities came to know each other as a result of previous collegial relationships through professional organizations as well as by reputation. Since mutual interest in integrated marketing communications was strong, members of the two faculties began to work collaboratively as early as 2001. Two SDSU faculty members were invited to teach in the University of Malta IMC program as visiting scholars for each of the first three cohorts (2002, 2004, and 2006). In 2004, a UM faculty member was awarded a Fulbright scholarship to pursue research in the area of integrated marketing communications. He spent several months in late 2004 in San Diego collaborating with SDSU faculty members.

As a result of the growing connections between the two faculties, discussions began to take place regarding the potential for development of a joint program. Early considerations included whether the program would be an undergraduate program (which was what SDSU offered at the time) or a post-graduate program (which was what UM offered at the time). Also under initial consideration was what might be the ideal location for the program (San Diego? Malta? Elsewhere?), or alternatively whether the program might logically be developed as a distance education offering.

It was recognized early on that mounting an undergraduate program would produce far greater challenges than a post-graduate program would. The US system of four year undergraduate degrees versus the European system of three year undergraduate degrees would be a significant hurdle if the former was to be pursued. Further, the need to account for general education requirements, the program length, and the commitment of younger students all suggested that the challenges provided by an undergraduate joint offering would likely prove to be insurmountable. A decision was made to further investigate the development of some form of collaborative program at the post-graduate level. This meant a shorter program and more directed requirements (i.e. no general education). Although SDSU did not offer a graduate degree program in integrated marketing communications at the time (and still does not) it appeared that the Master of Science in Business Administration, Marketing was flexible enough in its requirements to be easily adaptable to a focus on IMC.

The issue of delivery mode was another early consideration. Given the physical distance between the two campuses it might appear that delivery through a distance learning approach would be ideal. While the faculties of both universities agreed that including some distance education in the program could potentially be appropriate and practical, they also agreed that a fully online program was not part of their vision. Face-to-face was believed to be desirable and it was decided that this delivery mode would be a major part of each course delivered in the program. This decision was strongly supported by the Rector of UM.

Having decided to primarily emphasize face-to-face delivery, site location presented the biggest challenge amongst the early considerations. Because the two faculties had initially envisioned positioning the program with a strong European and Mediterranean emphasis, attempting to physically locate the program in southern California was less attractive. Further, the SDSU College of Business had experience offering face-to-face international programs (an active and successful graduate business program was in place in Taiwan) whilst University of Malta did not have such experience. Hence it was determined that locating closer to, if not on, the UM campus was preferred. While the campus of University of Malta might have clearly seemed the most logical option, early consideration focused on the University of Malta satellite campus in Rome, Italy. Rome was initially seen as offering the potential to draw from a larger pool of applicants than Malta. After some initial contacts and investigation it became apparent, however, that locating in the country of Malta was the better choice. The decision was strengthened by a new initiative at UM that was considering building a portfolio of joint masters programs with US universities as part of the new International Masters Programmes (IMP). This endeavor was aided by the fact that it had the full support and encouragement of the then ambassador of the US to Malta.

In order to develop the IMP portfolio of programs as a unique brand, the University of Malta made the decision to locate the IMP programs off its main campus and to utilize the historical campus of the University of Malta in Valletta that dated back to 1592. The historical, original building of the University in Valetta was targeted for renovations as it was envisaged that the renovated building would allow the IMP programs to operate near enough to the main UM campus to realize the services and other advantages of a large university campus while still offering a clearly distinct identity. The collaborative IMC program would be one of the first two IMP offerings.

CASE DESCRIPTION

Collaborative Degree Program Development and Approval

The road from the concept of a collaborative degree offered primarily through face-to-face delivery on the ground in Malta to the launch of that program's first cohort was long and complex, taking approximately seven years. The fact that San Diego State University is part of a 23 campus public university system in the state of California contributed significantly to the challenges as the bureaucracy of that system frequently created roadblocks. The bureaucracy of SDSU, however, was certainly not the only stumbling block along the way.

The process began with a proposal that detailed all aspects of the collaborative effort. This included the program's goals, vision and positioning, its requirements, the delivery plan, the responsibilities of each partner university in terms of teaching, administration, and logistical support, the plan for marketing and recruiting, the processes for application and admission, and a budget indicating the number of students needed to breakeven. Since the program was to operate on both campuses as a "stand alone" program that received no financial support from the state of California (on the SDSU side) or the government of Malta (on the UM side), it needed to be self sustaining. Such a detailed proposal required the two sides to engage in extensive talks that at times verged on negotiations as each university found it necessary to give and take in order to reach mutual accord. The final proposal would need to be approved by multiple entities on each campus.

Vision, Positioning, and Program Goals

As suggested previously, early considerations suggested a program emphasis on the Mediterranean region. As planning began in earnest, however, this emphasis expanded to a wider global focus. The prominence of integrated marketing communications growth in the United States and the program's physical location in Europe did result in a strong focus on these two areas however every effort was made during program development and is being made during program delivery to provide a broad global emphasis. This effort has ultimately been aided by the diverse, global student body that the program has attracted.

Student goals and learning outcomes for the program were identified early in the planning as:

Goal 1: Demonstrate effective analytical and critical thinking skills to evaluate marketing problems and develop solutions to them.

Learning Outcome:

1. Construct an analysis of marketing problems and issues facing companies and organizations.

Goal 2: Understand the role and practice of marketing within an organization including theoretical and applied aspects of the marketing discipline.

Learning Outcomes:

1. Recognize, describe, and analyze key concepts such as market segmentation, targeting, positioning, and branding; and the role of product/service planning, pricing, distribution, and promotion in the marketing process.
2. Explain and provide applications of how marketing decisions are influenced by various forces in the external business environment as well as significant trends and developments affecting current and future marketing practices.

Goal 3: Understand how to develop and evaluate strategic and tactical marketing plans and programs and assess marketing performance.

Learning Outcomes:

1. Develop and analyze marketing strategies and plans that include various elements of the marketing mix.
2. Analyze markets and customers utilizing primary and secondary sources of information.

Goal 4: Understand the role of and practice of integrated marketing communications including theoretical and applied aspects.

Learning Outcomes:

1. Explain how IMC decisions are influenced by internal and external environmental factors.
2. Describe the role of IMC in the overall marketing communications program.

Goal 5: Understand how to develop and evaluate strategic and tactical IMC plans and programs and assess communications effectiveness.

Learning Outcomes:

1. Develop and analyze IMC strategies and plans that include various elements of the promotional mix including advertising, public relations, sales promotion, direct marketing, and the Internet and interactive media.
2. Produce an integrated marketing communications plan.

Program Requirements

Perhaps one of the most challenging tasks of early program development was detailing the combined requirements that would satisfy the individual requirements for each of the two degrees on its respective campus while still allowing the program to be completed in a timely manner. The goal was to create a program that could be completed in a single calendar year. Efforts began with a detailed comparison of the existing UM MA in IMC degree requirements and the existing SDSU MSBA, Marketing degree requirements. Where was the overlap? What could be considered elective in each program? The challenge of finding the common ground was exacerbated by the challenge that came with the universities using different credit unit systems. UM participates in the European Credit Transfer System (ECTS). Credit units in this system equate to US credit units at a value of 1.75 ECTS = 1.0.

For courses that were an important part of both degrees (Research Methods for example) a determination needed to be made as to which university would teach the course. Per SDSU regulations, a maximum of 30% of courses taken to satisfy the SDSU degree could be transferred from UM. Many courses in both programs satisfied overlapping requirements however there were two courses and a program culminating dissertation required by University of Malta to earn its degree that were not required by SDSU. Further, SDSU required a shorter culminating experience that could not be satisfied directly by the dissertation that UM required. These individual requirements, of course, needed to remain in the program if students were to successfully earn both degrees. The process of satisfying all the varied requirements, both course-wise and in terms of number of transferable units and number of units required to complete the degree for both degree programs was challenging and at times tedious. The final result is shown in Tables 1 and 2.

Program Delivery

Having made the decision that a significant part of each course in the program was to be delivered in a face-to-face format, the program developers were then challenged to determine how to make this happen for a program delivered in Malta but in which approximately half of the courses would be taught by SDSU faculty members. A traditional delivery that found students taking multiple courses concurrently over the period of a 10 – 15 week term would not work. It was necessary to minimize the amount of time that any individual SDSU faculty member would spend in Malta while still allowing for full and complete delivery of courses. While this constraint did not exist for University of Malta faculty it was decided early on that the delivery of SDSU and UM courses should parallel each other as much as was practical in order to provide a coordinated approach.

Table 1. SDSU degree

Course Number	Course Name/Topic	UofM Course	SDSU Units	Taught by:
COMM 574	International Advertising		3	SDSU
MKT 729	Contemporary Topics in Marketing: Branding		3	SDSU
MKT 729	Contemporary Topics in Marketing: New Media		3	SDSU
MKT 762	Integrated Marketing Communications		3	SDSU
MKT 768	Internet Marketing & E-Commerce		3	SDSU
MKT 779	Advanced Marketing Strategy		3	SDSU
TRANSFER	Consumer and Organization Buying Behaviour	CCT 5580	3[1]	UM
TRANSFER	Research Methods	CCT 5570	3	UM
TRANSFER	Consumer in the Law	CCT 5552	1[2]	UM
TRANSFER	Ethics in the Market	CCT 5531	1	UM
TRANSFER	Consumer Protection	CCT 5552	1	UM
MKT 790	Directed Readings in Marketing (SDSU Culminating Experience)		3	SDSU
	Principles of Management and Organization	CCT 5542	Not Required	UM
	Corporate Reputation	CCT 5261	Not Required	UM
	Dissertation	CCT 5901	Not Required	UM
			30	

Source: Internally developed, UM/ SDSU

Notes:

1. This course and Research Methods are 6 ECTS at University of Malta which would transfer to SDSU at approximately 3.4 units. Since a maximum of 9 units of transfer credit is allowable, however, the student receives only 3 units of SDSU credit for each of these courses.

2. This course and Ethics in the Market and Consumer Protection are 2 ECTS at University of Malta which transfer to SDSU at approximately 1.15 units. Since a maximum of 9 units of transfer credit is allowable, however, the student receives only 1 unit of SDSU credit.

Table 2. UM degree

Course Number	Course Name/Topic	SDSU Course	ECTS	Taught by:
CCT 5580	Consumer & Organization Buying Behaviour		6	UM
CCT 5570	Research Methods		6	UM
CCT 5552	The Consumer and the Law		2	UM
CCT 5552	Consumer Protection		2	UM
CCT 5531	Ethics in the Market		2	UM
CCT 5542	Principles of Management & Organization		4	UM
CCT 5261	Corporate Reputation		2	UM
TRANSFER	Integrated Marketing Communications	MKT 762	6[1]	SDSU
TRANSFER	Advanced Marketing Strategy	MKT 779	6	SDSU
TRANSFER	Contemporary Topics: Branding	MKT 729	6	SDSU
TRANSFER	E-Commerce & Internet Marketing	MKT 768	6	SDSU
TRANSFER	International Advertising	COMM 574	6	SDSU
TRANSFER	Contemporary Topics: New Media	MKT 729	6	SDSU
	SDSU Culminating Experience	MKT 790	Not Required	SDSU
CCT 5901	Dissertation/Project		30	UM
			90	

Source: Internally developed, UM/SDSU

Note:

1. A 3 unit SDSU course would transfer to UM at 5.25 units however SDSU faculty add 5.4 hours of instruction to these courses so that they transfer to UM at 6 ECTS courses.

After considering a variety of possible approaches it was decided that program courses would be delivered in a modular form, with courses delivered one at a time in a sequence over the course of two terms (September through June) followed by the completion of the SDSU program culminating experience and the UM dissertation in the summer following the second term. Six ECTS/3 Unit courses (the majority of the courses in the program) would be delivered in three week blocks. For SDSU courses, Week #1 of the three weeks would be an intensive preparation week. Students would complete assignments during this week working independently or in groups. The course instructor, in San Diego, would provide guidance during the week and conduct two online sessions totaling three hours of time. Week #2 of each SDSU course was an in-class week. The SDSU faculty member would be on the ground in Malta and eight hour class sessions would take place daily for five days. This, combined with the three hours of online instruction in Week #1 allows for 43 hours of instructional time, the 37.5 hours required by SDSU for a 3 unit course plus the extra 5.4 hours that allow the course to be transferred to UM at 6 ECTS. Week #3 of each SDSU course was planned to be a finalization week. Students would be completing a project, paper, or other "take home" assignment for the course. The faculty member would again be available virtually to provide guidance to students. This delivery system allows SDSU faculty to be gone from SDSU for only one week. For UM courses, delivery would also fall into a three week block (UM courses less than 6 ECTS meet for proportionately shorter times). Since UM instructors have greater flexibility, the structure of the three week delivery system might vary. While some UM instructors choose to follow the same pattern used by the SDSU faculty, others choose to meet face-to-face with students over the two or three weeks of the course but for shorter daily sessions.

A decision was made to link the SDSU culminating experience requirement and the UM dissertation requirement rather to leave them as two distinct projects. The SDSU culminating experience for the program was designed to be a formal proposal including literature review for the research that would comprise the UM dissertation. Although the proposal would only receive credit towards the SDSU degree and the dissertation itself would only receive credit towards the UM degree, the overall effort would be guided throughout by two faculty members – one from the University of Malta and one from San Diego State University. Students would be encouraged to remain in Malta until the research proposal had been approved by both faculty members however completion of the dissertation could occur from a global location of the student's choosing.

Partner Responsibilities

Decisions regarding the teaching responsibilities of faculty from each university were mentioned in the previous section. These decisions were largely driven by requirements (for example, in the case of SDSU 70% of its 30 unit degree had to be taught by SDSU faculty), expertise of the various faculty members at the two universities, and preferences. Beyond teaching however there was a wide variety of other responsibilities that needed to be accounted for and split between the two institutions. Decisions regarding how to split these responsibilities were sometimes based on practical considerations. For example, on-the-ground logistical issues could really only be handled by UM. In other cases the split was based on initial beliefs regarding how the program would play out. In the initial breakdown, marketing for example, was assigned to the University of Malta because it was believed that the target market for the program was southern Europe, the Mediterranean basin, and northern Africa thus Malta was better positioned for these activities. The specific split of responsibilities as detailed in the program proposal was as follows:

San Diego State University

1. Select, support, and compensate faculty members to meet curriculum requirements of the seven (7) courses assigned to SDSU; including administrative support in the preparation of teaching materials. This will include travel and per diem expenses for SDSU faculty teaching in Malta.
2. Management of the admissions and registration processes for the SDSU degree for program applicants and students.
3. Procurement of all cases and classroom teaching materials for the seven (7) SDSU courses.
4. Award the Master of Science in Business Administration degree to the students who successfully complete the program.

University of Malta

1. Select, support, and compensate faculty members to meet curriculum requirements of the eight (8) courses assigned to University of Malta including administrative support in the preparation of teaching materials.
2. Provide lodging for the visiting SDSU faculty members while they are teaching in Malta.
3. Market the collaborative degree program in the Mediterranean region and solicit qualified applicants.
4. Collect and forward the necessary admissions information, including applications, transcripts, letters of recommendation, and resumes to the SDSU Graduate School of Business.

5. Assess non-native English speaker applicant's language ability through TOEFL scores.
6. Collect program fees from admitted students and send the appropriate portion in U.S. dollars to San Diego State University.
7. Manage and provide site location logistics including classroom availability and set-up and any required audio-visual and other technological needs.
8. Manage on-the-ground logistics for visiting SDSU faculty members – to include accommodations and ground transportation while in Malta.
9. Manage order and delivery of textbook and/or other required materials as well as library and computer access.
10. Manage other day-to-day operational details as they arise during weeks that face-to-face class is in session.
11. Award the Master of Arts in Integrated Marketing Communications degree to the students who successfully complete the program.

The more comprehensive list of University of Malta responsibilities accounts for its greater share of expenses which was reflected in the program budget.

Marketing and Recruiting

Since it was a goal to attract applicants not only from Malta but from the entire Mediterranean basin, Europe, North Africa, and ultimately from around the globe, it was believed that marketing and recruiting efforts would need to focus not only on the program itself but also on the country of Malta. Given the size of Malta, the smallest country in the European Union, those familiar with the islands would have to be persuaded that it was a good choice for a year's study. Further, outside of the European Union, especially in North America and other parts of the world, people often were totally unfamiliar with Malta.

It was agreed early on that the primary focus of the marketing activities for the IMP programs would be to push potential students to the IMP website. The website, it was reasoned was a relatively inexpensive means by which to introduce interested individuals to both the program and to Malta. In addition to the website, color brochures, flyers, and promotional cards were designed and printed. These were distributed within Malta and were downloadable from the Internet. The major objective of these items, however, was to lead people to the website.

Given the centrality of the website to the program's marketing and recruiting efforts, much effort went into building the site. This involved decisions not only about the front-end but more importantly the back-end structures required to sustain the site. The front-end aspects involved such things as the color scheme, the logo for the IMP programme and other design aspects, together with the wording to be used on the different pages. Content focused not only on the program but also on Malta and living and studying in Malta. Much effort also went into ensuring that the back-end side of the site functioned well. A critical decision, made early on, was to put in place the necessary structure to ensure that any communication received via the site or from anywhere else would be answered in a meaningful way within 24 hours.

Attracting traffic to the website was the key goal of all other marketing and recruiting efforts. These efforts varied across two geographic targets, within Malta and overseas. In targeting potential Maltese students two press campaigns were undertaken in the largest circulation English language newspapers supported by banner ads on the online version of the same newspaper. Given that this was the first time that Maltese students were being asked to pay for courses run by UM, the possibility that potential local applicants were eligible to apply for government scholarships intended for local students to pursue post graduate courses overseas was a key piece of information that needed to be communicated. Additionally a number of email campaigns to recent graduates of UM undergraduate programs in relevant disciplines occurred.

Efforts were also undertaken to drive potential applicants from overseas to the website. To this end efforts were directed at ensuring that the website appeared among the top five sites that would come up from a Google search when certain terms were entered. In addition, a list of targeted countries was compiled and use was made of key words in Google that, if searched, would trigger an ad on the Google page. Traffic to the site was regularly monitored and changes, adaptation, and experimentation were regularly employed to improve traffic.

For marketing activities of a more traditional nature the IMP received the support of the UM International Office. The International Office sought to promote the IMP programs at the fairs they visited and among the agents network of UM in different countries. A US academic was also specifically tasked to visit and promote a number of graduate fairs in the United States. Representation at a small number of graduate fairs around the world did suggest that this is potentially a fruitful means of marketing and recruiting. Hence, it is an area that will be receiving increased attention to leverage this resource better in future marketing and recruiting efforts.

In addition to the formal efforts just described, informal efforts and word-of-mouth proved to also be effective recruiting techniques. At SDSU for example, faculty discussed the program in undergraduate IMC classes and the program was highlighted on the SDSU College of Business website.

Once individuals indicated a strong interest and a commitment to apply to the program, social media were used to sustain that interest. A Facebook site was created for the IMP IMC program. The site allowed highly interested students to connect with each other. Further, the site was monitored regularly and postings were made. These postings were varied and included useful links, information about happenings in Malta (including such events as concerts) and information about housing and visa requirements. The back-end staff also saw to occasional postings of information about the programs in a number of other relevant networking sites. Finally, a number of webinar conferences were also held for interested persons located around the globe. Use was also made of online Skype facilities whereby persons that showed interest in the course could, during specific times, contact a person in program admissions to clarify issues and to sort out any administrative matter at hand. It is worth pointing out that Skype was also used as a coordination tool between administrative and academic faculties at both institutions as well as by academics with students during the reading phase in the three week SDSU studying blocks. It helped academics to direct the focus of the reading by students and to answer any queries that required clarification.

Admission Requirements

The two universities had different admission criteria for their existing programs. Since applicants needed to be successful in admission to both universities this meant that they would need to meet the admission criteria of both schools.

In the case of University of Malta, requirements for the existing MA in IMC were:

1. An honours first degree (4 year undergraduate course) at second class or better.
2. In the case of students with a lower classification, students must provide evidence of a minimum of five years relevant work experience.
3. In the case of students for whom English is a foreign language, a score on the IELS test (English as a second language) better than 6.5 is required for postgraduate students.

For the existing MSBA, Marketing degree at San Diego State University, requirements were:

1. A baccalaureate degree with a minimum grade point average (GPA) of 2.8.
2. Adequate performance on the Graduate Management Admissions Test (GMAT)
3. In the case of students for whom English is a foreign language, a score on the TOEFL exam of 650 or higher.

The first and third requirements for each university were roughly equivalent. In the case of UM's second requirement, however, SDSU did not allow for undergraduate performance compensation via work experience hence it would be necessary for applicants to meet the SDSU mandated minimum GPA regardless of their work experience. More problematic was SDSU's requirement of the GMAT exam. The University of Malta argued that in Europe and northern Africa, the anticipated source of most applicants, the GMAT was not a common requirement for post-graduate programs. Hence it was strongly believed that requiring the GMAT would render the program less competitive amongst program choices. The issue was further exacerbated by the fact that the country of Malta did not have a GMAT testing facility. The closest testing locations to Malta were Tunis, Tunisia and Rome, Italy.

It was decided to appeal to SDSU for a GMAT requirement waiver for the program. The request to waive the GMAT requirement for SDSU admission was made in the form of a proposal to the SDSU Graduate Council. This was a highly unusual proposal. Such a waiver did not exist for any graduate programs on the SDSU campus. The primary concern of the Graduate Council was how qualified applicants could clearly be identified through the admission process if this requirement was waived. To address this concern, program developers proposed that minimum required performance at the undergraduate level be raised from the standards in place in both universities' existing programs. The SDSU Graduate Council ultimately agreed to a three year trial waiver of the GMAT with the following requirement in place:

- The GMAT would be waived for applicants whose first/undergraduate degree was awarded at a second class upper or better (from universities with classification systems) or a 3.3 or higher cumulative GPA. The second class upper designation is generally equivalent to the 3.3 GPA.
- Applicants whose undergraduate performance fell below this level might still be admissible however they would be required to take the GMAT.

In addition to the admission requirements detailed above, the two partner universities further agreed on common requirements regarding work experience. Applicants would be expected to have two years of relevant experience. Additionally, two letters of recommendation would be required.

Application

The program was conceived and developed as a collaborative degree program meaning successful students earned two distinct degrees, one from each university, not a single joint degree. This means that applicants needed to be accepted independently at each university in order to participate in the program. Initial thinking regarding the application process was that applicants would need to complete and submit two separate applications, one to each university. The SDSU Admissions office, a stickler for traditional handling of processes strongly preferred this approach. Indeed, the initial program proposal identified this as the approach stating, "Each partner (SDSU and UM) will handle their own admissions decisions. Applicants to the proposed program will complete and submit separate applications to each of the two institutions. Applications will be processed individually at both institutions." As this approach was further considered, however, program developers concluded that applicants would see the program as uncoordinated and find the process cumbersome if asked to complete and submit two separate applications.

Ultimately a compromise was reached. Applicants would submit a single program application to the University of Malta. The application form was specially developed to include all information required by each of the two universities. Applicants were required to submit a single fee with their application thus allowing the process to appear seamless to the applicant. The IMP IMC program administrator in Malta, upon receiving an application, would submit an application online to SDSU on behalf of the applicant. The fee paid by the applicant was sufficient to cover both the fee charged by UM and the fee charged by SDSU. The SDSU application fee was paid by UM to SDSU out of the single fee paid by the applicant. The only exception to this seamless approach is that both universities required a full set of official transcripts. Applicants were required to submit two sets of official transcripts with their application. UM then forwarded one set to SDSU when the SDSU application was submitted on the applicant's behalf. Asking the applicant to request a set of official transcripts to be sent directly to SDSU (thus avoiding the intermediary step) while seemingly logical, might have resulted in transcripts arriving at SDSU prior to an application being submitted and potentially being misplaced or causing confusion.

Although each of the two universities made independent admission decisions, clearly an applicant needed to be successful in their admission efforts at both universities to be accepted to the collaborative program. It was the preference of the program developers that a single "You're admitted" letter be sent to successful applicants. SDSU's admissions procedures, however, were fairly inflexible hence admitted students were automatically sent a computer generated acceptance to SDSU once a decision was made. UM, on the other hand, did not send acceptances to students that they had admitted until it was confirmed that the applicant had already been accepted at SDSU. For applicants who had also been successfully admitted to UM, the University of Malta program administrator would then follow the SDSU acceptance e-mail with a letter stating that the applicant had also been accepted at UM and welcoming the applicant to the collaborative degree program.

Budget

As indicated previously, the program was to be a self-supporting, stand alone initiative on both campuses. As such, revenues from student fees needed to be sufficient to cover all program expenses including faculty salaries, administrative support, and marketing efforts. Although it was not the goal of either institution for the program to be a source of profits, the program would not be approved to launch by either campus unless it broke even. The initial budget indicated a breakeven requirement of 20 students.

With no history to help estimate the number of applicants and ultimately qualified students that would begin the program, the budget was amended multiple times throughout the initial development process in order to reduce the breakeven level. This was accomplished by working to reduce expenses with faculty salaries taking the biggest hit. Faculty on both campuses graciously agreed to teach for less in a desire to see the program launched. Ultimately the breakeven point for the initial year's cohort was 10 students. It is not anticipated, however, that this figure will hold constant. To operate in future years faculty salaries will almost certainly need to be increased thus raising the likely breakeven for cohorts beyond the first to approximately 18 – 20.

The Approval Process

During the program development process, visits by the principals involved and in some cases top university officials occurred on both sides of the Atlantic. The principal program developer from San Diego State University visited Malta to meet with the principal program developers on the UM campus as well as with the Rector of the university. The Rector of UM, the director of the UM Centre for Communications Technology, and The Pro-Rector who chairs the Programme Validation Committee (PVC) visited SDSU where meetings with the program developers, the dean of the SDSU College of Business Administration, and the SDSU Provost took place.

Once a full proposal, detailing all aspects of the program, was completed, it was required to be thoroughly vetted on both campuses. On the UM campus, the Program Validating Committee (PVC) is entrusted by the Senate to ensure that programs of study offered by the University are of the required academic standard, supported by the necessary resources and are responsive to national and market needs. Concurrently, on the SDSU campus the program was reviewed by a number of curriculum committees within the College of Business Administration and by the university Graduate Council.

Approval by the required on-campus committees at both universities, however, was not the end of the road in terms of program approval. Two additional hurdles remained: a formal Memorandum of Understanding between the two universities and approval by the Western Association of Schools and Colleges (WASC). The latter was required because SDSU is accredited by WASC. New programs that will be located more than 25 miles from a school's main campus must be approved in this manner.

The Memorandum of Understanding

The bureaucracy that is San Diego State University, part of the 23 campus California State University system began to clearly rear its head as a memorandum of understanding (MOU) was being prepared. The document was initially drafted by SDSU although not by the principal program developers. Rather, because of the technical language required by the state of California, the MOU was drafted by the legal department of the university using information provided in the program proposal. Once drafted the document was sent to Malta for consideration. At the University of Malta the MOU was vetted through the legal department. Significant back and forth occurred between the two campuses prior to final agreement. At that point the document was signed by the Rector of UM and returned to SDSU where signatures from five different individuals were required.

Approval by Western Association of Schools and Colleges (WASC)

The application for approval of an off campus program required by the accrediting agency, Western Association of Schools and Colleges (WASC) consisted of six distinct sections and was approximately 90 pages in length. It was prepared by the principal program developer at SDSU with help from others on both the SDSU and UM campuses. Following review of the application, WASC required a conference call that allowed for questions by the reviewers. Due to the volume of WASC's work, scheduling the call alone was a several month process. Following review and the conference call, WASC issued conditional approval of the application. Final approval did not occur until a site visit to University of Malta was made by a WASC representative. The program was required to cover all travel costs of the site visit as well as a site visit fee.

Recruiting a Cohort

Following delays as a result of the varied approvals required, recruiting for the Fall 2008 inaugural cohort began in February 2008 following a ceremonial MOU signing in Malta that served as a public relations launch for the program. Everyone concerned recognized that this was very late. By May 2008 it was determined that the number of applications received would not produce the required cohort size to breakeven. It was decided to postpone the launch of the program by one year and to gain an early start on the recruitment of a first cohort for Fall 2009.

Although disappointing, the postponement was a decision made for both of the IMP programs initially set to launch in Fall 2008. By waiting, both programs ultimately benefited from a significantly longer period of time for recruitment, application submission, and application processing. Given challenges encountered in application processing on the SDSU campus with the first IMC cohort the decision to wait was ultimately a wise one.

By the deadline of June 2009, twenty-three applications had been received for the IMC program. One of the early visions of the program was to have a global student base whose various cultural perspectives would contribute to the learning of the entire cohort. The geographic range of the applicants suggested that this vision was indeed proven true. This was exciting news. The countries of origin of the applicants represented in the inaugural applicant pool included: Bulgaria, China, Germany, India, Iran, Malta, Nigeria, Slovakia, and the United States. It was particularly surprising to have six American (US) applicants. This was definitely not anticipated in initial planning but clearly welcomed as was the case with the wide variety of nationalities represented by others in the applicant pool. A decision to focus greater marketing efforts on the US for subsequent cohorts was made. Of the twenty-three applicants, eighteen met the qualifications to be admitted to both universities. The admission process presented a number of unanticipated challenges due to the significant bureaucracy of the SDSU system. The admissions learning curve with the first cohort of applicants was very steep with many lessons learned about how to hopefully smooth the path for future intakes.

Of the eighteen admitted to the first cohort, twelve chose to start the program. While this number was certainly less than the initial vision for program size (ideally 20 -25) and less than the initial breakeven number of 20, it was above the revised breakeven level of ten. Further a two-thirds "show rate" amongst admitted applicants was considered good.

From Launch to Culmination

The first cohort of the program began classes in Valletta, Malta in October 2009. The first course was preceded by a two day orientation. The orientation introduced students to the program, the delivery mode, and covered essential issues related to the administration and logistics of the program. Further it included team building exercises designed to build community amongst the cohort of students. Social activities in the evenings worked further to achieve this goal. Faculty members from both SDSU and the University of Malta faculty participated in the orientation.

The students, upon completion of requirements, were eligible to participate in the graduation/commencement ceremonies of both San Diego State University and the University of Malta. Unfortunately, SDSU annual commencement occurs in May for those completing their degrees in spring and the following summer. The collaborative degree students were still in Malta, taking classes, at the time of SDSU commencement. The annual UM graduation ceremony occurs in November, following the summer session when the collaborative degree students finished their program. A few local individuals were in Malta and able to attend this ceremony, the majority of the students had left Malta by the time of the traditional UM November graduation however and could not attend. Due to these circumstances, a special recognition ceremony was held in Malta for the cohort in September – this timing coincided with the students' completion of their theses/dissertations and was before the departure from Malta of many of the international students.

CHALLENGES FACED

The challenges faced in the development and implementation of the collaborative program were varied. The main challenge came from both institutions trying to adapt to each others' requirements and culture. The UM has a long tradition that dates back to 1592 and has systems that have gone through adaptation in recent years to conform with the Bologna agreement that sought to offer a degree of standardization among EU universities. With the collaborative degree program the university (UM) found itself again trying to match its requirements, in this case to those of SDSU. SDSU of course faced a similar situation complicated perhaps by an even more rigid administration that at times saw the coordinators at either end struggling to arrive at a mutually acceptable solution.

A multicultural student group is undoubtedly enriching but it is not without its challenges. Although the orientation week that occurred at the very beginning of the program sought to acclimatize the students to the location, the institution, and to foster coherence among the cohort, misunderstandings among the students and with the administration could and did occur. The course coordinators sought to act jointly despite challenges in time zones to try and sort out issues as quickly as possible throughout the year.

The different traditions of the two institutions manifested themselves in many different ways. For example, the UM masters degree requires that students write a thesis/dissertation, something that is not always a requirement in the US tradition. Further, many students who obtained their undergraduate educations in Europe have experience in completing a research project as part of those degree requirements. Because North American students generally lack experience with this type of project, they have been found to be particularly apprehensive on this issue. Workshops and clinics were held that sought to offer reassurance, direction and building of confidence among students.

Finally, the need to have SDSU professors jet over to Malta has logistical implications and while these are normally manageable, nature in terms of one or two volcanic eruptions in Iceland during the spring of 2010 and the resultant ash clouds did create some headaches.

RECOMMENDATIONS AND CONCLUSION

The road to program launch was long, time consuming, and at many points frustrating. Likewise, the first year of implementation brought an additional set of challenges. The program developers frequently found it necessary to laugh and chock seemingly insurmountable problems up to different views. "It's a cultural thing" became both a mantra and a joke as one partner attempted to explain to the other why something could not be accomplished in the way it was envisioned. There were certainly points along the way when all involved sat back and wondered whether they would have ever begun the process had they been able to foresee the road ahead. The time and angst put into program development by all involved is difficult to quantify but was clearly significant. Other responsibilities for teaching, research activity, and other professional activities not to mention personal time were frequently sacrificed in the face of the next program challenge.

It would be too simplistic to say that every bit of these sacrifices went out the window as the program principals faced the first set of faces during the inaugural cohort's orientation or even by the time of the recognition ceremony that marked the end for the first cohort. Significant attempts have been made, however, to learn from past experiences and to make improvements as the program moves forward. Looking ahead to the second cohort and beyond, recruiting efforts have been improved, the application process has been refined, and ideas for a stronger and more informative orientation are planned.

All involved believe that the venture provides a win-win situation for both universities. It has brought in new students that would otherwise have gone elsewhere. The combination of the two universities made it possible to offer a distinctive and unique dual degree program in the middle of the Mediterranean, in English that has recognition in both the US and the EU. It tapped into a market that made it possible for prospective North American students to earn a US degree in an exotic location in a country that is a full member of the EU while also obtaining a second degree that is fully recognized in the EU. Concurrently, the program offered prospective students from the region both in mainland Europe to the North and others to the South and East the chance to complete a US degree without the need to go to the US.

The multicultural nature of the cohort allowed for interesting experiences to be shared and that has helped develop and enhance lecturing and learning capabilities that cater to the diversity in the group. In the medium term, it is envisaged that the interaction among the faculties from the two institutions could enable the development of joint research pursuits in areas of common interest with particular emphasis on cross cultural influences on different aspects of Integrated Marketing Communications. Undoubtedly it is one small, but tangible, step in the path of true and proper internationalization of either institution.

Despite the challenges that have presented themselves along the road, all involved still believe strongly in what has been accomplished. This innovative program represents a transnational partnership and collaboration of educational programs in its truest sense. Although the effort associated with its development and launch has been significant it is believed that this is the type of program needed as education is redefined in today's changing technological and global environment. As new technologies continue to create bold new worlds for the delivery of knowledge, this type of program contributes to the learning curve. Further, as it becomes increasingly critical that students and graduates worldwide not only appreciate and understand but have also experienced global perspectives, a program such as this one will become not only attractive but almost required for those desiring a competitive edge. While the road has been long, this program represents the type of innovation in educational programming that is needed today and in the future.

ADDITIONAL READING

de Wit, H. (2002). *Internationalization of higher education in the United States of America and Europe: A Historical, Comparative, and Conceptual Analysis*. Westport, CT, USA: Greenport Press.

Inoue, Y. (2010). *Cases on Online and Blended Learning Technologies in Higher Education: Concepts and Practices*. Hershey, PA: IGI Global.

Jürgen, E., & Oliver, F. (2002). *Higher education in a globalising world: international trends and mutual observation*. Netherlands: Kluer Academic Publishers.

McBurnie, G., & Ziguras, C. (2007). *Transnational education: issues and trends in offshore higher education*. London, New York: Routledge.

Peter, H., & Meeri, H. (2005). *Internationalizing higher education: critical explorations of pedagogy and policy*. Netherlands: Springer.

Wit Hans de, K.J.A. (1999). *Quality and internationalisation in higher education.* Organisation for Economic Co-operation and Development Organisation.

Zajda, J.I. (2005). *International handbook on globalisation, education and policy research.* Netherlands: Springer. doi:10.1007/1-4020-2960-8

KEY TERMS AND DEFINITIONS

Collaborative Degree: A program effort between two universities that results in successful students earning two independent degrees – one from each university.

Dual Degree: Term is used interchangeably with Collaborative degree in this document.

Integrated Marketing Communications: A concept of marketing communications planning that recognizes the added value of a comprehensive plan that evaluates the strategic roles of a variety of communication disciplines—for example, general advertising, direct response, sales promotion, and public relations—and combines these disciplines to provide clarity, consistency, and maximum communications impact. [Schultz, Don E. 1993, "Maybe Definition Is in the Point of View," *Marketing News*, January 18, P.17.]

International Masters Program: one of several programs developed by the University of Malta that seek to achieve a wider exchange of cultural viewpoints, networks and experiences and at the same time provide students with global work opportunities.

Malta: A small, independent, country located in the Mediterranean Sea south of Italy. Member of the European Union.

MSBA: Master of Science in Business Administration – a graduate degree in business offered by San Diego State University. The MSBA offers a more targeted emphasis that traditional MBA programs.

Chapter 8
A Multidisciplinary Project Integrating Marketing Research, Art and Spanish Language for Social Sciences

Manuel Cuadrado-García
University of Valencia, Spain

María-Eugenia Ruiz-Molina
University of Valencia, Spain

Lourdes Hernández-Martín
London School of Economics, UK

EXECUTIVE SUMMARY

In the framework of a collaboration agreement between the University of Valencia (UV) and the London School of Economics (LSE), students from both universities have had an opportunity to take part in an interdisciplinary project based on a real decision making process in the context of cultural management.

In this chapter we describe this interdisciplinary project focusing on the contribution in the teaching-learning process of students at the University of Valencia, in the context of the subject Marketing Research. Specifically, a series of photographs is selected in order to organize an exhibition in London and, to ensure the success of the exhibition, students of the subject Marketing Research have combined sources of secondary and primary data, and have become familiar with databases of business information from the Library of the University of Valencia as well as with the commonly used software for data processing. In general, students have very much appreciated this activity as a facilitator of learning in the field.

DOI: 10.4018/978-1-60960-599-5.ch008

ORGANIZATION BACKGROUND

An important trend in education in the last decades is a movement of the focus from that of teaching to that of learning (e.g. Bates, 1995; Oliver & Omari, 1999). An evidence of this change is the wide use of problem-based learning, an instructional learner-centered approach that empowers learners to conduct research, integrate theory and practice, and apply knowledge and skills to develop a viable solution to a defined problem (Savery, 2006). The learning effectiveness and the transfer of skills of problem-based learning requires activities valued in the real world (Bransford, Brown & Cocking, 2000).

In the present chapter, we assess the outcomes of a problem-based activity in a Content and Language Integrated Learning (CLIL) program. It is a project based on a multicultural, interdisciplinary and bilingual collaboration developed between two European universities, i.e. the University of Valencia (Spain) and the London School of Economics and Political Science (United Kingdom)

In this project, students have worked on linguistic aspects, economic and managerial contents as well as other social competences. In particular, the activity was held for LSE students taking an optional course such as Spanish Language and Society, which is oriented to non-Spanish-speaking students, and for students at UV taking a core course of the Business Administration degree (i.e. Marketing Research) in English, which is not the native language for most students. Students had to do several tasks in groups related to Business and Society (qualitative and quantitative research, including a survey, data collection and statistical analysis, and written reports). Language used by LSE students was Spanish, while UV students had to communicate in English.

A pinhole exhibition was proposed as a source of inspiration for multidisciplinary activities in Higher Education studies at the University of Valencia and the London School of Economics.

What is a pinhole photography? It is a photograph which is cooked inside a metal without lens, viewfinder and even without a shutter. The light enters through a tiny hole forming the image on a photosensitive paper. fotolateras.com

Thanks to a previous bilateral interuniversity agreement in force since 2006, the Marketing Department of University of Valencia (Spain) and the Spanish Section of the Language Centre in London School of Economics (UK), with the help of the photography artists Fotolateras.com[1], decided to implement several teaching-learning activities related to the subject of marketing research (for University of Valencia students) and Spanish language (for the London School of Economics students).

In order to assess the outcomes of this activity, both qualitative and quantitative approaches have been considered. Regarding the qualitative assessment, results have allowed us to conclude that this collaboration project enables students to obtain and to process information on other realities and to improve their language skills through a motivating online learning environment. In general, students' involvement and feedback seem to confirm the positive contribution of this problem-based, interdisciplinary and bilingual activity to the teaching-learning process.

Concerning quantitative analysis, a survey to measure the student assessment of this activity was performed among participants. In particular, the survey measured student assessment on the interest of this activity for the teaching-learning process, motivation, group interaction and use of technological tools. We also considered data about student participation in this activity and final grades. After statistical processing of student assessment, participation and grades, as well as the qualitative feedback obtained from student' comments, we obtained evidence supporting the relevance of this project in the teaching-learning process and its positive implication in students' results. Notwithstanding, the project failed at encouraging group interaction and involved difficulties in the use of technology. As a result, discussion about the importance of task definition and its influence on e-learning outcomes will need to be developed.

SETTING THE STAGE

Active learning environments, in comparison to traditional classrooms, have been associated with increased student motivation (Garcia & Pontrich, 1996, Stipek et al., 1998), contributing in this way to self-regulated learning (Young, 2005). In this sense, the cognitive theory states that student motivation and performance is influenced by the will to reach specific academic objectives, that can be learning-oriented or goal-oriented (Elliott & Dweck, 1988; Ames, 1992; Dupeyrat & Mariné, 2005). Additionally, student social motivations have been also proposed as antecedents of academic goal achievement (Wentzel, 1993; Urdan & Maehr, 1995; Covington, 2000; Humphrey, 2004). Thus, student motivation is closely related with participation (Martin, 2007).

To actively involve students in their learning process, Marketing lecturers have used various learning methods and activities such as team projects (Lilly & Tippins, 2002), documented class participation (Peterson, 2001), experiential learning exercises (Gremler et al., 2000), Internet-based projects (Siegel, 2000), case-study method (Kennedy et al., 2001) and, sharing certain characteristics with the latter, problem-based learning (Savery, 2006).

In particular, problem-based learning is an instructional approach focused on the student that develops the ability to carry out research, to integrate theory and practice, and to apply knowledge and skills to reach a viable solution to a problem (Savery, 2006). However, to ensure effective learning and transfer of skills, problem-based learning requires activities highly valued in the real world (Bransford et al., 2000). Mainly used in Medicine studies, this teaching-learning method has been applied successfully in the past decades and continues to gain acceptance in various disciplines. This method can be included among active and cooperative learning strategies that use students to help each other learn (Slavin, 1990).

CASE DESCRIPTION

A pinhole exhibition: Tinned Cities/Ciudades Enlatadas is part of the activities celebrating the 10-year anniversary of the LSE Language Centre and it is conceived as an inspiration for several multidisciplinary activities.

The project has been integrated in two courses in the academic year 2009-10:

- Marketing Research, core degree of the Business Administration degree, taught in English by Manuel Cuadrado-Garcia and María-Eugenia Ruiz-Molina, marketing lecturers at the University of Valencia.

In 2009-2010, students taking this course have developed a survey that has shown the real-life implementation of marketing research. Specifically, they have undertaken a quantitative research to select 23-black and white pinhole pictures by *fotolateras.com* to be shown in an exhibition at LSE in February 2010. Thus, students have fully understood the application of the theoretical concepts of Marketing Research.

- Spanish Language and Society (Beginners) course coordinated by Lourdes Hernández-Martín, Assistant Language Co-ordinator (Spanish) at LSE.

In 2009-2010, as a part of Spanish Language and Society (Beginners), students have followed a 20-hours activity called *Still Spanish*, a workshop which aims to provide students with a basic knowledge of documentary films. As their final

Figure 1. Torres de Serranos, Valencia. (© 2009, fotolateras.com. Used with permission.)

product, students have been asked to create a multimedia essay using pictures, text and audio under the title *Cityscape*.

The 23-pictures of *Tinned Cities/Ciudades Enlatadas* by *fotolateras.com* to be shown at the exhibition have been used as material for several activities for *Still Spanish*. Among those activities, students have written the captions of the pictures for the exhibition (with a translation in English).

Students have participated in a workshop given by *fotolateras.com* on photographic techniques.

All these activities have taken place in Spanish and they have been integrated into the curriculum of the course during Lent Term.

LSE students are exposed to research on cities through different programs or projects such as LSE Cities: Urban Age[2] or the Cities Programme[3]. Their work focuses on the problematic nature of 21st Century cities[4]. Politicians, investors, planners, architects, urban designers, engineers, public service workers and private sector leaders seem to be the only inhabitants of these complex spaces which need to be developed, organised, and managed.

fotolateras.com and their collection *Tinned Cities/Ciudades Enlatadas* will bring a different narrative of the urban spaces to LSE. Witnesses of a society which watches everything but does not look, *fotolateras.com* wander the urban landscapes as *baudelarian flaneurs* "cooking" new images in their tins where past and present mixed in a singular manner. *fotolateras.com* reminds us that cities can still be lived in and experienced as romantic and mysterious landscapes.

Aims of the project

For the Marketing Department, Faculty of Economics, UV

The aims of this project are linked to the basic principles, competences and skills of the University of Valencia strategic plan and the Bologna principles. Among them: cooperation, exchange, languages, cultures, new technologies, critical thinking, etc. Focused on the UV students, the project aims

Figure 2. Trafalgar Square, London. (© 2009, fotolateras.com. Used with permission.)

- To understand the role of marketing research in an organisation and in the society, and specifically in the context of arts.
- To develop individual and team working abilities, to improve informational and communicational skills, and to learn to search and analyse different types of information resources.
- To understand the problems or situations an organisation may face, and suggesting surveys and actions to start solving them.
- To make the teaching-learning process more interesting, motivating and satisfactory.
- To make students more aware of disciplines different to business, management and marketing.

For the Spanish Section, Language Centre, LSE

This project has offered the Spanish section a means to directly address some of LSE values and strategic priorities as stated in the *LSE Strategic Plan 2008-2013*[5]:

- to implement innovative ways of teaching and learning offering students educational experiences that are engaging and relevant.
- to address the whole student experience which encompasses their social, living, study and life experiences.
- to engage with the wider community through a diverse range of activities.

From a language point of view, this project fulfills fully the criteria of the Common European Framework of Reference for Languages (CEFR) for selecting language tasks which must be "purposeful and meaningful –perceived as real life[6] - for the learners, and involve them as fully as possible"[7].

The project has also provided students with an excellent opportunity to practise all their language skills through activities involving reception, production, interaction and mediation in real life.

The objectives of this project are linked to the basic principles, competences and skills of the Strategic Plan of the University of Valencia, as well as the key topics of the European Higher Education Area, among them being cooperation, exchange, languages, culture, information and communication technologies, critical thinking, etc.

Process/Stages

In order to achieve the above mentioned objectives, a real problem in cultural management is proposed to students to be solved. The following steps are followed:

21 September 2009- 15 December 2009

In the course Marketing Research in the International Group (taught in English) at the University of Valencia, students have carried out market research in order to select, among a large number of pinhole photographs by *fotolateras.com*, the most-liked 23 photographs to be shown in a public exhibition at LSE.

Qualitative and quantitative techniques have been developed to measure the level of attractiveness of the pictures. The research population, i.e. interviewees, has been potential visitors of an art exhibition in a university campus: students, administrative personnel and academics in the University of Valencia.

In particular, the University of Valencia students have developed six activities to conduct research from the research problem definition to survey, analyse data, and develop decision making skills. In order to provide a solution to the problem of choosing 23 photos out of 53, UV students had to conduct several activities:

- define management problem and research problem,

- define research questions,
- conduct qualitative research using secondary sources of information (i.e. documents already available, not elaborated by the researchers, such as institutional websites and market research databases of the UV library, that involve generalization, analysis, synthesis or data evaluation).
- conduct quantitative research through primary sources of information (i.e. first-hand information collected by researchers), that involved questionnaire elaboration and survey to collect data from 10 respondents by student,
- Conduct data analysis through statistical analysis software (SPSS version 17).

UV students had to deliver three written reports showing and explaining the results of their qualitative research (Report 1), data collection (Report 2) and data analysis (Report 3).

Report 1 consisted of a comparative study between United Kingdom (i.e. exhibition site) and Spain (country where the research is developed) about attendance to exhibitions, camera sales and additional data allowing inferences about the popularity of photography and cultural events related to this in United Kingdom and Spain. In order to complete this task, UV students made use of the databases available in the Virtual Library of the University of Valencia.

Report 2 involved for students to develop proposals of questionnaire that were later gathered by the lecturers to elaborate an official questionnaire that will be used by all the students in the field work. The objective of this questionnaire was to gather the assessment of a representative sample of members of the university community (i.e. target market of the exhibition) about the 53 pinhole photos with the final purpose of selecting 23 for the London exhibition. In order to achieve this aim, each student needed to collect 10 valid questionnaires.

Finally, Report 3 shows the results of the questionnaires once processed with the SPSS software. The students were invited to perform a series of statistical analyses that allow to choose the 23 most preferred pictures by respondents and to conclude the potential success of the pinhole exhibition to be celebrated in London.

For students at the University of Valencia, this project was proposed as a team and voluntary activity, whose full implementation might contribute to the student's final grade in a maximum of 1 point out of 10.

15 December 2009-10 January 2010

Fotolateras.com have organised the exhibition to be taken place in London according to the results of the research. In this sense, *Fotolateras.com* have sent copies of the 23 selected photographs via email to Lourdes Hernandez-Martin to be integrated in the activities of *Still Spanish*.

January 2010

Once the 23 photos were selected as a result of the research conducted by the students at the University of Valencia, the students of Spanish Language and Culture at the London School of Economics were invited to develop a caption and a text (in Spanish with a translation in English) to accompany each of the photographs in the exhibition in London, under the collaborative agreement between both the universities. The inter-university project was designed as a multicultural, interdisciplinary and bilingual project; each student at LSE was required to develop this task individually.

All activities have been performed in Spanish.

16-23 February

- Exhibition at LSE: Tinned Cities/Ciudades Enlatadas. Inauguration: 16 February

2010, Time: 19.30, Place: Atrium Gallery, Old Building.

- Workshop. The artists will give a 4-hours workshop to students of Spanish Language and Society (Beginners) in Spanish on photographic techniques focusing on pinhole techniques using tins.

Day: 17 February 2010, Time: 14.00-16.00

Weather permitted, students will have the opportunity "to *photo-tin*": 18 February 2010, Time: 9.00-11.00

METHODOLOGY FOR ANALYZING TEACHING-LEARNING OUTCOMES

With these activities we expect to increase student motivation, comprehension of the contents of the respective subjects and the involvement in class activities. In order to assess these expected outcomes, we have combined both qualitative and quantitative data. Regarding the former, we have considered the quality of the tasks developed by the students during the course, as well as the feedback received.

Figure 3. 5th Ave., New York. (© 2009, fotolateras.com. Used with permission.)

Regarding quantitative inputs, we have conducted a survey among students to assess motivation, group interaction, use of technology, and the suitability of problem-based learning. The items of the questionnaire have been adapted from Hazari et al. (2009) and proposed by the authors; data have been processed through SPSS statistical software to obtain descriptive statistics and contingence tables.

To evaluate the results of this pilot activity for the UV students, the first consideration was student participation in this activity, both quantitatively and qualitatively. In this sense, although this activity was voluntary and its contribution to the student final grade was scarce (i.e. 10% maximum), almost all enrolled students took part in this project. In particular, 57 out of 64 students (i.e. 89.06%) submitted at least one of the three reports under this activity. Regarding the quality of the reports submitted, it is quite high, being the average grade "outstanding".

Second, on the last day of the class a questionnaire based on the proposal of Hazari et al. (2009) was administered in order to gather students' evaluation of their perception of the educational contribution of this activity, their motivation for problem-based learning activities, the ability of this activity to encourage interaction within the group and the use of technology tools such as databases of the Digital Library of the University of Valencia and the statistical software SPSS. Additionally, classification questions were included.

Respondents were asked to rank each statement in a 5-point Likert scale according to their level of agreement or disagreement (1 = I totally disagree, 2 = I disagree, 3 = neutral, 4 = I agree, 5 = I totally agree). Results for 56 valid questionnaires are shown in Table 1.

Regarding the assessment of the pinhole activity by the UV students, the results obtained are encouraging, since the scores exceed the midpoint of the 5-point Likert scale (i.e., 3) for all items considered. In particular, high scores are obtained for the items "I would recommend classes that

Table 1. Students' assessment of the pinhole activity contribution to the teaching-learning process

	Mean	St. Dev.
1. The Pinhole Exhibition activities were overall easy to understand	3.95	0.796
2. I liked interacting with other students in the Pinhole Exhibition activity	3.73	0.842
3. I would prefer classes that use problem-based activities over other classes that do not use this kind of activities	3.36	1.227
4. Using SPSS was easy	3.02	0.981
5. The Pinhole Exhibition activities aided me in achieving course objectives	3.59	0.813
6. I stayed on the task more because of the Pinhole Exhibition activities	3.36	0.841
7. I would like to see problem-based activities used in other courses	3.79	0.825
8. Benefit of the Pinhole Exhibition activities is worth the extra effort & time required to work on them	3.45	0.807
9. I participated in the assignment more because of this problem-based activity	3.47	0.690
10. Benefits of using the SPSS outweighed any technical challenges of its use	3.27	0.952
11. The Pinhole Exhibition activities helped me interact more with students	3.64	0.841
12. Technical features of SPSS helped enhance my learning	3.36	1.103
13. Because of working on a real problem-based activity, my group was able to come to a consensus faster	3.59	0.910
14. I will retain more material as a result of taking part in the Pinhole Exhibition activity	3.47	0.790
15. I would recommend classes that use real problem-based activities to other students	4.16	0.811
16. Compared to SPSS, the Euromonitor database was easier to use	3.87	1.090
17. Development of a real marketing research promoted collaborative learning	3.96	0.687
18. I learned more because of information shared with other students in the Pinhole Exhibition activities	3.36	0.749
19. The Pinhole Exhibition activity enhanced my interest in the course	3.66	0.837
20. I will continue to explore use of databases for education	3.63	0.964

use real problem-based activities to other students" (4.16), "Development of a real marketing research promoted collaborative learning" (3.96) and "The Pinhole Exhibition activities were overall easy to understand" (3.95). Notwithstanding, the questionnaire also shows as the worst rated items those relating to the use of technology tools: e.g. " Benefits of using the SPSS outweighed any technical challenges of its use" (3.27) and "Using SPSS was easy" (3.02).

Grouping the items in Table 1 in the four factors identified by Hazari et al. (2009), i.e., Learning/ Pedagogy, Motivation, Group Interaction and Technology, we have estimated the average of the items included in each factors. Results are shown in Table 2.

The results obtained provide evidence in the sense that our problem-based activity is not encouraging group interaction as expected. Thus, although Reports 1 and 3 were to be developed in teams, it seems as if team members divided tasks and worked individually. This finding has relevant implications for task definition.

Furthermore, the resulting average for the Technology factor supports the difficulties experienced by some students with the technological

Table 2. Students' assessment of the pinhole activity contribution to their English command

Factor	Items no.	Mean	St. dev.
Technology	1, 4, 10, 12, 16	3.48	0.557
Motivation	3, 6, 8, 15, 20	3.71	0.491
Group Interaction	2, 11, 13, 17, 18	3.13	0.435
Learning/Pedagogy	5, 7, 9, 14, 19	3.60	0.493

tools used during the course. Notwithstanding, the high value of the standard deviation for this factor reflects the heterogeneity of the assessments expressed by students regarding this issue.

On the other hand, the high average scores for student motivation and the contribution of this activity to learning are encouraging. Therefore, the fact of conducting a real research project from the beginning to the end seems to have encouraged students to actively follow the course and to complete the different tasks, contributing positively to the assessment of their learning in this subject.Additionally, UV students were requested to contribute to this activity to improve their English command. Results of the comparison of their command at the completion of the project to the previous English command are shown in Table 3.

As a result, we observe that half of the students consider that taking part in this activity has positively contributed to the development of their communication skills in English. In particular, this improvement is assessed as more relevant to the improvement of the English command of the student. Therefore, we obtain evidence supporting a positive impact of the proposed problem-based activity on the teaching-learning of Marketing Research and on the student language skills.

Table 3. Students' assessment of the pinhole activity contribution to their English command

English	Pinhole activity contribution to English command			Total
command	None	Fair	Significant	
Intermediate	2 3.6%	10 17.9%	1 1.8%	13 23.2%
Advanced	19 33.9%	10 17.9%	2 3.6%	31 55.4%
Proficiency	5 8.9%	5 8.9%	0 0.0%	10 17.9%
Native	2 3.6%	0 0.0%	0 0.0%	2 3.6%
Total	28 50.0%	25 44.6%	3 5.4%	56 100.0%

Chi-squared: 10.807 (p-value: 0.095)

Finally, the questionnaire included an open question -"Any additional comments? (such as what you liked MOST/LEAST about the Pinhole exhibition marketing research)"- inviting students to provide qualitative feedback about their experience in this problem-based activity. Results are shown in Table 4.

Although this was the last question and was not as quick to answer as the preceding multiple choice or 5-point-scale questions, nearly a quarter of students developed and provided their impressions about this activity. In particular, 12.5% of students responded to this question with thankful and supporting comments, encouraging the lecturers to repeat this type of activity in further courses.

On the other hand, all negative comments were focused on complaints about the difficulties experienced with the use of SPSS software and the speed of computer processing. Regarding the latter, there were some problems with computers in some sessions due to a failure in the UV network. Notwithstanding, some students suggested the convenience of including an additional session to get familiar with the SPSS software before developing the required task and, thus, we shall take this idea into account for further courses.

CONCLUSION, LIMITATIONS AND RECOMMENDATIONS

A problem-based learning approach was adopted to design a Marketing Research course activity to be developed sequentially to enable students

Table 4. Students assessment of the pinhole activity contribution to their English command

Type of feedback	Number of students	%
Positive	7	12.5%
Positive & negative	1	1.8%
Negative	4	7.1%
None	45	78.6%

to achieve course objectives in a more efficient way in comparison with traditional methods. Following the evidence obtained for the UV Marketing Research course, we consider that the interdisciplinary collaboration between UV and LSE through this project has involved positive effects on students' motivation, involvement and performance. In particular, we have obtained results supporting that, even if there is a low extrinsic reward for the student because of his/her participation, he/she becomes actively implicated in the activities proposed if he/she considers them as exciting, challenging and useful for solving a real-world problem. This result has implications for the design of attractive teaching-learning activities that may stimulate student's participation therefore contributing to improve his/her final results. This evidence is in the line of Deci & Ryan (1985), who assumed that the activation of intrinsic motivation is determined to a great extent by characteristics of the task. In this sense, we agree with Bergin (1992) regarding the existence of a relationship between motivation, academic activities and leisure that the lecturer must take advantage of in favour of the teaching-learning process.

All in all, the results obtained for the students of University of Valencia seem to support the positive influence of this interdisciplinary activity in the students' performance and the use of learning methods that facilitate active and cooperative learning through problem-based activities. The collaboration project allowed students from two different disciplines and different universities not only to meet the learning objectives of their corresponding courses, but also to get information on other realities (i.e. arts management) and to improve their foreign language skills. Both the qualitative and quantitative results seem to confirm the positive contribution of this interdisciplinary problem-based learning activity to the teaching-learning process and, according to previous literature, the convenience of the use of this method in Higher Education classrooms.

However, the evidence is not conclusive, as it has been an exploratory research and the activity should be replicated in further years and for different courses. Regarding the quantitative data, the results obtained could be biased because some students' work in groups for Reports 1 and 3 that may find an incentive to act as "free riders", since the grade for these reports was common for all team members. On the other hand, causality between participation indicators and student's final grade has not been explored. In this sense, do students have better results because of their participation in this problem-based learning activity? Or do the "best" students tend to participate in this activity more than others? "Best" students might be more intrinsically motivated by these class activities and vice versa. In this sense, considering the performance of students in other subjects and qualitative analysis – e.g. interviews with students – might contribute to shed additional light on the results of this research.

REFERENCES

Ames, C. (1992). Classrooms: Goals, structures, and student motivation. *Journal of Educational Psychology*, *84*(3), 261–271. doi:10.1037/0022-0663.84.3.261

Bates, A. (1995). *Technology, open learning and distance education*. New York, NY: Routledge.

Bergin, D. A. (1992). Leisure activity, motivation, and academic achievement in high school students. *Journal of Leisure Research*, *24*(3), 225–239.

Bransford, J. D., Brown, A. L., & Cocking, R. R. (2000). *How people learn: Brain, mind, experience, and school*. Washington, DC: National Academy Press.

Covington, M. V. (2000). Goal theory, motivation and school achievement: An integrative review. *Annual Review of Psychology*, *51*, 171–200. doi:10.1146/annurev.psych.51.1.171

Deci, E. L., & Ryan, R. M. (1985). *Intrinsic motivation and self-determination in human behavior*. New York, NY: Plenum.

Dupeyrat, C., & Mariné, C. (2005). Implicit of intelligence, goal orientation, cognitive engagement, and achievement: A test of Dweck's model with returning to school adults. *Contemporary Educational Psychology*, *30*(1), 43–59. doi:10.1016/j.cedpsych.2004.01.007

Elliot, E., & Dweck, C. (1988). Goals: An approach to motivation and achievement. *Journal of Personality and Social Psychology*, *54*(1), 5–12. doi:10.1037/0022-3514.54.1.5

Garcia, T., & Pontrich, P. R. (1996). The effects of autonomy on motivation and performance in the college classroom. *Contemporary Educational Psychology*, *21*(4), 477–486. doi:10.1006/ceps.1996.0032

Gremler, D. D., Hoffman, K. D., Keaveney, S. M., & Wright, L. K. (2000). Experiential learning exercises in services marketing courses. *Journal of Marketing Education*, *22*(1), 35–44. doi:10.1177/0273475300221005

Hazari, S., North, A., & Moreland, D. (2009). Investigating pedagogical value of Wiki technology. *Journal of Information Systems Education*, *20*(2), 187–198.

Humphrey, N. (2004). The death of the feel-good factor? *School Psychology International*, *25*(3), 347–360. doi:10.1177/0143034304046906

Kennedy, E. J., Lawton, L., & Walker, E. (2001). The case for using live cases: Shifting the paradigm in marketing education. *Journal of Marketing Education*, *23*(2), 145–151. doi:10.1177/0273475301232008

Lilly, B., & Tippins, M. J. (2002). Enhancing student motivation in marketing classes: Using student management groups. *Journal of Marketing Education*, *24*(3), 253–264. doi:10.1177/0273475302238048

Martin, A. J. (2007). Examining a multidimensional model of student motivation and engagement using a construct validation approach. *The British Journal of Educational Psychology*, *77*(2), 413–440. doi:10.1348/000709906X118036

Oliver, R., & Omari, A. (1999). Using online technologies to support problem based learning: Learners' responses and perceptions. *Australian Journal of Educational Technology*, *15*(1), 58–79.

Peterson, R. M. (2001). Course participation: An active learning approach employing student documentation. *Journal of Marketing Education*, *23*(3), 187–194. doi:10.1177/0273475301233004

Savery, J. R. (2006). Overview of problem-based learning: Definitions and distinctions. *The Interdisciplinary Journal of Problem-based Learning*, *1*(1), 9–20.

Siegel, C. E. (2000). Introducing marketing students to business intelligence using project-based learning on the World Wide Web. *Journal of Marketing Education*, *22*(2), 90–98. doi:10.1177/0273475300222003

Slavin, R. E. (1990). *Cooperative learning*. New Jersey: Prentice-Hall.

Stipek, D. J., Salmon, J. S., & Givven, K. B. (1998). The value of practices suggested by motivation research and promoted by mathematics education reformers. *Journal for Research in Mathematics Education*, *29*(4), 465–488. doi:10.2307/749862

Urdan, T., & Maehr, M. L. (1995). Beyond a two-goal theory of motivation: A case for social goals. *Review of Educational Research*, *65*(3), 213–244.

Wentzel, K. R. (1993). Does being good make the grade? Social behavior and academic competence in middle school. *Journal of Educational Psychology*, *85*(2), 357–364. doi:10.1037/0022-0663.85.2.357

Young, M. R. (2005). The motivational effects of the classroom environment in facilitating self-regulated learning. *Journal of Marketing Education*, *27*(1), 25–40. doi:10.1177/0273475304273346

ADDITIONAL READING

Albanese, M. A., & Mitchell, S. (1993). Problem-based learning: A review of the literature on its outcomes and implementation issues. *Academic Medicine*, *68*(1), 52–81. doi:10.1097/00001888-199301000-00012

Appleton-Knapp, S. L., & Krentler, K. A. (2006). Measuring Student Expectations and Their Effects on Satisfaction: The Importance of Managing Students Expectations. *Journal of Marketing Education*, *28*(3), 254–264. doi:10.1177/0273475306293359

Association of College & Research Libraries. (2000). Information Literacy Competency Standards for Higher Education. Retrieved February 13, 2010, from http://www.ala.org/ala/acrl/acrlstandards/informationliteracycompetencystandards.cfm.

Boekaerts, M. (1997). Self-regulated learning: A new concept embraced by researcher, policy makers, educators, teachers and students. *Learning and Instruction*, *7*(2), 161–186. doi:10.1016/S0959-4752(96)00015-1

Denton, B. G., Adams, C. C., Blatt, P. J., & Lorish, C. D. (2000). Does the introduction of problem-based learning change graduate performance outcomes in a professional curriculum? *Journal on Excellence in College Teaching*, *11*(2&3), 147–162.

Garcia, T., & Pontrich, P. R. (1996). The effects of autonomy on motivation and performance in the college classroom. *Contemporary Educational Psychology*, *21*(4), 477–486. doi:10.1006/ceps.1996.0032

Gremler, D. D., Hoffman, K. D., Keaveney, S. M., & Wright, L. K. (2000). Experiential learning exercises in services marketing courses. *Journal of Marketing Education*, *22*(1), 35–44. doi:10.1177/0273475300221005

Hmelo-Silver, C. E. (2004). Problem-based learning: What and how do students learn? *Educational Psychology Review*, *16*(3), 235–266. doi:10.1023/B:EDPR.0000034022.16470.f3

Hmelo-Silver, C. E., & Barrows, H. S. (2006). Goals and strategies of a problem-based learning facilitator. *Interdisciplinary Journal of Problem-based Learning*, *1*(1), 21–39.

Hsu, J. (2007). Innovative Technologies for Education and Learning. *International Journal of Information and Communication Technology Education*, *3*(3), 70–89. doi:10.4018/jicte.2007070107

Kirschner, P. A., Sweller, J., & Clark, R. E. (2006). Why minimal guidance during instruction does not work: an analysis of the failure of constructivist, discovery, problem-based, experiential, and inquiry-based teaching. *Educational Psychologist*, *41*(2), 75–86. doi:10.1207/s15326985ep4102_1

Lilly, B., & Tippins, M. J. (2002). Enhancing student motivation in marketing classes: Using student management groups. *Journal of Marketing Education*, *24*(3), 253–264. doi:10.1177/0273475302238048

Loranger, A. L. (1994). The study of strategies of successful high school students. *Journal of Reading Behavior*, *26*(4), 347–360.

Merrill, M. D. (2002). A pebble-in-the-pond model for instructional design. *Performance Improvement*, *41*(7), 39–44. doi:10.1002/pfi.4140410709

Peterson, R. M. (2001). Course participation: An active learning approach employing student documentation. *Journal of Marketing Education*, *23*(3), 187–194. doi:10.1177/0273475301233004

Schmidt, H. G. (1993). Foundations of problem-based learning: some explanatory notes. *Medical Education*, *27*(5), 422–432. doi:10.1111/j.1365-2923.1993.tb00296.x

Siegel, C. E. (2000). Introducing marketing students to business intelligence using project-based learning on the World Wide Web. *Journal of Marketing Education*, *22*(2), 90–98. doi:10.1177/0273475300222003

Stinson, J. E., & Milter, R. G. (1996). Problem-based learning in business education: Curriculum design and implementation issues. In Wilkerson, L., & Gijselaers, W. H. (Eds.), *Bringing problem-based learning to higher education: Theory and practice. New Directions For Teaching and Learning Series, No. 68* (pp. 32–42). San Francisco, CA: Jossey-Bass.

Stipek, D. J., Salmon, J. S., & Givven, K. B. (1998). The value of practices suggested by motivation research and promoted by mathematics education reformers. *Journal for Research in Mathematics Education*, *29*(4), 465–488. doi:10.2307/749862

Sweller, J. (1988). Cognitive load during problem solving: Effects on learning. *Cognitive Science*, *12*(2), 257–285. doi:10.1207/s15516709cog1202_4

Sweller, J. (2006). The worked example effect and human cognition. *Learning and Instruction*, *16*(2), 165–169. doi:10.1016/j.learninstruc.2006.02.005

Sweller, J., Van Merrienboer, J., & Paas, F. (1998). Cognitive architecture and instructional design. *Educational Psychology Review*, *10*(3), 251–296. doi:10.1023/A:1022193728205

KEY TERMS AND DEFINITIONS

Content and Language Integrated Learning (CLIL): Lecturer and students of content subjects (e.g. History, Economics, Business, Political Sciences, etc.) use a foreign or second language as the medium of communication and instruction. In this sense, CLIL is a means of learning a language, and of introducing international aspects into the teaching of content subjects.

Cooperative Learning: Educational strategy through which students learn from others.

Problem-Based Learning: Instructional student-centered approach that empowers students to conduct research, integrating theory and practice, and applying knowledge and skills to develop a feasible solution to a problem proposed by the instructor.

ENDNOTES

1. For more information on their work, please visit the web page of the two artists http://www.fotolateras.com/.
2. http://www.urban-age.net/01_introduction/intro_idea.htm.
3. http://www.lse.ac.uk/collections/cities/.
4. In China, India, Africa, and Latin America, urban populations are exploding and cities are growing exponentially. At the same time, many developed cities are shrinking and being radically restructured as a result of shifting economic bases and new patterns of migration. (…)Urban policymakers are struggling to balance this massive growth in public and private investment with more sustainable forms of urban development. Questions regarding the shape, size, density and distribution of the city have become increasingly complex and politicised. … http://www.urban-age.net/01_introduction/intro_idea.html.

5 Planning and Corporate Policy Division, London School of Economics. LSE Strategic Plan 2008-2013. London, UK.

6 Common European Framework, http://www.coe.int/T/DG4/Portfolio/documents/Framework_EN.pdf, p.161.

7 Common European Framework, http://www.coe.int/T/DG4/Portfolio/documents/Framework_EN.pdf p. 153.

8 Common European Framework, http://www.coe.int/T/DG4/Portfolio/documents/Framework_EN.pdf p.14.

Chapter 9
A Four-Step Process to Reposition Small Schools as Sites within Teaching and Learning Networks

Ken Stevens
Memorial University of Newfoundland, Canada

EXECUTIVE SUMMARY

The international problem facing small high schools in rural communities of providing access to educational and vocational opportunities that approximate those available to urban students has been addressed by repositioning these institutions as sites within teaching and learning networks in the Canadian province of Newfoundland and Labrador. Four inter-connected dimensions of change are outlined (technological, pedagogical, organizational, and conceptual) whereby small rural schools in this Canadian province were repositioned as sites in teaching and learning networks thereby enhancing educational and vocational opportunities for senior students. There are implications in these changes for the professional education of high school teachers who are increasingly likely to be required to teach in networked classes as well as in traditional classrooms.

BACKGROUND

The decline of traditional rural education in the Canadian province of Newfoundland and Labrador coincided with a pan-Canadian initiative over a decade ago to prepare people across the country for the Information Age (Information Highway Advisory Council,1997; Ertl and Plante, 2004), providing impetus for the classroom application of emerging technologies. In rural Newfoundland and Labrador the introduction of the Internet and

DOI: 10.4018/978-1-60960-599-5.ch009

internet-based technologies has had a transforming effect on the capacity of small schools to deliver programs (Brown, et.al. 2000, Healey and Stevens, 2002; Stevens, 2001; 1999a). In other developed countries with substantial rural populations to be educated there have also been major changes in the configuration of small schools in isolated communities. In New Zealand (Stevens, 2000; 1999b), Finland (Tella, 1995), Iceland (Stevens, 2002), Russia (Stevens et al, 1999) and the USA (Dorniden, 2005; Glick, 2005; Schrum, 2005) a variety of communication technologies have been engaged to promote educational opportunities for students and more efficient ways of organizing and managing knowledge in collaborative electronic structures that have implications for regional economies.

The rapid growth and educational application of the Internet has led to a challenge to traditional ways of teaching and learning at a distance (Ben-Jacob et al, 2000) that were based on paper and the postal system. E-Learning is Internet-based and does not require the degree of central control that distance educators have traditionally employed within dedicated institutions. The growth of e-learning in schools has led to pedagogical considerations and to the development of new ways of managing knowledge that enable these institutions to assume extended roles in the regions they serve. These changes have implications for the professional education of teachers.

In the last decade two e-learning developments have changed the nature of education in rural Canada and, in particular, in the province of Newfoundland and Labrador, including the introduction of the opportunity to study online from schools located in remote communities and the possibility of enrolment in Advanced Placement (AP) courses from rural schools (see Note 1).

CASE DESCRIPTION

The Development of Collaborative Structures to Support Rural Canadian Schools

The search for appropriate new educational structures for the delivery of education to students in rural Newfoundland and Labrador has led to the development of school district intranets, within which virtual classes have been organized. In the process of developing e-teaching within school district intranets, several challenges have had to be met. The electronic linking of eight sites within the former Vista school district to collaborate in the teaching of AP Biology, Chemistry, Mathematics and Physics created a series of open classes in rural Newfoundland that became known as the Vista School District Digital Intranet (See Note 2). The creation of the Vista School District Digital Intranet was an attempt to use information and communication technologies to provide geographically-isolated students with extended educational and, indirectly, vocational opportunities. The development of the intranet within a single school district involved the introduction of an open teaching and learning structure to a closed one (See Note 3). Accordingly, adjustments had to be made in each participating site so that administratively and academically, AP classes could be taught. The Vista school district initiative challenged the notion that senior students in small schools have to leave home to complete their education at larger schools in urban areas. By participating in open classes in real (synchronous) time, combined with a measure of independent (asynchronous) learning, senior students were able to interact with one another through audio, video and electronic whiteboards.

In eight schools within the rural Vista school district of Newfoundland and Labrador, 55 students were enrolled in AP Biology, Chemistry, Mathematics and Physics courses. While AP courses are a well-established feature of senior secondary education in the United States and Canada, it was unusual for students to be able to enroll for instruction at this level in small schools in remote communities. The advanced nature of these courses requires highly qualified and experienced teachers who are often difficult to attract and retain in small schools in rural communities. Furthermore, small rural schools, because of their size, have few students who are able to undertake instruction at this level. This initiative was significant for rural Canadian education in that it was, as far as can be ascertained, the first time courses at this level were delivered to students who would otherwise not have had access to them because of the size and location of their schools. By introducing AP subjects to small schools in a remote region of Canada, a step was taken toward inclusion of rural people in the emerging knowledge economy. Several graduates of this program were subsequently able to enroll in science and engineering faculties at the local university with a small part of their post-secondary program already completed. Perhaps, more importantly, they entered universities with the knowledge that they could successfully compete academically with students anywhere in North America.

The major change for students in the first intranet in Newfoundland and Labrador was the opportunity to study advanced science subjects and mathematics as members of open classes from their small, remote communities. Students in the Vista school district intranet were frequently subject to scrutiny by their peers as they responded to one another through chat-rooms, audio and video as well as with their AP on-line teacher. The intranet provided students with access to multiple sites simultaneously, as well as the opportunity to work independently of a teacher for part of the day. The need to prepare for classes before going on-line became increasingly apparent to both teachers and students if the open, synchronous, science classes were to succeed.

The advent of the intranet had implications for students who began to interact with teachers and their peers in a variety of new ways. Many students experienced difficulty expressing themselves and, in particular, asking questions in open electronic classes when they did not know their peers from other small communities. The organization of social occasions for students learning science in open classes in the Intranet helped overcome these problems. As students became more comfortable with one another, inhibitions such as asking questions on-line were overcome. The e-teachers had little to guide their practice in teaching at this level for the first time. Each of the four AP science subjects was taught in a different way. For example, the physics and mathematics teachers had little need for video in their interactions with students, but access to electronic whiteboards was critical so that the development of equations and calculations could be managed interactively. For the e-teacher of chemistry experimental work posed a problem because of the dispersed locations of the students. Videos of experiments that were to be conducted in person, at designated sites and pre-arranged times, were found to be useful in preparing students for the laboratory component of the AP course.

In the process of developing e-teaching and e-learning within intranets in rural Newfoundland and Labrador, teachers, learners and administrators had to adapt to a new, electronic educational structure. In the open teaching and learning environment of an intranet, participating institutions academically and administratively interfaced for that part of the school day during which classes were taught. This was, for teachers and administrators, a different educational structure from the traditional and, by comparison, closed educational environment of the autonomous school with its own teachers and its own students.

There was potential conflict between the local school as an autonomous educational institution serving a designated area and schools that became, in effect, sites within electronic teaching and learning networks serving a particular region. Principals and teachers appointed to the closed, autonomous learning environments of traditional schools frequently discovered that the administration of knowledge required the development of open structures within which they were increasingly expected to collaborate with their peers located on a range of distant sites. Many discovered that the positions to which they were appointed in traditional (closed) schools became, in effect, locations within new (open) electronic schools.

The need for increased technical support for the new, open structure became increasingly urgent for teachers and students who were using information and communication technologies to teach and learn across dispersed sites. Both had to be provided with expert advice and instruction in the use of new applications. A problem that emerged was difficulty in securing and maintaining instructional design expertise in the preparation and upgrading of courses, although this issue is common in the development of on line courses at high school level. An essential aspect of the development of open electronic classes was the coordination of both hardware and software between schools. Without synchronized technology, schools cannot fully participate in electronic networks. However, the purchase of appropriate hardware and software was initially a matter of confusion for many Principals, teachers and school boards who had to seek expert advice and support. Many rural schools with open electronic classes realized that the successful administration of a network required shared local technical support. Unless adequate technical support systems could be established, electronic networked classes could, potentially, be curtailed by teachers who argued, with justification, that there was insufficient technical support for their investment in e-learning. While there were doubts by some teachers and administrators about the adequacy and robustness of the technology that was available, the solutions that were sought and the infrastructure that was implemented were at the regional rather than local school district level.

The changes that took place in the closed learning spaces of traditional rural schools in Newfoundland and Labrador with the introduction of an intranet and AP instruction online led to a ministerial inquiry into the implications of these developments for the future of rural education in the province. The provincial government, after a ministerial inquiry (Government of Newfoundland and Labrador, 2000) expanded the linking of schools through the creation of the Centre for Distance Learning and Innovation (CDLI) within the Newfoundland and Labrador Department of Education. CDLI (http://www.cdli.ca/) develops and administers online learning that complements traditional classes in schools throughout the province. Since its inception it has considerably extended e-learning throughout Newfoundland and Labrador.

A Four Step Process to Reposition Small Schools

The development of the first school district intranet in Newfoundland and Labrador involved a matrix of technological, pedagogical, organizational and conceptual change (Stevens, 2007). In rural Newfoundland and Labrador this matrix supported the creation of a rural school district intranet of four interconnected dimensions:

Technological	Pedagogical
Organization	Conceptual

Technologically, the development of the school district intranet was difficult. In many parts of the province the telecommunications infrastructure was barely adequate to link schools within such a structure. Minimum specifications were adopted for computer hardware and network connectivity. All schools involved in the project had DirecPC satellite dishes installed to provide a high speed down-link. In most rural communities in this part of Canada, digital telecommunications infrastructures do not enable schools to have a high speed uplink to the internet. Appropriate software had to be identified and evaluated for both the development of the resources and the delivery of instruction within the Intranet. Front Page 98 was selected as the software package. Additional software was used for the development of images, animated gifs and other dimensions of course development. These included Snagit32, Gif Construction Set, Real Video, and similar packages. Many software packages were evaluated and finally WebCT was selected. This package enabled the instructor to track student progress, it contained online testing and evaluation, private E-mail, a calendar feature, public bulletin board for use by both instructor and student, a link to lessons and chat rooms for communication between teacher and student. For real - time instruction, Meeting Point and Microsoft NetMeeting were selected. This combination of software enabled a teacher to present real-time interactive instruction to multiple sites. An orientation session was provided for students prior to the implementation of this project. Students had to learn how to communicate with each other and with their instructor using these new technologies before classes could begin.

Pedagogically the integration of schools in a single district meant teaching in ways that were different from traditional classroom practices. Instead of providing instruction exclusively within their own classrooms, teachers had to consider teaching collaboratively from one site to another in what became shared teaching and learning space. The challenge of teaching between rather than exclusively in schools focused attention on what Van Manen (2002) terms "the pedagogical task of teaching." For some teachers this was difficult to accept when a colleague on another site had the role of teaching AP students on line in his or her school, from another school in the district intranet. For those teachers who taught the initial AP subjects of Chemistry, Mathematics, Physics and Biology within the new collaborative structure (the school district intranet) there was little pedagogy to guide them other than, for one of the teachers, previous experience as a distance education instructor. Issues arose in the delivery of classes between schools (or sites) involving the balance of synchronous and asynchronous instruction, motivation, control, student lack of confidence based on inexperience in learning other than by formal classroom instruction and assessment. One of the first challenges for students was how to interact online, with peers they had not met. In some cases this led to awkwardness and embarrassment that threatened to impede learning. Teachers had to adjust to talking less during lessons and to prepare questions very carefully so that all students could participate. The development of judicious questioning by teachers helped students learn from one another as they all considered how to respond.

Organizationally, the integration of schools in a district intranet involved institutional collaboration beginning with the coordination of senior class timetables so that students located on multiple sites could be taught together online. Unlike earlier initiatives in New Zealand (Stevens and Moffatt, 2003), where self-governing schools do not have assistance and direction from school boards, Newfoundland and Labrador schools were organized in school districts in each of which there was a board office that provided administrative, curriculum and technological support. The first rural district digital network was organized by the board office, including the selection of online teachers together with technical and organizational support. During the first year of operation the issue of schools coordinating their timetables for senior classes was not fully resolved so that some classes had to be repeated. It became apparent during the initial year that students needed on site as well as on line support if they were to succeed. This was not understood before the intranet was established as the participating students were considered by everyone – teachers, parents and themselves to be "independent learners." In almost all cases AP students in each of the four initial science subjects reported that they needed help to stay "on task" to succeed. In subsequent years some teachers were appointed as "mediating" teachers (M-teachers) whose job, in addition to teaching traditional classes on site, was to mentor and assist where necessary and liaise with the e-teacher teaching from another site (Barbour and Mulcahy, 2005).

Conceptually, the development of a school district intranet involved a different way of thinking about teaching, learning and the organization of schools. The first conceptual change for teachers was that rather than being appointed to teach their own classes, in their own classrooms, in the schools to which they were appointed, a selected few were asked to teach other teacher's students, located in other classrooms beyond their own school and community, on-line. A second conceptual change that the first school district intranet initiated was the introduction of learning at a distance in traditional classrooms. In the first intranet in Newfoundland and Labrador some teachers were introduced to the notion of teaching both in a traditional classroom and on line, through the internet. This was an important step in the integration of virtual and actual teaching. Students were also introduced to the notion of learning both on site and on line during a school day. These were significant steps in the integration of on-site and on-line education or the merging of actual and virtual classes (Stevens, 2005; Stevens and Stewart, 2005). A third conceptual change was that schools that were small in terms of the number of students attending in person, on site, and the number of teachers who were appointed to them, could become relatively large schools in terms of the range of subjects they could offer with the addition of online instruction. Finally, there was a conceptual change in the realization by students, parents and teachers that school location was not necessarily a barrier to accessing areas of the curriculum that had not traditionally been provided on site in traditional classrooms. Advanced Placement subjects, taught in large urban schools throughout North America, could be made available to senior students in small and geographically-isolated schools.

Each of the four parts of the matrix was shaped though collaboration between each of the other parts. The organization of the intranet depended on the connectivity provided by internet-based technologies, assisted by the installation of satellite dishes in Newfoundland and Labrador schools. The technological dimension depended on the organizational skills of administrators in the school district office collaborating with on-site administrators and teachers. Several times during the first year of operation there were technological problems that were solved collaboratively by administrators and teachers working alongside technicians. Technological changes introduced by the internet and its application to school district organization to facilitate the administrative and academic linking of classrooms in small and dispersed schools, encouraged teachers to consider new, collaborative, ways of teaching in open learning environments. The introduction of the first school district intranet in Newfoundland and Labrador challenged the exclusivity of traditional classrooms in which a defined number of students were taught, in person, by a single teacher.

Changes in rural education in Newfoundland and Labrador can be further considered within a second matrix. The creation of school district intranets and the advent of e-learning led to the development of collaborative structures and processes, adaptation of innovative ways of using new technologies in schools, and, ultimately, the preservation of the distinct cultural identity of rural communities in Newfoundland and Labrador.

Collaboration	Innovation
Adaptation	Cultural Identity

Collaboration has been critical to the success of e-learning in rural schools in Newfoundland and Labrador. As rural schools changed from closed, autonomous institutions to become administratively and pedagogically open to other sites (schools) within intranets, collaborative teaching and learning was facilitated. Collaborative teaching and learning are not dependant on school size or location; neither are they dependent on school district intranets. The lesson for the global community from collaborative teaching and learning in Newfoundland and Labrador has been the creation of structures and processes to support this.

The creation of school district intranets was based on organizational and managerial *innovation* that led to the development of virtual educational structures to support traditional schools. Innovation that led to the creation of new educational structures and processes in Newfoundland and Labrador was grounded in the demise of the fishing industry and rural outmigration. The organizational and managerial response has been the development of extended learning opportunities for young people and, indirectly, for their families and communities.

Educational changes that have taken place in rural Newfoundland and Labrador have been based on the *adaptation* of existing structures and processes within which teaching and learning have been extended through the integration of traditional and virtual classrooms. In adapting traditional small rural schools to internet-based structures and processes, capacity building has taken place. Many small Newfoundland and Labrador schools have become, in effect, sites within extended teaching and learning environments.

Through collaboration, innovation and adaptation in Newfoundland and Labrador, sustainable rural schools have been created and an important aspect of the *cultural identity* of the province has been preserved. It could be argued that the Centre for Distance Learning and Innovation supports the cultural identity of the province and sustains rural communities through the creation of extended learning opportunities. Currently CDLI teaches 983 students in 103 schools in Newfoundland and Labrador. It employs 30 e-teachers, has 1774 course registrations and has developed 38 online courses with a further two under development.

The Professional Education of e-Teachers

The problems that have faced rural Newfoundland and Labrador over the last decade and the community response to them are of interest to educators and policy makers beyond the province. The above matrices show how schools and, indirectly through them, rural communities can be sustained.

There are four lessons from the Canadian province of Newfoundland and Labrador for the global community in the building of sustainable rural schools:

1. *Small schools can be large schools*. Schools that are small in terms of the number of students who attend, in person, on a daily basis, can become large educational institutions in the way they electronically access and disseminate teaching and learning. In Newfoundland and Labrador this has been achieved by the first two cells in the above matrices: acceptance of new technologies and using them in collaborative ways. A lesson for the rest of the world from this province is that school size and location are no longer important in educational terms.
2. *Virtual and actual teaching and learning can be integrated.* In rural Newfoundland and Labrador steps have been taken to integrate traditional and virtual teaching and learning within intranets and, more recently, through the Centre for Distance Learning and Innovation. Today many young people attend small schools in their rural communities in this province while also being taught by e-teachers employed by CDLI. In Newfoundland and Labrador virtual teaching and learning integration can be considered within the second cells of the above two matrices: pedagogical changes (eg, e-learning) combined with an innovative approach to the delivery of education such as the steps taken a decade ago in academically

and administratively linking small schools within intranets.

3. *Small schools can be sustained through the introduction of new structures and processes.* The third cells of the above matrices – organization and adaptation were applied in the development of the Vista School District Intranet. This structure introduced revolutionary change in the way education was delivered in the province. The intranet was organized around building increased teaching capacity in small schools through application of the first two lessons – accepting and adapting new technologies and making space for virtual teaching and learning in traditional classrooms.
4. *Newfoundland and Labrador is preparing its young rural people for the digital world by educating them within that world.* The fourth cells in the above matrices (conceptualization and cultural identity) together underpin a vision of how education can be organized in ailing rural communities. There was a vision by those who created the new educational structures and processes in this province that the distinctive rural dimension of Newfoundland and Labrador's cultural identity would not be compromised by the combined forces of the demise of the fishing industry and out-migration. Today young people can live and be educated in rural communities in Newfoundland and Labrador while participating in a global digital world.

CONCLUSION

Newfoundland and Labrador has undertaken changes in the organization of rural education to sustain rural schools. Two possible future directions can now be considered.

The first possible new direction is that e-learning in the province could possibly be extended to include e-living (Stevens, 2008). The horizontal linking of rural schools and the new pathways for high school students that have been created can now, possibly, be extended to include vertical integration so that links are forged between local schools and students' homes. The high technology beacons that many rural Newfoundland and Labrador schools have become may, in future, provide opportunities for adult learners to complete their schooling or extend it in new ways.

Second, Newfoundland and Labrador could usefully share its success in the application of advanced technologies to develop rural school e-learning with other parts of the world, particularly the developing world. Newfoundland and Labrador can be likened to Singapore, a city state that has grown rich by using its main resource - the talent and entrepreneurial drive of its citizens - to develop one of the highest standards of living in the world. People in Newfoundland and Labrador, like the Singaporeans, have applied their knowledge, skills and ingenuity to overcome problems of size and isolation by enhancing their provincial education system with e-learning. There are many places in the world in which the e-learning successes of this Canadian province could be shared by being replicated in culturally-appropriate ways. The development of new structures and processes that have transformed access to educational and, indirectly, vocational opportunities, in small and isolated communities in Newfoundland and Labrador, could, possibly, provide a template to be modified and introduced in other parts of the world.

REFERENCES

Barbour, M., & Mulcahy, D. (2005). The role of mediating teachers in Newfoundland's new model of distance education. *The Morning Watch*, September.

Ben-Jacob, M. G., Levin, D. S., & Ben-Jacob, T. K. (2000). The learning environment of the 21st century. *Educational Technology Review*, *13*, 8–12.

Brown, J., Sheppard, D., & Stevens, K. (2000). *Effective schooling in a tele-learning environment.* St. John's: NL, Centre for Tele-Learning and Rural Education, Faculty of Education, Memorial University of Newfoundland.

Dorniden, A. (2005). K-12 schools and online learning. In Howard, C., Boettcher, J. V., Justice, L., Schenk, K., Rogers, P. L., & Berg, G. A. (Eds.), *Encyclopedia of distance learning* (pp. 1182–1188). Hershey, PA: Idea Group Reference.

Ertl, H., & Plante, J. (2004). *Connectivity and learning in Canada's schools*. Ottawa, Canada: Statistics Canada, Government of Canada.

Glick, D. B. (2005). K-12 online learning policy. In Howard, C., Boettcher, J. V., Justice, L., Schenk, K., Rogers, P. L., & Berg, G. A. (Eds.), *Encyclopedia of distance learning* (pp. 1175–1181). Hershey, PA: Idea Group Reference.

Government of Newfoundland and Labrador. (2000). *Supporting learning: Report on the ministerial panel on educational delivery in the classroom*. St John's: NL, Department of Education.

Healey, D., & Stevens, K. (2002). Student access to Information Technology and perceptions of future opportunities in two small Labrador communities. *Canadian Journal of Learning and Technology, 28*(1), 7–18.

Information Highway Advisory Council. (1997). *Preparing Canada for a digital world.* Ottawa, Canada: Industry Canada.

Schrum, L. (2005). E-learning and K-12. In Howard, C., Boettcher, J. V., Justice, L., Schenk, K., Rogers, P. L., & Berg, G. A. (Eds.), *Encyclopedia of distance learning* (pp. 737–742). Hershey, PA: Idea Group Reference.

Stevens, K. (2000). Télé-enseignement et éducation en milieu rural en Nouvelle Zélande et à Terre Neuve. *Géocarrefour - Revue de Geographie de Lyon - Espaces Ruraux et Technologies de L'Information, 75*(1), 87–92.

Stevens, K. (2001). The development of digital Intranets for the enhancement of education in rural communities. *Journal of Interactive Instruction Development, 13*(3), 19–24.

Stevens, K. (2002). Making the world smaller -the electronic networking of small schools –some unseen connections of the Icelandic educational network in New Zealand and Canada. [Icelandic translation by Karl Erlendsson]. *Skólavarðan, 2*(2), 22–24.

Stevens, K., Sandalov, A., Sukhareva, N., Barry, M., & Piper, T. (1999). The development of open models for teaching physics to schools in dispersed locations in Russia and Canada. In V. Grementieri, A. Szucs & V. I. Trukhin (Eds.), *Information and communication technologies and human resources development: New opportunities for European co-operation*, Budapest, Hungary: European Distance Education Network, October, (pp. 148–154.)

Stevens, K. J. (1999a). A new model for teaching in rural communities – the electronic organisation of classes as Intranets. *Prism – Journal of The Newfoundland and Labrador Teachers'. Association, 6*(1), 23–26.

Stevens, K. J. (1999b). Telecommunications technologies, tele-learning and the development of virtual classes for rural New Zealanders. *Open Praxis, 1.*

Stevens, K. J. (2005).The integration of virtual and actual classes in sparsely populated regions. In Kinshuk, D. G. Sampson & P. Isaias (Eds.), *Cognition and exploratory learning in the digital age,*(pp. 517-520). IADIS Press.

Stevens, K. J. (2007). A matrix for e-collaboration in rural Canadian schools. In Kock, N. (Ed.), *Encyclopedia of e-collaboration* (pp. 444–449). Hershey, PA: IGI Global, Information Science Reference.

Stevens, K. J. (2008). From e-learning to e-living. *Newfoundland Quarterly, 100*(4).

Stevens, K. J., & Moffatt, C. *(2003). From distance education to tele-learning -the organization of open classes at local, regional and national levels. In J. Bradley (Ed.),* The open classroom – distance learning in and out of schools *(pp. 171-180). London, UK & Sterling, VA: Kogan.*

Stevens, K. J., & Stewart, D. (2005). *Cybercells – learning in actual and virtual groups*. Melbourne, Australia: Thomson-Dunmore Press.

Tella, S. (1995). *Virtual school in a networking learning environment*. Helsinki, Finland: University of Helsinki, Department of Teacher Education.

Van Manen, M. (2002). The pedagogical task of teaching. *Teaching and Teacher Education, 18*(2), 135–138. doi:10.1016/S0742-051X(01)00058-0

ADDITIONAL READING

Dorniden, A. (2005). K-12 Schools and Online Learning. In Howard, C., Boettcher, J.V., Justice, L., Schenk, K., Rogers, P.L and Berg, G.A. (Eds.), *Encyclopedia of Distance Learning,* Hershey: Idea Group Reference, pp. 1182-1188.

Ertl, H., & Plante, J. (2004). *Connectivity and Learning in Canada's Schools*. Ottawa: Statistics Canada, Government of Canada.

Lai, K.-W. (2005). *e-Learning Communities: Teaching and Learning With the Web*. Dunedin: University of Otago Press.

Ministry of Education. (2006). *Enabling the 21st Century Learner: An e-Learning Action Plan for Schools 2006-2010.* Wellington: Learning Media.

Stevens, K., & Stewart, D. (2005). *Cybercells - Learning in Actual and Virtual Groups*, Melbourne: Thomson - Dunmore Press, viii +150pp.

Stevens, K. J. (2003). E-Learning and the Development of Open Classes for Rural Students in Atlantic Canada. In Bradley, J. (Ed.), *The Open Classroom - Distance Learning In and Out of Schools, London and Sterling* (pp. 149–157). VA: Kogan Page.

Stevens, K. J. (2003). From Distance Education to TeleLearning – The Organization of Open Classes at Local, Regional and National Levels. In Bradley, J. (Ed.), *The Open Classroom – Distance Learning In and Out of Schools, London & Sterling* (pp. 171–180). VA: Kogan Page.

Stevens, K. J. (2010). Three Stages in the Social Construction of Virtual Learning Environments. In Ertl, B. (Ed.), *E-Collaborative Knowledge Construction Learning From Computer-Supported and Virtual Networks* (pp. 232–243). Hershey, PA: IGI Global.

Stevens, K. J. (2010). Regional, National and Provincial Stages in the Development of Open Learning Structures for Rural Communities. In Greene, V., & Cherrington, S. (Eds.), *Delving Into Diversity: An International Exploration of Issues of Diversity in Education* (pp. 311–320). New York: Nova Science Publishers.

KEY TERMS AND DEFINITIONS

Asynchronous: Also known as delayed time.

e-Teacher: Also known as internet-based teachers. e-teachers teach online.

m-Teacher: Also known as mediating teachers who support e-teachers in schools.

Rural: Also known as non-urban. Rural schools are sometimes known as country schools.

Synchronous: Also known as real time.

ENDNOTES

1. Advanced Placement (AP) courses enable senior students to begin undergraduate degrees with part of their program completed from high school if courses are passed at grade levels specified by the university of their choice.
2. The initial school district (District 8) contained 18 schools ranging in student enrolment from 40 to 650. The region in which the School District was located extends from Bonavista in the north, (the place where John Cabot landed in North America in 1497) to the Burin Peninsula in the South. It is a large geographic area covering about 7000 square kilometres. The region has a population of about 35,000 people and an economy supported by a diverse infrastructure including fishing, forestry, farming, mining, aquaculture and tourism. The School District was formed in 1996 and became a legal entity in January 1997. There were 5165 students enrolled in the 18 schools in the district who were taught by 366 teachers.
3. Intranets consist of schools that are academically and administratively internet-linked so that they can share teaching and learning between participating sites.

Chapter 10
Academic Freedom and the Ethics of Marketing Education

Francine Rochford
La Trobe University, Australia

EXECUTIVE SUMMARY

Academic freedom is acknowledged to both define the university and to protect its status. A commitment to academic freedom must be reflected in organisational structures and attitudes. However, many of the uses to which universities are put by the state, and the choices made by universities themselves, can erode the effective protection of academic freedom. The deployment of marketing techniques, including technological advances, to mimic the activities of private corporations, are frequently part of the wider systemic threat to the university 'system' in most modern economies – its deployment in instrumental economic goals. If these goals are pursued to the exclusion of other university goals, universities' raison d'être will be diminished. In particular, academic freedom as a corollary to scholarly practice and a model of inquiry will be threatened. The casualization of the university workforce is both a managerial mechanism to effect economic goals and a cause of growing instrumentalism in the sector. Universities' increasing deployment of casual staff presents a problem for the real exercise of academic freedom, and is an abandonment of the ethical role of the university.

BACKGROUND TO THE PROBLEM

Truth, like all other good things, may be loved unwisely – may be pursued too keenly – may cost too much. And surely ... the general evil of infusing reserve and dissimulation, uneasiness, and suspicion and fear, into those communications which must take place, and which, unless in a condition of perfect security, must take place uselessly or worse, is too great a price to pay for truth itself. (Pearce v Pearce 1846, p. 957)

DOI: 10.4018/978-1-60960-599-5.ch010

Lofty ideals are often espoused in absolutes, but are always constrained in application. This is particularly the case in relation to freedom of speech, (Fish, 1994) and subsidiary concept, academic freedom. Academic freedom, in particular, generates prolific supplemental commentary, frequently polemical in nature. However, even the most polemical advocate of academic freedom must concede that there are limits to its definition and scope, and indeed there is a great deal of commonality between conceptions of academic freedom and that academic freedom is a societal good (Rochford, 2003; Karran, 2009).

Academic tenure is frequently advocated as a means of preserving academic freedom. Conversely, tenure which does not have a role in supporting or maintaining proper academic freedom is insupportable (De George, 2003, p. 11). Academic freedom is typically advocated as particularly important in the development of knowledge – so that there can be no unjustified interference with the pursuit of avenues of inquiry. However, it is also arguably applicable to teaching (De George, 2003, p. 12). Short of academic tenure, however, employment contracts of sufficient length to enable a university teacher to be self-determining, in order to enable the radical-creative imagination (Marginson, 2008) would scaffold the connection between research and teaching, improve pedagogy and model processes of inquiry to students. Whilst a single failure to afford self-determination to an academic is of limited importance, and maybe a number of failures to do so can also be overlooked, a systemic failure to afford self-determination to teaching staff could have serious, systemic consequences.

It is the thesis of this chapter that it is the responsibility of an academic institution to create governance systems which are consistent with the exercise of academic freedom and to resist external and internal pressures which would compromise effective academic freedom. This is a question of systemic ethics, and it requires institutions to take an approach to their systems of governance which not only appreciates the nuanced idea of academic freedom, but is also alert to the daily application of systems of governance and the manner in which they can compromise academic freedom. The modern system of academic governance in Australia, however, is ill-adapted to this task; the primary drivers of forms of academic governance are accountability mechanisms steered by government funding models. In relation to the transmission of knowledge, the strategies adopted by institutions to create and maintain market share in the face of diminishing recurrent grants threatens an underclass of casualized academic staff exercising no academic freedom and unable to contest even the application of academic freedom to their teaching.

Using these observations as the starting premise, this case study considers the concept of academic freedom in the Australian higher education 'system', the diminishing contexts in which it is applicable to an academic's work, and in particular the degree to which it applies to university teaching of undergraduates. It then considers the models of service provision – that is, the models of delivery of undergraduate courses – in the Australian education market, and the power hierarchies established by these models, particularly in the provision of 'international' education. The silence of a casualized workplace in the negotiation of the appropriate space for academic freedom parallels and is a function of the powerlessness of the casual staff member in the negotiation of an academic contract. Information technology, it is argued, provides the mechanism by which internationalization of university courses can be provided at relatively little monetary cost, but it also may permit the creation of a teaching and learning environment which does not sufficiently model academic freedom.

Finally, this chapter considers the ethics of the individual university in negotiating the architecture of the university system, the architecture of internal governance, and in negotiating the contract of the casual staff member. The collective obligation of those enjoying academic freedom is to 'protect those whose academic freedom is threatened.' (De George, 2003: 14).

This is one of those areas of social discourse in which there is an incongruity between espoused principle and practice. Individual academics, universities, and state and federal legislatures advocate and support academic freedom. However, one of the primary means by which academic freedom was supported, university autonomy, can no longer be claimed. Individual academics, however, tend to act and react as if universities are capable of exercising autonomy. In this respect there is a deep conservatism in university culture. Not on its face, for it does appear to have absorbed an enormous shift in policy over the last fifty years. However, the deeper traditions and self-knowledge of those in the university sector have not kept pace.

> *The study of higher education policy is taken up with explaining and understanding what is, and with analysing the impact that policy-driven change and adjustment in selected dimensions of the enterprise have upon others closely related to them: access, finance, structural change, management, etc. ...[Yet] higher education remains an institution one of whose outstanding features is an immense and omnipresent organisational memory - a feature shared by few other social institutions, with the obvious exception of the churches, the law courts and the legislature. (Neave & Van Vught, 1991, p. ix)*

Neave and Van Vught suggest that there are a number of consequences of this 'institutional memory':

- present practices are shaped by previous rationalities;
- the power of institutional memory forms the bedrock on which concepts of academic autonomy rest;
- any institution whose identity and whose structures - whose legitimacy - is historically defined will tend to judge change according to whether it is sympathetic or antipathetic to ensuring continuity in the institution's mission, its responsibilities and its place in society. (Neave & Van Vught, 1991, p. x)

However, claims resting on these foundations are inarticulate in the face of new arguments based on 'the gods of technological development', of international competition, of market forces and to the final arrival upon this earth of that New Electronic Jerusalem - the information society, the learning society, or the communication society.' (Neave & Van Vught, 1991, pp. x-xi) Privatization will be accompanied by internationalization, ushered in by the neo-liberalism reflected in the policies dominant in the World Bank. 'As with many developments for which human experience provides little precedent, this latter-day technical millennialism brings with it massive hopes, claims, panaceas, in short, visions so vast and all-embracing that one can be sure of one thing - namely their guaranteed disappointment.' (Neave & Van Vught, 1991, p. xi)

The particular disappointment in this context may well be the capacity of the modern university to support academic freedom meaningfully, in ways that do not contribute to a gradual, incremental loss of its fundamental bases.

CONCEPTS AND CONCERNS

Academic freedom protects against intrusions by the state, and by universities themselves, which would impede the search for the truth and the communication of the outcomes of that search; and encourages others to do the same. (Rosborough, 2009) However, it is subject to restrictions; and whereas most would accept the general conception of academic freedom, the nature and extent of the restrictions on academic freedom are contentious and political.

A broad interpretation of the nature and extent of academic freedom threaten the modern university in a number of ways. Firstly, the university as employer wishes to be able to direct its employees. The indicia of an employment relationship carry consequences, and the capacity to control is one of the primary indicia of a common law employment relationship. Academic freedom is potentially contrary to that capacity. Secondly, the university as legal entity wants to be able to protect itself from litigation. The unrestricted exercise of academic freedom could render the employer liable vicariously. Thirdly, the university as corporate entity wants to attract external funding and maintain intellectual property (University of Western Australia v Gray, 2009). It is arguable that the academic freedom to pursue remunerative research removes funding and intellectual property from the university. Fourthly, the university as a recipient of government funding must comply with government accountability mechanisms and funding rules. Typically, the university will be required to demonstrate compliance with these rules and will accordingly put systems in place to require and record compliance mechanisms.

These multiple constraints create a number of – often conflicting – pressures on university governance structures. But the dominant trend is towards the legalisation of university relationships and a process of identification, contraction and atrophy of those relationships. (Rochford, 2008). Understandably, there is little substantive law which defines the concept in more than general terms, although developments in the United States may populate this absence. (Garcetti v Ceballos, 2006) United States' decisions have also been applied to university student speech to uphold the free speech rights of students and student organisations (Board of Regents of the University of Wisconsin System v Southworth, 2000) (Rosenberger v Rector and Visitors of the University of Virginia, 1995) (Widmar v Vincent, 1981) (Papish v Board of the Curators of the University of Missouri, 1973) (Healy v James, 1972), although cases have consistently held that schools have the right to regulate their students' speech. (Morse v Frederick, 2007) (Hazelwood School District v Kuhlmeier, 1988) (Bethel School District No 403 v Fraser, 1986) (Tinker v Des Moines Independent Community School District, 1969). However, these cases are litigated in the context of the rights afforded to United States' citizens by the First Amendment, which rights apply to all citizens, not faculty alone. In this section the modern understanding of academic freedom is considered, and its capacity to support what is required of it is assessed.

A Contested Concept

Academic freedom as a defining element of a university is asserted both at government level and within individual universities. It is, however, a contested concept. Auspiced at the behest of the then coalition-controlled Senate, the Senate Standing Committee on Education, Employment and Workplace Relations (SSCEEWR) conducted an Inquiry into Academic Freedom in 2008. (SSCEEWR, 2008) The inquiry was to investigate 'the level of intellectual diversity and the impact of ideological, political and cultural prejudice' in universities and schools in the context of allegations that students were subject to left-wing bias. (Gelber, 2008) However, the Committee noted in the Preface to the Report that:

Academic freedom is not in question in this inquiry and was given scant attention during the public hearings, except in relation to the idea of charters of academic freedom in the last of the terms of reference. (SSCEEWR, 2008, p. ix)

The Committee did attempt to set out the main principles of academic freedom, taking as its initial premise the results of a 2001 survey of the attitudes of social scientists which took academic freedom to mean the right to 'teach, research and publish on contentious issues; choose their own research colleagues; and speak on social issues without fear or favour in areas of their expertise... balanced by the responsible and disciplined exercise of scholarly expertise.' (Kayrooz, Kinnear, & Preston, 2001, p. 44). The Committee noted in particular the submission from the Australian Universities Quality Agency (AUQA):

Academic freedom is a necessary pre-condition in the development of a knowledge society and in the foundation of knowledge institutions such as universities. Institutional autonomy should be used to create the conditions to protect academic freedom both within the institution and to protect staff from pressures on academic freedom from the external environment. This includes protecting the academic freedom of staff from external government, public or private sector interference. (Australian Universities Quality Agency, 2008)

However, the Committee noted that, even without a clear conception of the limits of academic freedom, perceptions across political affiliations were that there were current threats to academic freedom. (Australian Universities Quality Agency, 2008, p. 33)

The Australian Federal Government is reported to be considering legislation to protect academic freedom (Healy, 2009; Riddiford, 2009). However, commentators have noted that:

[t]he idea of academic freedom is what Abraham Lincoln called a "glittering generality", that is, emotionally appealing words that invite acclaim, despite the absence of specifics.

These characteristics make academic freedom a useful device for soaring political rhetoric, but a far more dubious basis for the prosaic task of crafting legislation. (Riddiford, 2009).

Some university Acts already require 'the Governor in Council, the Minister and the Council [to have] regard to appointing members to the Council who have an appreciation of the values of a University relating to teaching, research, independence and academic freedom.'(See, for instance, Melbourne University Act 1958 (Vic), University of Ballarat Act 1993 (Vic), Swinburne University of Technology Act 1992 (Vic), Royal Melbourne Institute of Technology Act 1992 (Vic), Swinburne University of Technology Act 1992 (Vic). These provisions were added by the Higher Education Acts (Amendment) Act 2005 (Vic))). In addition, Bills have been introduced in a number of jurisdictions which, if passed, will require consideration of the same matters.

Whilst the Submissions to the enquiry reported a number of areas of concern, the Senate Committee Report reached no conclusion on whether there should be statutory protection of academic freedom, considering it a matter appropriate for the consideration of universities themselves. (SSCEEWR, 2008, p. 41).

The American Association of University Professors (AAUP) has been considered an authoritative source on the notion of academic freedom; its 1915 Declaration of Principles on Academic Freedom and Academic Tenure has been described as 'the greatest articulation of the logic and structure of academic freedom in America' (Post, 2006). The AAUP's 1940 Statement of Principles on Academic Freedom and Tenure (Association of American Colleges and Universities, 1940) has been similarly influential. (Rosborough, 2009). It begins with the assertion that Institutions of Higher Education are carried out for the 'common good' – not to further the interests of the individual teacher or of the institution; and that '[t]he common good depends upon the free search for truth and its free exposition.' (Association of American Colleges and Universities, 1940, p. 3):

Academic freedom is essential to these purposes and applies to both teaching and research. Freedom in research is fundamental to the advancement of truth. Academic freedom in its teaching aspect is fundamental for the protection of the rights of the teacher in teaching and of the student to freedom in learning. It carries with it duties correlative with rights. (Association of American Colleges and Universities, 1940, p. 3)

Generally speaking, therefore, academic freedom is acknowledged to be a 'good thing', consistent with the role of the university and its proper function in society. Few deny that academic freedom is subject to caveat and exemption; most acknowledge that academic freedom is not established to create a site free of restriction for the forwarding of personal vanity or institutional profit.

A Diminishing Space

However, the modern university is unlike the traditional university, particularly in the degree to which it is compelled to market its teaching function beyond its traditional constituency. As a result of Australian Government funding models, one of the most attractive non-traditional markets is the provision of educational services to overseas students located offshore.

This is a heavily regulated 'industry', but it is based on a market premise. The General Agreement on Trade in Services (GATS) applies to transnational education. McBurnie and Ziguras (2001) note that at a basic level GATS attempts to enable greater international trade by preventing two forms of discrimination: discrimination 'between incumbents and new entrants into a market (be they domestic or foreign)', (McBurnie & Ziguras, 2001, p. 87) and discrimination 'between domestic and foreign service providers'. (McBurnie & Ziguras, 2001, p. 88) GATS therefore advocates a tempering of restrictions on foreign providers through customers regulations, qualifications authorities and limitations of foreign ownership.

Nevertheless, industry regulation occurs at a national level in all of the countries into which education is 'exported'. Regulation also occurs at a state and a national level in the home jurisdiction. In Australia, Universities are typically established by State or Federal legislation. States and Territories prevent a person from operating as a university unless authorised. However, attempts to define the 'university' are more commonly directed to excluding usages which would reduce the marketability of the term, or to determine whether the organisation is subject to regulation. In Australia this preoccupation has been seen in several disputes. In one case a US-based distance education provider, Greenwich, established itself on Norfolk Island, prompting claims of 'reputational asset stripping'. (Illing & Richardson, 1999, p. 39)' In another, the Federal Court ordered the Australasian Institute to stop advertising or posting on its Web site claims that its global master of business administration was approved or sponsored by the University of Ballarat. The Institute claimed affiliation with a number of Australian universities. ('Order on web college claims, 1999, p. 35)

Attacks on the standing of Australian institutions have prompted government intervention. Federal, state and territory governments have agreed National Protocols for Higher Education Approval Processes for approving higher education institutions 'to set up a national accreditation and quality standard consistent across the two levels of government.' (Illing, Rules mean unis must measure up, 2000, p. 35) The criteria set down processes for admitting entrants into the market, and a quality assurance scheme for ongoing monitoring. The title 'university', however, is protected through business names and associations legislation and through the corporations law, and 'through legislation with consistent criteria and procedures. ... There [is] a common definition of an Australian university, common criteria for assessment of applications for university status and core elements for evaluating claims.' (Illing, 2000, p. 35) The criteria for recognition as a university in the Australian market include 'a 'culture of sustained scholarship', 'original creative endeavour', 'free inquiry', 'commitment of faculty to these values, and organisation structures and processes 'sufficient to ensure the integrity of the institution's academic programs'. (McBurnie & Ziguras, 2001, pp. 96-97). These requirements seem to import the indicia of academic freedom; however, rather than introducing a regulatory requirement of academic freedom, they appear to be primarily intended to ensure protection of the local market and maintenance of credibility of Australian providers in the international market. (McBurnie & Ziguras, 2001, p. 98)

However, in many of the countries to which Australia 'exports' education, the state restrictions on students or staff may be more rigorous. For instance, in Malaysia, whilst private sector universities are permitted, they are strictly regulated. Along with other requirements, including the necessity for an invitation by the Minister for Education and the incorporation of a local company with a structure determined by the Private Higher Educational Institutions Act 1996, each course of study must be assessed to determine whether it means minimum standards. In order to provide the basis for employment in the public sector, the course must also be accredited. McBurnie and Ziguras note that 'the government of Malaysia has not been willing to completely hand over power of cultural reproduction to the market, amid concerns that the type of education offered by foreign providers may not meet national objectives.' (McBurnie & Ziguras, 2001, p. 93) In addition to the requirement that a number of compulsory subjects be taught by private providers – including Islamic studies or moral education – the Private Higher Educational Institutions Act 1996 also requires the provider to 'include a provision in their constitution prohibiting students from becoming involved with any political organisations or 'expressing support or sympathy with or opposition to any political party or trade union'. Institutions are obliged to expel students that breach these conditions.' (McBurnie & Ziguras, 2001, p. 95, citing (Kementerian Pendidikan (Ministry of Education) Malaysia, 1997)) The consequence of providing courses in this market, therefore, would be the requirement to ensure that students did not engage in some forms of political discourse in the classroom, and would also be a constraint on the instructor from some forms of discourse.

Aside from the 'hard' regulations, universities in most western countries are subject to many of the financial and administrative practices of 'new public management'. Marginson notes that, in addition to laws, regulations and policies, scholars must also comply with 'techniques of government and managing, administrative and financial systems, publishing regimes [and] academic hierarchies'. (Marginson, 2008, p. 270)

'New public management' uses mechanisms such as 'funding-based economic incentives, user-driven production, product formats, the pricing and sale of outputs, entrepreneurial production, output monitoring and measurement, competitive ranking of personnel and of institutional, performance management, performance pay, contracts...with industry, and systems of accountability and audit'. (Marginson, 2008, p. 270)

For academics in their teaching roles, this may impact on their legitimate academic freedom in a variety of ways. Output monitoring and measurement requires identification of outputs. By introducing the language and techniques of audit the university is transformed by individualistic notions of learning, instead of participatory, community-based ideas. The individualistic learning strategy is reified by contractual form to produce transparent knowledge outcomes – outputs. (Rochford, 2008) This is reinforced by the armoury of risk management mechanisms which, designed to ameliorate risk, actually create risk. (Rochford, 2007) Practically, the generalised outcome of this is 'capture' by a set of planning and audit processes. Teaching staff on many campuses are obliged to submit curricula, reading lists and assessment pieces well in advance to ensure compliance with university planning timelines. In the case of courses taught in multiple locations, or offshore, staff may be obliged to comply with more rigorous requirements, including provision of lecture notes, presentation material, tutorial questions and answers and examinations to all sites at which the course is presented. From the perspective of the 'home' academic, this diminishes the temporal space within which the course can be subject to innovation; it becomes 'fixed' at a point in time well in advance of the presentation of the course. From the point of view of the presenter of each *version* of the course, the potential for innovation, or even deviation from the course, is significantly constrained by the fixed curriculum and by the existence of assessment material set by the primary lecturer.

THE TEACHING FUNCTION OF THE UNIVERSITY

Marginson discusses the role of 'self-determination' as a driver of the 'radical-creative imagination' under the influence of 'new public management' (Marginson, 2008, p. 269). Although he limits his arguments to the researcher or scholar, if we accept the proposition that teaching is also appropriate as a space for the exercise of academic freedom his argument can be extended to this function as well. It could be argued that this is a serious leap, and that there are quite significant differences between research and scholarship and teaching. However, traditional and well-accepted definitions of academic freedom, including those cited above, include the teaching function of the university as one of the protected spaces.

As with research and scholarship, teaching does not carry with it an unrestricted degree of academic freedom. (Rochford, 2003, p. 252) Teachers are obliged to comply with the law, codes of conduct, with various policies of the university, with directions of their employer. However, academics as employees have specialist knowledge, and it is not anticipated that their employer should be in a position to direct what is taught.

Academic freedom with respect to teaching is also a restricted right that carries with it obligations. It is the right to teach one's discipline in the way that one, because of his or her knowledge, deems best. If it is for one's knowledge that a university hires a teacher, it must presume that the teacher is the best qualified person it can find to teach the subject. If the administration knows more than the faculty and so can dictate what the faculty must teach in courses, then the institution is not the kind that requires academic freedom (De George, 2003, p. 14)

The application of the principles of academic freedom to the teaching function of an academic was tested in an incident involving Kevin Barrett, a University of Wisconsin-Madison academic. He presented to a talk-show host the view that the terrorist attacks on September 11 2001 were planned by the United States government and the Central Intelligence Agency. He said that he would be presenting that and a range of alternative views to his students. The resulting calls for his dismissal and threatened withdrawal of funding to the university by the state legislature were stared down by the university, which reviewed his course and asserted his right to present ideas to his students unconstrained by political pressure.

However, academic freedom in teaching duties was tested in the United States Supreme Court in Garcetti v Ceballos (2006). This case considered the continued application of the Pickering balancing test, which derived from Pickering v Board of Education (1968) to determine the constraints imposed on a public employee by the nature of their employment by the state. In Pickering and later cases, the United States Supreme Court had 'articulated a quite cogent process of analysis to determine whether speech by a public employee is protected by the First Amendment' (Rosborough, 2009). Garcetti did not involve an academic, but a deputy district attorney for the Los Angeles County District Attorney's Office; Richard Ceballos. His public servant status meant that, according to the Supreme Court, when he was speaking pursuant to his official duties he was not protected by First Amendment rights. The majority held that 'when public employees make statements pursuant to their official duties, the employees are not speaking as citizens for First Amendment purposes, and the Constitution does not insulate their communications from employer discipline.' (Garcetti v Ceballos, 2006, p. 421) According to Rosborough, this has implications for academics:

'[p]resumably, under the rule announced in Garcetti, a public university has the right to dismiss a professor solely becoause the administation disagreed with the content of his lectures, research, or publications because his speech would fall under the duties he was employed to perform. This would subject professors not only to institutional regulation through their Departments, but also to extensive regulation of the content of their scholarship.' (Rosborough, 2009, p. 14)

Similar concerns arise out of Australian litigation. A 2001 case (NTEIU v University of Wollongong, 2001) involving the sacking of a Wollongong University molecular biologist for his refusal to recant allegations of 'soft marking', although ultimately reinstating the academic, is troubling primarily because of the motivations of the university and the support it received from Australian Vice Chancellors. (Rochford, 2003, p. 249) Universities' primary motivation in a highly marketized environment appears to be preservation of a public image, and it has a wide range of tools, ranging from minor censure, reassignment and removal of privileges such as web access or email, but culminating in the device of dismissal.

Within this contested realm, what is the role of the casual academic? The casualization of Australian universities has frequently been described. Junor cites Department of Education, Science and Training (DEST) figures suggesting that 20 percent of academic and 13 percent of general staff are casual; but using head count figures 40 percent of academic staff are not casual employees. (Junor, 2004). This does not account for the number of casual academics employed under one or other of the models of service provision under which Australian universities service offshore students. It is reasonable to assume that a significant number of staff presenting programs offshore, or in alternative modes, will be casual staff members or will not be staff members of the university at all. The models of service provision for delivering courses at alternative venues do not support the use of tenured staff; contracts will be for a limited term, and salaries will not be allocated to recurrent funding. What is the effect of a predominantly casual or outsourced staff? The casualization of academic jobs is inversely related to job commitment (McClurg, 1999; Joiner & Bakalis, 2006) which can lead to difficulties in teaching quality. Reports of poor or biased teaching have been attributed to the prevailing conditions in the higher education sector, which has led to an increasing incidence of casual staff. (SSCEEWR, 2008) This is consistent with the trend across the Australian economy. (Welters & Mitchell, 2009)

The Senate Report noted that the conditions under which both casual staff and their deans and heads of departments work are detrimental to the mentoring of new staff. Students' reports of bias, or other types of complaints, are a function of this time-pressed environment. (SSCEEWR, 2008, p. 5) This critique of the effects of casualization on academic freedom is primarily an account of defects in professionalism of individuals. It does not focus on the diminished opportunity afforded to this category of staff to control their teaching and the potential effects of this on the promulgation of attitudes towards knowledge. However, as Marginson has pointed out, higher education is a market, that higher education is a 'positional good,' (Marginson, 2006, p. 3), and nearly everyone opts for prestige.' (Marginson, 2006, p. 3) A university focussed entirely on the market aspect of course delivery is not disadvantaged by failing to ensure premium delivery, and specifically is not disadvantaged by provision of courses through casual or outsourced staffing.

However, the provision of teaching using casual staff fails to model academic freedom. Casual staff are rarely employed for their research or scholarship, and in teaching they are frequently delivering a prepared course. The AAUP Statement of Principles on Academic Freedom and Tenure is explicit on the relationship between academic freedom and tenure. It notes that tenure forwards the purposes of freedom of teaching and research, and creates a sufficient degree of financial stability to make the profession attractive. Without tenure, it concluded, the institution cannot fulfil its obligations to students and to society. (Association of American Colleges and Universities, 1940, p. 3) Welters and Mitchell, investigating whether casual employment constitutes a 'stepping stone' to full time employment, concluded that casual employees tend to be 'locked in' to casual employment. (Welters & Mitchell, 2009, p. 11) There is no necessary progression from casual employment to tenure, or even contract, so casual staff are typically appointed for a semester, or term, or in some cases pursuant to contracts under which they are purportedly able to be dismissed at an hour's notice. In those circumstances the capacity of the staff member to exercise academic freedom is diminished. With no temporal, nor sometimes physical space within which to prepare, with a curriculum and assessment fixed well in advance, and sometimes with fixed lecture notes and timelines, the casual staff member is constrained to the delivery of another's course, without the means or opportunity to exercise any degree of freedom. The modern information technology environment has the capacity to sideline that staff member even more – perhaps by limiting their involvement to tutoring to recorded or virtual lectures.

MODELS OF SERVICE PROVISION IN THE MODERN AUSTRALIAN HIGHER EDUCATION MARKET

Background

Australia is a major exporter of higher education. It is acknowledged, along with America, New Zealand, the United Kingdom, and Canada, to be a 'world [leader] in export of higher education services.' (Shive, 2010) (Healey, 2008, p. 335) Models of service provision range from a 'franchising degree provision to international partners' (Healey, 2008, p. 333) to 'foreign direct investment as universities set up campuses in other countries.' (Healey, 2008, p. 333) Advances in information and communication technologies are some of the primary drivers of this expansion, along with mass air travel and the hegemony of English as the preferred instructional language. (Healey, 2008, p. 334)

Healey, following the Uppsala internationalization model, describes the incremental process of 'internationalization' of business as following four steps: exporting, licensing production, joint ventures and sole ventures. (Healey, 2008, p. 335) Exporting higher education is in the form of students studying on the home campus, or students studying on-line and taking a degree from the home campus. This group is of less concern in relation to academic freedom, as their teaching is (generally) main-stream and in the hierarchy of responsibilities the lecturer will tend to have a similar status as other on-campus staff. This is not to say that there is not potential for casualization of these staff, and concomitant difficulties with maintaining academic freedom; rather, this is not an issue peculiar to internationalization of higher education.

The second stage identified by Healey is the licensing, or franchising, of higher education, by sub-contract, to a local provider in another country. Healey reports that, on 2003 data, around 30% of all international students studying for an Australian program were doing so in a franchised degree program. (Healey, 2008, p. 338) The history of these programs has left a legacy of regulation, as the poor quality of some courses resulted in reputational damage. Quality assurance programs both in Australia and in the franchisee's country monitor activities.

Healey identifies joint ventures as the third stage of internationalization. This is particularly relevant where local regulation requires the involvement of a local partner, and is particularly attractive to governments aiming to improve their own capacity to deliver higher education. (Healey, 2008, p. 340)

The final, and probably tangential, phase of internationalization is the sole venture, set up as a wholly-owned branch campus. Of the few full examples of this style of education provision, Healey cites the University of New South Wales Asia, in Singapore. However, this campus closed only a few months after it had opened in 2007. (Forss, 2007)

Varghese finesses this final form, describing it as 'the presence of representatives in another country to provide the service.' (Varghese, 2008, p. 12) This may involve the physical presence of individual academic staff, as employees of a foreign university, or as part of an academic partnership, or, reflecting Healey's categorisation, to teach in a branch campus. Some instances of this rather more *ad hoc* set of arrangements may not attract the same concerns in relation to academic freedom.

Application of Academic Freedom to Offshore Private Education

The commercial benefits to the institution of exporting higher education prompt particular attention to the role of higher education and its benefits to the state – and the correlative place of academic freedom. As Shive puts it, '[a] public good deserves government support and will benefit the whole community over time. A private good mainly benefits the individual, and thus should pay for itself.' (Shive, 2010, p. 7) Internationalization of higher education purely for the commercial benefit of the institution does not attract the arguments for academic freedom from the perspective of a state engineering the regulatory space within which academic freedom can be practised. This is at issue in a relatively parlous environment for higher education, and an ascendancy of market-based instruments, as a consequence of which 'the reorientation of public policies shifted their emphasis from investments in social sectors to improve equity to investing in tradables in order to enhance growth...market-friendly reforms in education implied a diversion of public resources from education to productive sectors and a reduction of subsidies in education.' (Varghese, 2008, p. 10)

Looking beyond the immediate concerns of the 'exporting' university, however, the globalisation of higher education has other goals. Varghese notes that although universities are national entities they have traditionally been international. (2008, p. 10) 'Universities are institutions with dual characteristics – national and international. The content and knowledge imparted in universal and international, while the ownership, structure and organization have always been national.' (Varghese, 2008, p. 10) The arguments for subsidization of universities, based on market principles, will justify support of university internationalization if it can be seen to be in the economic interests of the nation – which it might very well be. However, do the same arguments apply to support for academic freedom as a socially engineered space? Is it imperative for the purposes of the nation that the principles of academic freedom *in teaching* be applied in the teaching of non-nationals? Should the state subsidise the purely financial goals of the university by allowing this space (relatively) free of regulation for academic freedom? More practically, should the state finance universities on a model generous enough to allow the adoption of practices generous enough to scaffold academic freedom, including the use of full time staff members instead of casual staff?

Varghese notes the use of foreign aid, including the funding of overseas students as a technique for the suppression of communism. 'The policy of disseminating scientific advances and sharing industrial progress with the developing world sought the help of higher education institutions.' (Varghese, 2008, pp. 12-13) This justification of subsidisation of overseas education resulted in a number of types of programs, including the funding of students from former colonies by colonial powers, study-abroad programs funded by cold war rivals, overseas education funded by bilateral and multilateral agencies, funding by national governments, and privately funded programs. (Varghese, 2008, p. 14) Where this is the justification for the export of higher education, the arguments that support state subsidisation of the costs of academic freedom, the adoption of teaching practices that do not fully support academic freedom fail both in philosophy and practice. Philosophically, the provision of teaching in an environment which fails to provide a space free for discourse, or demonstrates to the student that faculty are not free to explore alternative viewpoints, furthers a colonialist premise that the 'coloniser' knows best, and is once again imposing knowledge, rather than participating with the student in the quest for knowledge. Alternatively, it could be perceived as the manipulation of knowledge for strategic ends – propaganda, the converse of teaching. Practically, students' perceptions of the motives of the coloniser are instrumental in the success or failure of the dissemination of a democratic worldview.

It could be argued that failing to provide a quality learning experience, modelling the highest principles of academic freedom, could reduce the university's prestige. However, research does not support this assertion. Marginson notes that universities now operate in an environment of both national and global competition. (Marginson, 2006, p. 2) Citing Hirsch (1976), he notes that higher education is a 'positional good,' (Marginson, 2006, p. 3). He notes that 'when faced by choice between a prestigious university with known indifference to undergraduate teaching, and a lesser institution offering better classroom support, nearly everyone opts for prestige.' (Marginson, 2006, p. 3) By this measure, universities will attain the commercial advantage regardless of their attention to the quality of the discursive space offered to instructors and students in the classroom. Rather, the degree to which an instructor in an exported course has a degree of academic freedom, informing teaching and, perhaps, the teaching/research nexus, is an indication of the prestige of the institution, rather than a cause of the prestige: 'student-magnet institutions accumulate prestige, cashed out as tuition revenues and further leveraged to raise public and private monies that buy high-cost faculty and sustain research programs.' (Marginson, 2006, p. 5)

POWER AND POLITICS IN A CASUALIZED UNIVERSITY SECTOR

The meta-law, law, regulations, policies, codes and even practices are reasonably transparent when compared with the embedded hierarchies of power that actually motivate action in the higher education sector. Yet this is a critical question, as Scott notes, since '[a]cademic freedom was aimed at resolving conflicts about the relationship between power and knowledge, politics and truth, action and thought by positing a sharp distinction between them'. (Scott, 2009, p. 452) She posits some of her critique on the need to keep the research function of the university immune from the influence of funding and public opinion. However, the bulk of her thesis supports the application of academic freedom in teaching - part of the raison d'être of maintaining it in that context was the public good generated by 'stir[ring] students to think differently, to become "more self-critical," hence more likely to bring about change'. (Scott, 2009, p. 453) The 'transformative' function of teaching, particularly in the social sciences, rendered both staff and students vulnerable to disapproval and hence in need of protection from the influence of money (in the form of funding) and power.

The principles of academic freedom are readily applicable in cases involving the influence of University Councils (or Trustees), or politicians, or benefactors, or funding agencies on individuals. What is less identifiable, and hence more problematic, is the influence of internal hierarchies of power. In a sprawling, multi-campus institution, with multiple instances of individual subjects which must be taught consistently, where does the power in relation to delivery of the curriculum reside? Even absenting the desire to exert power, the role of the primary course convenor necessitates the silencing of other academics involved in the teaching of the course. As already discussed, the curriculum, teaching materials and assessment materials are typically settled well in advance as a result of the university's desire to fix and audit outcomes, and the scope for deviation from those materials is limited. For the casual staff member, whose appointment might co-incide with the start of the teaching period, the capacity to be involved in the settlement of the curriculum is limited. Additional factors, such as the representation of casual staff in faculty or university decision-making forums, the limited time and space afforded to casual staff, and the tenuous nature of casual employment in any event diminish casual staff members' power to solicit or implement change in curricula.

Where does that leave the primary motivation of academic freedom in teaching – the desire to produce, not orthodoxy, not ready-made opinion, 'but the propensity for new thinking in the next generation'? (Scott, 2009, p. 458) Scott cites the AAUP in the 1915 version: students should experience a "genuine intellectual awakening", (American Association of University Professors, 1915, p. 35) one which 'depends on the student's confidence in the intellectual integrity of the teacher:

It is clear, however, that this confidence will be impaired if there is suspicion on the part of the student that the teacher is not expressing himself fully or frankly, or that college and university teachers in general are a repressed an intimidated class who dare not speak with that candor and courage which youth always demands in those whom it is to esteem ... There must be in the mind of the teacher no mental reservation. He must give the student the best of what he has and what he is. (American Association of University Professors, 1915, p. 28)

Scott's examples all involve established faculty, not necessarily tenured, but at least in the position of members of faculty. 'Faculty autonomy' is readily conceded. Disciplinary proceedings against faculty, even after the publication of extreme or ludicrous claims, can still generate commentary on the need for academic freedom. For the well-populated underclass of casual staff members, disciplinary proceedings are unnecessary. They are not normally even members of faculty. They are effectively silenced. There is, therefore, a large cohort of students who are not attaining the advantages of the 'transformative education'. What is the ethical stance of the university towards these staff and these students?

ACADEMIC FREEDOM AND THE ETHICS OF THE INSTITUTION

Motivations for Casual Contracts

The 1998 Review of Higher Education Financing and Policy (the West Report) suggested an 'essential incompatibility' between a view of the world based on collegiate decision making, and one based on executive decision making. It suggested that a failure to change internal decision making would result in a failure to operate effectively in an environment of increasing competition and increasing student choice. (Department of Employment, Education, Training and Youth Affairs, 1998, p. 24) In response to criticism such as this, and steered by compelling market-based external mechanisms, universities have positioned themselves to take on a government-designated role in supporting economic growth.

St. George argues that it is a characteristic of this model to reduce of the role of government in higher education, and to create a market within which universities compete against each other. (St George, 2006). The role of the government is to create an 'enabling regulatory environment' and 'appropriate financial incentives.' (World Bank, 2002, p. 83) This trend is not confined to Australia; the 'remarkable congruity' (Kelsey, 1998, p. 53) in changes to higher education across many countries 'reflects a coherent policy agenda which is promoted through interlocking networks of international actors and agencies, which cross-fertilize with the officials, politicians, entrepreneurs and commentators who influence policy at the national level.' (St George, 2006, p. 53) As a result, we are no longer talking about an autonomous university, but a 'university system' which enables co-operative planning of higher education. (Shattock, 1996) The leverage, or steering mechanisms, employed to exert pressure on university decision-making to create a compliant higher education sector has resulted in the adoption of an increasingly 'managerial' approach to university management, sinking or limiting the scope of decisions made in a 'collegiate' environment.

There is no inherent incompatibility between academia and managerialism; rather, there are 'soft' and 'hard' managerialist approaches, and it is the incidents of 'hard' managerialism which attract criticism. The 'soft' approaches to management 'see higher education as an autonomous activity, governed by its own norms and traditions, with a more effective and rationalised management still serving functions defined by the academic community itself.' (Trow, 1994, p. 11) However, this is not the form adopted in Australia or in the United Kingdom. Hard managerialists 'are resolved to reshape and redirect the activities of [the academic] community through funding formulas and other mechanisms of accountability imposed from outside the academic community, management mechanisms created and largely shaped for application to large commercial enterprises.' (Trow, 1994, p. 12) The idea is to make universities sufficiently similar to commercial firms to enable assessment and management in roughly similar ways.

One consequence of this approach is that the university is remodelled to emulate other types of business organisation. This results in a transference of power from the academic, who had a voice in the collegiate decision making structure, to a new management class, which speaks of the organisation as an entity in its own right, which is mediated through 'new languages built around 'objective' social scientific research, concepts of economic efficiency, and accounts of organizational success in terms of profit and loss.' (Griffiths, 1992, p. 9) The scientists, 'technocrats', economists and accountants who speak those languages become powerful in the process.

Concepts of economic efficiency and accounts of organizational success in terms of profit and loss privilege decision-making which favours efficiency, organizational flexibility to ensure responsiveness to market signals, reduced on costs and reduced fixed costs. These considerations make the use of casual staff, where available, attractive in any event. Where the costs are related to a cost centre not attached to recurrent funding, such as an offshore partnership, these considerations become primary. University policies in relation to the use of casual staff typically do not require the long lead times required by university recruitment policies (see, for instance, (The University of Adelaide, 2005).

The use of casual staff who can be supported by contract-based or tenured 'home' staff provides flexibility and responsiveness to market conditions.

The Use of Bargaining Power

Casual staff have multiple motivations for entering into a casual teaching arrangement with a university. Welters and Mitchell have noted that casual employment does not, in the current environment, constitute a 'stepping stone' to full time employment. (Welters & Mitchell, 2009, p. 11) Indeed, a long-term casual employee is less likely to obtain non-casual employment. This data was not specific to academics; some studies have concentrated on particular staff segments in academic work. Universities themselves typically try to limit the use of casual staff by limiting the purpose for which they can be employed, for instance to cover staff absences, or to undertake short term projects. (The University of Adelaide, 2005)(University of Wollongong, 2008) However, the use of casual staff is accepted where the availability of work and/or funding is uncertain, (The University of Adelaide, 2005) as is frequently the case in marketing education to non-traditional constituencies. Codes of conduct or similar documents have been developed to deal with the policies and procedures for recruitment of casual staff, although in some cases these operate only in relation to on-shore programs. (University of South Australia, 2009) Many university policies define casual staff members in a manner which restricts their contribution to a semester or term; however, it is not unusual for casual staff to be employed in multiple consecutive periods (see, for instance, Brown, Goodman, & Yasukawa, 2006, p. 1), rendering their designation nominal.

The rights of casual staff are scaffolded by the law and by university policy, but these rights are of little functional use in the context of casual employment particularly where, as is often the case, the staff member wishes to continue to be employed at the institution. Casual staff members have no access to holiday or sick pay, study time, professional development, or paid public holidays. (Brown, Goodman, & Yasukawa, 2006, p. 4) They have no income security and as a result little bargaining power. If they are perceived to be 'troublesome' they may not be re-employed. Historically, the most powerful instruments for the protection of casual staff have been industrial processes such as the enterprise bargaining processes. Strategies employed by the National Tertiary Education Union (NTEU) to respond to the increasing casualization of the academic workforce have included raising the cost of casual staff, thereby making it a less attractive managerial strategy, and the limitation on the hours able to be taught by a casual employee. (Brown, Goodman, & Yasukawa, 2006, p. 10) However, these disadvantages did not offset the organisational advantages of casualization. The NTEU sought to introduce caps on casualization in the 2003 enterprise bargaining round, but in 2005 the Federal Government imposed Higher Education Workplace Relations Requirements which prohibited restrictions on the use of casual contracts. (Brown, Goodman, & Yasukawa, 2006, p. 10) NTEU policy now commits it to pursue the right of a casual academic staff member to convert to a tenured position. The degree to which casual staff members have attained that right varies according to the institution's enterprise bargaining arrangements.

However, these limited protections do not obviate the job security concerns of a casual staff member who is *reaching the point* where he/she could reasonably expect to be entitled to conversion. Nor, more particularly, to they address the difficulties of academic staff teaching offshore as part of a university's franchised offerings, or in similar arrangements. In these cases the university has effectively 'outsourced' its job security obligations.

The motivations of a fully qualified person to enter casual employment vary; some undertake it as an interesting and moderately remunerative addition to fully professional employment. Some are retirees, outside industry experts and self-employed. (Junor, 2003) Junor notes that a reasonable proportion of casuals amongst this group are happy to remain casual. Others, however, expressed a strong desire to have more than casual employment. This group included those seeking university careers. For these groups, a lack of bargaining power in the employment situation may be exacerbated by other situational disadvantages representing individual or social risks.

Modelling Ethical Behaviour

Most universities subscribe to codes of ethics, (see, for instance, The University of Western Australia, 2009; University of South Australia, 2004) and in general could be said to be reasonably good corporate citizens. Generally, however, universities' conduct must be more than beyond reproach. Both in research and in teaching universities are models, and should be models of good conduct. Particularly in relation to their offshore operations, given some of the putative justifications for engaging in export of education, universities should be modelling for their staff and their students staffing policies which comply with both the letter and the spirit of codes of conduct. Wheeler notes that 'the present position of multinationals offers a unique opportunity for them to become public actors in the sense of exercising responsibility'. (Wheeler, 2007, p. 5, citing Rondinelli, 2002) Failure to comply with an ethical code in relation to employment characterises the university as merely instrumental, diminishing its capacity to model ethical behaviour in teaching and abrogating its high ground in demanding academic freedom. In the non-academic context Lowry characterised a number of implications of casualized employment as ethical problems. She said that '[f]or casual workers, work scheduling and the availability of work hours are likely to be directly related to employees' remuneration, thus justice issues are important.' (Lowry, 2001, p. 56) Citing Rawls, she noted that [e]mployees are denied equality in 'liberty and opportunity, income and wealth, and the bases of self-respect', all essential elements of a just society.' (Lowry, 2001, p. 56, citing Rawls, 1971, p. 55) Wheeler takes this argument further. She asserts that neither collective bargaining strategies nor contractual protections can capture the social relationships within an employment relationship. She argues that 'an ethically constructed dialogue has the potential to recognise [the care, discretion and initiative required in the interaction between employer and employee] and allow it to be used to recognise values such as social democracy and equality.' (Wheeler, 2007, p. 4) Whereas individuals may be ethical in matters within their own compass, 'managers are frequently content to adopt a position of moral neutrality towards employees. The organisational structure of the corporation allows managers to distance themselves from the consequences of their decisions and to see themselves as remote from employees as individuals.' (Wheeler, 2007, p. 19) Where that is the case, it is insufficient for the organisation to have a code of ethics when the entirety of the organisation's processes press in a different direction. It is insufficient for universities to promulgate a code of ethics, whilst outsourcing teaching obligations to franchisees who are not obliged to comply with the same standards. More specifically, it is insufficient to have policies and procedures, and to enter into enterprise bargaining agreements, which protect casual staff members and regulate the proportion of the faculty employed on a casual basis when courses delivered offshore or in partnerships are not subject to these restrictions.

Returning to the thesis of this chapter, the proportion and conditions of casual employment are a direct risk to the capacity of the institution to comply with and model the proper exercise of academic freedom. Universities which allow academic freedom to be exercised by a diminishing proportion of tenured staff whilst allowing a growing number of casual staff to be the primary connection between the institution and its students risk a charge of hypocrisy.

Norm-Based Governance

Managerialism provides for universities a set of fixed regulatory mechanisms and compliance rules which will too often be proxy for appropriate resolution of norms. An institution such as a university, established and funded at least partially for critique, and enjoying special status as acknowledged sites of discursive freedom, cannot allow itself to apply procedural rules as norms of conduct. Norm-based governance must be applied by the university at four levels:

1. In negotiations with government, universities must not allow themselves to abandon the primary position that universities are not the same as profit-taking organisations. Whereas it is true that 'there is no 'idea of the university' free of historical contingency', (Rochford, 2006, p. 147) and that the state, paying the piper, may call the tune, that does not mean that universities are thereby exculpated from the duty of representing consistently their role and their responsibilities.
2. In formulation of partnerships other contractual arrangements with institutions or foreign states for the franchise or alternative offering of courses, universities must present and hold the position that academic freedom is not negotiable, and that staff members must be afforded sufficient time, resources and protections both to exercise and to model freedom to their students.
3. In preparation of codes of ethics, policies and procedures universities must be alive to both the theory and the practical effect of casualization, must apply protections to tenured and casual staff alike, and must not allow the managerial convenience and economy of casual staff to diminish by barely perceptible increments the already diminished space afforded to academic freedom.
4. In negotiations with staff, universities must be aware that front-line managers will not necessarily be applying normative criteria. Universities must not allow themselves to believe that the manager, as an individual, will not 'shelter behind the corporate ediface'. (Wheeler, 2007, p. 26) Policies and procedures should be interpreted at all times *subject to* the primary purpose of the institution, and the primary mechanism by which it is achieved – academic freedom.

CONCLUSION

Recent decades have shown a fundamental and political redefinition of universities and education, as part of a redefinition of public services in general. Social and political values have been subordinated to the economic value of producing profit and operating efficiently. Weber suggests that it is becoming anachronistic to speak of an 'idea' governing a university: rather, the prevailing tendency is to talk of the 'mission' of the university. The term 'mission' no longer has a religious or transcendent connotation, and 'instead is employed to suggest the dependence of the university on the prevailing economic system. The 'mission' of the university is thus increasingly understood as that of being 'accountable' to those who pay for it, whether these are understood to be large corporations, individual taxpayers or even students.' (Weber, 1996, pp. 53-4)

This sentiment has led to calls for the 'philosophical separation of the notions of *accountability* and *accounting.*' (Readings, 1996, p. 18) Readings argues that 'it is imperative that the University respond to the demand for accountability, while at the same time refusing to conduct the debate over the nature of its responsibility solely in terms of the language of accounting (whose currency is excellence).' (Readings, 1996, p. 19) Kelsey refers to the 'consensus-mongering' of global neo-liberalism as directly antipathetic to the traditional university, which is a source of critique and a breeding ground for radical ideas. The successful subjugation of the university in that form to the precepts of neo-liberal economics results in an intellectual closure, an absence of questioning, (Kelsey, 1998, p. 60) the very converse of academic freedom.

Universities are under significant pressure, arising from the costs associated with a mass higher education system, a clear expectation that the higher education sector is tied to the national economy, that an increasing expectation of participation higher education makes it more or a political issue, competing burdens on social services arising from changing demographics, and the development of the 'knowledge processing sector'. (Slaughter & Leslie, 1997, p. 6) Nevertheless, co-option of universities to the instrumental tasks presented by these pressures *to the exclusion* of a culture of inquiry is directly antithetical to the wider purposes to which these tasks are directed. In failing to hold their ground universities are on increasingly precarious ground.

REFERENCES

American Association of University Professors. (1915). General report of the Committee on Academic Freedom and Academic Tenure. *Bulletin of the AAUP*.

Association of American Colleges and Universities. (1940). *Statement of principles on academic freedom and tenure*. Retrieved January 20th, 2010, from http://www.aaup.org/AAUP/pubsres/policydocs/contents/1940statement.htm

Australian Universities Quality Agency. (2008). *Submission to the Senate Standing Committee on Education, Employment and Workplace Relations*. Commonwealth of Australia.

Bethel School District No 403 v Fraser, 478 US 675. *(1986)*.

Board of Regents of the University of Wisconsin System v Southworth, 529 US 217. *(2000)*.

Brown, T., Goodman, J., & Yasukawa, K. (2006). *Getting the best of you for nothing - casual voices in the Australian academy*. Retrieved January 27th, 2010, from http://www.nteu.org.au/getinvolved/categories/casual/papers/uts

Department of Employment, Education, Training and Youth Affairs. (1998). *Learning for life - review of higher education financing and policy. Final Report*. Canberra, Australia: Commonwealth of Australia.

Fish, S. (1994). *There's no such thing as free speech (and it's a good thing, too)*. New York, NY: Oxford University Press.

Forss, P. (2007, May 23rd). *Singapore News*. Retrieved January 22nd, 2010, from http://www.channelnewsasia.com/stories/sinaporelocalnews/view/277897/1/.html

Garcetti v Ceballos, 547 US 410. (2006).

Gelber, K. (2008). *Academic freedom in Australia*. Retrieved December 4, 2009, from http://www.australianreview.net/digest/2008/12/gelber.html

George, R. T. (2003). Ethics, academic freedom and academic tenure. *Journal of Academic Ethics*, *1*, 11–25. doi:10.1023/A:1025421706331

Griffiths, J. (1992). *Communicating the idea of a university in the public sphere - Habermasian social theory as a framework for critique*. Research paper, Deakin University.

Harmon, G. (2004). New directions in internationalizing higher education: Australia's development as an exporter of higher education services. *Higher Education Policy*, *17*(1), 101–120. doi:10.1057/palgrave.hep.8300044

Hazelwood School District v Kuhlmeier, 484 US 260. *(1988)*.

Healey, N. (2008). Is higher education really internationalising? *Higher Education*, *55*, 333–335. doi:10.1007/s10734-007-9058-4

Healy, G. (2009, October 7). Law to back academic freedom. *The Australian*. Retrieved December 4, 2009, from http://www.theaustralian.com.au/higher-education/law-to-back-academic-freedom/story-e6frgcjx-1225783534874

Healy v James, 408 US 169. (1972).

Higher Education Acts (Amendment). *(*2005*)*.

Hirsch, F. (1976). *Social limits to growth*. Cambridge, MA: Harvard University Press.

Illing, D. (2000, March 29). Rules mean unis must measure up. *The Australian*, (p. 35).

Illing, D., & Richardson, J. (1999, March 10). Greenwich forum call. *The Australian*, (p. 39).

Joiner, T. A., & Bakalis, S. (2006). The antecedents of organizational commitment: The case of Australian casual academics. *International Journal of Educational Management*, *20*(6), 439–452. doi:10.1108/09513540610683694

Junor, A. (2003). *Choice, risk and equity in casual university work: Implications for regulation*. Unpublished discussion paper.

Junor, A. (2004). Casual university work: Choice, risk, inequity and the case for regulation. *Economic and Labour Relations Review*, 276-304.

Karran, T. (2009). Academic freedom: In justification of a universal ideal. *Studies in Higher Education*, *34*(3), 263–283. doi:10.1080/03075070802597036

Kayrooz, C., Kinnear, P., & Preston, P. (2001). *Academic freedom and commercialisation of Australian universities: Perceptions and experiences of social scientists*. Australia Institute.

Kelsey, J. (1998). Privatizing the universities. *Journal of Law and Society*, *25*, 51. doi:10.1111/1467-6478.00079

Kementerian Pendidikan Malaysia. (1997). *Private higher educational institutions (expulsion of students) regulations*. Kuala Lumpur, Malaysia: Jabatan Pendidikan Swasta.

Lowry, D. (2001). The casual management of casual work: Casual workers' perceptions of HRM practices in the highly casualised firm. *Asia Pacific Journal of Human Resources*, *39*(1), 42–62. doi:10.1177/103841110103900104

Marginson, S. (2006). Dynamics of national and global competition in higher education. *Higher Education*, *52*, 1–39. doi:10.1007/s10734-004-7649-x

Marginson, S. (2008). Academic creativity under new public management: Foundations for an investigation. *Educational Theory*, *58*(3), 269–287. doi:10.1111/j.1741-5446.2008.00288.x

McBurnie, G., & Ziguras, C. (2001). The regulation of transnational higher education in Southeast Asia: Case studies of Hong Kong, Malaysia and Australia. *Higher Education*, *42*, 85–105. doi:10.1023/A:1017572119543

McClurg, L. N. (1999). Organizational commitment in the temporary-help service industry. *Journal of Applied Management Studies*, *8*(1), 5–26.

Melbourne University Act. (1958).

Morse v Frederick, 127 S Ct 2618. (2007).

Neave, G., & Van Vught, F. A. (1991). *Prometheus bound - the changing relationship between government and higher education in Western Europe. NTEIU v University of Wollongong, FCA 1069.* (2001).

Order on Web college claims. (1999, June 2). *The Australian*, (p. 35).

Papish v Board of the Curators of the University of Missouri, 410 US 667. *(1973).*

Pearce v Pearce, 63 Eng Rep 950. (1846).

Pickering v Board of Education, 391 US 563. *(1968).*

Post, R. (2006). The structure of academic freedom. In Doumani, B. (Ed.), *Academic freedom after September 11* (p. 61).

Rawls, J. (1971). *A theory of justice*. Cambridge, MA: Harvard University Press.

Readings, B. (1996). *The university in ruins*. Cambridge, MA & London, UK: Harvard University Press.

Riddiford, M. (2009, October 14). Academic freedom a political football. *The Australian*. Retrieved December 4, 2009, from http://www.theaustralian.com.au/higher-education/opinion-analysis/academic-freedom-a-political-football/story-e6frgcko-1225786422196

Rochford, F. (2003). Academic freedom as insubordination: The legalisation of the academy. In G. B. Palfreyman (Ed.), *Education and the Law, 15*(4), 249-262.

Rochford, F. (2006). Is there any clear idea of a university? *Journal of Higher Education Policy and Management, 28*(2), 147–158. doi:10.1080/13600800600750988

Rochford, F. (2007). The law of negligence in a risk society: Calculating ideas of reasonable risk. *Griffith Law Review*, 172-192.

Rochford, F. (2008). The contested product of a university education. *Journal of Higher Education Policy and Management, 30*(1), 41–52. doi:10.1080/13600800701745044

Rochford, F. (2008). The contested product of a university education. *Journal of Higher Education Policy and Management*, 41–52. doi:10.1080/13600800701745044

Rondinelli, D. (2002). Transnational corporations: International citizens or new sovereigns. *Business & Society, 107*, 391–413. doi:10.1111/1467-8594.00143

Rosborough, R. S. (2009). A great day for academic freedom: The threat posed to academic freedom by the Supreme Court's decision in Garcetti v Ceballos. *Albany Law Review*, 565–598.

Rosenberger v Rector and Visitors of the University of Virginia, 515 US 819. *(1995).*

Royal Melbourne Institute of Technology Act. *(1992).*

Scott, J. (2009). Knowledge, power and academic freedom. *Social Research*, 452–480.

Senate Standing Committee on Education. Employment and Workplace Relations. (2008). *Allegations of academic bias in universities and schools: Report.* Canberra, Australia: Commonwealth of Australia.

Shattock, M. (1996). *Creation of a university system*. Blackwell Publishing.

Shive, G. (2010, January). Exporting higher education services: An engine of growth for Hong Kong? *Hkjournal*. Retrieved January 22, 2010, from www.hkjournal.org/PDF/2010_spring/4.pdf

Slaughter, S., & Leslie, L. L. (1997). *Academic capitalism*. Baltimore, MD: Johns Hopkins University Press.

St George, E. (2006). Positioning higher education for the knowledge based economy. *Higher Education*, 589–610. doi:10.1007/s10734-005-0955-0

Swinburne University of Technology Act. (1992).

The University of Adelaide. (2005). *Casual employment guidelines*. Retrieved January 27th, 2010, from http://www.adelaide.edu.au/policies/689/?dsn=policy.document;field=data;id=2843;m=view

The University of Western Australia. (2009). *Code of ethics and code of conduct*. Retrieved January 27th, 2010, from http://www.hr.uwa.edu.au/publications/code_of_ethics#ceth

Tinker v Des Moines Independent Community School District, 393 US 503. *(1969)*.

Toben v Jones, FCAFC 158. (2002).

Trow, M. (1994). Managerialism and the academic profession: The case of England. *Higher Education Policy*, *7*, 11–18. doi:10.1057/hep.1994.13

University of Ballarat Act. (1993).

University of South Australia. (2004). *Code of ethical conduct*. Retrieved January 27th, 2010, from http://www.unisa.edu.au/policies/codes/ethics/ethics.asp

University of South Australia. (2009). *Protocols for the management of academic casual staff*. Retrieved January 27th, 2010, from http://www.unisa.edu.au/hrm/employment/recruitment/academic/protocols.asp

University of Western Australia v Gray, FCAFC 116. *(2009)*.

University of Wollongong. (2008). *Code of practice - casual academic teaching*. Retrieved January 27th, 2010, from http://www.uow.edu.au/about/policy/OUW058668.html

Varghese, N. V. (2008). *Globalization of higher education and cross-border student mobility*. Paris, France: International Institute for Educational Planning.

Weber, S. (1996). The future of the university: The cutting edge. In T. S. (Ed), *Ideas of the university* (pp. 43-76). Sydney, Australia: Research Institute for the Humanities and Social Sciences and Power Publications.

Welters, R., & Mitchell, W. (2009). *Locked in casual employment. University of Newcastle*. Newcastle, UK: Centre of Full Employment and Equity.

Wheeler, S. (2007). Ethics in the workplace. *Law and Critique*, *18*, 1–28. doi:10.1007/s10978-006-9008-9

Widmar v Vincent, 454 US 263. (1981).

World Bank. (2002). *Constructing knowledge societies: New challenges for tertiary education*. Washington, DC.

ADDITIONAL READING

Åkerlind, G., & Kayrooz, C. (2003). Understanding academic freedom: the views of social scientists. *Higher Research and Development*, *22*(3), 327–344. doi:10.1080/0729436032000145176

Altman, P. G. (2001). Academic freedom: International realities and challenges. *Higher Education*, *41*, 205–219. doi:10.1023/A:1026791518365

Anderson, D., & Johnson, R. (1998). *University Autonomy in Twenty Countries Higher Education Division Evaluations and Investigations Program*. Canberra: Australian Government Publishing Service.

Berdahl, R. (1990). Academic freedom, autonomy and accountability in British universities. *Studies in Higher Education*, *15*(2), 69–80. doi:10.1080/03075079012331377491

Brown, R. S., & Kurland, J. E. (1990). Freedom and Tenure in the Academy: The Fiftieth Anniversary of the 1940 Statement of Principles. *Law and Contemporary Problems*, *53*(3), 325–355. doi:10.2307/1191800

Daughtrey, W. (1990). The legal nature of academic freedom in United States colleges and universities. *University of Richmond Law Review. University of Richmond*, *25*(2), 233–271.

De George, R. (2003). Ethics, academic freedom and academic tenure. *Journal of Academic Ethics*, *1*(1), 11–25. doi:10.1023/A:1025421706331

European Universities Association. (1988). *Magna Charta Universitatum*. Bologna: EUA.

Kaplan, C., & Schrecker, E. (Eds.). (1983). *Regulating the Intellectuals: perspectives on academic freedom in the 1980s*. New York: Praeger.

Kaplin, W. A., & Lee, B. A. (2006). *The Law of Higher Education*. San Francisco: John Wiley & Sons.

Karran, T. (2007). Academic freedom in Europe: a preliminary comparative analysis. *Higher Education Policy*, *20*, 289–313. doi:10.1057/palgrave.hep.8300159

Lieberwitz, R. (2002–03). The corporatisation of the university: distance learning at the cost of academic freedom? *The Boston University Public Interest Law Journal*, *12*(1), 73–135.

Marginson, S. (1997). How Free is Academic Freedom? *Higher Education Research & Development*, *16*, 359–369. doi:10.1080/0729436970160309

Marginson, S., & Considine, M. (2000) *The Enterprise University*

Menand, L. (1996). *The Future of Academic Freedom*. Chicago: University of Chicago Press.

Metzger, W. P. (1969). *Dimensions of Academic Freedom*. Urbana: University of Illinois Press.

Olivas, M. A. (1993). *'Reflections on Professorial Academic Freedom: Second Thoughts on the Third "Essential Freedom"' Stanford Law Review, 45, (6) 1835-1858 O'Neil, R., (1997) Free Speech in the College Community*. Indiana University Press.

Pincoffs, E. L. (Ed.). (1975) *Conference on the Concept of Academic Freedom, University of Texas at Austin*. Austin: University of Texas Press

Poch, R. K. (1993). *Academic Freedom in American Higher Education: Rights, Responsibilities, and Limitations*. Washington, D.C.: George Washington University, School of Education.

Russell, C. (1993). *Academic Freedom*. London: Routledge.

Tierney, W. (2001). Academic freedom and organisational identity. *Australian Universities Review*, *44*(1), 7–14.

Tight, M. (1988). So What Is Academic Freedom? In Tight, M. (Ed.), *Academic Freedom and Responsibility*.

Trow, M. (1994). Managerialism and the academic profession: The case of England. *Higher Education Policy*, 7.

Turner, J. (1988). The Price of Freedom. In Tight, M. (Ed.), *Academic Freedom and Responsibility* (pp. 104–113). Buckingham: SRHE/OU Press.

White, L. (2000). Academic tenure: its historical and legal meanings in the United States and its relationship to the compensation of medical school faculty members. *Saint Louis University Law Journal*, *44*(1), 51–80.

Yeatman, A. (1996). The New Contractualism: Management Reform or a New Approach to Governance? In Weller, P., & Davis, G. (Eds.), *New Ideas*. Better Government.

KEY TERMS AND DEFINITIONS

Academic Freedom: This term is capable of many definitions and limitations, but in general it is autonomy to carry out research and scholarly activities in a university without constraints imposed by internal and external bodies.

Ethics: Ethics as a philosophical study deals with questions of morality.

Knowledge Society: this typically aspirational term refers to the situation in which knowledge forms the basis of the economy.

Managerialism: Managerialism is a (typically pejorative) term representing a shift in university management from a collegiate style to a top-down technique, largely to improve efficiency and accountability.

New Public Management: NPM has been introduced in the provision of governmental services, as well as to the management of universities. It applies a suite of techniques adapted from commercial practices such as the use of performance measures, concentration on outputs and the introduction of competition to develop efficiency in the provision of public services.

Tenure: Again, this term has multiple understandings. In general the system of tenure protects an academic against arbitrary dismissal. It is usually only afforded to academics once their general competence has been established.

University: An institution of higher learning historically, incorporated by authority (typically by legislation or charter) characterised by autonomous management, research as well as teaching, accepting students openly, and teaching one of the 'higher faculties'. The definition of the university in practice, of course, depends upon the legislative authority allowing a body to function as a university.

Chapter 11
Developing a Grassroots Cross-Cultural Partnership to Enhance Student Experiences

Iryna Pentina
University of Toledo, USA

Veronique Guilloux
UPEC IRG, France

EXECUTIVE SUMMARY

Increased globalization of the world economy makes international aspects of marketing an important priority. A growing number of business colleges provide cross-cultural experiences in marketing disciplines that help students better understand other cultures while applying their academic preparation to real-life settings. Today's students represent the first generation that has been born into the digital age, and freely use multiple technologies in preparing for classes, sharing notes, shopping, rating professors, and accomplishing multiple everyday tasks. This case discusses a class project on developing integrated marketing communications conducted by American and French cross-cultural student groups to promote environmentally-sustainable products in international markets. Modern social networking technologies were widely used both as tools for accomplishing the project, as means for presenting and displaying the results and as a medium for international marketing communications.

INTRODUCTION

Bringing real-world relevance into the classroom is a widely-acknowledged challenge for marketing educators (Bearden, Ellen, & Netemeyer, 2000). Media convergence and globalized markets present complex and unique problems to budding practitioners, requiring skills in innovativeness, problem-solving, resource optimization, and creativity. Business colleges and schools face more rigorous demands from both employers and students for adequate and cutting-edge workplace preparation. In addressing these challenges, marketing professors increasingly utilize innovative teaching methods that include simulations, qualitative interpretive research, interdisciplin-

DOI: 10.4018/978-1-60960-599-5.ch011

ary projects and innovative uses of technology (Albers-Miller, Straughan, & Prenshaw, 2001). Such emerging and rapidly developing content areas as corporate social responsibility, marketing ethics, digital and mobile marketing, globalization of marketing, and ecological sustainability are being incorporated in marketing curricula to reflect the changing business environment (Bridges & Wilhelm, 2008; Kelley, 2007; Jahan & Mehta, 2007). This chapter reports on designing and implementing a cross-cultural student team project that answers the calls for comprehensive, realistic, and relevant teaching tools in marketing classrooms, which promote collaborative problem-solving using available technological advancements, and broaden students' perspectives on the global economy.

SETTING THE STAGE

The idea for the project was developed by the instructors as a result of sharing research papers and data online: both the French and the American marketing professors were using qualitative research in their investigation, and observed substantial cultural differences in student responses to similar questions. This finding led to an idea of having student teams create marketing communications campaigns using qualitative research data collected by their international teams with the goal to introduce and emphasize the concept of cross-cultural marketing and comparative marketing. The existence and wide availability of the Internet, the availability of overlapping instructional calendar schedule, as well as the requirement for the French students in their program to fluently speak English helped avoid frequently mentioned challenges for cross-cultural collaborations. The choice of the content area for the project was mutual: environmental sustainability has become a globally urgent issue that has yet to find its way into the marketing curriculum. The intensifying development of "green" start-ups, investment firms, political initiatives and regulations creates an imperative for business schools to prepare graduates for the sustainable business activities and practices, strategies and tactics. The project was conducted in the fall semester of 2008, with one pilot class of 30-35 students in each of the participating universities (in France and in the US).

CASE DESCRIPTION

Cross-Cultural Marketing Education

Increased globalization of the world economy makes teaching international aspects of marketing an important priority. The demand for international literacy and sensitivity among the business sector job applicants is reflected in AACSB requirements for international focus in business curricula. The major reason cross-cultural marketing education is necessary is that although globalization facilitates homogenization of tastes and fashions, strong national and local differences exist among cultures that warrant separate and different marketing campaigns, and brand and product development efforts. The ease of offering a product globally does not imply its universal acceptance. That is why globalization necessarily presupposes marketing with cultural sensitivity and understanding (Kelley, 2007). According to Morris et al. (1999), society can be analyzed using two different interpretations. The inside view considers constructs and ideas from a specific local perspective. This is the Emic view which relies on internal member's society criteria. In the outside view, the point of vantage is external and is called Etic. From the latter position, culture can be analyzed with universal categories. The two approaches are seen as either dichotomous or complementary and alternate in the process of cultural investigation. Thus, the ultimate goal of teaching cross-cultural marketing would be to teach students to evolve to the Etic interpretation through comparing various Emic approaches.

Harris and Moran's (1987) view on culture as a learned, shared and interrelated set of symbols, codes and values that justify human behavior informed our definition of cross-cultural marketing. Marketing across cultures means marketing to consumers whose culture is different in at least one fundamental aspect, such as values, lifestyle, social norms, religion, or language. Therefore, the strategic process of cross-cultural marketing should involve researching, planning and implementing all elements of the marketing mix (product, price, promotion, and distribution). In addition to studying how a particular culture may affect any marketing initiative, it is also important to ascertain the extent to which a company's marketing efforts may affect this culture (Hall, 1976) and the consequences of such changes. This, in turn, makes the process of cross-cultural marketing continually evolving, and the need for teaching and learning this are particularly pressing.

A growing number of business colleges provide study abroad experiences in marketing disciplines that help students better understand other cultures while applying their academic preparation to real-life settings. Recent reports indicate drastic increases in the number of study abroad tours among American students (100% increase over the past 8 years), with the most valued activities cited by the students being cultural activities, experiencing day-to-day life, and communicating with the locals (Koernig, 2007). The literature on study abroad mentions numerous potential difficulties and problems that can be encountered during the trip: managing large groups, overindulgence in parties, balancing academic content and cultural activities, etc. (Koernig, 2007). Additionally, with rising energy prices and weakening economic situation, the trips tend to be shorter and present a very sketchy and superficial introduction to different cultures and business environments. It appears that other methods may be used to achieve international emphasis in teaching marketing, in particular those using the available technology to connect students across the world.

The Roles of Technology and Team-Based Collaborative Problem-Solving

With the Internet penetration reaching 63.6% in the US, and 16.6% of the worldwide population (International Telecommunications Union, 2007), communicating and working across political and geographical borders have become unproblematic and universal. Email and chat, gaming and brand virtual communities, as well as medical, professional, social networks and political forums and blogs are being widely used; electronic commerce is booming; and mobile communications are becoming more available and affordable. Today's students represent the first generation that has been born into the digital age, and freely use multiple technologies in preparing for classes, sharing notes, shopping, rating professors, and accomplishing multiple everyday tasks. Such social networks as the Facebook and My Space allow its participants to literally share their lives with the selected referents. Any of these interfaces can be used by the project teams to meet, share ideas, and jointly work on the project using available collaboration software to track changes and make comments.

Group projects are considered a very effective pedagogical technique in marketing (Hernandez, 2002). They are used extensively in virtually all marketing classes as both a short, one class period-long technique (ad hoc clusters to discuss a question or solve a problem), and as longer formations to complete a case study or write a paper. The benefits stemming from utilizing group projects in advertising, marketing research, personal selling, public relations, and other marketing courses include exposure to applied near-work experiences, ability to work on larger and more complex projects, and higher student motivation and interest (McCorkle et al., 1999, Williams et al., 1991). This project used formally assigned teams that were established for the whole duration of the assignment (from October until December of 2008). The teams were self-selected by the students and confirmed by instructors. Both the American and the French class formed 7 groups that were paired in cross-cultural teams according to their interest in one of the proposed "green" products (organic food, cosmetics, appliances, etc.). Thus, each joint cross-cultural group contained 4-5 American and 4-5 French students (for the total of 8-10 students). It has been noted that an optimal size for a team should be larger than 3 and fewer than 9 participants (Cooper, 1990; Smith, 1986). The suggested group size made in-country groups flexible enough to meet frequently, and cross-cultural groups – large enough to accomplish the assignment successfully. To avoid free-riding and prevent non-cooperation, peer evaluation was offered after the completion of the project, so that each member assessed the contribution of all members in their cross-cultural group. An additional benefit of using teams is an opportunity for inter-group competition. In this project, the marketing communications created by each team were subsequently rated by marketing students within respective Colleges of Business, and the winning cross-cultural team was announced and recognized within the College. Thus, the concept of cross-cultural virtual project teamwork has been created and implemented whereby technology (e-mail, social network, groupware) replaced face-to-face communications. In this type of project, cross-cultural teams are dedicated toward a target (here creation of an advertising) in delimited duration. The technology supports textual communication (e-mails) but also multimedia (through internet). Collaboration in this kind of environment requires trust and motivation to achieve the tasks.

Sustainability Marketing and its Role in Marketing Curriculum

Environmental concerns represent a prominent narrative in today's social, political, and economic life worldwide. The tasks of preserving and reproducing resources for future generations, reducing and eliminating toxic waste, and ensuring social justice are being put forward and prioritized by governments, non-governmental entities, and international bodies (Blackburn, 2007). In the business arena, firms are increasingly adopting a "green" image and employ public relations and advertising to promote and express their concern with the environment. More companies utilize independent certification and labeling in their products (e.g. organic, Energy-Star, natural, etc.) and release sustainability reports and accountability statements regarding key environmental performance indicators (Bridges & Wilhelm, 2008). Skills related to sustainability marketing and advertising appear to be in high demand by commercial and non-profit organizations.

For several decades the growing segment of environmentally-concerned consumers has presented both an opportunity and a challenge to marketers. Tracing its origin to the environmental activism of the 1960s and 1970s that led to the establishment of numerous environmental groups, creation of the Environmental Protection Agency, adoption of the Endangered Species Act, the Comprehensive Environmental Act (Menon & Menon, 1997), and other legislature, the concern about sustainable development has been steadily on the rise. The role of marketing in the process of social and environmental change was theoretically justified and legitimized in 1971. In the introduction to the *JM* special issue on the topic, Kelly (1971, p.1) stated:

Environmental deterioration is the social issue which will probably receive the greatest amount of business involvement. Business responsibilities toward improving the environment will become more important because a variety of ecological and social forces are stimulating a long-term national commitment to environmental protection.

In the same issue, Kotler and Zaltman introduced the concept of social marketing, which goes beyond influencing the acceptability of social ideas to "deal with the market's core beliefs and values" as opposed to "superficial preferences and opinions" (Kotler & Zaltman, 1971, p. 11). Since then, and in light of the increasing demand for environment-friendly products and more meaningful regulation policies and interventions, the need to understand the "green" consumers of the 21st century has become a priority for marketers. This understanding can help create meaningful marketing messages and help businesses modify their products and marketing strategies.

In accordance with a UN Human Environment report (World Commission on Environment and Development, 1987) on sustainable development, we define sustainable marketing as an integrative approach addressing environment, social equity, and economic/financial concerns in the development of marketing strategies (Bridges & Wilhelm, 2008). The concept of sustainable marketing incorporates environmentally sound vision, socially responsible business practices, and economic stability into traditional marketing strategies, tactics, and communications. A recent survey of business schools' commitment to teaching sustainability indicates that over half of the assessed business colleges require courses on sustainability. Among those courses there are a number of marketing electives that focus on new product and marketing communications sustainability; additionally, other marketing courses are adding content segments emphasizing environmental and social issues (Bridges & Wilhelm, 2008). Sustainable debates in France are emphasized, for example, by the ministry (Ministère de l'Ecologie, de l'Energie, du Développement durable et de la Mer) and through the implementation of the French law RNE (nouvelles régulations économiques) which imposes listed securities to write an annual report on their sustainable politics. Several research projects have been funded by the French government to analyze sustainable development. Academic association like Association Française du Marketing stimulates the creation of knowledge on that subject. Some French universities require pedagogical teams to integrate in each teaching module a session on sustainable development so that each student learns to be sensitive to ecological issues and to respect the planet. However, "current levels of student knowledge and comprehension regarding sustainability are low" (Bridges & Wilhelm 2008, p. 44) and calls are being issued to develop new pedagogical ideas, joint interdisciplinary projects and research endeavors that would move this content area to a more advanced level.

PROJECT OUTLINE

One Principles of Marketing Communications (US, 35 students) and one International Marketing Management (France, 40 students) class were selected for this cross-cultural project, the goal of which was to develop international and cultural understanding of environmental sustainability among future marketing professionals, promote analytical and creative thinking skills by engaging students in qualitative market research and interpretation, and provide hands-on opportunity to develop targeted marketing communications for international audiences and test their effectiveness. The selection of these classes was based on the objectives in their curricula emphasizing development of cross-cultural marketing understanding and skills. Additionally, the catalog descriptions of both classes emphasized the development of marketing communications campaigns as their intended deliverables. The project started in October and ended in December of 2008, the months during which academic schedules for both universities overlapped (Table 1).

At the beginning of the project, its objectives, structure, timeline, and the evaluation criteria were explained to both groups by their instructors (Figure 1).

They were then requested to voluntarily select their local team members based on common aca-

Table 1. Outline of the project

Date	Activity	Notes and Additional Readings
Oct 2008	Introduce the project and its goals	Students start selecting teams and product categories
	Module on Sustainability and its Global Implications	Clark 2007; McDonald et al. 2006; Mont and Plepys 2008; Oates et al. 2008;
	Confirm teams and products, assign international peer teams	Students establish electronic communications
	Module on Qualitative research and Depth Interviewing Techniques	McCracken 1988, LeCompte and Schensul 1999, Miles and Huberman 1994, Price, Arnould and Curasi et al. 2000, Pryor and Grossbart 2005
Nov 2008	Qualitative Research	Conduct depth interviews, record, translate and share transcripts
	Depth Interview Analysis	Code transcripts and analyze the results
	Work on Creative Campaigns	Students create marketing communications campaigns for both French and American audiences
Dec 2008	Compare US and French results and interpret them	Comparative analysis of campaign effectiveness and cultural differences

Figure 1.

This project provides you an opportunity to apply the concepts learned in this class to creating multi-cultural marketing communications campaigns for promoting "green" products. You will be working in international teams with marketing students in France (Paris). Initially you should select your local team members based on academic interests and logistical convenience (3-4 students), and then you will be paired with a French team based on common interests in particular "green" product categories. Each international team will then identify a product for which it will develop a **marketing communications campaign** embracing at least two communications venues (e.g. print and online) that would synergistically impact targeted consumers' behavior. Based on customer data obtained through depth interviews in both countries, each international team will develop one campaign for the American market, and one campaign for the French market.

The criteria for a successful marketing communications campaign are: proper audience selection and targeting, creativity, memorability, brand appeal, and competitive differentiation. In addition to a receiving grade, each campaign will be evaluated by other classes of marketing students in respective countries (or by actual target markets), based on brand recognition, brand recall, and purchase intentions. Winners in both countries will be recognized.

A proposal with your group's preliminary thoughts (no more than 1 page) is due no later than **October 25**. In the proposal you should: describe the selected "green" product (or service), describe the potential customers and competitors, and provide justification of your choice (e.g. changing consumption trends or technological breakthroughs).

Separate class meetings will focus on 1) sustainable consumption and its role in the world and 2) qualitative research techniques (specifically, on depth interviewing). Each team member will select a representative of the target market for their group's product and conduct a semi-structured depth interview (sample outline attached). French students should provide interview transcripts in English. Criteria for a good quality depth interview are: breadth of the domain tapped, number of new themes uncovered, information on motivations for acquiring the product, information on competitors' products perception, and suggestions for the group's Marketing communications creative and strategic solutions.

Table 2. List of the suggested environmentally sustainable product categories and the products selected

Product Category	Additional Information and Resources	Products Selected by Teams
Green Transportation	http://www2.ademe.fr http://www.cleanvehicle.org/ http://www.car-free.org/ http://www.sierraclub.org/transportation/	Tesla Roadster Honda Clarity Hybrid Ford Truck Solar-Powered Jet Skis
Personal care	http://www.greenpeople.org/OrganicSkinCare.html http://www.ecoseek.net/browse/personal-care/	Organic Cosmetics Bio-Detergent
Clothing and accessories	http://www.ams.usda.gov/AMSv1.0/nop http://www.buygreen.com/EcoGreenClothing.html http://www.ecoist.com/	Recyclable Flip-Flops Shoes from Tires Bio-Degradable Diapers
Organic Food Products	http://www.organic-europe.net http://www.organic.org/	Organic Beer
Household Products	http://www.guide-topten.com/ http://www.eco-label.com/default.htm http://www.ecohuddle.com/products/	Shower Filter Water Softener Solar Panels

demic interests and convenience. Subsequently, local teams were paired with the respective foreign teams based on their interest in a particular sustainable, fair or green product category (Arthus-Bertrand, 2008; Canfin, 2008) from the following list: green transportation, personal care, clothes and accessories, organic food products, and household products (Table 2). By the third week of the project progression, the cross-cultural teams had established communications via email, discussion boards, and social networking sites and finalized their selection of products within their preferred categories.

Concurrently with team formation, students in both countries were offered a content module on sustainable consumption that included one class lecture and a general online discussion board supported by the US University's distance learning platform. The discussion was moderated by the instructors, based on the suggested readings (Table 1), and emphasized cultural differences in views on sustainability. The sustainability module served as a background that facilitated team and product selection and as an initial reference for collecting secondary data, and doing research on target markets and competitive environment.

At the beginning of the second month of the project the students were trained in depth interviewing and practiced compiling interview guides (Table 1). They proceeded to conduct depth interviews with consumers in their respective countries, which they transcribed and shared within their teams via email. The interviews followed a structured interview guide (Figure 2) and focused on consumer attitudes towards the selected product, the concept of sustainability in general, and the motivations of buying "green", with suggested probing questions on the role of information, communication and advertising in affecting buying decisions. The whole team was responsible for coding and categorizing the transcribed materials, as well as for coming up with marketing communications theme and creative decisions. The analysis was completed and submitted to the instructors by the end of the second month of the project. The third month was dedicated to team collaborations on creating marketing communications (advertising, web advertising, or a website) to promote the product.

Figure 2.

This project provides you an opportunity to apply the concepts learned in this class to creating multi-cultural marketing communications campaigns for promoting "green" products. You will be working in international teams with marketing students in France (Paris). Initially you should select your local team members based on academic interests and logistical convenience (3-4 students), and then you will be paired with a French team based on common interests in particular "green" product categories. Each international team will then identify a product for which it will develop a **marketing communications campaign** embracing at least two communications venues (e.g. print and online) that would synergistically impact targeted consumers' behavior. Based on customer data obtained through depth interviews in both countries, each international team will develop one campaign for the American market, and one campaign for the French market.

The criteria for a successful marketing communications campaign are: proper audience selection and targeting, creativity, memorability, brand appeal, and competitive differentiation. In addition to a receiving grade, each campaign will be evaluated by other classes of marketing students in respective countries (or by actual target markets), based on brand recognition, brand recall, and purchase intentions. Winners in both countries will be recognized.
A proposal with your group's preliminary thoughts (no more than 1 page) is due no later than **October 25**. In the proposal you should: describe the selected "green" product (or service), describe the potential customers and competitors, and provide justification of your choice (e.g. changing consumption trends or technological breakthroughs).

Separate class meetings will focus on 1) sustainable consumption and its role in the world and 2) qualitative research techniques (specifically, on depth interviewing). Each team member will select a representative of the target market for their group's product and conduct a semi-structured depth interview (sample outline attached). French students should provide interview transcripts in English. Criteria for a good quality depth interview are: breadth of the domain tapped, number of new themes uncovered, information on motivations for acquiring the product, information on competitors' products perception, and suggestions for the group's Marketing communications creative and strategic solutions.

Each group worked on two types of communications: for French and for American audiences, analyzing and synthesizing their findings and realizing global advertizing principles learned in class. The final products of the project contained combinations of print, radio, video and/or social networks ads. They were posted online, and business students in both countries ranked them on quality and purchase intentions.

CHALLENGES FACING THE PROJECT

It is widely believed that college students learn better and report higher satisfaction with learning when they are actively involved in the process (Beckman, 1990). Working jointly on solving real-world problems fosters the development of communication and leadership skills, negotiation and persuasion abilities, as well as presentation and writing proficiencies (McCorkle et al., 1999). Being responsible for the group results stimulates independent contribution, increases student motivation to seek information and feedback from the instructor, and fosters organizational and time management capabilities (Paladino, 2008). Group projects are considered a very effective pedagogical technique in marketing (Hernandez, 2002). They are used extensively in virtually all marketing classes as both a short, one class period-long technique (ad hoc clusters to discuss a question or solve a problem), and as longer formations to complete a case study or write a paper. The benefits stemming from utilizing group projects in advertising, marketing research, personal selling, public relations, and other marketing courses include exposure to applied near-work experiences, ability to work on larger and more complex projects, and higher student motivation and interest (McCorkle et al., 1999, Williams et al., 1991). There are some potential downsides to utilizing project teams. Some frequently mentioned problems include potential lower exposure to the scope of the problem due to specialization of tasks, reduced quality of learning for free-riders (McCorkle et al., 1999), potential for inter-personal conflicts, etc. For a cross-cultural, electronically-mediated project, additional problems may arise with inability to get in touch, language and time differences, as well as cultural misunderstanding. Additionally, perceptions of sustainability have been historically different for Europe and the USA, with the European "green" movements enjoying much greater popularity and engagement among younger populations.

SOLUTIONS AND RECOMMENDATIONS

Participation in and fulfillment of this cross-cultural team assignment has provided students from both countries with hands-on experience with a foreign culture and understanding of the differences in approaches to sustainability, as well as analyzing different attitudes towards and expectations from marketing communications. For example, at the stage of product selection, French students reported that the market for pick-up trucks in France exists ONLY among small business owners, and is non-existent among general commuter drivers. Therefore, the French campaign was refocused to target small businesses with a hybrid pick-up truck. Similarly, the concept of solar-powered jet-skis was not familiar to the French students, and it took a sufficient amount of communications to be finalized as a "green" product of choice.

At the stage of interviewing and transcript sharing, the majority of teams found that the concept of sustainability and "green" consumption is perceived by the French markets as a duty, and by the American markets more in terms of convenience and savings these products may provide. Therefore, the campaigns for the French consumers overwhelmingly emphasized the cause-related appeals of saving the planet and making the country beautiful, while the same products for American consumers were focused on more pragmatic advantages, such as saving money and gas. It was also discovered that American respondents preferred learning about detailed and more technical product attributes and specifications (e.g. driving range of an electric vehicle or the number of shampoo bottles that one organic bar soap substitutes) while French customers were better persuaded by symbolic appeals and functional benefits within an ad (e.g. fashion for shoes from recycled tires and protesting animal testing for organic cosmetics).

The goals of the assignment were fulfilled: the cross-cultural groups created marketing communications campaigns, with the majority containing one social networks advertising and one print advertising, each utilizing the advantages of the respective medium and reflecting cultural differences of the target markets. In addition to formal grading by instructors, the campaigns were offered to other marketing students in both countries for comments that were subsequently discussed by the teams. The conclusions about campaign effectiveness were included into the final reports. While the project was very successful in achieving the pre-determined educational goals, there were some unexpected issues and challenges in its execution. At the initial stage, the students enjoyed establishing connections and technology-mediated communications by sharing their photographs and becoming friends on social networks. As the project progressed, some groups experienced difficulties with on-time submission and sharing of ideas, suggestions, and depth interview transcripts that led to frequent instructor interventions. A solution to this may be arranging the project into modules by establishing deadlines and enforcing the submission of each deliverable increment to instructors. However, this approach may reinforce the timeliness at the expense of closer student collaboration and group norms development. Due to differences in academic schedules and academic levels, the final stage of the project (comparison and analysis of results) was less beneficial for the American participants who did not have sufficient time to reflect upon the outcomes. This issue can be addressed by more closely matching the educational level of the cross-cultural teams.

In order to more objectively assess the success of the project from the point of view of the students, the average class evaluation grade for the U.S. class was compared to the evaluation grade for the same Principles of Marketing Communications class that was taught by the same instructor in the Spring 2009 semester and did not offer a cross-cultural project. The class that contained the innovative project received the average evaluation of 4.2 out of 5, and the class without the innovation 4.0 out of 5. Additionally, both French and American students provided their verbal assessments of the project in their written comments. The responses (quoted below) were overwhelmingly positive and addressed the following learning outcomes:

Educational value added:

- "when compared to a similar project in another class based solely on secondary research, this joint research approach was an invaluable experience in that it gave me an opportunity to develop and test ideas based on dialog with students from France"
- "we not only studied theory, but had to use personal reflection and personal action"
- "the level of commitment was higher and we understand better, we learn better"
- "very enriching, would be glad to do it again!"
- "in seven semesters at two different universities, I've never had another opportunity like that. I recommend the experience highly"
- "having the ability to do a project with direct contact to students in another country should be a part of every student's college experience"

Higher level of analytical skills:

- "in case studies method, solutions are within easy reach, this project makes us think and draw conclusions based on our observations"
- "we used the same methods (e.g. SWOT analysis), but had to adapt it to fit the local conditions: e.g. the concept of recycling tires to make shoes is not new for the American consumers, but is an innovation for the French, so the whole business environment analysis is different"
- "our ideas and work were compared, which helped to see different approaches in marketing and advertising in two countries"

High practical relevance and realism:

- "this project was a little bit like working for two different branches of the same company"
- "in the same project, there is not a sole answer but different ones linked to different cultures. French people want to dream while American advertising is more practically oriented – we achieve the same result by different means"
- "it was very enriching to perceive other views in a culture that seems very close to ours"
- "this project helped me to develop some skills in marketing and advertising for my scholarship in Bordeaux where I worked for a communications agency"

Intercultural competencies:

- "I got to know working habits of other cultures, which helps avoid ethnocentrism"
- "now I will go to London for an internship … I have understood that a "French way" is not the only best way…I am ready to go to this English firm and be open to other perspectives"
- "even in international business classes I have not been able to connect with another culture so easily and efficiently as in this assignment"

Some negative evaluations of the project concerned logistical difficulties mentioned above:

- "we did not have enough time in the course of the project to speak to our American colleagues"

- " the schedules did not allow us to compare the different reactions of both markets to the advertising campaigns"
- "the cultural objectives of the project were not clearly formulated ... but that was a first experience"

Based on the above comments, the instructional innovation can be considered a useful pilot test of cross-cultural collaborative teaching.

Due to the broad spectrum of skills it introduces and reinforces, this project can be successfully incorporated into International Marketing, Marketing Research, Marketing Strategy and other classes with various degrees of emphasis on its components. For example, instead of depth interviews, students can do secondary or survey research; instead of "green" products, non-profit services can be the focus; alternatively, the deliverables do not have to focus on communications campaign, but may be a marketing plan or a package design. A similar assignment can be offered to MBA classes, with the additional results assessment and analytical components. This project was intended to improve student knowledge and awareness in the areas of international marketing and advertising (e.g. standardization vs. localization), human values (universal vs. culture-specific, e.g. environmentalism), establishing comparability (emic and etic dilemma), and the emerging domain of online advertizing and marketing (Craig & Douglass, 2000). It also promoted research skills, creativity and accountability, as well as cross-cultural technology-mediated collaboration, ability to apply theoretical knowledge to practice, and capability to solve real-life problems. By addressing the above content areas and specific skills development, this project answered the calls for marketing educators to incorporate complex, real-life and creative assignments into marketing curriculum and prepare more aware and better marketing specialists. This cross-cultural study involved only two cultures (American and French). It could be interesting to conduct a similar project in countries that are more culturally distant from each other. Additionally, the idea of "sustainable development diffusion lag" between economically developed and developing countries (e.g. those in Africa) could be explored to better understand differential marketing approaches in those countries.

REFERENCES

Albers-Miller, N. D., Straughan, R. D., & Prenshaw, P. J. (2001). Exploring innovative teaching among marketing educators: Perceptions of innovative activities and existing reward and support programs. *Journal of Marketing Education*, *23*(3), 249–259. doi:10.1177/0273475301233010

Bearden, W. O., Scholder, P. E., & Netemeyer, R. G. (2000). Challenges and prospects facing doctoral education in marketing. *Marketing Education Review*, *10*(1), 1–14.

Beckman, M. (1990). Collaborative learning: Preparation for the workplace and democracy. *College Teaching*, *38*(4), 128–133.

Blackburn, W. R. (2007). *The sustainability handbook*. Washington, DC: Environmental Law Institute.

Bridges, C. M., & Wilhelm, W. B. (2008). Going beyond green: The why and how of integrating sustainability into the marketing curriculum. *Journal of Marketing Education*, *30*(1), 33–46. doi:10.1177/0273475307312196

Clark, G. (2007). Evolution of the global sustainable consumption and production policy and the United Nations environment programme's (UNEP) supporting activities. *Journal of Cleaner Production*, *15*, 492–498. doi:10.1016/j.jclepro.2006.05.017

Cooper, J. (1990). Cooperative learning and college teaching: Tips from the trenches. *Teaching Professor*, *4*(5), 1–2.

Craig, C., & Douglas, S. (2000). *International marketing research*. Wiley.

Hall, E. T. (1976). *Beyond culture*. New York, NY: Anchor Press-Doubleday.

Harris, P. R., & Moran, R. T. (1987). *Managing cultural differences* (2nd ed.). Houston, TX: Gulf.

Hernandez, S. (2002). Team learning in a marketing principles course: Cooperative structures that facilitate active learning and higher level thinking. *Journal of Marketing Education*, *24*(1), 73–85. doi:10.1177/0273475302241009

Jahan, K., & Mehta, Y. (2007). Sustainability across the curriculum. *International Journal of Engineering Education*, *23*(2), 209–217.

Kelley, C. A. (2007). Assessing the trends and challenges of teaching marketing abroad: A delphi approach. *Journal of Marketing Education*, *29*(3), 201–209. doi:10.1177/0273475307306885

Kelley, E. P. (1971). Marketing's changing social/environmental role. *Journal of Marketing*, *35*(3), 1–2.

Kotler, P., & Zaltman, G. (1971). Social marketing: An approach to planned social change. *Journal of Marketing*, *35*(3), 3–12. doi:10.2307/1249783

LeCompte, M. D., & Schensul, J. J. (1999). The ethnographic tool kit: *Vol. 5. Analyzing and interpreting ethnographic data*. Walnut Creek, CA: AltaMira Press.

McCorkle, D. E., Reardon, J., Alexander, J. F., Kling, N. D., Harris, R. C., & Vishwanathan, I. R. (1999). Undergraduate marketing students, group projects, and teamwork: The good, the bad, and the ugly? *Journal of Marketing Education*, *21*(2), 106–117. doi:10.1177/0273475399212004

McCracken, G. (1988). Lois Roget: Curatorial consumer in a modern world. In *Culture and consumption* (pp. 44–56). Bloomington, IN: Indiana University Press.

McDonald, S., Oates, C. J., Young, C. W., & Hwang, K. (2006). Toward sustainable consumption: Researching voluntary simplifiers. *Psychology and Marketing*, *23*(6), 515–534. doi:10.1002/mar.20132

Menon, A., & Menon, A. (1997). Enviropreneurial marketing strategy: The emergence of corporate environmentalism as marketing strategy. *Journal of Marketing*, *61*, 51–67. doi:10.2307/1252189

Miles, M. B., & Huberman, A. M. (1994). *Qualitative data analysis*. Thousand Oaks, CA: Sage.

Mont, O., & Plepys, A. (2008). Sustainable consumption progress: Should we be proud or alarmed? *Journal of Cleaner Production*, *16*(4), 531–537. doi:10.1016/j.jclepro.2007.01.009

Morris, M. W., Leung, K., Ames, D., & Lickel, B. (1999). Views from inside and outside: Integrating EMIC and ETIC insights about culture and justice judgment. *Academy of Management Review*, *24*(4), 781–796. doi:10.2307/259354

Oates, C., McDonald, S., Alevizou, P., & Hwang, K. (2008). Marketing sustainability: Use of information sources and degrees of voluntary simplicity. *Journal of Marketing Communications*, *14*(5), 351–365. doi:10.1080/13527260701869148

Paladino, A. (2008). Creating an interactive and responsive teaching environment to inspire learning. *Journal of Marketing Education*, *30*(3), 185–188. doi:10.1177/0273475308318075

Price, L. L., Arnould, E. J., & Folkman, C. C. (2000). Older consumers' disposition of special possessions. *The Journal of Consumer Research*, *27*(2), 179–201. doi:10.1086/314319

Pryor, S., & Grossbart, S. (2005). Ethnography of an American main street. *International Journal of Retail and Distribution Management*, *33*(11), 806–823. doi:10.1108/09590550510629400

Smith, K. A. (1986). Cooperative learning groups. In Schmoberg, S. F. (Ed.), *Strategies for active teaching and learning in university classrooms*. Minneapolis, MN: Office of Educational Development Programs, University of Minnesota.

Williams, D. L., Beard, J. D., & Rymer, J. (1991). Team projects: Achieving their full potential. *Journal of Marketing Education*, *13*(2), 45–53. doi:10.1177/027347539101300208

ADDITIONAL READING

Arthus-Bertrand, Y. (2008). *Le catalogue GoodPlanet.org 1000 façons de consommer responsable*, ed de La Martinière.

Canfin, P. (2008). *Consommer responsable*. Flammarion.

Carlson, L., Grove, S., Kangun, N., & Polonsky, M. (1996). An international comparison of environmental advertising. *Journal of Macromarketing*, *16*, 57–68. doi:10.1177/027614679601600205

KEY TERMS AND DEFINITIONS

Culture: A learned, shared and interrelated set of symbols, codes and values that justify human behavior.

Cultural Emic vs. Etic Perspectives: The Emic view relies on internal member's society criteria, while in the Etic view, the point of vantage is external. From the latter position, culture can be analyzed with universal categories. The two approaches are seen as either dichotomous or complementary and alternate in the process of cultural investigation.

Cross-Cultural Marketing: Marketing to consumers whose culture is different in at least one fundamental aspect, such as values, lifestyle, social norms, religion, or language.

Cross-Cultural Marketing Strategy: Researching, planning and implementing all elements of the marketing mix (product, price, promotion, and distribution).

Cross-Cultural Virtual Project Teamwork: Project in which technology (e-mail, social network, groupware) replaces face-to-face communications. In this type of project, cross-cultural teams are dedicated toward a target in delimited duration. The technology supports textual communication (e-mails) but also multimedia (through internet). Collaboration in this kind of environment requires trust and motivation to achieve the tasks.

Social Marketing Approach: Marketing that goes beyond influencing the acceptability of social ideas to deal with the market's core beliefs and values (as opposed to superficial preferences and opinions).

Sustainable Marketing: An integrative approach addressing environment, social equity, and economic/financial concerns in the development of marketing strategies.

Chapter 12
Using Text Mining for Improving Student Experience Management in Higher Education

Chong Ho Yu
Arizona State University, USA

Samuel DiGangi
Arizona State University, USA

Angel Jannasch-Pennell
Arizona State University, USA

EXECUTIVE SUMMARY

The objective of this case study is to illustrate how text mining of open-ended responses from a student survey could yield valuable information for improving student experience management (SEM). The concept of student SEM was borrowed from the notion of customer experience management (CEM), which aims for ongoing improvement of customer relations through understanding of the customer's point of view (Pine & Gilmore 1998). With the advance of text mining technology, textual data that were previously underutilized are found to be valuable in CEM. To illustrate how text mining can be applied to SEM, we discuss an example from a campus-wide survey conducted at Arizona State University. The purpose of this survey was to better understand student experiences with instructional technology in order for administrators to make data-driven decisions on its implementation. Rather than imposing the researchers' preconceived suppositions on the students by using force-option survey items, researchers on this project chose to use open-ended questions in order to elicit a free emergence of themes from the students. The most valuable lesson learned from this study is that students perceive an ideal environment as a web of mutually supporting systems. Specifically, online access should be augmented by use of laptops and availability of course materials, whereas virtual classes should be balanced by human interactions.

DOI: 10.4018/978-1-60960-599-5.ch012

ORGANIZATION BACKGROUND

Arizona State University (ASU) is the largest public research university in the United States under a single administration, with a 2009 student enrollment of 68,064 (ASU, 2009c). ASU is composed of four campuses spanning across the Phoenix Metropolitan Area (Tempe, West, Polytechnic, Downtown). In 2009 the total endowment supporting ASU is $407 million whereas the total assets of ASU Foundation worth $645 million (ASU, 2009b).

ASU was founded in 1885 as the Tempe Normal School by an act of the Thirteenth Territorial Legislature. Its name was changed to the Normal School of Arizona in 1901 and became Tempe State Teachers College in 1925. In 1945, the school was under control of the Arizona Board of Regents and was renamed Arizona State College. These changes resulted from expansions of the curriculum and degree offerings. By 1958 the school performed all the functions of a regular university. As a result, a statewide ballot led the school to adopt the current name Arizona State University. Although research endeavors preceded attainment of university status in 1958, the development of new academic programs and library holdings and the conferral of doctoral degrees in the 1960s led the Carnegie Foundation to grant ASU Research I status in 1994 (ASU, 2009d).

In 2002, Dr. Michael Crow became the university's 16th president. President Crow outlined his vision for transforming ASU into a "New American University," an open and inclusive source of learning opportunities for all types of. Crow has stated that ASU is in a unique position to evolve together with the city into one of the great intellectual institutions in the world. In order to build a New American University, ASU has undergone some radical changes over the last few years. Like many universities, ASU has added new buildings, hired new faculty and brought in new students. For instance, ASU admitted its largest and highest-quality freshman class ever in fall 2003 and has developed nationally recognized programs in a number of fields, including accounting, astrobiology, design science, creative writing, music, ecology and evolutionary biology, electron microscopy, nanotechnology, psychology, solid-state science, and supply chain management. In addition, ASU has embarked on an aggressive capital building effort. The university is adding one million square feet of research infrastructure, and is continuing its development and expansion of the West, Polytechnic and Downtown campuses (ASU, 2009a). More importantly, the core essence of New American University is open and inclusive. The preceding efforts might not yield the expected results if student experience is not well understood. Thus, under the leadership of Dr. Crow, the management style of ASU has become more data-driven, research-based, and student (customer)-oriented.

SETTING THE STAGE

Customer Experience Management

This case study illustrates the value of text mining of open-ended responses from student survey as a data source for improving student experience management (SEM). The concept of student SEM was borrowed from the idea of customer experience management CEM), which was introduced by Pine and Gilmore (1998, 1999). Before the introduction of this concept, American corporations were either production-oriented or market-oriented. Based on the belief that the process is as important as the product, Pine and Gilmore asserted that successful businesses are those that understand the customer's point of view so that ongoing improvement of customer relations is possible (Pine & Gilmore 1998). Pine and Gilmore (1999) differentiated between selling a product/service and selling an experience: "when a person buys a service, he purchases a set of intangible activities carried out on his behalf. But when he buys an experience, he pays to spend time enjoying a series of memorable events that a company stages—as in a theatrical play—to engage him in a personal way" (p.2).

Greenberg (2004) used his experience in International House of Pancake (IHOP) to vividly illustrate what "selling experience" means. Greenberg and his wife visited an IHOP in Manassas, Virginia, only to find a long line of customers at the restaurant waiting to be seated. Looking at the tag assigned to them by the staff, his wife saw that it had a name ("Ashley Judd") instead of a number. Then they heard the waitress call for "Tom Cruise." The assignation of "celebrity tags" amused the waiting customers and a potentially frustrating delay became an enjoyable experience.

Another well-known example is Starbucks. When Starbucks former CEO Howard Schultz was conceptualizing the proper marketing strategy for the company, he asked an interesting question: "What would happen if you took the quality coffee bean tradition of Starbucks and merged it with the charm and romance of the European coffeehouse?" (cited in Michelli, 2006, p.2) The implication is that the company should focus on customer experience in addition to the product and service quality. Every café or restaurant is capable of selling a variety of coffees to customers. Obviously, the success of Starbucks is not solely due to its coffees; rather, it is the enjoyable experience for which the Starbucks customer is willing to pay. In a typical American Starbucks café, customers are encouraged to stay as long as they wish. Far from being just a coffee shop, Starbucks has included an array of pastries, CDs, and many other items in its retail offerings (Forbes, 2005). Starbucks captures the emotional capital of their customers by creating a welcoming atmosphere that it has become a favorite meeting place. Wireless internet access is provided in many locations. Furniture at Starbucks is comfortable and conveniently arranged for individual reading or for chatting in pairs or small groups. In fact, DiJulius III (2008) suggested it would be possible for Starbucks to stop selling coffees and simply charge people admission for using their place to meet..

Despite the fact that CEM was introduced only a decade ago, it has become a fashionable acronym open to wide interpretation and confusion (Musico, 2009). One common misconception is that CEM is nothing more than a variant of custom relationship management (CRM) or customer service, but indeed there is a subtle difference between CEM and conventional CRM/customer service. Customer relationship management, by definition, is a strategy of managing a company's interactions with existing and potential customers in order to enhance marketing, customer service, and technical support (Thomson, 2009). Schmitt (2003) was so critical of CRM that he called CRM "the devil in disguise" (p.9). In his view, CRM is generally equated with databases and software programs used in call centers. CRM focuses on information the company perceives as important, such as transactional records (e.g. when the customer bought what; how much the customer spent in which store). These data are usually used for shaping customer behaviors. However, CRM data cannot be used to discern whether the customer has established an emotional bond with the brand. To remedy this, CEM subscribes to a different philosophy. Smith and Wheeler (2002) assert that CEM "is not about customers being loyal to you. It is about you being loyal to the customers. You earn loyalty by giving it" (p. 27). Simply put, CRM is about how a customer views a company whereas CEM is about how the company views the customer (SearchCRM.com, 2010). Instead of amending unpleasant experiences after the fact or manipulating the customer to act in the company's interest, CEM attempts to create enjoyable experiences for customers by listening to them. Some analysts related to CEM as CRM 2.0, which emphasizes the spontaneity of the customer ecosystem. With the explosive growth of communication technology, empowered customers are increasingly adamant about making their own choices and controlling the interactions between themselves and companies with which they do business. For example, rather than passively receive information from the vendor, many customers of Kana software Inc. successfully use blogs and wikis to change the knowledge-creation process itself (Lager, 2007).

One of the widespread slogans of CEM is: "If you can't measure it, you can't manage it." Therefore, it is no surprise to see that CEM is quantitative in nature. One common metric used to indicate positive customer experience is the Net Promoter Score (NPS) (Lager, 2007; Sevier, 2009). Nevertheless, with the advance of text mining technology, previously underutilized textual data can be valuable in CEM. Take call center data as an example: when Hewlett-Packard (HP) took over Compaq, HP discovered that Compaq's call center operators kept records with notes on customer interactions, business process issues or text from customer e-mails. In response to this opportunity, HP employed text mining to identify the concerns of its most valuable customers and to develop new customer service strategies based on these common threads (SAS Institute, 2008).

Student Experience Management

Experience management is a fairly new concept to educators because traditionally educators do not view students as customers. Sevier (2009) argued that CEM can be readily transformed into SEM by clarifying what it is that colleges and universities sell to students. He asserted that what schools sell is the sum of all the student experiences before, and opportunities he or she has after, graduation. Following this line of reasoning, it is logical to employ a tool to manage the experience of the students. Sevier used "the Depot" at Abilene Christian University (Texas, USA) to demonstrate the benefits of SEM. A series of focus groups uncovered student frustrations with the existing system of bill payment, parking ticket settlement, and other related services. In response, administrators set up a new office called "the Depot," a one-stop shop that provides students with convenient services, including financial aid, billing, registrar, ID cards, parking, dining services, and many others.

Student experience is multi-faceted -it includes the academic experience, the campus life experience, the resident life experience, the athletic experience, and many others. The academic experience can be split into 13 sub-elements (Sevier, 2009), including class availability, flexibility of class scheduling, advising, honors, registration, classroom and lab experience, technology, internships and co-ops, study abroad, academic assistance/tutoring/remediation, library, career planning and placement, and grad placement. For this case study, the researchers chose to focus on technology only.

Text Mining

In recent years educational data miners have recognized that research questions in the private sector and in higher education are indeed similar, and thus business analytical tools should be applicable to higher education (Luan, 2002). Some educational researchers (e.g. Luan, 2002) have mapped corresponding research questions between industry and higher education. For example, customer profile analysis is equivalent to student profile analysis. Web log analysis for website enhancement is similar to Web traffic analysis for online course improvement. Research on retaining loyal customers is almost exactly the same as student retention research.

While data mining is often used to analyze structured data, which is a small percentage of existing data sources, text mining is the ideal tool for tapping into under-utilized, unstructured data. As a survey-based researcher in political science, Nie was impressed by the effort survey researchers devote to developing open-ended questions and transcribing the responses, but was disappointed by how little use is actually made of the resulting data (SPSS Inc, 2006). One of the reasons why open-ended responses are underused is that analyzing such data is time-consuming and human coders must be well-trained in order to yield accurate classifications. With advances in computing technology, automated text analysis can alleviate much of the preceding problem.

While data mining procedures are designed for structured, numeric data, text mining is primarily for unstructured or semi-structured data. Weiss, Indurkhya, Zhang, and Damerau (2005) asserted that text mining and data mining for solving pattern-recognition and prediction problems are the same type of method, whether the data are structured or not. Thus, they contended that there is nothing unique about text mining that makes it different from data mining. If data mining is a suitable candidate for educational research by translating business-oriented questions into institutional research questions, there is no reason that text mining should not be widely adopted for advancing educational research.

Text Mining is typically defined as a process of extracting useful information from document collections through the identification and exploration of interesting patterns (Feldman & Sanger, 2007). It utilizes the technology of natural language processing (NLP), which is a subfield of artificial intelligence (AI) and computational linguistics (CL). The focus of NLP is on the automatic analysis of human language using algorithms that can handle "fuzzy" structures. Based on AI and CI theories, NLP aids text mining in information retrieval (Singhal, 2001) and automatic summarization (Mani, 2001). NLP aims to deal with the complexity and multiple connotations of natural languages. A single word can mean different things in different contexts. For example, "books" in the phrase "he books tickets" is completely different from the same word in the phrase "he reads books." Relying on a computer to conduct text analysis could be dangerous if the software is not well-written. As a remedy, text mining employs NLP in an attempt to "understand" the data in the same way that a human coder would.

Although text mining and information retrieval (IR) share the common ground built upon NLP, IR is not equated with text mining. Information retrieval is a branch of science developed in the 1950s and 1960s that aims to search for information in documents (Weiss et al. 2005). Specifically, common applications of IR are found in library systems and search engines. In the former the objective is to provide users with access to books, journals, and other documents, whereas in the latter, Web search engines, such as Google and Yahoo, return Web pages according to the key phrases entered by users. First, using pre-determined labels to retrieve information is in sharp contrast to the exploratory character of text mining. Text mining does not assume a pre-established taxonomy. Rather, the discovery engine examines the corpus each time a query is made and is therefore potentially capable of discovering previously unknown relationships and network nodes (Haravu & Neelameghan, 2003). More importantly, returning a list of search results in IR, which may or may not be relevant to the subject matter under study, does not make a substantive contribution to new knowledge discovery, a major goal of text mining. For example, it is estimated that Google, arguably the most powerful search engine, could return only 30% relevant documents out of all results. In other words, every time an inquirer conducts a search, more than 70% of the documents in the output are irrelevant (Rzhetsky, Seringhaus, & Gerstein, 2008). A successful text mining process, which aims to extract relevant information, is composed of the following three steps:

1. *Extraction*: As the name implies, this is the process of gleaning information to serve as the building blocks for categorization from the textual data. A typical extraction process returns three types of results, namely, terms, types, and patterns. Terms are words or phrases that carry important connotations. During the extraction process, many

frequently recurring but trivial words, such as "a," "an," "the," "is," "am," "are," "however," "although," "but," etc., are ignored. Types are semantic groupings of terms. For example, consider the "teacher" type groups terms: "professor," "faculty," "instructor," and "trainer." Patterns are composed of a combination of terms and built-in types (SPSS Inc., 2006).

2. *Categorization*: In text mining, categorization refers to the process of grouping related concepts, themes, or common threads. This process is data-driven and iterative. Specifically, some concepts are proposed based upon the initial findings of the text patterns. Afterwards, all subsequent responses are scanned to check whether any text falls into the existing categories. New categories may be created and existing ones may be updated during this process. But categorization is not mutually exclusive; the same passage can be assigned into several categories. This overlapping of memberships enables the next step, namely, concept linking (SPSS Inc., 2006).
3. *Concept linking*: In conventional statistical research, it is common for researchers to formulate a new hypothesis by visually inspecting a correlation matrix to determine potential linkage between variables. By the same token, after grouping responses into several concepts, the text miner can examine the relationships among these themes using concept maps. The classic examples of hypothesis generation via concept linking are a series of studies conducted by Swanson (1986, 1989b). Based on the idea of concept linking, Swanson carefully scrutinized the medical literature and identified relationships between some apparently unrelated events, namely, consumption of fish oils, reduction in blood viscosity, and Raynaud's disease. His hypothesis that there was a connection between the consumption of fish oils and the effects of Raynaud's syndrome was eventually validated by experimental studies (DiGiacomo, Kremer, & Shah, 1989). Using the same methodology, the links between stress, migraines, and magnesium were also postulated and verified (Swanson, 1988, 1989a; Thomas, Thomas, & Tomb, 1992). Since then, numerous studies set the goal of mimicking Swanson's process of hypothesis generation (e.g. Banerjee, Hu, & Yoo, 2005; Bekhuis, 2006; Weeber, et al., 2001, 2003).

CASE DESCRIPTION

To illustrate how text mining can be applied to SEM, an example from a campus-wide survey conducted at Arizona State University is discussed here. The purpose of this survey was to allow administrators to make data-driven decisions on implementation of instructional technology. As technology advances, universities across the United States struggle to find ways to incorporate the resulting changes in the educational experiences provided to students, while continuing to provide quality learning environments. Educators want students to find success after graduating and are cognizant of the benefits and importance of embracing new technologies. Universities are challenged to use technology to improve quality of instruction and academic success in addition to preparing students for careers that demand increasing knowledge of technology (Penuel, 2006). A study conducted by the EDUCAUSE Center for Applied Research examined the increasing role of information technology in the lives of undergraduate students (Caruso & Kvavik, 2005). Of all respondents, 90 percent reported use of broadband Internet access, with 98.4 percent reporting use of computers for email, writing documents, and browsing the Internet for coursework (2005). Additionally, students reported spending an average of 11-15 hours per week using computers (2005). Information technology is becoming increasingly important in the lives of all students and universities are assuming at least part of the responsibility, not only for delivery of current technology to students, but also for training them on how best to incorporate these technologies into their lives. However, existing technological policies and infrastructures of a university may not have kept pace with the explosive growth of technology and might not be capable of providing the students with an experience that enhances learning in an enjoyable manner. For example, many so-called "hybrid courses" are nothing more than a Blackboard site hosting the syllabus posted by the faculty. Technologically savvy students who have formed numerous virtual communities on their own via Facebook, MySpace, wiki, blog, and other Web 2.0 technologies are unlikely to be impressed or engaged by dated or underutilized technology.

Although the university intended to make user-driven decisions regarding integrating education with technology, a survey with mere force-option items was considered insufficient due to the fact that Web 2.0, which facilitates use of social software (e.g. Wiki, Google apps), has been shifting the tectonic plates of the Internet (Carpenter & Steiner, 2007). As discussed in the section "customer experience management," today many tech savvy customers use blogs and wikis in their own way to generate a customer ecosystem. By the same token, students also manipulate these technologies on their own terms, such as "Rate my professors." Further, like CEM, SEM should focus on how to create an enjoyable and ideal learning environment (as perceived by the students) rather than merely undoing negative experiences. Hence, the university sent students a survey with both force-option and open-ended items in an attempt to understand what they would consider an ideal learning environment in terms of educational technology. The focal point of this article is the analysis of open-ended responses by text mining.

Email invitations were sent to all currently enrolled students (n=62680). Of these email addresses, 62,095 were valid addresses; 708, a mere 1.12%, were returned as undeliverable. Eight thousands eight hundred and seventy-two students responded to the survey over a 3-week period, with 5,344 responding within the first 7 days. Since non-response bias has been acknowledged as a major threat to the validity of survey research (Ranney, Tveite, & Bradbury, 2006), two reminder letters were sent to non-respondents. The first reminder prompt was sent to the remaining sample pool on day 8. Two thousands one hundred and seventy-one students responded between day 8 and 14; a second prompt was sent on day 14. The overall response rate was 14.28%.

This article concentrates on one particular open-ended item only. For this question, concerning student attitudes on what would constitute an ideal learning environment in regards to instructional technology, the number of non-empty responses is 4,071. The software module employed in this project is *SPSS Text Analysis for Surveys* (SPSS Inc., 2006).

RESULTS AND CURRENT CHALLENGES

Themes

The following table is the final list of common themes with respect to the ideal learning environment extracted by text mining:

The meaning of each theme will be explained as follows. It is important to point out that these categories are not mutually exclusive. There is some degree of overlapping among these categories and therefore conceptual linking is possible.

1. **Class structure:** Class structure means how a class should be conducted, such as the mode of the class (physical or online) and installation of technology.
2. **Online access:** As the name suggests, "online access" is concerned with connection to the Internet, availability of online resources, and online classes.

Table 1. Themes extracted by text mining

Theme	Frequency
Class structure	1363
Online access	857
Technology	578
Laptop	317
Course material	285
Interaction	185
Video	75

3. **Technology:** This category refers to technology in a broad sense, including PowerPoint, static HTML pages, and projectors. Although "video" and "laptop" can also be classified into "technology," those two are treated as separate categories because potential applications of webcast (video) and mobile devices have become major concerns in the university strategic plan.
4. **Laptop:** This includes both conventional laptops and tablet PCs.
5. **Course materials:** This theme is concerned with how course materials are delivered.
6. **Interaction:** This refers to human interactions between faculty and students, and among students.
7. **Video:** With the rise in popularity of podcasts, it is surprising to see that "video" instead of "audio" emerges as a major theme. This will be discussed in detail later.

Concept Maps

Relationships among themes or concepts are presented in concept maps, as shown in Figures 1-7. In each map, there is a reference point so that the relative positions to the focal point of other concepts can be formulated. For example, in Figure 1, "class structure" is the focal point of interest and the strength of its associations with other concepts are presented. The strength of the relationship is indicated by the thickness of the line. A thick black line symbolizes the strongest relationship, a thick gray line shows a strong relationship, and a thin gray line denotes weaker relationship. Finally, the size of the circle signifies the popularity of the concept. The digit beside the label is the number of observations that are shared by the focal concept and the related concept. For instance, 1363 observations are classified into the category "class structure" and 323 observations belong to both "online access" and "class structure."

Figures 1 and 2 indicate that there is a strong link between class structure and online access. Where students desire more online classes and access to online course materials, there is also an implicit desire for changing the traditional class

Figure 1. Concept map of class structure

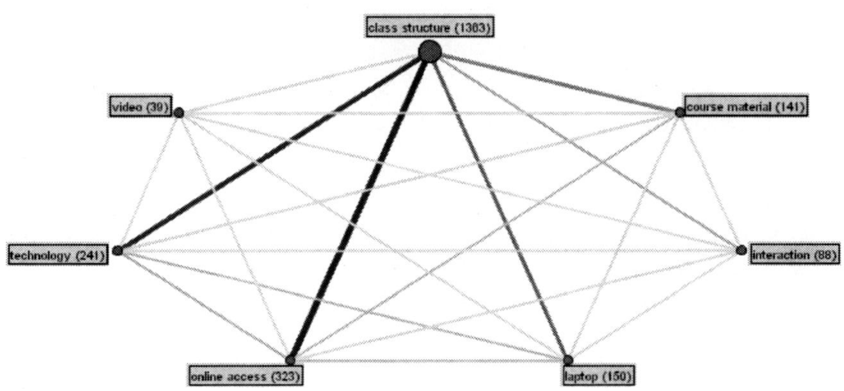

Figure 2. Concept map of online access

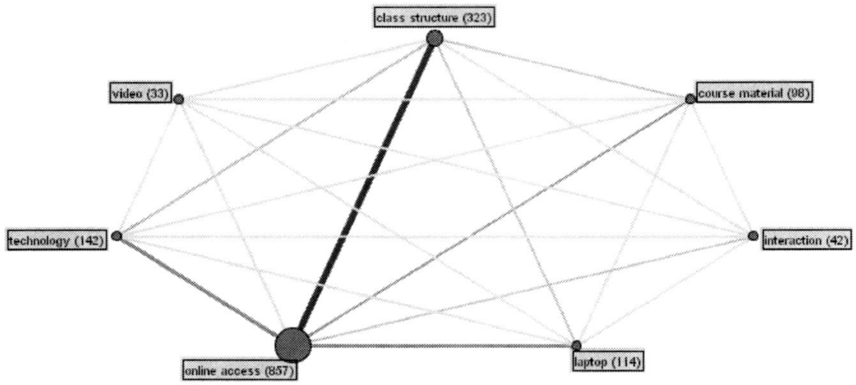

structure. For example, some students felt that course materials and lectures notes should be made available online beforehand, and thus more class time could be devoted to learning the material instead of simply copying notes. Some students felt that it should be possible to communicate with professors regardless of whether they were physically present in a classroom or not. They also believe that professors should make grades available online and have discussions online, as well as in class, in order to enhance the learning experience. In short, the demands of the availability of online access and the virtual classroom go together. Not surprisingly, online access is strongly associated with technology. Specifically, students see the need for supporting technologies for online access provided by the university, such as *Blackboard* (an online course management system) and wireless networking. The following are some typical examples:

"In my ideal learning environment all classes would incorporate some online element. For example, lecture courses would podcast their lectures so that if any student missed a class the lecture would be available. Also I feel that the library system pays a lot of money for internet database content; so I feel professors should be better trained to use more of this content to replace the textbooks. Professors and TA should also be encouraged to blog additional information and resources about what was covered in class."

"Tons of wireless internet. Personal laptops that are student-owned (they would be ultra-cheap if the school purchased thousands) and of the students' preference of OS (Mac, Windows, Linux). Technology integration from the very beginning, for everyone (not just sci, math, engineers). Free software (MATLAB and all the others that that cost an arm and leg). Lecture via podcast (for those missed 7am classes)!"

Figure 3 depicts the concept map for technology. It is important to point out that although many students see a positive role for technology in online access and class structure, some raised concerns about the potential problems with technology. For example, one student said that while everyone should have access to digital technology, a class should treat technology as a tool, never the main method of teaching. Also, some students found that classmates bringing their computers to class are more enthralled with Instant Messaging and browsing the Internet than with the lecture.

The concept map for "laptop" is shown in Figure 4. "Laptop" is separated from "technology" as a standalone category for two reasons. First, it

Figure 3. Concept map of technology

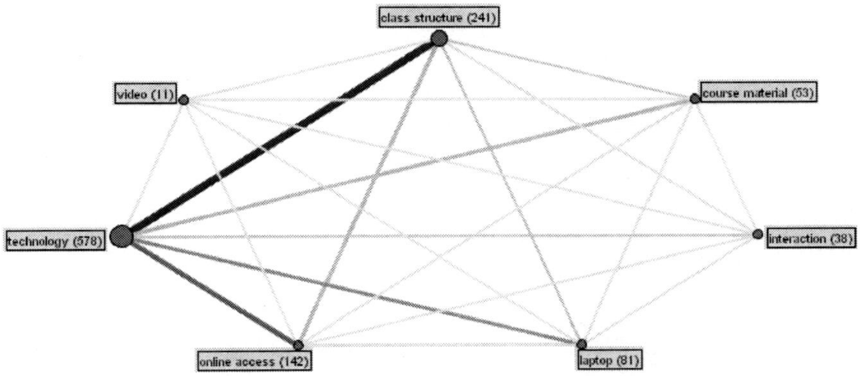

Figure 4. Concept map of laptop

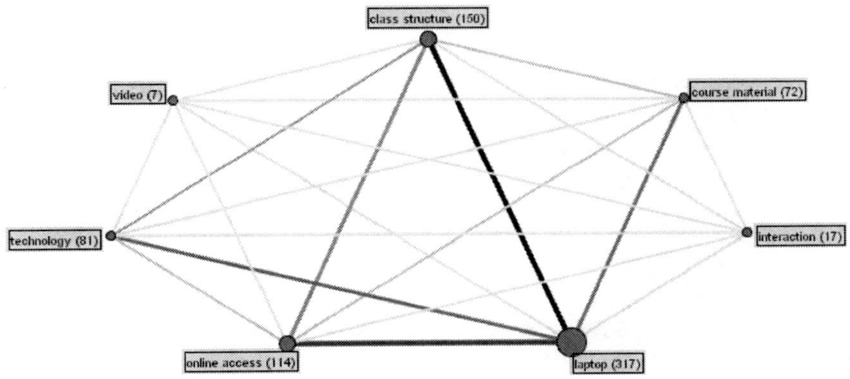

is owned by students rather than by the university. Second, the popularity of laptops among students creates a pressing demand of ubiquitous online access in general and access to course materials in particular. Some students bluntly said that they brought their laptop to the class to look for further information on the Internet about the subject matter in the lecture because they feel that the materials posted by the instructor pale by comparison.

It is important to point out that although many students embrace online access, the virtual classroom, and instructional technology, they do not ignore the human aspect in the class structure. Many of the survey respondents still regard face-to-face interaction with faculty and other students as an indispensable experience in learning, as shown in Figure 5. Also, in their view an ideal learning environment would be an academic setting in which students could participate in many cultural and social activities, and in which they could network and share ideas more fully than what is currently possible in an electronic-only format. The following are some typical responses with respect to human interaction:

"A small class with a great instructor. I don't think all this technology, much as I love it, makes that much of a difference. Sure, it's needed for lots of things. Heck, I study statistics, so I need lots of computing power. But it's all for naught if I don't

Figure 5. Concept map of interaction

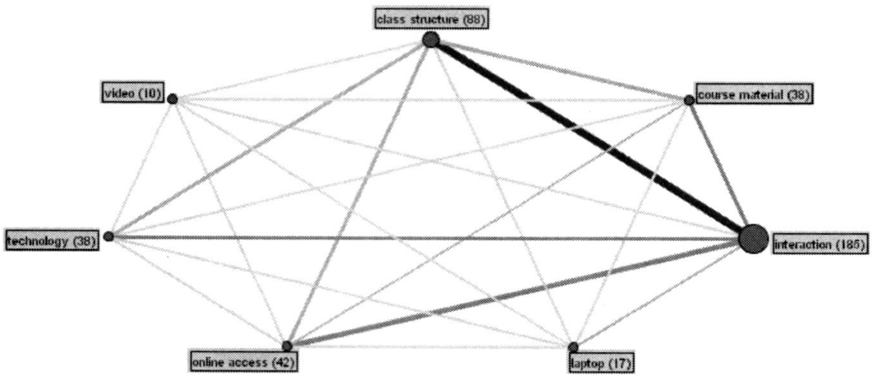

have good teachers. I would rather the university focus on that first."

"Smaller classes with more engaged professors. Many professors think that by using high tech presentations they will reach more students, but many of the professors overlook the need to use that technology to teach us something. I would like fewer laptops in the classroom, they are a distraction much more often than they are useful, and I would like the professors to consider podcasts of their lectures, but that may be detrimental to class attendance."

Again, Figure 6, the concept map for course materials, shows its stronger associations with class structure, online access, technology, and laptop. Interestingly, while most students were concerned with the issue of accessing course materials for their own courses, especially the *Blackboard* system, one forward-looking student suggested that the university adopt the open courseware model initiated by MIT so that all course materials can be freely accessible.

It is surprising to see that "video" instead of "audio" emerged as a common theme in the survey. Apple Computer has created a service allowing any university to distribute course content (both audio and video) for free via their *iTunes* software. Several universities, including Stanford, Berkeley, and the University of Michigan have already taken advantage of this service, making podcast versions of lectures available to anyone who accesses the respective sections of iTunes. Since June 2006 Arizona State University has been partnering with Apple Inc. to develop the *iTunes University*, a platform to podcast lectures in MP3 format. At present, a variety of audio courses are available through iTunes. It was expected to see "audio, "iTunes," "iPod," or "MP3" as common themes for students; however, it is clear that "video," instead of "audio," is the predominant interest in the domain of multimedia technology for survey respondents. In addition, there is a strong association among video, class structure, and online access. Simply put, many students would like to access lectures via online channels in video format. These findings suggest that further research with regard to the role of video and audio in instructional technology, as well as students' perceptions of these technologies.

In summary, the preceding text mining example extracts categories from the open-ended responses using algorithms of natural language processing. The importance of these categories, as measured by the frequency of occurrence in proper contexts, is ranked in a table. More importantly, text miners can visualize inter-relationships among these categories via the concept maps.

Figure 6. Concept map of course materials

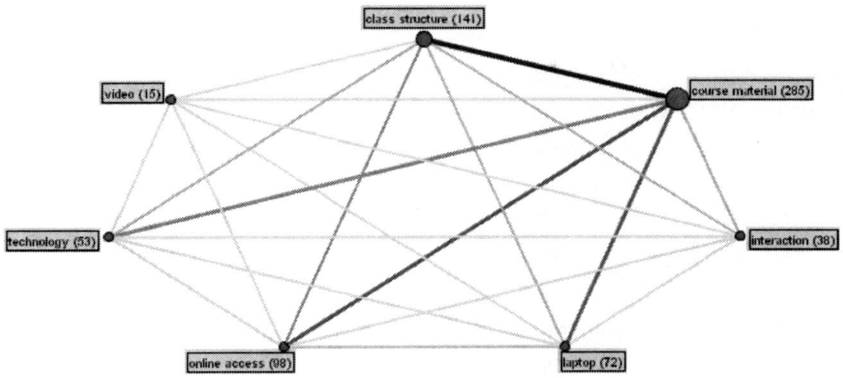

Figure 7. Concept map of video

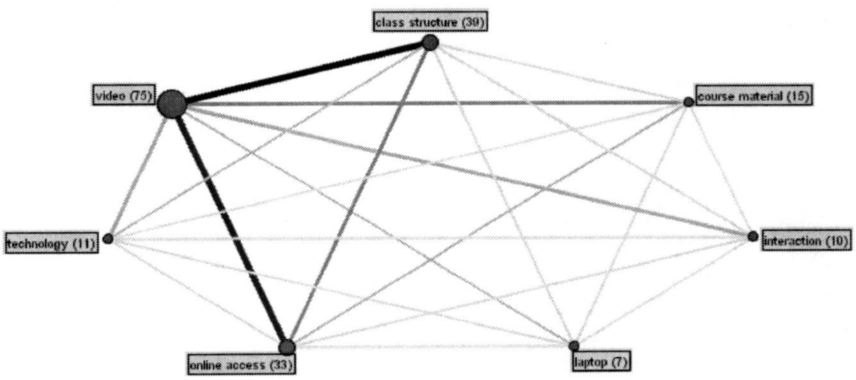

SOLUTIONS AND RECOMMENDATIONS

The results of this study can assist administrators in making informed decisions with regard to formulating campus-wide strategies on instructional technology. Unlike studies that impose the researcher's preconceived ideas on the students by using force-option survey items, in this project the researchers let the themes emerge freely from the students. The previous survey analysis concentrates on the quantitative data collected from force-option items (DiGangi, Kilic, Yu, Jannasch-Pennell, Long, Kim, Stay, & Kang, 2007). Technology (equipment and applications, as well as use and integration) is clearly a priority expressed by the respondents. Therefore, it was concluded that technology, such as use and ownership of mobile phones, computers, and many other computing devices, is important to a successful college experience.

The text mining project partially concurs with the quantitative analysis, but it reveals additional insight. Because mobile device ownership and usage is viewed by many students as an integrated component of online access and the virtual classroom, the university has de-emphasized the importance of computer labs. Rather, the university encourages all users have their own mobile multimedia digital devices that possess the capability of connecting to the Internet, such as an iPod, a laptop, a tablet PC, or an electronic book reader, as opposed to using the old computing model, in which desktop computers are stationed in a lab and shared by many students. To cope with this trend, the university has developed a program with Apple and Dell to encourage owning a laptop at the best possible price. With a laptop a student could potentially attend classes online and view online resources anywhere, anytime.

One salient difference between the text mining findings and the quantitative analysis is that responses to the text mining study indicated technology alone is not the final answer. In the opinion of the research team, the principal finding of this study is that students perceive an ideal learning environment as a web of mutually supporting systems. It is important to point out that "class structure," rather than use and ownership of technology, is the number one theme yielded from text mining. Technology alone would not improve learning if there is no structure to guide the proper use of technology. Participants' concern with class structure implies that current applications of instructional technology by faculty might be improper, or insufficient, or both. Indeed, this possibility is reinforced by another study conducted at the university regarding faculty adoption of Web 2.0 (Yu, Brewer, Jannasch-Pennell, & DiGangi,, 2010). It was found that full-time and tenured instructors devote less effort to producing Web 2.0 applications for teaching than their part-time and non-tenure counterparts. The implication for policy-making is that the initial promotion of technology use should not emphasize the production component, especially if the faculty support infrastructure is lacking. In response to the need to help faculty with class structuring or restructuring, various training programs for faculty have been under development at the university.

Further, the research team learned that online access is expected to be augmented by availability of course materials. Although the information students find on the Internet has long been known to be of questionable accuracy, the ease of a web search remains attractive. In response, the university is devoting efforts to developing new course management systems and databases in order to broaden the accessibility of academic-related materials. For example, currently Dublin City University and Arizona State University (2008) have been appointed as the lead academic partners in Global Grid for Learning (GGFL), a database containing a large collection of instructional materials, including text, graphics, and movie clips on various subjects. At the time of this writing, over 1.25 million resources from thousands of sources are available through Global Grid for Learning, including leading publishers and rights management organizations, such as Reuters, Corbis, Encyclopedia Britannica, and Cambridge University Press. The initiative aims to connect a billion digital education resources by 2018. Open source and open courseware are also under intensive development. Further, the university's technology support team has been providing new technology training to staff and faculty as necessary to improve skills and implement technology changes.

ACKNOWLEDGMENT

Special thanks to Elizabeth Farley-Metzger and Charles Kaprolet for their valuable input to this chapter.

REFERENCES

Arizona State University. (2009a). *A new American university*. Retrieved December 29, 2009, from http://newamericanuniversity.asu.edu/

Arizona State University. (2009b). *Financial charts 2009*. Retrieved December 29, 2009, from http://annualreport.asu.edu/investment/financial-charts.shtml

Arizona State University. (2009c). *Quick facts 2009*. Retrieved December 29, 2009, from http://uoia.asu.edu/sites/default/files/quickfacts/Quick_Facts_Fall_2009.pdf

Arizona State University. (2009d). *More ASU history*. Retrieved December 29, 2009, from http://www.asu.edu/about/history/more.html

Banerjee, P., Hu, X., & Yoo, I. (2005). Discovering the wealth of public knowledge: An approach to early threat detection. *AIS SIGSEMIS Bulletin*, *2*(3&4), 77–85.

Bekhuis, T. (2006). Conceptual biology, hypothesis discovery, and text mining: Swanson's legacy. *Biomedical Digital Libraries, 3*(2). Retrieved May 31, 2008, from http://www.bio-diglib.com/content/3/1/2

Carpenter, C., & Steiner, S. (2007). *Using Web 2.0 technologies to push e-resources*. Georgia Tech Institutional Repository. Retrieved May 8, 2008, from http://smartech.gatech.edu/bitstream/1853/13640/2/236-fri-11_05.pdf

Caruso, B., & Kvavik, R. (2005). *ECAR study of students and information technology, 2005: Convenience, connection, control, and learning*. Educause Center for Applied Research. Retrieved November 30, 2006, from http://www.educause.edu/LibraryDetailPage/666?ID=ERS0506

DiGangi, S., Kilic, Z., Yu, C. H., Jannasch-Pennell, A., Long, L., Kim, C., et al. Kang, S. (2007). 1 to 1 computing in higher education: A survey of technology practices and needs. *AACE Journal, 15*(4). Retrieved October 29, 2007, from http://www.editlib.org/index.cfm?fuseaction=Reader.ViewAbstract&paper_id=22813

DiGiacomo, R. A., Kremer, J. M., & Shah, D. M. (1989). Fish-oil dietary supplementation in patients with Raynaud's phenomenon: A double-blind, controlled, prospective study. *The American Journal of Medicine*, *86*(2), 158–164. doi:10.1016/0002-9343(89)90261-1

Dublin City University's Learning, Innovation and Knowledge Research Centre & Arizona State University's Applied Learning Technologies Institute. (2008). *Global Grid for learning*. Retrieved October 6, 2008, from http://www.globalgridforlearning.org/

Feldman, R., & Sanger, J. (2007). *The text mining handbook: Advanced approaches in analyzing unstructured data*. Cambridge, UK: Cambridge University Press.

Forbes, S. (2005, December 12). Who'da thunk it? Coffee is hot. *Forbes*, *176*(12), 33.

Gillam, L. (2006). *Sentiment analysis and financial grids*. Paper presented at National Centre for e-Social Science Workshop, Manchester, United Kingdom.

Haravu, L. J., & Neelameghan, A. (2003). Text mining and data mining in knowledge organization and discovery: The making of knowledge-based products. *Cataloging & Classification Quarterly*, *37*, 97–113. doi:10.1300/J104v37n01_08

Jurafsky, D., & Martin, J. (2000). *Speech and language processing: An introduction to natural language processing, computational linguistics, and speech recognition*. Upper Saddle River, NJ: Prentice Hall.

Kao, A., & Poteet, S. (Eds.). (2007). *Natural language processing and text mining*. London, UK: Springer. doi:10.1007/978-1-84628-754-1

Lager, M. (2007, December). It's coming 2.0gether. *Customer Relations Management Magazine*, *11*(12), 22–27.

Lavengood, K., & Kiser, P. (2007, May/June). Information professionals in the text mine. *Online*, *31*(3), 16–21.

Luan, J. (2002). Data mining and its applications in higher education. In Serban, A., & Luan, J. (Eds.), *Knowledge management: Building a competitive advantage in higher education* (pp. 17–36). San Francisco, CA: Josey-Bass.

Mani, I. (2001). *Automatic summarization*. Philadelphia, PA: J. Benjamins.

Manning, C., & Schütze, H. (1999). *Foundations of statistical natural language processing*. Cambridge, MA: MIT Press.

Mehler, A., & Köhler, R. (2007). *Aspects of automatic text analysis*. Berlin, Germany: Springer.

Michelli, J. (2006). *The Starbucks experience: Five principles for turning ordinary into extraordinary*. New York, NY: McGraw-Hill.

Musico, C. (2009, December). No substitute for experience. *Customer Relations Management Magazine*, *13*(12), 22–29.

Nasukawa, T. (2006). *Text analysis within the knowledge mining project and sentiment analysis*. Paper presented at National Centre for e-Social Science Workshop, Manchester, United Kingdom.

Natarajan, J., Berrar, D., Hack, C. J., & Dubitzky, W. (2005). Knowledge discovery in biology and biotechnology texts: A review of techniques, evaluation strategies, and applications. *Critical Reviews in Biotechnology*, *25*, 31–52. doi:10.1080/07388550590935571

Penuel, W. R. (2006). Implementation and effects of one-to-one computing initiatives: A research synthesis. *Journal of Research on Technology in Education*, *38*, 329–348.

Pine, B. J. II, & Gilmore, J. H. (1998). Welcome to the experience economy. *Harvard Business Review*, *76*, 97–105.

Pine, B. J. II, & Gilmore, J. H. (1999). *The experience economy: Work is theatre and every business a stage*. Boston, MA: Harvard Business School Press.

Ranney, G., Tveite, M., & Bradbury, I. (2006). *Misuse of statistical methodology*. Paper presented at the Joint Statistical Meeting, Seattle, WA.

Rzhetsky, A., Seringhaus, M., & Gerstein, M. (2008). Seeking a new biology through text mining. *Cell*, *134*, 9–13. doi:10.1016/j.cell.2008.06.029

SAS Institute. (2008). *Mining more than gold: HP soaring to the next level of CRM with SAS*. Retrieved May 30, 2008, from http://www.sas.com/success/hp.html

Schmitt, B. H. (2003). *Customer experience management: A revolutionary approach to connecting with your customers*. New York, NY: Wiley.

Search, C. R. M. com. (2010). *Significant differences between customer experience management (CEM) and CRM*. Retrieved January 5, 2010, from http://www/searchcrm.com

Sevier, R. A. (2009). Managing the experience. *University Business*, *12*(4), 37–39.

Singhal, A. (2001). Modern information retrieval: A brief overview. *Bulletin of the IEEE Computer Society Technical Committee on Data Engineering*, *24*(4), 35–43.

Smith, S., & Wheeler, J. (2002). *Managing the customer experience: Turning customers into advocates*. Upper Saddle River, NJ: FT Press.

SPSS Inc. (2006). *SPSS text analysis for surveys 2.0 user's guide*. Chicago, IL: Author.

Swanson, D. R. (1986a). Fish-oil, Raynaud's syndrome, and undiscovered public knowledge. *Perspectives in Biology and Medicine*, *30*(1), 7–18.

Swanson, D. R. (1986b). Undiscovered public knowledge. *The Library Quarterly*, *56*, 103–118. doi:10.1086/601720

Swanson, D. R. (1988). Migraine and magnesium: Eleven neglected connections. *Perspectives in Biology and Medicine*, *31*, 526–557.

Thomas, J., Thomas, E., & Tomb, E. (1992). Serum and erythrocyte magnesium concentrations and migraine. *Magnesium Research*, *5*(2), 127–130.

Thompson, E. (2009). What's hot in CRM applications in 2009. *Gardner Research*. Retrieved January 5, 2010, from http://www.gartner.com/DisplayDocument?&id=1004212

Weeber, M., & Klein, H., de Jong-van den, B., Lolkje T. W., & Vos, R. (2001). Using concepts in literature-based discovery: Simulating Swanson's Raynaud-fish oil and migraine-magnesium discoveries. *Journal of the American Society for Information Science and Technology*, *52*, 548–557. doi:10.1002/asi.1104

Weeber, M., Vos, R., Klein, H., De Jong-Van Den Berg, L. T., Aronson, A. R., & Molema, G. (2003). Generating hypotheses by discovering implicit associations in the literature: A case report of a search for new potential therapeutic uses for thalidomide. *Journal of the American Medical Informatics Association*, *10*, 252–259. doi:10.1197/jamia.M1158

Weiss, S. M., Indurkhya, N., Zhang, T., & Damerau, F. (2005). *Text mining: Predictive methods for analyzing unstructured information*. New York, NY: Springer.

Yu, C. H., Brewer, L., Jannasch-Pennell, A., & Digangi, S. (2010). Adopting Web 2.0 for instruction: The effects of faculty rank and employment status. *Journal of Technology Integration in Classroom*, *2*(2), 131–143.

ADDITIONAL READING

Ananiadou, S. (2006, April). *Terminology management for text mining applications*. Paper presented at National Centre for e-Social Science Workshop, Manchester, United Kingdom.

Bailor, C. (2006, September). Stocking the customer experience. *Customer Relations Management Magazine*, *10*(9), 15.

Brachman, J. M. (2007) *Text-mining Jihadi websites: Opportunities and pitfalls for analysts*. Paper presented at the annual meeting of the International Studies Association 48th Annual Convention, Chicago, IL, USA.

Carlzon, J. (1987). *Moments of truth*. Cambridge, MA: Ballinger.

Cohen, A., & Hersh, W. (2005). A survey of current work in biomedical text mining. *Briefings in Bioinformatics*, *6*, 57–71. doi:10.1093/bib/6.1.57

Corti, L. (2006, April). *The SQUAD project*. Paper presented at National Centre for e-Social Science Workshop, Manchester, United Kingdom.

Corti, L. (2006, May). *Mine your data: Contrasting data mining approaches to numeric and textual data sources*. Paper presented at IASSIST conference, Ann Arbor, MI.

DiJulius, J. R. III. (2008). *What's the secret: To providing a world-class customer experience*. New York, NY: Wiley.

Driggs, W. (2007, June). Making the pivot. *Customer Relations Management Magazine*, *11*(6), 48.

Gelbukh, A. (Ed.). (2007). *Computational linguistics and intelligent text processing: 8th international conference, Mexico City, Mexico, February 18-24, 2007 proceedings*. New York: Springer.

Gibbs, G. (2006, April). *Concordances and semi-automatic coding in qualitative analysis: Possibilities and barriers*. Paper presented at National Centre for e-Social Science Workshop. Manchester, United Kingdom.

Gillam, L. (2006, April). *Sentiment analysis and financial grids*. Paper presented at National Centre for e-Social Science Workshop, Manchester, United Kingdom.

Gilmore, J. H., & Pine, J. P. II. (2000). *Markets of one: Creating customer-unique value through mass customization*. Boston, MA: Harvard Business Press.

Greenberg, P. (2004). *CRM at the speed of light: Essential customer strategies for the 21st century*. New York, NY: McGraw-Hill/Osborne.

Hyken, S. (2009). *The cult of the customer: Create an amazing customer experience that turns satisfied customers into customer evangelists*. New York, NY: Wiley.

Jurafsky, D., & Martin, J. (2000). *Speech and language processing: An introduction to natural language processing, computational linguistics, and speech recognition*. Upper Saddle River, N.J.: Prentice Hall.

Kao, A., & Poteet, S. (Eds.). (2007). *Natural language processing and text mining*. London: Springer. doi:10.1007/978-1-84628-754-1

Lavengood, K., & Kiser, P. (2007, May/June). Information professionals in the text mine. *Online*, *31*(3), 16–21.

Lee, C., & Hu, C. (2004). Analyzing hotel customers' e-complaints from an Internet complaint forum. *Journal of Travel & Tourism Marketing*, *17*, 167–181. doi:10.1300/J073v17n02_13

Lewins, A. (2006, April). *The CAQDAS networking project*. Paper presented at National Centre for e-Social Science Workshop, Manchester, United Kingdom.

Mani, I. (2001). *Automatic summarization*. Philadelphia: J. Benjamins.

Manning, C., & Schütze, H. (1999). *Foundations of statistical natural language processing*. Cambridge, MA: MIT Press.

Mehler, A., & Köhler, R. (2007). *Aspects of automatic text analysis*. Berlin: Springer.

Michelli, J. A. (2008). *The new gold standard: Five leadership principles for creating a legendary customer experience courtesy of the Ritz-Carlton Hotel Company*. New York, NY: McGraw-Hill.

Miller, T. (2005). *Data and text mining: A business applications approach*. Upper saddle River, NJ: Pearson.

Nasukawa, T. (2006, April). *Text analysis within the knowledge mining project and sentiment analysis*. Paper presented at National Centre for e-Social Science Workshop, Manchester, United Kingdom.

Natarajan, J., Berrar, D., Hack, C. J., & Dubitzky, W. (2005). Knowledge discovery in biology and biotechnology texts: A review of techniques, evaluation strategies, and applications. *Critical Reviews in Biotechnology*, *25*, 31–52. doi:10.1080/07388550590935571

O'Sullivan, E. L., & Spangler, K. J. (1998). *Experience marketing: Strategies for the new millennium. State College*. PA: Venture.

Roberts, K. (2006). *Lovemarks: The future beyond brands*. New York, NY: PowerHouse.

Shaw, C. (2007). *The DNA of customer experience: How emotions drive value*. New York, NY: Palgrave Macmillan.

Shaw, C., & Ivens, J. (2004). *Building great customer experiences*. New York, NY: Palgrave Macmillan.

Singh, N., Hu, C., & Roehl, W. (2007). Text mining: A decade of progress in hospitality human resource management research: Identifying emerging thematic development. *Hospital Management*, *26*, 31–147.

Spasser, M. (1997). The enacted fate of undiscovered public knowledge. *Journal of the American Society for Information Science American Society for Information Science*, *48*, 707–717. doi:10.1002/(SICI)1097-4571(199708)48:8<707::AID-ASI4>3.0.CO;2-W

Swanson, D. R. (1987). Two medical literatures that are logically but not bibliographically connected. *Journal of the American Society for Information Science American Society for Information Science*, *38*, 228–233. doi:10.1002/(SICI)1097-4571(198707)38:4<228::AID-ASI2>3.0.CO;2-G

Swanson, D. R. (1989a). A second example of mutually isolated medical literatures related by implicit, unnoticed connections. *Journal of the American Society for Information Science American Society for Information Science*, *40*, 432–435. doi:10.1002/(SICI)1097-4571(198911)40:6<432::AID-ASI5>3.0.CO;2-#

Swanson, D. R. (1989b). Online search for logically-related noninteractive medical literatures: A systematic trial-and-error strategy. *Journal of the American Society for Information Science American Society for Information Science*, *40*, 356–358. doi:10.1002/(SICI)1097-4571(198909)40:5<356::AID-ASI9>3.0.CO;2-B

Swanson, D. R. (1990a). Medical literature as a potential source of new knowledge. *Bulletin of the Medical Library Association*, *78*(1), 29–37.

Swanson, D. R. (1990b). Somatomedin C and argine: Implicit connections between mutually isolated literature. *Perspectives in Biology and Medicine*, *33*(2), 157–186.

Swanson, D. R., & Smalheiser, N. R. (1997). An interactive system for finding complementary literatures: A stimulus to scientific discovery. *Artificial Intelligence*, *91*, 183–203. doi:10.1016/S0004-3702(97)00008-8

Swanson, D. R., & Smalheiser, N. R. (1999). Implicit text linkages between Medline records: Using Arrowsmith as an aid to scientific discovery. *Library Trends*, *48*(1), 48–59.

Temkin, B. (2009, December). Seven keys to customer experience. *Customer Relations Management Magazine*, *13*(12), 12.

Ukelson, J. (2007). *Structured, semi-structured and unstructured data in business applications*. Retrieved May 29, 2008, from http://exeedtechnology.com/structured-semi-structured-and-unstructured-data-in-business-applications

Wilburn, M. (2006). *Managing the customer experience: A measurement-based approach*. Milwaukee, WI: ASQ Quality Press.

KEY TERMS AND DEFINITIONS

Customer Experience Management: Customer experience management (CEM) is a set of coherent strategies that aims to understand the customer's point of view so that ongoing improvement of customer relations is possible.

Customer Relationship Management: Customer relationship management is a strategy for managing a company's interactions with existing and potential customers in order to enhance marketing, customer service, and technical support.

Data Mining: Data mining is the process of automatically extracting useful information and relationships from immense quantities of data using a cluster of techniques, including classification trees, neural networks, and K-mean clustering.

Natural Language Processing: Natural language processing (NLP) is a subfield of artificial intelligence (AI) and computational linguistics (CL). The focus of NLP is on the automatic analysis of human language with use of algorithms that can handle "fuzzy" structures.

Information Retrieval: Information retrieval (IR) is a branch of science that aims to search for information in documents using pre-determined taxonomies and terms. Common applications of IR are found in library systems and search engines.

Student Experience Management: Student experience management (SEM) is a concept borrowed from customer experience management. The applicability of CEM to SEM is based on the assertion that the products and services delivered to a student by the school include all the experiences that a student has and the opportunities he or she has after graduation, and thus SEM is also intended to provide students with positive experiences.

Text Mining: Text mining is a process of extracting useful information from document collections and open-ended responses from participants through the identification and exploration of interesting patterns.

Chapter 13
Innovations in Technology for Educational Marketing:
Stakeholder Perceptions and Implications for Examinations System in Rwanda

John Rutaisire
Rwanda National Examinations Council, Rwanda

EXECUTIVE SUMMARY

This chapter highlights the importance of educational marketing through modern innovative technologies. It explores how teachers who mark Rwandan primary and secondary examinations perceive the Rwanda National Examinations Council and what the implications are for the effective management of the examinations system. The chapter highlights the Rwandan context in which before the 1994 genocide, the education system was characterized by nepotism, corruption, discrimination and victimization based on ethnicity, regionalism, and gender. Thus, after 1994, the task of the education system was to reverse the imbalance in favor of equity, transparency, accountability and responsiveness in public service. In terms of national examinations, this demanded, among other things, a vigorous marketing strategy through innovation and technology. In spite of the relative success, however, the chapter acknowledges challenges associated with post-conflict educational reconstruction focusing mainly on human resource capacity development and management, and highlights some lessons learned as Rwanda looks forward to the future.

ORGANISATION BACKGROUND

The Rwanda National Examinations Council (RNEC) referred to as the 'Council' throughout this chapter was established in 1998, and law No 19/2001 of 12.3.2001 outlines its major responsibilities as follows: (i) to be responsible for national examinations for primary and secondary school (ii) establish rules regulating the conduct of national primary and secondary school examinations (iii) uphold transparency and justice in examinations'

DOI: 10.4018/978-1-60960-599-5.ch013

administration and other related issues (iv) award certificates or diplomas to successful candidates (v) place successful candidates in different secondary schools and higher education institutions.

The education system in Rwanda before 1994 had been guilty of discrimination, injustice and sowing seeds of division based on ethnicity, sex, regionalism (home background) and religion; and this form of injustice was mainly implemented through examinations (Rutaisire, 2007). Before 1994, entry to all government and assisted schools and tertiary institutions was determined mainly by "Ethnic and Regional" quotas. The results of primary and secondary schools were never published. Also, students' personal identification files known in French as *'fiches signeletiques'* were used to identify them as 'Tutsi, Hutu or Twa.' The purpose was to identify individuals and, or groups for discrimination and victimization (Rutaisire, etal, 2004). Thus after 1994, there was urgent need to redress this imbalance for purposes of promoting national reconciliation and healing the nation. This entailed reforming the examinations system by considering performance standards which are considered to be the obvious measures of outcome (Gipps and Storbart (1993). As a result, 'since its establishment, the Rwanda National Examinations Council has been improving transparency, accountability and responsiveness in the Rwandan public service' (United Nations Public Service Awards, 2009:174). The establishment of the Council after the 1994 genocide was in line with international best practice. For example, West et al (2000) argue in favour of the importance of self management because of the possibility it offers eventually to increased control over policies and resources and expanded scope for leadership. This has implications for effective management of the examinations system in Rwanda.

Management Structure

The recently revised law number 36/2007 of 02/09/2007 determines responsibilities, organization, functioning and powers of the Rwanda National Examinations Council for primary and secondary education. The law designates the Council as an autonomous institution supervised by the Ministry in charge of primary and secondary education. The Council is composed of a Board of Directors (policy making) which has full powers and responsibilities to take all decisions; and an Executive Secretariat (management) which runs day today affairs of the institution. The responsibilities of the Board of Governors are to: adopt the internal rules and regulations of the Council which shall be approved by the Order of the Minister in charge of primary and secondary school; provide a strategic vision and programme of action for the Council; consider and approve the annual draft budget before it is transmitted to relevant authorizes; monitor the performance of the Council in accordance with the plan of action and the budget; approve the activity and financial reports of the previous year; offer advice to the Council management and staff; participate in determining an effective general policy relating to primary and secondary examinations; institute directives on how examinations are to be conducted and on those relating to similar issues; and take decisions on persons who act contrary to this law and those who do not respect the directives relating to examinations.

The Executive Secretariat (management) has five professional units/departments namely: (i) Preparation & Administration of Examinations (test development); (ii) Orientation, Selection, Training and Documentation; (iii) Planning and Research (iv) ICT; and (v) Administration and Finance. It is responsible for the management of daily operations of the Council and has 69 members of the professional staff. Its responsibilities are to: coordinate and conduct all daily activities of the Council; represent the Council in everyday activities and take administrative decisions; establish relations and cooperate with other national and international agencies carrying out similar responsibilities; allocate successful candidates in

Table 1. Budget allocation from 2007 to 2011 in US Dollars

2007	2008	2009/2010	2010/2011
2,567,638.6	4,032,487.6	5,402,619.3	6,617,534.9

secondary schools, universities and other Higher Education Institutions; ensure measures of effective staff management according to competence, the nature of the work and the required numbers; make a report of the Coincil's activities and that of budget management; sign certificates and diplomas; issue certificates and diplomas to successful candidates who pass examination; sign contract with employees; and determine equivalence between certificates and diplomas issued abroad and those issued in Rwanda.

Candidates registering for national examinations come from a wide spectrum of primary and secondary schools. Some are government owned, government supported, while others are, private. We also have private candidates aspiring to complete high school diploma. Trends show that the number of candidates for examinations has been steadily increasing over the years and it will certainly go on increasing considering that Rwanda implemented a fee- free and compulsory 9 years of basic education in 2009. Additionally, there exists a strong government drive to promote Public-Private-Partnerships (PPP) as an incentive for entrepreneurship in the education sector which will certainly result into the creation of new schools ready to receive students at all levels of secondary and higher education.

Financial Considerations

Today's quality service delivery imperatives demand innovative strategies and reinforced inputs to be invested in the process. A number of measures that Council has been putting in place not only to improve the quality of services, but also generate some income include: speedy candidates' registration where forms are correctly filled out; properly done printing of registrations forms; timely availing of examination sheets for all the candidates throughout the country; comprehensive training of teachers on evaluation methods for all subject matters, in all primary and secondary schools, throughout the country; hiring the entire required staff and cutting down on outsourcing needs to preserve confidentiality of examinations; expanding logistic resources during examinations periods; availing to the staff opportunities to access knowledge development sources; investing in technology to take advantage of the most advanced ICT software and equipment; running its own printing press in order to cut down on costs of having examination questions and answer sheets printed outside the country while ensuring more security and confidentiality of documents; training of staff in a variety of subjects including evaluation methods and computer skills; compiling and disseminating old examinations syllabuses; and developing and disseminating models of answers. The following Table 1 shows the council's budget allocation from 2007 to 2011 in United States Dollars.

Against this background, the Council is determined to supplement the current budget funding mechanisms with its own income generating activities which include, but are not limited to the following: Online registration and publication of results where by the Council would share benefits with the service provider; increased candidate registration fees to match the Council's unit cost of running national examinations; operating Council's own printing press for income generation purposes; availing examination syllabuses and past papers for a fee; research and consultancy on assessment issues; and other service charges. The Council makes use of a financial management and accounting software known as SAGE Pastel which will soon be replaced by the "Smart Government" (SMART GOV) to harmonize with other government agencies. SMART GOV is a Ministry of Finance Accounting Software designed to manage government expenditure across all government public institutions including central ministries, autonomous agencies, provincial, districts and other local administration budget institutions. Staff trains on the job or takes advantage of various opportunities presented and organized by the Council, or the Ministry of Public Service and Labor. Budget preparation and execution, supply and logistics, office furniture, transport, etc are also executed in strict respect of government procedures and regulations. Requisition forms have been issued to facilitate and put order in the procurement process, while facilitating units and individual staff members' involvement in the execution of the budget. The Council works very closely with the Rwanda Public Procurement Authority (RPPA) to train the Internal Tender Committee (ITC) in procurement and tendering procedures and regulations. Also, the Council has a full-time internal auditor who ensures compliance with the national finance and procurement laws.

SETTING THE STAGE

The Council deals with an array of both internal (staff) and external stakeholders most notably schools whose relationship is the focus of this chapter. Therefore, it should be able to communicate to them its mission and activities to ensure they are fully aware of and understand the importance of working together for effective service delivery. Thus it is important that the Council examines its relationship with its stakeholders especially schools from a marketing perspective. One of its stated aims is to inform all the stakeholders especially schools about its mission and priorities and enable them to be involved in future direction, for networking, for dissemination of the Council's operations, and crucially for consulting with them about the way forward. For example, during the marking exercise, teachers can identify weaknesses and errors in student scripts. The Council can then use teachers' feedback to improve on the management of the examination process and marking as part of the overall management of the examinations system. In this way they have contributed immensely to its future direction.

Communicating the Council's mission and priorities is important because as Bush (1999) points out, the increased emphasis on external relations and the 'permeability of boundaries means that education managers cannot ignore the need for marketing their institution'. In the case of the Council, marketing is used here to mean the process through which it communicates and in fact, tries to 'sell' its reforms (products) to the teachers who should in turn communicate 'sell' the reforms to their communities. This is important if the reform is to be accepted and implemented. Thus the fact that the Council already has a relationship with schools is not in itself sufficient to create an environment in which schools feel comfortable with the post genocide examination products or packages. It is therefore important to improve the partnership and collaboration with schools. However, accepting change goes beyond improvements as it entails new ways and patterns of thinking (perceptions) by teachers which requires effective communication (marketing) on the part of the Council to 'sell' the reforms.

The Council regards schools as its customers, clients, partners or stakeholders. Anderson, et al (2004) distinguish between customers and clients; partnership and stakeholders. According to them customers and clients are people who seek a service, and they may be internal to the institution or external. Partnership involves 'a working relationship that is characterized by a shared sense of purpose, mutual respect and the willingness to negotiate.' This implies sharing of information, responsibility, skills, decision making and accountability. According to Warring (1999), stakeholders refer to 'all those who have a legitimate interest in the continuing effectiveness and success of an institution.' This implies that all clients and all partners are stakeholders, together with others who may have 'a legitimate interest'. Stakeholders may be internal (staff) or external, in this case, schools. However, Anderson, et al, (2004) argue that external stakeholders are said to 'rely to a very large extent, on past experience, or on information communicated to them by internal stakeholders' for their information about the institution.

The relationship between the Council and the schools which it serves may be analyzed within the context of institutional openness and what it regards as marketing to serve their needs. Anderson, et al, (2004, p. 58) cite Hoy and Miskel (1987) who argue that the open system concept highlights the 'vulnerability and interdependence of organizations and their environments'. I find this observation relevant to the Council because it implies that the environment is important as it affects the internal structures and processes of the Council. For example, in 2009, there were about 2700 primary and secondary school teachers involved in the marking of national examinations. Their views and perceptions regarding the way examinations are run are important because the Council should consider them during the process of organizing, coordinating and managing the examinations system. This is so because those who do the marking are the ones who can see and identify areas for improvement, for example in the way examinations are set, packaged, administered and graded. Teachers are on the front line of the examinations processing.

This process may be analyzed through the lens of the match between the institution and its environment and this phenomenon is not only limited to the Council. Viewed from a wider perspective especially from that of schools, Anderson, et al (2004) assert that schools and colleges may 'respond to external demands through planning and forecasting where likely changes and future pressures may occur'. They argue that 'the move towards having an institutional development plan may be seen in part, as a response to the demands and influences from outside the institution'. This argument holds for the Council as well because the impetus and urgency for its effective management has been dictated mainly by external circumstances. For example, in Rwanda, the recent financial law (2006) requires public institutions to design within their strategic plans income generating activities outside government budget. Thus the Council needs to generate income to cater for about 2700 teachers who participate in marking primary and secondary school national examinations each year. This requires a substantial amount of innovations in technology to enhance the marketing strategy.

Before 1994, institutional planning was minimal in Rwanda. Foskett (1999) argues that in the past 'building an external relations component into institutional planning or strategy was simply a matter for professional judgment'. In fact in Rwanda it was nonexistent. Even today in many institutions in Rwanda, its presence or absence depends on the management's view of the value of the relationship it wants to develop with its external stakeholders. In the case of the Council, it would seem inconceivable to ignore the significance of about 2700 teachers involved in its work. From this perspective, stakeholder perceptions of the Council's management of the examinations system become crucial. As Farnham (1993) observes, political and social change embedded in a commitment to 'the ideology of the market and of consumer choice in pursuit of economy, efficiency and effectiveness' has been steadily absorbed into the 'educational culture and given statutory authority through legislation.' However, in Rwanda as in many developing countries, this is for most educationists an imported, even alien concept.

Although the Council seeks to market itself, Foskett (1999) points out two important issues which complicate marketing in education. First, service industries, even in the private sector, have not traditionally taken a strong marketing perspective because service products are inherently intangible which makes their promotion difficult, particularly where the 'product' is long term in its rewards, such as education; services in the professional sector may see marketing as unethical, compromising the objectivity of their relationship with their 'client'; some service sectors experienced demand far in excess of their ability to provide it, such as in higher education, so promotion was unnecessary; most educational organisations have enjoyed monopoly power; and little professional guidance or training on adopting a marketing perspective has been available. Secondly, Foskett argues that traditional concepts of professionalism and public service in education do not sit easily with the notion of marketing; and that the view of the professional as 'expert' and the monitor of quality may be interpreted to mean that responsiveness to the market is unnecessary.

Gray (1991, p. 25) has suggested that 'the purpose for which public sector institutions such as schools were established goes far beyond mere customer satisfaction'. According to this view, educational institutions have 'public service duties and responsibilities to tackle real needs which may not be appreciated by these customers'. The argument here is that educational institutions have many different external links which go beyond transactional or exchange relationships and that while managing external relations is of great importance to the institution, each is embedded in its internal processes. However, Foskett (1999, p. 36) quotes Worcester (1985) who asserts that "no organization can sustain a good reputation that it does not deserve". This is relevant because in this case, it implies that each member of the Council, for example, ought to have a role.

Effective external relations will probably require significant internal marketing to support it and staff are key players within this process since their activities define the quality of the organization and they represent a key stakeholder group with whom management must manage relationships with great care. Earlier research by Foskett (1992) points out that external relations management relates to those aspects of an organization's activities that in any way cause it to relate to an audience beyond its own boundaries. This includes both processes with an overtly external connection and those processes which, while largely internal to the organization, have a direct impact on some external stakeholders. The implications are enormous because such processes need effective management. Johnson & Scholes (1993) argue that the whole concept of effective management comprises three components namely; strategic analysis, strategic choice and strategic implementation. Although a detailed discussion of each is beyond the scope of this chapter, suffice it is to say that each one of these may be identified with stakeholder relations components at the Council. For example, establishment of effective internal quality assurance systems in the Council should ensure that the service or product meets school expectations. It is also important to develop mechanisms for collecting external data using available technology on how the examination system in Rwanda is perceived as part of its marketing strategy.

The objective of attempting to gauge teacher perceptions is by all intents and purposes to establish an audit of the effective management of the examinations system which relates to how far the Council has been communicating its mission to teachers. From a schools' perspective, Knight (1993, p. 19) defines and illustrates educational effectiveness as 'the fullest possible attainment of the goals and objectives of the school'. Examples include improved performance, possibly against performance indicators such as improved examination results or test scores; improved student attitudes and behaviour; better parent and community relations and improved school environment. It may be reiterated that effectiveness is concerned with maximizing the benefits due to educational provision within the constraints of cost or resource availability. Mortimore et al (1994, p. 23) do not necessarily disagree but instead put it in another way by suggesting that 'cost effectiveness is concerned with selecting the least cost alternative for securing the desired outcome'. However, Thomas (1990) disagrees. He argues that the most cost-effective will be the 'least costly of the alternatives compared, but this is not necessarily the cheapest possible method of obtaining the objective'. In any case, the limits of experiences, knowledge and attitudes one is able to draw upon limits the decision.

To effectively manage the national examinations system in Rwanda, the Council will have to deal with organizational and institutional dilemmas if it has to develop and improve its own ratings by teachers. To improve teacher perceptions of the Council, the management should address crucial issues as highlighted by Middlewood & Lumby (2003) to include: Appropriate and effective communication process, full integration of all stakeholders, positive resolution of conflict, a code of conduct which reflects the organization's culture and appropriate degrees of stakeholder involvement in decision making. It should be acknowledged that the critical success factors in terms of the effective management of the examinations system in Rwanda is the linking together of the work of different operating units and stakeholders. Bush & Coleman (2002) argue that the coordination of such factors and the establishment of a culture which promotes them lies with the over all management and ethos of the institution. This is relevant to the Council considering that its stated goal and purpose is to support learning and teaching in Rwanda schools. Other researchers such as Briggs & Sommefeldt (2002) are of the view that the placing of different interest groups is open to debate according to the factors at play in a particular cultural, social and political situation and those external influences are said to impact on organizational effectiveness. Indeed with about 2700 teachers involved in the Rwandan examinations processes, the significance of their perceptions cannot be underestimated.

CASE DESCRIPTION

Experiences and Expectations: Players Involved and Their Roles within the Council

In April 2007, I was about to start my second year of the Doctorate in Education (EdD) at the University of Sussex, Brighton, (United Kingdom). The last assignment of year 1 of the Doctoral Programme required students to research or evaluate an educational institution. I decided to research my own institution. I selected three secondary schools in Kigali city whose medium of instruction is English. I did this because my previous experience with non –English speaking schools had proved problematic in terms translation from French or Kinyarwanda (mother tongue) into English. I had requested head teachers of each of the schools to select four teachers, where possible both male and female who mark national examinations. The combined number of teachers in the three schools was twelve. One school is a girls' school, another is a boy's only school and the third school is mixed sex. The girls' school is government supported (*libre subsidie)*, the boys' school is public and the mixed school is private. The intention was to create a variety in the hope that responses would be varied as well as to reinforce the trustworthiness of results.

Below, I summarise the findings according to each question:

To what extent has the Council marketed itself to ensure stakeholder understanding of its mission?

This question challenges the Council's identity which must be perceived and evaluated against societal needs and aspirations. The Council needs a clear sense of purpose that people understand. Here purpose and belonging are the two facets of identity. The Council's identity must spring from the organisation's own roots, its personality, its strength and weaknesses. It must be so clear that it becomes the yardstick against which its products, behaviour and actions are measured. Here, teacher perceptions put this identity through a magnifying glass. According to this lens, teachers in the sample stated that the mission of the Council was to set and mark examination and that they identified with it.

There were some common responses concerning how schools could contribute to the mission of the Council. They indicated that schools could contribute in a number of ways such as: (i) analysing student performance in national examinations (ii) covering the curriculum so that students do not fail national examinations (iii) each school having a secretariat that communicates to teachers about examination updates and issues (iv) evaluating students periodically before they seat national examinations in order to meet the Council's mission and providing feedback to the Council. Perhaps more intriguing was the teachers' suggestion that teachers should start examination departments in their respective schools. These departments would come up with mission statements that eventually lead to formulation of the Council's mission statement. This suggestion implies that school mission statements related to examinations should be integrated into the Council's own mission statement which has implications for the relationship between the Council and the schools.

Notwithstanding the teachers' declaration of their awareness of its mission and potential contributions to the Council's work, the same number also reported that although they have been marking national examinations for an average of five years, they were not aware of its plans and only responded when called upon to mark national examinations. If this had been a larger sample, it would have said much to the Council's identity as a national organisation. And in fact, it did since such a big number of the research sample said that the Council has had no formal ways of communicating its plans and activities to the very stakeholders who say they identify with it and have clearly indicated the roles they can play in contributing to its mission, then there exists a weakness on the part of the Council for its inability to tap into such a reservoir of knowledge and experience – the teachers.

There is therefore a need for a vigorous marketing (communication) strategy especially at this crucial time when the Council is in the process of transforming itself in the context of Rwanda's entry into the East African Community and now the British Commonwealth of Nations. The search for a marketing strategy cannot be ignored because marketing in this sense is seen as a means of enhancing the position and value of the Council as a whole. In this way, the institution begins to make a more proactive attempt to develop a reputation within the wider community especially with the teachers. Marketing here is measured through improving the image of the Council. It becomes a clear task of communicating information that will lead teachers to develop a better and more accurate picture of the Council.

What are the teachers' perceptions of the Council regarding its present management of the examinations system?

Analysis of the responses showed that teachers are an invaluable source of knowledge on the examinations system. They raised issues concerning timing of papers during setting. They said that three hour papers are too long and tiresome suggesting that two or more papers be introduced in future. This would give room for few hours' examinations and room to examine the whole subject content as in the curriculum of the particular course. What the teachers implied was that shorter time papers can examine students better. This raised the question of training not only for teachers but also for student's in attempting national examinations. Respondents wondered whether one paper per subject (current practice) could cover a whole syllabus. In fact, this seems to be a legitimate observation considered against the earlier concern about a three hour paper, which is long and given more time supposedly to ensure wide coverage of the curriculum. Respondents argued however, that shorter, but more papers would cover the syllabus better than one long one. This seems to be a legitimate argument since the examination is meant to measure skills rather than just how much knowledge one has acquired.

In terms of the examination papers and examiners, respondents pointed to some major weaknesses in the system. For example, there was constant reference to some questions not coming from clearly indicated topics of the subject curriculum and that the curriculum did not show clearly the examinable areas. This has implications for an examinations syllabus which is a responsibility of the Council. Here again considerations of a 'fair and transparent' system matched against practical and professional considerations become a challenge in terms of management of an examination system in conflict affected societies. I make this observation because it seems that the system might have concentrated its effort on the more 'political' concerns of justice, equity and reconciliation of a post – genocide educational reconstruction and less on practical and professional issues raised by the teachers in the study.

Another area of concern raised by the teachers was that of training. Again there was a general concern about examiners who should be trained teachers and experts in their area. Scoring was raised as an issue of concern in which respondents felt that depending on the technicality of the questions, scoring should be done professionally so as not to underscore or over score. Thus examiners require in service training on regular basis to set and mark to the expected standards. This issue relates to the one on coverage of syllabus content where a balance needs to be exercised during the setting of examinations so that some curriculum content is not over examined or under examined.

The issue of educational materials seemed to revolve mainly around those items used during examinations such as scientific calculators. Some teachers complained that there were many models nowadays of scientific gadgets. Many were unfamiliar to most students. This called for the need of specifying the models to be used in national examinations. I consider this to be a relevant observation. For an institution that prides its self of being fair to its stakeholders, it is a major weakness to set examinations without spelling out the relevance of different scientific models to the questions on which the models are to be applied or used, the availability of the models on the Rwandan market and the cost of the model, with considerations of whether or not it would be affordable to the common student considering the poverty levels of the country. This also means that teachers should be required to be conversant with the model and to train students accordingly.

What are the teachers' future expectations of the Council in terms of its management of the examinations system?

Responses here were mixed. The teachers thought that there was plenty of room for the Council to improve its image and services to schools. They referred to the Council's management of the examinations system as satisfactory and fair, but also pointed out that there were some areas which needed to be improved. They said that the Council should address the issues of the link between the curriculum and national examinations so that questions are not set outside the syllabus. The Council should ensure that examinations follow the order and sequence of the curriculum. Teachers also stressed the need for introduction of practical examinations especially in the natural sciences and setting application and other higher order questions covering the rest of the curriculum; and regular in service training of teachers involved in examination work. A majority of the teachers said that only teachers should set examinations and should be trained to become experts in their respective areas.

Secondly, the research revealed that Rwandan teachers were increasingly becoming aware of and making connections between their own school works with that of other educational institutions. The fact that teachers were able to link teaching and learning issues in the classroom with assessment at national level places a challenge to the Council as awareness of the interests of the teacher's demands a place in its policy and strategic plan. This is so because any reputation the Council attempts to present to external stakeholders must be based upon the reality of the situation. As a matter- of- fact, respondents in this research came out quite clearly by holding the Council 'accountable' through their perceptions which not only reinforces the need for creating partnership with them, but also puts new pressure on the Council to do so sooner rather than later as the institution transforms itself to meet the 21st century challenges.

What are the implications for effective management of the examinations system?

The research highlighted some interesting features. For example, the teachers wanted the Council to involve them more and more in its activities. That school perceptions happened to point to this direction is in itself a wakeup call for further investigation regarding how examinations are organised and managed, by whom and with what impact, and what relationship it has with the schools. The research revealed that teachers were seeking further involvement and participation in the life and activities of the Council which is an expression of a strategic partnership. This kind of partnership should be managed strategically and should be characterised by a shared sense of purpose, mutual respect and a willingness to negotiate. This implies sharing of information, responsibilities, skills, decision making and accountability. Here, the concern for the Council should be how such information might be shared and how the Council may gain respect from the schools and vice versa. The Council should be waking up to the reality that educational institutions, even in a developing country context like Rwanda can no longer work in isolation.

From this perspective, Anderson, et al (2004) argues that although the reputation of an institution may vary from a stakeholder group to another, it will always be based on the perceptions they hold. These perceptions may have very little basis in fact, or may be out dated and biased, but they must still be recognised as the views these particular groups hold. Thus the Council should as a matter of urgency develop a clear appreciation of the experiences, expectations and perceptions held by the different stakeholders especially teachers who are directly involved in its work. The Council should learn what various stakeholders are saying, what it wants them to say and how it can get them to say that.

Following that experience, I organised some in-house workshops in my institution to discuss the results of my research with all the 69 members of the professional staff. Consequently, in 2008, we were able to reform the way we set our examinations to make them more practical and skills oriented. We focussed especially on the science related examinations and since then laboratory and other practical work is a compulsory and major component of the examinations system. We also designed a table of specifications (Blue print) based on Benjamin Bloom's taxonomy of instructional objectives, so that in the humanities, we determined the number of questions per paper that demand recall of information, comprehension, application, analysis of a situation, synthesis and evaluation of outcomes. We also reviewed the way we mark and score and reformed the national grading system.

Guiding Questions

1. What do you think is the mission of the Council? Is this a mission you identify with? Why?
2. How can schools contribute to the mission of the Council?
3. How would you evaluate the way in which the Council manages the marking of secondary school national examinations? In your opinion, is it doing so fairly and accurately?
4. From your experience of marking national examinations, do you see areas where it can improve? How?
5. What is your opinion of the ways in which the Council places successful candidates in different schools?
6. From your experience, what do you see as some of the challenges the Council faces in managing the examinations system?
7. What should the Council do to improve its image and services to schools?
8. How can schools play a supportive role to the work of the Council, especially in improving the management of examinations?

Technology Concerns

In the national examinations process, the Council undertakes various massive tasks of registration of candidates, preparation of examinations, conducting of examinations, marks processing, grading and publication of results and then orientation of successful candidates to the next level of secondary and university education. These tasks involve processing of large databases and message exchanges through internal communications; and interaction with students, parents or guardians, teachers, heads of institutions and district education officers through announcements, rules and regulations governing the conduct of examinations. Engaging this array of stakeholders demands innovations in technology for educational marketing, in this case of national examinations reform products, such as the recently introduced 'Conveyor – Belt' Marking System, the new grading system based on the new curriculum, the introduction and emphasis on practical science examinations and the new changes in the content and format of certificates and diplomas. These products need relevant technology for effective and efficient marketing to various stakeholders. The next section describes the technologies that the Council has been trying to put in place to enhance not only service delivery, but the actual marketing of its products.

Technology Components

ICT Project (i)

The Council has a number of ICT equipment including two server machines, a fully wired computer network with fibre optic back borne, and an Optical Mark Reading Machine. In 2005, the Council signed a contract with HAMLET COMPUTER GROUP LTD, a United Kingdom based company to develop an examination processing application called FAIM running on SQL server and windows 2003 server. This has facilitated the RNEC to develop its ICT capability in order to deliver its services to the public much more efficiently and effectively. This also is necessitated by the fact that the number of candidates increases every year, hence ICT capability to deliver and meet the long term needs and expectations of Rwandan primary and secondary schools is essential. As a result of this initiative, the Council is able to carry out the following functions with relative efficiency.

Registration of Candidates

The ICT system captures candidate's surname, first name, sex, date of birth, father's name, mother's name, district name, district number, sector name, sector number, school number, subject combination, student number, language of examination, (candidates have been allowed to write their examinations in either English or French), disabilities, choices (candidates have 3 choices of schools and 3 choices of subject combinations). These data are usually collected in MS Excel and have to be integrated in the database. Marks are entered against the candidate details already in the data base and provision for marks entry is designed into the system.

As part of the process, lists and reports are produced which include lists of all registered candidates by school and by district with their full details for typing error corrections; list of candidates by sex; lists of grades for each candidate based on the weights of the subjects and the raw marks obtained, list of candidates by school and by district indicating marks in every subject and the average mark, list of first 20 candidates by their average mark, list of the first 20 candidates in each subject by their mark, list of the first 20 female students in the country, list of the first 20 female candidates in each subject by their mark, list of the first 20 schools by the average mark of all candidates in that school, list of the bottom schools by the average mark of all candidates in that school, the first 20 public schools by the average mark of all candidates in that school, the first 20 private schools by the average mark of all candidates in that school, the best candidate overall by average mark and his/her school, the best female candidate overall by average mark and her school, total number of candidates at registration, total number of candidates at registration by sex, total number of candidates who attended examinations in that year, total number of candidates who attended examinations by sex, total number of candidates who obtained a pass mark, total number of candidates who obtained a pass mark by sex, percentage of candidates who obtained a pass mark and percentage of candidates who obtained a pass mark by sex.

In this process, the ability to do selection of candidates to the Advanced Level of the secondary school cycle based on the available vacancies and the candidate choices that were recorded at registration is paramount. After this selection process, a number of lists and reports must be generated. These include lists of selected candidates by choice and allocated school, lists of selected candidates by district of the allocated school and lists of selected candidates by sex. The Ministry of Education and other stakeholders require different kinds of statistical data and the Council must have a facility to produce such data. The Council's success may be attributed in part to having generic report templates which are completed by providing input parameters and redefining the display layout which is very important for effective service delivery.

ICT Project (2)

In 2008, the Council signed a contract with AGILE LEARNING TECHNOLOGIES, an American company (which has acquired a licence to operate in Rwanda), to develop a web -based tool to enable the Council to improve the coordination and managements of high stake public examinations processes. The system / Project is known as the 'Rwanda Examinations Coordination and Management Information System' (RECMIS). As a result of the support emanating from this Public-Private-Partnership, AGILE LEARNING TECHNOLOGIES has helped develop local capacity at the Council through technology transfer and the Council was able to achieve the following targets in record time:

1. *Online registration of candidates, publication of results and SMS cell phone based system*

A highly secure online system for checking results was installed where students and parents or guardians can access Council's databases by providing their registration number and then their results are displayed in non modifiable format through web based application or SMS. The candidates can also register online through an interface that is linked to our data base. The Council has built an Online- Based- Results Information System that has been used to provide primary and secondary school leaving candidates with online access to their results through cell phones by SMS text and the Internet through the Web and provides other services such as registration verification by SMS text.

The Council has installed and configured the system to enable students query its databases by SMS text for their results as well as through the Web and also to verify their registration status. The Council has built all the necessary capacity needed to run, support and maintain the developed system. The system includes querying of examination timetables for all sets of examinations. We have developed a database that enables the collection of statistics on the traffic and usage of the SMS and Internet system. This is important for SMS service provider (a local company called MTN Rwanda) with which the Council signed a separate contract; and for monitoring purposes.

The Council has trained staff to develop a strategy of implementation for the marketing and public awareness of the system to ensure sustainability. One of the important features of the system is to conduct system requirements analysis, design and development, deployment, testing and providing a clear maintenance plan of the system comprising of both client and server system components and staff have been trained on its use. No effort has been spared to ensure effective and efficient server configurations including the implementation of SMS and Internet interfaces (gateway configuration) between the system and the selected mobile telecommunications operator. We have established a central database and server software for storage and retrieval of examination results information. This information has been correlated and aggregated in the manner required by the Council and its stakeholders.

An enhanced website has been in place for use to publish examination results and student registration details and additional promotional information about the system including but not limited to basic information about the Council. There exist built-in reporting mechanisms to support statistical analysis of examination results data. Data collected are summarized and made available through the website and other media formats (Tables, Graphic Charts, PDF, Spread sheets, GIS Maps, etc). Candidates are able to query the database using specific student codes such as registration numbers or other pin numbers to be determined in order to retrieve examination results either by SMS or directly from the website. Users, who use SMS to receive examination results, are charged a premium rate for the SMS messages by the service provider and the fee is shared with the Council equally. Queries are also made directly into the database through a web interface. Information retrieved from the website is also available for downloading. The system has the ability to create historical trend reports (annual reports on primary and secondary schools examination results) using the electronically stored data, to use in planning and reporting on the activities of the sector.

2. *Collaboration tool*

The RNEC has developed a collaborative tool to enhance marketing and communication amongst stakeholders. Below are some of the data/message elements collected by the RNEC which is utilized by this application. They include list of registered students, list of withdrawals from examinations, rules, regulations and guidelines to conducting examinations in centers and districts, announcements, reports on administration of examinations, lists of students selected for the next level of study, list of transferred candidates, urgent messages to centers and districts, internal messages by Examinations Council staff, where possible voice and video chats for virtual meetings and video conferencing and general chat. The content format is designed in such a way that the lists are either word processing documents or spread sheets, reports, rules, regulations and guidelines are word processing documents; announcements, urgent messages and live text chat are in text or html formats; and there is also some voiceXML and MPEG or Avi for video chats.

The user categories include systems administrator, regular user and moderator. Every district officer, Head of department and Chief Executive Officers can be upgraded to moderate their group chats. In addition a user may access the application by providing a user name and password that was previously set at registration by the system administrator. Then users are authenticated and only information related to their duties is made available to them. This means that (a) officers who head examination centers are now able to upload or download their own lists of students and reports, view rules and regulations, announcements, urgent messages, district and the Council's reports and also join chat sessions of their group or the general chat; (b) District officers are now able to upload or download their own lists of students and reports, view rules and regulations, announcements, urgent messages, district and the Council's reports and also join chat sessions of their group or the general chat and posting announcements and urgent messages; and the Council staff are now able to upload/download rules and regulations, lists of students and reports, view rules and regulations, announcements, urgent messages, also join chat sessions of their group or the general chat.

3. *Selection process*

This module enables the Council to gather important statistics as indicated below. Schools or institutions can now submit these vacancies online into the server indicating number of places available at Ordinary (lower secondary) and Advanced (upper secondary) school levels and at the University level; and the number of places available at A' level by option for candidates completing O' level. Very high degree of security and privacy is required.

4. *Examiners tracking system*

This module covers the following items using online interfaces that are well designed which make use of appropriate technology concepts: Registration of examiners, giving their personal details; the examinations an examiner sets and also the examination he/she marks; examiner/teacher's qualifications; the class a teacher teaches and the subject that he/she teaches including the team leader's comments. Very high degree of security and privacy is required

5. *School performance*

The Council is now able to track the results and examine the performance of schools. This system generates statistical data on the performance of each school.

Benefits

Owing to these technological innovations, the Council received media attention for a while for having gone 'high tech.' The leading and influential daily English news paper 'THE NEW TIMES' had on 26th January 2009 as its front page caption: 'EDUCATION MINISTRY REFORMS THE EXAMINATION SYSTEM'; and on 28th January 2009, the same paper carried an article on page 7 titled: 'THANKING THE EDUCATION MINISTRY FOR EXAMINATIONS REFORM'. Consequently, during the budget process in June/July 2009, in the midst of a global economic crunch (recession), the Council still received an additional six hundred million Rwandan francs equivalent to one million two hundred thousand United states Dollars for reforming the science examinations in that year. The funds came from '*internal re-allocations*' within the ministry of education in recognition of the Council as change agent in the Rwandan educational system.

CURRENT CHALLENGES

The Issue of Human Resource Development and Management

The main challenge facing the Council is the lack of sufficient human resource capacity. The Council has been struggling to develop and build a human resource base as a basis for spurring institutional growth and development. The Council needs to acquire such values as to enable them to be more effective and challenging in changing situations. They need to recognise that the Rwandan society and the Council in particular is under pressure to provide higher levels of quality service and value and that experience alone does not count anymore as the environment in the "global village" is changing fast. Middlewood & Lumby (2003, p. 5) are of the view that the quality of staff in an educational organisation "is an issue of both specification and development, and that quality is about much more than appointing the most suitable candidate". Professional development is an imperative. Bush and Bell (2002) also believe that this entails ongoing process of education, training and learning in either external or work based activities, proactive engagement and promotion of learning and development of professional knowledge, skills and values.

Recently, the focus has included learning to be able to influence, motivate and work in closer working relationships, in teams with vision that aligns with and contributes to the achievement of the overall vision of the Council. However, the whole concept of 'teamwork' presents a dilemma not only at the Council, but also in Rwandan educational institutions as a whole. At the Council, in spite of all the effort to create a team work environment, work ethic and a changed mindset, the results have not been as forthcoming as expected mainly owing to human resource capacity considerations. Wallace & Hall (1994) have suggested that team working can be fraught with difficulties over the balance between equity and hierarchy, meaning that not everyone wants to work in a team, yet the joint work that teamwork represents depends on the commitment of all involved. The challenge facing the Council therefore, is to analyse the effectiveness of its staff development provision in terms of its impact upon a 'learning organisation' that the Council aspired to be. This is no easy task as there is an urgent need for change and the Council cannot change unless the its staff develops an attitude to change of both mind and heart to enable them to see, make informed choices and take the opportunities that change brings (Middlewood, 1997c). This is fundamental to the improvement of organisational performance and therefore as a core task of the Council.

From this perspective, the Council needs to be careful not to take educational marketing for granted in terms of its impact on a learning organisation because of the challenges associated with developing the people responsible for such marketing. Bush & Middlewood (1997) suggest that such a programme has to be devised in the context of attempting to meet the varying and sometimes conflicting needs within the institution. Whatever the programme, the effectiveness of its components depends in part, upon the extent to which there is recognition of those factors which affect the learning of adults. Southworth (1984) sees the whole process as essentially adult education and warns that educational institutions need to be aware of the technological developments and organisational change which has gradually led some employers to realize that success relies on the skills and abilities of their employees. This has also been underscored by the rise in human resource management with its emphasis on the importance of people and the skills they possess in enhancing individual, team and organisational performance and efficiency (Armstrong, 2003; Beardwell & Holden, 2001; Summons, et al, 1995).

Educational marketing involves providing structures, resources and support which will help staff learn how to learn and all staff need to be involved in the collaborative learning. Nevertheless, external pressure, particularly financial pressure limits the scope of strategic planning in educational marketing. Thus the Council will need to create an environment in which people continually expand capacity to create the results they truly desire, where new and expansive patterns of thinking are nurtured, where collective aspiration is set free, and where people are continually learning how to learn together (Senge, 1990; 1993). Thus, if the speed of innovation means that the problems and solutions of the past are no longer an adequate basis on which to plan, then new ways of coping with change are imperative. New forms of learning are needed and the concept of the learning organisation appears an enticing goal (Burgoyne, 1994).

To do so, the Council has to overcome the challenge of developing the skills for identifying needs, designing activities, deciding on monitoring and allocating resources and this depends upon the evaluation of previous activity and includes consideration of the monitoring and subsequent review processes (Anderson, et al, 2004; Bush &Coleman, 2002; Briggs & Sommefeldt, 2002). In the prioritisation process, the opportunities that will be foregone will need to be considered in terms of their educational and resource impact. For example, Middlewood & Burton (2003) advise that the act of reprioritising the acquisition of one multi-media computer over the purchase of text-based reference materials for the same cost is one that needs to be judged in terms of the overall educational impact. This in fact, seems to be a leadership challenge because leaders are designers, stewards, and teachers. They are responsible for building organisations where people continually expend their capabilities to understanding complexity, clarify vision and improve shared mental models –that is, they are responsible for learning since they need to ensure that the learning is moved to those parts of the organisation which need it, valuing and rewarding learning and transforming the organisation through the application of its learning (Garret, 1994; Senge, 1990). This remains a challenge for educational marketing and technology development.

SOLUTIONS, RECOMMENDATIONS AND LESSONS LEARNED

Anderson, et al (2004) quote Beare, et al (1992, p. 235) as saying: 'image begets public esteem; esteem creates public support; public support begets political attention; and political influence begets finance and staff numbers and governmental priority.' I find this argument quite valid for the Council. For example, created in 1998 to redress injustice and discrimination that prevailed before the 1994 genocide, the young institution has seen public support grow from year to year largely due to the public image as a transparent, fair and accountable organisation. From the experience of the Council, education can win tangible public support and finance when respect for its operations and out puts is high; but as Anderson, et al (2004, p. 79) observe, 'kill community regard and in the same process one kills the supply of resources.' This means that stakeholders should be proactively engaged and their importance should not be underestimated.

Another consideration is that the Council has to change the way it does business with schools which requires regular communication so that they are not only aware of its new 'products', but support and feel they are co-owners for effective implementation and service delivery. According to Bush (1999, p. 4), educational institutions can no longer 'operate in isolation' and expectations of society whether expressed by individual parents, identifiable groups, or government legislation, mean that educational institutions need to be aware of views being expressed by stakeholders. Citing Bagley, et al (1996, p. 125), Bush points out that educational institution must take account of public perceptions of 'how well they are performing and be prepared to respond to those articulated concerns which are genuinely representative.'

There is therefore a need for closer stakeholder partnership and collaboration.

A lesson learned here is that once the Council has developed a clear concept of such a relationship, then the management of the examinations system will be clear. Also, there ought to be a change in the relationship between the Council and the schools. This calls for renewed power relations and a pragmatic approach has to be taken to work out more effective teacher participation beyond marking examinations. This implies an effective co-learning relationship with the teachers involved in its work.

REFERENCES

Anderson, A., Briggs, R. J., & Burton, N. (2004). *Managing finance, resources and stakeholders in education*. London, UK: Paul Chapman.

Armstrong, M. (2003). *A handbook of human resource management practice*. London, UK: Kogan Page.

Beardwell, I., & Holden, L. (2001). *Human resource management: A contemporary approach*. London, UK: Pearson Education Limited.

Briggs, A. R. J., & Sommefeldt, D. (2002). *Managing effective teaching and learning*. London, UK: Paul Chapman.

Burgoyne, J. (1994). Personnel management. In Armstrong, M. (Ed.), *A handbook of human resource management practices*. London, UK: Kogan Page.

Bush, T. (1999). The vanishing boundaries: The importance of effective external relations. In Lumby, J., & Foskett, N. (Eds.), *Managing external relations in schools and colleges*. London, UK: Paul Chapman.

Bush, T., & Bell, L. (2002). *The principles and practice of educational management*. London, UK: Paul Chapman.

Bush, T., & Coleman, M. (2002). *Leadership and strategic management in education*. London, UK: Paul Chapman.

Bush, T., & Middlewood, D. (1997). *Managing people in education*. London, UK: Paul Chapman.

Coleman, M., & Anderson, L. (2002). *Managing finance and resources in education*. London, UK: Paul Chapman.

Coleman, M., & Lumby, J. (2001). The significance of site-based practitioner research in educational management. In Middlewood, D., Coleman, M., & Lumby, J. (Eds.), *Practitioner research in education*. London, UK: Paul Chapman.

Cooksey, B. (1992). *Basic education sector review*. Kigali, Rwanda: UNICEF.

Farnhan, D. (1993). *Managing the new public services*. Basingstoke, UK: Macmillan.

Foskett, N. (1992). An introduction to the managing of external relations in schools. In Foskett, N. H. (Ed.), *Managing external relations in schools*. London, UK: Routledge. doi:10.4324/9780203415146_chapter_1

Foskett, N. (1999). Strategy, external relations and marketing. In Lumby, J., & Foskett, N. (Eds.), *Managing external relations in schools and colleges*. London, UK: Paul Chapman.

Garrat, B. (1994). Learning organisation . In Middlewood, D. (Eds.), *Practitioner research in education: Making a difference*. London, UK: Paul Chapman.

Gipps, C., & Stalbart, G. (1993). *Assessment: A teacher's guide to the issues* (2nd ed.). London, UK: Hodder and Stoughton.

Gray, L. (1991). *Marketing education*. Buckingham, UK: Open University.

Knight, B. (1993). *Financial management for schools: The thinking managers' guide*. Oxford, UK: Heinemann.

Lumby, J., & Forskett, N. (1999). *Managing external relations in schools and colleges*. London, UK: Paul Chapman.

Middlewood, D. (1999). Managing relations between schools and parents. In Foskett, N., & Lumby, J. (Eds.), *Managing external relations in schools and colleges*. London, UK: Paul Chapman.

Middlewood, D., & Burton, N. (2003). *Managing the curriculum*. London, UK: Paul Chapman.

Middlewood, D., & Lumby, J. (1998). *Strategic management in schools and colleges*. London, UK: Paul Chapman.

Middlewood, D., & Lumby, J. (2003). *Human resource management in schools*. London, UK: Paul Chapman.

Mortmore, (1994). *Managing associate staff: Innovation in primary and secondary schools*. London, UK: Paul Chapman.

Rutaisire, J. (2007) The role of teachers in social and political reconstruction in Rwanda, in, Leach, F. And Dunne, M. (eds) Education, Conflict and Reconciliation: International perspectives, pp. 115-129, Berne: Peter Lang.

Rutaisire, J., Kabano, J., & Rubagiza, J. (2004) Redefining Rwanda's future: The role of curriculum in social reconstruction, in Tawil, S. And Harley, A, (eds) Education, conflict and social cohesion, pp. 315-373, Geneva, IBE, UNESCO

Sammons, P. (1995). Key characteristics of effective schools: A review of school effectiveness. In *J. Bush & D. Middlewood (1997). Managing people in education*. London, UK: Paul Chapman.

Senge, P. (1990). The fifth discipline. In Middlewood, D. (Eds.), *Practitioner research in education*. London, UK: Paul Chapman.

Southworth, G. (1984). Development of staff in primary schools. In Bush, T., & Middlewood, D. (Eds.), *Managing people in education*. London, UK: Paul Chapman.

Southworth, G. (1994). The learning school. In Bush, T., & Middlewood, D. (Eds.), *Managing people in education*. London, UK: Paul Chapman.

Thomas, H. (1990). *Educational costs and performance: A cost- effective analysis*. London, UK: Cassell.

United Nations. (2009). *Good practices and innovations in public governance. United Nations public service awards winners and finalists, 2003-2009*. New York, NY: United Nations.

Wallace, M., & Hall, V. (1994). Inside the SMT: Teamwork in secondary school management. In Lumby, J., & Foskett, N. (Eds.), *Managing external relations in schools and colleges*. London, UK: Paul Chapman.

Warring, S. (1999). Finding your way: Sensing the external environment. In Lumby, J., & Foskett, N. (Eds.), *Managing external relations in schools and colleges*. London, UK: Paul Chapman.

West, M., Jackson, D., Harris, A., & Hopkins, D. (2000). Learning through leadership, leadership through learning: Leadership for sustained school improvement. In Riley, K. A., & Louis, K. S. (Eds.), *Leadership for change and school reform: International perspectives*. London, UK: Routledge Falmer.

ADDITIONAL READING

Ansoff, I. (1987). *Corporate Strategy*. London: Penguin Business.

Bargley, C., Woods, P. & Glatter, R. (1996). Scanning the Market: School Strategies for Discovering Parental Perspectives, *Educational management and Administration, 24*(2), pp.125-38

Bolman, L., & Deal, T. (1989). Organisations, Technology and Environment. In Glatter, R. (Ed.), *Educational Institutions and Their Environments: Managing the Boundaries*. Milton Keynes: Open University press.

Bull, T. (1989). Home-School Links: Family–oriented or Business Oriented. *Educational Review, 41*(2), 113–119. doi:10.1080/0013191890410203

Carlson, R. (1975). Environmental Constraints and Organisational Consequences: The Public School and its Clients. In Baldridge, J., & Deal, T. (Eds.), *Managing Change in Educational Organisations, Berkely: McCutchan*.

Christopher, M., McDonald, M., & Wills, G. (1980). *Introducing Marketing*, London: Pan

Cowell, D. (1984). *The Marketing of Services*. Oxford: Butterworth.

Davis, B., & Ellison, L. (1997). *Strategic Marketing for Schools*. London: Pitman.

Davis, P., & Scribbins, K. (1985). *Marketing Further and Higher Education*. Harlow: Longman for FEU.

Glarrer, R. (1994). What Future for School Cooperation? *Management in Education, 8*(3), 22–23. doi:10.1177/089202069400800309

Gray, L. (1991). *Marketing Education*. Buckingham: Open University Press.

Hall. V. (1994). *Further Education in the United Kingdom*, London: Collins Educational and the Staff College.

Hanson, E. M., & Henry, W. (1992). Strategic marketing for Educational Systems. *School Organization, 12*(2), 255–267.

Holland, G. (1998). Learning In The twenty-First century, New. *Childhood, 13*(1), 4–5.

Hornby, G. (1990). The Organisation of Parent Involvement, School *Organisation, 10*(2 and 3), 247-52.

Hughes, M. (1996). *Colleges Working With Industry, FE Matters, 1(3)*. Bristol: FEDA.

James, C., & Phillips, P. (1995). The Practice of Educational Marketing in Schools. *Educational Management and Administration, 23*(2), 75–88. doi:10.1177/174114329502300202

James, C. & Phillips, P. (1995). The Practice of Educational Marketing in Schools, *Educational management and Administration, 23*(2),75-88.

Johnson, G., & Scholes, K. (1993). *Exploring Corporate Strategy*, 3rd edition, Hemel Hempstead: Prentice-Hall.

Kogan, M. (1984). *Educational Accountability: An Analytic Overview*. London: Huchinson.

Kotler, P., & Fox, K. (1995). *Strategic marketing for Educational Institutions*, 2nd Edition, NewYork: Kotler, P. (1994). *Marketing Management: Analysis, Planning, Implementation and Control*, 8th Edition, London: Prentice-Hall.

Martin, Y. (1995). What Do parents Want? *Management in Education, 9*(1), 8–9. doi:10.1177/089202069500900104

Martinez, P. (1995). *Improving Student Retention: A Guide to Successful Strategies*. London: FEDA.

Martinez, P., & Murray, F. (1998). *9000 Voices: Completion and Drop – out in Further Education*. London: FEDA.

McDonald, M. (1995). Marketing Plans: How To Prepare Them, How To Use Them, 3rd Edition, London: Butter-worth-Heinemann.

Murgatroyd, S., & Morgan, C. (1993). *Total Quality Management and the School*. Buckingham: Open University Press.

Payne, A. Christopher, M., Clark, M. & Peck, H. (1995). *Relationship Marketing for Competitive Advantage: Winning and Keeping Customers*, Oxford: Butter-worth-Heinemann.

Pieda. (1996). *Labour Market Information for Further Education Colleges: A Handbook for Practitioners*, Manchester: Pieda

Riley, K. (1998). *Whose School Is It Anyway?*London: Falmer Press.

Sarason, S. (1990). *The Predictable Failure of Education Reform*. San Francisco: Jossey-Bass.

Smith, D., Scott, P., & Lynch, J. (1995). *The Role of Marketing in the University and College sector*. Leeds: Heist.

Woods, P., Bagley, C., & Glatter, R. (1998). *School Choice and Competition: Markets in the Public Interest?*London: Routledge.

KEY TERMS AND DEFINITIONS

Discrimination: This was a state of affairs in which the Tutsi and other social groups were systematically excluded from participation in the education system. Social discrimination included the exclusion of girls in favor of boys, and others based on religion and place of origin.

Education System: This refers to the Rwandan education system which provides for six years of primary (elementary) education, three years of the lower secondary education, known in East Africa and the British Commonwealth as the 'Ordinary Level', three years of the upper secondary education, known as the 'Advanced Level', and four years of University education (6+3+3+4).

Effective Management: Refers to the results oriented post-genocide paradigm shift in attitude and management practices in which the Council implements its policies and decisions to assist in directing its activities towards its specified goals and objectives. This includes monitoring and controlling of its activities, how we make our decisions, and how we control our resources.

Innovation and Technology: This refers to the improvements and changes in technology that the Council has instituted to assist in the effective management of the national examinations system for more cost-effective and cost-efficient delivery of its reform packages. It applies to the way candidates register for national examinations, in test development, marks processing, grading, and publication of results and in orientation of successful candidates to Ordinary and Advanced Levels of secondary schools, and to Universities and other Higher Education Institutions.

Marketing the Council: Refers to the efforts that the Council has been taking to communicate its vision, mission, goals and activities to its stakeholders. The last ten years have marked a series of reforms in the national examinations system which demanded among other things stakeholder consultation and making sure that they felt part of the ownership of the reform packages.

Nepotism: This refers to a phenomenon in which before 1994, for a learner to proceed from one level of the education system to another, they had to be related to, or be friends with the president of the republic, a government minister, or other government and political party officials regardless of performance at school.

Rwanda National Examinations Council: This institution was created after the 1994 Tutsi genocide in Rwanda to address the imbalances that obtained in the education system. These were based on inequities in the system related mainly to nepotism and discrimination which affected upward mobility of learners from the lowest level of the education system to the highest.

Chapter 14
When Going Online Isn't Going

Elizabeth Osika
Chicago State University, USA

Rochelle Johnson
Chicago State University, USA

Rosemary Buteau
Chicago State University, USA

EXECUTIVE SUMMARY

Over the last few years, Southern State University (SSU) has experienced a decline in enrollment and state funding. However, one aspect that holds promise, based on past enrollment data, is the potential movement towards providing online degree programs. While SSU provides rewards and encouragement for the development of online courses and programs, and students consistently are quick to fill the online sections, there has only been a small cohort of faculty who embrace teaching online. Therefore, there has been little to no growth in the number of online courses compared to other schools in the area, and not a single program has been established as being offered completely online. SSU is now faced with the issue of how to convince the heavily unionized faculty and other stakeholders that movement to the offering of online programs is a vital aspect of the university's future success.

INTRODUCTION

Online education has become commonplace in the educational market. According to Seaman and Allen (2010) more than twenty-five percent of all higher education students are enrolled in at least one online course. Their report also shows that as students continue to look for ways to balance their ever increasing schedules and react to the economic downturn, online courses and programs have sustained continued growth, even in light of the limited or reduced growth in traditional college enrollments. As universities continue to move towards online education, they are faced with a variety of responses from faculty including those who are resistant, if not opposed to the concept.

Even though many faculty members are now comfortable with technology, using email to communicate and other Internet tools for research and information, many are resistant when it comes to incorporating technology into their classrooms. Brill and Galloway (2007) noted two limitations

DOI: 10.4018/978-1-60960-599-5.ch014

to the use of technology in instruction: inadequate availability of technology, and technology that is not adequately supported. This information is important for universities moving into the online environment, as it shows that technology must be readily available and fully supported if faculty members are to integrate technology into their classrooms.

Other research has shown various factors that contribute to the decisions of faculty to adopt technology into his or her teaching: feelings, attitudes and perceptions towards technology (Albion & Ertmer, 2003; Christensen, 2002; Dusick, 1998) and the individual faculty member's teaching style (Grasha & Hicks, 2003; Ferguson, 2004). Fully understanding these feelings, perceptions, and teaching styles will be necessary to provide the type of environment that encourages faculty to explore the potential that technology can have on teaching and learning.

Additionally, research has found that instructors' beliefs about technology use are formed "during time spent in the classroom either as teachers or students" (Albion & Ertmer, 2003). Therefore, if faculty members form their pedagogical beliefs about using technology in instruction while they were students or early in their teaching career, efforts should be made to guarantee that new faculty members' experience with technology is successful. These early experiences should be positive and reinforce the benefits of technology integration.

Finally, research discusses how the lack of skills is another factor negatively influencing faculty members' motivation to adopt technology. This lack of skills is mainly due to faculty members not being trained or having technology properly modeled during their academic career (Ertmer, 2004; Ertmer, Conklin, & Lewandowski, 2003; Rosenfeld & Martinez-Pons, 2005). Consequently, creating technical competency among faculty through training, modeling, and mentoring is crucial if an organization wants to make technology an "organic" part of the learning environment.

All of these factors - availability and ease of use of technology and faculty members' attitudes, beliefs, and skills - contribute to the decision of faculty members whether or not to integrate technology into their courses. Therefore, a university wishing to expand or leverage technology use in teaching, such as online education, needs to develop a specific plan to "sell" the concept to the organization. In this plan, marketing will play a vital role.

When it comes to establishing a new idea or paradigm, such as online education, within the culture of a university, the fundamental principles of marketing cannot be overlooked. Even though the "customer" base is internal and policies can be put in place to force compliance, the intelligent organization will take a softer approach and create a plan that generates buy-in and approval. This is especially important when the customers are faculty members who are used to a high level of autonomy and self-governance.

Leveraging the 4P's of marketing with faculty members requires some adaption of the usual definition of product, price, place, and promotion. This starts by understanding the needs and the desires of the customers (Seybold, 2001). Once an understanding of the customers' needs is understood it quickly becomes as issue of showing how the new idea, in this case online education, can help them meet their needs.

For instance, the product of online learning must be shown as an effective tool that will help faculty accomplish the tasks involved in teaching more efficiently. The price of online education is not measured by faculty in terms of monetary cost but in time. How much time will be needed to incorporate the online tools determines the "price" of the tool. Placement for online education has to be shown as easily available to faculty members where ever and whenever they need it. Finally, the promotion of online education needs to be multifaceted and appeal not only to the individual faculty member's needs of effectiveness, efficiency, and ease of use, but it also must demonstrate how it will better serve the students and positively impact learning.

The following case demonstrates how a specific university's initial attempts at establishing an online educational program came up short and how through focusing on the needs of the customer it has tried to turn around the trend through marketing.

ORGANIZATION BACKGROUND

Southern State University (named changed for the sake of the case) has a rich background. Starting in the heart of an urban city, the school began as a teachers college using whatever space was available to meet. Over time, it grew to become a well known university serving a diverse population with several different colleges within the university, including education, sciences, business, health studies, pharmacy, and applied engineering.

Demographic Information

SSU is situated in the heart of the city where the primary student population is African-American (92%), female (58%), and a commuter student (93%). Many of the students enrolled at SSU are single parents struggling to meet their everyday needs in terms of housing, food, and security. To compound the issue, the vast majority of students are first-generation college students who have been academically prepared in the city school system resulting in the need for academic remediation for a significant portion of students. However, the students are generally serious about their studies and will work up the level of standards set for them, rising above the challenges they face.

The faculty at SSU is a highly unionized body comprised of a majority of African-American (57%) professors. There is a very low turnover in the faculty body. The majority of the faculty (72%) has been employed at SSU for more than 10 years, with 31% employed for over 20 years. Technology use among the faculty is limited. PowerPoint is the most popular instructional technology software, followed by loading supplemental materials in the course management system. A rather unstable technological infrastructure has caused faculty to distrust the network, as it is frequently down or slow.

Current Economic Factors

In 2009, the recession felt across the United States hit Southern State University, as it did most of the other academic institutions across the nation. SSU was faced with a dramatic decrease in state funding, as the state budgets were under the strain of reduced income and increased costs. In addition, financial aid was becoming less available. This was especially significant to SSU, as the vast majority of the students (87%) used some form of federal financial aid to support part, if not all, of their education.

The economic situation was also impacting the students' ability to attend courses. Many students now had to work second jobs or could no longer afford childcare, which kept them out of the classrooms on campus. During this time, SSU saw an increase in the number of students enrolled in the courses that were offered online, as this seemed to be one way of juggling academic, work, and family responsibilities.

SETTING THE STAGE

In the midst of the economic downturn and challenges that students faced, the administration needed to capitalize on systems and opportunities to increase enrollment and help students continue their education. One promising aspect was the enrollment trends of courses offered online through the Internet.

The recent national and state data on online enrollment has provided positive indicators as to the demand for courses in this format. Nationally, Allen and Seaman (2008) found that "online enrollment has continued to grow at rates far in excess of the total higher education student population, with the most recent data demonstrating no signs of slowing" (p. 1). Their survey revealed that over 3.9 million students are taking courses online, which is a 12 percent increase over the number reported the previous year. In addition, this 12 percent increase is dramatically above the slightly more than one percent (1.2%) increase in the overall higher education population.

When investigating why schools would invest in online courses and programs, Allen and Seaman (2007) reported the following from the participating institutions:

- 92% cited increased student access to courses
- 81% cited increased enrollment from students outside the traditional service area
- 72% cited increased rate of degree completion

This trend of increased enrollment in online courses and programs was also evident in the state in which Southern State University resides. Here the state saw a 24% increase in online course enrollment over the previous year.

When administrators at SSU began to investigate how online enrollment impacted their overall enrollment pattern, some mixed results were found. In terms of overall enrollment in online courses, SSU had only 9% of their students taking online courses compared to the national average of 20%. This lagging enrollment was also seen when comparing online enrollment with local schools with whom they competed for students. While SSU had approximately 9% enrollment in online courses, the two closest academic competitors had 21% and 20% online enrollment, due to the number of online courses available at each institution.

Availability of online courses and programs at SSU was limited; however, it was found that no online course sections were ever cancelled due to low enrollment. It was also determined that these online sections filled first and often had a waiting list. This data shows that students want and will take online courses if offered. However, the history of online course offerings shows a slow growth rate with an average of approximately 20 courses added each year. Table 1 shows the distribution of courses offered online by SSU colleges over the past four years.

Table 1. Online courses taught at SSU by college

College	2005	2006	2007	2008
Education	18	29	37	63
Arts and Sciences	9	19	23	31
Business	3	8	8	12
Health Studies	5	9	12	19
Total	39	65	80	125

Therefore, the administrators at SSU were faced with the following questions in order to capitalize on student demand for online courses. What can we do to increase the number of online courses? What factors were influencing faculty decisions whether or not to teach online? Which courses have the highest student demand? What support systems are currently in place, and what needs to be added? From these questions a systematic plan to market the benefits of online education needed to be developed to garner support and involvement from the faculty who teach the courses.

CASE DESCRIPTION

The administration's enrollment team, eager to reverse the decline in overall enrollment at the university, actively investigated what they could do to increase the number of online courses and programs available to students. Their investigation focused on two primary areas: 1) Factors influencing faculty members' decision to teach online and

2) Students' perceptions of, and needs related to, online courses. The results of their investigation are presented below.

Factors Influencing Faculty Decisions to Teach Online

Two faculty members and a graduate student conducted the study which investigated the factors that impacted a faculty member's decision whether or not to use technology in his instruction. The researchers conducting the survey did so separately from the influence of the administration. They simply reported aggregate findings to the university.

The methodology used to understand what influenced a faculty member's decision to teach with technology followed standard survey research methodology. The team developed a survey instrument to gather information on faculty perceptions of the usefulness and importance of online courses and what factors or barriers influenced the decision to use technology, specifically the online course management system. The instrument consisted of a four-page questionnaire comprised of 62 questions which were divided into the following five sections: 1) Perceptions of importance/validity of distance learning; 2) Usage of SSU's course management system; 3) Factors that influence the use or non use of the course management system; 4) General comments and suggestions; and 5) Demographics.

During the term the study was conducted, SSU employed 316 full time instructors, part time lecturers, and tenured and tenured-tracked faculty. Using a random selection process, 75 participants were selected from the list of instructional staff, which was approximately 25% of the total population. Once the sample was selected, each participant was assigned a random four-digit ID code to provide a confidential method to track participation. The sample population contained a distribution similar to that of the total population.

Each of the participants in the sample were sent a packet containing 1) a personal letter which described the purpose of the study, the need for participation, options for participating, and instructions for the handling of the survey, 2) a copy of the survey with the assigned four digit ID code affixed, and 3) an envelope to return the completed survey. Two follow-up reminders were sent to those participants who had not returned the survey.

Of the 75 survey packets mailed to sample participants, a total of 36 surveys were returned for a final response rate of 48%. Participant demographics presented a fairly accurate reflection of the distribution of the sample population and the total faculty population of the university, which provides some strong evidence that the results of the survey would also reflect the sample and total population.

Perceived Importance and Validity of Distance Learning Courses

Eighty-three (83%) percent of the survey participants indicated that a strong distance learning program was a requirement for the future success of the university; eighty-six percent (86%) felt that offering online courses should be a priority. Furthermore, all respondents (100%) agreed that distance learning courses allow students to have more flexible schedules, allowing some students to maintain attendance where they otherwise would not be able to. Participant responses suggest faculty are willing to embrace technology because they perceive a strong distance learning program is a necessity to the success of the university, as well as a way to better serve an increasing non-traditional student population. However, less than half of the faculty responding (48%) felt that online courses were of the same quality and rigor as traditional face-to-face courses.

Usage of the Online Course Management System

Several survey questions explored faculty use of SSU's current course management system (CMS). Seventy-nine percent (79%) of faculty reported using the CMS in their classes. Thirty-three (33%) percent of these faculty reported having instructed courses completely online, 14% reported having taught courses using a balance of online and face-to-face (hybrid) instruction, and 86% stated they have taught using traditional face-to-face methods along with online supplements (enhanced).

Factors Influencing Usage

Twenty four factors emerged from the review of literature as potentially contributing to faculty decisions to use or not use technology (Osika, Johnson, & Buteau, 2009). These factors included areas of support and training, comfort in use, monetary rewards, and pressure to use technology from students and colleagues. Faculty responses to these factors were measured on a scale ranging from strong positive influence to strong negative influence.

Success with other technologies (72%), flexibility (69%), and perceived need for online courses (66%), solicited the strongest positive responses as the influencing factors among respondents. On the other hand, issues with infrastructure (34%), student abilities (34%), and problems with technology (28%), solicited the strongest negative responses. Table 2 shows the faculty responses to each of the 24 factors.

Faculty who are successful using other technologies (email, PowerPoint, word processing tools, etc.) outside of instruction seem to be more inclined to use the course management system (CMS) in the delivery of course content. Flexibility in scheduling, another key factor that solicited positive responses from survey participants, allows faculty the freedom to teach at times and locations convenient for them. Another point to consider is that faculty who perceive a need for online courses are more willing to adopt technology into their pedagogy. Infrastructure issues and student abilities solicited the same percentage of negative responses from faculty. With regards to student abilities, faculty resent the amount of time required to assist students who cannot efficiently use the CMS. This leaves less time for faculty to learn how to better utilize the CMS themselves. The lack of technological support from the university further compounded this issue. If faculty cannot resolve technological issues, in real time, the delivery of online course content becomes more difficult and less attractive to faculty.

Faculty Who Use Technology

For further analysis, researchers separated the faculty who reported that they currently use the course management system from faculty who reported not using the technology. Among participants who reported using the CMS, past successes with other technologies (80%), the perceived need for distance learning courses (76%), and flexibility in scheduling (68%), rated as being the most positive influences on faculty decisions to use technology. Infrastructure issues (36%), problems with technology (36%) and student abilities (36%), had the most negative influence on faculty decisions to use technology.

These responses reiterate that faculty who are already comfortable using technologies in other areas of work are more inclined to use technology in online instruction. Furthermore, faculty who feel there is a need for technology, view flexibility as a positive factor in serving the needs of students who demand more online courses.

Faculty Who Do Not Use Technology

Several factors emerged from the data as having positive influences on the decisions of faculty who were not currently using technology in their courses. The most positive influence: Flexibility

Table 2. Factors influencing faculty decision to teach online

	Positive Influence	No Influence	Negative Influence
Past success with other technologies	72%	22%	6%
Ability to have flexibility in scheduling	69%	25%	6%
Perceived need for online courses	66%	28%	6%
Support from Online Services	56%	38%	6%
Training provided from Online Services	56%	44%	0%
Comfort level in using technology	56%	34%	9%
General opinion about online courses	50%	25%	25%
Challenge of teaching in a new environment	47%	44%	9%
Preference for teaching online classes	47%	44%	9%
Training provided by your college	44%	53%	3%
Availability of the CMS for all courses	44%	22%	34%
Perceived technical abilities of students	41%	25%	34%
Perceived technical resources of students	41%	31%	28%
Support from department to teach online	34%	66%	0%
Monetary reward for teaching online	34%	59%	6%
Pressure from administration to teach online	34%	56%	9%
The technology infrastructure at SSU	31%	34%	34%
Support from college to teach online	28%	72%	0%
Training received from department	22%	72%	6%
The size of the classes taught	22%	66%	13%
Pressure from students to use the CMS	19%	78%	3%
Pressure from peers to use the CMS	19%	78%	3%
Amount of time to teach online	19%	66%	16%
Ability to handle problems with the technology	16%	56%	28%

NOTE: Responses for Strong Positive Influence and Positive Influence were combined in the column labeled Positive Influence. Responses for Strong Negative Influence and Negative Influence were combined in the column labeled Negative Influence.

(71%), followed by monetary rewards (43%) and pressure from students (43%) rated the highest among this group. The only negative influence that impacted the decisions of faculty who do not use technology was the overall negative opinion (57%) faculty had of distance learning technology. This comment sums up the general consensus of faculty who do not teach online: "Impersonal; no-face-to-face; no discussion; no substitute for being in class."

The data suggest that faculty who do not use technology perceive flexibility (not having to be on campus to teach classes), monetary rewards and pressures from peers, administration and students, were positive motivating factors which would make them consider using technology. These are factors that could be used to further help influence faculty to consider using technology. Changing faculty's overall negative opinion about using technology seems to be the major hurdle to overcome in influencing this group to use the CMS in the delivery of course content.

Potential Responses to Increase Faculty Use of Technology

The results of the faculty study provided some insights for the administrators as to how they can work to encourage faculty to teach online courses. First, they want to focus on making sure faculty members are successful with other technologies, such as email, electronic classrooms, student information system, etc. This will mean having to improve the overall reliability of the network at SSU. These successes should help build the faculty members' confidence in using technology and encourage movement to more technology use in their courses.

In addition to working on guaranteeing success with standard technology tools, SSU administrators would like to address some of the issues raised in the survey. Suggestions included establishing an exemplary course contest to highlight the rigor and quality of online courses, providing an assessment to determine students' readiness to succeed in an online class, creating a marketing plan focusing on how quality online classes can address issues such as declining enrollment and scheduling needs of SSU's student population, and looking at the possibility of expanding the help desk, as well as the instructional support department, to meet the technological needs of students and faculty.

Students' Perception of and Needs Related to Online Courses

In order to gain a better understanding of students' interest in online courses and confirm what was seen in the enrollment data, a survey was developed and administered to students at SSU. The survey was administered through an online survey collection tool.

Students were informed of the survey in a variety of methods. An icon to the survey was placed on the SSU homepage. Messages were sent to individual student email accounts with a link to the survey. A system wide message was posted in the course management system. Finally, signs were posted throughout the computer labs asking students to take the survey.

At the close of the survey, there were 615 submissions, roughly 10% of the current student population. Of these, 64% (n=392) were undergraduate students, 28% (n=171) were graduate students, 3% (n=17) were students at-large or continuing education students, and the remaining 6% (n=35) selected Other to described their status.

Of the respondents, 95% (n=572) stated they had a computer in their home and 85% (n=522) stated that the computer was connected to the Internet through a DSL or cable connection. Six percent (n=36) stated they connected their computer to the Internet through a dial-up connection. The remaining stated they did not have Internet access at home.

Participation and Willingness to Participate in an Online Course

Approximately half the students responding to the survey (54%, n=325) stated they have previously taken an online course at SSU. More interesting, is that 88% of the respondents stated that they would possibly (22%, n=138) or definitely (66%, n=406) be willing to take an online course in the future, even though online courses currently have an extra $50 fee required from the student.

Only 4% (n=27) of the respondents stated that they would definitely not take an online course in the future. Of these 27, 13 had taken an online course at SSU in the past. The most prevalent reason presented by this group for not taking another online course was the lack of communication between the instructor and the student - an area that can be improved through education and effort.

When looking at the reasons for not taking an online course by those students who stated they would definitely want to take an online course in the future, the overwhelming reason was the lack of online courses offered at SSU. The courses most frequently mentioned as needing to be offered online included many of the general education requirements, such as English composition, psychology, sociology, history, and philosophy.

Potential Responses to the Student Survey

SSU administrators would like to see the development of a sequence of online courses that would satisfy the general education requirements of SSU. This could mean working with the faculty at SSU to develop and offer courses, or work through an existing consortium of schools to see if their online courses could be utilized for this purpose. Since all undergraduates have to take this sequence of courses, it makes sense to concentrate efforts here in order to get the greatest impact on the effort expended.

In addition, the Online Services Department would be asked to review the comments made by students regarding the quality of the courses they have taken. If applicable, the Online Services Department would develop training and support materials for faculty to help them better serve the academic needs of students in an online environment.

CURRENT CHALLENGES FACING THE ORGANIZATION

The challenges faced by SSU are similar in many ways to those faced by all other academic institutions during the current economic downturn. How can a university maintain or increase student enrollment during times of economic recession and reductions in state funding and federal financial aid? The administration of SSU is looking at an increase in online enrollment as one method to help stay the loss of credit hours at the university. This approach not only helps address the need for increased enrollment, it also allows students with demands of work, family, and economic related issues to attend to their courses at their convenience in their own homes.

However, adding more online course sections is not as easy as simply adding them to the course schedule. Given the current environment at SSU, there are several issues that need to be resolved prior to adding additional online courses. The most pressing are the limited budget, working with the union, maintaining quality in the courses, reliability of the campus network, and accreditation requirements.

First, as mentioned previously, SSU is experiencing significant budget cuts and constraints. Therefore, the funding available to support new initiatives is scarce. However, the administration knows that this area holds significant potential for the university, so it is willing to move budgets around to provide some additional dollars. Before any money is released, the administration wants a clear plan as to how it will be used and the return on the investment.

Second, all changes and proposals need to be vetted through the union, especially if it impacts faculty pay, working environment, or responsibilities. In the past, the union has been willing to work with the administration on programs that it saw as benefiting both the faculty and the university. In fact, in the last contract, the union and administration agreed to pay faculty a stipend equivalent to teaching one course for each online course developed. This monetary reward, put in place in 2005, helped generate some interest among the faculty, but did not have the impact on additional course offerings as expected. However, in addition to the compensation for developing an online course, the union negotiated a clause stating that no faculty member could be required to teach a course. This rule, coupled with the rule that a faculty member who has taught a course previously is given the first chance to teach it in the future, limits which courses the administration can move online.

Third, the administration is very concerned about the quality of online courses. While the majority of courses seem to be constructed and facilitated effectively, there have been issues in the past regarding the quality of individual courses. As important as it is to move more courses online, the school needs to guarantee that the quality of courses and programs is maintained.

Fourth, the university has to resolve the instability of the campus network. This is the single most important factor facing the integration of technology into the curriculum. Currently, faculty are highly skeptical of the network's performance based on a multitude of negative experiences. Some of these experiences have been the student information system failing during registration, the Internet unavailable during class hours, and a consistent slow response time. The administration understands the severity of these problems and has recently replaced the Chief Information Officer and several key personnel in the Information Technology department. However, it is too early to tell what impact these changes have had on the service provided.

Finally, according to the accreditation requirements of SSU, any program that is offered completely online requires approval from the accreditation body. This process requires a proposal to be created outlining what the program covers, how students will be accommodated in the online environment, and the qualifications of the instructors teaching in the program. While a somewhat time consuming process, it is doable.

As shown, while there is interest in moving more courses and programs online, there are several challenges that need to be addressed. Some of these challenges will take more time, effort, and money than is currently available, so creative solutions and a phased-in approach will need to be developed.

SOLUTIONS AND RECOMMENDATIONS

While there are a number of challenges, SSU believes there are several things that can be implemented quickly to encourage the growth of online courses and programs. The administration would like to move forward with the following, as soon as possible.

First, and foremost, the marketing of the benefits of online courses and programs to the campus needs to be implemented. From top administration to the faculty engaged in teaching online, consistent communication needs to occur regarding the benefits of online instruction to the students, school, and faculty members, themselves.

The marketing plan should focus on placing the tools for online education into the hands of the faculty and making the use of the tools easy to incorporate and well supported. Persuasive advertisements showing how online courses have positively impacted the lives of students and faculty need to be commonplace on campus. Additionally, demonstrations of how the online courses are equivalent or superior in rigor and quality to traditionally taught courses need to be communicated, in order to address the concerns raised in the faculty survey.

Finally, the administration needs to encourage faculty members to teach online by continuing to offer the current financial incentive for developing online courses, and by giving recognition for developing an online course that meets specific quality indicators. This recognition could become part of their promotion and tenure evaluation. Certificate programs that acknowledge a faculty member's commitment to learning how to incorporate technology into their courses could be launched. This would provide faculty members a way to demonstrate continued professional development, plus it provides the university a method to train faculty on the appropriate methods and techniques used to teach online. Also, in light of tight budgets, SSU could funnel a portion of the $50 per class online education fee back to the faculty member's department. This money could then be used to subsidize travel, research, or teaching needs of the faculty member.

The solutions here can be implemented right away without costing a great deal of money. What is necessary to succeed in generating more interest in providing online opportunities for students is a concerted, creative effort on the part of all involved.

REFERENCES

Albion, P. R., & Ertmer, P. A. (2002). Beyond the foundations: The role of vision and belief in teachers' preparation for integration of technology. *TechTrends*, *46*(5), 34. doi:10.1007/BF02818306

Allen, I. E., & Seaman, J. (2008). *Online nation: Five years of growth in online learning*. Needham, MA: Sloan Consortium.

Allen, I. E., & Seaman, J. (2009). *Staying the course: Online education in the United States, 2008*. Needham, MA: Sloan Consortium.

Allen, I. E., & Seaman, J. (2010). *Learning on demand: Online education in the United States, 2009*. Needham, MA: Sloan Consortium.

Brill, J. M., & Galloway, C. (2007). Perils and promises: University instructors' integration of technology in classroom-based practices. *British Journal of Educational Technology*, *38*(1), 95. doi:10.1111/j.1467-8535.2006.00601.x

Christensen, R. (2002). Effects of technology integration education on the attitudes of teachers and students. *Journal of Research on Technology in Education*, *34*(4), 411.

Dusick, D. M. (1998). What social cognitive factors influence faculty members' use of computers for teaching? A literature review. *Journal of Research on Computing in Education*, *31*(2), 123.

Ertmer, P. A. (2005). Teacher pedagogical beliefs: The final frontier in our quest for technology integration? *Educational Technology Research and Development*, *53*(4), 25. doi:10.1007/BF02504683

Ertmer, P. A., Conklin, D., & Lewandowski, J. (2003). Increasing preservice teachers' capacity for technology integration through the use of electronic models. *Teacher Education Quarterly*, *30*(1), 95.

Ferguson, P. (2004). *Faculty beliefs about teaching with technology*. Association for Educational Communications and Technology.

Grasha, A. F., & Yangarber-Hicks, N. (2000). Integrating teaching styles and learning styles with instructional technology. *College Teaching*, *48*(1), 2. doi:10.1080/87567550009596080

Osika, E., Johnson, R., & Buteau, R. (2009). Factors influencing faculty use of technology in online instruction: A case study. *Online Journal of Distance Learning Administration*, *12*(1). Retrieved from http://www.westga.edu/~distance/ojdla/spring121/osika121.html.

Rosenfeld, B., & Martinez-Pons, M. (2005). Promoting classroom technology use. *Quarterly Review of Distance Education*, *6*(2), 145.

Sybold, P. B. (2001). Get inside the lives of your customers. *Harvard Business Review*, *80*, 80–89.

ADDITIONAL READING

Bonk, C. J. (2001). *Online teaching in an online world*. Retrieved September 10, 2003, from http://www.courseshare.com/reports.php.

Chizmar, J. F., & Williams, D. B. (2001). What do faculty want? *EDUCAUSE Quarterly*, *1*, 18–24.

Cooper, J. (2006). The Digital Divide: The Special Case of Gender. *Journal of Computer Assisted Learning*, *22*(5), 320. doi:10.1111/j.1365-2729.2006.00185.x

Cuban, L. (1999). High-tech schools, low-tech teaching. *Education Digest*, *64*(5), 53.

Culp, G., Riffee, W., Starrett, D., Sarin, S., & Abrahamsen, A. (2001). Faculty rewards in digital environments. *Syllabus, 14* (6), 11-12 and 14.

Demiray, U., & Sever, S. (Eds.). (2009). *The challenges for marketing distance education in online environments*. Eskisehir, Turkey: Anadolu University.

Dillon, C. L., & Walsh, S. M. (1992). Faculty: The neglected resource in distance education. In Foster, L., Bower, B., & Watson, L. (Eds.), *Teaching and learning in higher education, ASHE Reader Series. 2001.*

Dusick, D. M., & Yildirim, S. (2000). Faculty computer use and training: Identifying distinct needs for different populations. *Community College Review, 27*(4), 33. doi:10.1177/009155210002700403

Ennew, C., & Fernandez-Young, A. (2006). Weapons of mass instruction? The rhetoric and reality of online learning. *Marketing Intelligence & Planning, 24*(2), 148–157. doi:10.1108/02634500610654008

Ertmer, P., & Ottenbreit-Leftwich, A. (2010). Teach technology change: How knowledge, confidence, beliefs, and culture intersect. *Journal of Research on Technology in Education, 42*(3), 255–284.

Granitz, N. (2003). Applying e-Marketing Strategies to Online Distance Learning. *Journal of Marketing Education, 25*(1), 16–30. doi:10.1177/0273475302250569

Grönroos, C. (2000). *Service Management and Marketing*. NY: John Wiley.

Howell, S., Williams, P., & Lindsay, N. (2003). Thirty-two Trends Affecting Distance Education: An Informed Foundation for Strategic Planning. *Online Journal of Distance Learning Administration*, 4(3). Retrieved February 25, 2005, from http://www.westga.edu/~distance/ojdla/fall63/howell63.html

Institute for Higher Education Policy. (2000). *Quality on the line: Benchmarks for success in internet-based distance education.* Washington, D.C.: The Institute for Higher Education Policy.

Johnstone, S. M., Ewell, P., & Paulson, K. (2002) Student Learning as Academic Currency. *ACE Center for Policy Analysis*. Retrieved February 25, 2005, from http://www.acenet.edu/bookstore/pdf/distributed-learning/distributed-learning-04.pdf

Kane, R., Sandretto, S., & Heath, C. (2002). Telling half the story: A critical review of research on the teaching beliefs and practices of university academics. *Review of Educational Research, 72*(2), 177. doi:10.3102/00346543072002177

Lorenzetti, J. (2005). A new approach to marketing strategies for distance education. *Distance Education Report, 9*(8), 1–5.

Lowerison, G., Sclater, J., Schmid, R. F., & Abrami, P. C. (2006). Are we using technology for learning? *Journal of Educational Technology Systems, 34*(4), 401. doi:10.2190/ER58-3H7P-Y8FK-U8F7

Lumpe, A. T., & Chambers, E. (2001). Assessing teachers' context beliefs about technology use. *Journal of Research on Technology in Education, 34*(1), 93.

Maguire, L. (2005). Faculty participation in online distance education: Barriers and motivators. *Online Journal of Distance Learning Administration, 8*(1). Retrieved from http://www.westga.edu/~distance/ojdla/spring81/maguire81.htm.

Osika, E. (2006). The concentric support model: A model for the planning and evaluation of distance learning programs. *Online Journal of Distance Learning Administration, 9*(3). Retrieved from http://www.westga.edu/~distance/ojdla/fall93/osika93.pdf.

Parker, A. (2003). Motivation and incentives for distance faculty. Retrieved on October 26, 2003 from www.westga.edu/~distance/ojdla/fall63/parker63.htm.

Peluchette, J. V., & Rust, K. A. (2005). Technology use in the classroom: Preferences of management faculty members. *Journal of Education for Business*, *80*(4), 200. doi:10.3200/JOEB.80.4.200-205

Rovai, A. P., & Childress, M. D. (2003). Explaining and predicting resistance to computer anxiety reduction among teacher education students. *Journal of Research on Technology in Education*, *35*(2), 226.

Shaik, N. (2005). Marketing distance learning programs and courses: A relationship marketing strategy. *Online Journal of Distance Learning Administration*, *8*(2). Retrieved from http://www.westga.edu/~distance/ojdla/summer82/shaik82.htm.

Spotts, T. H., Bowman, M. A., & Mertz, C. (1997). Gender and use of instructional technologies: A study of university faculty. *Higher Education*, *34*(4), 421. doi:10.1023/A:1003035425837

Teclehaimanot, B., & Lamb, A. (2005). Workshops that work: Building an effective, technology-rich faculty development program. *Journal of Computing in Teacher Education*, *21*(3), 109–115.

Wolcott, L. L., & Betts, K. S. (1999). What's in it for me? Incentives for faculty participation in distance education. Retrieved on October 26, 2003 from http://cade.athabascau.ca/vol14.2/wolcott_et_al.html.

KEY TERMS AND DEFINITIONS

Barriers to Use: Obstacles that keep or hinder instructors from using technology.

Distance Education: Education that takes place when the instructor and participant are separated by space and/or time.

Distance Learning: The process by which technology, typically the Internet, is used to present content and interaction between the instructor and the student. Distance learning allows individuals to participate in classes at times and locations that are convenient for them; thus, increasing access to education to individuals who otherwise may never have the opportunity to participate.

Enhanced Course: A face-to-face course which uses the course management system to share documents, make online office hours available, etc.

Hybrid Course: A course that sometimes meets face-to-face and sometimes online.

Instructional Quality: Assessment of whether or not a specific course or module of instruction meets the educational goals and objectives specified. It also relates to the amount and quality of interaction occurring in the course between faculty, students, and the content.

Instructional Technology: Technology used to assist in the teaching and learning process.

Technology Integration: The infusion of technology into the classroom to meet specific educational objectives.

Chapter 15
The Trends and Challenges of Higher Education in China

Shuyi Zhang
Shanghai Finance University, P. R. China

Li Zhao
Shanghai Finance University, P. R. China

EXECUTIVE SUMMARY

This case focuses on the challenges and trends of Chinese higher education. It analyzes the challenges that the Chinese higher education faces and discusses a couple of issues of internationalization of higher education, and finally, the case points out the future trends that Chinese higher education might encounter.

BACKGROUND

Since the foundation of People's Republic of China, gradually the Chinese government has established three national education strategies: Priority Development, Revitalization China in Term of Science and Education, and Reinvigoration China through Human Resource. China has shaped the socialist education system with characteristics of increasing scale, quality improvement, reasonable structure, and effectiveness enhancement. During the process of reform and development initiating in1980s, the deepening education structural reform has provided powerful impetus to the vitality of Chinese education. After years of exploration and practice, China has established its compulsory education system led by the State Council, planned and implemented by the provincial government, especially the local government. Such a system strengthens the government's duty, and plays a key role to push forward the compulsory education. With the advancement of building socialist democracy and legal system, China has set up preliminary education law and regularity system that composed of the central and local education law, administrative rules, which paved the way for the civil education right, the basic educational institute, and the improvement of reform and development (Yang, 2001).[1] In 2008, nationwide institutions of higher education numbered

DOI: 10.4018/978-1-60960-599-5.ch015

Table 1. The number of students at different educational level (in, 0,000)

Type of education	1949	1978	2008
primary school	2439	14624	10332
middle school	83	4995	5628
high school	44	1804	4546
University	12	228	2907

(Source: The number of students in different educational level in 1949, 1978, and 2008, available at http://www.moe.gov.cn/edoas/website18/41/info1251089001570241.htm)

2,663, including 2,263 regular higher education institutions, and 400 institutions of higher adult education. Among regular institutions of higher education, 1,079 were four-year undergraduate institutions, and 1,184 were polytechnic colleges. There were altogether 796 master's-degree-granting institutions in China, including 479 colleges and universities and 317 research institutes.[2]

China has just celebrated 60th anniversary in October, 2009 and looking back, the Chinese education has made a great progress along with the achievements in other industries. During the past 60 years, especially last three decades, the Chinese government has been improving educational level for general public and hence promoting the cultural and scientific quality for Chinese nation (Liu, 2009). By establishing the socialist education framework, Chinese education has fulfilled two historic stride leaps, namely, the universal of the nine-year compulsory education, and the mass higher education which contribute more to accelerating development of vocational education by insisting on the public welfare and equal access to education (Postiglione, 2005). The number of students in primary school, middle school, high school, and the universities respectively booms as shown in Table 1 below. The enrolment for institutions of higher education and the number of students attending school continued to increase.

Now, China is holding the largest education in the world with the aim to turn it into leading human resource nationally.

SETTING THE STAGE

The Achievements of Chinese Higher Education

Fostering Millions of Trained Talents

Since the national liberation in 1949, the Chinese education has trained billions of highly qualified labors, millions of specialized professionals and a host of outstanding innovative talents. In 1949, there were only 120 thousand undergraduate students altogether in China. Since then, the higher education has experienced tremendous development as illustrated in Table 2. The numbers nearly doubled since 1995 due to the college expansion plan in 1999.[3] In 2008 the total number of students in all kinds of higher education institutions reached 29,070,000 which is 243 times of students in 1949. The total number of students enrolled for regular

Table 2. The number of undergraduate students (1949-2008) (in, 0,000)

Year	1949	1965	1978	1980	1985	1990	1995	2000	2005	2008
Students	12	109	228	272	352	382	577	1230	2300	2907

(**Source**: The number of undergraduate students, available at http://www.moe.gov.cn/edoas/website18/37/info1252641418587437.htm)

Table 3. Number of undergraduate students (in, 000)

Year	1977	1998	2002	2008
Enrolled student	270	1,080	2,750	6,080

(Source: The number of entrant of undergraduate students, available at http://www.moe.gov.cn/edoas/website18/29/info1251088709483229.htm)

institutions of higher education reached 6,076,600, and the gross enrolment rate for higher education reached 23.3%. At the same time, the enrolments for postgraduates nationwide reached 446,400 in 2008, out of which 59,800 were doctoral candidates. The number of postgraduates attending school was 1,283,000 in 2008.

In 2008, there were 2,051,000 faculty and staff members at regular institutions of higher education, among them, the number of full-time teachers were 1,237,500, an increase of 69,200 over the previous year, and the number of faculty and staff members at institutions of higher education for adults was 89,900.

The higher education promotes the population quality and accordingly, among those who are more than 15 years old and the incoming labor force, the average educational age limit is more than 8.5 and 11 years respectively in 2008[4]. More than 82 millions of people have higher educational background, which takes the lead of developing countries.

The reasons why we have so many undergraduate students studying in university are owed to two critical changes: firstly, the increase of the enrollment in higher education, and secondly, the increasing number of universities (Table 3).

After 10 years suspension since 1966 because of the Chinese "cultural revolution",[5] only 270 thousand students enrolled as undergraduate in 1977, and 1.08 million and 2.75 million students enrolled in 1998 and 2002 respectively, and the number rocketed to 6.08 million in 2008. We could also find the increase in the number of regular institute higher education, adult colleges and graduate students.[6] Accordingly, there are more graduate students among 100 thousand inhabitants by level shown in Table 4. In 1999, there are 594 undergraduates among 100 thousand people, while in 2008, that number is 2042, which is 3.4 times of 1999.

As far as the number of universities is concerned, (Figure 1), China had 1080 institutes for higher education in 1994, while in 2008, the number reached to 2263 i.e. double of 1994. At the same time, because of the reforms in investment system, the ratio of university affiliated to Ministry of Education decrease gradually, while the ratio of university affiliated to Local Government and Provincial Educational Ministry increases accordingly.

Since 1980s, the Chinese government has sent tens of thousands of students studying abroad, i.e. more than 1.39 million students studying worldwide from 1978 to 2008. Supported by the government, many of them came back and started working in the universities, academic institutes, enterprises and government departments, etc. The Chinese government also establishes cooperating relationship with more than 180 countries and

Table 4. Student-teacher ratio during 2002-2008

Year	2002	2003	2004	2005	2006	2007	2008
Student-teacher ratio	19:1	17:1	16.22:1	16.22:1	17.93:1	17.28:1	17.23:1

(Source: Calculated by the authors according to [National Education Development Statistical Bulletin], Available at www.moe.gov.cn/edoas/website18/24/info1251088576880224.htm)

Figure 1. The number and its ratio of state and local universities (Source: The number and its ratio of state and local universities, available at http://www.moe.gov.cn/edoas/website18/30/info1252641129464430.htm)

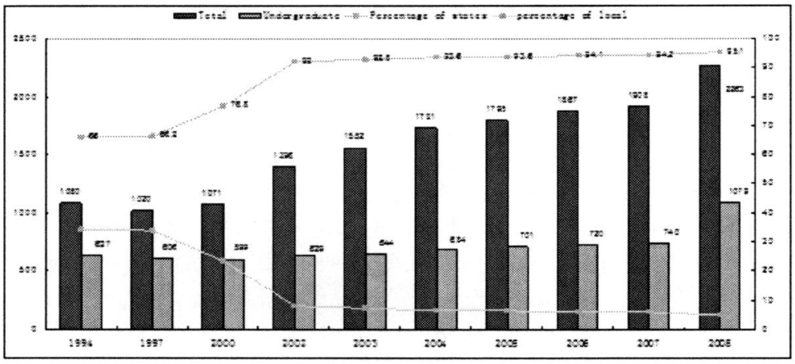

regions, and most of the Chinese universities have their overseas partner right now (Lin, 2009). Nearly every university in Shanghai has more than one partner called sister-university, and they share the educational idea, teaching method, textbook, transfer faculty and student, which benefit the Chinese university and their partners alike. For example, Shanghai Finance University (SFU) has the partners scattered in United States, Canada, Australia, Denmark, etc, and it has worked out several joint program, such as "1+2+1" dual-degree program with Towson University, which means after one year's studying in SFU, some students go to Towson for 2 years, and come back in the fourth year, both the Towson and SFC take the credit hours as granted mutually. The students are expected to get two Degree Certificates issued by the SFU and Towson respectively if they meet the requirements. So does the "2+2" joint program with Lakeland College. As for the junior college student, SFU has a "3+1" joint program with Niels Brock Copenhagen Business College of Denmark.

Another example is the post-doctoral, since its initiation in July, 1985, proposed by Tsung-Dao Lee, the Nobel laureate of physics in 1957,[7] the total number of post-doctor is now more than 60 thousand. Usually, the post-doctoral researcher does their research in the university or institute, or just work in the enterprises focusing on the specific problems the firm faces. At present, there are 1794 centers for post-doctoral research, which includes 12 disciplines and 88 branches of learning covering the fields of science, technology, agriculture, medicine, philosophy and social science, and there are 1670 post doctorate enterprise workstations distributed mainly in the fields of electronic information, information technology, biomedical, economics and finance, etc.

The Contributions to Science and Technology

According to the national strategy of "revitalization China through science and education", Chinese education paves the way for the economic and social development. Most of scientific achievements were made by the universities which belongs to 985 program launched by the Chinese government in May, 1998[8]; those which are listed in the program got the funding varying from 700 millions RBM to 1.2 billions RMB, which is equivalent of the amount of the Association of American University, or the average level of the eight-universities-alliances of Australia. The 985 program brings a remarkable achievement as following: firstly, advancing the capability of independent innovation rapidly with a lot of scientific research achievements, amongst the

Figure 2. The key achievements made by the universities (Source: The key achievements made by the universities, available at http://www.moe.gov.cn/edoas/website18/57/info1252643099201457.htm)

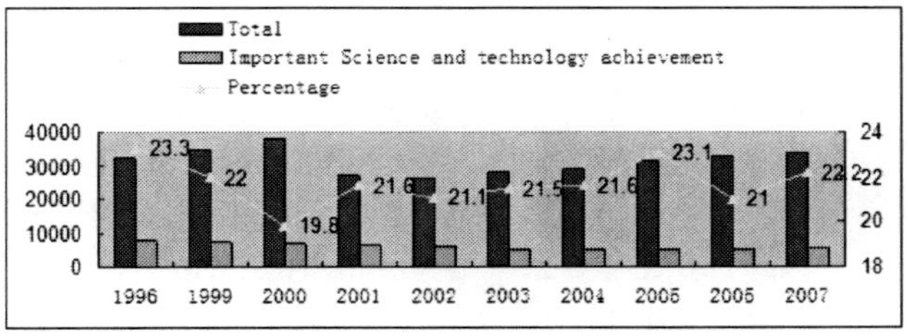

winners of the first prize of national science and technology progress, national technological innovation, and natural science, most of them are professors or scholars coming from "985 university". Secondly, the 985 universities undertook a multitude of national key science and technology program based on the science and technological platform; nearly half of the state key laboratories and half of first agents of the state key laboratory belong to "985 universities". Thirdly, the program has been recruiting a lot of young and middle aged scholars who are active on the frontier of international academic community, which in turn boosting the breakthrough of the various disciplines, and flourishing of humanities and social science alike. All in all, among the significant science and technology payoffs, nearly one fifth comes from the institution of higher learning, as illustrated in Figure 2.

Based on published papers in Thomson Reuters-indexed journals from January 1998 to August 31, 2008,[9] China is one of the "Top 20" out of a pool of 147, which published at least 10,000 papers across all fields during the period. The papers are ranked by three separate measures: total citations, number of papers, and cites per paper. China is ranked 10th and 5th in total citations and number of papers respectively.

If you look at the candidates who got their Ph.Ds in United States, most of them come from Tsinghua University and Peking University, which surpasses the University of California, Berkeley and Seoul University, illustrated in Figure 3.

Main Reasons for Achievements

Why China has made such a great achievements? There are four most accepted reasons. Firstly, led by the Communist Party of China and Chinese government, China established the educational development as the priority strategically; secondly, persevering in the final development is in the interest of the people, for the people and by the people, and insuring the equally sharing the educational achievement; thirdly, the education development relies on the instructor by giving them full play to arouse their enthusiasm, initiative and creativity; and finally, the various education branches insists upon taking the reform and opening outside as the impetus that activate the Chinese education business (Hare & Thomas, 2002; Mok, 2005). All the above are the valuable experiences which will

Figure 3. Baccalaureate origins of PhDs (Source: CPST analysis of SED, 2006)

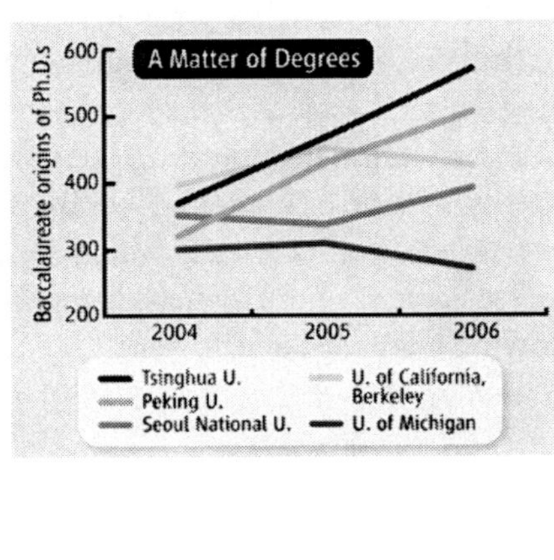

have a far-reaching impact on the further reform and development of Chinese education.

THE CHALLENGES OF CHINESE HIGHER EDUCATION

According to Martin Trow (1972, 1998), the famous American educational sociologist, higher education could be classified into three stages: elite, mass and popular, based on the ratio of enrolled undergraduate between 18 to 21 years old. Albeit the agreement remained miles apart, it is an influencing proposition. The elite education stage refers to gross enrollment rate less than 15 percent, mass education stage refers to the rate between 15 to 50 percent, while universal education more than 50 percent. The United States is the first country listed in the stage of universal education that boosts the gross enrollment rate of 82 percent. Although popularity of mass education in European countries is 10 years later compared with the USA, they entered into the mass education around 1970s, and the gross enrollment rate is more than 50 percent,[10] the rates of Japan, English, Germany, France, and South Korea are all more than 50 percent, much higher than the world average level of the 14.7 percent.[11]

What about China? According to the Action Plan to Vitalize Education in the 21st Century issued by the Ministry of Education in 1999, Chinese government planned to raise the gross enrollment rate of higher education to 15 percent by the end of 2010.[12] In 2002, China achieved a gross enrollment rate of 15 percent eight years ahead of the goal, and in 2009, the number is 23.3 percent, namely, Chinese higher education is in the mass education stage (Postiglione, 2005). Despite continued expansion of higher education, supply still lags behind demand. Meanwhile, on account of scale extension, Chinese higher education faces the following challenges.

Quality Assurance in Higher Education

The first challenge is the quality assurance, which is the heart of Chinese higher education. In fact, Chinese higher education is still far behind of the United States, European and other developed countries, especially after the expansion in 1999 (Ding, 2004). How to sustain and promote the higher educational quality has always been a challenge for the university, government, and the whole society alike.

Such a problem concerns not only the internal factors, such as size enlargement (Ding, 2004), but also the external factors stemmed from the university development itself. As for the internal factors, the main one is the size enlargement. The entrance threshold of university is comparatively lower than before because of more and more students having chance to enroll as the undergraduate (Chen, 2008). Usually, the higher quality goes along with the less quantity, this is also the question around the world during the 1960s and 1970s, with the education size increasing world widely, the higher education quality once was the focus of public, most people worried about whether higher education can sustain the appropriate level as before (Ouyang, 2006).

As for the financial factor (Liu, 2004), without considering the depreciation, the education expenditure is increasing rapidly (Figure 4) on the one hand, while the funding per capita is decreasing on the other. Because of the slope down of the economy especially the recent financial crisis, keeping the large amount of the education budget would be a burden for the government which bites off one can chew; many countries cut education budget accordingly. It is very difficult for educational sector to sustain the quality standard without sufficient financial support, let alone promoting the level. Government's budget is the main source of educational expenditure for Chinese university (Min and Ding, 2005); they seldom get the donation compared with that of USA. In 2008, the total

Figure 4. Education expenditure

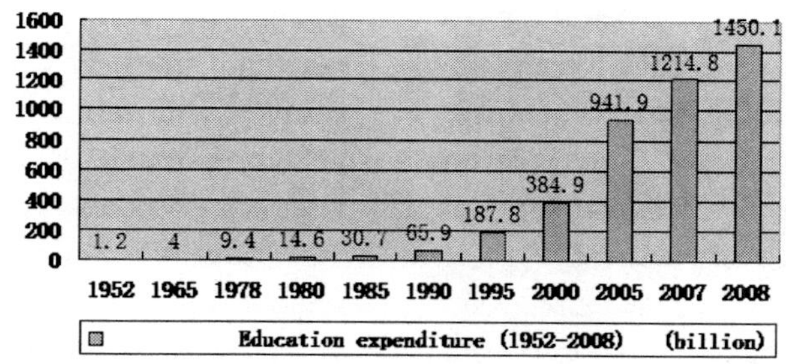

national education expenditure is 1450.1 billions Yuan RMB, in which 104.5 billions coming from the national budget that accounts 3.48% of GDP, which increases 0.26 percentage point than the previous year. Although the education expenditure out of the GDP has been growing for last three years, it has not yet reached the 4%, which is taken to be the average level world widely. The funding shortage caused lots of problems, one is the lack of needed resources to meet each student's demand, for example, in 1998, the average teaching administrative area is 12.5 square meters per student, after that the number decreased yearly, it is only 0.9 square meters in 2001, and it is not to reverse until 2007 with 13.6 square meters; the other one is the imbalance of student-teacher ratio because of the scale expansion shown as Table 4, usually, the increasing speed of instructor is much lower than that one of students.

In order to meet the higher quality demands, the Chinese educational administrative departments has established the scientific and normative appraisal system that is suited to Chinese national situations, including the pluralism of evaluation system for potential talents (Cen & Ross, 2009). Now the Chinese government encourages independent quality evaluation made by the specialized agency or intermediary. For example, as for evaluating the quality of business school, some universities had asked for certification of AACSB or EQUIS. For example, China Europe International Business School (CEIBS), and the Economic and Business School of Tsinghua University, had passed the certification of AASCB, and Guanghua Business School of Peking University had passed the EQUIS. Some universities or branches are exploring the possibility of cooperating with the well-known international educational appraisal institute, with the aim to issue the yearly report of university educational quality.

Cultivating the Innovative Talents

Because of the economic reform and opening policy, China has made a great achievement during the last three decades; one of the main reasons is to transfer the huge market with cutting-edge technology and advanced management initiated by Deng Xiaoping, the senior leader and the Chief Architect of the Chinese Economic Reform, and even goes farther to the extreme to rely on the foreign technology without paying more attention to the technology with Chinese intellectual property rights aftermath. Albeit, it is necessary and common for developing countries to focus on the imitation and transferring in their initiating stage, if such a situation lasts for a long time, China is always the follower rather than the leader, let alone the pioneer. It is the backward of technology that China emphases more on the independent innovation with an aiming of building the innovative country in the near future.

In fact, innovation is now popular around the world. The EU took the 2009 as "Year of creation and innovation" to build the creative and innovative atmosphere, the Germany government thinks that the scientific innovation is the only way to deal with the financial crisis with the proposal of investing 3 percent of GDP on the scientific research (NG and Li, 2000), and 7 percent on education; while United States presents the 500 million dollar of "creative investment" in the budget proposal of 2011, the most accepted road map, namely, from education to innovation, from innovation to growth, from growth to employment, from employment to harmony, from harmony to competency, is now the scheme for stirring the economics prosperity and development during the time of post finance crisis.

Changing the Pattern of Personnel Training

The one characteristics of traditional pattern of personnel training in Chinese higher education is the separation of learning from doing. On the one hand, most Chinese students study passively compared with western country, they just sitting in the classroom, taking notes, reciting the main content and answering the key points while taking the examination, they seldom discussing with instructor, let alone challenging the professor, which is no good for the "stomach" because of "eating" too much without thinking that will extinguish the curiosity gradually

The other characteristics is doing "on the paper" rather than on the site while students have their practice, they just imitate the real world rather than involve in it, the students rarely have chance to practice "using their own hand" on the account of insufficient supporting resources sponsored by the company, and there is also no incentive for the company to support the university. In fact, such a phenomenon was also very often in western countries 100 hundred years ago, and with the time elapse, it is now partially changed, which could be found in Canada and USA by means of "co-op", etc.

Why? On account of examination-oriented education system, the talent training pattern could not meet the needs of building the innovative country. There are several reasons for such a phenomenon, firstly, the capability of cultivating the high-quality talents is still weak for most Chinese university, they have not found the effective merit system for the appraisal for the creative talents; secondly, the capability of faculty and staff is still not strong, especially there is no leading professor in some universities, who is always the most wanted; thirdly, there is a gap between the structure of applied discipline and the industry needs, the company have no desire to participate the higher education because of the insufficient support coming from the government and society; and finally, it is deficient to communicate among various educational institute, there is much work to do to design the sharing system of public educational resource.

The one way to cultivate the creativity is to encourage the students to take part in seminar, which will arouse their criticizing thinking independently as well as safeguarding their point of view. On the one hand, the university should train students to have internal desire to be creative, innovative, and encourage them to discuss and communicate with the professor; on the other hand, the professor had better show student how to solve the practical problem, how to conduct the scientific research by giving them more opportunity to practice and share the joyfulness of research.

In order to fulfill the task above, Chinese higher education could take some effective measures including the creative education idea, active learning style and gradual institutional improvement. As for the educational idea, the university and educational administrative department had better to establish the full implementation so as to lead the students to focus on the scientific spirit, humanism accomplishment, and lifelong learning capability with an emphasis more on the social responsibility, innovative and practical ability. As far as the training style concerned, it is encouraged to do the self-reform in term of learning by doing, and advocating the heuristic and discussing method to stir the student's independent thinking, cultivate the capability of getting knowledge by collecting and processing the information, analyzing and solving the problem in term of teamwork and communicating. As for the institution improvement, it is very important to clarify the administrative duty of the officials, enlarge the autonomy right of the university (Yang et al., 2007), and explore to establish the modern institute of running university, and sustain the suitable environment of talent training.

Keep the Balance of Equity and Efficiency

The next challenge is the equity and efficiency, which is another dilemma for Chinese higher education. With the booming of Chinese higher education, a number of issues related to fairness and efficiency emerges (Jacob, 2006), such as fairness including opportunity fairness, process fairness, and regional fairness connected with college enrollment, effectiveness about the education cost, and so on. As for the opportunity fairness, the university is distributed significant different among various provinces and autonomous regions because of historical reasons. Since every Chinese has a resident status that belong to a specific provincial region, so the student who applies for college entrance examination must register in his/her hometown first, and then takes examination organized by the provincial educational administration sector. The number of student that the province or municipalities plan to recruit is assigned by the Ministry of Education according to the student number, the educational resources, such as the number of university, faculty and staff as well as the social and economic level, etc. On account of the different educational resources, the students who belong to the metropolitan, such as Beijing, Shanghai, have more opportunities to enrolled as undergraduate than underdeveloped province, for instance, the average college enrollment rate is more than 70% in Beijing, Shanghai, Tianjin right now, while the rate is less than 50% in Hebei, Anhui, Shandong and Sichuan province.

As far as the regional fairness concerned, the research shows that those who have a lower payment are sensitive to tuition and fees, they may quit when the tuition increasing, this is very often common in the countryside and rural region. A good example is that the rate of student coming from countryside in top universities has been decreasing recently, and those who choose the "hot" major usually come from middle-class or affluent family, they have more economic, social and cultural capital.

As for the efficiency, due to the scarce education resource, the higher education has the character of exclusiveness. With a given amount of students, someone going to the university means chance's loss of another one, that in turn will influence the revenue and social status in the future, which had been demonstrated by the human resource theory. It is said that the internal rate of return of Chinese higher education is around 18 percent, which is equivalent to that of middle income country, and a less lower than the developing countries.[13] Taking the tuition as an example, the student and his/her family hope get their maximum output of revenue by minimum education input, especially for those who coming from the countryside and rural region. To date, further reforming and perfecting the tuition system has to be done in the long run (Hare and Thomas, 2002), such as the deferent price system in the market-oriented education institute, namely, the private university (Mok, 2005), continuing education, post-secondary education and vocational training, professional degree, etc.

Internationalization of Higher Education

The fifth challenge is the educational internationalization that calls for Chinese higher education to reposition itself. All levels of Chinese education have undergone profound transformation in the last decade. Traditionally, the Chinese university is applicable for domestic students, while globalization means the university recruits international students as well as national students, which makes the Chinese university face several challenges (Hayhoe & Zha, 2004), such as operation mechanism, professional structures, management style, educational resources, target, and value orientation, etc. As a matter of fact, international commercialization has a huge impact on traditional Chinese higher education, for instance, a large number of foreign educational institutions are eager to set up shop in China, managing joint-run degree programs and franchising degrees to Chinese institutions.

It is reported that there were 250 thousand Chinese students go abroad for study at their own expense in the last decade. In fact, the tuition and living expenses is the huge investment for host country beyond all doubt. For those who stay in developed countries after their graduation, it means the loss for China. On the one hand, Chinese government provided free nine-year compulsory education, and the government pays much subsidy for undergraduate also, they are expect to contribute the parent country rather than host country after graduation, it wouldn't be the case if the number of stay abroad is smaller than the number of going abroad, as a matter of fact, the situation is just the opposite. It was said that there have been 1.06 million students studying abroad; only 275 thousand of them coming back, the 785 thousand students who stay abroad are equivalent to the 30 times of total undergraduate student studying in Beijing University and Tsinghua University, the most famous universities in China. Another example is the immigration, according to the report of Global Politics and Safety, issued by the Chinese Social Science Academy, China is listed number one for its brain drain of the elite, among which most of them have good higher education background.[14]

In fact, during the last three decades, the Chinese government took the education opening as the strategic action to promote educational reform, which shortens the distance between China and the developed countries (Lin, 2009). Insisting on the principle of "supporting studying abroad, encouraging the return home, free coming and going", Chinese education have formed the new pattern, which is the mixture of government subsidizing and self-supporting. At the same time, China will make every effort to attract more foreign students to further studies in China, more than 230 thousand students, coming from 200 countries and regions, are studying in Chinese university in 2009. China has launched 282 Confucius Institutes and 272 Confucius classrooms in 88 countries and regions, with total 250 thousand enrolled students, more than 40 million people are studying Chinese now (Lin & Liu, 2009).

Nevertheless, the breaking breakthrough has been found in the fields of macro structural adjustment on account of insistence of the educational public welfare, the Chinese education has established the new framework of higher education system with Chinese characteristics.

FUTURE STRATEGIES

Education, like other public policy areas, is affected by globalization process. Over the years of opening up to the world, China is aware of the importance of higher education to ensure the quality of the workforce and to carry out cutting-edge research (Vidovich et al., 2007).

Financial Support by the Government

In 1993, Chinese government first announced a major national initiative to give significant financial support to 100 universities aiming at achieving world-class status by the 21stcentury. It was nicknamed "the Project 211" (Hayhoe & Zha, 2004). The 100 universities have been given significant additional financial support. For ex-

Table 5. Proportion of project 211 universities' major resources out of national total

Resource Item	**Project 211 Universities' Proportion (%)**
Library book volume	25.65
Scientific equipment & instrumentation	38.70
Bachelor & sub-degree student enrolment	18.33
Master student enrolment	69.14
Doctoral student enrolment	86.01
International student enrolment	58.19
Ratio of full professors (national average 9.77)	18.85
Research funds	70.10
National key laboratories	100
National key programs	83.61
Patent registration	72.81

(Source: China's Higher Education, Vol.24, No.19 (2003), p.16)

ample, Peking university and Tsinghua university both received RMB 1.8 billion (USD 225 million), while Fudan, Zhejiang, and Nanjing Universities received RMB1.2 billion (USD 150 million) each. These 100 institutions in the top echelon of the system that benefit from the extra resources enjoy significant advantages, and carrying out most of the graduate education and research across the whole higher education system. This is evident from the statistics provided in Table 5. Rather than deciding the list of "key-point" institutions that would qualify for high-level support from the top, as had been done in the past, the State invited universities to put forward competitive proposals for acceptance into this elite group. This opportunity to gain recognition and significant financial enhancement unleashed a frenzy of activity around the country, as universities developed strategic plans to demonstrate the unique contribution they could make to the nation based on their particular strengths in areas of critical importance. From 1995 to 1998, China's most prestigious institutions competed for inclusion in "the Project 211", 100 institutions forming the core of China's world-class knowledge system, with distinguished chairs, competitive salaries, and high-tech parks and research grants to promote scholarship and university-enterprise collaboration.

University Restructuring and Merging

In order to improve the 'global competency' of its citizens and to make its higher education systems more efficient, higher education restructuring along the line of 'university merging' has been launched in the mid-1990s. In 1995, the State Education Commission (SEC), a central administrative organization responsible for higher education policy and management, issued a policy document entitled 'Suggestions on Deepening Higher Education Structural Reform' ('Suggestions', hereafter), recommending the four major restructuring strategies, namely, 'joint development' (gongjian), 'restructuring' (huazhuan), 'merging' (hebing) and 'cooperation' (hezuo) to reform its higher education systems (Mok, 2005).

Table 6 shows the number of higher education institutions involved in the restructuring processes, some of them have taken the restructuring strategy while the other are readjusted and transformed by other reform measures like 'joint development', 'merger' and 'cooperation'.

Mergers were to improve economies of scale and also act as a fast track to world class standards. A large number of mergers took place subsequently, in almost all cases resulting in more comprehensive types of universities, with a broad range of knowledge areas from basic arts and sciences to most fields of professional specialization. Zhejiang University is one of the most striking examples of these mergers. It had been one of China's top comprehensive universities in the 1930s and 1940s, while it had been dismembered in 1952 and made into a university of engineering sciences. It took the initiative to form a merger in 1997, and now ranks the fifth among China's

Table 6. Current developments of higher education restructuring in China

Types of structural change	*Joint Development (gongjian)*	*Restructuring (huazhuan)*	*Merging (hebing)*	*Cooperation (hezuo)*
1993	5	-	-	-
1994	15	-	4(2)	11
1995	40	5	70(28)	120
1996	56	7	103(42)	178
1997	100	16	162(74)	228
1998	114	177	258(105)	267
1999	197	226	304(125)	317
2000	-	509	556(232)	-

(Source: State Education Commission, 1994, 1995, 1996, 1997, 1998; Ministry of Education 1999, 2000, 2001)

top institutions[15]. Overall the sweeping trend for mergers has resulted in a remarkable diversification of the Chinese higher education system. There are many more comprehensive institutions of varied curricular emphases.

However, there also some universities identified the national push towards university amalgamations to create large, comprehensive institutions as a major weakness in strategies to achieve 'world-class' status. In fact, the problem is that all universities are aiming to be big and comprehensive, whereas the university should specialize in one or two subjects.

Eclecticism Mode

The internationalization of curriculum and research that took place in China was characterized by eclecticism, with curricular materials drawn from Western countries, and real efforts made to adapt them to China's own development needs.

There has been significant governmental support for study abroad over the past two decades, Chinese students and scholars have also been successful in gaining opportunities for privately sponsored study abroad. Several hundred thousand students have taken advantage of the open door to study abroad (Vidovich et al., 2007), with the largest concentration in North America but very significant numbers in Europe, Japan, Australia, New Zealand, and so on. Chinese official policy has wavered between sending younger students to gain higher degrees, and sending established scholars for opportunities to familiarize themselves with current developments in their field abroad, and take up opportunities for collaborative research. Just to give a sense of the scope and scale of this movement, officially published statistics indicate that 460,000 had been sent abroad since the late 1970s. The faculty in China's top universities are now as internationalized in outlook and experience as those in major Western universities, if not more so. One recent study indicated that 70% of full professors and 80% of associate professors at Peking University are returnees from the West, and 85% of the current heads of research institutes of the Chinese Academy of Sciences are returnees, as are 81% of academicians (Hayhoe & Zha, 2004).

To promote steady advancement of school administration cooperation with foreign partners, the Ministry of Education (MOE) issued the "Interim Measures Governing Universities and Colleges Engaged in Overseas Education" in 2002; meanwhile, "The Action Plan for Revitalizing Education from 2003 to 2007" clearly states that China intends to further expand access to its education market and promote international cooperation and exchange at a high level in a comprehensive and multiregional manner. However, the internationalization of higher education issues is closely linked to the question of its localization. According to the former president of Peking University, internationalization does not mean that the whole universities all over the world should adopt the same mode. Unified mode implies huge risks. We are all invariably drawing the American mode, but we must note that the successful American mode is not the only choice; we should learn other countries' successful experiences and also keep our own traditions.

Renew Degree Certification System

With respect to the issue of degree certification, the Chinese government has had positive negotiations with other countries and produced remarkable achievements, so far signing agreements on mutual degree recognition with twenty-six nations, including the United States, Germany, Britain, France, Australia, and New Zealand. At the same time, stringent rules have been formulated and implemented to manage degree conferment and maintain academic reputation. According to the "Notice on Conferment and Management of Academic Degrees for Chinese–Foreign Cooperation in Running Schools" issued in 1996, "Chinese institutions running schools or programs abroad in collaboration with foreign partners must abide by local laws, get consent from local education authorities as well as approval from the Academic Degree Commission of the State Council (China's cabinet) before conferring academic degrees; such degrees will be limited to disciplines with recognized academic content and rigorous conferment rules."

Networked Learning Environment

Presently more than 80 percent of Chinese universities are connected to the CERNET, The China Education and Research Network, which began operating in 1994 and has two gateways to the Internet. Many universities own their campus LAN (Local Area Network) centers and support the various online computer servers for the use of libraries, offices, and labs, as well as dormitories. Advanced information infrastructures help create a new learning environment, which forms the base of initial digital libraries and virtual universities. New learning environments make higher education expand beyond the university and operate more effectively and efficiently (Ding, 2004). This also enables higher education to collaborate with other social agencies all over the world.

Under the supervision of the Chinese Education Committee, information skills education in academic libraries has been well developed during the past twenty years. Also, many university libraries in China have built computer labs for instruction and information search practice. The library at Tsinghua University in Beijing presents a good example for teaching information and library skills utilizing credit courses. It offers ten credit courses related to library and information literacy and teaches them to more than 2,000 students, both undergraduates and graduates, on an annual basis, and they are taught on different levels and have different requirements. The textbooks and teaching materials have been written, edited, and reworked by the librarians who instruct the students. Statistical data indicates that more than 400 textbooks have been published during the past twenty years to teach the information skills courses.

CONCLUSION

China's higher education system is reacting to globalization and knowledge economy in ways common to what other countries have done. It has expanded enrollment, rationalized administrative structures, and encouraged the development of private colleges and universities (Mok, 2005). Problems resulting from the rapid expansion are now challenging existing education management system (Ding, 2004), which should be tackled in the coming years. Although Chinese university have fostered millions of students who are now the pillar of national economic and technological sector, the China's influence is still limited comparing with developed countries, the Chinese higher education has a long way to go. The trend of Chinese higher education is just as following.

First, the Chinese higher education should have the idea of training young people to be all-round personnel rather than the experts who is good at one or two techniques. Chinese university had better have a unique ethos and a clear rationale, and the students are expected to be curious to outside, active to learn something new with the right method, they are to be cultivated a citizenship capable of creativity, flexibility, independent thinking and innovative, and the students should broaden their mind and keep up with the everlasting changes.

Secondly, Chinese higher education should take effective reforms to meet the demand of market. In fact, a world-class university requires a style of administration which makes sure the rationale is implemented in all aspects of the university's operation. Chinese university are experiencing the big challenges of unfitness between what they have learnt inside-campus and what the society need outside-campus, which could be seen in two aspects of teaching and studying because of the constraint of the higher education management system. For example, although the students have learnt much more about the theory, they don't know how to apply their knowledge to serve the society; they are just follower rather than leader because of no creative desire to do something innovative.

Thirdly, highest importance must be given to issues of quality and benchmarking. With more and more Chinese young students have the chance to attend the college, once step into university; they need higher quality education accordingly, which is still far behind the needs of the students as well as their parent and the whole society alike. So the higher education institutes should focus on quality assurance by means of faculty and staff, textbook, teaching philosophy, and so on.

Last but not least, Chinese higher education will contribute to human civilization and well-being (Vidovich et al., 2007), as well as social and economic development on the national level. The intellectuals are the conscience of society. Chinese university not only trains the talents who have specific knowledge to serve the motherland, but cultivates them to serve the mankind also.

REFERENCES

Cen, Y., Ross, C., & Ross, H. (2009). Chinese higher education and evaluation in context. *Chinese Education & Society*, *42*(1), 3–7. doi:10.2753/CED1061-1932420100

Chang, J. (2006). Globalization and English in Chinese higher education. *World Englishes*, *34*(3/4), 513–525. doi:10.1111/j.1467-971X.2006.00484.x

Chen, X. (2008). *The study on quality assurance system for our mass higher education*. Unpublished Master dissertation, Zhejiang Sci-Tech University. (in Chinese).

Ding, X. (2004). The challenges faced by Chinese higher education as it expands in scale. *Chinese Education & Society*, *37*(1), 36–53.

Hayhoe, R., & Zha, Q. (2004). Becoming world-class: Chinese universities facing globalization and internationalization. *Harvard China Review, Spring*, 88-92.

Jacob, W. J. (2006). Social justice in Chinese higher education: Regional issues of equity and access. *Review of Education*, *52*, 149–169.

Jinhui, L., & Zhiping, L. (2009). New exploration in the development strategy of going out for Chinese-foreign cooperation in higher education. *Chinese Education & Society*, *42*(4), 78–87. doi:10.2753/CED1061-1932420406

Ka-Ho, M. (2005). Globalization and educational restructuring: University merging and changing governance in China. *Higher Education*, *50*, 57–88. doi:10.1007/s10734-004-6347-z

Liu, D. (2009). Chinese higher education changes during sixty years. [in Chinese]. *Higher Education Exploration*, *5*(5), 5–12.

Liu, X. (2004). Higher education budget financing and investing. *Journal of Capital Normal University (Social Science Edition)*, 176-179. (in Chinese).

Lu-ting, M. (2009). Structure framing of higher education system of Switzerland and the analysis of its features. [in Chinese]. *Comparative Education Review*, *7*, 1–6.

Ministry of Education. (1999). Action scheme for invigorating education towards the 21st century. [in Chinese]. *The China Higher Education*, *6*, 35–39.

Ouyang, H. (2006). Investigation and analysis on higher education quality. *Educational Development Study*, *11*, 26–29.

Postiglione, G. (2005). Higher education in China: Perils and promises for a new century. (pp. 138-143).

Trow, M. (1972). The expansion and transformation of higher education. *International Review of Education*, *1*, 61–63. doi:10.1007/BF01450272

Trow, M. (1998). *From mass higher education to universal access*. Paper of the meeting of the Japanese Society for Higher Education Research, Hiroshima, May 31, 1998.

Vidovich, L., Yang, R., & Currie, J. (2007). Dancing in a cage: Changing autonomy in Chinese higher education. *Higher Education*, *54*, 575–592. doi:10.1007/s10734-006-9009-5

Vidovich, L., Yang, R., & Currie, J. (2007). Changing accountabilities in higher education as China opens up to globalization. *Globalisation, Societies and Education*, *5*(1), 89–107. doi:10.1080/14767720601133447

Weifang, M., & Xiaohao, D. (2005). Financing Chinese higher education: Reforms and future challenges. *Harvard China Review*, 129-131.

Ying Chu, N. G., & Li, S. (2000). Measuring the research performance of Chinese higher educations: An application data envelopment analysis. *Education Economics*, *8*(2), 139–156. doi:10.1080/096452900410712

Yu, X. (2009). Faculty employment policy shift in Chinese higher education. *The Journal of Education*, 51-62.

Zhang, H., Dong, Y., & Chen, G. (2005). Educational technology training for higher education teachers in China and some suggestions for improving it. *Chinese Education & Society*, *38*(6), 69–78.

KEY TERMS AND DEFINITIONS

Higher Education: Post secondary education set up offered by Universities, polytechnic colleges in China.

Internationalization: Efforts by the Govt. of China to set standards in education at par with other developed and developing countries.

ENDNOTES

1. The special topic about the achievements of China during the last 60 years, available at http://www.moe.edu.cn/edoas/website18/zhuanti/200960years/2nd_1.htm
2. Statistical Communiqué on National Educational Development in 2008, Ministry of Education, 17 July 2009, available at http://www.moe.edu.cn/edoas/en/level3.jsp?tablename=1244015362633291&infoid=1250005986959241&title=Statistical Communiqué on National Educational Development in 2008

3. In 1999, Chinese government has launched a new plan to increase the undergraduate dramatically to train more talents for the nation development as well as meeting the demand of those who want to go to university.
4. The average years of educational more than 15 year old, available at http://www.moe.gov.cn/edoas/website18/42/info125108902
5. During the great proletarian Cultural Revolution from 1966 to 1976, Chinese government suspends the national examination.
6. Maofang Xiong, (2000), The thinking about the mass national higher education, Education Journal of Jimei University, (6), 65-69. (in Chinese)
7. Chinese government launched the post doctorate in 1985 because of the proposal by Tsung-Dao Lee, the Nobel laureate of physics in 1957, Lee suggest the post-doctoral in China while talking with Deng Xiao Ping, Deng promise to initiate the post doctorate, and since then, ten thousand of post doctorate have been conducting scientific research in the university, academic institute, as well as enterprises.
8. In May 4th, 1998, the former president Jiang Zeming declared to establish a number of world-class university in a speech delivered in memory of the 100th anniversary of Peking University.
9. Top 20 Countries in ALL FIELDS, 1998-August 31, 2008, available at http://sciencewatch.com/dr/cou/2008/08decALL
10. Wang Shimei, Quality: Life of Higher Education for Masses, Journal of Hubei Institute for Nationalities (Philosophy and Social Science), 2002, (1), 96-100.
11. Yang Deguan, the popularity, diversity and quality assurance of higher education--the conclusion report of 6th annual meeting of national academy of higher education, the Study of Higher Education, 2001, (7)
12. Ministry of Education, Action Scheme for Invigorating Education Towards the 21st Century, The China Higher Education, 1999.
13. Equality and efficiency, the double target and the pursuit of pricing about the higher education, June 6, 2010, available at http://news.163.com/10/0606/10/68G6DMKD000146BD.html
14. It is time for Chinese elite to immigrate abroad, June 4th, 2010, available at http://focus.news.163.com/10/0604/10/68B1H3JT00011SM9.html
15. The others are Nanjing University (4), Fudan University (3), Tsinghua University (2), and Peking University

Chapter 16
Transformation through Marketing: A Case of a Secondary School in South Africa

Tom Bisschoff
University of Birmingham, UK

Christopher Rhodes
University of Birmingham, UK

EXECUTIVE SUMMARY

A historically white school in a city setting in South Africa is faced with the demand from a newly democratically elected government to transform and become an agent of change in making its pupil profile more representative of the demographics of the country as a whole. This demand is driven by significant national contextual change from a position where schools had an allocated catchment based upon geographical area and ethnic group (before 1994) to a market oriented approach where every school must compete for pupil recruitment to ensure survival whilst also adhering to the government requirement to demonstrate a willingness to change existing mono-cultural pupil profiles to multi ethnic profiles and establish non-sexism and non-racialism as the dominating culture.

SCHOOL BACKGROUND

South Africa is finally beginning to overcome many of the difficulties caused by years of struggle against Apartheid and the country has viewed educational change as one of the major strands in enabling necessary transformation to take place. During the challenge to Apartheid, education was one of the vehicles used by liberation movements to render the country ungovernable with the outcome that certain sections of the education system, especially during the nineties, were left in chaos

DOI: 10.4018/978-1-60960-599-5.ch016

and disarray. It is only now with the transformation agenda in place that significant improvement is taking root throughout the system. White schools with the better funding under the old dispensation opened their doors to all racial groups and black schools, now with additional funding, are coming much closer to delivering education at an acceptable level (Bisschoff in Pashiardis, 2001).

This case study is about the transformation process at an established white school in Johannesburg and how it utilised its marketing plan to better serve the schooling requirements of whole community irrespective of any racial differences and how it addressed the challenge of change and moved away from the divisions' characteristic of schooling under Apartheid.

SETTING THE STAGE

To understand the case study school and the context within which it is situated, one needs to look closely at the Human Rights entrenched in The Constitution of South Africa (RSA, 1996a). Within those Human Rights, the government sets out to redress all the historic imbalances in South African society created as a result of the former Apartheid ideology and to eliminate the inequalities and inequities of the past. In particular, issues of inequality and inequity relating to race and gender are high on the priority list for Governmental action, with the result that both national and provincial administrations of the country are now active in addressing such issues as a matter of course.

The principal aim of the transformation process is to afford every previously disadvantaged person of colour an opportunity to take his/her rightful place in society and to obtain full benefit from all aspects of public administration, including education (Davies, 1999). The transformation of the education system was of necessity far-reaching, demanding both organisational and structural changes to redress the imbalances in provision and to break the former bureaucratic stranglehold prevalent within the system. After 1994, the new National Department of Education radically altered and redefined the vision of the education system in South Africa with a series of policy initiatives and new legislation to ensure a new and better direction. Importantly, these new national policy frameworks contain clear guidance for education planning and for effective educational management.

It should be borne in mind that prior to 1994, the management structures responsible for education in the country were a direct function of the political system that was in place at the time. Glaring injustices in the socio-political development of the country before the advent of the 1994 transformation were well rooted in a divisive education system. Separate education departments and separate schools for "blacks, coloureds, Indians and whites" existed in all those areas of the country including those that had been divided up into smaller homeland areas. The policy at this time resulted in no fewer than 18 education departments in all, not counting the department at national level which had to be further divided among nine newly established provinces.

South Africa is now engaged in a continuing process of transformation and improvement in teaching and learning, school management and in the way in which national and provincial education departments are organised, all with the purpose of creating a democratic, equitable and comprehensive national system of education. Emergent legislation to date has served to place the country on the road to a school-based system of management. Indeed, education management has been devolved from national to provincial levels and the establishment of new governing bodies with the support of provincial and district offices has enabled substantial decision-making authority and responsibility to reside within schools themselves.

Such initiatives from the central government have presented an opportunity for South Africa to reinventing its schooling. A new vision opposes the traditional separatist forms of education and attendant reproduction of inequality. It has been realised that pupils and teachers need to be exposed to schooling that embraces democracy in order to build an egalitarian society. Schooling is the key because it empowers all to exercise their democratic rights and shape their destiny (Department of Education, 2001). Democratic schooling has the potential to enable people to participate in public life, think critically and act in a responsible manner. However, democracy and schooling has it own controversies and it should be noted that social policy is not necessarily the panacea for all social ills (see Chubb and Moe, 1990). Indeed, Plank and Boyd (1994) point out that democratic governance is no a panacea for the problems of a schooling system. Nevertheless, the values of the schooling system in South Africa are rooted in the values located in the Constitution (RSA, 1996a). The ten fundamental values are:

- democracy;
- social justice;
- equality;
- non-racism and non-sexism;
- ubuntu (human dignity);
- an open society;
- accountability;
- rule of law;
- respect;
- reconciliation.

The new emergent school-based management model requires each school to compete for good pupils, good teachers and funding to ensure the delivery of quality education (Bisschoff et al., 2004; Davies and Ellison, 1991). Devolution of responsibility for these important tasks represents both opportunities and challenges for individual schools. In recognition of the need to build management capacity at school level commensurate with the education transformation agenda, the Minister of Education appointed the Task Team on Education Development early in 1996 with the directive to make proposals for a national strategy for school management development in South Africa (Department of Education, 1996). A focus on the quality of school leadership and school management within individual schools has now been established. Without local as well as regional and national intervention, transmission and implementation of the transformation agenda will be severely weakened. The pivotal role the principal and his/her management team in transformation is clearly stated in the following inaugural address given in 1997:

"Transformation in education is possible only if the political leaders' vision for education were shared by the people at grass-roots level and (only) if this vision were pursued in education. At present, this co-operation between the visionary leaders and the foot soldiers does not amount to much. Even though the vision for education in South Africa has been clearly defined in the policy frameworks and legislation ... It is not yet reflected in the ethos, structures and procedures of education. This stage of affairs also applies to the education management practices which form the basis of (one of the main) issues to b addressed in the presentation, namely does co-operative management hold a key to transformation" (Bisschoff, 1997, p. 2).

CASE DESCRIPTION

Location

The historically white Afrikaans (one of the 11 official languages in the country) secondary school that constitutes this case study is situated in one of the middle class suburbs of Johannesburg. It had a 2009 enrolment of 1,201 pupils from the 8th year of schooling up to the 12th year. After consultation with the local school governing body it was agreed that I would have unrestricted access to all documents and venues associated with the school's marketing plan. The plan was developed in 1997, the first year of the implementation of the new Schools Act (RSA, 1996b) and, although having received some revision, it is still in force up to the present time (July 2009). I agreed that I would use the data collected to develop a special case study for training purposes without revealing the actual name of the school.

The Origin of the Marketing Plan

I was fortunate enough to secure an interview with the principal who was a member of the original school marketing committee (SMC). The principal, in consultation with the School Governing Body (SGB – see key terms and definitions), had formed the committee in July 1997. The original SMC had a parent with a marketing background as chair (he was also a fully elected member of the SGB), it also comprised the principal, his deputy and the Head of Department (Commercial Subjects) from the academic staff and the most senior member of the support staff who acted as clerk to the committee.

At the meeting the principal presented the following introductory paper, here reproduced in its original format as part of the minutes:

"In the last three years there has been a gradual increase in the school population on the outskirts of the suburb where our school is situated but this has not seen a corresponding rise in the roll of our school. In the past two years one of the primary feeder schools has even increased its roll but our school did not gain a full transfer of children from this school.

The current policy of open enrolment means that if one school is perceived by a number of parents to be more attractive than another, the parents send their children to the 'better' school. This will eventually result in that school flourishing while the other may even have to be closed (due to poor enrolment figures). It is clear that parents seek quality in education. In order to improve that quality more resources are needed as regard the curriculum, staff members, and furniture and building maintenance. But if the school is in a falling roll situation because parents are sending their children elsewhere), the available funding is immediately diminished. This leads to a situation of fewer children, less cash and worsening of the quality of education.

Today we must consider three points. The first concerns our reputation. Prior to 1994, only the one Afrikaans medium primary school had a good reputation while the other two feeder primary schools had a poor reputation in the city. Unrest was common and many teaching days were lost as a result. In 1994, a new head teacher was appointed to one to the failing primary schools. Its reputation improved, and it began to flourish and gain pupil numbers. I was then appointed at this school. I feel we are gaining to enjoy a better reputation but that parents from other ethnic groups still perceive us as a predominantly white Afrikaans school.

The second point is that some of the children who transfer to other schools do so for logical reasons, such as parents relocating. But we have gained the same number of pupils as what we have lost and are making very little inroad into the other ethnic groups living close to the school.

A third point concerns children who transfer elsewhere at the end of the eight year because their parents decided that another school would be more suitable. The reasons are at this moment very vague and could be related to the strict discipline in the school.

We need to try to reverse the loss trend into a gain trend for the school; in particular, we should strive to secure the transfer of all children from the feeder primary schools. It is unavoidable that some pupils will be transferred elsewhere, but we should make every effort to focus on encouraging a net gain and avoid a net loss.

I think our aim should be to establish seven classes (35 pupils each) for every year of study within the next five years. We can do this by securing the confidence of the parents and gaining a reputation in the city for striving for excellence and quality in every respect".

The chair had, at that stage, the most knowledge about marketing in general, but from the minutes of the meetings at this time it was clear that even he had problems translating private sector practices to the marketing of a school. After the above mentioned presentation by the principal the chair presented the following action plan:

1. A whole day SWOT analysis with the staff and members of the SGB on a Saturday to establish the strengths, weaknesses, opportunities and threads for the future of the school.
2. Clarity on the government's intentions with state schools, especially on staff and pupil composition that should reflect the racial demographics of the feeding area of the school.
3. A survey amongst the parents to determine what their views are on what the school should look like in ten years time.
4. Developing a detailed budget for the marketing plan in the region of R10 000 (£900).

The debate that followed was interesting in the sense that there already existed two distinct camps on the committee. One was a force for change who considered that pupils should be involved in the marketing plan and that government policy on schooling should be accepted as a given. The other constituted a force for maintenance of the *status quo*. This group regarded the present situation as ideal and that the Afrikaans medium of instruction should remain and that changes in the pupil profile should not be encouraged beyond the normal influx of inhabitants in the areas around the school.

There were even members who insisted that marketing is a business practice and as such is inappropriate in the school context and they were adamant that that they had no inclination to venture into a field that they knew nothing about.

The chair, according to the minutes, argued in favour of a marketing approach to the problem facing the school and quoted directly from the South African Schools Act (RSA, 1996b) which places public schooling clearly within the domain of site-based management within a competitive environment. For schools to survive they must market themselves. Furthermore, he emphasised that in his view this seems to be an integral part of the present government's overall strategy. Esp (1989) was brought forward and quoted to support his argument:

"It is assumed that improved standards in schools and a responsive education service will only be achieved through consumer choice in the marketplace (1989, p.23).

The action plan was duly changed to also include a survey among the senior pupils (10, 11 and 12 year groups) about their views on this issue.

The records of the SWOT analysis were kept and I could locate and access the original flip chart pages used during the session.

On the 'Strengths' chart the following appeared in different handwritings and it was confirmed for me that the chair had asked each member at the meeting to move around and write down what they regarded as 'Strengths':

Well maintained buildings; enough sport fields (rugby, netball, athletics, cricket and hockey for the girls only); a sufficiently resourced gymnasium for Physical Training (PT); a functioning library with more than 5,000 books and five computer workstations to access the worldwide web; a 98% pass rate in the 12th year national examination with 38% entrance to university endorsements; well qualified teachers; a qualified librarian; two qualified PT teachers; a qualified guidance teacher; well disciplined pupils; a strict dress code for pupils; parental involvement.

Table 1. Income loss for changing pupil profile

	Total number of pupils	Fee per pupil per year	Number of exempted pupils	Total income
Present	1,201	£20	none	£24,020
If intake includes at least 10% from poor backgrounds	1,201	£20	120	£21,620
Loss of income				£2,400

The people who contributed were clearly proud of their school because the list of 'Weaknesses' was a short one:

Dwindling pupil numbers as the suburbs around the school get older and very few young couples moving into the suburbs; white middle class parents leaving the country; white middle class parents taking their kids to independent schools as more black pupils enter the school; being a target for the government to enforce their multicultural ideology on the existing parent community.

The 'Opportunities' plotted on the chart exhibit an optimism that forms a clear contrast to the 'Threats' that were recorded:

The school can be an agent of change to serve the wider schooling needs of the broader community; the school can be a model for other schools that need to transform; white pupils will now get an opportunity to engage with people of colour on school level; tolerance for other cultures could be cultivated.

The parent survey mirrored the divide on the committee with some parents hoping to retain all the old ways of doing things, for example, a focus on strict discipline (some even proposing the continuation of corporal punishment although this was made illegal after 1994), Afrikaans as the only medium of instruction, emphasis on a Christian ethos, cleanliness as a high priority and direct teaching from the teachers with little opportunity for pupils to be involved in discussion. However, a second group of parents represented by more progressive thinkers saw transformation a *fait complet* and saw change as inevitable. They took a stance that the school management should not resist change. Along with all the other requirements set out in the newly accepted Constitution (RSA, 1996a), this group accepted that strict discipline should make way for a more child-centred approach with a merit and demerit system and rights to appeal. There was a strong feeling amongst this group that the doors of the school must be immediately opened to take in children from previously disadvantaged groups. They acknowledged that such a change in enrolment might lead to a reduction in school fees because the Schools Act (RSA, 1996b) allows for parents who cannot afford school fees to be exempted from payment. One parent provided a Table (see Table 1 below) to explain this:

He assumed that if we take in 10% of the children from impoverished communities the implication for the existing school fee income would be as follows:

The survey undertaken amongst existing pupils in years 10, 11 and 12 did not bring any new insights because the existing pupils only wanted the present situation to continue without any change. It was clear that these pupils come from fairly conservative white families with no inclination to disrupt what has been going on in the school since it establishment in 1934.

The committee considered the results of all the data collected and came up with the following short and long-term action plans:

Short Term Action Plan

"An open day for all prospective 8th year pupils will be held on a Saturday – invitations will be sent out to all the feeder primary schools in the area including the black, coloured and Indian township schools within 10 miles of the school grounds.

A leaflet with all the subject choices and school rules will be handed out during the open day and teachers and governing body members will be available for question-and-answer sessions.

The principal will address whoever is present at 10h00 on the Saturday in the school hall putting forward the mission statement of the school.

The aim of this open day is to attract 250 pupils for the 8th year of schooling from a wide variety of backgrounds. At that stage it was clearly communicated that the only medium of instruction would be Afrikaans".

Long Term Action Plan

"Our mission statement for the school -

Our school being situated in an urban area with people of all cultures and socio-economic status living in its vicinity undertakes to serve the whole community who favours Afrikaans as the medium of instruction for their children by providing schooling in accordance with the requirements set by the National Department of Education.

Actions based on the mission statement:

- improve parents' perceptions of the quality of education provided by the school;
- raise awareness of parents of prospective pupils of the school's strengths and successes;
- increase the school roll: to ensure an annual intake of 8th year pupils of 250 moving towards a more multi ethnic pupil profile. Our culture -

The school is 63 years old. A number of the pupils are children of former pupils. There is some movement of population but also considerable stability. There is a high proportion of children from middle class white families who are enthusiastic about formal schooling for their children and see it as a way of a middle class existence and entry into the professions.

Our marketing mission -

to identify and promote awareness of the strengths and successes of the school;

to identify weaknesses and implementation strategies and to deal effectively with those of highest priority."

CURRENT CHALLEGES FACING THE SCHOOL

The challenges facing the school are to increase the enrolment of prospective 8th year pupils and to change the profile of the enrolment to include more pupils from previously disadvantaged sections of the population. Since 1998 when the original marketing plan was implemented the school was not successful in this while retaining Afrikaans as the only medium of instruction, as Table 2 indicates:

SOLUTIONS AND RECOMMENDATIONS

From the data collected it seems evident that the language policy of the school will have to change in order to attract pupils who prefer to be educated in English. The decision to do that will have to

Table 2. Intake of 8th year pupils since 1998-2008

Year	Intake					Change
	White	Black	Coloured	Indian	Total	
1998	194	5	8	1	208	
1999	190	7	12	1	210	+2
2000	185	11	17	2	215	+5
2001	192	10	18	0	220	+5
2002	210	8	15	1	234	+14
2003	205	7	18	3	233	-1
2004	202	12	16	2	232	-1
2005	208	10	13	2	233	+1
2006	208	8	15	3	234	+1
2007	207	5	16	2	230	-4
2008	203	12	17	3	235	+5

be preceded by a period of positive advocacy which clearly points out the benefits to emerge from such a decision. By changing the language of instruction there is a greater chance of tapping into new markets of pupils and increasing both overall pupil numbers and also a wider ethnic mix.

If the decision is taken to add English as a medium of instruction, future parents and pupils will have to be convinced that a new transformed ethos that will prevail in the school and that this will include greater tolerance towards other ethnic and religious groups.

The role of marketing in transformation is highlighted as important, and in this case essential in bringing about the desired change. Communication, image and choice are central in market oriented approaches to educational provision. This is true both for this case study and for many schools internationally who are working within an environment led by market accountability.

REFERENCES

Bisschoff, T., Du Plessis, P., & Smith, E. (2004). *Effective school marketing*. Pretoria, South Africa: Van Schaiks.

Bisschoff, T. C. (1997). *Co-operative education management: The key to transformation?* Johannesburg, South Africa: Rand Afrikaans University.

Bisschoff, T. C. (2001). South Africa – a new vision for education management and leadership. In Pashiardis, P. (Ed.), *International perspectives on educational leadership*. Hong Kong: University of Hong Kong, Centre for Educational Leadership.

Chubb, J., & Moe, T. (1990). *Politics, markets and America's schools*. Washington, DC: Brookings.

Davies, B., & Ellison, L. (1991). *Marketing the secondary school*. Harlow, UK: Longman.

Davies, B., & Ellison, L. (1997). *Strategic marketing for schools*. London, UK: Pitman.

Davies, E. H. (1999). *Administration of the education system and school governance*. Pretoria, South Africa: Centre for Education law and Education Policy (CELP).

Department of Education. (1996). *Changing management to manage change in education*. Pretoria, South Africa: Department of Education.

Department of Education. (2001). *Manifesto on values, education and democracy*. Cape Town, South Africa: Department of Education.

Esp, D. (1989). *Competencies for school managers*. London, UK: Kogan Page.

Plank, D. N., & Boyd, W. L. (1994). Antipolitics, education, and institutional choice: The flight from democracy. *American Educational Research Journal, 31*(2), 263–281.

RSA. (1996a). *The Constitution of the Republic of South Africa, Act 108 of 1996*. Cape Town, South Africa: Government Printers.

RSA. (1996b). *South African Schools Act 84 of 1996*. Cape Town, South Africa: Government Printers.

Squelch, J. (Author). Lemmer, E. (Ed.), (1999). *Contemporary education*. Sandton, South Africa: Heinemann.

ADDITIONAL READING

Ardley, B. (1994). College marketing and management of change. *Journal of Further and Higher Education, 189*(1), 7–28.

Barnes, C. (1993). *Practical marketing in schools*. Oxford: Blackwell.

Dennison, W. F. (1992). Performance indicators and consumers' choice. *International Journal of Educational Management, 4*(1), 8–11.

Devlin, T., & Knight, B. (1990). *Public relations and marketing for schools. A do-it-yourself manual*. Harlow: Longman.

Drysdale, L. (1999). Relationship marketing: A new paradigm for marketing of schools. *Principal Matters*. The official journal of the secondary principals' association of Australia. September, *36 & 37*.

Evans, I. G. (1995). *Marketing for schools*. London: Cassel.

Gerard, S. J. (1990). Creating a positive corporate image for your school. *The Practicing Administrator, 12*(2), 34–36.

Gray, L. (1997). *Marketing education*. Philadelphia: Open University Press.

Hanson, M. E. (1992). Educational marketing and the public schools: Policies, practices and problems. *Educational Policy, 6*(1), 19–34. doi:10.1177/0895904892006001002

Hardie, B. (1991). *Marketing the primary school: An introduction for teachers and governors*. Plymouth: North Cote House.

Kenway, J. (1993). Marketing education in the post modern age. *Journal of Education Policy, 8*(2), 105–122. doi:10.1080/0268093930080201

Marland, M., & Rogers, R. (1991). *Marketing the school*. Oxford: Heinemann Educational.

Michael, S. O. (1990). Marketing educational institutions: Implications for administrators. *International Journal of Educational Management, 4*(11), 123–130.

Oplatka, I., & Hemsley-Brown, J. (2004). The Research on School Marketing: Current issues and Future Directions. *Journal of Educational Administration, 42*(3), 375–400. doi:10.1108/09578230410534685

Pardey, D. (1997). *Marketing schools* (2nd ed.). London: Kogan Page.

Smedley, D. (1993). *Marketing schools to parents*. Loughborough: Loughborough University.

Stott, K. (1991). Marketing for educational managers. *The Practicing Administrator, 13*(4), 8–19.

Stott, K., & Parr, H. (1991). *Marketing your school*. London: Hodder & Stoughton.

Thomas, A. & Dennison, B. (1991). Parental or pupil choice: Who really decides in urban schools? *Educational management and Administration, 19*(4), pp. 12-15.

Torrence, L., & Waldron, C. (1995). Marketing tips for educators. *Education Digest, 61*(1), 50–53.

Walters, L. (1993). How and why customers choose a secondary school – Does the school fulfil their needs? Unpublished MSc dissertation. Glamorgan: University of Glamorgan.

Warner, L. (1994). *Promoting your school*. Thousand Oaks: Corwin.

KEY TERMS AND DEFINITIONS

School Governing Body (SGB): The promulgation of the South African Schools Act (RSA, 1996b) heralded a dramatic change in the legal status of public schools, in that public schools are now categorised as juristic persons. The term "juristic person" refers to an abstract legal entity that stands apart from the people who are members of it. A juristic person can, in itself, have rights and duties that have nothing to do with the rights and/or duties of its members. A juristic person can, therefore, engage in legal activities in its own name. It can do so through its organs or functionaries who act on its behalf. Unlike a natural person, however, a juristic person continues to exist as a legal entity despite any changes to any of its organs (Squelch in Lemmer, 1999).

The school governing body is made up of the head teacher in his/her official capacity (ex officio), elected parents representatives, elected teacher representatives, elected non-teaching representatives and in the case of a high school elected pupil representatives. The parents always form the majority on the school governing body.

The South African Schools Act (RSA, 1996b): Distinguishes between the terms "governance" and "professional management", assigning the former to the governing body and the latter to the head teacher of the school, in consultation with the School Management Team (SMT).

Chapter 17
Navigating a Pathway to Partnership through Turbulent Seas of Adversity

Paul Breen
INTO University of East Anglia, UK

Magdalena De Stefani
Instituto Cultural Anglo-Uruguayo, Uruguay

Achilleas Kostoulas
Technological Educational Institute of Epirus, Greece

EXECUTIVE SUMMARY

This chapter will endeavour to provide a rich description and detailed analysis of how an institution, in the British higher educational sector, has designed and provided a course of in-context doctoral study. The institution described in this chapter is a redbrick university situated in the north of England. The purpose of this chapter is not to cover the broad spectrum of higher education courses provided by distance means but rather to take one particular case as an illustration of how institutions can adapt and indeed need to adapt to the nature of society and education in the twenty first century.

Many adult professionals no longer have the time or finances to engage in full time, on site study, and as a consequence are seeking flexible alternatives. Some institutions have been slow to react to this change. The organisation described herein has been quicker to react but this movement towards change also poses its own unique issues. These issues are discussed and analysed by three students who have participated in a part-time programme of doctoral studies while embedded in their research context. But, one of the drawbacks of conducting a study such as this though is the contemporary lack of statistics on the actual dichotomy of provision between conventional and alternative modes of teaching in the higher education sector. The reason for this is that higher education organisations in Britain operate in a competitive and individualised manner rather than as a cohesive block.

DOI: 10.4018/978-1-60960-599-5.ch017

ORGANIZATIONAL BACKGROUND

Aside from a few ancient universities such as Oxford and Cambridge, the British higher educational sector itself can be divided into three main categories; 'red brick universities' formed in the 19th and early 20th centuries, 'plate glass universities' established in the 1960s, and 'new universities' created in the 1990s through an upgrading of the former Polytechnics to full university status. In total there are 166 Higher Education institutions in the United Kingdom, of which 116 are classified as universities (Higher Education Statistics Agency, 2009).

Although the education of teachers by distance means is hardly radical in itself, it could be argued that very few redbrick institutions have ventured so far as to provide studies at this level in a format that diverges significantly from traditional modes of delivery. This is not to say that there are no courses of high quality being delivered by a number of progressive British universities, exclusively by distance means. Rather, the amount and significance of these courses is limited at the present time and largely restricted in the number of participants. Those universities that have embraced distance courses are still fighting battles, often from within, to have them recognised as equal partners in terms of educational quality but in fighting such a battle, these organisations and the individuals at the forefront of such initiatives have placed themselves resolutely within the domain of modernity.

In this high tech age, if institutions are to remain at the forefront of innovation there is a need to meet the requirements and expectations of the society in which they operate. Today's digitally literate, globalised society has facilitated interaction on a scale unimaginable in times past. Organisations that survive in the new economic and socio-cultural milieu of British higher education, in the twenty first century, need to adapt and come up with radical programmes of study that lose none of their traditional pedagogic values but at the same time are versatile enough to meet the demands of a society that, for better or worse, is becoming increasingly corporate.

Degrees provided by distance are neither a new phenomenon nor a product of the digital age, either in the United Kingdom or overseas, and are often the source of considerable debate amongst educators and institutions, for both academic and economic reasons. Valentine (2002, p. 1) explains how distance learning courses have existed in the European context for over one hundred years. These original correspondence-style courses gradually evolved to incorporate audio and video formats in the middle of the century (ibid) before the advent of Web technologies in subsequent decades. Jim Taylor (2001, p. 12) asserts that educators have now reached a fifth generation mode of educational delivery by distance means, which is based around "the intelligent flexible learning model" (ibid). One of the chief affordances of these fifth, and even sixth, generation distance education courses is that they facilitate a transparent exchange of ideas and good practice within the university teaching profession as advocated by Laurillard and Mc Andrew (2002, p. 5). The reason for needing this open exchange of ideas and analysis is that the contemporary proliferation of distance degree courses has caused some scepticism about the benefits of distance education and the accreditation or value for money learning experience that it offers.

This undercurrent of scepticism featured strongly in the All-Africa Ministers' Conference of 2004 where Badat (2004, p. 2) made the assertion that in certain scenarios "developments may well be driven by technologists and business interests rather than by educators" with corporate representatives at the top of the hierarchical pyramid and teachers in a position of struggle at the bottom in what White (2003, p. 45) terms "a bifurcated system."

That scepticism too has been echoed by background voices in this particular context who fear that opening up the university's esteemed on-site research tradition to an online element could result in a lessening of standards and a narrowing of the gap between established universities and the contemporary plethora of organisations and bodies that claim to offer degree courses by distance. A Google search of the term 'PhD by distance learning', as of May 2010, brings up 1,490,000 results in 0.6 seconds. To be buried amongst that extensive list of names and courses is understandably not an appetising prospect for organisations that pride themselves on the strength of their supervised research tradition.

This chapter takes the position that although such fears may be justified in some instances, the argument fails to take into account one very vital factor at the heart of the educational equation. There is an absence of belief in the power of the student to meet the challenges of distance education courses and to take control of their own learning processes. Later stages of the chpater will demonstrate how limitations, in using technological affordances to their fullest capacity, were overcome by students making the most of the tools at their disposal.

Furthermore, the participants in this programme of in context education are not part of a new movement in the way that Prensky (2001, pp. 1-6) might classify today's learners into "digital natives" and "digital immigrants." These learners are part of an educational tradition which Murray (2000, p. 414) describes as "the traditional stepchild of most educational systems". A prime example of this fostering comes from Kanuka and Jugdev (2006, pp. 153-154) who, in discussing the roles of empathy and motivation for distance learners, analyse the history of MBA programmes from their initial delivery in the early twentieth century to some modern versions taught almost entirely by distance and aimed primarily at what Rocha Trindade et al. (2000, p. 4) might describe as "extra mural students." Yet, it is not just business courses that dominate the distance education 'market'. A significant statistic, referred to in Breen (2006), citing Yates (2004), reveals that in the early years of the twenty first century teacher training courses were seen to account for three quarters of all distance learning education courses in Francophone Africa and a half of all distance learning education courses in Anglophone Africa. This shows that distance education is a phenomenon that crosses continents as well as disciplines, but Britain, the locus of this study, has also been at the forefront of historical developments.

In earlier literature, prior to the digital age and the advent of online learning, Thorpe (1987, p. 56) describes the British tradition of Open Learning which is best illustrated by the existence of the Open University that was founded and funded by the UK government in 1969. Since its first enrolment of almost 50,000 students in 1971, the organisation has grown threefold and has not only become a leading provider of distance education courses but has also become prominent in the field of research into education and pedagogy. Contemporary relevant papers produced by Open University researchers include Laurillard and Mc Andrew (2002), Jones & Lea (2008), and Mc Andrew & Wilson (2008) where the authors argue for online projects to be freely shared amongst partner institutions.

Campion and Guiton (1991), as described in Holmberg (2000, p. 1), have divided distance education research into two broad categories. The first category emphasises "endogenous" categories, namely concerns within the actual work done in the provision of education by distance means. Such issues might include the methods and media used in the delivery process. Although there was little intensive research into distance education until the second half of the twentieth century (ibid), most researchers appear to have focused on these "endogenous" categories. In this chpater we have opted to focus on what Holmberg (2000: ibid) defines as Campion and Guiton's (1991) second category, of "exogenous" concerns. The reason for this focus is that we are more interested in aspects of its "economic, technological, demographic, cultural, political and social contexts."

The latter four categories, for purposes of this relatively short chapter, can be covered in a brief description of the institution, a large 'redbrick' university belonging to the Russell Group. Having ventured into providing Master degrees in the discipline of education at the turn of the last century, the university has begun an innovative project to allow a select group of students to undertake part time doctoral studies, while embedded in their research context as described in the next section.

This is essentially the type of "dual mode" system described by Rocha Trindade et al. (2000, p. 4) as the institution having introduced "distance learning methods in some programmes, aimed at extra-mural students, in parallel with their conventional operation." The aforementioned authors do go on to say that when the distance learning stream is offered in dual-mode institutions, "it tends to be assigned a lower priority and to be allocated fewer resources than the conventional stream" (2000, p. 5). They cite reasons for this as being "cultural inertia" of older institutions and a fear of "dangerous innovations" (ibid). Such fears may well only be eradicated with evidence of success in the delivery of these new courses.

However there is clearly a market for such courses as evidenced by the amount of students currently undertaking part time studies in UK Higher Education as evidenced by figure one in which it is apparent that the majority of students undertaking postgraduate degree courses are now enrolling on a part-time basis. This is most pronounced in Medicine *(or subjects allied to it)*, Business, Architecture, and Education which are all vocational subjects wherein theory is closely allied to practice in the workplace, and furthermore these are competitive professions in which it is often neither practical nor beneficial to take a long term career break.

SETTING THE STAGE

Michael Moore (1995, p. 1) describes how *The American Center for the Study of Distance Education* hosted the *Third Distance Education Research Symposium Conference*, in which a group of researchers were asked to consider "the effect of research on improving the quality of distance education practice". In setting out a framework for analysis, they identified "four key research areas: course design, instruction, policy and administration, and learners and learning" (p. 4). The following sections of this chpater draw on that framework as a means of analysis, with the main focus being placed upon the experience of learners and learning.

In this section we will concentrate on the course design aspect of Moore's (1995, p. 4) framework briefly and describe the concerns that led to the development of the in-context PhD programme, as well as the steps that were followed in what could be described as a joint effort by both former distance (DL) Masters students and some of their tutors.

The initiative to put together a programme that would allow successful DL Masters candidates to move on to doctoral studies was very much a bottom-up endeavour. Several members of the Faculty of Education, all of whom were tutors in the DL MA TESOL programme decided to join efforts in order to develop a proposal that would convince the university's authorities that offering 'in-context' PhD programmes would be a success both in financial and academic terms. Perhaps rather unsurprisingly, the main concern raised by the authorities at the time was related to the difficulties of effectively monitoring the academic progress of potential PhD candidates who would be geographically removed from the university premises most of the time. They argued that the quality of academic work might suffer if candidates were not campus-based and therefore not within easy reach of materials, courses, tutors and supervisors, echoing the aforementioned senti-

Table 1. Number of full-time and part-time higher education students by subject area at UK HEIs: 2007/08 (Higher Education Statistics Agency, 2009)

	First degree		Other undergraduate		Postgraduate		Total
	Full-time	Part-time	Full-time	Part-time	Full-time	Part-time	
Medicine and dentistry	43,440	110	380	50	7,670	10,160	**61,810**
Subjects allied to medicine	86,545	27,435	57,365	68,920	11,690	35,165	**287,120**
Biological sciences	107,890	17,310	3,800	6,010	16,650	9,940	**161,600**
Veterinary science	4,080	55	0	0	490	225	**4,850**
Agriculture & related subjects	7,140	425	2,910	4,540	1,640	1,025	**17,680**
Physical sciences	51,460	6,470	1,225	5,185	13,900	3,890	**82,130**
Mathematical sciences	22,270	3,725	500	2,505	3,600	1,520	**34,120**
Computer science	50,920	9,355	4,780	10,580	13,425	6,520	**95,580**
Engineering and technology	74,155	11,165	6,270	12,175	23,875	11,800	**139,440**
Architecture, building & planning	27,785	8,625	3,675	8,015	5,900	9,090	**63,090**
Social studies	105,135	19,605	5,565	28,925	24,325	15,315	**198,870**
Law	53,020	9,200	1,140	4,205	13,095	8,585	**89,245**
Business & administrative studies	145,470	17,440	11,300	37,715	47,455	51,075	**310,455**
Mass communications and documentation	34,240	1,510	1,510	1,520	5,705	3,485	**47,970**
Languages	75,690	9,590	2,345	33,380	9,890	5,155	**136,050**
Historical & philosophical studies	52,115	12,800	445	15,225	8,340	7,705	**96,630**
Creative arts & design	119,590	5,125	10,010	6,800	10,815	6,550	**158,890**
Education	42,830	9,755	8,900	47,780	29,780	63,250	**202,295**
Combined	4,915	28,460	1,205	81,285	135	2,300	**118,300**
Total	**1,108,685**	**198,155**	**123,320**	**374,810**	**248,380**	**252,755**	**2,306,105**

ments described in Rocha Trindade et al. (2000, p. 5). A major issue related to this concern was that of research methods training, given the fact that the university did not offer a DL MSc in Educational Research Methods, the completion of which was a pre-requisite for entry to doctoral programmes. Despite these apparent setbacks, the DL tutors decided the endeavour was worth pursuing.

In the knowledge that several former DL Masters candidates were quite keen to continue their studies at the same university, the tutors and some of these candidates decided to gather information on what other prestigious UK universities were offering along the lines of in-context PhD provision. This 'market research' endeavour had a two-fold purpose; it would allow candidates to contact other universities with a view to applying, and it would also help the tutors to present a more convincing case to their still somewhat sceptical employers.

After some more discussion, potential in-context PhD candidates were allowed to go through the formal application process. Should their research proposals meet the requirements and expected academic standards, they would receive offers and be allowed to enrol as part-time PhD students. These 'test cases' would negotiate the frequency and duration of their visits according to their training and supervisory needs. They were required to submit assignments towards the completion of the MSc modules, having to attend at least some classes at the beginning of each semester. It was also agreed that once they started, such candidates would be closely monitored and only allowed to continue if they could prove an ability to meet the same standards as on-site students.

In short, this was the bottom-up process that resulted in the creation of an in-context PhD programme at the university. In the next sections we will describe the experience of the in-context PhDs in terms of technological and affective affordances.

CASE DESCRIPTION

Technological Concerns and Solutions

This section discusses the technological solutions that are being used to address the administrative, pedagogical and support requirements of the programme, echoing the second and third steps of Moore's (1995, p. 4) framework, namely issues of "instruction" and "policy and administration." Davis (2004, p. 3) has written that "building the infrastructure for online learning requires that many factors be considered, so it is difficult to provide a straightforward checklist or recipe to follow" and that "an understanding of the technological background of the intended students is crucial". Since the participants had already been chosen on the basis of competence, the creation of an infrastructure could take precedence over what might be termed as a familiarisation stage. A non-exhaustive list of administrative needs included the delivery of important announcements, as well as receiving and responding to student queries. Pedagogical needs varied from module to module, but generally included the delivery of learning materials such as journal articles, notes etc. (input), the provision of a venue for students to engage in collaborative learning tasks, and the development of assessment procedures, as well as the facilitation of academic supervision. The latter of course is particularly salient to the success of any doctoral study. It is widely recognised in the academic world that good supervision is essential for eventual success when pursuing studies at this level. Finally, with regard to support, provision had to be made for delivering technical assistance to a geographically dispersed student body, as well as fostering a sense of community amongst participants. This emphasis on community is a cornerstone in the work of Gilly Salmon, one of the key theorists in the field, whose seminal (2000) five step framework on the development of e-learning projects cites online socialisation as being a prerequisite for progress towards further stages of information exchange and knowledge construction. White (2003, p. 147) makes a further assertion that "one of the key aspects of the initial experience of a distance or online learning environment is that of learner confidence" and that "a way of responding to the issue of learner confidence is to provide opportunities for interaction with other learners."

This socialisation could also be interpreted as playing a key role in Moore's (1995, p. 4) framework since shared learning can only occur between learners who have actually developed some form of relationship at the point of receiving their instruction.

The needs of learners, based around the theoretical construct of Moore's (ibid) framework and the practical experience of instruction and support, are summarized as follows.

Administrative
- Announcements
- Student queries

Pedagogical
- Supervision
- Input
- Collaborative learning
- Assessment

Supportive
- Technical
- Community-building

Table 2. Uses of the VLE in programme modules

Module	Administrative	Pedagogical			Supportive	
	Announcements	*Input*	*Collaborative learning*	*Assessment*	*Technical*	*Community building*
A		✓				
B	✓	✓				
C		✓	✓			✓
D	✓	✓				
E		✓				
F						
G		✓		✓	✓	
H		✓				✓

The main technological components that were being used to address these needs were an amalgamation of a Virtual Learning Environment (VLE), various email networks, IT support, a collection of electronic resources, such as electronic databases and online journals, available from the university library, and a blog shared by the programme participants.

The Virtual Learning Environment

The Virtual Learning Environment was primarily used to deliver learning materials to participants who were not physically located in the university premises. Essentially, the VLE is a web-based platform that gives participants access to different modules in which they are enrolled. Module tutors can use it as a repository for learning materials, such as handouts and presentations which can be downloaded by participants. In its most basic form this can mean the mere addition of lecture slides and lecture notes, but it is commonly recognised in the field that learning must have some form of interactivity in order for the VLE to facilitate a deeper construction of knowledge. A second important component is the online discussion forums, which are activated at the module tutors' discretion and enable communication among participants. Other optional features include a real-time chat applet for synchronous communication and assessment tools, such as online test generators and a submission tool which can be used by students to upload assignments, although these were not extensively used.

In practice, on this course, the use of the VLE varied from module to module, as can be seen in Table 2. Nearly all modules made extensive use of the VLE for delivery of learning materials in slide or note format. The tutors of one particular module, who formed part of a university unit with extensive experience in providing distance learning, used the VLE to host an extensive set of materials which were optimised for online access and self-study. However, in most cases, the learning materials available came merely in the form of handouts or presentations that were simultaneously being used in the onsite programme. Very often there was little consideration given, in their design, for the explicit needs of extra-mural students. This provision was not always received favourably by the distance students, as can be seen in the following email extract from one participant to his academic supervisor:

I feel that the support provided [...] is not consistent and definitely less than helpful in addressing my needs. To be fair, I have to acknowledge that they do send out all the [...] presentations

Table 3. Uses of email in the programme

Network	Administrative		Pedagogical			Supportive	
	Announcements	*Student queries*	*Super-vision*	*Collaborative learning*	*Assessment*	*Technical*	*Community building*
Administrative	✓	✓			✓	(✓)	
Tutors and supervisors		✓	✓			(✓)	✓
Peers				✓		✓	✓

used in the [onsite] lectures (if at somewhat irregular intervals), but I believe that these are rather poor substitutes for the input provided in the sessions. Also, there seems to be very little interest in replicating the practical tasks carried out onsite.

As hinted in the previous extract, only limited use was made of the VLE to implement collaborative learning activities. It is unclear to what extent this omission has impacted learning outcomes, but some students seemed to perceive this as an important limitation, or –in the words of one participant– 'it's as if I am paying to be assessed and do most of the teaching by myself'. Although the VLE did offer the possibility for both asynchronous and synchronous communication, it was not generally used for announcements, support or social interaction. Similarly, very limited use was made of the VLE for assessment purposes. Indeed, a feature of the institution studied herein has been that previous work on the VLE, in areas such as discussion boards, counts for nothing in terms of final assessment. This led one participant to often ask the question of what particular purpose was served by assigning tasks to classes/groups and then rewarding those who did them no more favourably than those who did not. It seemed to contradict the whole ethos and purpose of creating a vibrant VLE. In summary, as evidenced below, there was graphic contradiction in the utilisation of a resource that ought to have been at the heart of the distance/extra-mural learning experience.

Email Networks and Mailing Lists

Apart from the VLE, the technology component that proved most helpful in generating and maintaining cohesion among the programme participants was email communication. Within the programme, three communication networks appeared to have gradually achieved this: (a) a network connecting students to the school administration, which mostly carried formal communications pertaining to administrative issues and assessment; (b) a network connecting students to their tutors or academic supervisors, which mainly carried information pertaining to pedagogical matters; and (c) a network connecting students to their peers, which was mainly used for academic collaboration and mutual support (Table 3).

Official communication between the school and in-context participants was conducted almost exclusively by email. Most of the communications were disseminated by means of mailing lists to which both onsite and in-context students were included, without differentiation. Some examples of topics covered by this communication were: registration and fees, training opportunities, conferences and seminars as well as social events. Student queries regarding administrative and technical matters were also usually dealt with through this channel of communication, although telephone was occasionally used. In addition to the above, the assignments that were used to assess the participants' progress were generally submitted by email to the school administration, although –paradoxically– feedback was provided in the form of hard copies that were sent to the participants by mail.

Communication between participants and their tutors and academic supervisors was also conducted primarily using email. Some indicative topics discussed included the students' academic progress and topic-specific queries, with occasional advice provided on technical matters. The frequency and effectiveness of this communication varied greatly, depending on the individual preferences of the persons involved. According to an informal feedback document submitted by a participant, this process 'is without doubt the most reliable source of support in terms of ease of access, timeliness and comprehensiveness of the responses'. In the view of the same person, 'the amount of support I have come expect from tutors has not been consistently high' but was nevertheless 'empowering with regard to working independently'. On the whole, there were only a few instances of sporadic breakdowns in this communication, and such occasional frustrations did not appear to have long-term effects on the progression of the participants.

Arguably the most vibrant aspect of the programme was the use of email communication between the participants. Although the scope of this communication precludes generalisations, two salient themes included collaborative learning activities alongside the psychological bulwark of mutual support. Figure 1 depicts the average number of email messages generated by each participant over a typical month of the programme. Furthermore, it is anecdotally attested that such activity tended to increase in the weeks immediately prior to the deadlines for the submission of assessed work, as participants exchanged views about their research and provided peer review for each other's assignments. The regular exchange of numerous messages partially replicated similar interaction opportunities enjoyed by the onsite learner community, and generated a rich and lively educational discourse focussing on the participants' research. In other words, email seemed

Figure 1. Average number of email messages / student generated by the 2008 cohort between 30 September and 30 October 2008

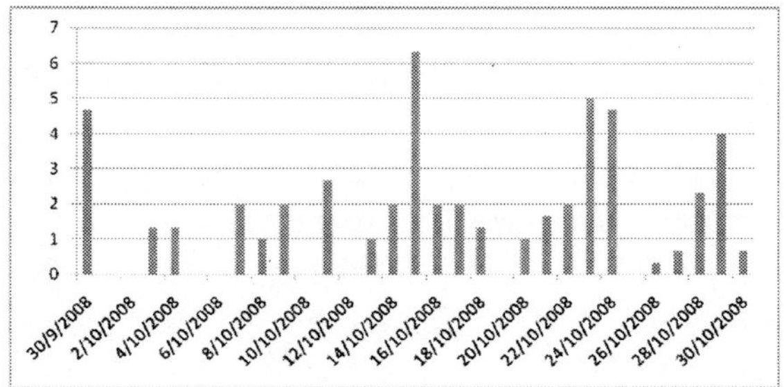

to complement the VLE by addressing perceived lacunae in the provision for collaborative learning activities and support.

IT Support

Providing adequate IT support to a geographically dispersed student body constitutes a major challenge as acknowledged in Salmon's (2000) framework where she asserts that the first stage of online course development is access and motivation. Generally speaking, the students' IT needs include the delivery of required software and the provision of IT support to facilitate the installation and operation of the software. Breen (2007) has highlighted how lack of access to resources in the context of developing countries can hinder online educational programmes. Yet lack of access is not restricted to developing countries alone. Lack of access does not solely refer to hardware issues. It can also refer to inability to access the required software or entrance to particular sites or domains of study.

The pedagogical and research requirements of this programme required that the students had access to a wide variety of electronic tools, including a word processing package, statistical analysis software, Computer Assisted Qualitative Data Analysis Software (CAQDAS) as well as various ancillary computer programmes, such as a Virtual Private Network (VPN) client, etc. In order to meet these needs, licensed versions of software packages were made available for distribution to the programme participants through direct download from the university website, with protective measures in place to limit exterior or unlicensed access.

Unfortunately, it appears that many programme participants experienced considerable difficulties in downloading and installing the software packages. These difficulties might be attributed, at least in part, to the technically demanding nature of the installation process. For example, the installation of the recommended statistical analysis package on a new computer presupposes the download, installation and configuration of the VPN client and a utility for reading.iso computer files, followed by four separate downloads and installations for the actual software package and subsequent patches. These difficulties were amplified by the fact that the participants tended to use diverse hardware running localised versions of computer operating systems. Further confounding the situation was the fact that the university IT support staff appeared to operate best when providing assistance on a face-to-face basis, whereas their competence in diagnosing problems and communicating solutions using alternative means of communication was not uniform. Aside from this, they also tended to have difficulties relating to the whole concept of the needs of extra-mural students.

Due to such technical difficulties and occasional licensing restrictions, several participants resorted to alternative means in order to procure the required software, leading to a pronounced lack of standardization. For instance, at a time a single cohort of students was using two different CAQDAS packages, three different versions of the recommended statistical software and two only partially compatible versions of a popular word processing program. This heterogeneity created additional demands on IT support and the teaching staff, and placed certain limits to the participants' ability to collaborate effectively. One participant had to seek guidance from their own workplace rather than the institution providing the degree, after having travelled in vain to the provider in order to get technical support. In Moore's (1995, p. 4) framework, this appears to cause some tension between issues of providing administrative support and facilitating ease of use for learners and learning.

Other Resources

Access to relevant literature formed a requisite for successful participation in the programme. To address this need, the university library boasts an extensive collection of electronic resources, ranging from electronic databases and e-books to online access to most major journals pertinent to the participants' research. Access to these resources is provided through the VPN for reasons of data security. Although training in the use of these resources appears to have been designed with the needs of onsite students in mind, access seems to have been unproblematic for all participants, judging from the lack of reported difficulties in our data.

A recent addition to the technological components which support the programme has come in the form of a blog shared by faculty and students (onsite and in-context). By providing a space where current and former students can share insights and useful information, it is hoped that the blog will help to reinforce the sense of community among programme participants. In addition, the blog provides outreach to a broader research community and may prove helpful in terms of recruiting future cohorts of students. At the time of writing, the blog is a relatively new development, so it is not at the moment possible to draw inferences regarding the participants' attitudes towards it, or its effectiveness in addressing its goals.

Table 4. Summary of the uses of technological components

Component	Administrative		Pedagogical				Supportive	
	Announcements	*Student queries*	*Supervision*	*Input*	*Collaborative learning*	*Assessment*	*Technical*	*Community building*
VLE	(✓)			✓	(✓)	(✓)		(✓)
Email	✓	✓	✓		✓	✓	✓	✓
IT support							✓	
Library e-resources				✓				
Blog	(✓)							✓

Concluding Remarks on Technological Concerns and Solutions

In this section, we described how the programme made use of various technological components in order to address the participants' administrative, pedagogical and support needs. This information is summarized in Table 4.

As can be seen in Table 4, the various technology components were used flexibly to complement each other. For instance, email communication emerged as an alternative way to implement collaborative learning activities and provide social support, as the relevant provisions in the VLE (online forums) proved to be less effective in these functions. Similarly, the development of a shared blog while the programme was already underway constitutes an example of a flexible adaptation to a perceived lack in the provision for fostering a sense of community.

A second inference that can be made from the table is that a strong tendency exists to use relatively unsophisticated technological solutions, even though more elaborate technological components are in place. This is lucidly demonstrated in the students' pronounced preference for email as a vehicle for collaborative learning, even in cases where online discussion boards had been deployed by the course tutors. Although the data at our disposal does not help to explain the reasons why the VLE boards did not appeal to students, it is possible that the directness and confidentiality inherent in email communication weighed on their preferences. A similar reluctance to abandon 'tried and tested' methods can be observed in the university policy of using email for important announcements and assessment purposes, even though it is possible to use the VLE for such purposes. Another manifestation of this trend towards technological conservativism is in evidence in the learning materials which have been made available through the VLE: in most cases, to date, these materials were in the form of presentations and handouts, and had not been optimised for online access.

Drawing on the above, it would appear that the University has not been entirely successful in fully exploiting the potential offered by the technological components at its disposal. This limitation is counterbalanced, however, by flexible adaptation practices and by the emergence of a vibrant online community which has made full use of the potential of relatively unsophisticated tools.

Furthermore, in terms of the marketability of this course, the study herein is not designed to denigrate its worthiness in any way. It is purely designed to provide a comprehensive analysis of the successes and failures because as Breen (2007), citing Davis (2004) states, the greatest failure of online learning ventures at the present time is that so many of them are "doomed to succeed", which essentially means that there is a lack of honest analysis about what has actually been delivered and how successful that delivery has been. Courses such as this one have huge potential, particularly at a time when there is such an emphasis on advanced professional training, but in order to realise that potential it is important for them to ensure that the technological elements of instruction and support are fully addressed. If they are not then essentially the project becomes stunted at the point of Salmon's (2000) first step in the pyramid of advancement towards the successful delivery of an online learning course. This would be a great waste and a serious issue with regard to the management of the course because the energy and synergy of the participants has demonstrated that extra mural students, as referred to throughout the work of Rocha Trindade et al. (2000), can play a vital role in the life of any contemporary institution providing third level education, regardless of academia's inherent cultural inertia (ibid, p. 5). There are clearly challenges that need to be addressed and technology, by the very nature of distance learning, is at the core of them.

Developing Collaborative Strategies

As acknowledged by many authors such as Keegan (1990), the distance mode of education is often a fragile one, even more so if the programme is not yet well-established, as was the case with the in-context PhD the three authors of this chapter embarked upon. Therefore, the affective and social aspects of taking part in such a venture undoubtedly played a major role in participants' perceptions of its effectiveness and their personal success. In this light, this section describes the impact of the social and academic strategies for collaboration developed by the three candidates, which at times compensated for what was perceived as insufficient or inadequate academic support.

At the start of the programme, candidates were introduced virtually and communication was encouraged by their respective PhD supervisors, who explained their hope was to 'build up an interactive and mutually supportive group of PT/DL candidates' (e-mail communication, August 2008). Despite the lack of geographical proximity which is said to play a key role in the effectiveness of collaboration (Kraut et al. 1988), the development of a sound personal and professional relationship was marked by several features of the communication that took place between them. For the sake of clarity, we have divided the strategies into academic and social ones, although such distinction is an artificial one and it could be argued that some contain elements of both categories.

The Academic Strategies

We have labelled 'academic' all those strategies which enabled candidates to make progress in terms of academic work. We will now describe each of these academic strategies by drawing on examples from our e-mail data.

Virtual Immediacy

Despite the asynchronous, mediated nature of e-mail, the fact that the authors were online daily and made a point of replying swiftly contributed to developing a sense of immediacy, giving the communication a certain feel of synchronicity. This can be seen in the extracts from one of their e-mail conversations taking place over a few hours on May 7, 2009:

'Forgive me for being slow, but just to help me understand: in the provinces, the private sector is served by some 300 teachers, most of whom are employed by the institute you work for. There are few teachers who are either self-employed or who work for smaller institutes. Am I getting this right?'

'Yes, that's right. In fact there aren't many small institutes, in many places this is the only one. But there are a few Ts who work for secondary state

schools. Hope this is clearer - my earlier message was messy!'

'OK I get it now. It's just that it's different from what happens in [...] More often than not, teachers are poorly trained and their schools, which are marginally profitable, cannot afford professional development programmes. Then there's the public school system, [...]'

This virtual immediacy was a key academic strategy in that it helped candidates to make progress with their work without undue delays. However, applying it also contributed to building the social aspects of the relationship, in that it helped to build a sense of trust.

Reflection on Learning

Throughout their conversations, candidates monitored their academic progress and critically evaluated the quality of their learning experience. This 'group monitoring' of their learning contributed to their academic work and also to developing a sense of trust. The following exchanges took place over a few hours of the same day (July 9, 2009), once again evidencing the frequency, swiftness and quality of the communication:

'I actually spoke to a guy who I work with who is a mathematician and his suggestions made far more sense in terms of starting out with Excel, using that to calculate means and standard deviations. I have to honestly say that in five minutes of talking to him things made far more sense than six months of trying to work things out for myself on the basis of the lecture notes on Blackboard.'

'I really understand your feelings about deep and surface knowledge. I myself feel that with this assignment I have proved to myself that I am capable of starting from scratch and learning quite a lot about something very specific (factor analysis), though I don't think I have managed to learn much more than that... Hardly deep learning as you say...'

'Before sending this email off, let me just add that you make a very good point when comparing the different forms of input (your mathematician friend and the online materials). I wonder how much of this difference is due to problems inherent in distance learning, and how much is due to the structure and provisions of this particular programme. I am also curious as to how this programme we are in would fit in the taxonomy of distance learning / blended learning / e-learning etc. Interesting questions, which we may well revisit at some future time.'

This metacognitive strategy was obviously an academic asset in itself, but had an added value in that reflections were shared among the three candidates. This public articulation of thoughts facilitated the finding of solutions and therefore the quality of the learning experience.

Detailed Feedback

Despite the fact that the students were often juggling their jobs, studies and personal lives, they were always keen to offer each other detailed feedback on assignments and other pieces. An example of this kind of feedback is illustrated in the extract below, which forms part of an email dated March 6, 2009, discussing an article one of the students was preparing:

'At the same time, I recognize some tension between your desire as an objective researcher to maintain some distance from the subject studied, and perhaps to respect issues of anonymity on the one hand, and the qualitative demand for greater transparency on the other. This was quite evident in the opacity surrounding your role (really, how did

you get involved in this?), and the not-too-specific references to [a university]. I am not suggesting that you should have done something differently, just saying that I appreciate how difficult it must have been to find a proper balance between these conflicting demands.'

As they became more and more involved in their colleagues' work, they also came to rely increasingly on each other's critical advice and comments, as can be seen in the following e-mail exchanges taking place on May 7, 2009:

'This is some very limited feedback on your assignment. As I say I have been hampered by the failure to get [the recommended statistical analysis software] at an earlier stage and therefore have concentrated on a few methods only. Therefore a lot of this is still all Greek to me as they say. I hope this is useful in some form or another.'

'Thanks so much, your feedback is extremely useful!!! I am planning to make some changes to my assignment over the weekend based on both your comments and [...]'s. I promise to have a look at your assignment tonight when I get back from work.'

For some candidates, this mutual help was clearly linked to their academic success, as expressed in the words of one of them on June 23, 2009:

'it was 75% so phew! And thanks to both of you - this is also yours:-) I honestly couldn't have done it without your feedback and advice!'

Collaborative Work

The quality of communication was sound enough for candidates to work collaboratively on tasks for the research training courses, as can be seen below in an e-mail dated October 14, 2008, at a moment when a task to be presented to one of the university tutors was being prepared:

'Let's go ahead with this content analysis of the Guardian articles. Would I need to analyse the article before [the tutor's] class tomorrow? Shall I select one myself and look for occurrences of the kinds of collocations [the tutor] was mentioning earlier? As a back-up plan, if we don't feel we are ready tomorrow, I could simply tell [the tutor] about our work in progress and then show him the finished product next Wednesday?' (October 14, 2008)

Such collaborative tasks were always of a high standard and thus provided some evidence to the otherwise unaware outside world of the university about how effective their collaboration was. It was difficult to ascertain though whether or not this collaboration was being recognised in any formal capacity by those responsible for design and delivery of the course, and whether or not this altered any of the inherent inertia shown towards distance learning.

The so-called academic strategies described above were supported by others of a more social nature, which we outline below.

The Social Strategies

We have defined as social those strategies which provided the necessary affective support for the collaborative relationship to develop effectively. Like previously, we will now describe such strategies by drawing on our data.

Transactional and Interpersonal Elements

At first communication was mostly transactional, dealing with all kinds of academic matters, although it soon came to incorporate interpersonal elements as well, which helped the candidates to get to know one another better and therefore develop a sense of trust. Although the purpose of most exchanges was to complete some kind of academic transaction, the writers generally included interpersonal elements which were not just formulaic openings but showed an honest interest in each other's personal lives, as can be seen below (October 13, 2009):

'At the moment I'm having a bit of a hard time deciding what to do next year. After [daughter] and the family, the PhD is my number one (two) priority, so I don't want to have too many classes to teach.'

'The good thing, I suppose, is that you have completed data collection and analysis is moving along, so you will probably have done most of the substantive work before [daughter] is born (...) Of course, if there is anything I can do to help with the workload you will always let me know:-)'

None of the candidates ever referred to their relationship as a friendship, probably because of its academic foundations and essentially virtual nature. However, it is fair to say that certain behaviours such as offering unconditional support and advice coincided with traditional friendship values.

Advice and Opinions

As their collaborative relationship developed, candidates offered each other useful advice and opinions which were often related to their academic lives but sometimes had an impact that went beyond the strictly academic, as seen in the following extracts (November 26, 2008):

'I can see why you might be feeling apprehensive, and I do sympathise, but I think that this apprehension you are feeling may be preventing you from assessing the true dimensions of the problem and from seeing the range of possible solutions.'

'I believe you need to step back and not view this in such a self critical light. All that has happened is that you have changed direction. You now need to reshape the assignment around that change.'

'Thanks, thanks and thanks again for helping me put this into perspective, and for all the helpful advice [...] It's good to know you two are out there to help when I panic:-)'

Humour

The occasional use of humour was also a feature of some exchanges, helping to strike a balance between the seriousness and dedication to academic work and the lighter social aspects of communication, as can be seen in the e-mail extract below (October 4, 2009):

'On a lighter note, between our studies, I just wanted to clarify that today's newspaper stories about [city] have absolutely no link to me visiting [football stadium] on Tuesday afternoon. I cut and pasted an extract in case you haven't heard the news and then added a picture "those arrested in [city] over recent days were planning attacks at key targets in the city and had been seen photographing themselves outside some well known landmarks there". I can categorically deny that I was planning any attempt to sabotage the second most successful soccer team (...)'

Many instances of humour and bantering like the one above occurred throughout the data-collection period, increasing in frequency as the relationship developed and candidates got to know one another better.

Figure 2. Compensatory mechanism which led to the development of an effective collaborative relationship between the candidates

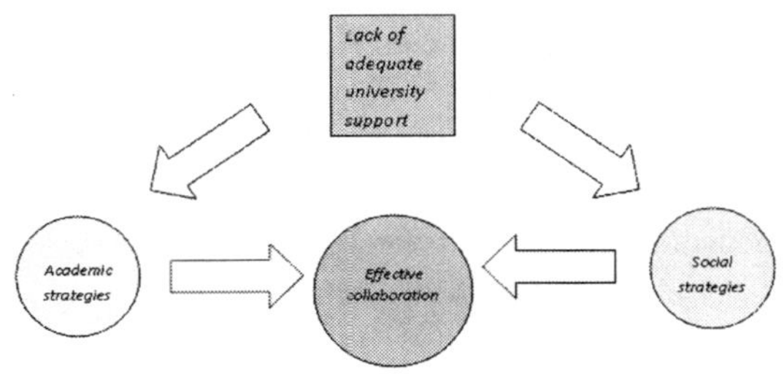

Concluding Remarks on Collaborative Strategies

Both the academic and social strategies described in this section contributed to building a mutually supportive collaborative academic relationship, the success of which came about as a result of the efforts made by the candidates themselves rather than the university.

The effectiveness of such collaboration was not only essential in terms of academic progress, but also compensated for the lack of social contact with other students and the occasional inadequacy or absence of academic support. It is worth mentioning that although the three authors spent short periods of time on campus every year, they did not develop solid academic or social relationships with other on-site students. Also, their visits did not always coincide, with the result that only one of them succeeded in briefly meeting the other two, so their collaborative relationship was developed mostly over e-mail contact. Also, the social and academic strategies developed by the three authors was in many ways seen as going beyond the expectations for effective face-to-face collaboration, as expressed by one of them (August 19, 2009):

'Like you, I honestly doubt that on-site students interact more profitably than we do! Certainly worth further investigation:-)'

If there is any degree of truth in the above statement then it clearly challenges the notion that education, on campus, somehow remains superior to an extra mural education even in the so called digital age. At a point when the British government is ushering in radical changes to funding for the university system there is a need for institutions to adapt to changing circumstances. Distance education can be a core component of this adaptation. From the data/dialogue transcribed herein it could even be argued that the onus is not on distance students to prove that their system of study can be equally effective, but rather on those who doubt its feasibility to offer reasons more substantial than the mere fact of tradition.

CURRENT CHALLENGES FACING THE ORGANISATION

The experience of delivering this programme has demonstrated the feasibility of conducting in-context PhD studies without making sacrifices in terms of academic rigour. As can be expected of a pilot programme, it has also highlighted certain aspects of the pedagogical and supportive provision where improvements are possible.

One such challenge pertains to the structure of the programme, and the provision for research training in particular. As was seen above, students registered for PhD studies are required to complete research training in the form of several 15-credit modules focussing on a variety of topics ranging from the generation to the analysis of both qualitative and quantitative data. An inherent challenge exists in reconciling the breadth of this coverage with the specific in-depth needs of conducting doctoral research. This challenge has been amplified by the modular structure of the research training provision, which seemed to discourage mixed-method research and encourage fragmentation (e.g. by artificially dividing data collection and analysis). It seems fair to claim that, as a result, some students have experienced difficulty in making the assessed work that was produced for these modules relevant to their particular research needs.

Despite the best of intentions of faculty and students, the tuition and supervision of the pilot cohort has not been entirely unproblematic. Some difficulties may be attributed to the fact that not all faculty members were adept or experienced in delivering tuition to 'extra-mural' students or monitoring their progress. Furthermore, it would appear that, at least in some cases, the expectations of students and tutors were at variance. For example, there are some indications in the data that some students expected a more involved role from the module tutors than was actually provided, and that some faculty members may have been uncomfortable with the low frequency of meetings with the students. In view of the above, finding a workable balance between these expectations and requirements and enhancing the tutors' ability to support and monitor the progress of the students constitute requisites for the successful continuation of the programme.

A final challenge that the programme will need to address is the development of a cohesive student community providing synchronic links between in-context students and their onsite counterparts, as well as diachronic links between different cohorts of students. This is necessary for affective reasons, as it will help to counter the feelings of isolation that can hinder the student's progression, and for pedagogical reasons, as it can lead to the productive cross-fertilisation of ideas. Previously, it was argued that the online forums which could contribute towards this goal were underutilised, and that alternatives such as email communication and, more recently, a blog, have been developed. Paradoxically, the success of the pilot cohort in maintaining group cohesion may be attributed to the small number and shared interests of the students in it. However, as the number of participants grows with the influx of new student cohorts, this cohesion may be threatened. It is therefore imperative that technological and other solutions are explored to address these needs.

SOLUTIONS AND RECOMMENDATIONS

In the previous sections, it was pointed out that the design and the implementation of the programme was typified by the emergence of bottom-up processes which allowed the programme participants to flexibly adjust to the challenges that inhere in in-context PhD studies. In this section we will make a number of additional suggestions which build on this finding, and which we believe will be helpful in addressing the challenges outlined above.

First, it would probably prove useful for the university authorities to rethink the structure of the research training programme for subsequent cohorts. Rather than prescribing a standardised regimen of research training modules to all students, it should be possible for each student to negotiate a research training path that is tailored to the specific needs of their own research. It is expected that such a change will have a major impact on addressing the perceived lack of congruence between the current research training programme and the research interests of the individual students. It would also empower students by giving them responsibility for designing research plans, identifying requisite skills and working towards acquiring them. Of course, the students' needs for in-depth training will have to be counterbalanced with the university policy for developing a comprehensive research competence. Extensive input from the students' academic supervisors delivered at an early stage may be helpful in striking a proper balance between these conflicting needs.

On the question of supervision, it may be necessary to rethink some aspects of supervisory and tuition arrangements, as they have on occasion proved less than ideal. One possible change would be to replace the current system of *ad hoc* communication between the students and their academic supervisors with a framework of regular contacts (e.g. face-to-face meetings, telephone communications, email exchanges). Considering the occasional communication break-downs between students and module tutors, it may also be helpful to establish formal communication channels between these two groups. It is expected that these changes should increase the level of support available to students, while providing more opportunities for faculty to identify and voice possible concerns regarding the students' progress.

To address the challenge of maintaining and expanding the vibrant online community that emerged within the programme, it is imperative that support is given to initiatives that connect in-context students to the university and e-replicate to a certain extent the sense of community shared by onsite participants. Furthermore, in order to enhance the bonds between students who belong to different cohorts, it should be possible to pair existing students with new intakes through a mentorship project. In addition to the obvious practical and affective benefits for new students, it is expected that such an initiative will provide programme participants with valuable experience in assuming responsibility for a younger, less experienced researcher.

This research has shown that the teaching and learning at higher level are moving towards a better utilization of ICT as means of exploration, rather than just a tool. We believe that this case study has demonstrated how an innovative educational project can be designed and implemented effectively through bottom-up processes that make full use of relatively straightforward technological means to address valid concerns raised by sceptics. We strongly feel that the continued success of such a pioneering programme depends, to a great extent, on the adoption of a flexible and open-minded attitude which embraces initiative and innovation. Thankfully universities appear to be moving in this direction, and the institution described herein, should be commended on striving towards an adoption of practices suited to the digital age, and changing needs of contemporary society.

REFERENCES

Badat, S. (2004). *The diversity of higher educational provision: Propositions on distance higher education policy and regulation towards equity, access, quality and social and economic responsiveness.* Paper Presented at the 2004 All Africa Ministers Conference on Distance Education, Cape Town, South Africa.

Breen, P. (2006). Coming out of the darkness of the past. *Turkish Online Journal of Distance Education, 7*(4).

Breen, P. (2007). Lessons from an international e-learning project. *International Review of Research in Open and Distance Learning, 8*(3).

Campion, M., & Guiton, P. (1991). Economic instrumentalism and integration in Australian external studies. *Open Learning, 6*(2), 12–20. doi:10.1080/0268051910060203

Davis, A. (2004). Developing an infrastructure for online learning. In T. Anderson & F. Elloumi (Eds.), *Theory and practice of online learning.* Athabasca, AB: AUPress. Retrieved April 7, 2007, from http://cde.athabascau.ca/online_book/ch4.html

Higher Education Statistics Agency. (2009). *Students in higher education institutions 2007/2008.* Retrieved on May 30, 2010, from http://www.hesa.ac.uk/

Holmberg, B. (2000). *Status and Trends of Distance Education.* Retrieved 21 February 2010 from: www.eden-online.org/papers/rw/holmberg_article_for_web.pdf.

Jones, S., & Lea, M. R. (2008). Digital literacies in the lives of undergraduate students: Exploring personal and curricular spheres of influence. *The Electronic Journal of E-Learning, 6*(3), 207–216.

Kanuka, H., & Jugdev, K. (2006). Distance education MBA students: An investigation into the use of an orientation course to address academic and social integration issues. *Open Learning*, *21*(2), 153–166. doi:10.1080/02680510600715578

Keegan, D. (1990). *Foundations of distance education* (2nd ed.). London, UK: Routledge.

Kraut, R., Egido, C., & Galegher, J. (1988). *Patterns of contact and communication in scientific research collaboration*. Association for Computing Machinery. Retrieved February 21, 2010, from http://www.cos.ufrj.br/~jano/CSCW2005/kraut_1988.pdf

Laurillard, D., & Mc Andrew, P. (2002). Virtual teaching tools: Bringing academics closer to the design of e-learning. *Conference Proceedings for Network Learning 2002: A Research Based Conference on e-Learning in Higher Education and Lifelong Learning*, (pp. 11–16). Sheffield, UK: University of Sheffield.

Mc Andrew, P., & Wilson, T. (2008). *Pocketing the difference: Joint development of open educational resources*. In ICALT 2008: The 8th IEEE International Conference on Advanced Learning, Technologies. Learning technologies in the Information society, 1-5 July 2008, Santander, Cantabria, Spain.

Moore, G. M. (1995). The 1995 distance education research symposium: A research agenda. *American Journal of Distance Education*, *9*(2), 1–6. doi:10.1080/08923649509526884

Murray, D. (2000). Protean communication: The language of computer mediated communication. *TESOL Quarterly*, *34*(3), 397–421. doi:10.2307/3587737

Prensky, M. (2001). Digital natives, digital immigrants. *Horizon*, *9*(5), 1–6. doi:10.1108/10748120110424816

Rocha Trindade, A., Carmo, H., & Biddara, J. (2000). Current developments and best practice in open and distance learning. *International Review of Research in Open and Distance Learning*, *1*(1).

Salmon, G. (2000). *E-moderating: The key to teaching and learning online*. London, UK: Kogan Page.

Taylor, J. (1995). Distance education technologies: The fourth generation. *Australian Journal of Educational Technology*, *11*(2), 1–7.

Thorpe, M. (1987). Adult learners in open learning. In Thorpe, M., & Grugeon, D. (Eds.), *Open learning for adults* (pp. 72–82). Harlow & Essex, UK: Longman.

Valentine, D. (2002). Distance learning: Problems, promises and possibilities. *Online Journal of Distance Learning Administration*, *5*(3).

White, C. (2003). *Language learning in distance education*. Cambridge, UK: Cambridge University Press. doi:10.1017/CBO9780511667312

Yates, C. (2004). *Teacher education at a distance: Lessons and experience from Sub-Saharan Africa*. Paper presented at the All-Africa Minister's Conference on Open Learning and Distance Education, 2004, Cape Town, South Africa.

ADDITIONAL READING

Ali-Choudhury, R., Bennett, R., & Savaniet, S. (2009). University marketing directors' views on the components of a university brand. *International Review on Public and Nonprofit Marketing*, *6*(1), 11–33. doi:10.1007/s12208-008-0021-6

Bates, A., & Bates, T. (2005). *Technology, e-learning and distance education*. New York: Routledge.

Becher, T., & Kogan, M. (1992). *Process and structure in higher education*. United Kingdom: Routledge.

Bettman, J., Thompson, K., Padykula, N., & Berzoff, J. (2009). Innovations in doctoral education: Distance education methodology applied. *Journal of Teaching in Social Work*, *29*(3), 291–312. doi:10.1080/08841230903018397

Bourdeau, J., Henri, F., & Ozkan, N. (2002). Doctorate at a distance (D@D): In search of serendipity. In *Proceedings of world conference on e-learning in corporate, government, healthcare, and higher education: 2009-2012*. Chesapeake, VA: AACE.

Bruce, C. (2004). 'Information Literacy as a Catalyst for Educational Change. A Background Paper.' In P. A. Danaher (Ed.). *Proceedings "Lifelong Learning: Whose responsibility and what is your contribution?" The 3rd International Lifelong Learning Conference* (pp. 8-29). Yeppon, Queensland.

Calvert, J. (2005). Distance education at the crossroads. *Distance Education*, *26*(2), 227–238. doi:10.1080/01587910500168876

Christensen, E. W., Anakwe, U. P., & Kessler, E. H. (2001). Receptivity to distance learning: The effect of technology, reputation, constraints and learning preferences. *Journal of Research on Computing in Education*, *33*(3), 263–279.

Coe, J. A. & Gandy, J. (2000) Perspectives from consumers (students) in a distance education program. *Journal of Technology in Human Services 16(2,3),* 161-174.

Davis, H., & Fill, K. (2007). Embedding blended learning in a university's teaching culture: Experiences and reflections. *British Journal of Educational Technology*, *38*, 817–828. doi:10.1111/j.1467-8535.2007.00756.x

Dawson, S. (2006). A study of the relationship between student communication interaction and sense of community. *The Internet and Higher Education*, *9*(3), 153–162. doi:10.1016/j.iheduc.2006.06.007

Discenza, R. (2002). *The design and management of effective distance education programs*. London: Idea Group Publishing.

Fedoruk, P. (2009). Standards in distance learning. *Proceedings of the 8th IASTED International Conference on Web-based Education, WBE 2009*, 216-220.

Finegold, A., & Cooke, L. (2006). Exploring the attitudes, experiences and dynamics of interaction in online groups. *The Internet and Higher Education*, *9*(3), 201–215. doi:10.1016/j.iheduc.2006.06.003

Franklin, S., & Peat, M. (2001). Managing change: The use of mixed delivery modes to increase learning opportunities. *Australian Journal of Educational Technology*, *17*(1), 37–49.

Guendoo, L. (2008). Community colleges friendlier to online PhDs. *Online Journal of Distance Learning Administration*, *11*(3).

Kelsey, K., & D'Souza, A. (2004). Student motivation for learning at a distance: does interaction matter? *Online Journal of Distance Learning Administration*, 7(2). Retrieved February 21, 2010 from http://www.westga.edu/~distance/ojdla/.

Laurillard, D. (1993). *Rethinking university teaching: A conversational framework for the effective use of learning technologies*. London: Routledge.

Lindner, J. R., Dooley, K. E., & Kelsey, K. D. (2002). All for one and one for all: relationships in a distance education program. *Online Journal of Distance Learning Administration,* 5(1). Retrieved February 21, 2010 from http://www.westga.edu/~distance/ojdla/spring51/linder51.pdf.

Littleton, K., & Whitelock, D. (2005). The negotiation and co-construction of meaning and understanding within a postgraduate online learning community. *Learning, Media and Technology*, *30*(2), 147–164. doi:10.1080/17439880500093612

Maddux, C. D., Ewing-Taylor, J., & LaMont Johnson, D. (2002). *Distance Education: Issues and Concerns*. Binghampton, NY: The Haworth Press, Inc.

Marginson, S., & Rhodes, G. (2002). Beyond national states, markets, and systems of higher education: A glonacal agency heuristic. *Higher Education*, *43*(3), 281–309. doi:10.1023/A:1014699605875

Maringe, F., & Gibbs, P. (2008). *Marketing higher education*. Maidenhead, UK: Open University Press.

Milstead, J., & Nelson, R. (1998). Preparation for an online asynchronous university doctoral course: lessons learned. *Computers in Nursing*, *16*(5), 247–258.

Moore, M. (2007). *Handbook of Distance Education* (2nd ed.). New Jersey: Lawrence Erlbaum Associates, Inc.

Park, C. (2007). Redefining the doctorate. *Higher Education Academy Discussion Paper.* Retrieved February 21st from http://www.heacademy.ac.uk/news/detail/Redefining_the_doctorate_report.

Pearson, M., & Ford, L. (1997). *Open and flexible PhD study and research. Centre for Educational Development and Academic Methods, The Australian National University*. Evaluations and Investigations Program, Higher Education Division.

Rooney, D., Hearn, G., & Ninan, A. (2005). *Handbook on the knowledge economy*. Cheltenham: Edward Elgar Publishing Limited.

Rovai, A. (2010). (article in press). Why some distance education programs fail while others succeed in a global environment. *The Internet and Higher Education*. doi:10.1016/j.iheduc.2009.07.001

Rovai, A. P. (2002). Building sense of community at a distance. *International Review of Research in Open and Distance Learning*, *3*(1), 74–85.

Rovai, A. P., & Jordan, H. M. (2004). Blended learning and sense of community: A comparative analysis with traditional and fully online graduate courses. *International Review of Research in Open and Distance Learning* 5(2). Retrieved February 21, 2010 from http://www.irrodl.org/index.php/irrodl/issue/view/18.

Silver, H. (2009). Martin Trow on British higher education. *Studies in Higher Education*, *34*(7), 751–763. doi:10.1080/03075070902737425

Sunderland, J. (2002). New communication practices, identity and the psychological gap: The affective function of e-mail on a distance doctoral programme. *Studies in Higher Education*, *27*(2), 233–246. doi:10.1080/03075070220120047

Thomerson, J., & Smith, C. (1996). Student perceptions of the affective experiences encountered in distance learning courses. *American Journal of Distance Education*, *10*(3), 37–48. doi:10.1080/08923649609526939

Wisker, G., Robinson, G., & Shacham, M. (2007). Postgraduate research success: Communities of practice involving cohorts, guardian supervisors and online communities. *Innovations in Education and Teaching International*, *44*(3), 301–320. doi:10.1080/14703290701486720

KEY TERMS AND DEFINITIONS

Blended Learning: A mode of learning which combines face-to-face contact with elements of distance education.

Extramural: Referring to studies removed from the physical campus of a university or college.

In-Context Research: Research conducted at close proximity with the studied phenomena, rather than at a remove from them (e.g. from the confines of a university campus).

Virtual Learning Environment (VLE): A software platform used to support learning over the Internet. Typically, a VLE will host online learning materials, online discussion boards and assessment tools.

Virtual Private Network (VPN): A secure computer network which is overlaid on a public network such as the Internet, and which is used to connect remote locations in an organisation.

Chapter 18
Exploration of Multi-Cultural Teaching and Learning in a Collaborative Virtual Environment

Gonca Telli Yamamoto
Okan University, Turkey

Michael D. Featherstone
Jacksonville State University, USA

Faruk Karaman
Istanbul Aydin University, Turkey

Patricia C. Borstorff
Jacksonville State University, USA

EXECUTIVE SUMMARY

This chapter presents an experiential case study of a multicultural virtual team project conducted by educators at two countries of three universities whose students came from very different cultural backgrounds. The authors suggest that new technologies present businesses and the institutions charged with training business professionals with a significant paradigm shift. Among the devices enterprises now employ to compete in the global business environment are virtual teams. We submit that it is incumbent upon educational institutions to formulate processes by which students may gain experience in the virtual work environment.

The chapter details the experiences both students and instructors encountered in creating and participating in a cross-cultural virtual team conducted predominantly in a virtual environment. We describe problems encountered and often (though not always) overcome. Students learned both the rewards and the frustrations such teams experience as they learned to participate in and contribute to the collective intelligence of the team.

DOI: 10.4018/978-1-60960-599-5.ch018

SETTING THE STAGE

Educational Institutions are being transformed by technological innovations and they have made vital contributions to the process. Institutions must continue to constantly innovate if they are to maintain their relevance. These efforts may have different objectives such as advancing their standing in the educational field, reaching better students, learners, increasing enrollments, enhancing the institutional brand, and/or providing reasonable pricing.

In transnational classes, cooperative efforts and projects provide a richer set of experiences for the educators and learners. As we prepared the class we utilized several collaboration tools such as groupware, Skype, team rooms, instant messaging and presence awareness software. The Yahoo Groups pages worked well as did email, Skype, instant messaging and individual team pages. Synchronous and asynchronous communication methods allowed the teams to connect seamlessly.

Today, virtual teams represent an important constituent for successful and adaptive organizations. Our aim was to develop the abilities of the students to collaborate effectively using virtual tools in a multi-cultural environment and to understand the different circumstances which occurred naturally during the course of the project.

The students of Jacksonville State University in Jacksonville, Alabama shared their experiences with students from Okan University, and Marmara University, both in Istanbul, Turkey in their "Virtual Enterprise"(USA) and"Marketing Management"(Turkey) classes that were offered in the fall of 2006. The professors chose the objectives for the students and established processes for making initial contact and engaging in communication events. The students learned to work with several collaboration tools and with one another emulating a work environment similar to that of international company managers.

INTRODUCTION

The advent of the World Wide Web has created an entirely new environment for the conduct of business. One attribute of any business which chooses to enter this environment is this; the business becomes a de facto international business. Markets once unreachable are now readily accessible. Working relationships which only a few short years ago may have been the dominion of only the largest of enterprises are now within the realm of any business – no matter the size – which has a Web presence. In addition, changes in information technology have made global communications virtually cost-free to most businesses.

The full impact of this rapidly evolving new business environment upon management is unclear. Equally nebulous are the best practices for utilizing the new communications tools for strategic advantage. What has been made abundantly clear is that businesses now interact in a global multicultural business environment (Benson-Armer & Hsieh 1997; Borstorff et al. 2006; Clausen et al. 2009; Duarte & Snyder 2006; Gatlin-Watts et al. 2007; Jarvenpaa & Leidner 1998; Johnson 2009; Lisak & Erez 2009; Mihhailova & Piiriste 2008; Powell, Piccoli & Ives 2004; VanRyssen & Godar 2000; Vinaja 2003; Yamamoto & Karaman 2006).

Because of the increasing importance of the globalization phenomenon, it is vital that companies adapt to these changes, or they risk losing their competitive standing. While this environment represents challenges for businesses hoping to compete in the global business arena, it also represents a unique opportunity for business schools who train the next generations of business leaders. Those business schools which recognize this and are transforming curricula to educate managers for the specific challenges of this new environment assume the risk but also gain the advantage of early adaptors. (Featherstone, Ellis & Borstorff 2004). On the other hand, not only the business schools but all universities and/or the institutions that provide the universal information/knowledge are facing different business environments than they were used to. Their marketing environment is also affected by these changes.

Not only for the developed countries but also all countries' educational and professional training systems do not sufficiently deliver the 21st century skills needed to ensure workforce competitiveness and economic innovation according to the EU ICT Task Force Report (2006). This means there needs to be a sufficiently educated workforce to implement and employ these innovations.

Chaotic competition occurred during the transition into the information society. Educational Institutions are being transformed by technological innovations and they have made vital contributions to the process. Institutions must continue to constantly innovate if they are to maintain relevance and survive. These efforts may have different objectives such as obtaining a sound place in the educational field, reaching more qualified students, increasing enrollments, enhancing the institutional brand, and/or providing reasonable pricing. These efforts can, in short, be defined as the adoption of the marketing approach. Educational Institutions should develop new methodologies and a new perspective. They will need to carefully choose the best communication tools in order to best meet their needs and those of the faculty and students.

However, the education sector seems to be slow in adapting to new changes. The current education system has been in use for such a long period of time that it is unthinkable for the veterans to replace these classical methods with new ones. This is because of a "resistance to change" in the educational system. In other words, the system has a sort of "inertia" which inhibits any kind of change. It is surprising that, nearly everyone talks about the fascinating new technologies and their possible implications in education, but few schools can really alter the old-fashioned ways of transferring knowledge to younger generations.

Educational Institutions increasingly employ modern tools in addition to conventional ones for promotion and success. However, conventional tools may sometimes be inefficient. Educational Institutions have to revise their promotional strategies and develop their plans and programs as means to reach their objective based on the educational institutions' particular condition (e.g. budgeting, staff, etc.). Recently, educational institutions have adopted various strategies in Internet marketing, mobile marketing and in other virtual environments as a necessity due to strict competition. Competitiveness and interactive marketing are transforming education into a global growing industry.

New technologies give educational institutions an opening to change the way they manage their teaching, learning and marketing. Therefore these technologies require the educational institutions to rethink these dynamics because we have faced several options to use familiar or some new approaches. Virtual teams are one of the new options for institutions. The mechanisms of a direct marketing or promotional vehicles are useful however indirect efforts also influence the structure of the education and human applications. Because content of the education is not detached from the applications while the applications are becoming more widely utilized. This kind of experience also utilizes social marketing for ideas and knowledge and uses other forms of interaction. This also engages the students and adds variety to the learning environment.

CASE DESCRIPTION

Innovations in Educational Marketing

Educational Institutions increasingly employ contemporary tools in addition to conventional ones for promotion and success. Conventional tools may no longer be sufficient. The promotional tools employed in educational institutions for marketing are: the web page, e-mail, mobile communication, and other virtual communication as well as the telephone and public relations.

The marketing-directed activities are mainly included within the scope of public relations or student affairs/relations. The importance of increasing the efficiency of the marketing function of the activities performed by these units is continuously increasing. Because every educational institution wants to be in the front ranks of student preferences and so, each educational institution aims at advertising and promoting itself in the best way possible to increase the number of qualified students possible. Educational institutions employ the tools in the marketing environment in order to present their efforts and reach their goals in the competitive environment. And they take advantage of the written, audio and visual communication tools and make use of any marketing communication tool which may be of benefit.

In some countries like Turkey, universities advertise in newspapers, create television programs, publicize on mass transport vehicles or billboards especially before the Student Election and Placement Tests (OSYM) and in some countries, they advertise before or after the registration periods, so many marketing communication elements are retained by educational institutions. With those activities, the universities aim at being in the front ranks of the student population with a more intensive image. These factors along with the marketing approach and their integrated evaluation has become highly important.

Such activities are actively practiced by the foundation and state educational institutions in Turkey and likewise invitations are sent to draw students to fair organizations, to websites in the Internet era, and banners to let the candidates of the educational institutions have an idea about the educational institutions with the hope that these will influence their selections.

Educational institutions select magazines, newspapers, TV, radio, Internet as mass communication environments and also integrate one-to-one communication environments such as personal interviews based on the marketing opportunity and combine these with their promotional activities. Thus, they spread the intended message around and continue with their image while developing their activities.

These are some formal tools that are deployed for educational institutional marketing, however there are some informal tools which can also be used. Some of these tools are virtual. In this chapter we give some details about usage of the virtual class and its affects on students.

According to the needs and desires of the market, how the messages are delivered and communicated in the series of promotional activities prepared in line with the characteristics of the educational institution is highly important. As in all other professional organizations, work of high quality should be carried out. These are the activities to be performed by educational institutions according to their strategic plans. Furthermore, making use of written, oral, audio and visual tools in these activities in an appropriate and systematic way is an important issue. The messages should be delivered to the target audience according to the educational institutions' advertising policies which should be well-defined and should influence the features of these messages such as content, language used, terminology, and means of communication and these issues should be considered in detail. Attention should be paid on delivering the right message to the right candidates, to the right influencers, and to society. These are important in protecting the integrity of the educational institution and its messages. Furthermore, the tools the educational institution should use while building its communication with the environment should be the ones with the highest accessibility rate and ease as tools of marketing communication.

In educational marketing, technological innovation, transnational innovations diversification and other marketing practices may be acknowledged as major enhancements (see Figure 1). First of all different applications of distance education can be considered. The simplest sort

Figure 1. Innovations in educational marketing ©2010 Gonca Telli Yamamoto

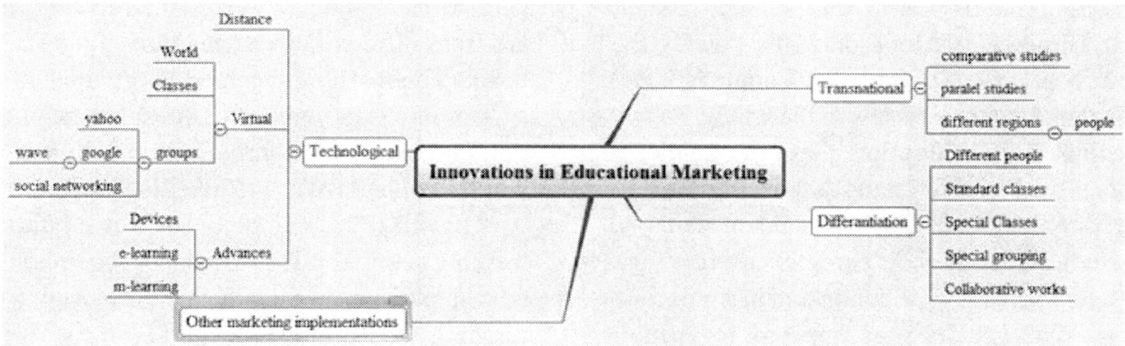

of these applications are distance, e-learning, m-learning and ubiquitous learning (Yamamoto, Ozan and Demiray, 2010). At the beginning of this applications are virtual classrooms, virtual world interactions (social networking) and virtual groups. Virtual groups are mainly groups that are supported by Wiki's, Google or Yahoo Groups or new applications such as Google Wave. These kinds of applications could be even more effective with the development of multifunctional mobile devices like Amazon's Kindle, Apple's new iPad or PDA's.

Innovations in Educational marketing also convey the differentiation. Some of the samples of these differentiations are;

- reaching different people, groups or geographies
- ease of use of standard applications
- special or specific projects
- targeted efforts in these projects with different groups.

In transnational studies, comparative or parallel efforts or projects would provide different experiences for the educators and learners.

Publications of business practitioner increasingly cite the utility of improving collaboration skills as well. "The ability to collaborate effectively using virtual tools may now become an increasingly important skill as technology offers more options than, say, video conferencing" (Tutton, 2009). According to Morten Brante, the HP Business Operations Regional Leader for the Americas, Nokia's development of a typical mobile device involves teams from nine different office locations. While at Hewlett-Packard, 40% of its USA workforce, and 60% of its non-USA workforce do not reside in the same office facility as their managers (Brante, 2010). This highlights the growing importance of student training in collaboration skills as a necessary preparation for competing in the multinational workspace.

Powell, Piccoli and Ives (2004) note that virtual teams represent a building block for successful and adaptive organizations. They further note that "While the findings of team research in the traditional environment may provide useful pointers, the idiosyncratic structural and contextual issues surrounding virtual teams call for specific research attention." (p. 6). There is a particular need for research on the interplay of information technology, multi-cultural interaction and team performance (Mihhailova & Piiriste, 2008).

As the importance of these new workplace paradigms increase, business universities and other educational institutions find incentive to train students to participate in a virtual environment. Given the increasing call for more innovative models in business school curricula *(AACSB 2010)*, a review of these articles focusing on university utilization of virtual teams seems appropriate.

Several articles argue in favor of the need for such research, either explicitly or implicitly (AACSB 2010; Biseda 2007; Johnson 2009; Powell, Piccoli & Ives 2004; Yamamoto & Karaman, 2006).

In their literature review of the article, Powell, Piccoli & Ives (2004) note that most studies of multicultural virtual teams (especially those of short duration) were done with student teams. All the studies cited in their comprehensive review, sixty-five percent were conducted in a university setting using students as opposed to business organization using employees.

Organizing Paradigm

A useful organizing paradigm for previous research on virtual teams is Saunders' (2000) life cycle model, which includes four general categories of variables. These are Input processes, Socio-Emotional processes, Task Processes, and Output processes. Each of these four general categories is sub-divided as follows: Input processes include items such as design, culture, technical, and training; Task processes include communication, coordination, and task-technology-structure fit; Socio-Emotional processes incorporate relationship-building, cohesion, and trust; Outputs include performance and satisfaction (Powell, Piccoli & Ives, 2004).

A team is a collection of individuals who are interdependent in their tasks, who share responsibility for outcomes, who see themselves and who are seen by others as an intact social entity embedded in one or more larger social systems (for example, business unit or the corporation), and who manage their relationships across organizational boundaries (Cohen & Bailey, 1997). Virtual teams frequently cross time, distance and organizational boundaries (Duarte & Snyder, 2006). They are geographically dispersed and rely on technology mediated communications rather than face to face interaction to accomplish tasks (Kirkman & Mathieu, 2004; Zakaria, Amelinckx & Wilemon, 2004). A multi-cultural team is a team whose members have different cultural backgrounds, for instance because they are from different countries (Vinaja 2003). The development of both synchronous groupware and asynchronous groupware has enabled collaboration between people from different parts of the world (Mihhailova & Piiriste, 2008).

Kimball (2001) emphasized that facilitating learning communities at a distance requires some new approaches to the practice of managing the teaching and learning process. This means if faculty start with a completely new mind set about where technology fits into the equation, it will be effective and bring some qualitative advantages. In addition to managing the delivery of the content to their courses, faculty teaching skills are developing such as to manage a new set of variables which determine the extent to which the courses are effective including: metaphor, meaning, culture, roles, time, awareness and collaboration. Virtual teams are supported from technologies that operate in multiple modes including having face to face meetings when possible in virtual world. According to Kimball (1997), managing virtual team means managing the whole spectrum of communication strategies and project management techniques as well as human and social processes in ways which support the team.

Communication

Communication in virtual teams has been among the most frequently documented categories due to the primacy of communications in moving toward goal achievement. The seminal article by Jarvenpaa and Leidner (1998) focuses on communication issues in global teams. Communication issues may represent a particular challenge in multicultural virtual teams. Problems may arise from "breakdowns due to cultural variances, unresolved conflicts among culturally different members, limited hours allowed to be worked and different holidays" (Vinaja 2003, p. 341). Some studies note that cultural dispersion within a team may exacerbate these issues, and the impact of different languages upon effective communication (Cramton, 2001).This means an individual could face several challenges that might affect his/her work such as limited hours, cultural gaps and impact of language in multicultural situations.

Other studies assert that communication is enhanced in virtual teams "Such teams not only have a wider variety of communication channels at their command but also are free of many of the psychological and practical obstacles to full and effective participation that hobble their traditional counterparts" (Majchrzak et al., 2004). The learning curves associated with the various communication tools might inhibit some, but in the university context, the professors may act as mentors in helping overcome this problem. However the evidence is that students are increasingly adept at accessing and using a variety of digital media (Dretzin, 2010)

In these classes, the most frequently used communication devices are currently computers and the internet. However, as 3G mobile devices become more pervasive, they will become more important tools. 3G technologies will augment the Internet and will narrow the difference between Internet (classical +mobile) and the real life. The Internet applications will become indistinguishable from the real life experiences. This will increase the adoption rates. Although, there is an increasing concern about the health related consequences due to use of mobile technologies, but it is impossible to get rid of them. Apparently, the real physical world goes nowhere but it is being enriched by the Internet and mobile technologies. Apparently, the education will also be transformed by these powerful technologies.

Trust

Effective communication is viewed as a tool to facilitate trust in virtual teams. Team members must feel open to express their view points without fear of criticism from other team members. This problem can be further complicated if team members have never met each other, or know little about the person other than their position on the team, or if they are not conversant to their team members native language. It is critical that team members strive to make a good first impression with their team. Usually there will not be a second chance for a good impression. This first impression will greatly increase the chances of developing this trust among team members (Jarvenpaa, 2001).

Jarvenpaa & Leidner (1998) note that global teams may form a type of swift trust but that such formulations may be transient and they identified nine specific behaviors to facilitate trust (Johnson, 2002). The role of trust is also identified as a necessary ingredient in the formulation of social capital in virtual teams (Biseda, 2007).

A poorly executed first impression can inhibit the interpersonal relationship and trust dynamic needed for effective communication within the team. Electronic communication channels initially lower relational intimacy. The members of virtual teams can develop ways of exchanging socio-emotional communication, including group feelings and attitudes over a period. Research has shown that members of a group using computers will gradually develop close relational ties, but it does take considerably more (Warkentin & Beranek, 1999).

Trust in a virtual group is accumulated over time. Over the Internet, you communicate with people you have never seen before and much of the time you do not see their pictures. This is especially true for our case since we mainly used Yahoo Groups. In more recent applications, such as Face book, a richer multimedia content is used and there is a greater opportunity for more robust interaction. However, classical Internet groups may be better suited for more uses that are formal. In these groups, it is interesting to note that trust can be formed over the Internet just by means of exchange of messages. If the goal of the group is to exchange ideas and participate in discussions such level of trust may be sufficient.

Successful teams need to form a collective identity that promotes a shared commitment to a common goal. This responsibility lies with management and is nurtured through the communication of the project status and the role that each team member is playing in developing a final solution. This must be continued throughout the project to ensure that each member understands the relative roles and responsibilities (Chinowsky & Rojas, 2003). Relying exclusively on e-mail as a primary mode of communication may result in a decrease in trust amongst team members (Majchrzak et al. 2004). Enthusiasm and desire to be a team member are important.Also the match between the nature of the task and choice of modality of communications are other factors that affect performance and trust.

Social Presence

Social presence also becomes a factor concerning trust and communication. Social presence refers to the ability of a communication medium to allow a group member to feel the presence of other group members and the feeling that the group is jointly involved in communicative interaction. The extent of social presence seems to rely on ability of the communication medium channels to transmit rich information such as verbal cues, facial expressions, gaze, gestures, posture, physical proximity, and back channeling cues. According to Andres (2002), as the variety of these channels decrease in a communication medium, less attention is paid to the presence of other participants engaged in a communications session. If team members are not able to see these non-verbal cues, the result is that the social distance between team members increases (Hakkinen, 2004).

Virtual communication requires that strategies be developed to account for the lack of nonverbal cues. Some researchers, such as Mehrabian (1981), theorize that communication is predominately nonverbal. Individuals who are about to become part of a virtual teaming experience should be sensitized to the importance of nonverbal cues (Roebuck, Brock & Moodie, 2004). Johnson (2009) suggests that immersive computer generated virtual environments may enable a deeper cultural understanding and might be a desired first step in preparation for participating in a multicultural virtual team project.

Newer technologies such as Skype also afford the team synchronous visual communications, Second Life allows avatar representations to meet and talk synchronously, and even simple instant messaging software allows the inclusion of emoticons to facilitate a deeper level of nuance in the participants' messages.

Experiential (Case Studies)

Experiential articles are prevalent in the literature. Experiential articles frequently follow a case study format and present the specific experience along with 'lessons learned' (Majchrzak et al. 2004; Mihhailova & Piiriste, 2008; VanRyssen & Godar, 2000; Vinaja, 2003). These case studies show that multicultural teams require special training, and that when working with student populations provide valuable team learning experiences, as well as personalizing the difficulties with regard to cross cultural communications (VanRyssen & Godar, 2000; Vinaja, 2003).

TRANSITION TO THE CASE STUDY

This segment describes a case study of a university level course entitled "The Virtual Enterprise" which was offered in the fall of 2006 'at' Jacksonville State University in Jacksonville, Alabama and shared with students from Okan University, and Marmara University, both in Istanbul, Turkey. Perhaps the use of the preposition 'at' is *a lucus a non lucindo*, for the act of trying to describe precisely where a "virtual" class takes place can be a more daunting task than may be assumed at casual first glance. This is because the students rarely interacted in the traditional classroom, but frequently met within the confines of each student's computer screen, at once a more confining and yet liberating environment.

Delaying some three years to discuss our experience has some merit, for a while we lose the shiny gloss of being among the first to document our exploration of a trendy new topic, we gain the patina that only a shared reflection over time can bestow on such an event.

Conception and Implementation

The professors chose the following objectives for the students and study: make initial contact with one another and engage in communication events with one another; learn to work with several collaboration tools such as groupware, Skype, team rooms, instant messaging and presence awareness software; have a multi-cultural learning experience; identify and resolve the problems of communication and working in virtual teams; complete a jointly developed paper; and evaluate the virtual experience.

Virtual Team Project

Over a period of one semester, American and Turkish college students collaborated on a common assignment using the web, email and Yahoo group team rooms. The primary aim of the project was for students to experience working in a virtual environment with multi-cultural team members. The students would experience differences in culture, social structure, educational systems, communication, time sensitivity, and languages. There is precedence for such an endeavor with students interacting across curriculum and culture (VanRyssen & Godar, 2000; Vinaja 2003).

We wanted the students to experience multiple learning opportunities by using their classroom, the internet, email, virtual teams, and team oriented websites, such as Wikis. Integrating the virtual team experience into the class allowed us to examine the attitudes and behaviors of students with the ambiguity and unstructured aspects of experiential learning. We were interested in the students' perception of the effectiveness of virtual teams as well as the advantages and drawbacks of such experiences.

The class was instructed as follows: You will choose a partner in your local class and choose a tentative topic for research from a list of suggested topics; then you will invite a Turkish team to join you by communicating in our Yahoo group. Once you have a complete team and jointly decide the final research topic, you will communicate on your own with one another. At the end of the semester, you will turn in a finished research paper. We did not offer any suggestions on what to expect as we wanted them to approach the assignment *tabula rosa.* The American students were quite enthusiastic about the exercise as it led to them being perceived as the innovators in their class. This also brought another focus to the students of their differentiation from their other colleagues at the same university. Turkish students were also enthusiastic about the opportunity to use their international skills such as language. Even though they have studies at schools they now had an opportunity to connect without going abroad. Some of them added this experience to their CV's after the class.

The plan was for all groups to choose a research topic together and submit their research to both professors in Turkey and the USA. In actuality, the USA students chose a topic and then attempted to find Turkish team mates. The respective professors graded their own students' work. The project was part of their semester grade. When using this methodology in future classes, we plan to have the project be the majority of the course's grade.

Communication of Professors

Featherstone and Yamamoto communicated often via email, Yahoo Groups, Skype, and land lines. Both used the Internet extensively in classes; both were experts in developing Web sites and navigating the Web. They both understood groupware and language translation software which was expected to facilitate in this undertaking. The professors initially had more input into the process as it unfolded. However, once students developed their own team pages for communication, the students did not come back to the original Yahoo Groups page. This led to the professors having little knowledge of the exact processes each team followed. We developed an evaluation template that the students used after each communication event. These evaluation checklists gave insight into successes and frustrations as they unfolded. Students who experienced problems had ready access to the professors who served as virtual team advisors/mentors.

Initially, we had little previous research to follow for our undertaking. Our thought was this would be a good 'hands-on' learning experience for the students. As we became immersed in the virtual teams, we discovered that others had used such techniques successfully.

Communication in Yahoo

The setting up of the mechanics of communication was readily accomplished. In one day, Dr. Faruk Karaman of Turkey set up two Yahoo Groups pages. The first was easily accessible by both students and professors; the second was exclusively for faculty communication. We experienced few problems with the technology. The Yahoo Groups pages worked well as did email, Skype, instant messaging and individual team pages. These synchronous and asynchronous communication methods allowed the teams to connect seamlessly, although they were separated by 7,000 miles. In spite of this, students often complained about the lack of timeliness in responses from their international teammates.

Yahoo Groups are excellent for asynchronous communication. This increases the message quality especially if they are moderated. In the instant communication tools the messages are transferred as they first appear in mind. However, in groups there is ample time to revise and fine-tune the message. This increase in quality is gained by accepting the delay. Even in very crowded groups you can not expect to get answers in minutes. You should allow a few days. This is very similar to telegraph communication in terms of its speed. However, this communication is very efficient given that the receiver can read the message any time and write a response. This may be one of the reasons that classical Internet groups persists even in the existence of more capable rivals such as Face book.

The professors were able to post information and updates at the Yahoo site. Team information, project updates, and time schedules were posted. Students could communicate as well as share their experiences with one another. The students did what they had to do for the research project. Few took the time to post personal reflections or suggestions for virtual teams. Professors communicated with one another through email, groupware and Skype. The time differences posed a challenge for synchronous communications media such as Skype and land line calls. In fact, the only time that worked for conversation by the professors was very early mornings in USA when it was late afternoon in Turkey. The time difference was eight hours with Turkey being in the next day. The inexperience of the U.S. students operating in a global environment was abundantly clear. Some of the Turkish students were aware of this kind of environment because they had some kind of apprenticeship/part time work in international firms however most of them were about the same as American students.

Student Project Planning and Execution

The students, for the most part, chose their teams. The Americans chose their teams first. Concurrently, Turkish students were selecting their preferred team mates as well. Like the Americans, they often chose team members who were personal friends American students were instructed to post messages on the Yahoo group to find Turkish partners. We suggested that they share some personal information and something about their chosen project topic. The students appeared to be quite shy during this 'dating' process. Some postings to the group site were no more than "My name is X and I am a student at Y University". Even with encouragement from the respective professors, the personal communication was sparse. If they shared photos, it was done at their own web page. In fact, one American student did not realize for over a month that one partner in Turkey was female. He had just assumed the student was male and that assumption was not corrected for a month.

Some teams worked quite well together. They seemed to have chosen well and completed an excellent project. They were able to quickly settle on a topic. Some groups using computers gradually developed close relational ties and had further relationship after the class. Other teams were less successful. For example, some of the teams never settled on a combined project and the American students turned their project in without Turkish input. These could be taken as personal or interpersonal interference. Such as low communication skills or complacency.

The project was to have been collaborative between the two international groups. The papers were sent by email which worked with few problems. The communication was in English because none of the American students could speak Turkish. In fact, only one American student spoke a second language at all, which meant finding a common language other than English was not feasible. The Turkish students either spoke English or used a language program such as Babelfish. There were several Turkish students that spoke other languages such as French, German and Russian (In Turkey because of the young population there is a very harsh competition to have a good job after graduation therefore several students are trying to differentiate themselves with these language or computer skills). The software program results were mediocre at best as far as accurate translation of Turkish into English.

The American students complained to their professor about the slow reply from their partners. Turkish students made exactly the same complaint to their professor. Some of the teams wrote curt notes to their foreign colleagues concerning timeliness, work effort, and follow up. Then the professor informed the students that the Turkish students were celebrating Ramadan Festival, their Holy month which included daily fasting. This oriented the students toward greater concern the other cultures. Few of our students had taken the time to study the Turkish culture in depth. They knew of Ramadan but were unaware of the fasting requirements and sacredness of the occasion. Our next attempt at virtual teams will begin with more required study of culture, such as the cultural dimensions developed by Hofstede (2005), It took prodding and talking on the part of the professors to keep some students on task. Unfortunately, this is not unique to only a virtual team class.

Towards the end of the semester, the Americans celebrated Thanksgiving. It came as a surprise to our students that they would need to communicate during their holiday. The Turkish students did not understand the absence of their teammates at this time.

Then in the first of December, the American semester ended. The Turkish students kept asking their professor where the Americans were. Evidently, the Americans just quit when the class was over without properly ending the experiment.

CURRENT CHALLENGES WITH THE VİRTUAL TEAM PROJECT

This project was an experiment. We felt that the learning objectives could be achieved despite the anticipated problems during the virtual execution and this project offered students the opportunity to experiment with innovative business tools, an experience they would be unlikely to have in a traditional classroom environment. Our main problems dealt with student issues, the group site was not initially understood by some students, and technical errors in using the Internet, groupware, Skype and IMs inevitably occurred. All these caused time delays which were critical due to the short duration of the project.

Student Problems

Students themselves were a challenge. Occasionally, they gave themselves time off, not only cutting classes but also taking time away from the virtual communication and project. They didn't feel accountable for an end product as employees would in a work setting. Interestingly, in virtual teams, the students found more opportunities to disperse blame or accountability for problems in more directions; i.e., it was the other countries' fault, or the technology, etc. Although their grade was tied to the project, there were other opportunities to make points to help their final grade.

In addition, students having problems did not report them in a timely manner. In fact, sometimes problems were only discovered by the professors interrogating the student about their not meeting goals and objectives of the class. If the professors had been notified at the inception of a problem, the problem would have been resolved quicker.

The U.S. students were quick to criticize the lack of speed in the process. They adopted the American attitude of "time is money." They had a project that needed to be completed so they wanted "to get down to business and get it out of the way." They were neither sensitive to building a relationship with team members nor with other cultural nuances. *One U.S. team dismayed the U.S. professors by the following. This team, apparently, trying to fill space on a communications event log, informed us of their profound discovery that, "In Turkey, they speak Turkish." This was a low point for the U.S. professors during the experiment. However, the second low point was a student admitting that he didn't speak another language and that Kurdish would have been helpful!

Although the students were frustrated at times with the process, the evaluations were consistently positive. The students scored their satisfaction level as 'very high.' Several noted that the experiment had taught them about functioning in a virtual environment which they expected to experience in their careers. Other students were pleased with learning about and using Yahoo Groups and Skype. And others commented on their satisfaction with "just being in an environment where the training is linked to the future of business."

Another student wrote that "I am satisfied because of the life lessons I have learned about business communication. You can not learn things in the normal classroom environment that we learned this semester. If someone walks out of this class without lessons that will help them in their business careers, then they were not paying attention."

Teams that were working well together had more problems with the unscheduled breaks (Ramadan and Thanksgiving). After such a break, some teams had trouble finding their 'groove' again. We eventually instructed the students to do project work whether they felt that their team mates were contributing or not. The U.S. students interpreted a break in communication from their team mates as a mini-vacation.

Time was an issue in the experiment for some U.S. students. Though students were required to develop Excel spreadsheets highlighting the different time zones, a few reported the time difference to be six hours, 15 hours, and even 20 hours. In fact, a couple of students explained that they didn't need to post a message as the student would not receive it due to the time differences. The schedules of the semesters of the universities were not concurrent and this presented yet another obstacle for the timing of the students.

Technical Problems

The major challenge here included servers being down, a virus shutting down one of the university's servers; In addition, various levels of technology were available on some of the campuses. The Turkish students did not have unlimited access to the computer lab, resulting in some glitches in communication. Skype and Grouper was not commonly known in Turkey at that time, resulting in some students' hesitation to use the technology. It was also new to the U.S. students; however, the students were quick to try it on their teams and anyone else they could find. None of these problems were fatal. However, combined with the lack of motivation on the part of some students, it presented a challenge to the leaders.

Cultural Problems

Admittedly, students were not knowledgeable about the other country's culture. Initially, we had assumed that language would be a huge problem. Yet programs such as Babelfish and custom translation software available in Turkey allowed the Turkish students to translate their messages (if only approximately) into English. Some Turkish students rated their English "good" so many didn't use translation software. For those using the translation software, there would be stilted language which required several readings for comprehension.

The American students did not always understand the English in the postings. They were typical in that none of the American students spoke Turkish so they had little appreciation of the challenge of communicating in a second language. All professors associated with the students spoke at least two languages. Some students commented on ineffective communication as an 'abundant problem.' They also realized that trust was an issue but didn't seem to be able to make the inferential leap to learning about the Turkish culture as a solution. One wrote of "the constant pressure of unintentionally offending someone." Another student wrote about "the inability to put a face with a name. I communicate better when I am least know what people look like. There are countless problems in virtual teams but I can see the potential in the business frontier."

Limitations

The time constraint was a significant limitation in our experiment. We had less than one semester and this was not enough time to allow us to complete all our objectives. In addition, we were not prepared for the magnitude of the impact of cultural differences. While students were encouraged to investigate the cultural dimensions of the two countries, it is our belief that this was only superficially done. Again, due to time constraints and the ad hoc nature of the project, we did not have exercises available prior to the beginning of the virtual team experiment.

The characteristics of the communication medium influenced the communication behaviors (Straus & McGrath 1994). Perhaps the context was contrived by limiting teams to electronic communication. However, it allowed us to investigate pure virtual interaction free from the influences of face-to-face interaction. We believe that this assists us in better understanding the challenges of working virtually and in providing better team design and group instruction, leading to more successful virtual interaction.

SUGGESTIONS AND RECOMMENDATIONS

Virtual teams are often the only choice companies have when their organizations are facing global challenges. Classes such as the case above give students an opportunity to gain valuable experience working in a virtual environment, as well as studying and learning with students from a different cultural background.

When the students try to build a team which includes members from different countries they definitely face some challenges. The challenges are mostly about language, communication barriers, cultural diversity and project management. There were several problems which occured due to the different holidays between the countries. Time zones represent another issue to deal with. Because time delays are an important problem for the students who have limited time to accomplish project goals.

Another challenge was the available technology. The current state of the technology is such that virtual teams can technically function well in many parts of the world. However, some employees living in different regions may not have access to new communications infrastructures like Skype, especially in rural areas, and employees in other countries may not have access to later release dates for software. Some other problems include incompatible networks, inadequate infrastructure, slow computers, and traffic on the network.

During communication in multi-cultural teams people are using different languages. Different language competency levels may exacerbate this issue. Such as misspelled names or lack of gender recognition may create dissension. It was sometimes not possible to connect to some email addresses. However these are all surmountable issues. Communication with people abroad might be enjoyable but working with them on a specific project which is time constrained is difficult. Maturity levels amongst the teams may vary.

Over insistence and/or lack of immediacy could also create some problems when communicating. There could be lack of separation of a project or some update problems during the project. While we did not encounter this problem, there exists the possibility that one could interfere in another's private life.

Priorities are also important for this kind of studies. When team members share the responsibility for detailed planning and task completion, team relations are greatly enhanced.

Virtual teams were almost unheard of a decade ago, but today they are an integral part of every organization and they have received considerable attention in the literature. We examined the use of virtual teams which aims to carry out projects through information technology and globalization. "Virtual teams" are becoming more and more common place in the business life and in educational settings. This kind of approach is not a fad for the educational institutions. To the readiness for the multicultural working /cultural environment it is very useful to practice before. Multi-cultural virtual teams are important in these days due to the increasing globalization of organizations.

In fact, virtual teams are more common than it is thought. The networking sites such as Face book and LinkedIn offer their own group applications. Especially in Turkey, it seems that groups replace non-governmental organizations (NGO) as a way to form interest groups. This is because, groups are very easy to enter and exit. With groups, one can virtually do everything a classical club or association could accomplish with a very negligible burden. For that reason, political parties, clubs, foundations all started their own discussion groups.

Some of the problems that multi-cultural virtual teams experience include the following: time delays in replies, lack of synergy among cross-cultural team members, communications breakdowns due to cultural variances, unresolved conflicts among culturally different members, limited hours allowed to be worked and different holidays.

It is not easy to coordinate an overseas project. This study was undertaken as a multi-cultural virtual team pilot project to better to enable us to better understand the global virtual world. Therefore students have to communicate students whom they have never seen and most probably they will not see again in the future.

There are a many different cultures existing in the world. Every person has different characteristics even though they inhabit the same country, in the same culture and even same family it is very common to face with a problem in a different cultural background.

Especially when it is a project and both sides have deadlines to submit the projects, this issue gains high importance. Unfortunately, in general one of the sides may have a lack of sense about this issue. Some factors may affect the lack of sense. It may be something regarding priorities. When you leave the small group initiative last minute calls were also causes the problems.

There should be team leaders and triggers to do this kind of projects. There is also a need for rules that the groups should follow. In this study the students had network contacts with each other, learned to work with group software in virtual world. They also learn to work with different cultures and explored some dimensions of these cultures. They had experience the problems of working in virtual team. In this study the most useful trigger was the records that a student get.

The idea of extending the project is a possibility with several different groups and countries. In future this kind of relationships and studies will be all around the world it will also preparedness for the virtual business world. This kind of studies will give a differential advantage to the students who involved in this kind of projects.

Team learning is a global strategy used by cross-functional teams to provide the best results within a tight deadline. Managers, whether in Turkey or in the United States, must define and develop universal strategies to communicate across borders by forming virtual business teams and by understanding the different culture dimensions and social contexts that are present in each country. This ability, or inability, to communicate and understand the different dimensions of culture will ultimately decide just how effective and successful the organization will be.

Having an opportunity to participate in a multicultural virtual teams class can go a long way in preparing workers to have the open mindedness and flexibility necessary to be successful in a virtual world. Virtual communication training may prove to be a valuable tool if it can help people develop the skills that they need to communicate effectively. Also virtual communication should be admit as tool for understanding different cultures which gives the students multinational experience as an indirect reputation of the person and the educational institution.

Lastly, the current virtual group applications are limited in functionality and more robust and powerful applications are too expensive. A powerful virtual group application with a reasonably low fee could gain wide acceptance. People do so many things with these groups that there is room for a professional virtual group company.

REFERENCES

AACSB. (2010). Management on a mission. *Biz Ed*, *9*(1), 28.

Benson-Armer, R., & Hsieh, T. Y. (1997). Teamwork across time and space. *The McKinsey Quarterly*, *4*, 19–27.

Biseda, M. (2007). *Building social capital in virtual environments* (pp. 1–18). Los Angeles, CA: Claremont Graduate University.

Borstorff, P., Featherstone, M., Camp, L., & Newton, S. (2006). Virtual teams: The challenges of communication. *E-Business Review*, *6*(1), 16–19.

Brante, M. (2010). Mobile facts. Personal communication with M. Featherstone.

Chinowsky, P. S., & Rojas, E. M. (2003). Virtual teams: Guide to successful implementation. *Journal of Management Engineering*, *19*(3), 98–106. doi:10.1061/(ASCE)0742-597X(2003)19:3(98)

Clausen, L., Soerderberg, A.-M., Worm, V., & Zolner, M. (2009). Cultural intelligence as a strategic resource in multicultural teams. *Proceedings of the International Workshop on Intercultural Collaboration*, Palo Alto, California Association for Computing Machinery.

Cohen, S., & Bailey, D. (1997). What makes teams work: Group effectiveness research from the shop floor to the executive suite. *Journal of Management*, *23*(3), 239. doi:10.1177/014920639702300303

Cramton, C. D. (2001). The mutual knowledge problem and its consequences for dispersed collaboration. *Organization Science*, *12*(3), 346–371. doi:10.1287/orsc.12.3.346.10098

Dretzin, R. (2010). *Digital nation*. Frontline PBS.

Duarte, D. L., & Snyder, N. T. (2006). *Mastering virtual teams*. San Francisco, California: Josey-Bass Business & Management Series.

Featherstone, M., Ellis, A., & Borstorff, P. (2004). The role of e-commerce in business education. *Australasian Journal of Business and Social Enquiry*, *2*(2), 1–12.

Gatlin-Watts, R., Carson, M., Horton, J., Maxwell, L., & Maltby, N. (2007). A guide to global virtual teaming. *Team Performance Management*, *13*(1/2), 47–52. doi:10.1108/13527590710736725

Hofstede, G. (2005). Geert Hofstede™ cultural dimensions. Retrieved on September 1, 2005, from http://www.geert-hofstede.com/

Jarvenpaa, S. L., & Leidner, D. E. (1998). Communication and trust in global virtual teams. *Journal of Computer-Mediated Communication*, *3*(4).

Johnson, C. (2002). Managing virtual teams. *HR Magazine*.

Johnson, W. L. (2009). Developing intercultural competence through videogames. *Proceedings of the International Workshop on Intercultural Collaboration*, Palo Alto, California Association for Computing Machinery.

Kirkman, B. L., & Mathieu, J. E. (2004). The role of virtuality in work team effectiveness. *Proceedings of the Academy of Management Annual Meeting, Louisiana Academy of Management*.

Lisak, A., & Erez, M. (2009). Leaders and followers in multi-cultural teams: their effects on team communication, team identity and team effectiveness. *Proceedings of the International Workshop on Intercultural Collaboration*, Palo Alto, California Association for Computing Machinery.

Majchrzak, A., Malhotra, A., Stamps, J., & Lipnack, J. (2004). Can absence make a team grow stronger? *Harvard Business Review*, *82*(5), 131–137.

Mehrabian, A. (1981). *Silent messages: Implicit communication of emotions and attributes* (2nd ed.). Belmont, CA: Wadsworth.

Mihhailova, G., & Piiriste, G. (2008). *Management and leadership challenges due to using virtual work in multi-cultural organisations: Cases of two service sector companies*.

Powell, A., Piccoli, G., & Ives, B. (2004). Virtual teams: A review of current literature and directions for future research. *ACM SIGMIS Database*, *35*(1), 6–36. doi:10.1145/968464.968467

Roebuck, D. B., Brock, S. J., & Moodie, D. R. (2004). Using a simulation to explore the challenges of communication in a virtual team. *Business Communication Quarterly*, *67*(3), 359–367. doi:10.1177/1080569904268083

Saunders, C. S. (2000). Virtual teams: Piecing together the puzzle. In Zimud, R. W. (Ed.), *Framing the domain of IT management: Projecting the future through the past*. Cincinnati, OH: Pinnaflex.

Straus, S. G., & McGrath, J. E. (1994). Does the medium matter: The interaction of task and technology on group performance and member reactions. *The Journal of Applied Psychology*, *79*, 87–97. doi:10.1037/0021-9010.79.1.87

Tutton, M. (2009). *Going to the virtual office in Second Life*. Retrieved from http://www.cnn.com/2009/BUSINESS/11/05/second.life.virtual.collaboration/

VanRyssen, S., & Godar, S. H. (2000). Going international without going international: Multinational virtual teams. *Journal of International Management*, *6*, 49–60. doi:10.1016/S1075-4253(00)00019-3

Vinaja, R. (2003). *Major challenges in multicultural virtual teams*. Retrieved on October 26, 2005, from http://www.sbaer.uca.edu/research/swdsi/2003/Papers/068.pdf

Warkentin, M., & Beranek, P. M. (1999). Training to improve virtual team communication. *Information Systems Journal*, *9*(4), 271–289. doi:10.1046/j.1365-2575.1999.00065.x

Yamamoto, G. T., & Karaman, F. (2006). The death of the nation-state and the need for global collaboration. *E-Business Review*, *6*(1), 170–173.

Yamamoto, G. T., Ozan, O., & Demiray, U. (2010). *Drugstore for learners: Learning vitamins D-E-M-T-U learning*. 3rd International Future-learning Conference, 10-14 May 2010, Istanbul, Turkey.

Yamamoto, G. T., Telli, A., Featherstone, M., & Borstorff, P. (2006). *Virtual environments, virtual works, virtual lives?* PICMET'06 (Portland International Conference on Management Engineering and Technology), 8-13 July 2006, Istanbul.

Zakaria, N., Amelinckx, A., & Wilemon, D. (2004). *Working together apart? Building a knowledge-sharing culture for global virtual teams*. SSRN eLibrary.

ADDITIONAL READING

Anctil, E. J. (2008). Selling Higher Education: Marketing and Advertising America's Colleges and Universities. *JB ASHE Higher Education Report Series (AEHE)*. Jossey Bass; *34*,(2).

Bok, D. (2004). *Universities in the Marketplace: The Commercialization of Higher Education*. Princeton University Press.

Clark, B. R. (1998). *Creating Entrepreneurial Universities: Organizational Pathways of Transformation (Issues in Higher Education)*. Pergamon.

Gibbs, P., & Knapp, M. (2001). *Marketing Higher and Further Education: An Educator's Guide to Promoting Courses, Departments and Institutions (Creating success)*. Routledge.

Guruz, K. (2008). *Higher Education and International Student Mobility in the Global Knowledge Economy,* State University of New York Press. Karaman, F. & Yamamoto, G.T (2007). Controlling the Pace and Direction of Technological Change. *E-Business Review,* Vol. *7*.

Maringe, F., & Gibbs, P. (2008). *Marketing Higher Education: Theory and Practice*. Open University Press.

Petrides, L. A. (2000). *Case Studies on Information Technology in Higher Education: Implications for Policy and Practice*. Idea Group Publishing.

Yamamoto, G. T. (2006). University Evaluation - Selection: A Turkish Case. *International Journal of Educational Management*, *20*(6-7).

Yamamoto, G.T.& Karaman, F. (2010). Education 2.0. On the Horizon (OTH) invited article for special issue on "Does 'Old Main' have a future?" (scheduled to print 2010).

Yamamoto, G. T., & Karaman, F. (2006). *ICT, New Working Elite, and Social Implications* (*Vol. 6*). E-Business Review.

KEY TERMS AND DEFINITIONS

Experiential Learning: Is learning through reflection on doing that engages the learner at a more personal level by addressing the needs and wants of the individual.

Learning: Is acquiring new knowledge, behaviors, skills, values, preferences or understanding, and may involve synthesizing different types of information.

SKYPE: A software applicationsoftware application that allows users to make voice calls over the Internetvoice calls over the Internet.

Ubiquitous Learning (U-Learning): Is equivalent to some form of simple mobile learning, e.g. that learning environments can be accessed in various contexts and situations.

Virtual Environment: A computer generated, three-dimensional representation of a setting, need only suggest a real or imagined space and does not have photorealism and a sense of total immersion a primary goal.

Virtual Groups: A group that established in the virtual environment either formal or informal.

Virtual Teams: A group of individuals who work across time, space, and organizational boundaries with links strengthened by webs of communication technology.

Chapter 19
Marketing Services Globally:
The Benefits of E-Learning

Felicia Blacher-Wilson
Southeastern Louisiana University, USA

Evan G. Mense
Southeastern Louisiana University, USA

Michael D. Richardson
Southeastern Louisiana University, USA

EXECUTIVE SUMMARY

E-learning and distance learning technologies have accelerated tremendously during the last decade. Changes in development and delivery include altered instructional methods and the expansion of support services for e-learning activities. Many business and political leaders speculate that globalization is indeed connecting international political, economic, cultural, and social life. These new Information Technologies significantly affect most aspects of higher education. Changes in teaching/learning and administration have impacted everyone associated with applying technology to global delivery of services. E-learning has increasingly become the vehicle of choice for many corporate clients who are actively engaged in creating diverse international markets for their goods and services.

INTRODUCTION

The United States is facing a new and unique demographic shift in population. The population change coupled with the globalization of the world's economy has now created new opportunities, as well as challenges for the United States and the world. These challenges have become the new mission of many institutions of higher learning, some of which are uniquely placed to become the change agents of the future in a diverse, multicultural and global society (Teichler, 2003).

In the United States, the traditional path to obtaining a college degree is quickly becoming the exception rather than the rule (Adams & Eveland, 2007). In short, universities are now faced with providing educational opportunities to not only

DOI: 10.4018/978-1-60960-599-5.ch019

more students, but to a more diverse population of students (Bates, 2000). To realize their purpose, university administrators construct rigorous analysis to ensure that educational opportunities are available to underrepresented or non-represented groups (Bratianu, 2008). Universities implement practices to bridge the educational gap using creative activities to reach out to nontraditional students and a diverse and global population (Bates & Poole, 2003). Universities are constantly turning to technology as one of the primary means for initiating and maintaining contact with a diverse student population (Blin & Munro, 2008).

Higher education institutions are now confronting a very complex society characterized by eight ominous patterns: (1) Lack of funding for higher education; (2) increased demand for educational services; (3) changing relationships between government and education; (4) changes in the development and articulation of knowledge; (5) an increasingly global society with increasing educational demands; (6) dramatically increased accountability for services and productivity; (7) increased diversity of clients and providers; and (8) increased competition for scare resources. (Altbach & Balan, Brown, 1997; Etzkowitz & Leydesdorff, 1998; Keegan, 1986; Marginson, 2002; Stofer & Meyer, 2006; Teichler, 2003).

Alexander (1999, p. 415) stated, "governments increasingly view postsecondary education as a stakes game too important to leave to the universities themselves or to traditional peer faculty and governance processes." Since the mid-1900s, universities have displaced knowledge from a public good to an economic good. The knowledge-based society accents skilled labor prepared by new techniques and strategies. Due to the incomparability of knowledge as commodity, higher educations institutions have become entrepreneurial (Baldwin & James, 2000).

SETTING THE STAGE

Technology

"Technology is constantly changing and new technology developments can have profound effects on education, as in the case of the web" (Bates, 2005, p.1). Technology has been present for more than a century, but vast and rapid changes have made the utilization of technology the "in thing" for colleges and universities (Berge & Muilenburg, 2001). " There is a revolution which the Information Communications Technologies (ICT) are presently driving, moving in many cases from print at the core of a variety of media, to the virtual environments carried through the Web, computer-mediated conferencing (CMC), and CD-Rom" (Tait, 2000, p. 288). With this rapid expansion of network access worldwide, vast arrays of distance learning programs permit educators to reach a more globally diverse clientele (Altbach, 2004). Advancements in technology have created opportunities for higher education institutions to extend educational opportunities beyond the traditional "brick and mortor" buildings and deliver educational services to geographically and culturally diverse audiences internationally (Antonelli, Geuna & Steinmueller, 2000).

With this new technology for distance learning programs, higher education institutions are faced with the challenge of competing globally for diverse clientele (Baker & LeTendre, 2005). In order for a program to be marketable, higher education institutions need to take into consideration: students, instructors, evaluations, cost and maintaining the academic quality of distance learning courses to insure the comparability and quality of the degree, as well as the higher education institution's philosophy of distance learning (Bartlett, Fredrick & Gulbrandsen, 2004).

The New Student Population and the Need for Change

The internet is a new and innovative medium for E-learning that can provide students with a low-cost, flexible option to expand into global markets (DiRamio & Kops, 2004). By 2004 almost two million higher-education students in the United States alone were engaged in some form of E-learning which allowed them to take courses independent of time and location constraints (Allen & Seaman, 2004).

Following 9/11, universities began eliminating online courses. Temple University and New York University shut theirs in 2001. Two years later, Columbia University closed down Fathom, its once-vaunted online venture. The courses were never able to attract enough students to justify the millions of dollars invested in them (Michailidou & Economides, 2003). The post-9/11 economy did not help. However, the need and demand for an advanced degree is expanding in the United States and throughout the world. It was estimated that by 2025, 150 million people would seek an advanced degree (Allen & Seaman, 2003). Much of this demand is due to the change in the culture of employment. Society requires higher levels of skills and gone are the days where a job for life was the norm (Balotsky & Christensen, 2004). With this new need the virtual campus is re-emerging. But the new speculators are public universities, and instead of creating commercial, online branches like their predecessors, they are embracing a not-for-profit model (Clark, 1998). Public universities are quickly realizing that their name recognition and credibility, along with lower tuition rates, afford them an advantage over for-profit universities (Bourner & Flowers, 1997). By all accounts, demand for online education is expanding. About 3.2 million students took at least one online course during the fall of 2005. That's 39 percent more than the 2.3 million the previous year (Bates & Poole, 2003). Higher education institutions are beginning to change in response to providing academic opportunities to a very diverse population of students (Bok, 2003).

CASE DESCRIPTION

Historical Developments: The Paradigm of E-Learning in Higher Education

Technologically, the television was the initiator of a new and powerful means of experiencing knowledge and events. The advent of the video cassette recorder (VCR) allowed the storing and viewing of images at different times, thus removing constraints of space and time (Hurt, 2008).

With the invention of the first computer conferencing in the early 1980s the first online teaching began. In early E-learning programs technology was not creative but was limited to the development of computer networks (Allen & Seaman, 2003). Despite the many limitations of E-learning in the early years of the concept, this new process provided more educational opportunities for more students globally (Altbach, 2004). Computer mediated communication enabled asynchronous communication between individuals. One of the first institutions to offer teaching through computer conferencing was the New Jersey Institute of Technology in the USA (Evans, 2002).

In 1988, the British Open University was one of the first institutions to use online learning for students who were not on campus. Online learning became more accessible with the advent of the World Wide Web and the spread of the internet in homes. It was not until 1995 that the first web-based university courses appeared at the University of British Columbia in Vancouver, Canada (Bates, 2000). During that same time, the University of British Columbia developed an innovative software package called WebCT which was specifically designed to allow universities to offer web based courses over the internet. The 1990s brought much-needed improvements to E-learning specifically with the introduction of designed course management systems which fostered a collaborative learning process (Gilbert, Morton & Rowley, 2007). These new systems employed conferencing, chat and assessment tools, and were specifically designed to support collaborative learning, knowledge building, and multiple representations of ideas and knowledge structure (Rowley, Lujan &Dolence, 1998). Since that time, especially in North America, there has been a huge expansion of online learning. According to Allen and Seaman (2003), over 1.6 million students in degree-granting higher education institutions in the USA took at least one online course in the fall semester of 2002 (11% of all U.S. higher education students), and over 500,000 took all their courses online. The current age of information and communication technology has forced institutions to redefine the process of information access and delivery (Dunn, 2000).

E-Learning: A Different Approach to Teaching a Diverse Population

Given the change in student populations, there is a greater need to find more creative, cost and time effective ways to draw students to institutions of higher learning. One such way of reaching a more diverse population is through the use of distance education or E-learning (Brown, 2006). The power of the Web is universal. Additionally, most students globally have access to the internet. The design of E-learning allows information to be accessed by everyone regardless of their location or disability (Margine, 2006). The general mission of E-learning is to fully extend quality educational opportunities to a very diverse population of learners who either prefer or have a special need of alternative methods of delivery (Frydenberg, 2002). For this population, removing the walls of a classroom provides greater opportunities for learners to achieve their goals even while continuing to fulfill the demands of their every day schedules. Hemsley-Brown and Oplatak (2006),. assert that universities will be left behind if they do not embrace the opportunities afforded them by new trends in technology.

Higher education, as well as E-learning and distance education, is facing rapid changes as the result of the many changes in technology and the changes in students' profiles (Johnson, 2001). New technology has drastically changed the method of instruction employed at higher learning institutions (Milheim, 2002). E-learning, which has several names, including: distance education, distributed learning, online education and Web learning, first appeared as a viable concept in the form of a correspondence course in the 19th century. In the 1970s there was a resurgence of this concept through the use of videotapes, broadcast satellite and cable production (Samuels, 2004). Today's concept of distance education refers specifically to the use of computers, video and audio tapes (Thursby & Kemp, 2002). Universities may use site-based, synchronous activities, which are activities conducted in real time or at specified times such as videoconferencing and telecourses (Learning Peaks, 2001). Or they may employ asynchronous activities which do not require participation at the same time, such as internet/online or teleweb (Rockwell, Schauer, Fritz & Marx, 1999),.

Universities have generally been seen as beacons of hope by families they serve. However, as society becomes more mobile and diverse, and the cost of traditional educational opportunities increases, universities must seek unique ways to market programs and service clients not only locally but also globally (Jayasurya, 2001; Lynch, 2006).

Marketing Services Globally: The Benefits of E-Learning

Introducing new services on the educational market represents an important contribution to society. Most economic researchers speculate that there are two methods of attaining new market share.

The first method refers to the saturation of the market, or the reach of the marketing concept. The second method refers to the adoption process, whereby the consumer accepts or rejects the new concept. The two concepts, *diffusion* and *adoption*, are connected to two levels: microeconomic and macroeconomic (Naidoo, 2003).

The development and delivery of e-learning is not a new concept, but it is innovative. There are two dimensions to innovation: *symbolic dimension* and *technological dimension*. Symbolic innovation refers to changing social meanings that are unclear or unknown. Technological innovation refers to creating a change resulting from a new technology or the adaption of an existing technology (Pituch & Lee, 2006). For a university technological innovation is expensive, in contract to symbolic innovation where cost is significantly lower (Hawkes & Cambre, 2000). From the economical point of view, two macro factors seem to underlie the trend toward globalization (Fletcher, 2004); (1) eliminating barriers to flow of goods, services and capital that has occurred since the end of World War II; and (2) the dramatic technological developments in recent years. Many economists postulate that services are conceptually different from products, but many higher education institutions provide both products and services (Oravec, 2003). E-learning being one of those services.

Marketing promotions by universities to students are almost identical to marketing promotions in any customer service environment (Kittle & Ciba, 2001).. However, academics face revolutionary changes in technology, financing and student recruitment (Pentina & Neeley, 2007). Both the external and internal environments of the university create upheaval resulting from technological changes, global competition, demographic transfer, and the shifting context of society, including diversity (Klassen & Sitzman, 2000). Academic educators worldwide are leading the technological revolution by their research and by applying the technologies in the classroom to increase academic credibility (Opoku, Hultman, & Saheli-Sangari, 2008).

There are many benefits to both traditional learning and E-learning. Traditional learning is generally linear in sequence and provides synchronous communication (Pahl, 2003). It is mainly structured by time and space. Traditional learning tends to be taught from textbooks only. E-learning provides not only synchronous communication but also asynchronous learning and is independent of time while having an open learning environment. However, the major benefits of E-Learning are flexibility in terms of time, distance and affordability (Ostlund, 2008). E-learning is becoming an attractive alternative for many students because of the great flexibility and diversity of course offerings and how their time must be spent. E-learning allows students more accessibility to course offerings. Students can actively engage in course work and study online from virtually anywhere in the world and at a time that is convenient to the student (Saheb, 2005. E-learning also permits students to communicate and study with peers worldwide (Richardson & Swan, 2003). This type of flexibility allows students to work their academic schedule into their existing work and family schedules rather than having to take time away from work or family to complete assignments (Hawkes & Cambre, 2000). Through E-learning, nontraditional students no longer have to choose between their education and their career.

Technology is the catalyst for changing educational delivery through the use of E-learning. Through E-learning, students can learn in their own way and at their own pace. Most E-learning courses can be viewed, printed out or simply listened to. E-learning can promote a different kind of communication between student and instructor (Shaik, 2005). Students are no longer restricted to asking questions simply during an assigned class period. Through the use of message boards, asynchronous online discussions, synchronous online discussions, instant messages and emails, the instructor, as well as other classmates, are easily available to the student (Evans, 2002).

E-learning programs provide the opportunity to create "virtual communities". Virtual communities are defined as designed communities using current networked technology, whereas communities of practice emerge within the design community via the ways their participants use the designed community (Salmi, 2003). To overcome student obstacles in distance learning providers are turning to "virtual communities." Forming these communities in distance learning can effect student satisfaction, retention, and learning (Bolotsky & Christenson, 2004).

E-learning programs generally have a more diverse student body which allows students to interact with students of all ages, from many different walks of life or in foreign countries (Allen & Seaman, 2003). Such diversity will enrich the learning process and be reflected in discussions, assignments and projects. E-learning programs tend to be win-win for the student and for the institution (Brown, 2001). Online classes cost the university less as classes are held in 'virtual' classrooms which do not require desks, chairs and building space. Additionally, students do not have costs generally associated with classes at a physical college such as parking and housing (Hara & Kling, 2002; Hawkes & Cambre, 2000).

Tait states, "Information Communications Technologies presents enormous opportunities to rethink student support in ways that are not yet fully understood, in particular with regard to time and place, and the social dimension of learning which can be enhanced or diminished" (2000, p. 288). The separation of student and teacher imposed by distance removes a vital "link" of communication between the two parties. In order for distance learning to be viable, certain obstacles will need to be overcome in order for distance learning to be marketable for students (Sife, Lwaga & Sanga, 2007; Stodel, Thompson & McDonald, 2006).

CONCLUSION

University administrators can be certain about the future of E-learning but also must remember that E-learning is not a panacea for all forms of distance education. E-learning should be aimed at the masses with particular attentions given to those students who are typically excluded from traditional forms of education. As technology becomes more developed there will be a greater need to enhance online instruction as more and more prospective students will enroll in institutions of higher learning that have demonstrated their ability to provide beneficial, practical and engaging learning opportunities.

Well designed E-learning programs provide timelines and goals for students and have good monitoring systems in place to ensure student success. E-learning has had a fundamental impact on the existing structure of higher education. The diversity of new student populations demands that institutions strategically develop programs that will address a broad range of learning requirements in the most time, space and cost effective ways possible. E-learning is not without limitations. Instructors have to be more creative and more individualized in the delivery of instruction.

Additionally, E-learning demands a greater maturity from the student than that of traditional learning which may cause stress to the student and to the instructor. E-learning does not allow for spontaneous responses and limits the amount of social interaction found in traditional learning environments. However, when implementing E-learning services university administrators must remember that: (1) E-learning is not necessarily the same as distance learning; (2) there are several ways of delivering e-learning besides online and, (3) E-learning should also incorporate other media or technologies such as textbooks. E-learning allows institutions and students to benefit from a global consumer base. E-learning now allows institutions of higher education to reach a more diverse student population and holds many advantages that traditional learning does not. E-learning not only can reach more students but it also can make education convenient. As the field of technology advances, the Web will be a major player in education. The world access to the internet moves non-traditional educational programs to a new, more advanced level.

REFERENCES

Adams, J., & Eveland, V. (2007). Marketing online degree programs: How do traditional-residential programs compete? *Journal of Marketing for Higher Education*, *17*(1), 67–90. doi:10.1300/J050v17n01_06

Alexander, J. (1999). Collaborative design, constructivist learning, information technology immersion, and electronic communities: A case study. *Interpersonal Computing and Technology*, *7*(1-2).

Allen, E., & Seaman, J. (2004). *Entering the mainstream: The quality and extent of online education in the United States*. Needham, MA: Sloan Center for Online Education.

Allen, I. E., & Seaman, J. (2003). *Seizing the opportunity: The quality and extent of online education in the United States: 2003 and 2003*. Needham, MA: Sloan Center for Online Education.

Altbach, P. G. (2004). Globalization and the university: Myths and realities in an unequal world. *Tertiary Education and Management*, *10*(1), 3–25. doi:10.1080/13583883.2004.9967114

Altbach, P. G., & Balan, J. (Eds.). (2007). *World class worldwide: Transforming research universities in Asia and Latin America*. Baltimore, MD: Johns Hopkins University Press.

Antonelli, C., Geuna, A., & Steinmueller, W. E. (2000). Information and communication technologies and the production, distribution and use of knowledge. *International Journal of Technology Management*, *20*(1-2), 72–94. doi:10.1504/IJTM.2000.002853

Baker, D., & LeTendre, G. (2005). *National differences, global similarities: World culture and the future of schooling*. Stanford, CA: Stanford University Press.

Baldwin, G., & James, R. (2000). The market in Australian higher education and the concept of student as informed consumer. *Journal of Higher Education Policy and Management*, *22*(2), 139–148. doi:10.1080/713678146

Balotsky, E. R., & Christensen, E. W. (2004). Educating a modern business workforce: An integrated educational information technology process. *Group & Organization Management*, *29*(2), 148–171. doi:10.1177/1059601103261353

Bartlett, L., Frederick, M., & Gulbrandsen, T. (2004). The marketization of education: Public schools for private ends. *Anthropology & Education Quarterly*, *33*(1), 5–29. doi:10.1525/aeq.2002.33.1.5

Bates, A. W. (2000). *Managing technological change: Strategies for college and university leaders*. San Francisco, CA: Jossey-Bass.

Bates, A. W. (2005). *Technology, e-learning and distance education*. New York, NY: Routledge.

Bates, A. W., & Poole, G. (2003). *Effective teaching with technology in higher education: Foundations for success*. San Francisco, CA: Jossey-Bass.

Berge, Z. L., & Muilenburg, L. (2001). Obstacles faced at various stages of capability regarding distance education in institutions of higher education. *TechTrends*, *45*(4), 40–45. doi:10.1007/BF02784824

Blin, F., & Munro, M. (2008). Why hasn't technology disrupted academics' teaching practices? Understanding resistance to change through the lens of activity theory. *Computers & Education*, *50*, 475–490. doi:10.1016/j.compedu.2007.09.017

Bok, D. (2003). *Universities in the marketplace: The commercialization of higher education*. Princeton, NJ: Princeton University Press.

Bourner, T., & Flowers, S. (1997). Teaching and learning methods in higher education: A glimpse of the future. *Reflections on Higher Education*, *9*, 77–102.

Bratianu, C. (2008). Strategies for lifelong learning and organizational knowledge. *Review of International Comparative Management*, *9*(2), 5–15.

Brown, J. S. (2006). New learning environments for the 21st century: Exploring the edge. *Change*, *38*(5), 18–24. doi:10.3200/CHNG.38.5.18-24

Brown, P. (1997). Education, globalization and economic development. *Journal of Education Policy*, *11*(1), 1–25. doi:10.1080/0268093960110101

Brown, R. E. (2001). The process of community-building in distance learning classes. *Journal of Asynchronous Learning Networks*, *5*(2).

Clark, B. (1998). *Creating entrepreneurial universities: Organizational pathways of transformation*. New York, NY: Pergamon Press.

Davies, D. (1998). The virtual university: A learning university. *Journal of Workplace Learning*, *10*(4), 175–213. doi:10.1108/13665629810213935

DiRamio, D. C., & Kops, G. C. (2004). Distance education and digital intellectual property issues. *Planning for Higher Education*, *3*(2), 37–46.

Dunn, S. L. (2000). The virtualizing of education. *The Futurist*, *34*(2), 34–39.

Etzkowitz, H., & Leydesdorff, L. (1998). The endless transitions: A triple helix of university-industry-government relations. *Minerva*, *36*(3), 203–208. doi:10.1023/A:1004348123030

Evans, C. (2002). Lifelong learning through the virtual university. *Campus-Wide Information Systems*, *19*(4), 127–134. doi:10.1108/10650740210438810

Fletcher, G. (2004). The future of e-learning. *T.H.E. Journal*, *32*(2), 2–3.

Frydenberg, J. (2002). Quality standards in e-learning: A matrix of analysis. *International Review of Research in Open and Distance Learning*, *3*(2).

Gilbert, J., Morton, S., & Rowley, J. (2007). E-learning: The student experience. *British Journal of Educational Technology*, *38*(4), 560–573. doi:10.1111/j.1467-8535.2007.00723.x

Hara, N., & Kling, R. (2000). *Students' distress with a Web-based distance education courses: An ethnographic study of participants' experiences*. Retrieved from http://scholarworks.iu.edu/dspace/bitstream/handle/2022/1092/wp00

Hawkes, M., & Cambre, M. (2000). The cost factor. *Technological Horizons in Education*, *28*(1), 26.

Hemsley-Brown, J., & Oplatak, I. (2006). Universities in a competitive global marketplace. *International Journal of Public Sector Management*, *19*(4), 316–338. doi:10.1108/09513550610669176

Hurt, J. (2008). The advantages and disadvantages of teaching and learning on-line. *The Delta Kappa Gamma Bulletin*, *74*(4), 5–11.

Jayasurya, K. (2001). Globalization and the changing architecture of the state: The regulatory state and the politics of negative coordination. *Journal of European Public Policy*, *8*(1), 101–123. doi:10.1080/13501760010001859

Johnson, C. M. (2001). A survey of current research online communities of practice. *The Internet and Higher Education*, *4*(1). doi:10.1016/S1096-7516(01)00047-1

Keegan, D. (1986). *The foundations of distance learning*. London, UK: Croom Helm.

Kittle, B., & Ciba, D. (2001). Using college websites for student recruitment: A relationship marketing study. *Journal of Marketing for Higher Education*, *11*(3), 17–37. doi:10.1300/J050v11n03_02

Klassen, M., & Sitzman, E. (2000). At the intersection of demand creation and demand fulfillment: Which schools are getting there first and why. *Journal of Marketing for Higher Education, 10*(1), 43–53. doi:10.1300/J050v10n01_04

Lynch, K. (2006). Neo-liberalism and marketisation: The implications for higher education. *European Educational Research Journal, 5*(1), 1–17. doi:10.2304/eerj.2006.5.1.1

Margine, F. (2006). University and course choice. *International Journal of Educational Management, 20*(6), 466–479. doi:10.1108/09513540610683711

Marginson, S. (2006). Dynamics of national and global competition in higher education. *Higher Education, 52*, 1–39. doi:10.1007/s10734-004-7649-x

Michailidou, A., & Economides, A. (2003). E-learn: Towards a collaborative educational virtual environment. *Journal of Information Technology Education, 2*, 131–152.

Milheim, W. (2002). Faculty and administrative strategies for the effective implementation of distance education. *British Journal of Educational Technology, 32*(5), 535–542. doi:10.1111/1467-8535.00223

Naidoo, R. (2003). Repositioning higher education as a global commodity: Opportunities and challenges for future sociology of education work. *British Journal of Sociology of Education, 23*(2), 249–259. doi:10.1080/01425690301902

Opoku, R. A., Hultman, M., & Saheli-Sangari, E. (2008). Positioning in market space: The evaluation of Swedish universities' online brand personalities. *Journal of Marketing for Higher Education, 18*(1), 124–144. doi:10.1080/08841240802100386

Oravec, J. A. (2003). Some influences of online distance learning on US higher education. *Journal of Further and Higher Education, 27*(1), 89–103. doi:10.1080/03098770305628

Ostlund, B. (2008). Prerequisites for interactive learning in distance education: Perspectives from Swedish students. *Australasian Journal of Educational Technology, 24*(1), 42–56.

Pahl, C. (2003). Managing evolution and change in Web-based teaching and learning. *Computers & Education, 40*(2), 99–114. doi:10.1016/S0360-1315(02)00100-8

Pentina, I., & Neeley, C. (2007). Differences in characteristics of online versus traditional students: Implications for target marketing. *Journal of Marketing for Higher Education, 17*(1), 49–65. doi:10.1300/J050v17n01_05

Pituch, K. A., & Lee, Y. (2006). The influence of system characteristics on e-learning use. *Computers & Education, 47*(2), 222–244. doi:10.1016/j.compedu.2004.10.007

Richardson, J. C., & Swan, K. (2003). Examining social presence in online courses in relation to students' perceived learning and satisfaction. *Journal of Asynchronous Learning Networks, 7*(1), 68–88.

Rockwell, S. K., Schauer, J., Fritz, S. M., & Marx, D. B. (1999). Incentives and obstacles influencing higher education faculty and administrators to teach via distance. *Online Journal of Distance Learning Administration, 2*(4).

Saheb, T. (2005). ICT, education and digital divide in developing counties. *Global Media Journal, 4*(7).

Salmi, J. (2003). Constructing knowledge societies: New challenges for tertiary education. *Higher Education in Europe, 28*(1), 65–69. doi:10.1080/0379772032000110125

Samuels, R. (2004). The future threat to computers and composition: Nontenured instructors, intellectual property, and distance education. *Computers and Composition, 21*(1), 63–71. doi:10.1016/j.compcom.2003.08.006

Schofer, E., & Meyer, J. (2006). The world-wide expansion of higher education in the twentieth century. *American Sociological Review*, *70*(6), 898–920. doi:10.1177/000312240507000602

Shaik, N. (2005). Marketing distance learning programs and courses: A relationship marketing strategy. *Online Journal of Distance Learning Administration*, *8*(2).

Sife, A. S., Lwoga, E., & Sanga, C. (2007). New technologies for teaching and learning: Challenges for higher learning institutions in developing countries. *International Journal of Education and Development Using ICT*, *3*(2).

Stodel, E. J., Thompson, T. L., & McDonald, C. (2006). Learners' perspectives on what is missing from online learning: Interpretations through the community of inquiry framework. *International Review of Research in Open and Distance Learning*, *7*(3).

Tait, A. (2000). Planning student support for open and distance learning. *Journal of Open and Distance Learning*, *15*(3), 287–209. doi:10.1080/713688410

Teichler, U. (2003). The future of higher education and the future of higher education research. *Tertiary Education and Management*, *9*(3), 171–185. doi:10.1080/13583883.2003.9967102

Thursby, J. G., & Kemp, S. (2002). Growth and productive efficiency of university intellectual property licensing. *Research Policy*, *31*(1), 109–124. doi:10.1016/S0048-7333(00)00160-8

ADDITIONAL READING

Abdon, B. R., Ninomiya, S., & Raab, R. T. (2007). E-Learning in higher education makes its debut in Cambodia: Implications of the provincial Business Education Project. *International Review of Research in Open and Distance Learning*, *8*, 1.

Abrami, P. C. (2001). Understanding and promoting complex learning using technology. *Educational Research and Evaluation*, *7*(2-3), 113–136. doi:10.1076/edre.7.2.113.3864

Abrami, P. C., Bernard, R. M., Wade, A., Schmid, R. F., Borokhovski, E., Tamim, R., & Peretiatkowicz, A. (2006). A review e-learning in Canada: A rough sketch of the evidence, gaps and promising directions. *Canadian Journal of Learning and Technology*, *32*(3).

Aczel, J. C., Peake, S. R., & Hardy, P. (2008). Designing capacity-building in E-learning expertise: Challenges and strategies. *Computers & Education*, *50*(2), 499–512. doi:10.1016/j.compedu.2007.07.005

Adeoye, B., & Wentling, R. M. (2007). The relationship between national culture and usability of an E-learning system. *International Journal on E-Learning*, *6*(1), 119–146.

Ambe-Uva, T.N. (2006). Interactivity in distance education: The National Open University of Nigeria experience, *The Turkish Online Journal of Distance Education*, 7(4).

Barajas, M., & Gannaway, G. J. (2007). Implementing e-learning in the traditional higher education institutions. *Higher Education in Europe*, *32*(2/3), 111–119. doi:10.1080/03797720701840609

Bates, A. W., & Bates, T. (2005). *Technology, e-learning and distance education*. New York, NY: Routledge.

Beldarrain, Y. (2006). Distance education trends: Integrating new technologies to foster student interaction and collaboration. *Distance Education*, *27*(2), 139–153. doi:10.1080/01587910600789498

Bhalalusesa, E. (2001). Supporting women distance learners in Tanzania. *Open Learning*, *16*(2), 155–168. doi:10.1080/02680510120050316

Bollag, B., & Overland, M. A. (2001). Developing countries turn to distance education. *The Chronicle of Higher Education*, *47*(40), A29–A22.

Boud, D., & Prosser, M. (2002). Appraising new technologies for learning: A framework for development. *Educational Media International*, *39*(3-4), 237–245.

Brown, S. A., Fuller, R. M., & Vician, C. (2006). *Individual Characteristics and E-learning: The Role of Computer Anxiety and Communication Apprehension*. Bloomington: Indiana University Press.

Burn, J., & Thongprasert, N. (2005). A culture-based model for strategic implementation of virtual education delivery, *International Journal of Education and Development using Information and Communication Technology*, 1(1), 32-52.

Caplan, D. (2005). The development of online courses. In Anderson, T., & Elloumi, F. (Eds.), *Theory and practice of online learning* (pp. 175–194). Creative Commons, Athabasca University.

Castle, S., & Neu, B. (2006, November). *The onset, evolution, and growth of online education: A case study of National University's School of Education*. A paper presented at the Asia-Pacific Educational Research Association (APERA) International Conference, Hong Kong.

Castle, S. R., Dang, B., McGuire, C. J., & Tyler, C. E. (2007, May). *Online education: Consideration of andragogy vs. pedagogy.* A paper presented at the Redesigning Pedagogy Conference: Culture, Knowledge and Understanding, The Centre for Research in Pedagogy and Practice (CRPP), Singapore.

Cook, D. A. (2009). The failure of e-learning research to inform educational practice, and what we can do about it. *Medical Teacher*, *31*(2), 158–162. doi:10.1080/01421590802691393

Crichton, S., & Kinsel, E. (2000). Communities in transition: Technology as a tool for change. *Education Canada*, *40*(3), 44.

Damoense, M. Y. (2003). Online learning: Implications for effective learning for higher education in South Africa. *Australian Journal of Educational Technology*, *19*(1), 25–45.

de Boer, W., & Collis, B. (2002). A changing pedagogy in E-learning: From acquisition to contribution. *Journal of Computing in Higher Education*, *13*(2), 87–101. doi:10.1007/BF02940967

Dunn, P. (2008). Beyond localization: Effective leaning strategies for cross-cultural e-learning. In Rahman, H. (Ed.), *Developing Succesful ICT Strategies: Competitive Advantages in a Global Knowledge-Driven Society* (pp. 155–164). UK: Networked Learning Design.

Friesner, T., & Hart, M. (2004). A cultural analysis of E-learning for China, *Electronic Journal on e-Learning*, 2(1), 81-88.

Gulati, S. (2008). Technology-enhanced learning in developing nations: A review. *International Review of Research in Open and Distance Learning*, *9*(1).

Gunga, S. O., & Ricketts, I. W. (2006). Facing the challenges of e-learning initiatives in African universities. *British Journal of Educational Technology*, *38*(5), 896–906. doi:10.1111/j.1467-8535.2006.00677.x

Guri-Rosenbilt, S. (2005). Eight paradoxes in the implementation process of e-learning in higher education. *Higher Education Policy*, *18*, 5–29. doi:10.1057/palgrave.hep.8300069

Guri-Rosenblit, S. (2005). 'Distance education' and 'e-learning': Not the same thing. *Higher Education*, *49*(4), 467–493. doi:10.1007/s10734-004-0040-0

Heeks, R. (2002). Information systems and developing countries: Failure, success and local improvisations. *The Information Society*, *18*(2), 101–112. doi:10.1080/01972240290075039

Hezel, R. T., & Mitchell, J. (2006). *Developing a global E-Learning program: From conceptualization to implementation*. Syracuse, NY: Hezel Associates.

Hiltz, S.R., & Turoff Murray. (2005). Education goes digital: The evolution of online learning and the revolution in higher education. *Communications of the ACM*, *48*(10), 59–64. doi:10.1145/1089107.1089139

Horton, W., & Horton, K. (2003). *E-learning tools and technologies*. Indianapolis: Wiley.

Kasworm, C. E. (2003). Setting the stage: Adults in higher education. *New Directions for Student Services*, *102*, 3–10. doi:10.1002/ss.83

Keller, J. M., & Suzuki, K. (2004). Learner motivation and e-learning design: A multinationally validated process. *Journal of Educational Media*, *29*(3), 229–239.

Kennedy, G. E., Judd, T. S., Churchward, A., Gray, K., & Krause, K. L. (2008). First year students' experiences with technology: Are they really digital natives? *Australasian Journal of Technology*, *24*(1), 108–122.

Kim, K., Zeng, T., Son, S. J., Teng, Y., & Oh, E. J. (2003). The future of blended learning in corporate and other training settings in the UK, US, China, Taiwan, and Korea. In E. Pearson & P. Bohman (Eds.), *Proceedings of World conference on Educational Multimedia, Hypermedia and Telecommunications 2006* (pp.80-82). Chesapeake,VA: AACE.

Kinuthia, W. (2004, October). *Impediments to faculty engaging in web-based instruction: Clarification of governing policies*. Paper presented at the Association for Educational Communications and Technology Conference, Chicago (ERIC Document Reproduction Service No. ED485016).

L'Allier, J., & Lacoff Resner, S. (2004). The competency gap: Aligning education. *Chief Learning Officer Journal,* 34-37.

Ladyshewsky, R. K. (2004). E-learning compared with face to face: Differences in the academic achievement of postgraduate business students. *Australasian Journal of Technology*, *20*(3), 316–336.

Levy, Y. (2007). Comparing Dropouts and Persistence in E-Learning Courses. *Computers & Education*, *48*(2), 185–205. doi:10.1016/j.compedu.2004.12.004

MacDonald, C. J., & Thompson, T. L. (2005). Structure, content, delivery, service and outcomes: Quality e-learning in higher education. *International Review of Research in Open and Distance Learning*, *6*(2).

Martey, A. (2004). ICT in Distance Education in Ghana. *Library Hi Tech News*, *21*(5), 16–18. doi:10.1108/07419050410546356

McLean, N. (2003). *Towards global e-learning standards for interoperability*.

Melinda De la Pena, B. (2007). Impact of ICTs on open and distance learning in a developing country setting: The Philippine experience. *International Review of Research in Open and Distance Learning*, *8*(1).

Meredith, S., & Newton, B. (2004). Models of e-learning: Technology promise vs learner needs literature review. *The International Journal of Management Education*, *4*(1), 43–56.

Morris, D. (2008). Economies of scale and scope in e-learning. *Studies in Higher Education*, *33*(3), 331–343. doi:10.1080/03075070802066164

Olaniran, B. (2007). Challenges to implementing e-learning in lesser developed countries. In Edmundson, A. (Ed.), *Globalized E-Learning Cultural Challenges* (pp. 18–34). Hershey, PA: IGI Global.

Oliver, R. (2006). Exploring a technology-facilitated solution to cater for advanced students in large undergraduate classes. *Journal of Computer Assisted Learning*, *22*, 1–12. doi:10.1111/j.1365-2729.2006.00155.x

Pagram, P., & Pagram, J. (2006). Issues in e-learning: A Thai case study. *The Electronic Journal of Information Systems in Developing Countries*, *26*(6), 1–8.

Pawlowski, J. M., & Richter, T. (2010). A methodology to compare and adapt e-learning in the global context. In Breitner, M. H., Lehner, F., Staff, J., & Winand, U. (Eds.), *E-Learning 2010* (pp. 3–13). Heidelberg, Germany: Physica-Verlag HD. doi:10.1007/978-3-7908-2355-4_1

Pérez Cereijo, M. V. (2006). Attitude as predictor of success in online training. *International Journal on E-Learning*, *5*(4), 623–639.

Ranieri, M. (2009). E-learning methodological models and typologies. In Cartelli, A., & Palma, M. (Eds.), *Encyclopedia of Information Communication Technology* (pp. 249–255). Hershey, PA: IGI Global.

Robinson, C. C., & Hullinger, H. (2008). New benchmarks in higher education: Student engagement in online learning. *Journal of Education for Business*, *84*(2), 101–108. doi:10.3200/JOEB.84.2.101-109

Safavi, A. A. (2008). Developing countries and e-learning program development. *Journal of Global Information Technology Management*, *11*(3).

Samarawickrema, G., & Stacey, E. (2007). Adopting web-based learning and teaching: A case study in higher education. *Distance Education*, *28*(3), 313–333. doi:10.1080/01587910701611344

Schuetze, H. G., & Slowey, M. (2002). Participation and exclusion: A comparative analysis of non-traditional students and lifelong learners in higher education. *Higher Education*, *44*(3/4), 309–327. doi:10.1023/A:1019898114335

Selim, H. M. (2005). Critical success factors for e-learning acceptance: confirmatory factor models. *Computers & Education*, *49*(2), 396–413. doi:10.1016/j.compedu.2005.09.004

Shapiro, B. (2002). Higher education in the new century: Some history, some challenges. *Education Canada*, *42*(1), 12.

Sharpe, R., & Benfield, G. (2005). The student experience of e-learning in higher education: A review of the literature, *Brookes eJournal of Learning and Teaching, 1*(3).

Siemens, G. (2005). Connectivism: A learning theory for the digital age. *International Journal of Instructional Technology and Distance Learning*, *2*(1), 3–10.

Sife, A., Lwoga,E., & Sanga C. (2007). New technologies for teaching and learning: Challenges for higher learning institutions in developing countries. *International Journal of Education and Development using ICT, 3*(2).

Siritongthaworn, S., Krairit, D., Dimmitt, N. J., & Paul, H. (2006). The study of e-learning technology implementation: A preliminary investigation of universities in Thailand. *Education and Information Technologies*, *11*(2), 137–160. doi:10.1007/s11134-006-7363-8

Sorenson, E. K. (2008). Design of dialogic elearning-to-learn: Meta-learning as pedagogical methodology. *International Journal of Web Based Communities*, *4*(2), 244–252. doi:10.1504/IJWBC.2008.017675

Sun, P. C., Tsai, R. J., Finger, G., Chen, Y. Y., & Yeh, D. (2008). What drives a successful e-learning? An empirical investigation of the critical factors influencing learner satisfaction. *Computers & Education*, *50*(4), 1183–1202. doi:10.1016/j.compedu.2006.11.007

Symposium de Versailles, France, 19th March. [Online]. Available: http://www.initiatives.refer.org/Initiatives-2003/_notes/_notes/McLean.htm [14th February,2006].

Tastle, W. J., White, B. A., & Shackleton, P. (2005). E-learning in higher education: The challenge, effort, and return on investment. *International Journal on E-Learning*, *4*(2), 241–251.

Wu, J., Tsai, R. J., Chen, C. C., & Wu, Y. (2006). An integrative model to predict the continuance use of electronic learning systems: Hints for teaching. *International Journal on E-Learning*, *5*, 2.

KEY TERMS AND DEFINITIONS

Distributed Learning: Distributed learning is an instructional model that allows instructor, students, and content to be located in different, non-centralized locations so that instruction and learning occur independent of time and place.

E-Learning: E-learning comprises all forms of electronically supported learning and teaching, which are procedural in character and aim to effect the construction of knowledge with reference to individual experience, practice and knowledge of the learner. Information and communication systems, whether networked or not, serve as specific media to implement the learning process

Globalization: It is the growing economic interdependence of countries worldwide through increasing volume and variety of cross-border transactions in goods and services, free international capital flows, and more rapid and widespread diffusion of technology.

Marketing Services: the process of researching and promoting to a market with nonphysical goods known as services.

Online Education: There are many terms for online education such as virtual education, Internet-based education, Web-based education, and education via computer-mediated communication (CMC). It is characterized by the separation of teachers and learners which distinguishes it from face-to-face education; the influence of an educational organization which distinguishes it from self-study and private tutoring; the use of a computer network to present or distribute some educational content; and the provision of two-way communication via a computer network so that students may benefit from communication with each other, teachers, and staff.

Web Learning: Web-based learning entails content in a Web browser (not just activities), and actual learning materials delivered in Web format. In this, Web-based learning is analogous to textbooks, where the content determines whether a book is a novel, a report, or a textbook. Simply offering computer-based training (CBT) for download from a Web site is not Web-based learning since there is no learning content in Web format). Web browsing the learning content (even linearly) is the key feature of Web-based learning. Web-based learning content is typically retrieved from a Web site, but alternative solutions are acceptable (a hypertext Web does not require Internet or networks).

Compilation of References

AACSB. (2010). Management on a mission. Biz Ed, 9(1), 28.

Abdullah, F. (2006). Measuring service quality in higher education: HEdPERF versus SERVPERF. Marketing Intelligence & Planning, 24(1), 31–47. doi:10.1108/02634500610641543

Adams, J., & Eveland, V. (2007). Marketing online degree programs: How do traditional-residential programs compete? Journal of Marketing for Higher Education, 17(1), 67–90. doi:10.1300/J050v17n01_06

Akridge, A., DeMay, J., Braunlich, L., Collura, M., & Sheaha, M. (2002). Retaining adult learners in a high-stress distance education learning environment: The Purdue University Executive MBA in Agribusiness. In V. Phillips, B. Elwert, L. Hitch, & C. Yager (Eds.), Motivating and retaining adult learners online. Essex Junction, VT: Geteducated.com. Retrieved from http://www.geteducated.com/images/pdfs/journalmotivateretain.pdf

Albers-Miller, N. D., Straughan, R. D., & Prenshaw, P. J. (2001). Exploring innovative teaching among marketing educators: Perceptions of innovative activities and existing reward and support programs. Journal of Marketing Education, 23(3), 249–259. doi:10.1177/0273475301233010

Albion, P. R., & Ertmer, P. A. (2002). Beyond the foundations: The role of vision and belief in teachers' preparation for integration of technology. TechTrends, 46(5), 34. doi:10.1007/BF02818306

Alexander, J. (1999). Collaborative design, constructivist learning, information technology immersion, and electronic communities: A case study. Interpersonal Computing and Technology, 7(1-2).

Allen, I. E., & Seaman, J. (2008). Online nation: Five years of growth in online learning. Needham, MA: Sloan Consortium.

Allen, I. E., & Seaman, J. (2009). Staying the course: Online education in the United States, 2008. Needham, MA: Sloan Consortium.

Allen, I. E., & Seaman, J. (2010). Learning on demand: Online education in the United States, 2009. Needham, MA: Sloan Consortium.

Allen, E., & Seaman, J. (2004). Entering the mainstream: The quality and extent of online education in the United States. Needham, MA: Sloan Center for Online Education.

Allen, I. E., & Seaman, J. (2003). Seizing the opportunity: The quality and extent of online education in the United States: 2003 and 2003. Needham, MA: Sloan Center for Online Education.

Altbach, P., & Knight, J. (2007). The internationalization of higher education: Motivation and realities. Journal of Studies in International Education, 11(3/4), 290–305. doi:10.1177/1028315307303542

Altbach, P. G. (2004). Globalization and the university: Myths and realities in an unequal world. Tertiary Education and Management, 10(1), 3–25. doi:10.1080/13583883.2004.9967114

Altbach, P. G., & Balan, J. (Eds.). (2007). World class worldwide: Transforming research universities in Asia and Latin America. Baltimore, MD: Johns Hopkins University Press.

American Association of University Professors. (1915). General report of the Committee on Academic Freedom and Academic Tenure. Bulletin of the AAUP.

Ames, C. (1992). Classrooms: Goals, structures, and student motivation. Journal of Educational Psychology, 84(3), 261–271. doi:10.1037/0022-0663.84.3.261

Anctil, E. (2008). Marketing and advertising higher education. ASHE Higher Education Report, 34(2), 19–30.

Anderson, J. C., & Gerbing, D. W. (1988). Structural equation modeling in practice: A review and recommended two-step approach. Psychological Bulletin, 103(3), 411–423. doi:10.1037/0033-2909.103.3.411

Anderson, A., Briggs, R. J., & Burton, N. (2004). Managing finance, resources and stakeholders in education. London, UK: Paul Chapman.

Andrews, C. P. (2007). Service learning: Applications and research in business. Journal of Education for Business, 83(1), 19–26. doi:10.3200/JOEB.83.1.19-26

Angelino, L. M., Williams, F. K., & Natvig, D. (2007). Strategies to engage online students and reduce retention rates. Journal of Educators Online, 4(2), 1–14.

Antonelli, C., Geuna, A., & Steinmueller, W. E. (2000). Information and communication technologies and the production, distribution and use of knowledge. International Journal of Technology Management, 20(1-2), 72–94. doi:10.1504/IJTM.2000.002853

Anyon, J. (1980). Social class and the hidden curriculum of work. Journal of Education, 162(1), 67–92.

Apple Computer Inc. (1989). HyperCard stack design guidelines. Cupertino, CA: Apple Computer Inc.

Arizona State University. (2009a). A new American university. Retrieved December 29, 2009, from http://newamericanuniversity.asu.edu/

Arizona State University. (2009b). Financial charts 2009. Retrieved December 29, 2009, from http://annualreport.asu.edu/investment/financial-charts.shtml

Arizona State University. (2009c). Quick facts 2009. Retrieved December 29, 2009, from http://uoia.asu.edu/sites/default/files/quickfacts/Quick_Facts_Fall_2009.pdf

Arizona State University. (2009d). More ASU history. Retrieved December 29, 2009, from http://www.asu.edu/about/history/more.html

Armstrong, M. (2003). A handbook of human resource management practice. London, UK: Kogan Page.

Ashby, A. (2004). Monitoring student retention in the Open University: Definition, measurement, interpretation and action. Open Learning, 19(1), 65–77. doi:10.1080/0268051042000177854

Association of American Colleges and Universities. (1940). Statement of principles on academic freedom and tenure. Retrieved January 20th, 2010, from http://www.aaup.org/AAUP/pubsres/policydocs/contents/1940statement.htm

At a Glance. (2008). The University of Melbourne. Retrieved from http://www.unimelb.edu.au/publications/docs/AtAGlance.pdf

Australia Education International. (2007). International students in higher education-comparison of main English speaking destination countries.

Australia Education International. (n.d.). Market information package. Retrieved on February 3, 2009, from http://www.aei.gov.au/AEI/MIP/Default.htm

Australian Universities Quality Agency. (2008). Submission to the Senate Standing Committee on Education, Employment and Workplace Relations. Commonwealth of Australia.

Badat, S. (2004). The diversity of higher educational provision: Propositions on distance higher education policy and regulation towards equity, access, quality and social and economic responsiveness. Paper Presented at the 2004 All Africa Ministers Conference on Distance Education, Cape Town, South Africa.

Baker, D., & LeTendre, G. (2005). National differences, global similarities: World culture and the future of schooling. Stanford, CA: Stanford University Press.

Baldwin, G., & James, R. (2000). The market in Australian higher education and the concept of student as informed consumer. Journal of Higher Education Policy and Management, 22(2), 139–148. doi:10.1080/713678146

Balotsky, E. R., & Christensen, E. W. (2004). Educating a modern business workforce: An integrated educational information technology process. Group & Organization Management, 29(2), 148–171. doi:10.1177/1059601103261353

Banerjee, P., Hu, X., & Yoo, I. (2005). Discovering the wealth of public knowledge: An approach to early threat detection. AIS SIGSEMIS Bulletin, 2(3&4), 77–85.

Banks, M., Oslen, A., & Pearce, D. (2009). Global student mobility: An Australia perspective five years on. Retrieved December 14, 2009, from http://www.idp.com/pdf/GSM_Brochure_Oct07.pdf

Barbour, M., & Mulcahy, D. (2005). The role of mediating teachers in Newfoundland's new model of distance education. The Morning Watch, September.

Bartlett, L., Frederick, M., & Gulbrandsen, T. (2004). The marketization of education: Public schools for private ends. Anthropology & Education Quarterly, 33(1), 5–29. doi:10.1525/aeq.2002.33.1.5

Baskin, C., & Williams, M. (2006). ICT integration in schools: Where are we now and what comes next? Australiasian Journal of Educational Technology, 22, 455 - 473. Retrieved 12 October, 2009, from http://www.ascilite.org.au/ajet/ajet22/baskin.html

Bates, A. (1995). Technology, open learning and distance education. New York, NY: Routledge.

Bates, A. W. (2000). Managing technological change: Strategies for college and university leaders. San Francisco, CA: Jossey-Bass.

Bates, A. W. (2005). Technology, e-learning and distance education. New York, NY: Routledge.

Bates, A. W., & Poole, G. (2003). Effective teaching with technology in higher education: Foundations for success. San Francisco, CA: Jossey-Bass.

Bateson, G. (1985). Mind and nature: A necessary unity. London, UK: Fontana Paperbacks.

Bayraktaroglu, G., & Atrek, B. (2010). Testing the superiority and dimensionality of SERVQUAL vs. SERVPERF in higher education. The Quality Management Journal, 17(1), 47–59.

Bearden, W. O., Scholder, P. E., & Netemeyer, R. G. (2000). Challenges and prospects facing doctoral education in marketing. Marketing Education Review, 10(1), 1–14.

Beardwell, I., & Holden, L. (2001). Human resource management: A contemporary approach. London, UK: Pearson Education Limited.

Beaver, C. (2009). The UK's international education strategy. Retrieved June 5, 2009, from http://www.iienetowrk.org/page/116258

Beckman, M. (1990). Collaborative learning: Preparation for the workplace and democracy. College Teaching, 38(4), 128–133.

Bedford, L. (2009). The professional adjunct: An emerging trend in online instruction. Online Journal of Distance Learning Administration, 12(3). Retrieved from http://www.westga.edu/~distance/ojdla/fall123/bedford123.html

Bekhuis, T. (2006). Conceptual biology, hypothesis discovery, and text mining: Swanson's legacy. Biomedical Digital Libraries, 3(2). Retrieved May 31, 2008, from http://www.bio-diglib.com/content/3/1/2

Bekkering, E., & Engelland, B. (2002). Extending quality assessment beyond the classroom: The campus computer lab scale. Journal of Advancement of Marketing Education, 2(1), 18–24.

Ben-Jacob, M. G., Levin, D. S., & Ben-Jacob, T. K. (2000). The learning environment of the 21st century. Educational Technology Review, 13, 8–12.

Benson-Armer, R., & Hsieh, T. Y. (1997). Teamwork across time and space. The McKinsey Quarterly, 4, 19–27.

Berge, Z. L., & Muilenburg, L. (2001). Obstacles faced at various stages of capability regarding distance education in institutions of higher education. TechTrends, 45(4), 40–45. doi:10.1007/BF02784824

Bergin, D. A. (1992). Leisure activity, motivation, and academic achievement in high school students. Journal of Leisure Research, 24(3), 225–239.

Berry, G. R., & Workman, L. (2007). Broadening student societal awareness through service-learning and civic engagement. Marketing Education Review, 17(3), 21–32.

Bethel School District No 403 v Fraser, 478 US 675. (1986).

Binsardi, A., & Ekwulugo, F. (2003). International marketing of British education: Research on the students' perception and the UK market penetration. Marketing Intelligence & Planning, 21(5), 318–327. doi:10.1108/02634500310490265

Biseda, M. (2007). Building social capital in virtual environments (pp. 1–18). Los Angeles, CA: Claremont Graduate University.

Bisschoff, T., Du Plessis, P., & Smith, E. (2004). Effective school marketing. Pretoria, South Africa: Van Schaiks.

Bisschoff, T. C. (1997). Co-operative education management: The key to transformation?Johannesburg, South Africa: Rand Afrikaans University.

Bisschoff, T. C. (2001). South Africa – a new vision for education management and leadership. In Pashiardis, P. (Ed.), International perspectives on educational leadership. Hong Kong: University of Hong Kong, Centre for Educational Leadership.

Blackburn, W. R. (2007). The sustainability handbook. Washington, DC: Environmental Law Institute.

Blin, F., & Munro, M. (2008). Why hasn't technology disrupted academics' teaching practices? Understanding resistance to change through the lens of activity theory. Computers & Education, 50, 475–490. doi:10.1016/j.compedu.2007.09.017

Block, C. C., Gambrell, B. L., & Pressley, M. (2002). Improving comprehension instruction: Rethinking research, theory, and classroom practice. Jossey-Bass.

Board of Regents of the University of Wisconsin System v Southworth, 529 US 217. (2000).

Bobbitt, L. M., Inks, S. A., Kemp, K. J., & Mayo, D. T. (2000). Integrating marketing courses to enhance team-based experiential learning. Journal of Marketing Education, 22(1), 15–24. doi:10.1177/0273475300221003

Bohm, A., Davis, T., Meares, D., & Pearce, D. (2002). Global student mobility 2025: Forecasts of global demand for international higher education. IDP Education Australia.

Bok, D. (2003). Universities in the marketplace: The commercialization of higher education. Princeton, NJ: Princeton University Press.

Borstorff, P., Featherstone, M., Camp, L., & Newton, S. (2006). Virtual teams: The challenges of communication. E-Business Review, 6(1), 16–19.

Bourner, J., Hughes, M., & Bourner, T. (2001). First-year undergraduate experiences of group project work. Assessment & Evaluation in Higher Education, 26(1), 19–39. doi:10.1080/02602930020022264

Bourner, T., & Flowers, S. (1997). Teaching and learning methods in higher education: A glimpse of the future. Reflections on Higher Education, 9, 77–102.

Bove, L. L., & Davies, W. M. (2009). Teaching marketing research using client-sponsored projects: Method, challenges and benefits. Journal of Marketing Education, 31(3), 230–239. doi:10.1177/0273475309344999

Bransford, J. D., Brown, A. L., & Cocking, R. R. (2000). How people learn: Brain, mind, experience, and school. Washington, DC: National Academy Press.

Brante, M. (2010). Mobile facts. Personal communication with M. Featherstone.

Bratianu, C. (2008). Strategies for lifelong learning and organizational knowledge. Review of International Comparative Management, 9(2), 5–15.

Breen, P. (2007). Lessons from an international e-learning project. International Review of Research in Open and Distance Learning, 8(3).

Breen, P. (2006). Coming out of the darkness of the past. Turkish Online Journal of Distance Education, 7(4).

Bridges, E. (1999). Experiential learning and customer needs in the undergraduate marketing research course. Journal of Marketing Education, 21(1), 51–59. doi:10.1177/0273475399211007

Bridges, C. M., & Wilhelm, W. B. (2008). Going beyond green: The why and how of integrating sustainability into the marketing curriculum. Journal of Marketing Education, 30(1), 33–46. doi:10.1177/0273475307312196

Briggs, A. R. J., & Sommefeldt, D. (2002). Managing effective teaching and learning. London, UK: Paul Chapman.

Brill, J. M., & Galloway, C. (2007). Perils and promises: University instructors' integration of technology in classroom-based practices. British Journal of Educational Technology, 38(1), 95. doi:10.1111/j.1467-8535.2006.00601.x

British Council Hong Kong. (n.d.). About us. Retrieved January 14, 2010, from http://www.britishcouncil.org/hongkong

Brochado, A. (2009). Comparing alternative instruments to measure service quality in higher education. Quality Assurance in Education, 17(2), 174–190. doi:10.1108/09684880910951381

Brown, R., Pressley, M., van Meter, P., & Schuder, T. (1996). A quasi-experimental validation of transactional strategies instruction with low-achieving second-grade readers. Journal of Educational Psychology, 88, 18–37. doi:10.1037/0022-0663.88.1.18

Brown, J., Sheppard, D., & Stevens, K. (2000). Effective schooling in a tele-learning environment. St. John's: NL, Centre for Tele-Learning and Rural Education, Faculty of Education, Memorial University of Newfoundland.

Brown, J. S. (2006). New learning environments for the 21st century: Exploring the edge. Change, 38(5), 18–24. doi:10.3200/CHNG.38.5.18-24

Brown, P. (1997). Education, globalization and economic development. Journal of Education Policy, 11(1), 1–25. doi:10.1080/0268093960110101

Brown, R. E. (2001). The process of community-building in distance learning classes. Journal of Asynchronous Learning Networks, 5(2).

Brown, T., Goodman, J., & Yasukawa, K. (2006). Getting the best of you for nothing - casual voices in the Australian academy. Retrieved January 27th, 2010, from http://www.nteu.org.au/getinvolved/categories/casual/papers/uts

Burgoyne, J. (1994). Personnel management. In Armstrong, M. (Ed.), A handbook of human resource management practices. London, UK: Kogan Page.

Bush, T., & Bell, L. (2002). The principles and practice of educational management. London, UK: Paul Chapman.

Bush, T., & Coleman, M. (2002). Leadership and strategic management in education. London, UK: Paul Chapman.

Bush, T., & Middlewood, D. (1997). Managing people in education. London, UK: Paul Chapman.

Bush, T. (1999). The vanishing boundaries: The importance of effective external relations. In Lumby, J., & Foskett, N. (Eds.), Managing external relations in schools and colleges. London, UK: Paul Chapman.

Camisón, C., Gil, M. T., & Roca, V. (1999). Hacia modelos de calidad de servicio orientados al cliente en las universidades públicas: El caso de la Universitat Jaume I. Investigaciones Europeas de Dirección y Economía de la Empresa, 5(2), 69–92.

Campion, M., & Guiton, P. (1991). Economic instrumentalism and integration in Australian external studies. Open Learning, 6(2), 12–20. doi:10.1080/0268051910060203

Capelleras, J. L. L., & Veciana, J. M. (2004). Calidad de servicio en la enseñanza universitaria: desarrollo y validación de una escala de medida. Revista Europea de Dirección y Economía de la Empresa, 13(4), 55–72.

Carman, J. M. (1990). Consumer perceptions of service quality: An assessment of the SERVQUAL dimensions. Journal of Retailing, 66(1), 33–55.

Carnevale, D. (2004). For online adjuncts, a seller's market. The Chronicle of Higher Education, 50(34).

Carpenter, C., & Steiner, S. (2007). Using Web 2.0 technologies to push e-resources. Georgia Tech Institutional Repository. Retrieved May 8, 2008, from http://smartech.gatech.edu/bitstream/1853/13640/2/236-fri-11_05.pdf

Carrington, R., Meek, V. L., & Wood, F. Q. (2007). The role of further government intervention in Australian international education. Higher Education, 53, 561–577. doi:10.1007/s10734-005-8755-0

Cartwright, V., & Hammond, M. (2007). Fitting it in: A study exploring ICT use in a UK primary school. Australiasian Journal of Educational Technology, 23, 390-407. Retrieved 12 October, 2009, from http://ascilite.org.au/ajet/ajet23/cartwright.html

Caruso, B., & Kvavik, R. (2005). ECAR study of students and information technology, 2005: Convenience, connection, control, and learning. Educause Center for Applied Research. Retrieved November 30, 2006, from http://www.educause.edu/LibraryDetailPage/666?ID=ERS0506

Casanueva, C., Periáñez, R., & Rufino, J. E. (1997). Calidad percibida por el alumno en el servicio docente universitario: Desarrollo de una escala de medida. In XI Congreso Nacional AEDEM (pp. 27-34). Spain: Lleida University.

Cen, Y., Ross, C., & Ross, H. (2009). Chinese higher education and evaluation in context. Chinese Education & Society, 42(1), 3–7. doi:10.2753/CED1061-1932420100

Chang, J. (2006). Globalization and English in Chinese higher education. World Englishes, 34(3/4), 513–525. doi:10.1111/j.1467-971X.2006.00484.x

Chen, X. (2008). The study on quality assurance system for our mass higher education. Unpublished Master dissertation, Zhejiang Sci-Tech University. (in Chinese).

Cheng, Y. C., Ng, S. W., Cheung, A., Choi, P. L., Tang, Y. F., & Yuen, W. Y. (2009). A technical research report on the development of Hong Kong as a regional education hub. Hong Kong: Hong Kong Institute of Education.

Cheng, Y. C. (2000). CMI-triplization paradigm for reforming education in the new millennium. International Journal of Educational Management, 14(4), 156–174. doi:10.1108/09513540010371975

Cheung, A., Yuen, W. W., & Yuen, Y. M. (2008). Exporting Hong Kong's higher education in Asian markets: Strengths, weaknesses, opportunities, and threats. International Journal of Educational Reform, 17(3), 308–326.

Cheung, A., Yuen, W. W., Yuen, Y. M., & Cheng, Y. C. (in press). -a). Promoting Hong Kong's higher education to Asian markets: Market segmentations and strategies. International Journal of Educational Management.

Cheung, A., Yuen, W. W., Yuen, Y. M., & Cheng, Y. C. (in press). -b). Strategies and policies for Hong Kong's higher education in Asian markets: Lessons from the United Kingdom, Australia, and Singapore. International Journal of Educational Management.

Chinowsky, P. S., & Rojas, E. M. (2003). Virtual teams: Guide to successful implementation. Journal of Management Engineering, 19(3), 98–106. doi:10.1061/(ASCE)0742-597X(2003)19:3(98)

Chow, P., & Marcus, R. (2008). International student mobility and the United States: The 2007 open doors survey. Retrieved from www.bc.edu/bc_org/avp/soe/cihe/newsletter/Number50/p13_Chow_Marcus.htm

Christensen, R. (2002). Effects of technology integration education on the attitudes of teachers and students. Journal of Research on Technology in Education, 34(4), 411.

Chubb, J., & Moe, T. (1990). Politics, markets and America's schools. Washington, DC: Brookings.

Clark, R. E. (1983). Reconsidering research on learning from media. Review of Educational Research, 53(4), 445–459.

Clark, G. (2007). Evolution of the global sustainable consumption and production policy and the United Nations environment programme's (UNEP) supporting activities. Journal of Cleaner Production, 15, 492–498. doi:10.1016/j.jclepro.2006.05.017

Clark, B. (1998). Creating entrepreneurial universities: Organizational pathways of transformation. New York, NY: Pergamon Press.

Clausen, L., Soerderberg, A.-M., Worm, V., & Zolner, M. (2009). Cultural intelligence as a strategic resource in multicultural teams. Proceedings of the International Workshop on Intercultural Collaboration, Palo Alto, California Association for Computing Machinery.

Cohen, S., & Bailey, D. (1997). What makes teams work: Group effectiveness research from the shop floor to the executive suite. Journal of Management, 23(3), 239. doi:10.1177/014920639702300303

Coiro, J. (2003). Exploring literacy on the Internet. The Reading Teacher, 56(5), 458–464.

Coleman, M., & Anderson, L. (2002). Managing finance and resources in education. London, UK: Paul Chapman.

Coleman, M., & Lumby, J. (2001). The significance of site-based practitioner research in educational management. In Middlewood, D., Coleman, M., & Lumby, J. (Eds.), Practitioner research in education. London, UK: Paul Chapman.

Comm, C. L., & Mathaisel, D. F. (2000). Assessing employee satisfaction in service firms: An example in higher education. Journal of Business and Economic Studies, 6(1), 43–53.

Cooksey, B. (1992). Basic education sector review. Kigali, Rwanda: UNICEF.

Cooper, J. (1990). Cooperative learning and college teaching: Tips from the trenches. Teaching Professor, 4(5), 1–2.

Covington, M. V. (2000). Goal theory, motivation and school achievement: An integrative review. Annual Review of Psychology, 51, 171–200. doi:10.1146/annurev.psych.51.1.171

Craig, C., & Douglas, S. (2000). International marketing research. Wiley.

Cramton, C. D. (2001). The mutual knowledge problem and its consequences for dispersed collaboration. Organization Science, 12(3), 346–371. doi:10.1287/orsc.12.3.346.10098

Cronin, J. J., & Taylor, S. A. (1992). Measuring service quality: A reexamination and extension. Journal of Marketing, 56, 55–68. doi:10.2307/1252296

Csikszentmihalyi, M. (1993). The evolving self: A psychology for the third millennium. New York, NY: HarperCollins Publishers, Inc.

Daly, S. P. (2001). Student-operated Internet businesses: True experiential learning in entrepreneurship and retail management. Journal of Marketing Education, 23(3), 204–215. doi:10.1177/0273475301233006

Davies, B., & Ellison, L. (1991). Marketing the secondary school. Harlow, UK: Longman.

Davies, B., & Ellison, L. (1997). Strategic marketing for schools. London, UK: Pitman.

Davies, D. (1998). The virtual university: A learning university. Journal of Workplace Learning, 10(4), 175–213. doi:10.1108/13665629810213935

Davies, E. H. (1999). Administration of the education system and school governance. Pretoria, South Africa: Centre for Education law and Education Policy (CELP).

Davis, A. (2004). Developing an infrastructure for online learning. In T. Anderson & F. Elloumi (Eds.), Theory and practice of online learning. Athabasca, AB: AUPress. Retrieved April 7, 2007, from http://cde.athabascau.ca/online_book/ch4.html

Deci, E. L., & Ryan, R. M. (1985). Intrinsic motivation and self-determination in human behavior. New York, NY: Plenum.

Department of Education. Employment and Workplace Relations. (2009). Importance of literacy and numeracy. Retrieved from http://www.deewr.gov.au/Schooling/LiteracyandNumeracyPilotProject/Pages/ImportanceL-andN.aspx

Department of Education. (1996). Changing management to manage change in education. Pretoria, South Africa: Department of Education.

Department of Education. (2001). Manifesto on values, education and democracy. Cape Town, South Africa: Department of Education.

Department of Employment, Education, Training and Youth Affairs. (1998). Learning for life - review of higher education financing and policy. Final Report. Canberra, Australia: Commonwealth of Australia.

DiGangi, S., Kilic, Z., Yu, C. H., Jannasch-Pennell, A., Long, L., Kim, C., et al. Kang, S. (2007). 1 to 1 computing in higher education: A survey of technology practices and needs. AACE Journal, 15(4). Retrieved October 29, 2007, from http://www.editlib.org/index.cfm?fuseaction=Reader.ViewAbstract&paper_id=22813

DiGiacomo, R. A., Kremer, J. M., & Shah, D. M. (1989). Fish-oil dietary supplementation in patients with Raynaud's phenomenon: A double-blind, controlled, prospective study. The American Journal of Medicine, 86(2), 158–164. doi:10.1016/0002-9343(89)90261-1

Dillon, W. R., & Kumar, A. (1994). Latent structure and other mixture models in marketing: An integrative survey and overview. In Bagozzi, R. P. (Ed.), Advanced methods of marketing research (pp. 295–351). Cambridge, MA: Blackwell Business.

Ding, X. (2004). The challenges faced by Chinese higher education as it expands in scale. Chinese Education & Society, 37(1), 36–53.

DiRamio, D. C., & Kops, G. C. (2004). Distance education and digital intellectual property issues. Planning for Higher Education, 3(2), 37–46.

DMEF. (2010). DMEF collegiate ECHO direct & interactive marketing challenge. Retrieved January 18, 2010, from http://www.directworks.org/uploadedFiles/Students/COMEPTITIONS_and_AWARDS/Collegiate_ECHO/Bing%20ECHO%20Competition%20Case%20Study%2008-25-09.pdf

Doren, D. V., & Corrigan, H. B. (2008). Designing a marketing course with field site visits. Journal of Marketing Education, 30(3), 189–206. doi:10.1177/0273475308318071

Dorniden, A. (2005). K-12 schools and online learning. In Howard, C., Boettcher, J. V., Justice, L., Schenk, K., Rogers, P. L., & Berg, G. A. (Eds.), Encyclopedia of distance learning (pp. 1182–1188). Hershey, PA: Idea Group Reference.

Drea, J., Engelland, B. T., & Singh, M. (1997). Using experiential learning in a principles of marketing course: An empirical analysis of student marketing audits. Marketing Education Review, 7(2), 53–59.

Dretzin, R. (2010). Digital nation. Frontline PBS.

Duarte, D. L., & Snyder, N. T. (2006). Mastering virtual teams. San Francisco, California: Josey-Bass Business & Management Series.

Dublin City University's Learning, Innovation and Knowledge Research Centre & Arizona State University's Applied Learning Technologies Institute. (2008). Global Grid for learning. Retrieved October 6, 2008, from http://www.globalgridforlearning.org/

Dunn, S. L. (2000). The virtualizing of education. The Futurist, 34(2), 34–39.

Dupeyrat, C., & Mariné, C. (2005). Implicit of intelligence, goal orientation, cognitive engagement, and achievement: A test of Dweck's model with returning to school adults. Contemporary Educational Psychology, 30(1), 43–59. doi:10.1016/j.cedpsych.2004.01.007

Dusick, D. M. (1998). What social cognitive factors influence faculty members' use of computers for teaching? A literature review. Journal of Research on Computing in Education, 31(2), 123.

Dutton, J. E., Dukerich, J. M., & Harquail, C. V. (1994). Organizational images and member identification. Administrative Science Quarterly, 39(34), 239–263. doi:10.2307/2393235

Edwards, D., & Hardman, L. (1989). Lost in hyperspace: Cognitive mapping and navigation in a hypertext environment. In McAleese, R. (Ed.), Hypertext: Theory into practice (pp. 105–125). London, UK: BSP.

Elam, E. L., & Spotts, H. E. (2004). Achieving marketing curriculum integration: A live case study approach. Journal of Marketing Education, 26(1), 50–66. doi:10.1177/0273475303262351

Elliot, E., & Dweck, C. (1988). Goals: An approach to motivation and achievement. Journal of Personality and Social Psychology, 54(1), 5–12. doi:10.1037/0022-3514.54.1.5

eMarketer. (2008). US online advertising spending, 2006-2012. Retrieved January 10, 2010, from http://www.marketingcharts.com/wp/wp-content/uploads/2008/03/emarketer-us-online-advertising-spending-2006-2012.jpg

Engelland, B. T., Workman, L., & Sing, M. (2000). Ensuring service quality for campus career services centers: A modified SERVQUAL scale. Journal of Marketing Education, 22(3), 236–245. doi:10.1177/0273475300223007

Ertl, H., & Plante, J. (2004). Connectivity and learning in Canada's schools. Ottawa, Canada: Statistics Canada, Government of Canada.

Ertmer, P. A. (2005). Teacher pedagogical beliefs: The final frontier in our quest for technology integration? Educational Technology Research and Development, 53(4), 25. doi:10.1007/BF02504683

Ertmer, P. A., Conklin, D., & Lewandowski, J. (2003). Increasing preservice teachers' capacity for technology integration through the use of electronic models. Teacher Education Quarterly, 30(1), 95.

Esp, D. (1989). Competencies for school managers. London, UK: Kogan Page.

Etzkowitz, H., & Leydesdorff, L. (1998). The endless transitions: A triple helix of university-industry-government relations. Minerva, 36(3), 203–208. doi:10.1023/A:1004348123030

Evans, C. (2002). Lifelong learning through the virtual university. Campus-Wide Information Systems, 19(4), 127–134. doi:10.1108/10650740210438810

Farnhan, D. (1993). Managing the new public services. Basingstoke, UK: Macmillan.

Featherstone, M., Ellis, A., & Borstorff, P. (2004). The role of e-commerce in business education. Australasian Journal of Business and Social Enquiry, 2(2), 1–12.

Feldman, R., & Sanger, J. (2007). The text mining handbook: Advanced approaches in analyzing unstructured data. Cambridge, UK: Cambridge University Press.

Ferguson, P. (2004). Faculty beliefs about teaching with technology. Association for Educational Communications and Technology.

Fish, S. (1994). There's no such thing as free speech (and it's a good thing, too). New York, NY: Oxford University Press.

Flaherty, T. B., Jansen, B. J., Hofacker, C., & Murphy, J. (2009). Insights on the Google Online Marketing Challenge and its successful classroom implementation. MERLOT Journal of Online Learning and Teaching, 5(2), 446–457.

Fletcher, G. (2004). The future of e-learning. T.H.E. Journal, 32(2), 2–3.

Forbes, S. (2005, December 12). Who'da thunk it? Coffee is hot. Forbes, 176(12), 33.

Fornell, C., & Larcker, D. F. (1981). Evaluating structural equation models with unobservable variables and measurement error. JMR, Journal of Marketing Research, 28, 39–50. doi:10.2307/3151312

Forrest, S., & Peterson, T. (2006). It's called andragogy. Academy of Management Learning & Education, 5(1), 113–122.

Forss, P. (2007, May 23rd). Singapore News. Retrieved January 22nd, 2010, from http://www.channelnewsasia.com/stories/sinaporelocalnews/view/277897/1/.html

Foskett, N. (1992). An introduction to the managing of external relations in schools. In Foskett, N. H. (Ed.), Managing external relations in schools. London, UK: Routledge. doi:10.4324/9780203415146_chapter_1

Foskett, N. (1999). Strategy, external relations and marketing. In Lumby, J., & Foskett, N. (Eds.), Managing external relations in schools and colleges. London, UK: Paul Chapman.

Foss, C. L. (1989). Tools for reading and browsing hypertext. Information Processing & Management, 25(4), 407–418. doi:10.1016/0306-4573(89)90068-X

Fountas, I., & Pinnell, S. G. (2001). Guiding readers and writers grades 3-6: Teaching comprehension, genre, and content literacy. Portsmouth, NH: Heinemann.

Freeman, R. E. (1984). Strategic management: A stakeholder approach. Boston, MA: Pitman.

Fry, E. (1977). Fry's readability graph: Clarifications, validity, and extension to level 17. Journal of Reading, 21, 242–252.

Frydenberg, J. (2002). Quality standards in e-learning: A matrix of analysis. International Review of Research in Open and Distance Learning, 3(2).

Fuentes, M., & Gil, I. (2006). Segmenting university students on the basis of their expectations. Journal of Marketing for Higher Education, 16(1), 25–45. doi:10.1300/J050v16n01_02

Fuentes, M., Gil, I., Berenguer, G., & Moliner, B. (2007). Expectations as the basis for predictive segmentation of university service quality. International Review of Public and Non Profit Marketing, 4(1/2), 47–64.

Gamoran, A. (1995). Effects of schooling on children and families. Family-school links: How do they affect educational outcomes? Hall, R. (1992). The strategic analysis of intangible resources. Strategic Management Journal, 13, 135–144.

Garcetti v Ceballos, 547 US 410. (2006).

Garcia, T., & Pontrich, P. R. (1996). The effects of autonomy on motivation and performance in the college classroom. Contemporary Educational Psychology, 21(4), 477–486. doi:10.1006/ceps.1996.0032

Garland, M. R. (1993). Student perceptions of the situational, institutional, dispositional, and epistemological barriers to persistence. Distance Education, 14(2), 181–198. doi:10.1080/0158791930140203

Garrat, B. (1994). Learning organisation. In Middlewood, D. (Eds.), Practitioner research in education: Making a difference. London, UK: Paul Chapman.

Garrett, R. (2008). Marketing online programs: Differentiation versus technique. Sloan-C View, 5(7). Retrieved from http://www.sloan-c.org/publications/view/v7n5/viewv7n5.htm

Gatlin-Watts, R., Carson, M., Horton, J., Maxwell, L., & Maltby, N. (2007). A guide to global virtual teaming. Team Performance Management, 13(1/2), 47–52. doi:10.1108/13527590710736725

Gelber, K. (2008). Academic freedom in Australia. Retrieved December 4, 2009, from http://www.australianreview.net/digest/2008/12/gelber.html

George, R. T. (2003). Ethics, academic freedom and academic tenure. Journal of Academic Ethics, 1, 11–25. doi:10.1023/A:1025421706331

Gibbons, H. S., & Wentworth, G. (2002). Processes for motivating online learners from recruitment through degree completion. In V. Phillips, B. Elwert, L. Hitch, & C. Yager (Eds.), Motivating and retaining adult learners online. Essex Junction, VT: Geteducated.com. Retrieved from http://www.geteducated.com/images/pdfs/journalmotivateretain.pdf

Gil, I. (1996). La evaluación de la calidad de servicio percibida y limitaciones de la herramienta SERVQUAL. Revista Europea de Dirección y Economía de la Empresa, 2, 19–32.

Gilbert, J., Morton, S., & Rowley, J. (2007). E-learning: The student experience. British Journal of Educational Technology, 38(4), 560–573. doi:10.1111/j.1467-8535.2007.00723.x

Gilbert, W. L., & Andrew, J. W. (2004). Real world problems bringing life to course content. Proceedings of the 5th Conference on Information Technology Education, Salt Lake City, UT.

Gillam, L. (2006). Sentiment analysis and financial grids. Paper presented at National Centre for e-Social Science Workshop, Manchester, United Kingdom.

Gipps, C., & Stalbart, G. (1993). Assessment: A teacher's guide to the issues (2nd ed.). London, UK: Hodder and Stoughton.

Glick, D. B. (2005). K-12 online learning policy. In Howard, C., Boettcher, J. V., Justice, L., Schenk, K., Rogers, P. L., & Berg, G. A. (Eds.), Encyclopedia of distance learning (pp. 1175–1181). Hershey, PA: Idea Group Reference.

Google. (2009a). Student guide 200. Retrieved January 15, 2010, from www.google.com/onlinechallenge/files/student_guide.pdf

Google. (2009b). Marketing and advertising using Google, 2nd ed. Retrieved January 15, 2010, from http://www.google.com/onlinechallenge/files/MarketingAndAdvertisingUsingGoogle2.pdf

Google. (2010). About the challenge. Retrieved January 15, 2010, from http://www.google.com/onlinechallenge/about.html

Govekar, M. A., & Rishi, M. (2007). Service learning: Bringing real-world education into the B-school classroom. Journal of Education for Business, 83(1), 3–10. doi:10.3200/JOEB.83.1.3-10

Government of Newfoundland and Labrador. (2000). Supporting learning: Report on the ministerial panel on educational delivery in the classroom. St John's: NL, Department of Education.

Grasha, A. F., & Yangarber-Hicks, N. (2000). Integrating teaching styles and learning styles with instructional technology. College Teaching, 48(1), 2. doi:10.1080/87567550009596080

Gray, L. (1991). Marketing education. Buckingham, UK: Open University.

Greasser, A. C. (2007). An introduction to strategic reading comprehension. In McNamara, D. S. (Ed.), Reading comprehension strategies: Theories, interventions, and technologies (pp. 3–26). Abingdon, UK: Lawrence Erlbaum Associates.

Gremler, D. D., Hoffman, K. D., Keaveney, S. M., & Wright, L. W. (2000). Experiential learning exercises in services marketing courses. Journal of Marketing Education, 22(1), 35–44. doi:10.1177/0273475300221005

Griffiths, J. (1992). Communicating the idea of a university in the public sphere - Habermasian social theory as a framework for critique. Research paper, Deakin University.

Grönroos, C. (1984). A service quality model and its marketing implications. European Journal of Marketing, 18, 36–44. doi:10.1108/EUM0000000004784

Hair, J. F., Anderson, R. E., Tatham, R. L., & Black, W. C. (1999). Análisis multivariante. London, UK: Prentice Hall.

Hall, E. T. (1976). Beyond culture. New York, NY: Anchor Press-Doubleday.

Hamer, L. O. (2000). The additive effects of semistructured classroom activities on student learning: An application of classroom-based experiential learning techniques. Journal of Marketing Education, 22(1), 25–34. doi:10.1177/0273475300221004

Hara, N., & Kling, R. (2000). Students' distress with a Web-based distance education courses: An ethnographic study of participants' experiences. Retrieved from http://scholarworks.iu.edu/dspace/bitstream/handle/2022/1092/wp00

Haravu, L. J., & Neelameghan, A. (2003). Text mining and data mining in knowledge organization and discovery: The making of knowledge-based products. Cataloging & Classification Quarterly, 37, 97–113. doi:10.1300/J104v37n01_08

Harmon, G. (2004). New directions in internationalizing higher education: Australia's development as an exporter of higher education services. Higher Education Policy, 17(1), 101–120. doi:10.1057/palgrave.hep.8300044

Harris, P. R., & Moran, R. T. (1987). Managing cultural differences (2nd ed.). Houston, TX: Gulf.

Hawes, J. M., & Foley, L. M. (2006). Building skills with professional activity reports. Marketing Education Review, 16(1), 35–40.

Hawkes, M., & Cambre, M. (2000). The cost factor. Technological Horizons in Education, 28(1), 26.

Hawtrey, K. (2007). Using experiential learning techniques. The Journal of Economic Education, 38(2), 143–152. doi:10.3200/JECE.38.2.143-152

Hayhoe, R., & Zha, Q. (2004). Becoming world-class: Chinese universities facing globalization and internationalization. Harvard China Review, Spring, 88-92.

Hazari, S., North, A., & Moreland, D. (2009). Investigating pedagogical value of Wiki technology. Journal of Information Systems Education, 20(2), 187–198.

Hazelwood School District v Kuhlmeier, 484 US 260. (1988).

Healey, D., & Stevens, K. (2002). Student access to Information Technology and perceptions of future opportunities in two small Labrador communities. Canadian Journal of Learning and Technology, 28(1), 7–18.

Healey, N. (2008). Is higher education really internationalising? Higher Education, 55, 333–335. doi:10.1007/s10734-007-9058-4

Healy v James, 408 US 169. (1972).

Healy, G. (2009, October 7). Law to back academic freedom. The Australian. Retrieved December 4, 2009, from http://www.theaustralian.com.au/higher-education/law-to-back-academic-freedom/story-e6frgcjx-1225783534874

Helms, M., M., Mayo, D. T., & Baxter, J. T. (2003). Experiential learning: The benefits of trade shows for marketing students and faculty. Marketing Education Review, 13(3), 17–25.

Hemsley-Brown, J., & Oplatak, I. (2006). Universities in a competitive global marketplace. International Journal of Public Sector Management, 19(4), 316–338. doi:10.1108/09513550610669176

Hernandez, S. (2002). Team learning in a marketing principles course: Cooperative structures that facilitate active learning and higher level thinking. Journal of Marketing Education, 24(1), 73–85. doi:10.1177/0273475302241009

Higher Education Acts (Amendment). (2005).

Higher Education Statistics Agency. (2009). Students in higher education institutions 2007/2008. Retrieved on May 30, 2010, from http://www.hesa.ac.uk/

Hirsch, F. (1976). Social limits to growth. Cambridge, MA: Harvard University Press.

Hirschhorn, L. (1988). The workplace within. Cambridge, MA: MIT Press.

Hofstede, G. (2005). Geert Hofstede™ cultural dimensions. Retrieved on September 1, 2005, from http://www.geert-hofstede.com/

Holland, J. H. (1995). Hidden order. Reading, MA: Addison-Wesley.

Holmberg, B. (2000). Status and Trends of Distance Education. Retrieved 21 February 2010 from: www.eden-online.org/papers/rw/holmberg_article_for_web.pdf.

Humphrey, N. (2004). The death of the feel-good factor? School Psychology International, 25(3), 347–360. doi:10.1177/0143034304046906

Humphreys, M. A. (1981). Client-sponsored projects in a marketing research course. Journal of Marketing Education, 3(10), 7–12. doi:10.1177/027347538100300203

Hurt, J. (2008). The advantages and disadvantages of teaching and learning on-line. The Delta Kappa Gamma Bulletin, 74(4), 5–11.

IAB. (2009). IAB Internet advertising revenue report. PricewaterhouseCoopers, March 2009.

Illing, D. (2000, March 29). Rules mean unis must measure up. The Australian, (p. 35).

Illing, D., & Richardson, J. (1999, March 10). Greenwich forum call. The Australian, (p. 39).

Information Highway Advisory Council. (1997). Preparing Canada for a digital world. Ottawa, Canada: Industry Canada.

Institute of International Education. (2007). Open doors 2007: Report on international educational exchange. New York, NY: Institute of International Education.

Institute of International Education. (2008a). Global destinations for international students at the post-secondary (tertiary) level, 2007. Retrieved Nov 11, 2008, from http://www.atlas.iienetwork.org/?p=48027

Institute of International Education. (2008b). IIE study abroad white paper series. New York: NY Institute of International Education.

Institute of International Education. (2008c). Open doors: Statistics on international study mobility. New York, NY: Institute of International Education.

Institute of International Education. (2009). Global destinations for international students at the post-secondary (tertiary) level, 2008. Retrieved April 17, 2009, from http://www.atlas.iienetwork.org/?p=48027

Intrator, S. M. (2000). Click, click, click... what do we know about reading hypertext? Knowledge Quest, 28(4), 31–34.

Jacob, W. J. (2006). Social justice in Chinese higher education: Regional issues of equity and access. Review of Education, 52, 149–169.

Jahan, K., & Mehta, Y. (2007). Sustainability across the curriculum. International Journal of Engineering Education, 23(2), 209–217.

Jansen, B., & Spink, A. (2006). How we are searching the World Wide Web? A comparison of nine search engine transaction logs. Information Processing & Management, 42(1), 248–263. doi:10.1016/j.ipm.2004.10.007

Jansen, B. J., Hudson, K., Hunter, L., Liu, F., & Murphy, J. (2008). The Google Online Marketing Challenge: Classroom learning with real clients, real money, and real advertising campaigns. Journal of Interactive Advertising, 9(1). Retrieved November 22, 2009, from http://www.jiad.org/article109

Jaques, E. (1952). The changing culture of the factory. London, UK: Tavistock.

Jarvenpaa, S. L., & Leidner, D. E. (1998). Communication and trust in global virtual teams. Journal of Computer-Mediated Communication, 3(4).

Jaschik, S. (2006). Adjuncts and graduation rates. Inside Higher Ed. Retrieved from http://insidehighered.com/layout/set/print/news/2006/10/16/parttime

Jayasurya, K. (2001). Globalization and the changing architecture of the state: The regulatory state and the politics of negative coordination. Journal of European Public Policy, 8(1), 101–123. doi:10.1080/13501760010018 59

Jinhui, L., & Zhiping, L. (2009). New exploration in the development strategy of going out for Chinese-foreign cooperation in higher education. Chinese Education & Society, 42(4), 78–87. doi:10.2753/CED1061-1932420406

Johnson, D. W., Johnson, R. T., & Smith, K. A. (1991). Active learning: Cooperation in the college classroom. Edina, MN: Interaction Book Company.

Johnson, C. M. (2001). A survey of current research online communities of practice. The Internet and Higher Education, 4(1). doi:10.1016/S1096-7516(01)00047-1

Johnson, C. (2002). Managing virtual teams. HR Magazine.

Johnson, W. L. (2009). Developing intercultural competence through videogames. Proceedings of the International Workshop on Intercultural Collaboration, Palo Alto, California Association for Computing Machinery.

Johnson-Sheehan, R., & Baehr, C. (2001). Visual-spatial thinking in hypertexts. Technical Communication, 48(1), 22–30.

Joiner, T. A., & Bakalis, S. (2006). The antecedents of organizational commitment: The case of Australian casual academics. International Journal of Educational Management, 20(6), 439–452. doi:10.1108/09513540610683694

Jonassen, D. H. (1991). Evaluating constructivist learning. Educational Technology, 31, 28–33.

Jones, S., & Lea, M. R. (2008). Digital literacies in the lives of undergraduate students: Exploring personal and curricular spheres of influence. The Electronic Journal of E-Learning, 6(3), 207–216.

Jöreskog, K. G., & Sörbom, D. (1993). Lisrel 8 structural equation modeling with the Simplis command language. Chicago, IL: Scientific Software International.

Joseph, M., & Joseph, B. (1997). Service quality in education: A student perspective. Quality Assurance in Education, 5(1), 26–37. doi:10.1108/09684889710156549

Joseph, M., Yakhou, M., & Stone, G. (2005). An educational institution's quest for service quality: Customers' perspective. Quality Assurance in Education, 13(1), 66–82. doi:10.1108/09684880510578669

Junor, A. (2003). Choice, risk and equity in casual university work: Implications for regulation. Unpublished discussion paper.

Junor, A. (2004). Casual university work: Choice, risk, inequity and the case for regulation. Economic and Labour Relations Review, 276-304.

Jurafsky, D., & Martin, J. (2000). Speech and language processing: An introduction to natural language processing, computational linguistics, and speech recognition. Upper Saddle River, NJ: Prentice Hall.

Ka-Ho, M. (2005). Globalization and educational restructuring: University merging and changing governance in China. Higher Education, 50, 57–88. doi:10.1007/s10734-004-6347-z

Kalamas, M., Laroche, M., & Cézard, A. (2002). A model of the antecedents of should and will service expectations. Journal of Retailing and Consumer Services, 9, 291–308. doi:10.1016/S0969-6989(02)00016-4

Kanuka, H., & Jugdev, K. (2006). Distance education MBA students: An investigation into the use of an orientation course to address academic and social integration issues. Open Learning, 21(2), 153–166. doi:10.1080/02680510600715578

Kao, A., & Poteet, S. (Eds.). (2007). Natural language processing and text mining. London, UK: Springer. doi:10.1007/978-1-84628-754-1

Karns, G. L. (2005). An update of marketing student perceptions of learning activities: Structure, preferences, and effectiveness. Journal of Marketing Education, 27(2), 163–171. doi:10.1177/0273475305276641

Karns, G. L. (2006). Learning style differences in the perceived effectiveness of learning activities. Journal of Marketing Education, 28(1), 56–63. doi:10.1177/0273475305284641

Karran, T. (2009). Academic freedom: In justification of a universal ideal. Studies in Higher Education, 34(3), 263–283. doi:10.1080/03075070802597036

Katims, S. D., & Harris, S. (1997). Improving the reading comprehension of middle school students in inclusive classrooms. Journal of Adolescent & Adult Literacy, 41(2), 116–123.

Katula, R. A., & Threnhauser, E. (1999). Experiential education in the undergraduate curriculum. Communication Education, 48(3), 238–255. doi:10.1080/03634529909379172

Kayrooz, C., Kinnear, P., & Preston, P. (2001). Academic freedom and commercialisation of Australian universities: Perceptions and experiences of social scientists. Australia Institute.

Keegan, D. (1990). Foundations of distance education (2nd ed.). London, UK: Routledge.

Kegan, R. (1982). The evolving self: Problems and process in human development. Boston, MA: Harvard University Press.

Kehm, B. M., & Teichler, U. (2007). Research on internationalisation in higher education. Journal of Studies in International Education, 11(3-4), 260–273. doi:10.1177/1028315307303534

Kelley, C. A., & Gaedeke, R. M. (1990). Student and employer evaluation of hiring criteria for entry-level marketing positions. Journal of Marketing Education, 12, 64–71. doi:10.1177/027347539001200309

Kelley, C. A. (2007). Assessing the trends and challenges of teaching marketing abroad: A delphi approach. Journal of Marketing Education, 29(3), 201–209. doi:10.1177/0273475307306885

Kelley, E. P. (1971). Marketing's changing social/environmental role. Journal of Marketing, 35(3), 1–2.

Kelsey, J. (1998). Privatizing the universities. Journal of Law and Society, 25, 51. doi:10.1111/1467-6478.00079

Kementerian Pendidikan Malaysia. (1997). Private higher educational institutions (expulsion of students) regulations. Kuala Lumpur, Malaysia: Jabatan Pendidikan Swasta.

Kennedy, E. J., Lawton, L., & Walker, E. (2001). The case for using live cases: Shifting the paradigm in marketing education. Journal of Marketing Education, 23(2), 145–151. doi:10.1177/0273475301232008

Kintsch, W. (1995). Discourse comprehension: Essays in honor of Walter Kintsch (Weaver, C. A. III, Mannes, S., & Fletcher, C. R., Eds.). Hillsdale, NJ: L. Erlbaum.

Kirkman, B. L., & Mathieu, J. E. (2004). The role of virtuality in work team effectiveness. Proceedings of the Academy of Management Annual Meeting, Louisiana Academy of Management.

Kirschner, P. A., Sweller, J., & Clark, R. E. (2006). Why minimal guidance during instruction does not work: An analysis of the failure of constructivist, discovery, problem-based, experiential, and inquiry-based teaching. Educational Psychologist, 41(2), 75–86. doi:10.1207/s15326985ep4102_1

Kittle, B., & Ciba, D. (2001). Using college websites for student recruitment: A relationship marketing study. Journal of Marketing for Higher Education, 11(3), 17–37. doi:10.1300/J050v11n03_02

Klassen, M., & Sitzman, E. (2000). At the intersection of demand creation and demand fulfillment: Which schools are getting there first and why. Journal of Marketing for Higher Education, 10(1), 43–53. doi:10.1300/J050v10n01_04

Kletzien, S. B. (2009). Paraphrasing: An effective comprehension strategy. The Reading Teacher, 63(1), 73–77. doi:10.1598/RT.63.1.7

Knight, B. (1993). Financial management for schools: The thinking managers' guide. Oxford, UK: Heinemann.

Kolb, A. Y., & Kolb, D. A. (2005). Learning styles and learning spaces: Enhancing experiential learning in higher education. Academy of Management Learning & Education, 4(2), 193–212.

Kolb, D. (1984). Experiential learning. Englewood. Cliffs, NJ: Prentice Hall.

Kolb, A. Y., & Kolb, D. A. (2009). Experiential learning theory: A dynamic, holistic approach to management learning, education and development. Retrieved January 15, 2010, from http://www.learningfromexperience.com/images/uploads/ELT-Hbk-MLE&D-LFE-website-2-10-08.pdf

Kotler, P., & Zaltman, G. (1971). Social marketing: An approach to planned social change. Journal of Marketing, 35(3), 3–12. doi:10.2307/1249783

Kraut, R., Egido, C., & Galegher, J. (1988). Patterns of contact and communication in scientific research collaboration. Association for Computing Machinery. Retrieved February 21, 2010, from http://www.cos.ufrj.br/~jano/CSCW2005/kraut_1988.pdf

Kupczynski, L., & Hooper, B. (2006). The internet as a path to adult learning. New Horizons for Learning Online, 12(3). Retrieved from http://www.newhorizons.org/journal/journal50.htm

Lager, M. (2007, December). It's coming 2.0gether. Customer Relations Management Magazine, 11(12), 22–27.

Landow, G. (2006). Hypertext 3.0: Critical theory and new media in an era of globalisation (3rd ed.). Baltimore, MD: The Johns Hopkins University Press.

Lapp, D., Flood, J., & Ranck-Buhr, W. (1995). Using multiple text formats to explore scientific phenomena in middle school classrooms. Reading and Writing Quarterly: Overcoming Learning Difficulties, 11, 173–186.

Laurillard, D., & Mc Andrew, P. (2002). Virtual teaching tools: Bringing academics closer to the design of e-learning. Conference Proceedings for Network Learning 2002: A Research Based Conference on e-Learning in Higher Education and Lifelong Learning, (pp. 11–16). Sheffield, UK: University of Sheffield.

Lavengood, K., & Kiser, P. (2007, May/June). Information professionals in the text mine. Online, 31(3), 16–21.

Lavin, M., Van Alstine, L., Scott, A., Oliver, J., & Murphy, J. (2009). The Google Online Marketing Challenge: Fostering student learning of search advertising. Journal of Advertising Education, 13(1), 38–43.

LeClair, D. T., & Stöttinger, B. (1999). Using an intensive living case in graduate marketing courses: Experiences from an international project. Marketing Education Review, 9(3), 31–40.

LeCompte, M. D., & Schensul, J. J. (1999). The ethnographic tool kit: Vol. 5. Analyzing and interpreting ethnographic data. Walnut Creek, CA: AltaMira Press.

Levisohn, B. (2009, February 9). Web work: Searching for hitmakers. Business Week.

Lewis, A. (2008). A new look for the teaching profession. Phi Delta Kappan, 89(7), 467–468.

Lilien, G. L., & Rangaswamy, A. (1998). Marketing engineering: Computer-assisted marketing analysis and planning. Reading, MA: Addison Wesley Educational Publishers.

Lilly, B., & Tippins, M. J. (2002). Enhancing student motivation in marketing classes: Using student management groups. Journal of Marketing Education, 24(3), 253–264. doi:10.1177/0273475302238048

Ling, P. (2008). The first global Google Online Marketing Challenge 2008: Perspectives of ECU student participants. ECULTURE 2008, Joondalup, Australia, November 5. Retrieved January 15, 2010, from http://www.ea.ecu.edu.au/staffdir/data/tmp/lingecu_google_participants_2008.pdf

Lisak, A., & Erez, M. (2009). Leaders and followers in multi-cultural teams: their effects on team communication, team identity and team effectiveness. Proceedings of the International Workshop on Intercultural Collaboration, Palo Alto, California Association for Computing Machinery.

Liu, D. (2009). Chinese higher education changes during sixty years. [in Chinese]. Higher Education Exploration, 5(5), 5–12.

Liu, X. (2004). Higher education budget financing and investing. Journal of Capital Normal University (Social Science Edition), 176-179. (in Chinese).

Long, P. D., Tricker, T., Rangecroft, M., & Gilroy, P. (2000). Satisfaction with distance education: Evaluation of a service template. Total Quality Management, 11(4/6), 530–536.

Lowry, D. (2001). The casual management of casual work: Casual workers' perceptions of HRM practices in the highly casualised firm. Asia Pacific Journal of Human Resources, 39(1), 42–62. doi:10.1177/103841110103900104

Luan, J. (2002). Data mining and its applications in higher education. In Serban, A., & Luan, J. (Eds.), Knowledge management: Building a competitive advantage in higher education (pp. 17–36). San Francisco, CA: Josey-Bass.

Luck, E., & Chalmers, W. (2007). Making education relevant. A SMART collaborative project: School marketing and real-world teaching. Proceedings of the Australian and New Zealand Marketing Academy (ANZMAC) Conference 2007, Dunedin, New Zealand. Retrieved January 20, 2010, from http://eprints.qut.edu.au/13097/1/13097.pdf

Luke, C. (2005). Capital and knowledge flows. Global Higher Education Markets, 25(2), 159–174.

Lumby, J., & Forskett, N. (1999). Managing external relations in schools and colleges. London, UK: Paul Chapman.

Lu-ting, M. (2009). Structure framing of higher education system of Switzerland and the analysis of its features. [in Chinese]. Comparative Education Review, 7, 1–6.

Lynch, K. (2006). Neo-liberalism and marketisation: The implications for higher education. European Educational Research Journal, 5(1), 1–17. doi:10.2304/eerj.2006.5.1.1

MacBeath, J., Gray, J. M., Cullen, J., Frost, D., Steward, S., & Swaffield, S. (2007). Schools on the edge: Responding to challenging circumstances. London, UK: Paul Chapman Publishing.

Madrid, R. I., Van Oostendorp, H., & Melguizo, M. C. P. (2009). The effects of the number of links and navigation support on cognitive load and learning with hypertext: The mediating role of reader order. Computers in Human Behavior, 29, 66–75.

Magidson, J., & Vermunt, J. K. (2002). Latent class models for clustering: A comparison with K-means. Canadian Journal of Marketing Research, 20, 37–44.

Majchrzak, A., Malhotra, A., Stamps, J., & Lipnack, J. (2004). Can absence make a team grow stronger? Harvard Business Review, 82(5), 131–137.

Malone, L. D., & Mastropieri, M. A. (1992). Reading comprehension instruction: Summarisation and self-monitoring training for students with learning disabilities. Exceptional Children, 58, 279–279.

Mani, I. (2001). Automatic summarization. Philadelphia, PA: J. Benjamins.

Manning, C., & Schütze, H. (1999). Foundations of statistical natural language processing. Cambridge, MA: MIT Press.

Margine, F. (2006). University and course choice. International Journal of Educational Management, 20(6), 466–479. doi:10.1108/09513540610683711

Marginson, S. (2006). Dynamics of national and global competition in higher education. Higher Education, 52, 1–39. doi:10.1007/s10734-004-7649-x

Marginson, S. (2007). Global position and position taking: The case of Australia. Journal of Studies in International Education, 11(1), 5–32. doi:10.1177/1028315306287530

Marginson, S. (2006). Dynamics of national and global competition in higher education. Higher Education, 52, 1–39. doi:10.1007/s10734-004-7649-x

Marginson, S. (2008). Academic creativity under new public management: Foundations for an investigation. Educational Theory, 58(3), 269–287. doi:10.1111/j.1741-5446.2008.00288.x

Marketshare.hitslink.com. (2009). Top search engine share trend. Retrieved January 30, 2010, from http://profitadz.com/pdf/MarketShare.pdf

Marshall, C., & Rossman, G. B. (2006). Designing qualitative research (4th ed.). Thousand Oaks, CA: Sage Publications.

Martin, A. J. (2007). Examining a multidimensional model of student motivation and engagement using a construct validation approach. The British Journal of Educational Psychology, 77(2), 413–440. doi:10.1348/000709906X118036

Mastropieri, M. A., & Scruggs, T. E. (1997). Best practice in promoting reading comprehension in students with learning disabilities. Remedial and Special Education, 18, 197–213. doi:10.1177/074193259701800402

Matulich, E., Papp, R., & Haytko, D. L. (2008). Continuous improvement through teaching innovations: A requirement for today's learners. Marketing Education Review, 18(1), 1–7.

Mayer, R. E. (2004). Should there be a three-strikes rule against pure discovery learning? The case for guided methods of instruction. The American Psychologist, 59(1), 14–19. doi:10.1037/0003-066X.59.1.14

Mazzarol, T. W. (1994). A model of sustainable competitive advantage for service exporters. Perth, Australia: Curtin University of Technology.

Mazzarol, T. W., Soutar, G., Smart, N., & Choo, D. (2001). Perceptions, information and choice: Understanding how Chinese students select a country for overseas study. Commonwealth of Australia: Australian Education International. Department of Education, Training and Youth Affairs.

Mazzarol, T., & Soutar, G. N. (2002). Push-pull' factors influencing international student destination choice. The International Journal of Education, 16(2), 82–90.

Mc Andrew, P., & Wilson, T. (2008). Pocketing the difference: Joint development of open educational resources. In ICALT 2008: The 8th IEEE International Conference on Advanced Learning, Technologies. Learning technologies in the Information society, 1-5 July 2008, Santander, Cantabria, Spain.

McBurnie, G., & Ziguras, C. (2001). The regulation of transnational higher education in Southeast Asia: Case studies of Hong Kong, Malaysia and Australia. Higher Education, 42, 85–105. doi:10.1023/A:1017572119543

McCarthy, J. (2001). Basic marketing: A managerial approach. Homewood, IL: Irwin.

McClurg, L. N. (1999). Organizational commitment in the temporary-help service industry. Journal of Applied Management Studies, 8(1), 5–26.

McCorkle, D. E., Reardon, J., Alexander, J. F., Kling, N. D., Harris, R. C., & Vishwanathan, I. R. (1999). Undergraduate marketing students, group projects, and teamwork: The good, the bad, and the ugly? Journal of Marketing Education, 21(2), 106–117. doi:10.1177/0273475399212004

McCracken, G. (1988). Lois Roget: Curatorial consumer in a modern world. In Culture and consumption (pp. 44–56). Bloomington, IN: Indiana University Press.

McDonald, M., & Dunbar, I. (2004). Market segmentation: How to do it, how to profit from it?Amsterdam, The Netherlands: Elsevier.

McDonald, S., & Stevenson, R. (1996). Disorientation in hypertext: Effects of three structures on navigation performance. Applied Ergonomics, 27(1), 61–68. doi:10.1016/0003-6870(95)00073-9

McDonald, S., Oates, C. J., Young, C. W., & Hwang, K. (2006). Toward sustainable consumption: Researching voluntary simplifiers. Psychology and Marketing, 23(6), 515–534. doi:10.1002/mar.20132

McEachern, R. W. (2001). Problems in service learning and technical / professional writing: Incorporating the perspective on nonprofit management. Technical Communication Quarterly, 10(2), 211–225. doi:10.1207/s15427625tcq1002_6

McGee, M. (2010). Experian gitwise: Google passes 72% U.S. market share. Retrieved January 20, 2010, from http://searchengineland.com/google-passes-72-us-market-share-33545

McIntyre, F. S., Webb, D. J., & Hite, R. E. (2005). Service learning in the marketing curriculum: Faculty views and participation. Marketing Education Review, 15(1), 35–45.

McKeachie, W. J. (2002). McKeachie's teaching tips: Strategies, research, and theory for college and university teachers (11th ed.). Boston, MA: Houghton Mifflin.

McNabb, M. (2005. (2006). Navigating the maze of hypertext. Educational Leadership, (December - January): 76–79.

McNamara, D. S., Ozuru, Y., Best, R., & O'Reilly, T. (2007). The 4-pronged comprehension strategy framework. In McNamara, D. S. (Ed.), Reading comprehension strategies: Theories, interventions, and technologies (pp. 465–496). Abingdon, UK: Lawrence Erbaum Associates.

Mehler, A., & Köhler, R. (2007). Aspects of automatic text analysis. Berlin, Germany: Springer.

Mehrabian, A. (1981). Silent messages: Implicit communication of emotions and attributes (2nd ed.). Belmont, CA: Wadsworth.

Melbourne University Act. (1958).

Menon, A., & Menon, A. (1997). Enviropreneurial marketing strategy: The emergence of corporate environmentalism as marketing strategy. Journal of Marketing, 61, 51–67. doi:10.2307/1252189

Merriam, S. B. (1995). What can you tell from an N of 1?: Issues of validity and reliability in qualitative research. PAACE Journal of Lifelong Learning, 4, 51–60.

Michailidou, A., & Economides, A. (2003). E-learn: Towards a collaborative educational virtual environment. Journal of Information Technology Education, 2, 131–152.

Michelli, J. (2006). The Starbucks experience: Five principles for turning ordinary into extraordinary. New York, NY: McGraw-Hill.

Middlewood, D., & Burton, N. (2003). Managing the curriculum. London, UK: Paul Chapman.

Middlewood, D., & Lumby, J. (1998). Strategic management in schools and colleges. London, UK: Paul Chapman.

Middlewood, D., & Lumby, J. (2003). Human resource management in schools. London, UK: Paul Chapman.

Middlewood, D. (1999). Managing relations between schools and parents. In Foskett, N., & Lumby, J. (Eds.), Managing external relations in schools and colleges. London, UK: Paul Chapman.

Mihhailova, G., & Piiriste, G. (2008). Management and leadership challenges due to using virtual work in multi-cultural organisations: Cases of two service sector companies.

Miles, M. B., & Huberman, A. M. (1994). Qualitative data analysis. Thousand Oaks, CA: Sage.

Milheim, W. (2002). Faculty and administrative strategies for the effective implementation of distance education. British Journal of Educational Technology, 32(5), 535–542. doi:10.1111/1467-8535.00223

Milliken, T. F., & Jurgens, J. C. (2008). Assessing the needs of human services adjunct faculty: Uncovering strategies for retaining quality instructors. Human Service Education, 28(1), 29–43.

Ministry of Education. (1999). Action scheme for invigorating education towards the 21st century. [in Chinese]. The China Higher Education, 6, 35–39.

Mok, K. H. (2008). Positioning as regional hub of higher education: Changing governance and regulatory reforms in Singapore and Malaysia. International Journal of Educational Reform, 17(3), 230–250.

Mont, O., & Plepys, A. (2008). Sustainable consumption progress: Should we be proud or alarmed? Journal of Cleaner Production, 16(4), 531–537. doi:10.1016/j.jclepro.2007.01.009

Moore, G. M. (1995). The 1995 distance education research symposium: A research agenda. American Journal of Distance Education, 9(2), 1–6. doi:10.1080/08923649509526884

Morris, M. W., Leung, K., Ames, D., & Lickel, B. (1999). Views from inside and outside: Integrating EMIC and ETIC insights about culture and justice judgment. Academy of Management Review, 24(4), 781–796. doi:10.2307/259354

Morse v Frederick, 127 S Ct 2618. (2007).

Mortmore, (1994). Managing associate staff: Innovation in primary and secondary schools. London, UK: Paul Chapman.

Mossenson, L., Hill, P., & Masters, G. (1987). Tests of reading comprehension: Manual. Australian Council of Educational Research.

Mullins, G., Quintrell, N., & Hancock, L. (1995). The experiences of international and local students at three Australian universities. Higher Education Research & Development, 14(2), 201–231. doi:10.1080/0729436950140205

Munoz, C., & Huser, A. (2008). Experiential and cooperative learning: Using a situation analysis project in principles of marketing. Journal of Education for Business, 83(4), 214–220. doi:10.3200/JOEB.83.4.214-220

Munro, J. (1996). Teaching reading strategies. Australia: Hawthorn.

Munro, J. (2002). Leading learning communities. Jolimont, Australia: Incorporated Association of Registerd Teachers of Victoria.

Murphy, J., Hudson, K., Hunter, L., & Neale, L. (2009a). The Google Online Marketing Challenge: Hands on teaching and learning. Journal of Hospitality and Tourism Education, 21(1), 44–47.

Murphy, J., Hudson, K., & Hunter, L. (2008). Google AdWords: Case study. In Summers, J., Gardiner, M., Lamb, C. W., Hair, J. F., & McDaniel, C. (Eds.), Essentials of marketing (3rd ed.).

Murphy, J., Hunter, L., Hofacker, C., Lavin, M., Voorhees, C., & Canhoto, A. I. (2008). The Google Online Marketing Challenge: A global teaching and learning initiative. Special Session at the American Marketing Association Summer Educator's Conference, August 10, San Diego, CA.

Murphy, J., Tuzovic, S., Ling, P., & Mullen, L. (2009b). Incorporating the Google Online Marketing Challenge into classes. Special Panel at the Marketing Educators' Association Conference, April 23-25, Newport Beach, CA. Retrieved August 5, from 2009http://www.google.com/onlinechallenge/research_files/MEA_Google_Challenge_Incorporating.pdf

Murray, D. (2000). Protean communication: The language of computer mediated communication. TESOL Quarterly, 34(3), 397–421. doi:10.2307/3587737

Musico, C. (2009, December). No substitute for experience. Customer Relations Management Magazine, 13(12), 22–29.

Nadiri, H., Kandampully, J., & Hussain, K. (2009). Students' perceptions of service quality in higher education. Total Quality Management & Business Excellence, 20(5), 523–535. doi:10.1080/14783360902863713

Naidoo, R. (2003). Repositioning higher education as a global commodity: Opportunities and challenges for future sociology of education work. British Journal of Sociology of Education, 23(2), 249–259. doi:10.1080/01425690301902

Nash, R. D. (2005). Course completion rates among distance learners: Identifying possible methods to improve retention. Online Journal of Distance Learning Administration, 8(4). Retrieved from http://www.westga.edu/distance/ojdla/.

Nasukawa, T. (2006). Text analysis within the knowledge mining project and sentiment analysis. Paper presented at National Centre for e-Social Science Workshop, Manchester, United Kingdom.

Natarajan, J., Berrar, D., Hack, C. J., & Dubitzky, W. (2005). Knowledge discovery in biology and biotechnology texts: A review of techniques, evaluation strategies, and applications. Critical Reviews in Biotechnology, 25, 31–52. doi:10.1080/07388550590935571

National Center for Education Statistics. (2008). Digest of educational statistics. U.S. Department of Education Institute of Education Sciences. Retrieved from http://nces.ed.gov/programs/digest/d08/tables/dt08_248.asp

Navarro, P. (2008). The MBA core curricula of top-ranked U.S. business schools: A study in failure? Academy of Management Learning & Education, 7(1), 108–123.

Neale, L., Treiblmaier, H., Henderson, V., Hunter, L., Hudson, K., & Murphy, J. (2009). The Google Online Marketing Challenge and research opportunities. Journal of Marketing Education, 31(1), 76–85. doi:10.1177/0273475308329534

Neale, L., Hofacker, C., Hunter, L., Hudson, K., Canhoto, A. I., & Murphy, J. (2008). The Google Online Marketing Challenge: A global real-world teaching and learning tool. In Kehoe, W. J., & Whitten, L. K. (Eds.), Advances in marketing: Issues, strategies and theories (p. 30). Tuscaloosa, AL: Society for Marketing Advances.

Neave, G., & Van Vught, F. A. (1991). Prometheus bound - the changing relationship between government and higher education in Western Europe. NTEIU v University of Wollongong, FCA 1069. (2001).

Nichols, M. (2010). Student perceptions of support services and the influence of targeted interventions on retention in distance education. Distance Education, 31(1), 93–113. doi:10.1080/01587911003725048

Nunnally, J. C. (1987). Teoría psicométrica. Mexico: Trillas.

O'Hara, B. S., & Shaffer, T. R. (1995). Details and student perceptions of an experiential program for personal selling and purchasing classes. Journal of Marketing Education, 17(Spring), 41–49. doi:10.1177/027347539501700106

O'Neill, M. A., & Palmer, A. (2004). Importance-performance analysis: A useful tool for directing continuous quality improvement in higher education. Quality Assurance in Education, 12(1), 39–52. doi:10.1108/09684880410517423

Oates, C., McDonald, S., Alevizou, P., & Hwang, K. (2008). Marketing sustainability: Use of information sources and degrees of voluntary simplicity. Journal of Marketing Communications, 14(5), 351–365. doi:10.1080/13527260701869148

Obst, D. (2008). National policies for international education. Retrieved Nov 8, 2008, from http://www.iienetwork.org/page/116248

OECD. (2007). Share of tertiary foreign students in OECD countries. Retrieved October 11, 2007, from http://www.oecd.org/document/54/0,3343,en_2649_37455_38082166_1_1_1_37455,00.html

Oldfield, B. M., & Baron, S. (2000). Student perceptions of service quality in a UK university business and management faculty. Quality Assurance in Education, 8(29), 85–95. doi:10.1108/09684880010325600

Oliver, R., & Herrington, J. (1995). Developing effective hypermedia instructional materials. Australian Journal of Educational Technology, 11(2), 8–22.

Oliver, R., & Omari, A. (1999). Using online technologies to support problem based learning: Learners' responses and perceptions. Australian Journal of Educational Technology, 15(1), 58–79.

Opoku, R. A., Hultman, M., & Saheli-Sangari, E. (2008). Positioning in market space: The evaluation of Swedish universities' online brand personalities. Journal of Marketing for Higher Education, 18(1), 124–144. doi:10.1080/08841240802100386

Oravec, J. A. (2003). Some influences of online distance learning on US higher education. Journal of Further and Higher Education, 27(1), 89–103. doi:10.1080/03098770305628

Order on Web college claims. (1999, June 2). The Australian, (p. 35).

Osika, E., Johnson, R., & Buteau, R. (2009). Factors influencing faculty use of technology in online instruction: A case study. Online Journal of Distance Learning Administration, 12(1). Retrieved from http://www.westga.edu/~distance/ojdla/spring121/osika121.html.

Ostlund, B. (2008). Prerequisites for interactive learning in distance education: Perspectives from Swedish students. Australasian Journal of Educational Technology, 24(1), 42–56.

Ouyang, H. (2006). Investigation and analysis on higher education quality. Educational Development Study, 11, 26–29.

Owlia, M. S., & Aspinwall, E. M. (1998). Quality in higher education: A survey. Total Quality Management, 7(4), 161–171.

Pahl, C. (2003). Managing evolution and change in Web-based teaching and learning. Computers & Education, 40(2), 99–114. doi:10.1016/S0360-1315(02)00100-8

Paladino, A. (2008). Creating an interactive and responsive teaching environment to inspire learning. Journal of Marketing Education, 30(3), 185–188. doi:10.1177/0273475308318075

Papish v Board of the Curators of the University of Missouri, 410 US 667. (1973).

Parasuraman, A., Zeithaml, V. A., & Berry, L. L. (1985). A conceptual model of service quality and its implications for future research. Journal of Marketing, 43, 41–50. doi:10.2307/1251430

Parasuraman, A., Zeithaml, V. A., & Berry, L. L. (1988). SERVQUAL: A multiple-item scale for measuring consumer perceptions of service quality. Journal of Retailing, 64, 39–48.

Parasuraman, A., Zeithaml, V. A., & Berry, L. L. (1994). Alternative scales for measuring service quality: A comparative assessment based on psychometric and diagnostic criteria. Journal of Retailing, 70(3), 201–230. doi:10.1016/0022-4359(94)90033-7

Patton, M. (2002). Qualitative research and evaluation methods (3rd ed.). Thousand Oaks, CA: Sage Publications.

Pearce v Pearce, 63 Eng Rep 950. (1846).

Pearson, P. D. (1984). Direct explicit teaching of reading comprehension. In Duffy, G. G., Roehler, L. R., & Mason, J. (Eds.), Comprehension instruction: Perspectives and suggestions (pp. 222–233). New York, NY: Longman.

Pentina, I., & Neeley, C. (2007). Differences in characteristics of online versus traditional students: Implications for target marketing. Journal of Marketing for Higher Education, 17(1), 49–65. doi:10.1300/J050v17n01_05

Penuel, W. R. (2006). Implementation and effects of one-to-one computing initiatives: A research synthesis. Journal of Research on Technology in Education, 38, 329–348.

Peterson, R. M. (2001). Course participation: An active learning approach employing student documentation. Journal of Marketing Education, 23(3), 187–194. doi:10.1177/0273475301233004

Petkus, E. (2000). A theoretical and practical framework for service-learning in marketing: Kolb's experiential learning cycle. Journal of Marketing Education, 22(1), 64–70. doi:10.1177/0273475300221008

Pickering v Board of Education, 391 US 563. (1968).

Pine, B. J. II, & Gilmore, J. H. (1998). Welcome to the experience economy. Harvard Business Review, 76, 97–105.

Pine, B. J. II, & Gilmore, J. H. (1999). The experience economy: Work is theatre and every business a stage. Boston, MA: Harvard Business School Press.

Pituch, K. A., & Lee, Y. (2006). The influence of system characteristics on e-learning use. Computers & Education, 47(2), 222–244. doi:10.1016/j.compedu.2004.10.007

Plank, D. N., & Boyd, W. L. (1994). Antipolitics, education, and institutional choice: The flight from democracy. American Educational Research Journal, 31(2), 263–281.

Post, R. (2006). The structure of academic freedom. In Doumani, B. (Ed.), Academic freedom after September 11 (p. 61).

Postiglione, G. (2005). Higher education in China: Perils and promises for a new century. (pp. 138-143).

Powell, A., Piccoli, G., & Ives, B. (2004). Virtual teams: A review of current literature and directions for future research. ACM SIGMIS Database, 35(1), 6–36. doi:10.1145/968464.968467

Prensky, M. (2001). Digital natives, digital immigrants. Horizon, 9(5), 1–6. doi:10.1108/10748120110424816

Pressley, M. (1998). Reading instruction that works: The case for balanced teaching. New York, NY: Guilford Press.

Pressley, M., Brown, R., El-Dinary, P. B., & Afflerbach, P. (1995). The comprehension instruction that students need: Instruction fostering constructively responsive reading. Learning Disabilities Research & Practice, 10, 215–224.

Pressley, M. (2000). What should comprehension instruction be the instruction of? In Kamil, M., Mosenthal, P., Pearson, P. D., & Barr, R. (Eds.), Handbook of reading research (Vol. 3, pp. 545–562). Hillsdale, NJ: Erlbaum.

Price, L. L., Arnould, E. J., & Folkman, C. C. (2000). Older consumers' disposition of special possessions. The Journal of Consumer Research, 27(2), 179–201. doi:10.1086/314319

Prugsamatz, S., Pentecost, R., & Ofstad, L. (2006). The influence of explicit and implicit service promises on Chinese students' expectations of overseas universities. Asia Pacific Journal of Marketing and Logistics, 18(2), 129–145. doi:10.1108/13555850610658273

Pryor, S., & Grossbart, S. (2005). Ethnography of an American main street. International Journal of Retail and Distribution Management, 33(11), 806–823. doi:10.1108/09590550510629400

Puzziferro, M., & Shelton, K. (2009). Supporting online faculty: Revisiting the seven principles (A few years later). Online Journal of Distance Learning Administration, 12(3). Retrieved from http://search.ebscohost.com/login.aspx?direct=true&db=eric&AN=EJ864301&site=ehost-live.

Radder, L., & Han, X. (2009). Service quality of on-campus student housing: A South African experience. The International Business & Economics Research Journal, 8(11), 107–119.

Ranney, G., Tveite, M., & Bradbury, I. (2006). Misuse of statistical methodology. Paper presented at the Joint Statistical Meeting, Seattle, WA.

Rawls, J. (1971). A theory of justice. Cambridge, MA: Harvard University Press.

Readings, B. (1996). The university in ruins. Cambridge, MA & London, UK: Harvard University Press.

Richardson, J. C., & Swan, K. (2003). Examining social presence in online courses in relation to students' perceived learning and satisfaction. Journal of Asynchronous Learning Networks, 7(1), 68–88.

Riddiford, M. (2009, October 14). Academic freedom a political football. The Australian. Retrieved December 4, 2009, from http://www.theaustralian.com.au/higher-education/opinion-analysis/academic-freedom-a-political-football/story-e6frgcko-1225786422196

Robinson, R., & Doverspike, D. (2006). Factors predicting the choice of an online versus a traditional course. Teaching of Psychology, 33(1), 64–68. doi:10.1207/s15328023top3301_10

Rocha Trindade, A., Carmo, H., & Biddara, J. (2000). Current developments and best practice in open and distance learning. International Review of Research in Open and Distance Learning, 1(1).

Rochford, F. (2006). Is there any clear idea of a university? Journal of Higher Education Policy and Management, 28(2), 147–158. doi:10.1080/13600800600750988

Rochford, F. (2008). The contested product of a university education. Journal of Higher Education Policy and Management, 30(1), 41–52. doi:10.1080/13600800701745044

Rochford, F. (2003). Academic freedom as insubordination: The legalisation of the academy. In G. B. Palfreyman (Ed.), Education and the Law, 15(4), 249-262.

Rochford, F. (2007). The law of negligence in a risk society: Calculating ideas of reasonable risk. Griffith Law Review, 172-192.

Rockwell, S. K., Schauer, J., Fritz, S. M., & Marx, D. B. (1999). Incentives and obstacles influencing higher education faculty and administrators to teach via distance. Online Journal of Distance Learning Administration, 2(4).

Roebuck, D. B., Brock, S. J., & Moodie, D. R. (2004). Using a simulation to explore the challenges of communication in a virtual team. Business Communication Quarterly, 67(3), 359–367. doi:10.1177/1080569904268083

Rondinelli, D. (2002). Transnational corporations: International citizens or new sovereigns. Business & Society, 107, 391–413. doi:10.1111/1467-8594.00143

Rosborough, R. S. (2009). A great day for academic freedom: The threat posed to academic freedom by the Supreme Court's decision in Garcetti v Ceballos. Albany Law Review, 565–598.

Rosenberger v Rector and Visitors of the University of Virginia, 515 US 819. (1995).

Rosenfeld, B., & Martinez-Pons, M. (2005). Promoting classroom technology use. Quarterly Review of Distance Education, 6(2), 145.

Rosenshine, B. (1986). Synthesis of research on explicit teaching. Educational Leadership, 43, 60–69.

Rosenshine, B., & Stevens, R. (1984). Classroom instruction in reading. In Pearson, P. D. (Ed.), Handbook of reading research (pp. 745–798). New York, NY: Longman.

Rosso, M., McClelland, M. K., Jansen, B. J., & Fleming, S. W. (2009). Using Google AdWords in the MBA MIS course. Journal of Information Systems Education, 20(1), 41–50.

Royal Melbourne Institute of Technology Act. (1992).

RSA. (1996a). The Constitution of the Republic of South Africa, Act 108 of 1996. Cape Town, South Africa: Government Printers.

RSA. (1996b). South African Schools Act 84 of 1996. Cape Town, South Africa: Government Printers.

Rundle-Thiele, S. R., & Kuhn, K.-A. L. (2008). Challenging first year marketing students using a tournament style competition. Proceedings of the 2008 Annual Conference of the Academy of Marketing Science: Creating Value in a Global Marketplace, May 28-31, 2008, Vancouver, BC, Canada.

Russell, M. (2005). Marketing education: A review of service quality perceptions among international students. International Journal of Contemporary Hospitality Management, 17(1), 65–77. doi:10.1108/09596110510577680

Russell, R., Atchison, M., & Brooks, R. (2008). Business plan competitions in tertiary institutions: Encouraging entrepreneurship education. Journal of Higher Education Policy and Management, 30(2), 123–138. doi:10.1080/13600800801938739

Rutaisire, J. (2007) The role of teachers in social and political reconstruction in Rwanda, in, Leach, F. And Dunne, M. (eds) Education, Conflict and Reconciliation: International perspectives, pp. 115-129, Berne: Peter Lang.

Rutaisire, J., Kabano, J., & Rubagiza, J. (2004) Redefining Rwanda's future: The role of curriculum in social reconstruction, in Tawil, S. And Harley, A, (eds) Education, conflict and social cohesion, pp. 315-373, Geneva, IBE, UNESCO

Rzhetsky, A., Seringhaus, M., & Gerstein, M. (2008). Seeking a new biology through text mining. Cell, 134, 9–13. doi:10.1016/j.cell.2008.06.029

Saheb, T. (2005). ICT, education and digital divide in developing counties. Global Media Journal, 4(7).

Salmeron, L., Canas, J. J., Kintsch, W., & Fajardo, I. (2005). Reading strategies and hypertext comprehension. Discourse Processes, 40(3), 171–191. doi:10.1207/s15326950dp4003_1

Salmi, J. (2003). Constructing knowledge societies: New challenges for tertiary education. Higher Education in Europe, 28(1), 65–69. doi:10.1080/0379772032000110125

Salmon, G. (2000). E-moderating: The key to teaching and learning online. London, UK: Kogan Page.

Sammons, P. (1995). Key characteristics of effective schools: A review of school effectiveness. In J. Bush & D. Middlewood (1997). Managing people in education. London, UK: Paul Chapman.

Samuels, R. (2004). The future threat to computers and composition: Nontenured instructors, intellectual property, and distance education. Computers and Composition, 21(1), 63–71. doi:10.1016/j.compcom.2003.08.006

Sánchez, M., Sánchez, R., Marín, G., & Gázquez, J. C. (2007). Service quality in public services as a segmentation variable. The Service Industries Journal, 27(4), 355–369. doi:10.1080/02642060701346771

SAS Institute. (2008). Mining more than gold: HP soaring to the next level of CRM with SAS. Retrieved May 30, 2008, from http://www.sas.com/success/hp.html

Saunders, C. S. (2000). Virtual teams: Piecing together the puzzle. In Zimud, R. W. (Ed.), Framing the domain of IT management: Projecting the future through the past. Cincinnati, OH: Pinnaflex.

Savery, J. R. (2006). Overview of problem-based learning: Definitions and distinctions. The Interdisciplinary Journal of Problem-based Learning, 1(1), 9–20.

Schibrowsky, J. A., & Peltier, J. W. (1995). The dark side of experiential learning activities. Journal of Marketing Education, 17(1), 13–24. doi:10.1177/027347539501700103

Schmitt, C. M., & Baumann, F. J. (1986). How to incorporate comprehension monitoring strategies into basal reader instruction. The Reading Teacher, 40, 28–31.

Schmitt, B. H. (2003). Customer experience management: A revolutionary approach to connecting with your customers. New York, NY: Wiley.

Schnitzer, M., & Crosby, L. (2003). Recruitment and development of online adjunct instructors. Online Journal of Distance Learning Administration, 6(2). Retrieved from http://www.westga.edu/~distance/ojdla/summer62/crosby_schnitzer62.html.

Schofer, E., & Meyer, J. (2006). The world-wide expansion of higher education in the twentieth century. American Sociological Review, 70(6), 898–920. doi:10.1177/000312240507000602

Schroeder, R. (2008). Teaching and learning: What does technology have to do with it? Sloan-C View, 7(1). Retrieved from http://www.sloan-c.org/publications/view/v7n1/viewv7n1.htm

Schrum, L. (2005). E-learning and K-12. In Howard, C., Boettcher, J. V., Justice, L., Schenk, K., Rogers, P. L., & Berg, G. A. (Eds.), Encyclopedia of distance learning (pp. 737–742). Hershey, PA: Idea Group Reference.

Scott, J. (2009). Knowledge, power and academic freedom. Social Research, 452–480.

Search, C. R. M. com. (2010). Significant differences between customer experience management (CEM) and CRM. Retrieved January 5, 2010, from http://www/searchcrm.com

Senate Standing Committee on Education. Employment and Workplace Relations. (2008). Allegations of academic bias in universities and schools: Report. Canberra, Australia: Commonwealth of Australia.

Senge, P. (1990). The fifth discipline. In Middlewood, D. (Eds.), Practitioner research in education. London, UK: Paul Chapman.

Sevier, R. A. (2009). Managing the experience. University Business, 12(4), 37–39.

Shaik, N. (2005). Marketing distance learning programs and courses: A relationship marketing strategy. Online Journal of Distance Learning Administration, 8(2).

Shakeshaft, C. (2002). The shadowy downside of adjuncts. The School Administrator. Retrieved from http://www.interactiveinc.org/Publications/downsideofadjuncts.pdf

Shank, M. D., Walker, M., & Hayes, T. (1995). Understanding professional service expectations: Do we know what our students expect in a quality education? Journal of Professional Services Marketing, 13(1), 71–89. doi:10.1300/J090v13n01_08

Shattock, M. (1996). Creation of a university system. Blackwell Publishing.

Shelton, K., & Saltsman, G. (2006). An administrator's guide to online education. University Business, 8(9), 73–76.

Shiffman, C. (2009). The emerging academician: The rise of the online adjunct faculty. Dissertation Abstract International, 70(2). (UMI No. AAT 3344730).

Shin, N. (2002). Beyond interaction: The relational construct of transactional presence. Open Learning, 17(2), 121–137. doi:10.1080/02680510220146887

Shin, N. (2003). Transactional presence as a critical predictor of success in distance learning. Distance Education, 24(1), 69–86. doi:10.1080/01587910303048

Shive, G. (2010, January). Exporting higher education services: An engine of growth for Hong Kong? Hkjournal. Retrieved January 22, 2010, from www.hkjournal.org/PDF/2010_spring/4.pdf

Siegel, C. E. (2000). Introducing marketing students to business intelligence using project-based learning on the World Wide Web. Journal of Marketing Education, 22(2), 90–98. doi:10.1177/0273475300222003

Sife, A. S., Lwoga, E., & Sanga, C. (2007). New technologies for teaching and learning: Challenges for higher learning institutions in developing countries. International Journal of Education and Development Using ICT, 3(2).

Simmons, D. C., Kuchs, D., Fuchs, L. S., Hodge, J. P., & Mathes, P. G. (1994). Importance of instructional complexity and role reciprocity to classwide peer tutoring. Learning Disabilities Research & Practice, 9, 203–212.

Simpson, O. (2004). The impact on retention of interventions to support distance learning students. Open Learning, 19(1), 79–95. doi:10.1080/0268051042000177863

Simpson, M. C., & Pham, K.-Q. (2007). The creative campus: Experiential learning by short study-abroad courses. Paper presented at 32nd Improving University Teaching Conference, Jaén, Spain.

Singapore Education. (n.d.). Roles and responsibilities of Education Services Division. Retrieved February 3, 2009, from http://www.singaporeedu.gov.sg/htm/abo/abo01.htm

Singhal, A. (2001). Modern information retrieval: A brief overview. Bulletin of the IEEE Computer Society Technical Committee on Data Engineering, 24(4), 35–43.

Slaughter, S., & Leslie, L. L. (1997). Academic capitalism. Baltimore, MD: Johns Hopkins University Press.

Slavin, R. E. (1990). Cooperative learning. New Jersey: Prentice-Hall.

Smith, G. S., Smith, A., & Clarke, A. (2007). Evaluating service quality in universities: A service department perspective. Quality Assurance in Education, 15(3), 334–351. doi:10.1108/09684880710773200

Smith, S., & Wheeler, J. (2002). Managing the customer experience: Turning customers into advocates. Upper Saddle River, NJ: FT Press.

Smith, K. A. (1986). Cooperative learning groups. In Schmoberg, S. F. (Ed.), Strategies for active teaching and learning in university classrooms. Minneapolis, MN: Office of Educational Development Programs, University of Minnesota.

Southworth, G. (1984). Development of staff in primary schools. In Bush, T., & Middlewood, D. (Eds.), Managing people in education. London, UK: Paul Chapman.

Southworth, G. (1994). The learning school. In Bush, T., & Middlewood, D. (Eds.), Managing people in education. London, UK: Paul Chapman.

Spoehr, K. T. (1994). Enhancing the acquisition of conceptual structures through hypermedia, in classroom lessons: Integrating cognitive theory and classroom practice. Cambridge, MA: Mcgilly.

SPSS Inc. (2006). SPSS text analysis for surveys 2.0 user's guide. Chicago, IL: Author.

Squelch, J. (Author). Lemmer, E. (Ed.), (1999). Contemporary education. Sandton, South Africa: Heinemann.

St George, E. (2006). Positioning higher education for the knowledge based economy. Higher Education, 589–610. doi:10.1007/s10734-005-0955-0

Stanovich, K. E., & Siegel, L. S. (1994). Phenotypic performance profile of children with learning disabilities: A regression-based test of phonological-core variable-difference model. Journal of Educational Psychology, 86, 24–53. doi:10.1037/0022-0663.86.1.24

Steenkamp, J. B., & Van Trijp, H. C. M. (1991). The use of Lisrel in validating marketing constructs. International Journal of Research in Marketing, 8(4), 283–299. doi:10.1016/0167-8116(91)90027-5

Stevens, K. (2001). The development of digital Intranets for the enhancement of education in rural communities. Journal of Interactive Instruction Development, 13(3), 19–24.

Stevens, K. (2002). Making the world smaller -the electronic networking of small schools –some unseen connections of the Icelandic educational network in New Zealand and Canada. [Icelandic translation by Karl Erlendsson]. Skólavarðan, 2(2), 22–24.

Stevens, K. J. (1999a). A new model for teaching in rural communities – the electronic organisation of classes as Intranets. Prism – Journal of The Newfoundland and Labrador Teachers'. Association, 6(1), 23–26.

Stevens, K. J., & Stewart, D. (2005). Cybercells – learning in actual and virtual groups. Melbourne, Australia: Thomson-Dunmore Press.

Stevens, K. J. (2007). A matrix for e-collaboration in rural Canadian schools. In Kock, N. (Ed.), Encyclopedia of e-collaboration (pp. 444–449). Hershey, PA: IGI Global, Information Science Reference.

Stevens, K. (2000). Télé-enseignement et éducation en milieu rural en Nouvelle Zélande et à Terre Neuve. Géocarrefour - Revue de Geographie de Lyon - Espaces Ruraux et Technologies de L'Information, 75(1), 87–92.

Stevens, K. J. (1999b). Telecommunications technologies, tele-learning and the development of virtual classes for rural New Zealanders. Open Praxis, 1.

Stevens, K. J. (2005).The integration of virtual and actual classes in sparsely populated regions. In Kinshuk, D. G. Sampson & P. Isaias (Eds.), Cognition and exploratory learning in the digital age,(pp. 517-520). IADIS Press.

Stevens, K. J. (2008). From e-learning to e-living. Newfoundland Quarterly, 100(4).

Stevens, K. J., & Moffatt, C. (2003). From distance education to tele-learning -the organization of open classes at local, regional and national levels. In J. Bradley (Ed.), The open classroom – distance learning in and out of schools (pp. 171-180). London, UK & Sterling, VA: Kogan.

Stevens, K., Sandalov, A., Sukhareva, N., Barry, M., & Piper, T. (1999). The development of open models for teaching physics to schools in dispersed locations in Russia and Canada. In V. Grementieri, A. Szucs & V. I. Trukhin (Eds.), Information and communication technologies and human resources development: New opportunities for European co-operation, Budapest, Hungary: European Distance Education Network, October, (pp. 148–154.)

Stipek, D. J., Salmon, J. S., & Givven, K. B. (1998). The value of practices suggested by motivation research and promoted by mathematics education reformers. Journal for Research in Mathematics Education, 29(4), 465–488. doi:10.2307/749862

Stodel, E. J., Thompson, T. L., & McDonald, C. (2006). Learners' perspectives on what is missing from online learning: Interpretations through the community of inquiry framework. International Review of Research in Open and Distance Learning, 7(3).

Straus, S. G., & McGrath, J. E. (1994). Does the medium matter: The interaction of task and technology on group performance and member reactions. The Journal of Applied Psychology, 79, 87–97. doi:10.1037/0021-9010.79.1.87

Strauss, A., & Corbin, J. (2007). Basics of qualitative research: Techniques and procedures for developing grounded theory (3rd ed.). Thousand Oaks, CA: Sage Publications.

Stutts, M. A., & West, V. (2003). Competitive learning: Beyond project-based classes. Retrieved January 15, 2010, from http://www.sbaer.uca.edu/research/acme/2003/papers/new/29.pdf

Sutherland-Smith, W. (2002). Weaving the literacy web: Changes in reading from page to screen. The Reading Teacher, 55, 662–669.

Swanson, P. N., & De La Paz, S. (1998). Teaching effective comprehension strategies to students with learning and reading disabilities. Intervention in School and Clinic, 33, 209–219. doi:10.1177/105345129803300403

Swanson, D. R. (1986a). Fish-oil, Raynaud's syndrome, and undiscovered public knowledge. Perspectives in Biology and Medicine, 30(1), 7–18.

Swanson, D. R. (1986b). Undiscovered public knowledge. The Library Quarterly, 56, 103–118. doi:10.1086/601720

Swanson, D. R. (1988). Migraine and magnesium: Eleven neglected connections. Perspectives in Biology and Medicine, 31, 526–557.

Sweeters, W. (1994). Multimedia electronic tools for learning. Educational Technology, 34(5), 47–52.

Swinburne University of Technology Act. (1992).

Sybold, P. B. (2001). Get inside the lives of your customers. Harvard Business Review, 80, 80–89.

Tabachnik, G. B., & Fidell, S. L. (1996). Using multivariate statistics. New York, NY: Harper Collins College Publishers.

Tait, A. (2000). Planning student support for open and distance learning. Journal of Open and Distance Learning, 15(3), 287–209. doi:10.1080/713688410

Tam, W. M. (2007). Rethinking school and community relations in Hong Kong. International Journal of Educational Management, 21(4), 350–366. doi:10.1108/09513540710749555

Tapicro, I. (2007). Situational models and levels of coherence: Towards a definition of comprehension. Abingdon, UK: Lawrence Erlbaum Associates.

Task Force on Economic Challenges. (n.d.). Six economic areas identified by task force on economic challenges for further development. Retrieved April 29, 2009, from http://www.fso.gov.hk/tfec/eng/press.html

Taylor, J. (1995). Distance education technologies: The fourth generation. Australian Journal of Educational Technology, 11(2), 1–7.

Teas, R. K. (1993). Expectations, performance evaluation and consumers' perceptions of quality. Journal of Marketing, 57(4), 18–34. doi:10.2307/1252216

Teichler, U. (2003). The future of higher education and the future of higher education research. Tertiary Education and Management, 9(3), 171–185. doi:10.1080/13583883.2003.9967102

Tella, S. (1995). Virtual school in a networking learning environment. Helsinki, Finland: University of Helsinki, Department of Teacher Education.

Testa, B. (2010). No mere perk: Flex-work as a strategic tool. Workforce Management, 89(3), 4.

The Hong Kong Government. (2007). Report on economic summit on China's 11th five-year plan and the development of Hong Kong. Retrieved September 22, 2009, from http://www.info.gov.hk/info/econ_summit/eng/pdf/tb_aa.pdf

The University of Adelaide. (2005). Casual employment guidelines. Retrieved January 27th, 2010, from http://www.adelaide.edu.au/policies/689/?dsn=policy.document;field=data;id=2843;m=view

The University of Western Australia. (2009). Code of ethics and code of conduct. Retrieved January 27th, 2010, from http://www.hr.uwa.edu.au/publications/code_of_ethics#ceth

Thomas, J., Thomas, E., & Tomb, E. (1992). Serum and erythrocyte magnesium concentrations and migraine. Magnesium Research, 5(2), 127–130.

Thomas, H. (1990). Educational costs and performance: A cost- effective analysis. London, UK: Cassell.

Thompson, E. (2009). What's hot in CRM applications in 2009. Gardner Research. Retrieved January 5, 2010, from http://www.gartner.com/DisplayDocument?&id=1004212

Thorpe, M. (1987). Adult learners in open learning. In Thorpe, M., & Grugeon, D. (Eds.), Open learning for adults (pp. 72–82). Harlow & Essex, UK: Longman.

Thursby, J. G., & Kemp, S. (2002). Growth and productive efficiency of university intellectual property licensing. Research Policy, 31(1), 109–124. doi:10.1016/S0048-7333(00)00160-8

Thurstun, J. (2004). Teaching and learning the reading of homepages. Prospect, 19(2), 56–71.

Times Higher Education. (n.d.). Times higher education - QS world university ranking 2009. Retrieved January 14, 2010, from http://www.timeshighereducation.co.uk/Rankings2009-Top200.html

Tindale, J. (2006). Reading print and electronic texts. In Murray, D. (Ed.), Navigating to read - reading to navigate (pp. 2–15). Sydney, Australia: Sydney AMEP Research Centre.

Tinker v Des Moines Independent Community School District, 393 US 503. (1969).

Tipple, R. (2010). Effective leadership of online adjunct faculty. Online Journal of Distance Learning Administration, 13(1). Retrieved from http://www.westga.edu/~distance/ojdla/spring131/tipple131.html.

Toben v Jones, FCAFC 158. (2002).

Tolhurst, D. (1995). Hypertext, hypermedia, multimedia defined? Educational Technology, 15(2), 21–26.

Trivellas, P., & Dargenidou, D. (2009). Organisational culture, job satisfaction and higher education service quality. The case of Technological Educational Institute of Larissa. The TQM Journal, 21(4), 382–399. doi:10.1108/17542730910965083

Trow, M. (1994). Managerialism and the academic profession: The case of England. Higher Education Policy, 7, 11–18. doi:10.1057/hep.1994.13

Trow, M. (1972). The expansion and transformation of higher education. International Review of Education, 1, 61–63. doi:10.1007/BF01450272

Trow, M. (1998). From mass higher education to universal access. Paper of the meeting of the Japanese Society for Higher Education Research, Hiroshima, May 31, 1998.

Tutton, M. (2009). Going to the virtual office in Second Life. Retrieved from http://www.cnn.com/2009/BUSINESS/11/05/second.life.virtual.collaboration/

Tuzovic, S. (2009). Google mania in higher education: Sharing the excitement and the nuts and bolts of incorporating the Google Online Marketing Challenge in the classroom (pp. 73-82). In D. Gómez Chova, M. Belenguer, & I. Candel Torres (Eds.), Proceedings of EDULEARN 09: International Conference on Education and New Learning Technologies, July 6-8, 2009, Barcelona, Spain: International Association of Technology, Education and Development.

Ueltschy, L. C. (2001). An exploratory study of integrating interactive technology into the marketing curriculum. Journal of Marketing Education, 23(1), 63–72. doi:10.1177/0273475301231008

United Nations. (2009). Good practices and innovations in public governance. United Nations public service awards winners and finalists, 2003-2009. New York, NY: United Nations.

University of Ballarat Act. (1993).

University of South Australia. (2004). Code of ethical conduct. Retrieved January 27th, 2010, from http://www.unisa.edu.au/policies/codes/ethics/ethics.asp

University of South Australia. (2009). Protocols for the management of academic casual staff. Retrieved January 27th, 2010, from http://www.unisa.edu.au/hrm/employment/recruitment/academic/protocols.asp

University of Western Australia v Gray, FCAFC 116. (2009).

University of Wollongong. (2008). Code of practice - casual academic teaching. Retrieved January 27th, 2010, from http://www.uow.edu.au/about/policy/OUW058668.html

Urdan, T., & Maehr, M. L. (1995). Beyond a two-goal theory of motivation: A case for social goals. Review of Educational Research, 65(3), 213–244.

Vaidya, S. R. (1999). Metacognitive learning strategies for student with learning disabilities. Education, 120, 186–189.

Valentine, D. (2002). Distance learning: Problems, promises and possibilities. Online Journal of Distance Learning Administration, 5(3).

Van Manen, M. (2002). The pedagogical task of teaching. Teaching and Teacher Education, 18(2), 135–138. doi:10.1016/S0742-051X(01)00058-0

VanRyssen, S., & Godar, S. H. (2000). Going international without going international: Multinational virtual teams. Journal of International Management, 6, 49–60. doi:10.1016/S1075-4253(00)00019-3

Varghese, N. V. (2008). Globalization of higher education and cross-border student mobility. Paris, France: International Institute for Educational Planning.

Vidovich, L., Yang, R., & Currie, J. (2007). Dancing in a cage: Changing autonomy in Chinese higher education. Higher Education, 54, 575–592. doi:10.1007/s10734-006-9009-5

Vidovich, L., Yang, R., & Currie, J. (2007). Changing accountabilities in higher education as China opens up to globalization. Globalisation, Societies and Education, 5(1), 89–107. doi:10.1080/14767720601133447

Vinaja, R. (2003). Major challenges in multi-cultural virtual teams. Retrieved on October 26, 2005, from http://www.sbaer.uca.edu/research/swdsi/2003/Papers/068.pdf

Voon, B. H. (2006). Linking a service-driven market orientation to service quality. Managing Service Quality, 16(6), 595–619. doi:10.1108/09604520610711927

Wallace, M., & Hall, V. (1994). Inside the SMT: Teamwork in secondary school management. In Lumby, J., & Foskett, N. (Eds.), Managing external relations in schools and colleges. London, UK: Paul Chapman.

Warkentin, M., & Beranek, P. M. (1999). Training to improve virtual team communication. Information Systems Journal, 9(4), 271–289. doi:10.1046/j.1365-2575.1999.00065.x

Warring, S. (1999). Finding your way: Sensing the external environment. In Lumby, J., & Foskett, N. (Eds.), Managing external relations in schools and colleges. London, UK: Paul Chapman.

Watson, T., & Hempenstall, K. (2008). Effects of a computer based beginning reading program on young children. Australiasian Journal of Educational Technology, 24(3), 258–574.

Way, J., & Webb, C. (2007). A framework for analysing ICT adoption in Australian primary schools. Australiasian Journal of Educational Technology, 23, 559-582. Retrieved 12 October, 2009, from http://www.ascilite.org.au/ajet/ajet23/way.html

Weber, S. (1996). The future of the university: The cutting edge. In T. S. (Ed), Ideas of the university (pp. 43-76). Sydney, Australia: Research Institute for the Humanities and Social Sciences and Power Publications.

Webster, C. (1989). Can consumers be segmented on the basis of their service quality expectations? Journal of Services Marketing, 3(2), 35–53. doi:10.1108/EUM0000000002485

Wedel, M., & DeSarbo, W. S. (2002). Market segment derivation and profiling via a finite mixture model framework. Marketing Letters, 13(1), 17–25. doi:10.1023/A:1015059024154

Wedel, M., & Kamakura, W. A. (2000). Market segmentation. Conceptual and methodological foundations. London, UK: Kluwer Academic Publishers.

Weeber, M., & Klein, H., de Jong-van den, B., Lolkje T. W., & Vos, R. (2001). Using concepts in literature-based discovery: Simulating Swanson's Raynaud-fish oil and migraine-magnesium discoveries. Journal of the American Society for Information Science and Technology, 52, 548–557. doi:10.1002/asi.1104

Weeber, M., Vos, R., Klein, H., De Jong-Van Den Berg, L. T., Aronson, A. R., & Molema, G. (2003). Generating hypotheses by discovering implicit associations in the literature: A case report of a search for new potential therapeutic uses for thalidomide. Journal of the American Medical Informatics Association, 10, 252–259. doi:10.1197/jamia.M1158

Weifang, M., & Xiaohao, D. (2005). Financing Chinese higher education: Reforms and future challenges. Harvard China Review, 129-131.

Weiss, S. M., Indurkhya, N., Zhang, T., & Damerau, F. (2005). Text mining: Predictive methods for analyzing unstructured information. New York, NY: Springer.

Welters, R., & Mitchell, W. (2009). Locked in casual employment. University of Newcastle. Newcastle, UK: Centre of Full Employment and Equity.

Wentzel, K. R. (1993). Does being good make the grade? Social behavior and academic competence in middle school. Journal of Educational Psychology, 85(2), 357–364. doi:10.1037/0022-0663.85.2.357

West, M., Jackson, D., Harris, A., & Hopkins, D. (2000). Learning through leadership, leadership through learning: Leadership for sustained school improvement. In Riley, K. A., & Louis, K. S. (Eds.), Leadership for change and school reform: International perspectives. London, UK: Routledge Falmer.

Wheeler, S. (2007). Ethics in the workplace. Law and Critique, 18, 1–28. doi:10.1007/s10978-006-9008-9

White, C. (2003). Language learning in distance education. Cambridge, UK: Cambridge University Press. doi:10.1017/CBO9780511667312

Widmar v Vincent, 454 US 263. (1981).

Williams, D. L., Beard, J. D., & Rymer, J. (1991). Team projects: Achieving their full potential. Journal of Marketing Education, 13(2), 45–53. doi:10.1177/027347539101300208

Williams, J. P., & Atkins, J. G. (2009). The role of metacognition in teaching reading comprehension to primary schools. In Hacker, D. J., Dunlosky, J., & Graesser, A. C. (Eds.), Handbook of metacognition in education (pp. 26–43). Hoboken, NJ: Routledge.

Wilson, C. (2010). Fighting back: The human cost of layoffs. Academe, 95(4).

Wolfinger, N., Mason, M., & Goulden, M. (2009). Stay in the game: Gender, family formation and alternative trajectories in the academic life course. Social Forces, 87(3), 1591–1621. doi:10.1353/sof.0.0182

Wood, J. (2000). Literacy: Charlotte's Web meets the World Wide Web. In Gordon, D. T. (Ed.), The digital classroom (pp. 117–126). Boston, MA: Harvard Education Letter.

World Bank. (2002). Constructing knowledge societies: New challenges for tertiary education. Washington, DC.

Yamamoto, G. T., & Karaman, F. (2006). The death of the nation-state and the need for global collaboration. E-Business Review, 6(1), 170–173.

Yamamoto, G. T., Ozan, O., & Demiray, U. (2010). Drugstore for learners: Learning vitamins D-E-M-T-U learning. 3rd International Future-learning Conference, 10-14 May 2010, Istanbul, Turkey.

Yamamoto, G. T., Telli, A., Featherstone, M., & Borstorff, P. (2006). Virtual environments, virtual works, virtual lives? PICMET'06 (Portland International Conference on Management Engineering and Technology), 8-13 July 2006, Istanbul.

Yates, C. (2004). Teacher education at a distance: Lessons and experience from Sub-Saharan Africa. Paper presented at the All-Africa Minister's Conference on Open Learning and Distance Education, 2004, Cape Town, South Africa.

Ying Chu, N. G., & Li, S. (2000). Measuring the research performance of Chinese higher educations: An application data envelopment analysis. Education Economics, 8(2), 139–156. doi:10.1080/09645290041 0712

Yonezawa, A. (2007). Strategies for the emerging global higher education market in East Asia: A comparative study of Singapore, Malaysia and Japan. Globalisation, Societies and Education, 5(1), 125–136. doi:10.1080/14767720601133561

Young, M. A. (2002). Experiential learning = hands-on + minds-on. Marketing Education Review, 12(1), 43–51.

Young, M. R. (2005). The motivational effects of the classroom environment in facilitating self-regulated learning. Journal of Marketing Education, 27(1), 25–40. doi:10.1177/0273475304273346

Yu, C. H., Brewer, L., Jannasch-Pennell, A., & Digangi, S. (2010). Adopting Web 2.0 for instruction: The effects of faculty rank and employment status. Journal of Technology Integration in Classroom, 2(2), 131–143.

Yu, X. (2009). Faculty employment policy shift in Chinese higher education. The Journal of Education, 51-62.

Zabkar, V. (2008). Advertising education in Central and Eastern Europe: A case study. Retrieved January 15, 2010, from http://www.eacaeducation.eu/download/pdf/Vesna_Zabkar.pdf

Zakaria, N., Amelinckx, A., & Wilemon, D. (2004). Working together apart? Building a knowledge-sharing culture for global virtual teams. SSRN eLibrary.

Zeithaml, V. A., & Bitner, M. J. (1996). Services marketing. New York, NY: McGraw-Hill.

Zhang, H., Dong, Y., & Chen, G. (2005). Educational technology training for higher education teachers in China and some suggestions for improving it. Chinese Education & Society, 38(6), 69–78.

About the Contributors

Purnendu Tripathi, an International Research Fellow of Open University Business School (2009) at Open University (UK), has a PhD in management and a master's degree in distance education. He was associated with Arab Open University Saudi Arabia Branch for three years as a faculty member in Business Administration. In his parent institution IGNOU (India), he is Assistant Director, looking after academic management and student support services with aspects in open and distance learning. He has co- edited teaching case books and contributed articles in standard national and international journals, as well as presented papers in national and international conferences. Dr. Tripathi is a member of review committees for numerous international conferences and journals. His current research interests include academic program life cycle (APLC) and educational marketing.

Siran Mukerji is Jawahar Lal Nehru scholar for her doctorate in HRD and also has master's degree in distance education and public administration. She has been International Research Fellow of Open University Business School (2009) at Open University (UK). She was associated with Arab Open University Saudi Arabia Branch for three years as a faculty member in Business Administration. She has co-edited teaching case books and contributed articles in standard national and international journals and also presented papers in national and international conferences. Dr. Mukerji is a member of review committees for numerous international conferences and journals. Her current research interests include performance management and HRM in open and distance learning institutions. In her parent institution IGNOU (India) she is Assistant Director.

* * *

Laurie Bedford is an adjunct faculty member in online education and an instructional development consultant. She has worked with all levels of education promoting effective instructional design, faculty development, and curriculum implementation. Working with both public and proprietary education, she has written articles, developed course materials, and facilitated faculty development focused on quality instructional strategies and best practices for supporting faculty. Dr. Bedford has a Ph.D. in Adult Education from the University of Wyoming. She also holds a Master of Science degree in Administrative Studies and a Bachelor of Arts degree in Social Work from the University of South Dakota.

Tom Bisschoff is a senior lecturer in the School of Education within the College of Social Sciences at the University of Birmingham. He is an emeritus professor of the University of Johannesburg in South Africa and a Visiting Professor of the Vaal University of Technology. He has authored and co-authored nine books on school management, of which one of the more recent ones is on Effective School Marketing. He is an established researcher according to the National Research Foundation (NRF) of South Africa, and publishes widely in the field of school leadership.

Felicia Blacher-Wilson holds a Doctorate in Educational Administration from Iowa State University and has been an active part of the education community working in five different states. She has served as a teacher of regular, special needs, and gifted students; as an elementary school counsellor, assistant principal, principal; an Assistant Superintendent for Elementary Schools; Director of Elementary Schools and Programs, and Assistant Professor and Dean of Education at a major university. Dr. Blacher-Wilson is currently an Assistant Professor in the Department of Educational Leadership and Technology at Southeastern Louisiana University in Hammond, Louisiana. Her research interests are: (1) spirituality and leadership; (2) non-traditional superintendents in urban school districts and (3) personnel performance evaluations for administrators and teachers.

Patricia Borstorff is an Associate Professor of Management at Jacksonville State University. She holds a PhD from Auburn University in human resource management and international business. She served as an invited member of the 40-member Oxford Round Table at Oxford University in England in 2004. She serves on the state council of the Society for Human Resource Management and has held all offices plus being a board member of Calhoun County SHRM. She has taught over 1,000 human resource professionals in a human resource certification study course and offers seminars and training in local and state industries. Dr. Borstorff has completed graduate international business studies in Japan, the Czech Republic, and Hungary, and has studied post-doctoral classes at the University of South Carolina in international management and international business.

Paul Breen is a lecturer and Programme Manager in the field of English for Academic Purposes/Study Skills and is currently working in the British higher education sector, having also worked in South Korea, Australia, and Japan. He has a Postgraduate Certificate of Education, as well as a Masters in Education in the fields of English Language Teaching and Educational Technology, and is currently pursuing doctoral studies in Education. His research interests are primarily in the fields of teacher education, English for academic purposes, and student interaction with virtual learning environments. Currently, his main professional interests are in designing courses that integrate technology into both the classroom teaching and self-study components, and training teachers to use technology effectively in the classroom.

Rosemary Buteau is the Chair of the Department of Reading, Elementary, Middle School, and Bilingual Education at Chicago State University. She holds a Bachelor's degree in Elementary Education, Master's degree in the Teaching of Reading (Reading Specialist), certificate in Educational Technology, and doctorate in Adult Education. In addition to serving as faculty in the Graduate Reading Program and continuing to serve students as an academic advisor, Dr. Buteau served seven years as the Technology Director for the College of Education. Her research interests include literacy development of children and adults, including technology literacy, and continued investigation into how universities can adapt to and better serve the increasing number of non-traditional students.

Alan C. K. Cheung is an Associate Professor in the Department of Educational Policy and Administration at the Hong Kong Institute of Education, Hong Kong SAR, China. His areas of specialization include large-scale assessment, research reviews, research methods, and private education.

Albert Caruana is Professor of Marketing at the University of Malta, Malta and Visiting Professor at the University of Bologna. His research interests focus primarily on market orientation and marketing communications. Dr. Caruana undertook post doctoral research as Fulbright Fellow in the US during 2004, as Commonwealth Research Scholar in 2000, and has been on various research fellowships in Australia. His work includes papers in the *Journal of Advertising, Journal of Business Research, International Journal of Advertising, European Journal of Marketing, and Industrial Marketing Management.* Dr. Caruana has also pursued numerous teaching invitations in various countries.

Yin Cheong Cheng is the Vice-President (Research and Development) and Chair Professor of Leadership and Change of the Hong Kong Institute of Education. His research is mainly in the areas of management reform, teacher education, education effectiveness, and school leadership. He has published internationally over 200 book chapters and journal articles and 20 academic books. Some of his publications have been translated into Chinese, Hebrew, Korean, Spanish, Czech, Thai, and Persian languages.

Manuel Cuadrado-García is an Associate Professor in the Department of Marketing and Market Research, University of Valencia, and is responsible for the International Exchange Office at the Faculty of Economics. He has been leading several research projects and teams of teaching-learning innovation. His projects have been financed by the Spanish Ministry of Education as well as by the University of Valencia. The results of his research have been published in several international journals and presented in global conferences. His current research interests are the outcomes of e-learning, as well as consumer behaviour in cultural settings.

Michael D. Richardson is the Hibernia Endowed Professor of Educational Leadership and Head of the Department of Educational Leadership and Technology at Southeastern Louisiana University. He completed Bachelor's and Master's degrees in Education at Tennessee Technological University and was awarded the Doctorate of Education from the University of Tennessee. Dr. Richardson served as Founding Editor of the Journal of School Leadership, an internationally refereed journal of educational leadership, as Editor of The Journal of At-Risk Issues, and Founding Editor of Contemporary Issues in Educational Leadership and The Mercer Journal of Educational Leadership. He has authored or edited fourteen books, published more than one hundred articles in professional journals, and made more than one hundred and fifty presentations to regional, national, and international professional organizations.

Magdalena De Stefani has been working as a teacher of English as a Foreign Language since 1997, when she obtained her Diploma in TEFL. She holds a Masters of Education in English Language Teaching and is currently working towards a PhD in Education. Her main research focus is on teacher development and ICT, although she is currently conducting research in the fields of intercultural communication, academic collaboration, and reflexivity. She is involved in pre- and in-service teacher training and also teaches students in preparation for Cambridge ESOL examinations in her hometown of Montevideo in Uruguay.

Samuel DiGangi is Associate Vice President of University Technology at Arizona State University (ASU), Associate Professor of Education specializing in technology integration, and Executive Director of ASU's Applied Learning Technologies Institute (alt^I). His research activities focus on infusing effective components of instructional design with emerging technology in education. In addition to extensive use of computer-mediated instruction in his teacher preparation courses, Dr. DiGangi directs several sponsored research projects examining implementation of high technology telecommunications and international networking in the classroom. Dr. DiGangi has taught numerous courses devoted to evaluation and assessment of the impact of technology on education.

Michael Featherstone is an Assistant Professor of Management at Jacksonville State University (JSU). He earned his BS and MPA degrees at Wayne State University in Detroit, Michigan, and completed his Doctor of Business Administration degree at Southern Cross University's Graduate College of Management, New South Wales, Australia. Prior to coming to JSU, he served as a manager at the IBM e-Business Innovation Center in Atlanta, Georgia. The center developed websites for prestigious events such as the Grammy Awards, the Tony Awards, the Wimbledon Tennis tournament, the Roland Garros Tournament, and the US Masters Golf tournament. He has also served as the Chief Executive Officer of two software development companies, Software Research Corporation and Advanced Training Technologies, Inc. His research interests include virtual teams, search engine marketing, and the impact of social media.

Maria Fuentes-Blasco is an Assistant Professor of Marketing at the University of Pablo de Olavide (Spain). Her main teaching and research interests include services marketing, marketing for higher education, business to consumer marketing, and marketing research. Dr. Maria has taught these topics in undergraduate and postgraduate courses, and has published articles in several international journals such as *Journal of Marketing for Higher Education, International Review of Public and Non profit Marketing, The International Review of Retail, Distribution and Consumer Research, Industrial Marketing Management, International Journal of Hospitality Management, The Service Industries Journal, Industrial Management & Data Systems Journal,* and *Journal of Services Marketing,* among others.

Evan G. Mense is an Assistant Professor in the Department of Educational Leadership and Technology and is currently serving as Director of the Masters in Educational Leadership Program at Southeastern Louisiana University. Dr. Mense has extensive background in Educational Administration and Leadership as a public school administrator in Missouri. Dr. Mense holds a Doctorate in Educational Leadership from Saint Louis University-Saint Louis, a Master of Science degree in Administration from Pittsburg State University – Pittsburg, Kansas, and a Bachelor of Science degree in Education from Missouri Southern State University – Joplin.

Irene Gil is Professor of Marketing at the University of Valencia (Spain). Her main teaching and research interests include business-to-business marketing, services marketing, consumer behaviour, and retailing. Dr. Gil has taught these topics in undergraduate and postgraduate courses and has published articles in several international journals such as *Annals of Tourism Research, The International Review of Retail, Distribution and Consumer Research, Industrial Marketing Management, International Journal of Hospitality Management, Tourism Management,* and *International Journal of Service Industry Management,* among others.

Veronique Guilloux (Ph.D. I.A.E. de Poitiers) is an Assistant Professor of Marketing at Université Paris XII. Her research interests include business education methods, new communication technologies, and consumer behavior.

Lourdes Hernández-Martín is Assistant Coordinator for Spanish and responsible for Arabic at the Language Centre, London School of Economics (London). She is part of the Spanish in Motion Team/ Language Centre project (http://spanishinmotion.wordpress.com/). Her research focuses on how the use of cinema techniques and global simulations can contribute towards enhancing motivation and learning during the acquisition of Spanish as a modern foreign language for specific purposes (i.e. social, political, and economic sciences).

Chong Ho Yu has a Ph.D. in Educational Psychology with an emphasis on Measurement, Statistics, and Methodological Studies, and a Ph.D. in Philosophy with a concentration on History and Philosophy of Science. Currently, he is Director of Research and Assessment at Applied Learning Technologies Institute, Arizona State University (ASU), USA. His research activities include philosophical foundations of research methodologies, exploratory data analysis, data visualization, data mining, psychometrics, and cognitive aspects of instructional technology.

Angel Jannasch-Pennell is Assistant Vice President of University Technology at ASU, and Director of Research and Outreach initiatives in alt^I. She directs collaborative projects across colleges and centers, and also integrates community-based endeavours and university partnerships. She brings a research-driven and application-oriented focus to the Institute, coordinating teams of researchers, faculty, and technical experts toward the proposal, development, and implementation of technology innovation. Dr. Angel's research activities include human interface of instructional technology, innovative applications of instructional technology across different contexts, and large-scale educational assessment.

Rochelle Johnson works as an Instructional Support Specialist in the Department of Technology and Learning Resources at Chicago State University where she assists faculty and staff with incorporating technology into the curriculum. She coordinates the Center for Teaching and Research Excellence Lab and provides technology workshops for staff and students to help them become successful consumers of technology. Ms. Johnson is currently working on her doctorate in Instructional Technology at Northern Illinois University. Her interests lie in effectively using technology, especially online technology, in higher education, and in finding ways to assist instructors and students to effectively use technology in the educational process. Her thesis focus, "Factors Influencing Faculty's Decision to Use Technology," sheds light on the factors revolving around instructors limited use of technology in the delivery of course content.

Faruk Karaman holds a B.S. in Electrical and Electronics Engineering from the Bosphorus University, Istanbul-Turkey. He also has MBA and DBA degrees from the Marmara University, Istanbul-Turkey. His work experience spans diverse industries such as investment banking, consulting, ICT, and academia. He has taught e-Business/e-Commerce, CRM, SCM, technology strategy, and ethics lectures at both graduate and undergraduate levels. Currently, he is the head of the Foreign Trade department at Gedik Vocational University, Istanbul-Turkey. He has numerous publications in the fields of e-business/e-commerce, technology strategy and social impacts.

Achilleas Kostoulas is a graduate of the Department of English Language and Literature of the National and Kapodestrian University of Athens, where he specialised in Theoretical and Applied Linguistics and English Language Teaching (ELT). He holds an MA in Teaching English to Speakers of Other Languages and is currently working towards a PhD in Education. His research focuses on the ways ELT is shaped by globalised and locally-situated dynamics in the Greek context. He has worked as a research associate in the Research Centre for Modern Greek Philosophy in the University of Ioannina (Greece), and has held numerous teaching, management, teacher education and advisory posts, both in the public and private education systems in Greece.

Kathleen A. Krentler, DBA, is Director of Assessment in the College of Business Administration, San Diego State University. She also directs the Undergraduate Program in her college and is a Professor of Marketing. Her current research focuses primarily on assurance of learning. She is involved in other educational issues including distance learning, curriculum innovation, and course pedagogy. Her research has been presented in a variety of sources including the *Journal of Business Research, Journal of the Academy of Marketing Science, and Journal of Marketing Education.* She is past president of the Academy of Marketing Science. She received her Bachelor's and Master's degrees in Business Administration from Wayne State University in Detroit, Michigan and her DBA from the University of Kentucky.

Paula Kwan, trained in the field of Business Management and Marketing, and having worked in the commercial sector in HK prior to teaching, is particularly interested in investigating the application of business theories and practices in educational contexts. Her most recent research projects include the work lives and job satisfaction of vice principals, principal recruitment and selection, and organizational culture.

Beatriz Moliner-Velázquez is an Assistant Professor of Marketing at the University of Valencia (Spain). Her current research interests are consumer behaviour and services marketing, and Dr. Beatriz has taught these topics in undergraduate and postgraduate courses. Her studies are published in several international journals such as *International Review of Retail, Distribution and Consumer Research, International Journal of Service Industry Management, The Service Industries Journal, Innovar, and Journal of Services Marketing,* among others.

John Munro is Head of Studies in Exceptional Learning and Gifted Education in the Melbourne Graduate School of Education at The University of Melbourne. Prof. Munro is a trained primary and secondary teacher and a psychologist. His research interests, teaching, and publications are in the areas of literacy learning and learning difficulties, maths learning disabilities, learning internationally, gifted learning and learning disabilities, gifted learning in African and Asian cultures, gifted mathematics learning, and in instructional leadership and school improvement. He is a consultant to several school improvement projects is Victoria. He was chairperson of the College of Educational and Developmental Psychologists (Aus) and a Life Member of the Learning Disabilities Australia.

Jamie Murphy is a Professor at the University of Western Australia Business School. His industry experience includes owning restaurants, serving as the European Marketing Manager for Greg LeMond Bicycles and PowerBar, and freelance reporting for The New York Times and The Wall Street Journal. Dr. Murphy's academic experience includes almost 200 refereed publications; full-time positions in the

United States and Australia; visiting positions in Austria, Canada, France, and Switzerland, and invited presentations on five continents. His latest initiative is co-founder and academic lead for Google's biggest business student initiative, the Google Online Marketing Challenge.

Iryna Pentina is an Assistant Professor of Marketing at the University of Toledo. Dr. Pentina's research interests include marketing pedagogy, consumer behavior, Internet marketing, and marketing communications.

Elizabeth Reed Osika is an Associate Professor in Technology and Education at Chicago State University's College of Education, where her focus is on the development of completely online graduate programs. Dr. Osika has a varied background in the use of technology in education, especially in terms of online instruction. She received her doctorate degree in Educational Technologies at Purdue University, West Lafayette, and also holds Masters degrees in Instructional Design from Purdue Calumet and in Human Resources from University of Illinois. Dr. Osika's academic interests include helping faculty develop their technical skills, investigating best practices in online instruction, and exploring various assessment strategies.

Christopher Rhodes worked in schools and colleges for 14 years prior to taking up a post in higher education. He has held a variety of senior leadership positions and was a school inspector in both the primary and secondary sectors. Dr. Rhodes was formerly Principal Lecturer and Director of Postgraduate and Professional Development in the School of Education at the University of Wolverhampton, UK. He presently holds the post of Senior Lecturer in Educational Leadership in the School of Education at the University of Birmingham, UK. He directs the EdD degree in Leaders and Leadership in Education and holds the post of Head of the Department of Professional Learning and Development.

Francine Rochford is a Senior Lecturer at La Trobe University, based at their Bendigo campus. Her work on the law and policy of higher education includes her doctorate dealing with the *Liability of the University in Negligence* at the University of Melbourne and a number of articles and book chapters dealing with aspects of the law and policy of higher education published in the international journals, books and conference proceedings. She also writes in the area of water policy and management, and in 2010, was the International Visiting Environmental Law Scholar at Lewis and Clark Law School, Portland Oregon.

María-Eugenia Ruiz-Molina is an Assistant Professor in the Department of Marketing and Market Research, University of Valencia, and consultant at Catalonia Open University (UOC). Together with Professor Manuel Cuadrado, she has been teaching in several Marketing courses in English. Dr. Ruiz-Molina's current research interests are the effects of the use of technology in language and marketing teaching-learning process, as well as consumer behaviour in retailing.

John Rutaisire is the Executive Secretary of the Rwanda National Examinations Council. He was senior lecturer of education at Tonota College of Education in Botswana before returning to Rwanda in 1999, where he has led and coordinated the development of a range of educational policies. He is currently pursuing his Doctorate in Education (Ed.D) at the University of Sussex, Brighton (U.K).

Ken Stevens is a New Zealander and a Professor of Education at Memorial University of Newfoundland where he was appointed to a chair in e-learning, funded by Industry Canada. His previous appointments were at James Cook University in Queensland, Australia, and at Victoria University of Wellington in New Zealand. In Australia, New Zealand, and Canada, he has specialized in the provision of education in rural communities and the application of Information Technologies for teaching and learning in and between schools in sparsely-populated areas. Currently he is cross-appointed from Memorial University of Newfoundland as Adjunct Professor of Education at Victoria University of Wellington.

Frank Wai-ming Tam has worked as a secondary school teacher, science panel chairperson, secondary school principal, lecturer, and program developer in local tertiary institutions. Dr. Frank's recent research interests include parent-school relationship, change management, knowledge management in schools, and action learning of teachers and school administrators.

Gonca Telli Yamamoto is an Associate Professor in the School of Applied Sciences at Okan University, Turkey. She is the head of Information Sciences and Technologies Department. She is also coordinating Okan University Distance Education Center at present. She currently teaches, consults, and conducts research on mobile and integrated marketing, and new learning technologies in business. She has been studying integrated marketing, technological developments, and customer value, and is more than a decade in the academic field. She has some books and chapters related to sales, integrated and mobile marketing, and IT ethics. Several of her articles have been published in several national and international journals. She has also received two outstanding paper awards from the International Academy of E- Business.

Sven Tuzovic is an Assistant Professor of Marketing at Pacific Lutheran University, School of Business, Tacoma, WA. He was a Visiting Professor in Marketing at Murray State University (2006/07) and at the University of New Orleans (2005/06). He holds a Doctoral Degree in Marketing from the University of Basel in Switzerland, a Diploma in Business Administration ("Diplom-Kaufmann") from the Catholic University of Eichstätt-Ingolstadt, Germany, and a BBA from Georgia Southern University, Statesboro, GA. His research has been published in *Managing Service Quality*, the *Journal of Services Marketing*, the *International Journal of Business Performance Management,* and in several international conference proceedings.

Elena Verezub (BEd., Candidate of Science in Ed. Psych., PhD in Education (Melb)) is a Language and Academic Skills Advisor at Swinburne University of Technology, Australia. Currently she develops, teaches, and evaluates workplace communication skills programs for international students. She has over 15 years of teaching experience in TESOL, education, and educational psychology, both in Australia and Ukraine. Elena's professional and research interests include e-learning and hypertext literacy; study expectations in TAFE and higher education environments; language and academic skills; and psychological aspects of text memorisation.

Lyle R. Wetsch is an Assistant Professor of Marketing at Memorial University of Newfoundland, St. John's, Newfoundland, Canada. Since joining the Faculty of Business Administration in July 2003, he has taught a variety of marketing courses at both the undergraduate and graduate level (MBA). His classes typically employ innovative teaching elements such as social media, blogs, virtual worlds

('Second Life'), and real world applications such as Google AdWords and "Marketing Survivor" that allow students to interact and work with real companies in their classes. With over 50 presentations and publications in the past 10 years, his research has been published in the *Marketing Education Review*, the *Journal of Advertising*, the *Journal of Virtual World Research*, the *Journal of Relationship Marketing,* and the *International Journal of Electronic Marketing and Retailing*.

Timothy Yuen graduated from the University of Hong Kong as a social science major and obtained his doctoral degree from the University of Durham. Dr. Yuen is now serving as an assistant professor in the Hong Kong Institute of Education. His research interest comprises inter alia, social analysis of education policies, and civic / political education. His recent publications can be found in *Compare*, *Citizenship, Social and Economic Education: An International Journal*, *Citizenship Teaching and Learning*, and *International Journal of Educational Reform*.

Celeste Yuen is an Associate Professor in the Department of Education Policy and Leadership at The Hong Kong Institute of Education. She taught in primary schools for several years before joining the Institute. Her two higher degrees are both in curriculum studies. Her work includes research on intercultural education, Chinese cross-boundary and new arrived students, and special and inclusive education. She has published in various journals including *Teaching and Teacher Education, Compare, Intercultural Education,* and *Pacific-Asian Education (PAE) Journal.*

Shuyi Zhang is full time Professor and Dean of School of Business Administration at Shanghai Finance University. He obtained his doctorate in Management Science and Engineering from the Southwest Jiaotong University, P. R. China after an extensive career in education and business. He has published more than 40 papers covering education study, technology management, and strategic alliance, and has made numerous conference papers presentations besides completing several programs sponsored by the government.

Li Zhao is a teaching assistant of Department of Human Resource Management, School of Business Administration at Shanghai Finance University. She obtained her doctorate in Human Resource Management and Entrepreneurship from Fudan University, P. R. China. As a participator, she has completed a couple of projects sponsored by the national and provincial founding program of China, and published several papers on human resource management and entrepreneurship. Besides this, she also works as a consultant for some companies.

Index

P

Q

R

S

T

CPSIA information can be obtained at www.ICGtesting.com
262871BV00003BA/13/P

9 781609 605995